Fundamentals of Learning

Fundamentals of Learning: A Behavioral Approach discusses the basic mechanisms of learning. It highlights how most behaviors are learned through minimal amounts of cognitive processing and acquired through associations between stimuli, such as observed in classical and operant conditioning (associative learning) and repeated experiences with a single stimulus (nonassociative learning).

Together, in combination with innate or instinctual behaviors, these forms of learning account for the acquisition of an impressively wide range of behaviors and played a crucial role in the evolution of species, as it permitted them to adapt to changing environments. The book begins by tracing the history of learning theory, acquainting students with the philosophers and early researchers who contributed to learning theory. It then goes on to cover theoretical explanations of the basic learning mechanisms, including theories of classical and operant conditioning. The modular approach of the book enables students to link the concepts they learn about in the text to their own behavior. The book concludes with a discussion of the role of cognition in learning, covering behaviors that are considered less automatized and mediated by cognitive processes, such as the formation of spatial maps and the processes involved in decision-making and motivated behaviors.

The book is written with the student in mind throughout, featuring real-life case studies, key terms, and learning objectives. It is also accompanied by additional resources to further support student learning. It will be a must-read for all students of learning and behavior or animal learning.

Stéphane Gaskin has served as a Psychology Professor at Dawson College in Montreal since 2006. He also gives lectures at McGill University and has previously taught at Concordia University. He obtained his PhD in Psychology from McGill in 2007 and his MA from Concordia in 2002. His postdoctoral work includes positions at the University of California, San Diego, and at Concordia University. Dr. Gaskin's research mainly focused on the behavioral neuroscience of learning and memory.

Fundamentals of Learning

A Behavioral Approach

Stéphane Gaskin

Routledge
Taylor & Francis Group
NEW YORK AND LONDON

First published 2026
by Routledge
605 Third Avenue, New York, NY 10158

and by Routledge
4 Park Square, Milton Park, Abingdon, Oxon, OX14 4RN

Routledge is an imprint of the Taylor & Francis Group, an informa business

ISBN: 978-1-032-79410-5 (hbk)
ISBN: 978-1-032-79404-4 (pbk)
ISBN: 978-1-003-49182-8 (ebk)

DOI: 10.4324/9781003491828

Typeset in Sabon
by Apex CoVantage, LLC

Access the support materials: www.routledge.com/9781032794044

To my lovely and supporting wife Marilyn and
my wonderful children April and Sam

Contents

Module 1

The Evolution of Learning Science

Introduction

Humans have always been fascinated by the study of behavior, reflecting a desire to understand ourselves, others, and our interactions with the world around us. Our behavior shapes social interactions and plays a crucial role in our adaptability to the environment. In this introductory module, we will explore the fundamental principles of learning that are central to acquiring new behaviors and facilitating behavior change. In Chapter 1, you will learn about the philosophical and historical roots of learning research, from Aristotle to the contrasting perspectives of rationalism and empiricism, underscoring the notion that observable behavior should take precedence over studying unobservable mental processes. We will also investigate the roles of neuroscience and artificial intelligence in enhancing our understanding of learning mechanisms.

In Chapter 2, we will build on these foundations. You will learn to differentiate between learning and performance, as well as the key scientific principles guiding learning research. Additionally, you will uncover the major theoretical perspectives from which learning is studied, along with the importance of animal research in this field. These foundational chapters will provide you with a framework for understanding the discussions surrounding the learning process that occupy the remainder of the textbook, including classical conditioning and operant conditioning, and how the behavioral adaptations arising from these processes contribute to survival. You will find that establishing a solid grounding in the fundamental principles of learning will deepen your appreciation of the intricate mechanisms that drive behavior in both humans and animals.

Chapter 1: Exploring the Pathways of Learning: From Aristotle's Laws of Association to Artificial Intelligence

Chapter 2: Fundamental Concepts: Mapping the Terrain of Learning

DOI: 10.4324/9781003491828-1

1 Exploring the Pathways of Learning

From Aristotle's Laws of Association to Artificial Intelligence

Learning Objectives

- Describe the significance of humans' inherent interest in understanding behavior and how this understanding aids in social interactions, adaptation, and therapeutic interventions for psychological disorders.
- Understand Aristotle's Laws of Association, including contiguity, similarity, and contrast, and how they govern the formation of associations between events.
- Explain René Descartes's philosophical position of dualism, emphasizing the distinction between mind and body and the role of reason in acquiring knowledge.
- Analyze the principles of associationism as advocated by British associationists like Thomas Hobbes, John Locke, David Hume, and David Hartley, focusing on the formation of ideas through sensory experiences and their associations within the mind.
- Explore the neurological basis of learning, including synaptic plasticity, as proposed by Donald Hebb and supported by studies on long-term potentiation (LTP), using techniques like fMRI and PET imaging.
- Discuss the principles of machine learning, including supervised learning, unsupervised learning, semi-supervised learning, and reinforcement learning, and their applications in various fields such as medicine, psychology, customer service, education, and language learning.

About the Learning Class

Giang and her friend Evert were having a discussion just outside their university's bookstore. It centered around the first chapter of the textbook that Evert just bought for his learning class. Giang, who took the course during the previous semester, was telling him about how she found that learning about some of the history behind the study of learning in the first chapter was quite useful in understanding the ideas and experiments presented in the course. Seeming a little unmotivated, Evert replied, "That is just because of your interest in history." "No," she answered. "I truly have a deep interest in learning." She also told Evert that she thought it remarkable that today's learning theories go back to Aristotle, whom she recently read about in an introductory philosophy class.

"Is he the only philosopher discussed?" he asked.

"No," she replied.

DOI: 10.4324/9781003491828-2

Source: IStock photo ID:1835665869.

There is also Descartes and a group of philosophers known as the British associationists, who lived between the 16th and 18th centuries. Evert knew about Descartes because he learned about him in high school and his introductory psychology class. "But who were the British associationists?" he asked. "Well," she replied. "They laid down what they believed to be the laws of learning, which included a description of how we form associations." Giang went on to explain how their ideas influenced a group of psychologists that sought to explain learning by only considering an organism's experiences with the environment, an idea known as behaviorism. "Behaviorism!" exclaimed Evert, as his eyes grew wide open. "We briefly studied it in introductory psychology. It's about people like Watson and Skinner, isn't it?" "Exactly," replied Giang. Giang went on to explain how the first chapter didn't only mention famous figures in the history of psychology but also how their ideas influenced learning research throughout the years to the present day, where scientists are investigating the neurobiological mechanisms of learning and whether computers can be made to learn like humans. "Pretty awesome," replied Evert.

1.1 Exploring Learning and Behavior: The Journey Begins

How often do you think of your behavior and the behavior of others? When I ask this question to my students, the answer I never fail to get is "all of the time." Indeed, humans seem to have an inherent interest in behavior. For example, how often have you wondered why you acted in a way that got you in trouble with another person, be it a friend, teacher, boss, or spouse? Also, think about the routine tasks that have become so automatized that you perform them with little attention or conscious awareness. You may have also wondered why people acted the way they did towards you and whether it was in response to something you did or said. What about when behavior goes awry? Humans become especially curious about the causes of behavior when it falls outside the norms. These types of behaviors are symptomatic of psychological disorders such as phobias, obsessive-compulsive disorder (OCD), depression, or schizophrenia.

As you may have already surmised, understanding your behavior and the behavior of others is important for regulating your interactions with others by helping you predict their reactions to events in their environments, which may also include you. Knowing about your behavioral responses to the environment, which may include other people, is also important in that it permits you to adjust your behavior so that it is more adaptive. But how are behaviors acquired in the first place?

The answer is that many of your behaviors are acquired through learning. You interact with others in specific ways and understand their behaviors because you have learned to do so. Learning is also the process by which you avoid dangerous situations or escape them when finding yourself in them, come to associate the ringing of a doorbell with someone waiting at the door, and acquire whatever skill you possess, whether it is expressed in artistic creations such as painting or playing a sport. The range of activities that a person can develop through learning is enormous. Learning is, of course, also important not only for the acquisition of new behaviors but also for the modification of behavior. For example, after noticing that a specific action elicits a negative response from a friend, family member, or spouse, you may want to modify your behavior to maintain healthy relationships with them. You may also change how you perform a task to be more efficient. People who have psychological disorders may have acquired maladaptive responses to their environment, which can be modified through what is known as behavioral therapy. Hence, learning is defined as a process by which new behaviors are acquired or modified through experiences with the environment.

However, it is important to understand that learning is not the only way behaviors are acquired and modified. For example, animals, but not humans, have genetically preprogrammed instincts that allow them to adapt to their environments. Both animals and humans also possess reflexes, which are inborn automatic reactions triggered by specific environmental stimuli. So, learning is often influenced by instincts and reflexes to produce behavior, and we will return to the contribution of instincts and reflexes in Chapter 3.

This textbook is about basic forms of learning. Notice that the behaviors we have been discussing are not about learning the subjects taught at school, such as arithmetic, grammar or geography, although many of the principles you will learn in this textbook could be applied to that. Instead, it is mainly about the basic associative mechanisms which have allowed animals to survive across evolutionary time. The rest of this chapter is dedicated to giving you an idea of the historical background that led to our knowledge of the basic associative process involved in learning and a little bit about how the study of learning evolved to also trying to understand its brain mechanisms and to build computers that can mimic human learning.

Critical Thinking Spot Check 1.1

1. Describe some everyday tasks that you perform in an automatized way, meaning that they require little to no attention or conscious awareness.
2. Why is it important for humans to understand their behavior as well as the behaviors of others?
3. In what ways, in addition to learning, can behaviors be acquired?

1.2 Aristotle's Laws of Association

Contiguity, Similarity, and Contrast

You might know we can learn by associating environmental events because you have experienced this phenomenon countless times. This was also the case for philosophers living in ancient Greece and relatively recent times. However, these philosophers were not content with observing the phenomenon; they wanted to discover the rules governing the formation of these associations. The ancient Greek philosopher Aristotle (384–322 B.C.) was most interested in this question (Beare, 2010).

Aristotle was interested in many aspects of human behavior, including sleep, emotions, ethical behavior, and memory. He recognized that two types of memories existed: recognition and recollection. He believed that animals could memorize by recognition, which involved matching a stimulus being experienced to one already imprinted in memory, such as when you recognize your schoolbag when you see it or recognize a song when you hear it. However, he believed that only humans were capable of memory by recollection, which involved triggering the image of a stimulus not presently experienced through the senses, such as remembering what you had for breakfast. He thought that recollection required one's soul to trigger a chain of associations, which he thought were a series of mnemonic movements which ended when the desired mental image was encountered.

Unlike his teacher, Plato (429?–347? B.C.), who believed knowledge was innate, Aristotle believed knowledge was acquired through experience. The way by which this knowledge was acquired was governed by three laws (Figure 1.1). By the **law of contiguity**, he believed associations between events were more likely to be created when linked by their proximity in time (temporal contiguity) or space (spatial contiguity). For example, we learned to associate thunder with lightning because they tend to occur close together in time (temporal contiguity) and chairs with tables because they are often found close together in space (spatial contiguity). By the **law of similarity**, he believed associations were created between stimuli resembling each other. For example, you recognize a laptop as a laptop because it resembles the ones you have seen before. Finally, by the **law of contrast** or opposition, he believed that experiencing one stimulus triggered the image of its opposite. For example, thinking of warmth triggered the thought of cold, the idea of danger triggered the thought of safety, and so on. With exception of the law of contrast, Aristotle's laws of association are still accepted in learning theory.

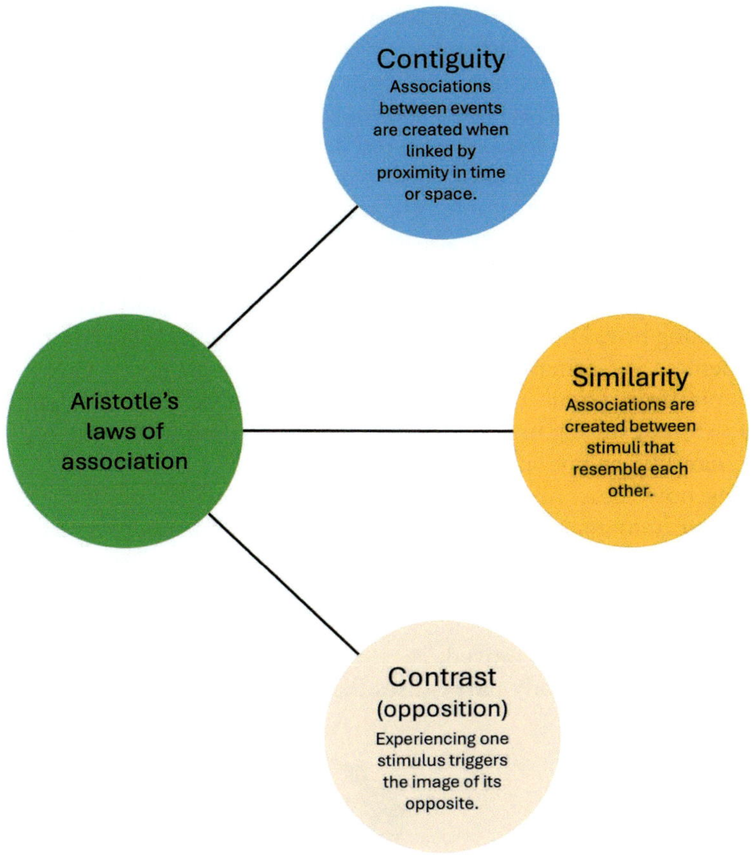

Figure 1.1 Aristotle's laws of association.

Critical Thinking Spot Check 1.2

1. What did early philosophers, such as Aristotle, want to find out about how learning occurred?
2. What two types of memories did Aristotle identify? Briefly describe each one and how he differentiated between humans and animals in their possession of one kind of memory versus the other.
3. Name and explain Aristotle's laws of association.

1.3 Philosophical Positions: Rationalism and Empiricism

Rationalism

Descartes's Dualism and Fluid Mechanical Theory

Contrary to Aristotle, French philosopher and mathematician René Descartes (1596–1650) believed all knowledge came from reason rather than experience, a philosophical position known as **rationalism** (Descartes, 1986). Descartes also thought that the mind and the body were composed of two distinct substances, the body being material and the mind being immaterial. This idea raised questions about how the immaterial mind could interact with a material body. Many positions regarding the relationship between mind and body have been proposed. Descartes's position, in which the mind and the body were distinct and could exist independently, is known as **dualism**.

Descartes thought that only humans possessed a mind. According to the **fluid-mechanical theory**, he believed that nonhuman animals were mere automata whose actions could be likened to robots and driven by simple reflexes. He explained these reflexes by describing the movement of fluids, called animal spirits, through hollow tubes in the body.

In the 17th century, automata that took the form of hydraulically operated moving statues were installed in the public gardens of cities across Europe and mainly served as entertainment. As a young boy, Descartes became fascinated with such automata when he visited the Royal Gardens at St-Germain in France. While walking through a garden, a person may step on a small platform. Upon stepping on the platform, a valve would open, causing water to flow into a piston, resulting in a threatening figure to swing out of the bushes or perform some other human-like behavior.

After learning how these automata worked, Descartes wondered if the seemingly automatic behaviors of humans and animals could be generated similarly, for example, when one seems to automatically withdraw a limb from an aversive stimulus such as a flame (Figure 1.2). Descartes's reasoning was as follows:

1. Muscles swell when a limb is moved.
2. External stimulation of a body part causes the nerves under the skin's surface to stretch.

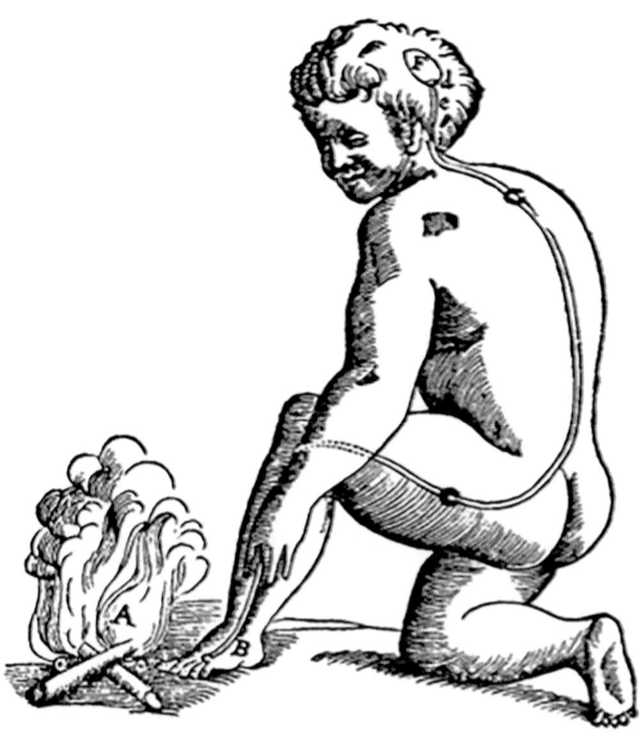

Figure 1.2 Descartes's conception of a reflex.

Source: Image in the public domain (https://commons.wikimedia.org/wiki/File:Descartes-reflex.JPG).

3. When stimulated, these nerves may act as strings that open valves located in the brain.
4. Opening these valves causes fluids to flow from the brain to the muscles, causing them to swell and resulting in the movement of the limbs.

Since animals lacked minds, Descartes thought that they could not reason, lacked self-consciousness, and were incapable of language. For Descartes, all of the qualities we think of as being distinctively human required a God-given soul (or mind), which he believed animals lack. He believed that the immaterial soul interacted with the pineal gland, which conferred on humans the unique abilities to have free will and to perform voluntary actions. He thought the pineal gland was ideal for interacting with the soul because it is a singular structure sitting at the brain's midline. He also felt that its being suspended, small, and light made it easy to be moved by the immaterial soul. He believed that, in response to sensory experiences and innate ideas, the soul caused the pineal gland to tip, releasing and directing animal spirits through the nerves to control the body. You probably remembered by now that Descartes was the philosopher Giang was referring to in the opening vignette of the chapter.

Empiricism

Empiricism refers to the philosophical school of thought that all knowledge stems from sensory experience. One problem with the claim of empiricism is that it is difficult to conceive that sensory experience alone can account for the complex chains of thoughts we are capable of. So, if not from direct sensory experience alone, how are these complex chains of thought created? One possible resolution to the problem lies in the position that thoughts derived from an animal's sensory experiences can become associated. This philosophical position is known as **associationism**, which is fundamental to the study of learning.

The British Associationists

Associationism is attributed to a group of philosophers known as the **British associationists,** also known as the British empiricists (Boring, 1950). The most prominent of these were Thomas Hobbes (1588–1679), John Locke (1632–1704), David Hume (1711–1776), and David Hartley (1705–1757). In this section, we will briefly explore those philosophers' momentous contributions to the study of learning.

Thomas Hobbes

Contrary to Descartes, who believed that an immaterial soul moved the body, Hobbes believed that only matter could affect matter. He thought that the strength of association between objects in memory depended on the *frequency* at which they were experienced together (Hobbes, 1968). For example, you formed strong associations between wheels and cars because you frequently experienced seeing wheels with vehicles. Hobbes also believed that associations are formed through experiencing cause-and-effect relationships. For example, if a spoiled food is the cause of an illness, spoiled food will subsequently make you think of the illness, and subsequent illness will make you think of the spoiled food.

John Locke

Locke thought that the mind did not possess innate ideas, as believed by Descartes and other rationalists, but that it originated as a blank slate (tabula rasa), onto which the objects of sensory experiences were imprinted. He believed in two categories of ideas: *simple ideas* and *complex ideas*. **Simple ideas** were those directly derived from the sensory experiences of objects. **Complex ideas** were formed by associating simple ideas within the mind. According to Locke, the mind had the ability to operate on ideas in different ways (Locke, 1948). First, in what he called **combining**, he thought that the mind could combine simple ideas into complex ideas. Second, in what he called **relating**, he thought that the mind could bring two ideas together, simple or complex, without combining them so that each could be considered simultaneously. Third, in what he called **abstracting**, he thought that the mind could separate ideas from time and place. For example, the idea of a dog, with its characteristics, can be grouped under the abstract idea of animal.

John Locke believed that the mind was a blank slate at birth onto which the objects of sensory experience were imprinted.

Sources: John Locke: https://commons.wikimedia.org/wiki/File:John_Locke.jpg Blank slate: IStock photo ID:175518424.

David Hume

Hume believed that the mind could combine simple ideas into an infinite number of complex ideas. He also believed that ideas were not associated at random but that they did so according to three laws of association (Hume, 1779). These were the laws of *resemblance*, *contiguity in time and place*, and *causation* (or cause and effect). For example, seeing a picture of a laptop makes you think of your own (resemblance); thinking about a soccer match you played in reminds you of an injury suffered during the game (contiguity), and thinking about studying makes you think of good grades because studying and good grades are linked by cause and effect.

David Hartley

David Hartley was the first to propose a form of psychobiological associationism. In other words, he proposed a way by which psychology and biology could be combined to explain how associations were created in the brain (Buckingham and Finger, 1997). More specifically, he proposed that, when stimulated, sensory organs caused a chain reaction of vibrations in particles located in the nerves that connected the organs to the brain. Hartley also proposed that the nerves from different sense organs followed distinct paths to enter the brain at different locations, which he thought explained the different qualities of the senses. This was because the nerves from different sense organs were differentially sensitive to the different types of environmental stimuli. He believed that simple ideas were created when repeated presentations of sensory stimuli left behind traces in the brain and that complex ideas were formed when less intense vibrations, which he called *vibranticules*, linked the traces of simple ideas together.

An astonishing aspect of Hartley's ideas is that they foreshadowed 19th- and 20th-century physiological models of perception, learning, and memory, such as the doctrine of specific nerve energies proposed by Johannes Peter Müller (1801–1858), which states that the information from different senses follows independent pathways to connect to specific brain areas (Isaac, 2019), and connectionism, in which learning a memory occurs through changes in the strength of connections in networks of neurons (Kassirer and Kopelman, 1990).

Critical Thinking Spot Check 1.3

1. Explain the philosophical position known as associationism and its importance in the study of learning.
2. How did Thomas Hobbes believe ideas became most strongly associated?
3. Distinguish between John Locke's simple and complex ideas.
4. Which of the laws of association did David Hume believe to be the most important and why?
5. Describe and give an example of how David Hartley believed that John Locke's simple ideas became associated to form complex ideas.

1.4 Behaviorism

Behaviorism refers to a branch of psychology that seeks to explain behavior without resorting to the mind, consisting of mentalistic concepts such as beliefs, desires, will, drive, personality, and attitudes. It comes into sharp contrast with the introspective method used by Wilhelm Wundt (1832–1920), who prioritized the study of inner conscious phenomena, or that of Sigmund Freud (1856–1939), for whom behavior could be explained by conflicts between hypothetical entities buried deep within the subconscious (i.e., Id, Ego, Superego).

There are many types of behaviorisms (Schneider and Morris, 1987; Innis, 1999; Strapasson and de Freitas Araujo, 2020), in fact, too many for each type to be described here. For our purposes it is sufficient to distinguish between three types of behaviorism: analytical behaviorism, methodological behaviorism, and radical behaviorism (also known as psychological behaviorism), and dispense of the deeper philosophical underpinnings. For those interested, the references just cited will guide you through a deeper dive into its different types, history, and philosophy. In terms of important figures in behaviorism, we will focus mainly on John B. Watson, B.F. Skinner, and Edward Tolman. Other names associated with its development, such as Edward Lee Thorndike (1874–1949) and Clark Hull (1884–1952), are discussed in various sections of the textbook.

Analytical Behaviorism

Analytical behaviorism, often attributed to philosophers Ludwig Wittgenstein (1889–1951) and Gilbert Ryle (1900–1976), is a philosophical position in which mental concepts are behavioral tendencies or dispositions to behave and must be translated into behavioral terms (Ryle, 1949; Wittgenstein, 1953). For example, according to analytical behaviorism, if we say that someone "desires" a piece of cake, what is referred to is the person's disposition to act in a certain way such as reaching for it when available. Speaking of someone feeling fear means that the person is disposed to exhibit observable behaviors such as fleeing from or avoiding a threatening situation. In another example, saying that someone feels pain could be translated into a withdrawal response, such as quickly removing one's hand from a hot stove.

Although analytical behaviorism had a significant influence on the development of the other two types of behaviorism, that is, methodological and radical behaviorisms, it is to those two types that we now turn, as they are most relevant to the bulk of the experiments described in this textbook.

Methodological Behaviorism

Methodological behaviorism is mainly attributed to psychologist John B. Watson (1878–1958). According to methodological behaviorism, a natural science of behavior, on equal footing with physics and chemistry, is possible. Therefore, it follows that psychology should only concern itself with observable behavior while completely ignoring mental states (i.e., beliefs, desires, will, drive, personality, and attitudes) or anything we would call consciousness, the mind, or private events such as thoughts or feelings. Watson also made no distinction between people and animals in an effort to come to a unified theory of behavior (Watson, 1913).

Because mental states [subjective experiences, thoughts, feelings, beliefs and desires] are unobservable, methodological behaviorists viewed them as unworthy of study. For example, a methodological behaviorist studying rats learning to find food on a maze would only study their observable behavior, such as recording their sequences of right and left turns and their eventual avoidance of blocked alleys over successive trials. The methodological behaviorist would not be interested in a rat's motivation, the rat's belief about where the food might be located, or any other mental state. Similarly, in studying the social interaction between two people, the methodological behaviorist might focus on observable responses such as eye contact, smiles, laughter, crying, and mannerisms, without ever considering their mental states, such as feelings of joy, sadness, frustration, thoughts, or intentions.

To help you understand this idea, consider the following in explaining why a person, who skipped lunch, is eating a large supper. One explanation for why she is eating such a large supper is that she feels very hungry. To the methodological behaviorist, stating that she feels hungry is unimportant because the feeling of hunger is a mental state, which is unobservable. That she is eating a big supper (an observable behavior) can be explained by the fact that she skipped lunch and that people that have not eaten in a long time (i.e., by having skipped a meal) tend to eat more when given the opportunity to do so. Hence, methodological behaviorists found the cause for behavior in external events, not in anything that might be going on in an animal's or person's mind. That is, they explained behavior as responses elicited by environmental events or stimuli.

Watson eventually became so extreme in his view that he did away with the very existence of the mind (Lashley, 1923; Schneider and Morris, 1987). He first publicly expressed this idea in 1913 during a lecture entitled "Psychology as a Behaviorist Views It," also known as "The Behaviorist Manifesto" (Watson, 1913). In it, he stated that 1) psychology should be an objective branch of the natural sciences, 2) its goals should be the prediction and control of behavior, 3) introspection should form no part of its methods, and 4) explanations of behavior in terms of consciousness should be rejected.

Apart from a few innate reflexes, Watson's belief that all behaviors were learned through experience with the environment is expressed in the following quote:

> Give me a dozen healthy infants, well-formed, and my own specified world to bring them up in and I'll guarantee to take any one at random and train him to become any type of specialist I might select—doctor, lawyer, artist, merchant-chief and, yes, even beggar-man and thief, regardless of his talents, penchants, tendencies, abilities, vocations, and race of his ancestors. I am going beyond my facts, and I admit it, but so have the advocates of the contrary, and they have been doing so for many thousands of years.
>
> (Watson, 1930)

Radical Behaviorism

Radical behaviorism is attributed to psychologist B.F. Skinner (1904–1990). Radical behaviorism agrees with methodological behaviorism that a natural science is possible. However, Skinner disagreed with methodological behaviorism in its treatment of private events. Contrary to methodological behaviorism, Skinner believed that private events, such as inner speech, emotions, and physiological sensations, were actually physical phenomena that occurred within the body, which could be included in the analysis of behavior (Skinner, 1974). This is because he believed that these private events could be observed indirectly in that they could be inferred by their effects on observable behavior. He believed that they could be used as discriminative stimuli that influence behavior by interacting with the environment.

The same could not be said about what is commonly referred to in psychology as the mind, which includes beliefs, desires, and intentions. He considered those unobservable entities which could not be measured objectively, making them unusable for scientific analysis. Skinner called the contents of the mind **explanatory fictions** used to account for observable behavior.

Instead, Skinner believed that a science of behavior would only include an empirical approach including only how environmental stimuli controlled behavior. He coined the term operant conditioning to denote how animals operate on their environment by responding to it in ways that produce consequences that either increase (reinforcement) or decrease (punishment) the probability of those responses.

He showed how operants could be used to shape complex behaviors by reinforcing successive approximations of the desired behavior and that different patterns of response can arise depending on the schedule on which animals are reinforced or punished for their behaviors. Skinner also proposed the concept of stimulus control to explain how, for example, a behavior that was reinforced in the presence of certain environmental cues is more likely to recur when the animal again finds itself in the presence of those cues. In what he called the three-term contingency (antecedent, behavior, and consequence), these environmental cues are antecedents that set the occasion in which a particular response will produce a reinforcer, as when raising your hand in class (behavior) occurs in response to the teacher saying, "Any questions?" (the antecedent) so that you can get an answer (the consequence). Skinner's ideas are covered in details in Chapters 12 and 15.

Purposive Behaviorism

In contrast to the methodological and radical behaviorisms of Watson and Skinner, respectively, *purposive behaviorism*, proposed by psychologist Edward Tolman (1886–1959), states that behavioral acts are selected by goals or purposes which guide sequences of behaviors until the goals or purposes are attained. This may come as a surprise to some, as Tolman was a behaviorist. Because of this, Tolman's theory is considered a cognitive theory of learning. It clearly opposed behaviorism, the dominant learning theory of his day.

He also believed that behavior was molar, in that it could only be considered as an integrated whole. It could not, according to him, be understood at the molecular level, that is, by studying every particular aspect of it, such as individual muscle contractions and glandular secretions (molecular) (Tolman, 1922). To make this distinction clearer, describing someone's behavior as individual footsteps and the series of physical and physiological events that compose them is a molecular analysis of the behavior. Describing it as the integrated act of walking is a molar analysis (Baum, 2004).

Tolman believed that molar behavior could be specified by three characteristics:

1. Animals acquire patterns of responses that lead them toward or away from a goal, and these persist until the goal is achieved.
2. These response patterns are consistent in that they are replicated on various occasions for achieving the same goal.
3. Animals select the most effective means of achieving the same goal out of several options.

Tolman also discovered that the behavior of rats in mazes could not be explained only by stimulus-response associations, as proposed by the behaviorists of his day. Instead, he proposed that they formed **cognitive maps** of the environment, which was in stark contrast with the behaviorist idea that mental processes were irrelevant in explaining behavior. Tolman also introduced the concept of **latent learning**, in which information could be acquired without conscious effort, attention, awareness, intention, or reinforcement and used only when the need to use the information arises. By the same token, Tolman's research also permitted him to draw a distinction between learning and performance (Tolman, Ritchie and Kalish, 1946a; Tolman, 1948). Tolman's work, which brought him to propose these ideas, is discussed in detail in Chapter 21.

Objective Psychology

An important influence on the development of behaviorism was *objective psychology*, developed by Russian physiologists who, in the early 1900s, proposed a scientific program for psychology. By objective psychology, they meant that behavior could strictly be understood in terms of reflexes and their underlying physiology. The most prominent of these scientists were Ivan Sechenov (1829–1905), Ivan Petrovitch Pavlov (1849–1936), and Vladimir Bechterev (1857–1927).

Sechenov believed that thoughts did not cause behavior but that they were mental reflexes generated by physiological processes, which were themselves elicited by environmental stimuli (Clower, 1998). He also believed that throughout development, certain areas of the human brain acquired the capacity to inhibit reflexes through what he called *central inhibition* (Stuart, 2014).

Based on Sechenov's ideas, Pavlov, who won the 1904 Nobel Prive in medicine for his studies on digestion, believed that all physiological functions resulted from the activity in the nervous system, a theory known as *nervism* (Razran, 1958). He showed that reflexes, thought to be inflexible responses to specific environmental stimuli, could be modified by learning (Pavlov, 1902, 1927). In a series of classic experiments, he and his collaborators showed how initially neutral stimuli, such as buzzers, tones, and lights, could be used to modify the salivation reflexes in dogs by creating an association between these stimuli and food, which naturally elicits the salivation reflex. Pavlov's ideas are referred to in various sections of this textbook, but his classic experiments are discussed in Chapter 5.

Critical Thinking Spot Check 1.4

1. Compare methodological to radical behaviorism.
2. Explain purposive behaviorism. How does it differ from methodological and radical behaviorism?
3. Explain objective psychology. In your opinion, in what way(s) do you think it influenced the development of behaviorism?

1.5 The Rise of Neuroscience in the Study of Learning

Long-Term Potentiation

Although, as you read above, a psychobiological theory of learning had already been proposed by David Hartley in the 18th century, scientific investigations of the neural processes involved in learning took off with influential theories put forward in the 19th and 20th centuries. One main idea that developed during the 19th century was that learning depended on changes in the strength of connections between neurons (synaptic strength) which are induced by experience (Refer to the "What in the Brain?" box in Chapter 2 for the basic structure and functions of neurons). This idea was proposed by Santiago Ramón y Cajal (1852–1934) in 1913 (Cowan and Kandel, 2001; Cajal and Azoulay, 1995). It was also anticipated by Sigmund Freud (1856–1939) (Centonze et al., 2004), who, as you probably know, is mostly known for his psychodynamic theory (Berlucchi and Buchtel, 2009).

However, it was Canadian psychologist Donald Hebb (1904–1985) who proposed the most influential theory of learning based on changes in synaptic strength between neurons (Hebb, 1949). Hebb famously stated that learning occurred when a neuron (neuron A) persistently activated another neuron (neuron B). He thought that this persistent activation facilitated the ability of neuron A to activate neuron B. His model, which became known as the Hebbian synapse, led to arguably the most famous quote in neuroscience, "neurons that fire together wire together," which is best explained in Hebb's own words:

> When an axon of cell A is near enough to excite cell B and repeatedly or persistently takes part in firing it, some growth process or metabolic change takes place in one or both cells such that A's efficiency, as one of the cells firing B, is increased.
>
> Hebb, (1949, p. 62)

Evidence for the Hebb synapse was found in the 1970s by neuroscientists Timothy Bliss and Terje Lømo. They found that when they repeatedly electrically stimulated the axons of neurons, the response of the neurons with which they communicated was enhanced. They also found that this enhanced response persisted for hours, days, or weeks (Bliss and Lomo, 1973). This observed increase in the efficiency of a synapse following high-frequency electrical stimulation became known as long-term potentiation (LTP) and became an accepted model for the neurobiological basis of learning (Douglas and Goddard, 1975).

Neuroscience and Learning Today

Today, many neuroscientists are interested in the neurobiological basis of learning, as can be attested by the many "What in the brain?" boxes throughout this textbook. Today's neuroscientists can study learning processes using a variety of imaging methods to measure the brain's activity while a person or animal is engaged in a learning task or to observe the brain changes that may have occurred after learning. These include visual imaging of the brain with magnetic resonance imaging (MRI), functional magnetic resonance imaging (fMRI), and positron emission tomography (PET); measuring brain waves such as with electroencephalography (EEG); and several others (Figure 1.3). Neuroscientists can also experimentally lesion specific brain areas or interfere with their functioning by pharmacological inactivation, which involves injecting a drug directly into the brain, to then observe the effects on a learning of a task (Gaskin and White, 2010, 2013). Neuroscientists can also use a method known as optogenetics in which the genes of animals are manipulated so that their neurons are capable of responding to light signals of different frequencies, enabling researchers to turn them on or off at will as animals perform a learning task (Pokala and Glater, 2018; Bimpisidis, Konig and Wallen-Mackenzie, 2020).

In a burgeoning field of interest, neuroscientists are trying to uncover the brain processes that participate in the acquisition of new information during sleep. For example, using fMRI, researchers found that activity in the brain's language areas as well as the hippocampus, a part of the brain important for the formation of memories, was involved in forming associations between new foreign words and their meanings in participants while they were sleeping (Züst et al., 2019).

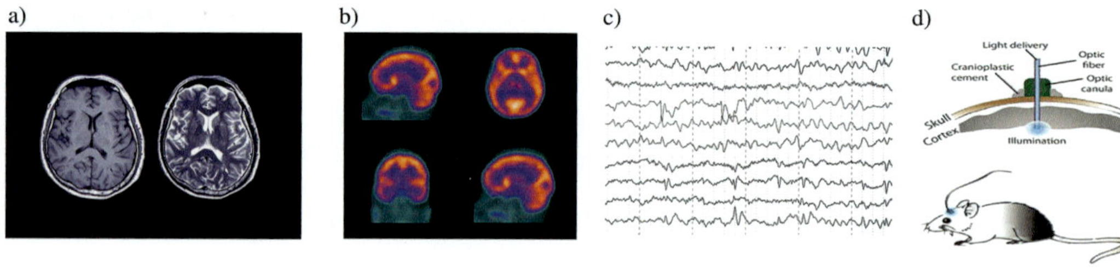

Figure 1.3 a) Magnetic resonance imaging (MRI). b) Positron emission tomography (PET). c) Electroencephalograph (EEG). d) Optogenetics.

Okami, P. (2017). *Psychology: contemporary perspectives*. Oxford University Press Academic US. (Figure 1.34.)

Sources: a) IStock photo ID:1165138015 b) IStockphoto ID:178076322 c) Stock photo ID:973873398 d) Pama E.A. Claudia, Colzato Lorenza, Hommel Bernhard—http://journal.frontiersin.org/article/10.3389/fpsyg.2013.00610/full Creative commons: https://en.wikipedia.org/wiki/Optogenetics#/media/File:Optogenetic_stimulation_consists_of_several_steps.png.

Critical Thinking Spot Check 1.5

1. What idea did Santiago Ramón y Cajal and Freud anticipate regarding learning?
2. Describe the Hebb synapse.
3. Who provided evidence for the Hebb synapse and how was it done?
4. How does knowing about long-term potentiation increase your understanding of how learning occurs?

1.6 Can Computers Think and Learn Like Humans?

Artificial Intelligence

Artificial intelligence (AI) is a branch of computer science that aims to simulate the capabilities of the human mind (Garnham, 2017; Ertel, 2018). It can be subdivided into two types: *weak AI or artificial narrow intelligence (ANI)* and *strong AI or artificial general intelligence (AGI)*.

Weak AI

The term weak AI is an unfortunate one. That is because it is not weak. If you have used virtual assistants on your phone or computer, smart speakers, or social media platforms, you have made use of weak AI. Weak AI also drives autonomous vehicles and operates email spam filters. This means that weak AI is already here, has been here for several years, and is getting better all the time.

Autonomous vehicles, social media, and smart speakers all make use of weak AI.

Source: Autonomous vehicle: IStock photo ID:1037080322; Social media: IStock photoID:1201792304 Smart speaker: IStock photo ID:1150572105

Strong AI

In contrast to weak AI, strong AI is science fiction and theoretical. A machine operating on strong AI would possess human intelligence. It would have the same problem-solving abilities and the ability to plan. It would also be self-aware and capable of experiencing emotions. Strong AI is depicted in movies such as *Ex Machina, Transcendence, Her,* and *The Matrix*.

Machine Learning

Machine learning is a branch of AI that focuses on imitating human learning. The accuracy of machine learning is gradually improved with the use of data and algorithms. An algorithm is a set of rules to be followed to solve a problem or a step-by-step way of doing things that is repeated every time. If you have ever baked a cake, put together furniture, or found a book in the library, you have followed an algorithm. Algorithms may also contain "if-then" statements. For example, while driving, you may have learned the rule "<u>If</u> there is too much traffic <u>then</u> get off the highway and take the alternate road indicated." Machine learning is divided into different subtypes. These are *supervised learning*, *unsupervised learning*, *semi-supervised learning*, *reinforcement learning*, and *deep learning*.

Deep learning is given special consideration and is discussed in this chapter's "Focus On" box. The subdivisions of machine learning are illustrated in Figure 1.4.

Supervised Learning

In **supervised learning**, the specific steps to carry out a task, specified by an algorithm, are compared to a set of instructions composed of *labeled data*. Labeled data are data that have been marked with specific properties or characteristics to which other data can be compared. In an example of supervised learning, identifying pictures of dogs as being of different breeds can be done by comparing a dog's features to those of pictures of different breeds contained in a dataset. Supervised learning can also be used to make predictions, such as the price of a house based on its location, square footage, and proximity to public transport by comparing it to houses with the same features stored in a database.

Unsupervised Learning

In **unsupervised learning**, no labeled data exist to which the steps specified by the algorithm can be compared for accuracy. Imagine being given an unlabeled box containing all the parts needed to build a specific piece of furniture with no instructions and no picture of the final product. You would have to do your best to find the pieces that best fit together. This method is known as *clustering* and is used by computers to put information from a dataset together based on similarities between features. For example, it may put different individual features of dogs together to represent a specific breed. Credit card companies use computers capable of unsupervised learning to detect anomalous transactions such as one made in New York City minutes after one was made in Los Angeles so that you can be alerted of a potential fraud. Unsupervised learning also includes learning by association. For example,

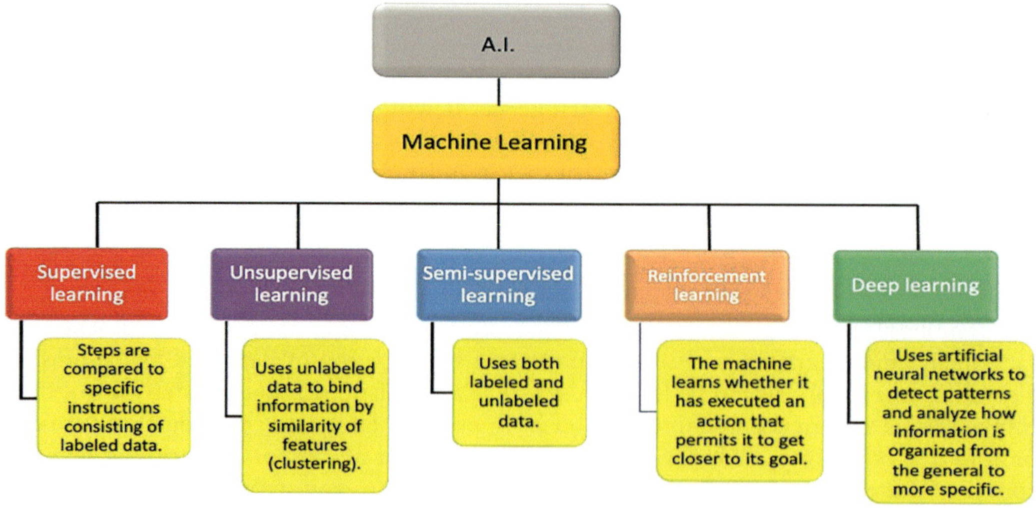

Figure 1.4 Machine learning is a branch of AI that includes supervised learning, unsupervised learning, semi-supervised learning, reinforcement learning, and deep learning. See accompanying text for details (deep learning is discussed in this chapter's "Focus On" box).

if you have recently bought a tablet and subsequently saw ads for laptop computers, you have experienced the power of unsupervised learning.

Semi-Supervised Learning

It can be very time consuming to label data to represent every property and characteristic of an object as is done in supervised learning. This is where **semi-supervised learning** comes in. In semi-supervised learning, both labeled data and non-labeled data coexist. However, if enough data are labeled, a computer can compare the data it collects to existing labeled data to improve its accuracy. There are many applications of semi-supervised learning. For example, internet search engines use semi-supervised learning to classify webpages because labeling every type of webpage available on the internet to be compared to is impossible. Semi-supervised learning is also used in speech analysis in which labeling every possible pattern of speech would be impossible.

Reinforcement Learning

Reinforcement learning does not make use of labeled data. Rather, the machine learns whether it has executed an action that permits it to get closer to a goal. Think about what happens when you play certain video games. When you first start playing, you have no idea of the specific sequences of actions that will lead you to a goal. However, by trial and error, some of your actions are rewarded by positive feedback, and other actions are followed by negative feedback. You tend to repeat the actions that were followed by positive feedback and avoid performing the actions followed by negative feedback. The same can be said of machine reinforcement learning. The feedback, whether positive or negative, can take the form of positive or negative points, respectively. The applications of reinforcement learning include its use in finance to evaluate the value of investment strategies and chemistry in the optimization of chemical reactions.

Chatbots

When combined with other forms of machine learning such as supervised learning (described previously) and deep learning (described in this chapter's "Focus On" box), reinforcement learning can be used to produce powerful and useful computer software such as **chatbots**. A chatbot is an artificially intelligent computer program able to simulate human conversations in natural language (i.e., ordinary human language) (Adamopoulou and Moussiades, 2020). Chatbots can be accessed through any type of online computer systems. Interacting with a chatbot can include text messaging, audio, speech recognition, or email.

Chatbots have a wide range of applications. For example, they could be used in medicine for monitoring a patient's health through text message communication (Schario et al., 2022), to deliver psychotherapy (Lim et al., 2022), to detect cognitive impairments in the elderly (de Arriba-Perez et al., 2022), for the gamification of learning (Gonzalez-Gonzalez et al., 2023), in customer service (Hsu and Lin, 2023), and for learning languages (Huang, Hew and Fryer, 2022). Chatbots known as chat generative pre-trained transformers (GPT) are also available on the internet for professionals, academics, and the general public (Lund and Ting, 2023).

Chatbots are also used in education to enhance student experiences and can be adapted to various teaching methods. However, you must also realize the shortcomings of chatbots when used for educational purposes (Kuhail et al., 2023). For example, they often possess limited training datasets, which can result in frustration of students looking for answers to their questions. In addition, chatbots can give incorrect responses. Another limitation of chatbots is that the students' personalities and learning styles are often not included in their design. It was also found that students can lose interest in chatbots over time. Chatbots were also found have limited ability to provide feedback, which is an important aspect of learning. Finally, chatbots often have distracting elements such as external web links and pop-ups.

Focus On

Deep Learning

Deep learning is a subtype of machine learning. Deep learning uses algorithms (i.e., procedures for solving problems) to analyze the way information is organized from the general to the more specific (Fan, Ma and Zhong, 2021). It detects the relationships between data points to identify patterns and classify different types of information. This is something humans do all the time. In fact, deep learning mimics the organization of the human brain in what is known as *artificial neural networks* (ANNs). Deep learning has applications in speech recognition, customer service, recommendation engines, stock trading, and medicine. In one study, a deep learning algorithm was used to predict depression from language referring to depressive symptoms used by people on a social media platform (Eichstaedt et al., 2018). In another study, deep learning was used to predict the outcome of children and adolescents treated with antidepressants (Athreya et al., 2022).

The Structure of ANNs

Nodes, Layers, and Edges

Artificial neural networks are made up of several layers of artificial neurons called *nodes* (Figure 1.5). All ANNs contain at least one *input layer,* one or more *hidden layers*, and at least one *output layer.* The term "deep" in deep learning refers to the number of hidden layers in the ANN. A deep learning network has at least three layers, including the input and output layers.

The nodes in each layer connect with nodes of the next layer by what are known as *edges,* which mimic axons. Nodes have varying levels of activation. A node's level of activation is usually represented by numerical values. However, in Figure 1.5, the activation level of a node is indicated by its shade of color, with darker shades representing higher levels of activation.

Weights and Biases

Whereas neurons form connections of varying strength with other neurons through their axons (see the section on long-term potentiation), nodes form connections of varying strength with other nodes via their edges. The strength of connection between nodes is referred to as its *weight,* which is usually represented by numerical values that vary between 0 and 1. In Figure 1.5, the strength of connection between nodes is represented by the thickness of the edges. Thicker edges represent more heavily weighed connections than thinner edges.

The activation value of a node in the input layer depends on low-level components of the stimulus. The activation value of a node in the hidden and output layers consists of the combined activation values of the nodes connected to it from the previous layer and the weight of each of their connections. A node must reach a minimal level of activation, represented as a numerical value known as *bias*, to activate nodes in the next layer. The bias mimics a neuron's threshold of activation.

A Simple Example

Suppose we wanted to train an ANN to recognize the faces of famous psychologists. We would begin by uploading a *training dataset* consisting of pictures of famous psychologists labeled with their names into a computer. We would then train the ANN by repeatedly presenting it with individual pictures of famous psychologists (e.g., Freud as shown in the figure on the left). At the beginning of training, the network would make many mistakes by outputting names of psychologists that would not match the name of the psychologist to be recognized. However, through a process of self-correction, the outputted name would eventually match the name of the correct psychologist. The beauty of deep learning is that the ANN goes through this procedure by itself, without human intervention. This process and the role played by each layer of the ANN are explained in the following and illustrated in Figure 1.5.

The Input Layer

In our example, the image would activate each node of the input layer at varying degrees, depending on the pattern of bright and dark pixels in the image.

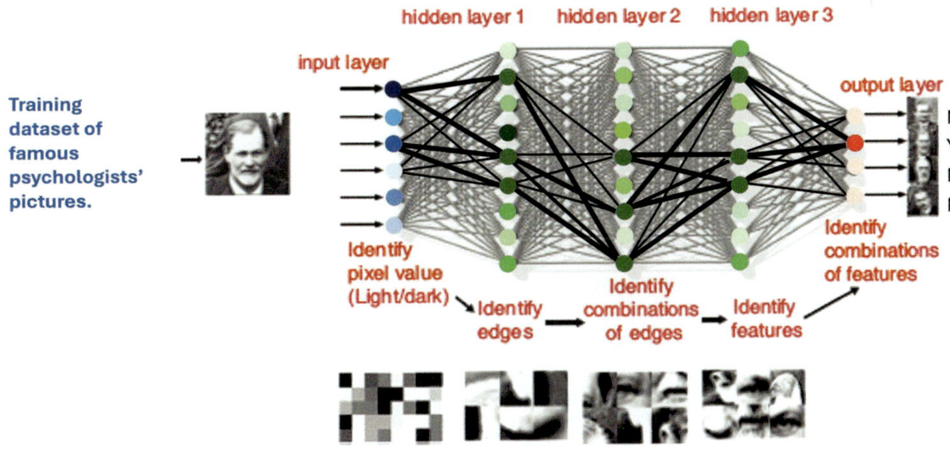

Figure 1.5 Identification of a picture from a training dataset by an artificial neural network. See accompanying text for details.

Source: IStock photo ID:886313714. The pictures of psychologist is creative commons (https://en.wikipedia.org/wiki/Sigmund_Freud#/media/File:Hall_Freud_Jung_in_front_of_Clark.jpg).

Hidden Layer 1 (HL-1)

The pattern of activity in the input layer would trigger a pattern of activity in HL-1 nodes. Each of the nodes activated in HL-1 would thus represent the combined activity of nodes in the input layer, and it would use HL-1 to identify contours.

Hidden Layer 2 (HL-2)

The activated nodes in HL-1 would in turn activate a pattern of nodes in HL-2. Because the nodes in HL-2 would each receive information from nodes that represent a contour in the image, each HL-2 node would identify a combination of contours.

Hidden Layer 3 (HL-3)

The activated HL-2 nodes, each representing a combination of contours, would activate a pattern of nodes in HL-3, which would each identify features from the combination of contours they receive.

The Output Layer

The activated HL-3 nodes, which represent individual features, would activate a pattern of nodes in the output layer, which would combine the features to identify a face. The degree of activation of each output node would indicate whether a picture was correctly identified. The node with the greatest activation level would reveal the correct match between the image being processed with that of the image in the training dataset.

Are You Thinking Critically?

1. How is an artificial neural network similar to a neural network in the brain?
2. Describe the role played by each of the layers in the network.
3. Think of another example that you can put through the artificial neural network. How would it work?

Critical Thinking Spot Check 1.6

1. Distinguish between weak AI and strong AI.
2. Distinguish between supervised, unsupervised, semi-supervised, and reinforcement learning.
3. Give an example of how each type of machine learning is used.

Chapter Summary

Each of the following bullet points aligns with the learning objectives outlined at the beginning of the chapter.

- Humans have an inherent interest in knowing about their own behavior as well as about the behavior of others. This is important for the formation and maintenance of social interactions. Humans have a special interest in behaviors that deviate from the norm in the form of psychological disorders. Learning is an adaptive mechanism that has permitted animals to survive across evolutionary time. It is a mechanism by which new behaviors are acquired and existing behaviors modified. Knowing about the mechanisms of learning is important for modifying one's behavior so that it is more adaptive. It also proved important for the modification of the behaviors of people suffering from psychological disorders in the form of psychotherapy.

- Aristotle believed that knowledge was acquired through experience and governed by a set of laws. These laws are the law of contiguity, which states that events that occur in close temporal or spatial proximity are more likely to be associated than events that are not; the law of similarity, which states that stimuli that are similar to each other are more likely to be associated than stimuli that are dissimilar; and the law of contrast, which states that the experience of one stimulus triggers the experience of its opposite. French philosopher and mathematician René Descartes believed that all knowledge derived from reason rather than experience and that mind and body were composed of two distinct substances. This philosophical position is known as dualism. He believed that only humans had a mind and that animals were mere automata driven by simple reflexes. Descartes originated what is known as the fluid mechanical theory in which he explained reflexes by the movement of animal spirits through hollow tubes in the body. Descartes believed that the reflexive behaviors of humans occurred in the same way but that distinctively human behaviors occurred because of a God-given soul.
- In a philosophical position called associationism, thoughts are derived from the association of sensory experiences. The ideas of associationism were espoused and promulgated by a group of philosophers known as the British associationists. These include Thomas Hobbes, who believed that the strength of association between stimuli depended on the frequency at which they were experienced together. John Locke believed the mind was a blank slate at birth and two categories of ideas existed: simple ideas, which were formed by the sensory experiences formed by objects in the environment, and complex ideas, which were formed by the association of simple ideas within the mind.
- Although Locke believed the mind to be a blank slate, he did believe that the mind had an innate capacity to perform certain actions on complex ideas, for example, to combine simple ideas into complex ideas, combining ideas in a way that they can be compared, and separating ideas from time and place in a process called abstraction. David Hume proposed three laws of association. These were the laws of resemblance, contiguity in time and space, and cause and effect. He believed the most powerful of these laws was that of cause and effect, which he believed permits us to predict the consequences of our actions. David Hartley incorporated physiology into a theory of associations. He believed that the medium for all sensations was the brain and that the stimulation of sensory organs triggered a chain reaction of vibrations from the sensory organs to their respective brain areas. He believed that simple ideas were created by traces of the vibrations left over from the repeated stimulation of sensory organs. He also believed that complex ideas were created when less intense vibrations, which he called vibranticules, linked simple ideas together.
- Neuroscientists believe that learning occurs in the brain through changes in the strength of synapses. This was anticipated by Santiago Ramón y Cajal and Sigmund Freud. A process by which this may occur was hypothesized by Donald Hebb in the late 1940s, which was immortalized by the quote "neurons that fire together wire together." Hebb's hypothesis was supported by studies conducted by Timothy Bliss and Terje Lømo in the 1970s. They found that repeatedly stimulating a neuron strengthens the connection between it and the neurons with which it is communicating. This became known as long-term potentiation. Today's neuroscientists make use of methods such as functional magnetic

resonance imaging, positron emission tomography, experimental brain lesions, inactivation, and optogenetics to answer questions about the brain areas involved in learning.
- Artificial intelligence refers to the ability of machines to mimic the human mind. There are two forms of AI, weak AI or artificial narrow intelligence and strong AI. Weak AI is not really weak, as it drives many useful and powerful applications such as those used in smartphones, social media, online shopping, and autonomous vehicles. Weak AI has become an integral part of our everyday lives. On the other hand, strong AI, which refers to machines that can think, feel, have self-awareness, and emotions like humans, is science fiction. Machine learning is a form of AI which can be subdivided into supervised learning, unsupervised learning, semi-supervised learning, and reinforcement learning. Chatbots are artificially intelligent computer programs able to simulate human conversations in natural language. They have many applications such as in medicine, psychology, customer service, education, and the learning of new languages.

Glossary

Abstracting A mental operation where the mind separates ideas from their specific time and place to form general concepts or categories.

Artificial intelligence (AI) A branch of computer science that aims to simulate the capabilities of the human mind.

British associationists Philosophers who believed that knowledge and thought arise from associations between experiences.

Chatbots AI-driven programs that simulate conversation and interact with users in a human-like manner.

Cognitive maps Mental representations of spatial environments used to navigate and recall locations.

Combining A mental operation where the mind joins simple ideas together to create complex ideas.

Complex ideas Ideas formed by combining or associating simple ideas within the mind.

Deep learning A subtype of machine learning that uses algorithms to analyze the way information is organized from the general to the more specific.

Dualism The idea that the mind and body are distinct, separate entities.

Explanatory fictions Skinner's term for hypothetical internal states (like "mind" or "will") invented to explain behavior but which are merely inferred from the behavior they claim to explain; circular pseudo-explanations.

Fluid-mechanical theory A historical theory proposing that bodily functions operate like hydraulic systems.

Latent learning Learning that occurs without immediate reinforcement and is later demonstrated when needed.

Law of contiguity The principle that ideas or events experienced close together in time or space become associated in the mind, so that experiencing one tends to recall the other.

Law of contrast The principle that experiencing one stimulus can evoke the thought of its opposite.

Law of similarity The principle that associations form between stimuli that resemble each other.

Machine learning A branch of AI that focuses on imitating human learning.

Rationalism A philosophical approach emphasizing reason as the primary source of knowledge.

Reinforcement learning Type of machine learning that does not make use of labeled data. Rather, the machine learns whether it has executed an action that permits it to get closer to a goal.

Relating A mental operation where the mind brings two ideas together for simultaneous consideration without merging them.

Semi-supervised learning Type of machine learning in which both labeled data and non-labeled data coexist.

Simple ideas Ideas directly derived from sensory experiences of objects; the basic building blocks of thought that cannot be broken down further.

Supervised learning Type of machine learning in which the specific steps to carry out a task specified by an algorithm, are compared to a set of instructions composed of labeled data.

Unsupervised learning Type of machine learning in which no labeled data exist to which the steps specified by the algorithm can be compared for accuracy.

2 Fundamental Concepts
Mapping the Terrain of Learning

Learning Objectives

1. Define learning and identify instances of behavioral changes that are not due to learning.
2. Recognize the significance of studying learning across domains like child rearing and therapy.
3. Distinguish between learning and performance, acknowledging latent behavior capacity.
4. Apply hypothetico-deductive reasoning in studying learning processes.
5. Critically evaluate the limitations of the general process approach to learning.
6. Understand the principles and applications of behaviorism, including radical behaviorism and behavior analysis.
7. Justify the use of animal models in learning research.

Dakota and Her Son Nash

IStock photo ID: Stock photo ID:1339162494

In a conversation with her new friend Avery, Dakota explained that she started worrying about her son Nash when, at the age of three, he could not put words together

DOI: 10.4324/9781003491828-3

in a sentence like other children his age. Not knowing Nash, Avery asked, "What else?" to which Dakota replied, "He does not play with other children. He just doesn't seem interested." With a hint of sadness and desperation in her voice, Dakota added, "He doesn't make eye contact when I try to engage him." This piqued the curiosity of Avery, who had been volunteering at a center for children with developmental problems. "I don't want to be intrusive," Avery said, "but does Nash engage in odd kinds of behaviors?" Dakota did find the question intrusive, but since she already opened up to Avery, she answered, "Well, when he wants a toy, he doesn't just point at it as other children do but screams until I give it to him." Dakota continued, "He also often lines up his toy cars on the floor and rearranges their order over and over again." Avery had seen children behave in similar ways at the center where she volunteers. She didn't know how much insight Dakota had into Nash's behavior. Being as sensitive as she could, Avery asked Dakota, "Do you know what might be going on?" "Of course," Dakota answered. "Nash was diagnosed with autism spectrum disorder when he was 18 months old." Wanting to show Avery that she knew what she was talking about, she said, "Autism spectrum disorder, or ASD, is a neurodevelopmental disorder characterized by deficits in communication and social interaction. Children with ASD may also engage in repetitive patterns of behaviors." After nodding in agreement, Avery asked Dakota, "Have you ever thought about applied behavior analysis?" "I have," answered Dakota.

2.1 The Basics

What Is Learning?

Learning refers to a process by which new information or behaviors are acquired through experiences with the environment and often involves practice and observation. Learning can also result in the modification (change) of existing behaviors. Take a moment to think about how much information, how many new behaviors, and how many times you have modified your existing behaviors through learning. What are you learning at this very moment? Consider also how much of what you have learned came from experiences with your environment. Keep this in mind as you read through the chapter.

Overt and Covert Behaviors

Learned behaviors can be **overt behaviors** or **covert behaviors**. Overt behaviors can readily be observed. Playing a sport, running for the bus, and taking notes in class are examples of overt behaviors. Overt behaviors can be problematic, as is sometimes the case of children with autism spectrum disorder (ASD) such as Nash in the opening vignette of this chapter. In contrast, covert behaviors are private events (i.e., they cannot be observed directly), which include paying attention, remembering, planning, and engaging in self-talk, such as when you use positive affirmations (positive statements you tell yourself) such as "I can do it" or "I am a really good person." Covert behaviors also include physiological functions such as heart rate, respiratory rate, and blood pressure.

Emotions

Both covert and overt behaviors can affect and be affected by emotions. This means that the relationship goes both ways. Emotions can influence behavior. For example, you might become anxious (emotion) and start thinking about how difficult an upcoming exam is going to be (covert behavior). Fear (emotion) might make you think that you are going to fail at a task (covert behavior). Feeling sad (emotion) might make you cry (overt behavior).

Behaviors can also trigger emotions. For instance, if you trip and fall in public (overt behavior), you might feel embarrassed (emotion). When you think about an upcoming oral presentation (covert behavior), you might feel anxious (emotion). Emotions involve physiological responses too. You might notice physical changes in your body that are connected to your emotions and thoughts, such as feeling your heart "beating out of your chest" or experiencing changes in heart rate and blood pressure while thinking about that presentation.

Behaviors can be overt or covert, both of which can be affected by and affect emotions. Top (left): It is obvious from their overt behavior that these people are learning to bake in a cooking class. Top (right): This man could be thinking about his future or remembering his weekend. It is difficult to tell because these are covert behaviors. Bottom (left): Physiological processes such as heart rate and blood pressure can only be accurately measured with specialized instrumentation. Bottom (right): An overt expression of emotions.

Source: (top left) IStock photo ID:1194472286 (bottom left) IStock photo Stock photo ID:1243547667 (top right IStock photo ID:1253877157 (bottom right) Stock photo ID:667103984.

Learning Occurs Through Experience With the Environment

To be considered to be due to learning, the acquisition or modification of a behavior must result from experience with the environment. The acquisition or modification of behaviors that are due to drugs, fatigue, illness, maturation, or instincts are not considered to result from learning. For example, a usually quiet person who becomes loud and belligerent after a few drinks does so because of the alcohol's effects, not because she has learned to do so, and a person may become less talkative due to fatigue or illness but not to learning.

Maturation refers to the process of growth and change throughout life. Although changes in behavior due to maturation are not considered to be due to learning, maturation can facilitate or set limits to what can be learned. For example, a child's brain may not be sufficiently developed to learn math or her musculature not sufficiently developed to learn to throw a ball.

Behaviors such as nest building, flying, and the caching of nuts by squirrels are thought to be due to instincts rather than learning. However, it is important to note that it is now accepted that in certain cases the acquisition or change of a behavior is due to a combination of **instincts**, which can be defined as innate fixed patterns of behaviors elicited by a particular environmental stimulus and learning. Instincts will further be discussed in Chapter 3.

Learning Occurs in Multiple Contexts

The first thing that might come to your mind when you think about learning is the way in which it occurs in context of formal education. This is understandable, as you have been exposed to it for most of your life. However, learning occurs in many other contexts. Think of all you learned before you went to school, including playing video games, singing songs, playing hopscotch, painting, drawing, and the new skills you are currently acquiring outside of school such as operating the cash register at a part-time job in a fast-food restaurant or those necessary for the practice of a new sport. In addition, getting along with others, controlling your emotions, and having a positive outlook on life is learned in the context of various life experiences. The point is that learning is an integral part of life.

The Learning Performance Distinction

Imagine watching a co-worker perform a task day after day without ever having to perform it yourself. Now imagine that one day your boss asks you to perform your co-worker's task after she has called in sick. While watching your work, your boss is amazed at how quickly you picked up the task without ever having been trained on it. This type of learning, which is acquired without conscious effort or intent and that remains unmanifested until the need for it arises is known as latent learning. That is, in this example, you never knew that you could perform your coworkers' job because you never previously had a chance to perform it. Hence, a distinction between learning and performance can be shown in examples of latent learning.

As explained in Chapter 1, Edward Tolman proposed that latent learning forms the basis of the acquisition of cognitive maps which can be used to later navigate through the environment (Tolman, 1948). For example, aimlessly strolling through the university campus shortly after you were admitted permitted you to quickly locate your classrooms on the first day of class. In another example, you may readily be able to drive to various destinations shortly after getting a new car because of the years you spent passively getting to the same places as a passenger. You will learn about the details of Tolman's findings and their significance in Chapter 22.

Critical Thinking Spot Check 2.1

1. Define learning.
2. List the conditions under which the acquisition or modification of an existing behavior is not due to learning.
3. Describe how learning occurs across multiple contexts.
4. Explain the learning performance distinction.

2.2 Why Study Learning?

Studying learning will help you understand how changes in one's environment can lead to changes in behavior. For example, if you have trouble studying because there are too many competing and more pleasurable activities at home, you might decide to study at the library.

Knowing How People and Animals Learn Is Useful

An understanding of basic learning principles can serve many other practical applications. Some of these are listed in the following.

- Helping parents find more effective ways to teach their children.
- Helping managers become more effective at teaching employees.
- Helping coaches become more effective at teaching athletes.
- Helping teachers become more effective at teaching students.
- Teaching your pets tricks.

Understanding of Psychological Disorders and Their Treatments

Psychological disorders are studied by researchers from different perspectives. From the biological perspective, or medical model, psychological disorders are partly caused by genetic predispositions and faulty or altered biological mechanisms, which can include imbalances in brain chemicals, damage to the brain, or degenerative processes within the brain (Barlow and Durand, 1995). In fact, it was found that a large percentage of the variability of ASD cases such as Nash in the opening vignette can be accounted for by genetic variability (Betancur, 2011; Chahrour et al., 2016) and that brain differences may account for some of the symptoms (Ha et al., 2015; Li et al., 2022). From the cognitive perspective, psychological disorders can be explained by faulty thought processes. For example, in depression, this may mean an exaggerated sense of hopelessness or a negative view of the self, world, and future (Dozois and Beck, 2011; Marchetti and Possel, 2022).

From the learning or behavioral perspective, certain psychological disorders can be explained by associations between environmental cues and events. This type of association is observed in posttraumatic stress disorder and phobias, in which exposure to environmental cues that have been associated with a terrifying event can trigger a fear response similar to the one experienced during the event itself (Mineka and Oehlberg, 2008). In drug addiction, people experience strong cravings for a drug when exposed to the environment in which a drug is often taken (Berridge and Robinson, 2016). In addition, the formation of inappropriate associations may account for some of the symptoms of schizophrenia (Jensen et al., 2008). It is also possible that Dakota in the opening vignette maintains Nash's screaming behavior when he wants a toy by rewarding him with it when he screams.

The therapeutic approach used in the treatment of psychological disorders is consistent with the perspective from which they are viewed. Within the medical model, treatment may include restoring chemical balance, electrical brain stimulation, or medication aimed at slowing down the impact of a degenerative process. Cognitive therapy can be aimed at helping people change their negative interpretation of the world, their future, and the opinion they have of themselves. This may also include challenging people's irrational beliefs (David et al., 2018).

From the learning perspective, the aim is to alter a person's behavioral responses to environmental stimuli. For example, a person who has a fear of dogs because they were once bitten by one has associated dogs with getting a bite and therefore now experiences intense fear in the presence of dogs or even when imagining or seeing a picture of a dog. In this case, the goal of one type of therapy, known as *behavioral therapy*, would be to get the person to associate dogs with a pleasant experience so that dogs no longer trigger a fear response (Wolpe, 1958). Another method would consist of repeatedly exposing a person to a feared stimulus until the fear induced by it is alleviated (Joseph and Gray, 2008).

Today many psychologists opt to treat psychological disorders by combining the cognitive and behavioral approaches by helping people modify their thoughts and behavioral patterns. This is known as **cognitive-behavioral therapy**, which is shown to be an effective method of treating various psychological disorders (Hofmann et al., 2012). Various therapy approaches are described in Module 3's application.

Critical Thinking Spot Check 2.2

1. Discuss the reasons the study of learning is important.
2. Explain how the learning perspective can help in understanding the development of psychological disorders.
3. Explain how the learning perspective is involved in the treatment of psychological disorders.

2.3 The Scientific Study of Learning?

Science in a Nutshell

Science can be defined as the application and pursuit of knowledge about the world following a systematic (step-by-step) methodology. The study of learning is a science because researchers engage in its study by following the scientific method. The scientific method involves what is known as the hypothetico-deductive method, illustrated in Figure 2.1. The first step in the hypothetico-deductive method consists of a researcher making informal observations on a topic of interest, which may present a practical problem. She then performs a literature search (i.e., reading through research journals) to find out whether others have made the same observations. She then generates a testable hypothesis, which is an

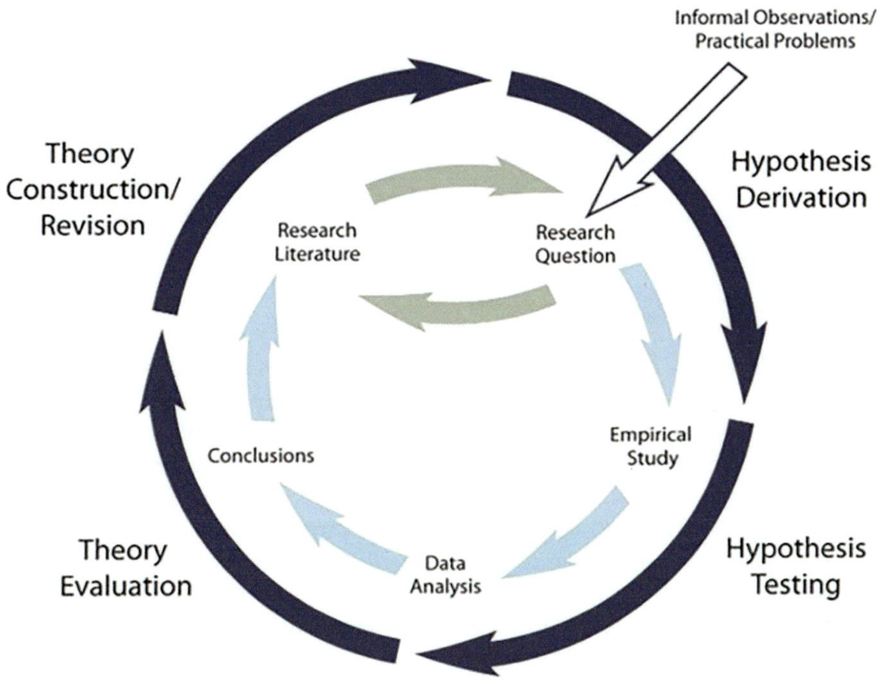

Figure 2.1 The hypothetico-deductive method.

educated guess or preliminary explanation for what is being observed. Next, she designs an empirical study (i.e., based on direct observations), in which she will conduct experiments that test her hypothesis. She will then analyze the data obtained from the experiment and conclude whether her hypothesis was supported. Her results may trigger an evaluation of existing theories or contribute to the generation of a new theory or to the revision of existing theories. Finally, more research questions may be generated by her findings, leading her to further search the literature and generate new research questions. Throughout this textbook, you will read about hypotheses and theories of learning that have been generated through this process.

Guiding Principles in Learning Research

In addition to following the scientific method, learning researchers abide by a set of philosophical guiding principles (Table 2.1). These include empiricism, determinism, the law of parsimony, and replicability.

Empiricism

Learning researchers based their interpretations of behavior on **empirical evidence**, which refers to knowledge acquired through observation or experimentation. Empiricism was discussed in Chapter 1, where the views of a group of philosophers known as the British associationists are contrasted to those of René Descartes, who as a rationalist believed that knowledge was innate.

Table 2.1 Guiding principles in learning research.

Empiricism	Knowledge is acquired through observation and experimentation.
Determinism	The antecedent(s) of any behavior can be found.
Parsimony	If several explanations for a phenomenon are available, choose the simplest.
Replicability	Other researchers arrive at the same results using similar methods.

Determinism

Determinism refers to the idea that every event in the universe is caused by previous events and that the relationship between these events is orderly and lawful. Learning researchers are for the most part proponents of determinism. They believe that no behavior occurs by chance and that through observation and experimentation, the antecedent (what came before a behavior) to any behavior or behavioral trait can be found to be determined by one's heredity, experiences, and environment. For example, your decision to get a higher education would have been determined by factors such as your genetic inheritance, your parents' educational level, their attitude towards education, your high school grades, the influence of teachers, and the neighborhood you grew up in. This occurred regardless of whether you were consciously aware of it or not.

Many people do not like the idea of determinism because they believe it absolves people of responsibility for their behaviors. They also find it difficult to accept that we might be helplessly at the mercy of genetic and environmental influences. Instead, they espouse the idea of **free will.** Proponents of free will believe that people are free to choose and that they are the cause of their behaviors. This means that they believe that in addition to heredity and the environment, a third force, call it the mind, soul, or self, must be involved in producing one's behavior. Free will is fundamental to most Western religions.

Determinism is also difficult to accept because it is so contrary to everyday experience. For example, it seems obvious to you that you willfully decide to study for your exams and that you are in control of the kind of music you choose to listen to, the people you choose to hang out with, and the foods you decide to eat. You also feel that you decide on more complex choices such as a program of study or the career path you wish to follow.

However, many studies and even personal experience show that behavior is determined by factors that do not include free will. For example, the study of consumer behavior has shown that people's decisions about the brands of the products they purchase are not guided by a rational and conscious assessment of their needs. Rather, people have little to no insight into the processes that lead them to decide (Bargh, 1994; Martin and Morich, 2011). One such process is mimicry, in which humans unconsciously and automatically copy the behavior of others around them. For example, in one study, participants were presented with two snack options, goldfish crackers and animal crackers, while seated in front of a confederate (an individual who secretly works for the experimenter) presented with the same choice of crackers. It was found that the participant ate more goldfish crackers when the confederate ate more goldfish crackers and ate more animal crackers when the confederate ate more animal crackers (Tanner et al., 2008).

Another unconscious process that was shown to influence behavior is stereotype activation, in which a stereotype attributed to a group of people is unconsciously activated. This was shown in a classic study in which participants were subliminally (below one's level of conscious awareness) exposed to words related to older people such as gray or bingo (Bargh, Chen and Burrows, 1996). The words were embedded in a task where the elements of sentences were presented in a scrambled manner and had to be descrambled by the participants to form a sensible sentence. It was found that when leaving the building in which they performed the task, participants exposed to the words related to older people walked more slowly than the participants not exposed to these words, showing that they behaved in a way that was consistent with an elderly stereotype.

Habits are probably the most effective in unconsciously controlling one's behavior. Habits are behaviors that have been gradually acquired by repetition through associating a stimulus and a response. I was often confronted with the power of habits in determining behavior when driving to one place when my goal was to get to another. For example, I have more than once found myself driving to Dawson College (where I teach) on a morning when I had a doctor's appointment, which required me to take a different route. The stimuli consisted of the stop signs, traffic lights, gas stations, or various other cues that became associated with the responses consisting of a series of right and left turns.

I like to explain such behavior as being due to being taken over by my "zombie system." Others may prefer the term "autopilot." Unfortunately, habits not only lead to such innocuous events but can also be part of psychological disorders in which an individual experiences a loss of control such as in compulsive gambling or substance abuse disorder. Habit learning, also known as stimulus-response (S-R) learning, is discussed in greater detail in Chapter 13.

The Law of Parsimony

The **law of parsimony,** also known as Occam's razor after the philosopher William of Occam (1285–1347), is the principle that when several explanations for a phenomenon are available, then the explanation must be the one that requires the fewest unverified assumptions or resorts to the fewest number of constructs unsupported by evidence (Elliott, 2015). For example, sightings of unidentified flying objects (UFOs), also known as unidentified areal phenomena (UAP), can mean that we are being visited by aliens from distant galaxies. However, to believe this, one must assume that aliens do indeed exist and that these aliens are able to travel astronomically long distances far beyond the ones we are able to travel, which would require that they possess technologies that are significantly more advanced than ours. In addition, one must assume that they were able to find our planet among billions of stars and that once they did, they were interested enough in it to come and visit. Alternatively, you might believe that UFOs or UAPs have earthly causes, including unmanned aerial vehicles, balloons, natural atmospheric phenomena, and optical illusions. Which of these two explanations is more parsimonious?

When applied to consciousness or the behavior of animals, the law of parsimony is embodied in **Morgan's canon,** named after ethologist and psychologist Conwy Lloyd Morgan (1852–1936), which states that the behavior of animals should not be interpreted as being a result of the operations of higher mental faculties if it can be interpreted as being a result of some other faculty lower on the psychological scale.

Replicability

As in all natural sciences, the results of experiments conducted by learning researchers are written up in articles published in scientific journals. One of the main characteristics of the articles submitted to these journals is that they are subjected to **peer review**, which consists of the evaluation of the quality of the research by researchers in the same field or "peers." For an article to be published in a scientific journal, the methods used by the researcher to investigate a research question must be clear and precise. Such clarity and precision of the methods are necessary for other researchers interested in verifying the published results by conducting their own experiments. **Replicability** means that other researchers arrived at the same results as the original experiment using the same or similar methodology. Replicability is an important concept in science because replicable results increase the probability that they can be relied upon to guide future research and be applied to real-world problems. A lack of replicability may raise questions such as the possibility that the original results were due to poor methodology, fraud, error, and questionable research practices in general (Peels, 2019).

The General Process Approach to Learning

The **general process approach** to learning refers to the supposition that the same principles of learning apply to all animals in a wide variety of situations. The aim of the general process approach is to derive general laws of learning from experimentation. To the proponents of this approach, having generalized laws of learning placed the study of learning on the same footing as sciences such as physics or chemistry, which state that laws that are universally applicable such as Newton's laws of motion or Lavoisier's law of conservation of mass.

Biological Constraints

The general process approach to learning ran into significant challenges when researchers realized that some of the general laws that were believed to govern the way in which learning takes place do not hold for all species in all circumstances. For example, it was found that **biological constraints** might make it difficult for animals to perform behaviors that are too far removed from the ones they perform in their natural environment. For example, gorillas and chimps can be taught the gestures used in sign language, but they cannot be taught to speak because they have not evolved the necessary vocal anatomy. However, as you know, parrots can be taught to produce speech sounds. This is because they have evolved the necessary vocal pathways (Jarvis, 2004).

Instinctual Drift

Instinctual drift occurs when animals trained to perform a task revert to instinctual behaviors. Several examples of instinctual drift were provided by psychologists Keller and Mariam Breland (1961) while training animals to perform in television commercials, shows, and tourist attractions. In one instance, they tried to train a racoon to deposit coins in a metal container, with the goal of later training it to deposit coins in a piggy bank. However, they gave up in trying to do so because the racoon would pick up the coins and incessantly rub them together and dip them into the container without releasing them. Where did this behavior come from? In nature, racoons wash their food by rubbing it with their paws and dunking it in a water source. Other challenges to the general process approach are discussed in detail in Chapter 7.

What in the Brain?

Neurons: The basic functional units of the nervous system

A deeper understanding of learning can be achieved by knowing about its neurobiological basis. The basic functional units of the nervous system, which includes the brain, spinal cord, and the nerves that control the muscles and organs of the body, are cells known as neurons. A prototypical neuron is shown in Figure 2.2a.

Like other types of cells, neurons have a cell body, also known as soma, which contains the nucleus. The nucleus contains deoxyribonucleic acid (DNA), which codes for proteins assembled by molecular machinery that resides outside the nucleus. Neurons can be differentiated from other types of cells by the projections from the cell body called neurites. There are two types of neurites: dendrites and axons. Neurons typically have many dendrites and a single axon. Dendrites receive messages from other neurons.

The axon transmits messages to other neurons or other types of cells such as muscle cells and the cells of organs and glands in the form of electrochemical currents called action potentials. The axon is covered by a fatty tissue called the myelin sheet, which improves the conductivity of the current. Action potentials are electrochemical because they are generated by the exchange of the ions (sodium and potassium) in and out of the neuron through specialized channels. Action potentials travel down the axon, changing the voltage of the neuron as they go along until they reach the axon terminals. This change in voltage in the neuron is known as depolarization, which means that the inside of the neuron becomes electrically less negative relative to the outside.

When action potentials arrive in the axon terminals, the change in voltage triggers the release of a chemical called neurotransmitter, stored in what are called synaptic vesicles, onto receptors located on the dendrites of the receiving neuron (Figure 2.2b[inset]). The point at which this occurs is called a synapse, and the tiny gap (nanometers wide) into which the neurotransmitter is released is known as the synaptic cleft.

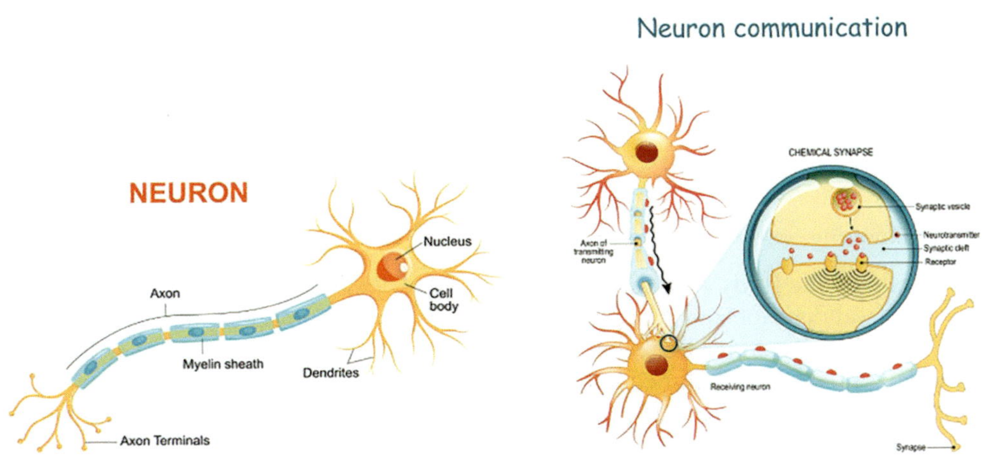

Figure 2.2 a) A prototypical neuron. b) The chemical synapse.

([a] Stock illustration ID:1153647071, [b] Stock illustration ID:1163216973).

There are many types of neurotransmitters which are associated with many different functions. Each binds to its own type of receptor in "lock-and key" fashion. Neurotransmitters can be subdivided into two broad types, excitatory and inhibitory, which are synthesized, stored, and released by different neurons. The release of an excitatory neurotransmitter on the receptors of the receiving neuron will cause that neuron to depolarize; this is known as an excitatory post-synaptic potential (EPSP). An action potential will be generated only if a certain threshold of depolarization occurs. However, the binding of an inhibitory neurotransmitter will cause the inside of the neuron to become relatively more negative on the inside than on the outside. This is known as an inhibitory post-synaptic potential (IPSP), which will limit that neuron's ability to trigger action potentials by reducing the probabilities that the threshold will be reached.

The brain contains about 86 billion neurons (Herculano-Houzel, 2012; Gaskin, 2020). Each neuron can form up to 10,000 connections. A receiving neuron can receive a combination of both excitatory and inhibitory messages. Whether it will fire an action potential depends on the summation of all excitatory and inhibitory messages it receives from transmitting neurons. If the sum is positive and depolarization reaches the threshold, an action potential will be generated. However, an action potential will not be generated if the sum does not reach the threshold.

Learning is believed to occur when the connections between neurons (or synapses) are strengthened through repeated stimulation in a process known as long-term potentiation (LTP). This means that the more a stimulating neuron activates a receiving neuron, the easier it becomes for that stimulating neuron to activate the receiving neuron (Lømo, 2003; Malenka, 2003). This is how a new motor skill, which may be difficult at first, becomes better with practice (Rioult-Pedotti et al., 1998; Kida and Mitsushima, 2018).

Are You Thinking Critically?

1. Why is it important to know about the brain to have a better understanding of learning?
2. Describe how neurons communicate with each other.
3. What is LTP? Why is it thought to be important for learning?

Critical Thinking Spot Check 2.3

1. Explain why the study of learning is a scientific endeavor.
2. Imagine and describe an experiment that would demonstrate the importance of learning in the acquisition of a new behavior or in the modification of an existing behavior by following the hypothetico-deductive method.
3. Describe the general process approach and explain why it is inadequate to explain learning across different species.
4. Explain the concepts of instinctual drift and biological constraints and their influences on learning.

2.4 Theories of Learning

There Are Several Theories of Learning

Several theories of learning exist, which include behaviorism, cognitivism, and constructionism. Most of the theories you will learn about in this textbook are grounded in behaviorism (explained subsequently). However, a full account of learning is impossible without knowing about other perspectives that are considered foundational. Hence, knowing about them may prove useful should you decide to pursue your studies of learning beyond the course you are currently taking. Therefore, they are summarized in the following sections as well as in Table 2.2.

Behaviorism

Behaviorism is the learning perspective in which all behaviors can be explained by experiences with the environment. You have already been introduced to some of the ideas of behaviorism in Chapter 1. Remember that behaviorists believe that behavior can be explained without reference to mental constructs such as will, emotions, and motivation. Major concepts in behaviorism include **reinforcement, punishment**, and **stimulus control.** Remember also that reinforcement refers to the phenomenon by which a behavior that is followed by an *appetitive stimulus* (something pleasant) is likely to be repeated, whereas punishment refers to the phenomenon by which a behavior that is followed by an *aversive stimulus* (something unpleasant) is not likely to be repeated. Stimulus control refers to the phenomenon by which the environmental stimuli present when a behavior is followed by a consequence come to control the occurrence of the behavior. For example, if your boss lets you leave work early only when she appears to be in a good mood, you are likely to ask her to leave early only when she appears to be in a good mood but not when she appears to be in a bad mood. Skinner's radical behaviorism led to the development of two other subfields of behaviorism. These are **experimental behavior analysis (EBA)** and **applied behavior analysis (ABA)**, both of which are discussed subsequently.

Table 2.2 Foundational theories of learning.

Theory	*Definition*	*Concepts*	*Major Figures*
Behaviorism	Learning can be explained by experiences with the environment.	Reinforcement, punishment, stimulus control.	Ivan Pavlov John Watson B.F. Skinner
Cognitivism	Learning occurs through mental operations.	Information processing, perceptual processing, attention, beliefs, problem solving, decision-making, and the retrieval of stored memories.	Ulrich Neisser Georges Miller Noam Chomsky
Constructivism	Learning is the construction of meaning from experiences.	Reality depends on the experiences and interactions that an individual has had with the world.	Jean Piaget Lev Vygotsky

Experimental Behavior Analysis

Experimental behavior analysis focuses on studying and discovering the principles that influence behavior. In EBA, researchers observe behavior and seek to explain it by analyzing the data obtained through experimentation. The results of these experiments permit them to predict the probability of a behavior occurring given a certain set of circumstances. Once the predictive value of these circumstances has been established, they can then be used to control behavior.

Applied Behavioral Analysis

In applied behavior analysis, the principles of learning and behavior uncovered in EBA are used to solve real-world problems (Virues-Ortega et al., 2014). Applied behavior analysis is mostly known for the treatment of children with ASD, which, as you read about in the opening vignette, is characterized by problems with communication, social interactions, and repetitive behaviors (Roane, Fisher and Carr, 2016; Yu et al., 2020). However, ABA is also applied to a range of other fields. As you will read in the applications section of this module, ABA is applied in organizational behavior in which problems related to productivity, occupational injuries, and skills acquisition are addressed (Wilder, Austin and Casella, 2009). It is also used for the improvement of sports performance (Luiselli and Reed, 2015), the prevention of medical problems (Allen and Hine, 2015), the treatment of problem gambling (Hoon et al., 2008), and the treatment of drug addiction (Silverman et al., 2011). Regardless of the field, the role of behavior analysts is to understand how behavior is under the control of environmental stimuli so that they can design interventions to increase the probability of desirable behaviors and decrease the probability of undesirable behaviors. We discuss ABA in several "Focus On" boxes throughout the textbook.

Cognitivism

In the 1950s, the idea that learning consisted of the direct interaction between stimuli and responses without postulating the influence of mental constructs as proposed by behaviorists was challenged by the proponents of a perspective which became known as **cognitivism** (Clark, 2018; Khan, Jamil and Sethi, 2020). The proponents of cognitivism were influenced by the rise of computer science and applied the information processing model of computers to the brain. That is, they believed that the brain processed information much in the way of computers by encoding, storing, and retrieving information. They believed that learning did not occur through the direct interaction between stimuli and responses but that mental operations such as information processing, perceptual processing, attention, beliefs, problem solving, decision-making, and the retrieval of stored memories intervened between them. The psychologists who played a central role in the rise of cognitivism include Ulrich Neisser (1928–2012), who coined the term cognitive psychology in the first textbook on cognitivism (Olivetti Belardinelli, 2012); Georges Miller (1920–2012), who studied the limits in our abilities to process information (1956); and Noam Chomsky, who wrote a rebuttal to one of Skinner's books entitled "Verbal Behavior" (Skinner, 1957), in which he explains his behaviorist perspective on language learning (1959).

Constructivism

In a branch of cognitivism known as **constructivism**, people build (construct) their understanding of the world on what they already know (Naylor and Keogh, 1999). They believe learning to be the construction of meaning from experiences. Hence, contrary to both behaviorism and cognitivism, which believe that the acquisition of knowledge is grounded in the individual's external reality, constructivists believe that individuals interpret incoming information to construct their own reality. To the constructivists, this explains why different individuals exposed to the same reality can interpret that reality in different ways. It follows that to constructivists, there is no objective reality but that reality depends on the experiences and interactions that an individual has had with the world.

One of the strongest influences of constructivism was psychologist Jean Piaget (1896–1980), who believed that children were active participants in their own cognitive development. To Piaget, children learn about the world by forming representations of objects and events in the world that surrounds them, called schemas. According to Piaget, schemas are expanded and created by the processes of *assimilation* and *accommodation* (Beilin and Fireman, 1999). For example, a schema for dogs is formed once a child has observed its general characteristics. This "dog schema" can then be used in the future to identify animals with similar characteristics as dogs. Each time an animal that fits the general characteristics of a dog is encountered, it is assimilated into the schema, even if that specific breed of dog was never encountered, thus expanding the "dog schema." However, if during a car trip the child points to cows in a field and utters "dog," one of the parents may correct the child by saying, "No, those are cows." In this case, Piaget believed that the child experiences a state of *disequilibrium* and will accommodate by creating a new schema that includes animals that share some of the characteristics of dogs but that differ on others, called "cows." Another psychologist associated with constructivism is Lev Vygotsky (1896–1943), who believed that children learned by interacting with more experienced members of society in what he called the *zone of proximal development* (Cong-Lem, 2022).

Critical Thinking Spot Check 2.4

1. Name and describe the different forms of behaviorism.
2. Distinguish experimental behavior analysis and applied behavior analysis.
3. Imagine and describe a situation in which you have learned something. Explain your learning from the behavioral, cognitivist, and constructivist perspective.

2.5 Animal Models in Learning Research

What Is an Animal Model?

Throughout this textbook you will read about many studies involving animals. In reaction to this, students often ask about the relevance of studying animals when we are really trying to understand human behavior. The answer to this is that animals are used as models for human behavior. In research, a **model** can be defined as a simplification of reality so that a particular phenomenon can be isolated, studied, and better understood. Models exist in every field of science. In learning research, animal models are used to study the basic mechanisms of behavior in simpler living systems to draw generalizations to human behavior (Moore, 2004).

Justifications and Advantages of Using Animal Models

The use of animal models can be justified by several homologies that exist between humans and animals. That is, similar behaviors found in animals and humans can to some degree be accounted for by a similar genetic makeup that has been transmitted through evolution, which, in turn, partly accounts for similar brain structures (Dunkelberger, Serway and Steven de Belle, 2008).

Another advantage of using animal models in the study of basic learning mechanisms is that they are uncomplicated by the variety of factors that differentiate humans from one another such as income, educational level, personality characteristics, and cultural differences. In contrast, animal studies can be conducted with genetically similar animals raised in controlled laboratory environments, which allows researchers to minimize confounding variables and more clearly identify cause-and-effect relationships in learning mechanisms. Studies using animal models can also be done relatively cheaply, often involving the need for fewer resources.

Animal models can also be used to answer questions about behavior that cannot be answered by conducting experiments on humans because of the invasiveness of the procedures involved. As you will read in many of the "What in the Brain?" boxes through this textbook, many animal models developed by learning researchers are used to investigate the role played by various brain areas in specific types of learning. In these studies animals can be subjected to experimental brain damage after which their performance on tasks that test a certain type of learning is assessed. The results of such studies are extremely useful in understanding the cognitive impairments observed in people who suffer from the effects of a stroke, Alzheimer's disease, Parkinson's, schizophrenia, attention deficit and hyperactivity disorder (ADHD), autism spectrum disorder (ASD), and many others. Keep in mind, however, that researchers using animal models are required to abide by a strict code of ethics (Smith, 1991; Jackson, 2013; Mandal and Parija, 2013).

Critical Thinking Spot Check 2.5

1. Explain what animal models are and why they are used.
2. How can learning researchers justify the use of animal models?

Chapter Summary

Each of the following bullet points aligns with the learning objectives outlined at the beginning of the chapter.

- Learning refers to a process by which the acquisition of new behaviors or the modification of existing behaviors occurs through experience with the environment. Behaviors that are readily observable are referred to as overt, and behaviors that are not readily observable are referred to as covert. Both overt and covert behaviors can influence and be influenced by emotions. To be considered to be due to learning, the acquisition or change of behavior must not be due to drugs, fatigue, maturation, illness, or instincts.
- The study of learning is important to the understanding in many domains, which include child rearing, management, coaching, teaching, and study skills. The study of learning is also important to the understanding of certain psychological disorders and their treatments, which includes cognitive-behavioral therapy.
- It is important to distinguish between learning and performance. That is, it is possible that learning does not result in behaviors that reflect this learning. This is because the capacity to perform a behavior may remain latent until it is required.

- Researchers who study learning follow the scientific method, which includes hypothetico-deductive reasoning. This means that they make observations on a topic of interest, generate hypotheses based on those observations, and test their hypotheses by conducting experiments. They also abide by the principles of empiricism, determinism, parsimony, and replicability.
- The general process approach refers to the idea that a set of general principles can be applied to how all animals learn in a wide variety of situations. However, this approach is widely rejected, as learning is limited by both the biological constraints of various species and instinctual drift, which refers to the tendency of animals to revert to instinctual behaviors. Different theories of learning exist. These include behaviorism, which can be subdivided in methodological behaviorism, analytical behaviorism, and radical behaviorism. Radical behaviorism forms the basis for behavior analysis, which includes applied behavior analysis and experimental behavior analysis.
- Experimental behavior analysts believe that knowledge comes from observation and experimentation. This is known as empiricism. They also believe that every behavior has a cause and that behavior is lawful. This is known as determinism. Experimental analysts also believe in the law of parsimony, which states that when several explanations for a phenomenon are available, then the simplest of the explanations must be chosen. This is also known as Occam's razor, which, when applied to the behavior of animals, is known as Morgan's canon. Experimental behavior analysts also value the replicability findings and that the studies from which findings are obtained are subjected to peer review. Applied behavior analysis is the field that uses behavioral principles uncovered by experimental behavior analysts to solve real-world problems such as the treatment of children suffering from autism spectrum disorder. Cognitivism is a field in which researchers believe that learning occurs through mental operations such as information processing, perceptual processing, attention, beliefs, problem solving, and the retrieval of stored memories. Constructivism is the field in which researchers believe that people build their understanding of the world on what they already know and that children are active participants in their own learning.
- An animal model is a simplified representation of reality used in research to isolate and study specific phenomena, such as behavior, to gain a better understanding. Animals serve as models for human behavior, with studies conducted on them allowing researchers to draw generalizations to human behavior. Justifications for using animal models include similarities in genetic makeup and brain structures between humans and animals, as well as the ability to control variables that differ among humans, such as income and cultural differences. Additionally, animal studies are often more cost effective and allow for investigations into behaviors that cannot be studied invasively in humans. These studies are crucial for understanding cognitive impairments observed in various neurological disorders. However, researchers using animal models must adhere to strict ethical guidelines.

Glossary

Applied behavior analysis (ABA) The practical application of behavioral principles to improve social and learning outcomes.

Behaviorism A psychological approach focusing on observable behaviors and their relationship to environmental stimuli.

Biological constraints Limitations in learning due to inherited traits or evolutionary influences.

Cognitivism A psychological perspective focusing on mental processes such as thinking, memory, and problem-solving.

Constructivism A learning theory emphasizing active engagement and knowledge construction through experience.
Covert behaviors Internal mental processes, such as thoughts and emotions, that are not directly observable.
Determinism The philosophical belief that all events, including human actions, are determined by prior causes.
Empirical evidence Information or data obtained through direct observation, measurement, or experimentation, rather than through theory, opinion, or speculation.
Experimental behavior analysis (EBA) A scientific approach studying behavior under controlled experimental conditions.
Free will The ability to make choices independent of external or predetermined influences.
General process approach to learning The idea that learning mechanisms are universal across species and situations.
Instinctual drift The tendency for learned behaviors to revert to innate behaviors over time.
Latent learning Learning that occurs without immediate demonstration but is revealed when needed.
Law of parsimony The principle stating that the simplest explanation is often the best.
Learning A process by which new information or behaviors are acquired through experiences with the environment and often involves practice and observation.
Model A representation or framework used to understand or predict behavior and processes.
Morgan's canon A rule in psychology emphasizing that animal behavior should not be explained using complex cognitive processes if simpler explanations suffice.
Overt behaviors Observable actions or responses that can be measured externally.
Peer review Evaluation of the quality of research by researchers in the same field or "peers."
Punishment A stimulus that decreases the likelihood of a behavior being repeated.
Reinforcement A stimulus that increases the likelihood of a behavior being repeated.
Replicability The ability to reproduce scientific findings under similar conditions to confirm reliability.
Stimulus control The process by which behavior is influenced by environmental cues.

Module Summary

In this module, you have examined the essential elements of behavior and learning. You began by understanding that studying behavior is a vital human pursuit necessary for fostering social interactions and comprehending psychological disorders. You learned how learning enables the acquisition of new behaviors and the modification of existing ones, with Aristotle's laws of association illustrating that knowledge is derived from experience. Next, you explored the philosophical viewpoints that have influenced psychological research on learning. René Descartes's rationalism introduced the notion that knowledge is inherent and the reflex concept. This contrasts with empiricism, which asserts that knowledge is acquired through sensory experiences, a perspective British associationists support.

You gained insight into behavior analysis solely through observation, without engaging the mind. You also studied the origins and ongoing development of experiments to uncover the neurobiological foundations of learning, which led to discussions about artificial intelligence and computer-based learning. You learned to define learning and differentiate between overt and covert behaviors.

Another key focus was applying the scientific method in learning research. You explored concepts such as empiricism, determinism, parsimony, and replicability, gaining an understanding of why the general process approach to learning is frequently dismissed. Numerous learning theories were introduced, including behaviorism, which features experimental and applied behavior analysis, as well as various forms of cognitivism. The discussion concluded with a review of animal models in learning research, highlighting their justifications and benefits. Together, these chapters have laid a strong foundation for comprehending the mechanisms and theories underlying behavior and learning, providing vital insights for further investigation in the field.

Module 1

Application

The Foundations of Learning in Education

Structured Learning Versus Experiential Learning

You may be surprised to learn that the philosophical debate between rationalism and empiricism explored in this module remains vibrant in education (Bailey et al., 2013). A relevant example of this debate is the differing preference for structured versus experiential learning. Structured learning embodies a rationalist approach, emphasizing the importance of logical reasoning and abstract thinking. In contrast, experiential learning, characterized by hands-on activities and real-world applications, aligns with the empiricist perspective. The following examples will assist you in differentiating between these two educational methods.

Structured Learning (Rationalism)

A psychology professor skilled in structured learning, teaching students about the principles of memory, may ask the students to consider memory as a vast filing system and question what might occur if they retrieved the wrong file. This illustrates an abstract concept, encouraging students to envision and contemplate ideas or objects that are not physically present. The professor may also prompt students to reflect on the consequences of losing their long-term memory while retaining a functioning short-term memory, which will require students to logically analyze a hypothetical situation.

Experiential Learning (Empiricism)

A different professor, who passionately advocates for experiential learning, would engage students in this topic in a dramatically different manner. For example, she might inspire half of the students to actively absorb a list of words by rehearsing them silently while encouraging the other half to vocalize their rehearsal, creating a dynamic and interactive classroom experience. She would then compare the results by testing all the students on their memory of the word list, providing empirical evidence of auditory encoding.

She may also ask students to interview family members about significant personal life events and to analyze how they differ in their ability to recall this information compared to their ability to remember facts about the world, demonstrating real-world differences in people's memory retention for different types of memories. Additionally, she may ask

DOI: 10.4324/9781003491828-4

students to compare the process of memorizing a list of grocery items through repetition versus creating a story that connects the items.

The Behavioral Approach (Behaviorism)

Adopting a behavioral approach can dramatically enhance student outcomes. By effectively shaping students' behaviors through observable actions and their responses to external stimuli, we can create an environment where positive behaviors thrive (Leung and Shek, 2020). Educators must harness the power of positive reinforcement and strategically implement consequences for undesired behaviors. This approach not only encourages students to embrace actions that lead to success but also helps them understand the impact of their choices, fostering a more conducive learning atmosphere.

For example, a professor skilled in this method might allow students to earn points for accurately recalling elements from the previous week's lesson. This exemplifies positive reinforcement and fosters a culture of studying and strategic thinking, motivating students to develop better study habits aimed at maximizing their points. Furthermore, the professor can introduce gamification into the learning process, allowing students to compete in teams in memory challenges. This collaborative aspect not only makes learning engaging but also motivates them to improve, showcasing how the behaviorist approach can lead to more effective and interactive educational experiences.

The Cognitive Approach (Cognitivism)

The cognitive learning approach is a powerful method that revolutionizes how we understand and engage with information. By emphasizing the critical role of mental activities like attention, memory, and problem-solving, this approach profoundly enhances the learning experience (Yilmaz, 2011). It encourages students to dive deep into their thought processes, actively engaging with new knowledge in a way that connects it to what they already know. This is far more effective than mere memorization; it's a pathway to true understanding and lasting knowledge. Embracing cognitive learning empowers students to take charge of their education, fostering a generation of critical thinkers and problem solvers who are equipped for the challenges of tomorrow.

For example, a professor with such an inclination might employ an elaborative encoding exercise wherein they connect new memory concepts to personal experiences. She may also use peer teaching, allowing students to form groups and practice teaching memory concepts to one another, thereby deepening the level at which they process the information. Additionally, she may encourage problem-solving strategies that require students to analyze the effectiveness of their study methods and make necessary adjustments if those methods prove ineffective.

A Holistic Approach

An educator advocating a more holistic approach may integrate elements from the previously mentioned methods to teach her students. For instance, she might have students study memory models and abstract concepts (structured learning/rationalism), encourage them to test memory concepts in real-life situations (experiential/empiricism), establish a points system for retaining learned concepts (behaviorist approach), and encourage them to relate memory concepts to their personal life experiences (cognitive approach).

Module 2

Innate Behaviors and Nonassociative Learning

Introduction

Welcome to this captivating module, where we unravel the intricate interplay between innate behaviors, learning principles, and adaptive responses to environmental stimuli. Understanding the complexities of learning requires us to appreciate the foundational role of innate (inborn) responses, which are automatic reactions programmed within organisms.

Our exploration begins in Chapter 3, where we delve deep into innate behaviors. These behaviors, categorized into reflexive and instinctual responses, have been fundamental to species' survival throughout evolution. Reflexes, such as withdrawing your hand from a hot surface, demonstrate immediate and automatic responses crucial for avoiding harm. On the other hand, instincts drive species-specific behaviors, shaping how animals interact with their environments. We will uncover the nuances of these innate responses, their variations, and how they are modifiable through learning and environmental influences.

In Chapter 4, we focus on fundamental forms of learning shaped by repeated exposure to stimuli. We will explore how animals and humans adapt their responses based on the predictive value or meaningfulness of stimuli encountered. We will thoroughly examine simple forms of learning, such as habituation, where responses decrease with repeated non-meaningful stimuli, and sensitization, where responses intensify with significant stimuli. We will also discuss how these basic learning processes contribute to adaptive behaviors essential for survival.

Moreover, we will reflect on the delicate balance between adaptive responses and the role of innate behaviors in shaping behavioral flexibility. By understanding how innate responses can be modified through learning, we will gain insights into the dynamic nature of behavior and the capacity of organisms to adapt effectively to changing environments.

By the end of this module you will have gained a comprehensive understanding of innate behaviors, various forms of learning, and their implications for adaptive behaviors. This knowledge will broaden your insights into human and animal behavior and provide a framework for understanding the intricate mechanisms governing behavioral responses in diverse environments.

DOI: 10.4324/9781003491828-5

3 Unveiling Nature's Blueprint for Learning

Exploring Innate Behaviors

Learning Objectives

- Understand the distinction between innate behaviors, reflexes, and instincts.
- Describe the physiological basis of reflex arcs and specific innate responses such as taxis, kinesis, and primitive reflexes.
- Explain the concept of instincts and modal action patterns.
- Evaluate the impact and significance of supernormal stimuli and recognize their application in various industries.
- Compare and contrast the ethological and behavior systems approaches in understanding animal behavior.

Boyang and Luis Discuss Innate Behaviors

Source: IStock photo 1371775427

DOI: 10.4324/9781003491828-6

On a warm summer night, Boyang and Luis relaxed on the porch of Boyang's parents' country house. Fascinated by insects, Boyang was transfixed by the moths attracted to a light hanging from the roof. Luis, lying on a long chair, trying to identify the constellations of stars, noticed Boyang's enthrallment with the moths. "What are you doing?" he asked. "What do you mean?" Boyang replied. "You keep staring at those moths," Luis answered. Boyang jumped on the occasion to show off what he had just learned in his learning class. "Positive phototaxis," he said. "They can't help it," he added. "It's innate behavior." "I see," said Luis. Boyang explained that other insects display negative phototaxis when escaping light. "Why do they do this?" asked Luis, to which Boyang answered, "Several hypotheses have been put forward. One is that moths use stars and moonlight for orientation. They fly at a straight angle to them to maintain a straight flight path. However, when the light source is too close, they fly right up into it," he continued. "So, it's a reflex," replied Luis. Wanting to show that he had also learned something new, Luis continued, "In my developmental psychology class, we learned that humans are born with many reflexes; some disappear, and others persist throughout life." "I know that," said Boyang, "and we also have many instincts," he continued. Luis replied, "You mean stereotyped and rigid patterns of behavior elicited by specific stimuli?" "I guess," replied Boyang. "No . . . no . . . no," said Luis, "instincts can explain many of the behaviors of animals, but when it comes to humans, our behaviors are much too complex to be explained by instincts." "Is that so?" replied Boyang. "Yep! And even in animals, instincts can be shaped by learning and environmental factors," replied Luis.

3.1 What Are Innate Behaviors?

The bulk of this textbook focuses on learned behaviors, which are acquired through interactions with the environment. However, learning theorists distinguish learned behaviors from **innate behaviors**, which are genetically programmed and occur automatically and stereotypically (i.e., always in the same way) in response to specific stimuli. Researchers believe innate behaviors can be shaped and modified by interactions with the environment and learning. This chapter will explore the two types of innate behaviors: reflexes and instincts.

Reflexes

Reflexes are simple innate responses requiring only a connection between a sense organ and the muscles needed to perform the response. Reflexes can explain many simple behaviors animals perform, but they can also be shaped by learning and the environment in ways that permit animals to adapt to particular situations. In addition, the same reflex may be adaptive in one situation but maladaptive in another (Axel Gorostiza, Colomb and Brembs, 2015). For example, a reflex that causes an animal to be highly sensitive to movement in its environment could be adaptive when the animal seeks food, as it helps the animal quickly detect and capture prey. However, the same reflex could be maladaptive when the animal is looking for a mate because it might cause it to misinterpret the movements of potential mates as threats, leading to missed mating opportunities or unnecessary aggressive behavior.

Some Simple Reflexes

We will next explore some of the simplest reflexes, known as taxis and kinesis, which can be observed in insects.

Taxis

Taxis refers to an active directional response to a stimulus. It can either be positive or negative. It is positive when the movement is directed towards a stimulus and negative when it is away from a stimulus. For example, honeybees, fruit flies, moths, and beetles show *positive phototaxis* (Figure 3.1a) when attracted to light (Yamaguchi and Heisenberg, 2011). In contrast, earthworms and some types of salamanders display *negative phototaxis* (Figure 3.1b) in that they are repelled by light and move in a direction away from light (Cecala, Noggle and Burns, 2017). Remember that this is precisely what Boyang explained to his friend Luis in the chapter's opening vignette. Several other types of taxis exist (Gardiner and Atema, 2007). These include *chemotaxis*, which refers to movement towards or away from a chemical stimulus, and *thigmotaxis*, which refers to the tendency of certain animals to stay near or away from the edges of fields.

Kinesis

Kinesis is similar to taxis except that the organism's response to the stimulus is non-directional. There are two types of kinesis: *orthokinesis* and *klinokinesis*. In *orthokinesis*, the intensity of a stimulus influences the speed of an organism's movements. The more uncomfortable the stimulus, the greater the speed of movement. When a comfortable environment has been reached, the movement speed is reduced. For example, cockroaches display a type of orthokinesis known as *negative photokinesis* (Figure 3.1c), which causes them to run

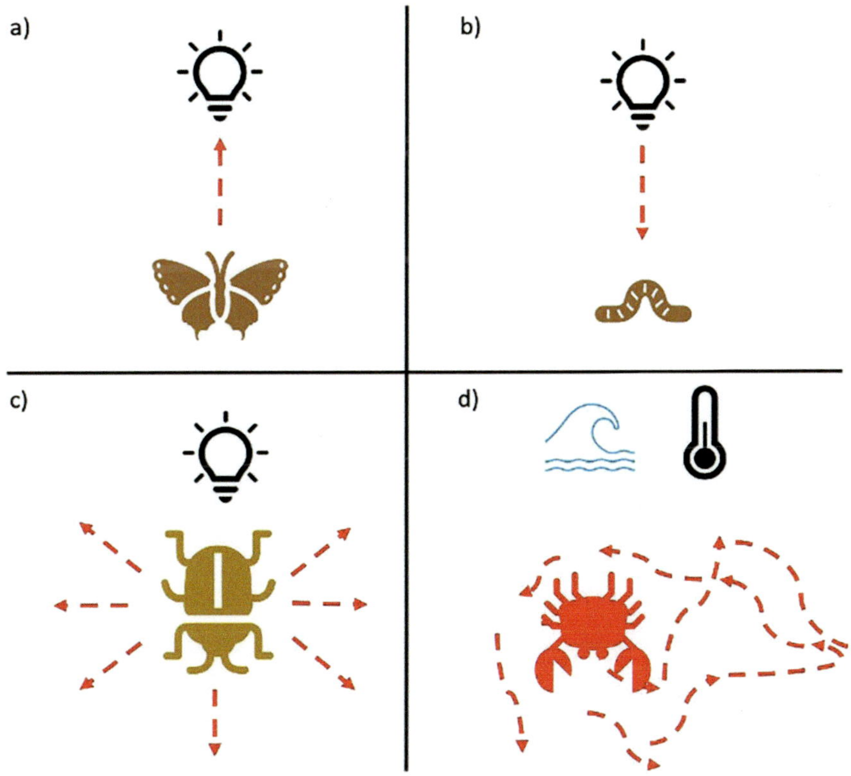

Figure 3.1 a) Positive phototaxis. b) Negative phototaxis. c) Negative photokinesis. d) Negative thermokinesis.

in all directions when a light is turned on. In *klinokinesis*, stimulus intensity affects the rate at which organisms execute random turns to escape or move toward an environment. The turning rate is high when in an uncomfortable environment and low in a comfortable environment. For example, crustaceans display a type of klinokinesis known as *negative thermokinesis* (Figure 3.1d) to avoid areas of extreme water temperatures due to their inability to regulate their body temperature (Lagerspetz and Vainio, 2006).

The Reflex Arc

In the previous sections, you learned that certain behaviors can be explained by simple mechanisms that mediate between an organism's sensory and behavioral systems. However, after reading the examples, you might think, "But I am not an insect." Indeed, you are not an insect, but you must understand that many of your behaviors are similarly elicited.

This is the case for the **withdrawal reflex**, which is a quick and automatic response to a painful stimulus. It involves a sudden movement away from the stimulus, requiring fast coordination between nerves and muscles. As illustrated in Figure 3.2, the withdrawal reflex occurs through a reflex arc, which consists of a neural circuit comprising an afferent neuron (sensory), which transmits nerve signals from a receptor to the spinal cord. Within the spinal cord, the sensory neuron directly connects to an interneuron, which is, in turn, connected to an efferent neuron (motor) that signals a muscle (effector) to contract.

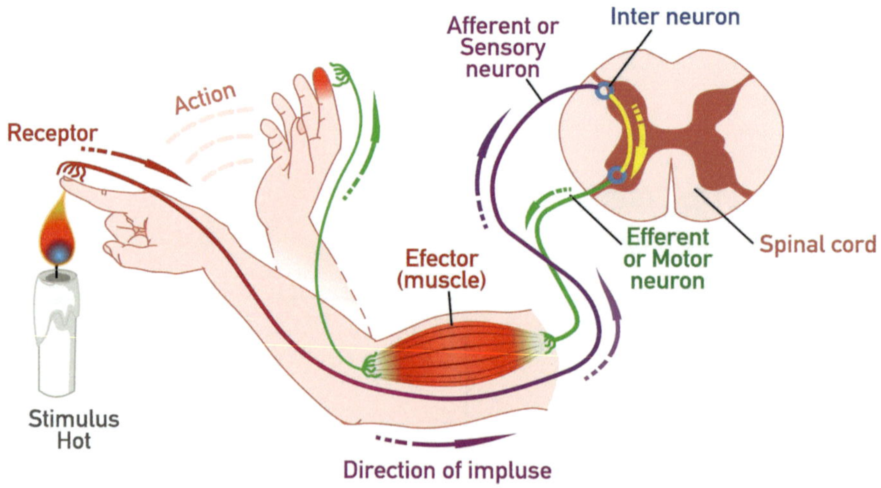

Figure 3.2 A reflex arc.

Source: Breedlove, S. M. (2015). *Principles of Psychology*. Sunderland, MA: Sinauer Associates/Oxford University Press, Figure 3.4.

Primitive Reflexes

Some reflexes, known as **primitive reflexes**, are present in newborn humans but disappear with maturation (Schott and Rossor, 2003). These are the reflexes to which Boyang's friend Luis was referring in showing off the new things he learned. Many types of primitive reflexes exist, which are too numerous to enumerate here (Hultborn, 2006; Zehr and Stein, 1999). However, they are discussed in this chapter's "Focus On" box.

Focus On

Newborn reflexes

Humans are born with various reflexes, known as primitive or newborn reflexes. A number of these reflexes are described in Table 3.1. As you can see, different types of stimuli elicit specific reflexive responses. You can also see in Table 3.1 that most primitive reflexes disappear early in life. However, others persist throughout the entire lifespan. Remember that the list of primitive reflexes in Table 3.1 is not exhaustive. At least 27 primitive reflexes are believed to exist (Futagi, Toribe and Suzuki, 2009).

The Functions of Primitive Reflexes

Primitive reflexes have survival value. The absence of these reflexes in our evolutionary ancestors would have meant certain death. Some of them, such as the rooting and sucking reflexes, were essential for newborns to fulfill the most fundamental need of feeding. Other primitive reflexes assisted in survival by forming the basis for more complex motor skills. These include the palmar reflex, which prepares for the voluntary grasping of objects; the stepping reflex, which prepares for voluntary walking; and the tonic neck reflex, which prepares for voluntary reaching. Others, such as the Moro reflex, promote the formation of bonds through gratifying interactions between infants and parents. Yet others, such as the startle and eyeblink reflex, protect from potentially dangerous stimuli.

As the brain matures, most primitive reflexes become inhibited, giving way to voluntary behaviors and motor development (Rousseau et al., 2017). The persistence of primitive reflexes beyond the expected period may indicate neurological problems. For example, studies showed that it may indicate cerebral palsy, a group of disorders caused by damage to the developing brain in which children may show unusual posture, spasticity, floppiness of the limbs, and unsteady walking (Gulati and Sondhi, 2018). The persistence of primitive reflexes has also been associated with attention-deficit/hyperactivity disorder (ADHD) and autism spectrum disorder (ASD) (Sigafoos et al., 2021).

Table 3.1 Newborn reflexes.

Reflex	*Stimulation*	*Response*	*Function*	*Age of disappearance*
Eye blink	Bright light or handclap near the head.	Quick eyelid closure.	Protects from strong stimulation.	Remains
Rooting	Stroking of cheek.	Turning of the head towards the source of stimulation.	Finding the mother's nipple.	3 weeks (becomes voluntary)
Sucking	Finger placed in the mouth.	Rhythmic sucking of fingers.	Feeding.	4 months (becomes voluntary)
Moro	Sudden drop.	Embracing motion.	Clinging to the mother.	6 months
Palmar grasp	Finger pressed against the palm.	Spontaneous grasping of fingers.	Prepares for voluntary grasping.	3–4 months
Tonic neck	Turning a baby's head to one side.	Adoption of a fencing position with one arm extended in front of the eyes.	Prepares for voluntary reaching.	4 months
Stepping	Bare feet touching flat surface.	Lifting of one foot after the other.	Prepares for voluntary walking.	2 months (depending on weight)
Babinski	Stroking the sole of the foot from toe to heel.	Fanning out of toes.	Unknown.	8–12 months
Startle	Sudden noise.	Throwing out the arms and arching back.	Protection.	Remains in different forms

Are You Thinking Critically?

1. Why are primitive reflexes necessary?
2. Why is the persistence of primitive reflexes beyond the expected timescale a concern?
3. Why do some of the primitive reflexes disappear early in life, whereas others persist?

The Ethological Approach

Ethology is defined as the study of animal behavior in its natural environment. Hence, the ethological approach is a method of studying behavior that emphasizes observing animals in their natural habitats, analyzing their actions as biological adaptations evolved to promote survival.

Instincts

Instincts are innate patterns of stereotyped, species-specific behaviors that occur in response to specific stimuli (Lorenz, 1958). Many animal behaviors are believed to be instinctual, including spinning webs by spiders, nest building and migratory behaviors in birds, and making cocoons by caterpillars. For **ethologists** like Konrad Lorenz (1903–1989) and Nikolaas Tinbergen (1907–1988), who studied animal behavior in natural environments, a behavior was considered instinctual only if it was fully developed at birth and consistently performed in the same manner. They also believed the behavior must manifest in animals raised in isolation from others, be species specific, and be elicited by environmental cues. However, it is important to recognize that contemporary ethologists also consider the influence of reciprocal interactions between genes and the environment in shaping behavior.

DO HUMANS HAVE INSTINCTS?

A recurring question I get from students is whether humans have instincts. Charles Darwin (1809–1882) was the first to propose that instincts were the source of an animal's motivation to behave (1859). Psychologist William James (1842–1910) suggested that a wide range of instincts could explain human behavior (1890). He believed that instincts were predispositions to act or impulses and that the proper environmental stimuli turned the instinctual impulses into action. For example, seeing an older woman struggling with grocery bags may trigger the sympathy instinct, making you rush over to help her; hearing a police siren outside your window may trigger the curiosity instinct, making you look out the window; hearing your favorite song triggers your tapping instinct, making you tap your feet, and so on. Later, William McDougall (1871–1938) took the extreme view that without instincts, humans would be useless bodies with no impulses to act (1914, 1919).

With many researchers subscribing to instinctual theories of behavior, the number of proposed instincts grew and eventually numbered in the thousands to the point where virtually any behavior could be attributed to an instinct. Another problem is that pointing to an instinct to account for what motivates behaviors is not an explanation for that motivation; it simply relabels the behavior. Such an explanation is circular because it attempts to define a term by using the term itself. For example, explaining looking out the window after hearing a police siren by postulating a curiosity instinct is circular because looking out the window, in this case, is the same as saying that you are curious (Tolman, 1923). For these reasons, most psychologists abandoned theorizing about human instincts. As Luis told Boyang in the opening vignette, human behavior may be too complex to be explained by instincts.

Fixed/Modal Action Patterns

Lorenz (1950) conceived of a species-specific and predictable behavior pattern he called **fixed-action pattern (FAP)** that is elicited by **sign stimuli** present in an animal's environment (Lorenz, 1982; Lorenz and Tinbergen, 1938; Tinbergen, 1952). These are similar to instincts, except that the stimuli that provoke them and the responses they generate are more specific. Lorenz believed that FAPs were fully developed at birth, required no practice to execute, and unfolded to completion once initiated, even if the sign stimulus that elicited the FAP was removed. Because of this, Lorenz designated these behaviors as instinctive.

However, you should know that George Barlow (1927–2009), one of Tinbergen's students, proposed replacing the term fixed action pattern with **modal action pattern** (MAP), which is mostly used today. This is because Barlow did not believe that the patterns of behaviors observed by Lorenz and Tinbergen were fixed but could be altered by changing environmental contexts and experiences.

Both Lorenz and Tinbergen provided classic examples of what they called FAPs. One of these examples is the egg-retrieving behavior of graylag geese (Lorenz and Tinbergen, 1938). If a mother goose sees an egg rolling out of its nest, it reacts by a series of movements permitting it to retrieve the egg. It first extends its head towards the egg while keeping its eyes fixated upon it and then stands up to walk towards it. Once near enough, it extends its neck downwards until the egg rests on its bill's underside and rolls it up between its legs back into the nest. The sequence of movement unfolds to completion once initiated, even if the egg is removed in an attempt to stop it. In another example, Tinbergen and Perdeck (1950) newly hatched herring gull chicks in which the mother regurgitates half-digested food in reaction to the chicks pecking at the sight of a red spot on its bill.

Tinbergen also described the courtship behavior of the three-spined stickleback fish which he observed in nature and in fish tanks (Tinbergen, 1952). Once its territory is established, the male stickleback drives away any potential intruder. It also builds a nest by digging a hole in the sandy bottom and covering it with weeds. After coating the weeds with a sticky substance secreted by its kidneys, it shapes them into a mound through which it digs a tunnel that becomes a nest. It then changes its colors, becoming bright red on its underbelly. It then engages in courtship behavior towards a female with a large underbelly from being filled with eggs. Tinbergen (1952) identified the stages of the stickleback's courtship behavior, which are illustrated in Figure 3.3.

Tinbergen performed several experiments to discover the sign stimuli that elicited the FAPs of several species. In one study, he presented sticklebacks with models of intruders in a fish tank (Tinbergen, 1951). The models differed in shape, size, color, and movement. As shown in Figure 3.3, he found that each stage of the stickleback's courtship ritual was elicited by a specific sign stimulus. For example, seeing a model with a distended abdomen initiated the courting behavior of males, and the sight of a model with a red underbelly moving in zigzags caused females to follow it wherever it led.

In another set of experiments, Tinbergen and Perdeck (1950) compared the reaction of herring gull chicks to different cardboard models of herring gull heads. They found that a spot of any color on the mother's bill elicited a higher frequency of pecking by the chicks than by a bill with no spot. They also compared the reaction elicited by bills uniformly painted different colors and found that a bill elicited the highest frequency of pecking, indicating that the sign stimulus for pecking was the presence of red on the bill.

THE INNATE RELEASING MECHANISM

Tinbergen (1951) believed that every FAP was controlled by a specific neural system. This neural system was inhibited by another system called the **innate releasing mechanism (IRM)**. The IRM's role was to filter out irrelevant environmental stimuli and only let through the sign stimuli that released its corresponding neural center from inhibition, hence the reason sign stimuli are also referred to as releasing stimuli.

SUPERNORMAL STIMULI

It was discovered that exaggerated versions of a sign stimulus could be more effective at eliciting a FAP (or MAP) than the sign stimulus encountered in nature. Such a sign stimulus is known as a **supernormal stimulus** (Tinbergen, 1951). A supernormal stimulus can be

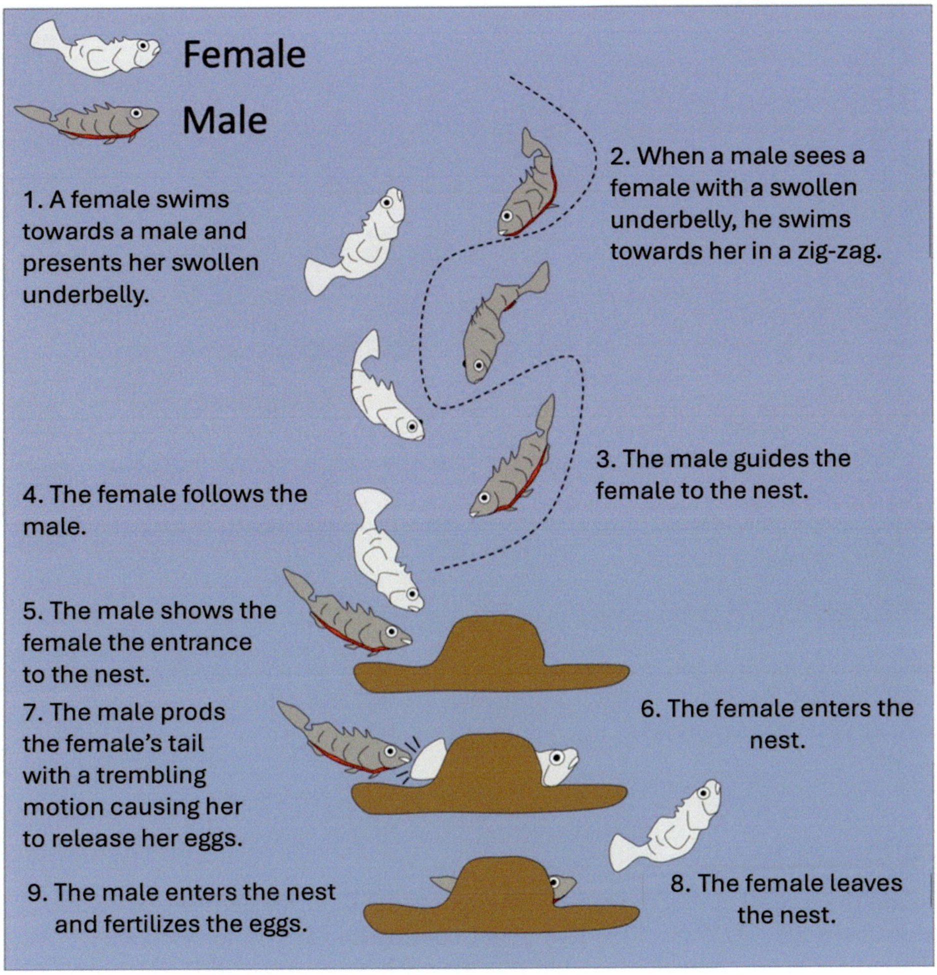

Figure 3.3 The male stickleback's courtship ritual.

produced by enhancing several effective features of a natural sign stimulus. For example, when presented with a pair of artificial eggs of different sizes and number of speckles, herring gulls chose to retrieve the larger and more speckled egg than normal (Baerends and Kruijt, 1973).

You may wonder if supernormal stimuli play a role in evoking more intense responses in humans. According to psychologist Deidre Barrett, supernormal stimuli are used in profusion in the media. Think about cartoon characters with exaggerated facial features, such as ultra-wide eyes, actors with bodies tremendously more muscular than those usually encountered, and supernatural feats performed by superheroes and villains. Also, think about movies in which the size and extent of natural disasters, such as tornadoes or earthquakes, are greatly exaggerated (Barrett, 2015). Barrett also suggested that the food industry bombards us with supernatural versions of the foods humans consumed in the distant past as hunters and gatherers. This is evident in the foods' high sugar and fat contents and their presentation. She believes these supernormal foods and their easy availability contribute significantly to obesity rates (Barrett, 2007).

Fast food advertisements often show supernatural versions of an actual product to produce a more significant response in consumers than a picture of what they will get.

Source: IStock photo ID-1157345589.

Critical Thinking Spot Check 3.1

1. Explain the typical characterization of innate behaviors by scientists.
2. Break down the reflex arc, identifying and naming its various components.
3. Differentiate between instinctual and reflexive behaviors, providing illustrative examples for each.
4. Apply the concept of modal action patterns by providing an example and specifying the associated sign stimulus.
5. Elaborate on the role of an internal releasing mechanism, using the example of the previously mentioned modal action pattern.

3.2 The Sequential Organization of Behavior

Appetitive and Consummatory Behaviors

Another contribution of the ethological approach to understanding the control of behavior was to propose that it was sequentially organized. This means that it suggests that behavior unfolded in logical successive steps included in two classes of behavior: **appetitive behaviors** and **consummatory behaviors** (Craig, 1917). Appetitive behaviors are species-specific, organized sequentially to get an animal progressively closer to a goal, such as a food source or potential mates. Consummatory behaviors consist of the consummatory act itself. It is essential to know that the term consummatory in the present context does not necessarily mean to eat. It also refers to any behavior that accomplishes a specific end. For example, the act of a tiger fatally biting its prey's neck is consummatory, as is chewing and swallowing after having found food or copulating after having found a mate (Bowers, 2020).

This is an essential ethological concept because it was thought to reconcile the fixity of behaviors observed in FAPs and the variability of other behaviors across species. Within this framework, consummatory behaviors such as chewing or copulating are fixed and highly stereotypical. However, appetitive behaviors can be highly variable and subject to environmental factors and learning.

The Behavior Systems Approach

The appetitive and consummatory distinction described previously is embedded in what is known as the **behavior systems approach** developed by William Timberlake (2001) and Timberlake and Lucas (1989). According to the behavior systems approach, the needs of animals, such as feeding, reproduction, and defense, are satisfied by activating particular behavior systems. The behavior systems approach has also been applied to playing (Freestone and Balcı, 2019), reasoning (Bowers and Timberlake, 2018), and emotions. It has also found support in mathematical models of decision-making (Freestone and Balci, 2019).

Two critical features underlie the behavior systems approach: 1) *systems*, *subsystems*, and *modes*, which are motivational processes that initiate, organize, and maintain behaviors aimed at fulfilling the needs of animals, and 2) perceptual-motor *modules* that link specific environmental stimuli to specific response components.

Systems and Subsystems

The system is the first or highest of four hierarchically organized control levels, which include a subsystem, mode, and module (Figure 3.4 [system level not shown]). The activation of a system is responsible for an animal's motivational state. The subsystem (the second level in the hierarchy) begins to fulfill the system's function by linking the animal's motivational state to appropriate stimulus–response relationships. For example, a moving object (stimulus) activates the feeding system's predation (response) subsystem, whereas stationary foods such as seeds or fruits activate the browsing subsystem. In addition, once activated, the appropriate subsystem inhibits the activation of subsystems that form irrelevant associations between stimuli and responses.

Modes

The third level in the hierarchy is that of the mode, which includes three possible behavioral patterns. The first two modes, general search and focal search, bring the animal close to the system's goal. For example, suppose no stimuli that predict food are detected within the feeding system. In that case, the general search mode is initiated when the animal does not know where food is located. If stimuli that indicate the presence of food are detected, the focal search mode is initiated. Finally, the handle/consume mode is initiated in the presence of food.

Modules

Modules, which represent the fourth level in the hierarchy, are filters tuned to specific stimuli to which animals emit species-specific responses. The modes initiate the modules'

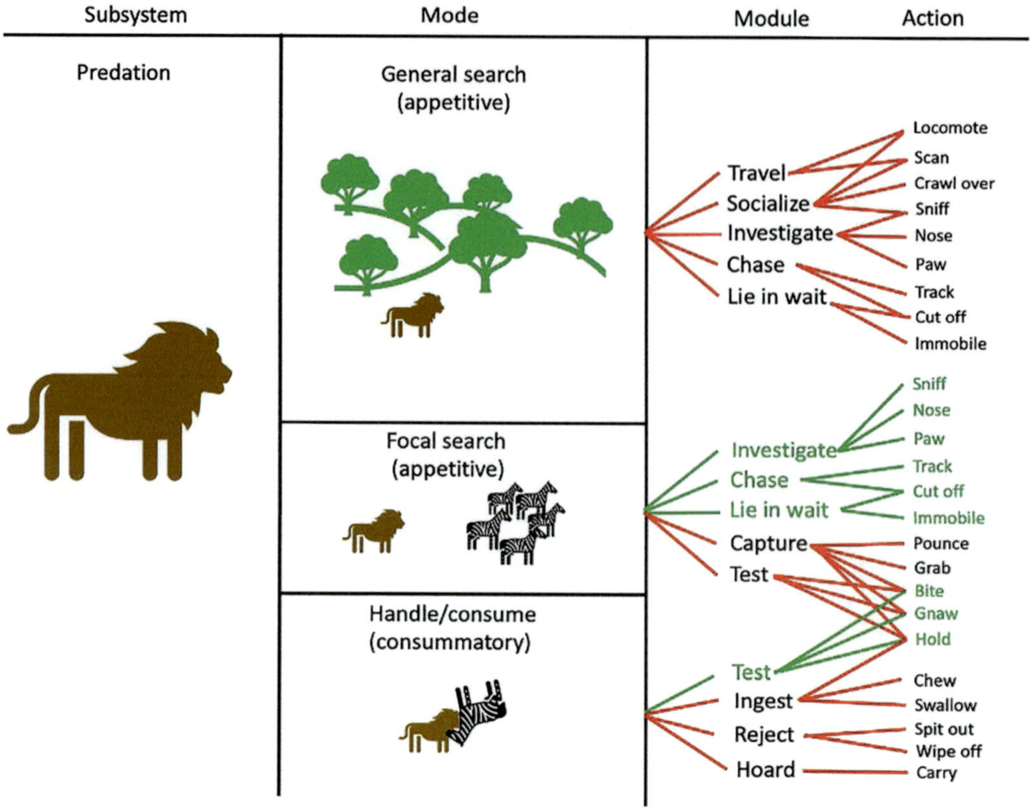

Figure 3.4 The behavior systems approach. See accompanying text for details.

responses. For example, in the predating subsystem, the general search mode can initiate traveling, socializing, investigating, chasing, and lying in wait. More specific action patterns carry out the responses initiated by the modules. For example, socializing may consist of locomotion, scanning, crawling, and sniffing. Considerable overlap between the action patterns associated with different modules may exist.

Although the responses initiated by the modules are primarily innate, learning can fine-tune them. However, at the same time, what an animal can learn is constrained by the interaction between these preexisting species-specific modules and the environmental stimuli that activate them. This differs from the general process approach, in which general rules of learning can be applied across species using arbitrary stimuli such as buzzers, lights, or electric shocks, which are never encountered in an animal's natural environment.

Behavior Systems in Humans

After reading the previous section, you may ask yourself whether human behavior is similarly hierarchically organized into systems. Before I answer this question, remember, as mentioned at the beginning of the chapter, that human behavior is relatively complex. Thus, in addition to the possibility that the behavior systems proposed by Timberlake and Lucas (1989) exist in humans, human systems also include factors such as a person's environment, experiences, direct and indirect social interactions with others, and culture (Darling, 2007). However, models of hierarchical learning in humans, including the involvement of specific brain areas, exist and can be more or less mapped onto the behavior systems approach (Diuk et al., 2013; Ribas-Fernandes et al., 2011). Unfortunately, describing these models is well beyond the scope of this textbook.

Nevertheless, we can extrapolate from the behavior systems approach to explain a simple instance of human behavior (Figure 3.5). Imagine being starved because you have not taken time to eat lunch during a day of studying, activating your feeding system, leading to the activation of the "browsing for food" subsystem. You then enter the general search mode (appetitive), in which the module of using a food delivery application is activated, leading to the action of swiping through the food-option images with your finger. You then enter the focal search mode (appetitive), in which the module of selecting a specific food category (e.g., pizza) is activated, leading to the action of clicking on the food category icon (e.g., pizzerias). After ordering a pizza from a specific restaurant, it is delivered hot and fresh to your door. At this point, you enter the handle/consume mode (consummatory), during which the module of handling the food with fork and knife or hands to bring it to your mouth is activated, leading to the actions of chewing and swallowing.

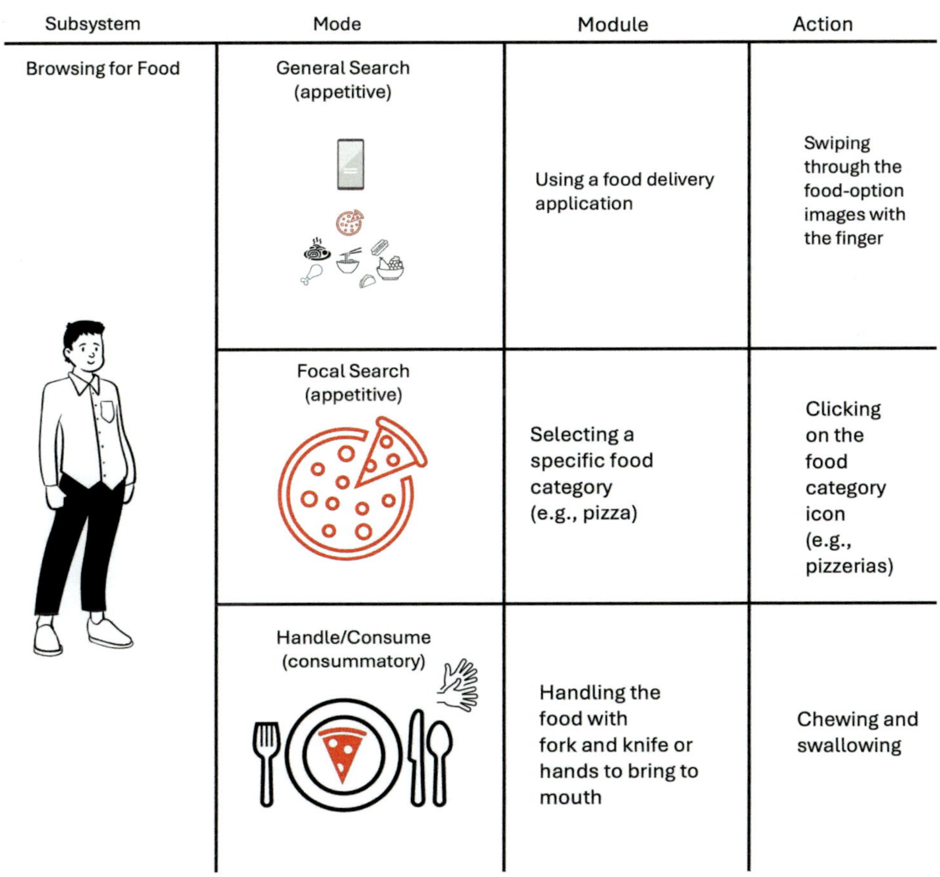

Figure 3.5 The behavior systems approach is extrapolated to human behavior.

Critical Thinking Spot Check 3.2

1. How do appetitive and consummatory behaviors relate to fixed action patterns (FAPs)?
2. How might the behavior systems approach influence our understanding of animal decision-making?
3. How could the behavior systems approach provide insights into complex behaviors like playing or reasoning?
4. How does the hierarchical model in the behavior systems approach explain behavioral complexity and flexibility?
5. How does the behavior systems view of learning constraints differ from the general process approach?

Chapter Summary

Each bullet point aligns with the learning objectives outlined at the beginning of the chapter.

- Innate behaviors are genetically programmed to occur automatically and stereotypically in response to an environmental stimulus. Most scientists believe that learning and environmental factors can modify innate behaviors. Innate behaviors include reflexes and instincts. Direct links between physiology and behavior can explain reflexes, which include taxis, kinesis, and primitive reflexes. The reflex arc, which includes the withdrawal reflex, can be explained by the activation of sensory neurons by an external stimulus and their connections with motor neurons within the spinal cord, which generate a response.
- Instincts are unlearned, highly stereotyped species-specific behaviors in response to a stimulus. Instincts are believed to be responsible for many of the behaviors of animals. However, most psychologists believe that the behavior of humans is too complex to be explained by instincts. A prototypical example of instincts is known as the modal action pattern. Modal action patterns are elicited by specific environmental stimuli known as sign (or releasing) stimuli. Modal action patterns have been observed in many natural and laboratory species. A modal action pattern is controlled by specific neural systems, which are inhibited by what is known as an innate releasing mechanism. Releasing stimuli remove the innate releasing mechanism's inhibition of the modal action pattern.
- Exaggerated versions of sign stimuli, called supernormal stimuli, elicit more vigorous responses than natural stimuli. The media and food industry use supernormal stimuli to enhance people's reactions to products.
- According to the ethological approach, behavior can be subdivided into appetitive and consummatory behaviors. Appetitive behaviors consist of organized sequences aimed at progressively bringing an animal closer to its goals, while consummatory behaviors consist of the consummatory act itself.
- According to the behavior systems approach, animals achieve their needs by activating specific systems. A system is the highest of four levels of control, which include a subsystem, which controls an animal's motivational state and is responsible for eliciting a general class of responses that bring the animal closer to its goal; modes that trigger more specific responses; and modules that fine-tune those responses to particular stimuli, which result in specific actions. Although it is thought that the responses elicited by systems are primarily innate, it is also believed that they can be modified by learning. The behavior systems approach is contrasted with the general process approach, in which general learning rules can be applied across species responding to arbitrary stimuli.

Glossary

Appetitive behaviors Actions performed to approach or seek out a goal, often leading to consummatory behaviors.

Behavior systems approach A framework suggesting that behaviors are organized into systems shaped by evolution and biological needs.

Consummatory behaviors Final, goal-directed actions that complete a behavioral sequence, such as eating or mating.

Ethologists Scientists who study animal behavior, particularly instinctive and evolutionary behaviors.

Fixed-action pattern (FAP) A sequence of innate behaviors that, once triggered, follow a specific, unchangeable pattern.

Innate behaviors Actions or responses present at birth, not learned, and often crucial for survival.

Innate releasing mechanism (IRM) A neural system proposed by Tinbergen that inhibits fixed action patterns until triggered by specific environmental stimuli; acts as a gatekeeper for species-typical behaviors.

Instincts Complex, inherited behavioral patterns that occur naturally in response to environmental triggers.

Kinesis Non-directional movement in response to a stimulus, where speed or activity level changes.

Modal action pattern (MAP) A species-typical behavioral sequence that is relatively stereotyped but shows some variability across individuals; the preferred modern term replacing "fixed action pattern."

Primitive reflexes Early reflexes seen in infants, often disappearing as the nervous system matures.

Reflex arc The neural pathway controlling reflex actions, involving sensory input, processing, and motor response.

Reflexes Automatic, involuntary responses to specific stimuli, such as blinking or knee-jerk reactions.

Sign stimuli Specific environmental cues that trigger instinctive behaviors or fixed-action patterns.

Supernormal stimulus An exaggerated version of a natural stimulus that elicits a stronger behavioral response.

Taxis Movement toward or away from a stimulus, often seen in organisms responding to environmental cues.

Withdrawal reflex An automatic reaction pulling a body part away from a painful or harmful stimulus.

4 Exploring Nonassociative Learning

Nonassociative Learning

Learning Objectives

- Define nonassociative learning and its two types: habituation and sensitization.
- Explain habituation and differentiate it from sensory adaptation.
- Explain why habituation to one stimulus does not generalize to other stimuli.
- Identify the factors that lead to an increase in responding to repeated stimuli.
- Compare the effectiveness of the comparator model versus the dual-process theory in explaining habituation and sensitization.
- Describe a hypothetical scenario where dishabituation can affect the behavioral response to a stimulus.
- Explain how the opponent process theory is believed to be involved in regulating emotions and drug addiction.

A Pre-Class Discussion

Stock photo ID 1369355839

DOI: 10.4324/9781003491828-7

Elena is an undergraduate psychology student planning to go to graduate school. However, she has yet to decide on the field of psychology she wants to study. After she brought up the topic as they were waiting for a class to begin, her friend Noor suggested that she volunteer in a laboratory to help her find out. In addition, Noor explained that volunteering in a laboratory was a great way to gain valuable experience that would increase her chances of getting accepted into graduate school. Elena could barely contain her excitement at the prospect and asked, "How do I start?" Before meeting Elena that day, Noor began exploring her options and told Elena that she had a meeting set up with Dr. Korvacina at the end of the day to inquire about the possibility of volunteering in her lab. "Oh! I heard of her," Elena said. "What would you be working on in her lab"? "I still haven't had time to read up on her research, but I think it would have something to do with habituation," replied Noor. "Ah! I remember," said Elena. "A reduction in responding to a stimulus after repeated exposures. I remember that from the general psychology class." "Does she work with humans or rats?" asked Elena. "Rats," answered Noor. Elena and Noor hadn't noticed that Jared, a classmate always sitting near them, was overhearing their conversation. He exclaimed unsolicited, "They do something similar with human babies." However, not being interested in that topic, he showed off that he presently worked in a lab and added, "In the lab I work in now, we study behavioral sensitization, which is somewhat the opposite of what you're talking about." "What's the point?" asked Noor. "It's about substance abuse," he answered. However, before explaining, the professor signaled that the class had begun.

4.1 What Is Nonassociative Learning?

Habituation and Sensitization

Nonassociative learning is a process by which information is acquired without forming associations between stimuli or between a stimulus and a response. This chapter focuses on two types of nonassociative learning: habituation and sensitization.

Habituation

As Elena seems to understand in the opening vignette, habituation refers to a decrement in a response's frequency, magnitude, or duration due to repeated stimulation (Harris, 1943; Humphrey, 1933; Rankin et al., 2009; Sokolov, 1963). Habituation is one of the simplest forms of learning and has been observed across species, including single-cell organisms such as amoeba and protozoa (Harris, 1943). Habituation permits animals to filter out irrelevant stimuli, preventing them from incurring the cost of unnecessarily responding to non-threatening stimuli (Lima, 1998). To be considered habituation, the decrease in the frequency of a response with repeated stimulation must not be due to muscle fatigue. It should also not be due to **sensory adaptation**, the process through which a sensory system adapts to a consistent stimulus by increasing the threshold at which the stimulus is perceived (Adibi and Lampl, 2021; Boudreau and Ferster, 2005; Dalton, 2000; Pellegrino et al., 2017). This means that a constant stimulus must be more intense than usual to be detected by sensory receptors.

Sensory adaptation is evident when, despite constant exposure to a stimulus, such as an odor, an individual becomes less aware of it over time. This occurs when continuous exposure elevates the threshold at which olfactory sensory receptors respond, diminishing the ability to perceive the smell. The receptors' sensitivity returns after a period of non-exposure to the stimulus.

Habituation Is Common

Habituation is common in animals. For example, newly acquired pets such as hamsters and birds are easily startled by taps on their cages or noises in the house but stop reacting to them once they learn they do not pose a threat. Similarly, a kitten may initially shy away from its owner reaching out to touch it but eventually becomes accustomed to it. Habituation is also common in humans. For example, you may initially get annoyed by your neighbor's loud music when trying to study but readily habituate to it. Note again the difference here between habituation and sensory adaptation. In all these cases, there is no loss in the ability to perceive the stimulus.

Habituation often explains how city animals, such as birds and squirrels, adapt to cohabiting with humans (Chapman, Rymer and Pillay, 2012; Rodriguez-Prieto et al., 2008). However, it was shown that such an adaptation may not always be due to habituation but to a range of other factors. For example, city animals may have remained in an area populated by humans not because they have habituated to their presence but because it is being tolerated. Because of factors such as the availability of resources, risk of predation, and suitable habitats, the cost of fleeing the area may have been greater than remaining in it (Bejder et al., 2009; Samia et al., 2015). Hence, being able to differentiate between habituation and tolerance is essential to the understanding of human activity on wildlife.

Behavioral Characteristics of Habituation

SPONTANEOUS RECOVERY

In habituation, **spontaneous recovery** refers to the return of a response due to withholding the stimulus during a period after which the response has been habituated. For example, if you have habituated to the loud music played by your neighbor, you will probably get annoyed by it again if she starts it up again the following morning.

LONG-TERM HABITUATION AND SHORT-TERM HABITUATION

A decrement in response when repeated stimulus presentations occur close together in time, called *massed exposures*, is known as **short-term habituation**. A decrement in responding when repeated stimulus presentations occur relatively further apart in time, called *spaced exposures*, is known as **long-term habituation**. Short-term habituation is associated with a more sudden decrement in the response than long-term habituation but also results in more immediate spontaneous recovery. In contrast, long-term habituation proceeds more slowly than short-term habituation, resulting in more delayed spontaneous recovery. In both cases, spontaneous recovery becomes progressively less evident with repeated cycles of habituation.

The difference in the extent to which long-term and short-term habituation relate to spontaneous recovery was shown experimentally in a study that examined habituation of the **startle response** in rats (Leaton, 1976). The startle response refers to an unlearned reaction to a sudden and unexpected intense stimulus, such as a loud noise. It is thought to serve a protective function. It includes forcefully closing the eyes, grimacing, hunching the head and body, and increased muscle tension (Wilkins, Hallett and Wess, 1986). The magnitude of a rat's startle response to a stimulus such as a tone can be measured by an apparatus known as a *stabilimeter,* illustrated and briefly described in Figure 4.1a, which measures sudden movements by detecting the changes in pressure exerted on the floor of the apparatus.

The experiment consisted of three phases. In Phase 1 (long-term habituation), the rats were presented with a 98-db tone (approximately the loudness of a food processor) once

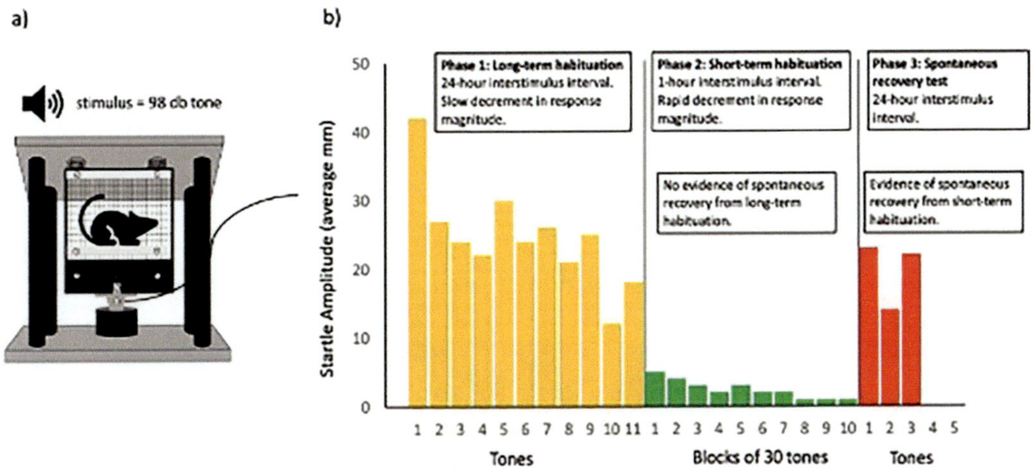

Figure 4.1 a) Representation of the stabilimeter used in the Leaton (1976) experiment. It consists of a wire mesh cage suspended within a wooden frame. The cage is sandwiched between four springs attached to the top of the frame and a rubber cylinder on which a device called an accelerometer is located. The rats' movements cause the cage to move, which causes the accelerometer to send out signals about the movements to be analyzed by an external device. b) Results of the Leaton (1976) experiment on long-term and short-term habituation. See text for details.

Source: Graph modified from Leaton, R. N. (1976). Long-term retention of the habituation of lick suppression and startle response produced by a single auditory stimulus. *J Exp Psychol Anim Behav Process*, 2(3), 248–259 (Figure 3, Page 255).

a day on 11 consecutive days (24-hour interstimulus interval). In Phase 2 (short-term habituation), which began 24 hours following the last test session of Phase 1, the rats were presented with ten blocks of thirty 98-db tones that occurred one second apart (1-second interstimulus interval). In Phase 3 (spontaneous-recovery test), which occurred 24 hours after the last test session of Phase 2, the tones were presented with a 24-hour interstimulus interval on three consecutive days.

The results are shown in Figure 4.1b. The decrement in startle magnitude was relatively slow during Phase 1, with the 24-hour interstimulus interval. By the first trial of Phase 2, the response had reached rock bottom, with no sign of spontaneous recovery despite the 24-hour rest period. The response magnitude remained suppressed throughout Phase 2, with the 1-second interstimulus interval. However, contrary to what occurred during the first trial of Phase 2, spontaneous response recovery occurred during the first trial of Phase 3.

Why does recovery from habituation more readily occur after short-term than long-term habituation? The key lies in understanding that these two forms of habituation involve different underlying mechanisms. Long-term habituation, established through widely spaced trials (24-hour intervals in Phase 1), produces a relatively stable and enduring suppression of the response. This explains why no spontaneous recovery occurred at the beginning of Phase 2—the long-term habituation was too robust to dissipate after just 24 hours of rest. In contrast, short-term habituation, established through massed trials (1-second intervals in Phase 2), produces a more temporary and labile form of response suppression. This form of habituation decays with the passage of time, which is why spontaneous recovery occurred at the beginning of Phase 3 following the 24-hour rest period. The Leaton (1976) study thus demonstrates that habituation is not a single process but rather involves distinct short-term and long-term mechanisms with different properties and temporal dynamics.

STIMULUS SPECIFICITY

Another characteristic of habituation is that it is stimulus specific. For example, you may have ceased to be annoyed by the sound of your neighbor's loud music while studying but be startled by a loud knock at the door. Stimulus specificity shows habituation is a central process, not at the sensory receptor level. If it were due to the deactivation of receptors, you would also not react to the knock at the door. Figure 4.2 shows another example of the stimulus specificity of habituation.

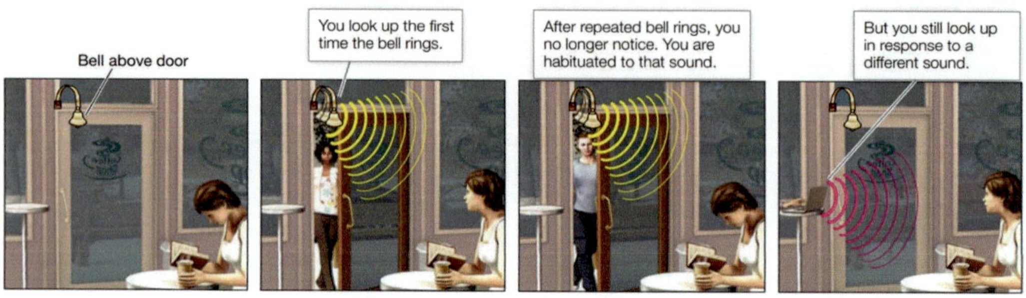

Figure 4.2 Depiction of the stimulus specificity of habituation. See accompanying text for details.

Source: Breedlove, S. M. (2015). *Principles of Psychology*. Sunderland, MA: Sinauer Associates/Oxford University Press, Figure 8.2a.

DISHABITUATION

Dishabituation refers to the return of a habituated response to a stimulus due to exposure to another stimulus. For example, you may have habituated to the music playing from the headphones of another student in the library. However, it may annoy you again after hearing other students chatting in a nearby book aisle. This also shows that dishabituation is not stimulus specific. Contrary to habituation, any stimulus can be a dishabituating stimulus to a habituated response, as shown by another example in Figure 4.3.

Figure 4.3 Depiction of habituation and dishabituation. See text for details.

Source: Breedlove, S. M. (2015). *Principles of Psychology*. Sunderland, MA: Sinauer Associates/Oxford University Press, Figure 8.3a.

HABITUATION CAN BE USED AS A TOOL TO ASSESS MEMORY

Various methods exist to assess memory in humans and animals, several of which are described in Chapter 10. However, assessing memory in preverbal infants (infants who have not yet developed speech) and animals can be challenging because they cannot verbally report what they remember. Therefore, models were developed to assess memory by observing behavioral responses. One of these models is the visual paired comparison test (VPC) (Fagan and Detterman, 1992).

The VPC test takes advantage of the natural propensity of human infants and animals to explore novelty. This propensity may have evolved for infants to continually increase their knowledge database. For animals, novel stimuli can signal a new food source or the presence of a predator. The VPC as administered to infants is illustrated in Figure 4.4a–b. It consists of a familiarization and test phase. During the familiarization phase, an infant is shown two identical images, each presented on a separate computer screen. The infant is permitted to look at the pictures until a significant decrease in time looking at the photos, decreased heart rate, and reduced respiration rate occurs. At this point, the infant is believed to be habituated to the images. During the test phase, a new image is presented along with the one to which the infant has habituated. Infants spend significantly more time looking at the novel image (recovery of responding) than at the image to which it has habituated. This is taken as an indication that the familiar image was recognized. Infants can show recovery of responding to the novel image with delays of up to seven weeks between familiarization and testing when the stimuli used were clips of women performing familiar and novel actions (Bahrick, Gogate and Ruiz, 2002). This is the procedure Jared, Elena and Noor's obtrusive classmate, seemed to know something about in the opening vignette.

The VPC test can also assess memory for objects and places in animals (Mumby et al., 2002). The VPC procedure for animals also called the novel object preference test (NOP), is shown in Figure 4.4c–d. For the familiarization phase, an animal, typically a rat, is permitted to explore two identical objects in an open field for a predetermined period, normally

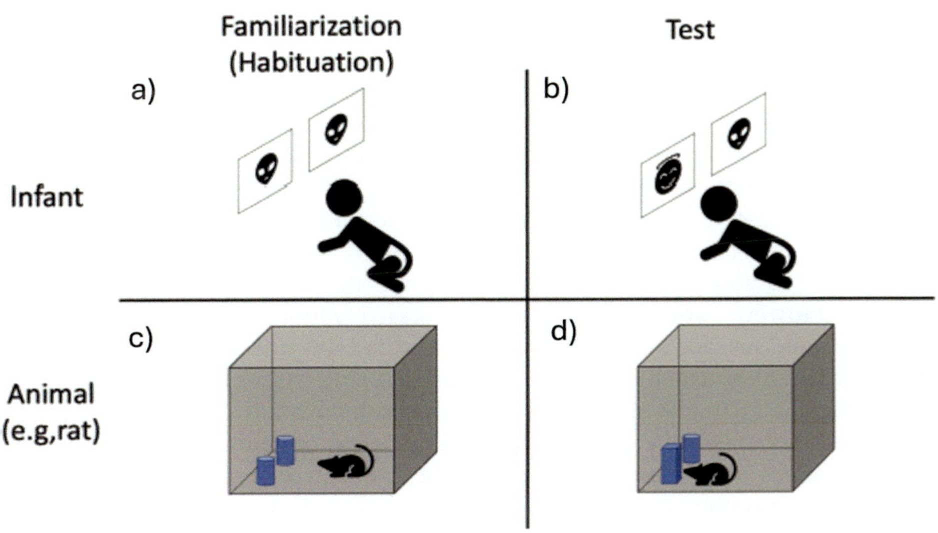

Figure 4.4 (a–b) The visual paired comparison test (VPC) for human infants and (c–d) animals. See text for details.

two to five minutes. Next, the animal is removed from the open field for a retention interval. Finally, the animal is placed back into the open field, but this time, the familiar object is presented along with a novel object.

Similarly to human infants, animals will spend significantly more time exploring the novel object than the familiar object, indicating that they recognize the familiar object. In another version of the test, memory for places can be assessed by presenting the copies of the objects explored in the familiarization phase, but with one of the copies placed in a novel location. Which of the two copies do you think will be explored the most? If you guessed the one in the novel location, you are correct. As you have gathered, these procedures were likely used by Dr. Korvacina, for whom Noor, in the opening vignette, was considering working.

The VPC and its variants can be used to assess the effects of damage to different brain areas on memory for objects, places, and contexts (Broadbent et al., 2010; Gaskin et al., 2009; Gaskin et al., 2010). It can also provide researchers with valuable information in their understanding of the memory impairments observed in brain degenerating diseases such as Alzheimer's so that better treatments may be discovered (Ali et al., 2022; Gaspar et al., 2022; Tropea et al., 2022)—more on this in Chapter 20.

Sensitization

Under certain circumstances, repeated occurrences of a stimulus cause an increase in the strength of the response to the stimulus. This phenomenon is known as **sensitization** (Groves and Thompson, 1970). The following example illustrates sensitization. Imagine someone initially startled by the loud and sudden honking of a car horn near their home. In the beginning, every "honk" triggers a noticeable startle response, which consists of protective reactions against sudden or intense stimuli, such as closing the eyes, furrowing the brows, compressing the lips, lowering the head, hunching the shoulders, and bending the trunk and knee (Davis, 1984). As this scenario repeats, the individual's startle response intensifies, and protective behaviors become more pronounced.

Sensitization to environmental events, such as the sounds of predators or their scents following painful injuries from an attack, is vital for animal survival. This sensitization enhances the likelihood of animals surviving future encounters with predators. For example, one study demonstrated that chronic pain sensitized the hypervigilance response of mice to a predator's scent. In another study, defensive behaviors in squids were intensified after they suffered non-lethal injuries.

An interesting fact about sensitization is that it can occur with the same stimuli to which one becomes habituated. One factor that might determine whether one habituates or sensitizes to a stimulus is a person's initial state or level of responsiveness. For example, you might habituate to your roommate's nagging comments about how messy you are when you are calm. However, you might become progressively more sensitive to those comments when you feel anxious (for instance, after having a bad day at school).

You might also habituate to the sound of music coming from a classmate's earbuds while studying in the library but become sensitized to it if you are annoyed by other students chatting in a nearby book aisle. In another example, one's fear of being stung by a bee intensifies as it buzzes around one's head if the sight of the bee causes anxiety. Conversely, another person who remains calm upon seeing a bee experiences a decrease in fear as the bee buzzes around. In each of these instances, sensitization to a stimulus depends on the individual's state, such as anxiety. Sometimes, a source of stress that alters one's state can be identified. Such a stimulus (e.g., the students chatting in the book aisle in the previous example) is referred to as a **sensitizing stimulus.**

The effect of a sensitizing stimulus was demonstrated in a classic experiment in which researchers tested whether the startle response could be sensitized (Davis, 1974). In the experiment, two groups of rats were placed in a stabilimeter, the apparatus described previously in the context of Leaton's (1976) experiment on habituation (Figure 4.5). One group of rats (60-db group) was subjected to a series of 110-decibel (dB) tones (equivalent to the loudness of a car horn) at 30-second intervals. The 110-db tone was sounded against the background of a continuous 60-db white noise (equivalent to the loudness of an electric toothbrush). For the other group of rats (80-db group), the 110-db tone was sounded against an 80-db continuous white noise (equivalent to the loudness of an alarm clock). The experimenter aimed to determine whether the intensity of the background noise affected the sensitization of the rats' startle response to the tones. As shown in Figure 4.5, they found that the startle response of the 60-db group habituated across ten trial blocks, each consisting of ten tone presentations. However, the reaction of the 80-db group sensitized over the same number of trials. The results demonstrated that both habituation and sensitization can occur in response to the same stimulus, depending on the circumstances under which the stimulus is presented.

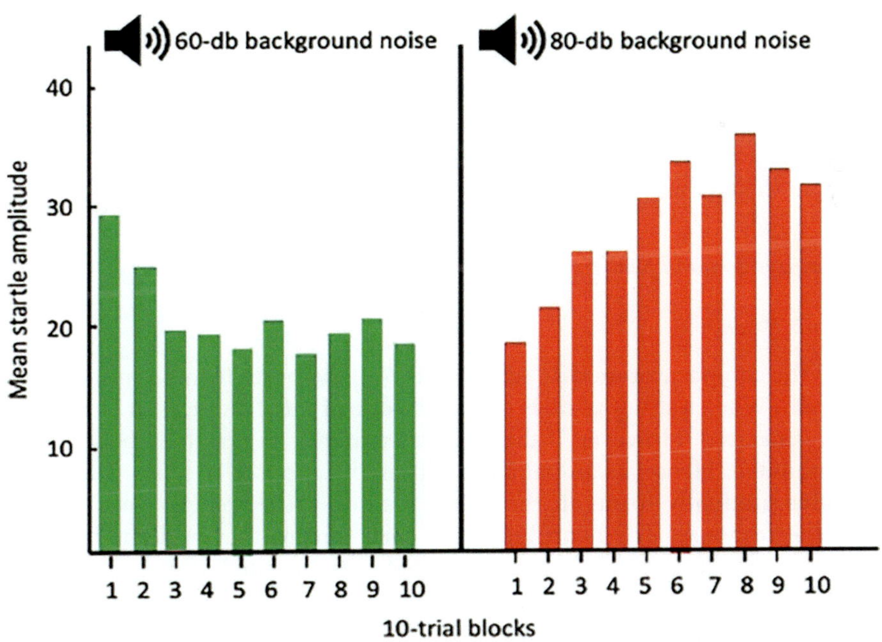

Figure 4.5 Results of the Davis (1974) experiment (see text for details).

Source: Davis, M. (1974). Sensitization of the rat startle response by noise. *J Comp Physiol Psychol*, 87(3), 571–581. https://doi.org/10.1037/h0036985 (Figure 1, Page 572).

Sensitization Is Not Stimulus Specific

Similar to dishabituation, sensitization is not specific to a particular stimulus. For instance, the students chatting in a nearby book aisle in the dishabituation example could also serve as a sensitizing stimulus. In the experiment described earlier, any range of stimuli, aside from the tone and 80-dB white noise, could have been used to sensitize the rats' startle response.

In a type of sensitization known as **behavioral sensitization**, a long-lasting increase in the sensitivity to the locomotor effects of drugs such as cocaine, amphetamine, and several others occurs with repeated exposures (Cadoni et al., 2001; Eikelboom and Stewart, 1982; Stewart, 1983). It is also believed to play an important role in drug addiction by inducing drug-seeking behavior and cravings in humans (Leyton, 2022; Robinson and Berridge, 1993; Steketee and Kalivas, 2011).

Another aspect of behavioral sensitization is that the effects of one drug may potentiate the effects of another. For example, nicotine (Smith et al., 1999) and caffeine (Ferreira, Abrahao and Souza-Formigoni, 2013; Kunin et al., 2000) have been shown to potentiate the effects of alcohol. This is concerning in terms of the development of alcoholism, considering the trend of mixing caffeinated drinks with alcohol (Reissig, Strain and Griffiths, 2009). This is notwithstanding the fact that the stimulant effects of caffeine may overshadow the depressant effects of alcohol, giving the user a sense that they can engage in activities that require skills that are still being impaired by the alcohol, such as driving (Marczinski et al., 2011).

It is also important to know that sensitization to the effects of drugs may also be induced by prolonged stress, which can explain higher rates of drug abuse in people who have certain psychological disorders such as depression (Alam and Chaudhary, 2020; Camarini, Marianno and Rae, 2018). Interestingly, behavioral sensitization was also induced by repeated exposure to food cues (Le Merrer and Stephens, 2006), which may explain overeating behavior in humans (Bonder and Davis, 2022; Temple, 2016). In other words, when exposed to these cues, people can become progressively more likely to act on their compulsion to eat. Behavioral sensitization was the phenomenon of interest in the laboratory for which Jared, in the opening vignette, was volunteering.

Theories of Habituation and Sensitization

The Comparator Model

According to the **comparator model** (Sokolov, 1960), the brain forms a model of frequently repeated stimuli. When a stimulus does not match one of these models, an orienting response towards it is generated. However, if the stimulus matches any of the models, the orienting response is inhibited. Hence, as an animal is repeatedly exposed to a new stimulus, a model of the stimulus gradually forms in the brain, leading to decrements in the frequency or intensity of the response. The neurobiological mechanisms that underlie habituation and sensitization are discussed in this chapter's "What in the Brain?" box.

The Dual-Process Theory of Habituation and Sensitization

According to the **dual-process theory** of habituation and sensitization, whether an organism's response habituates or sensitizes to a stimulus depends on the relative activation of a stimulus-response system (**S-R system**), which provides the fastest route between the stimulus and the response and a **state system** (note that this was briefly illustrated by the examples at the beginning of the section on sensitization), which determines the animal's degree of arousal (Groves and Thompson, 1970). According to the dual-process theory, activity in the S-R system promotes habituation, whereas activity in the state system promotes sensitization. The S-R and state systems are activated when presented with a new stimulus. A decrement in response to a stimulus is observed if activation of the S-R system is greater than that of the state system. However, greater activation of the state system relative to the S-R system results in sensitization.

Hence, the same stimulus can induce habituation or sensitization depending on the organism's state of arousal. This was shown by the experiment performed by Davis (1974) described previously, in which the startle reflex of rats both habituated and sensitized to a tone of the same frequency. The loudness of the background noise determined whether they were habituated or sensitized. According to the dual-process theory, sensitization occurred with the loudest of the two background noises (80 db) because of the greater physiological arousal it produced via the greater activation of the state system relative to the S-R system. The same can be said about the example of the student studying in the library. With no students chit-chatting in the book aisle, the S-R system was activated to a greater degree than the state system, resulting in habituation. However, students chatting in the book aisle led to greater activation of the state system relative to the S-R system. This led to sensitization to the music coming from the classmate's earbuds. In the other example, sensitization of the fear created by the buzzing bee was due to a greater activation of the state system relative to the S-R system created by the high anxiety levels at the sight of the bee. Figure 4.6 illustrates a situation where a student is exposed to traffic sounds while studying.

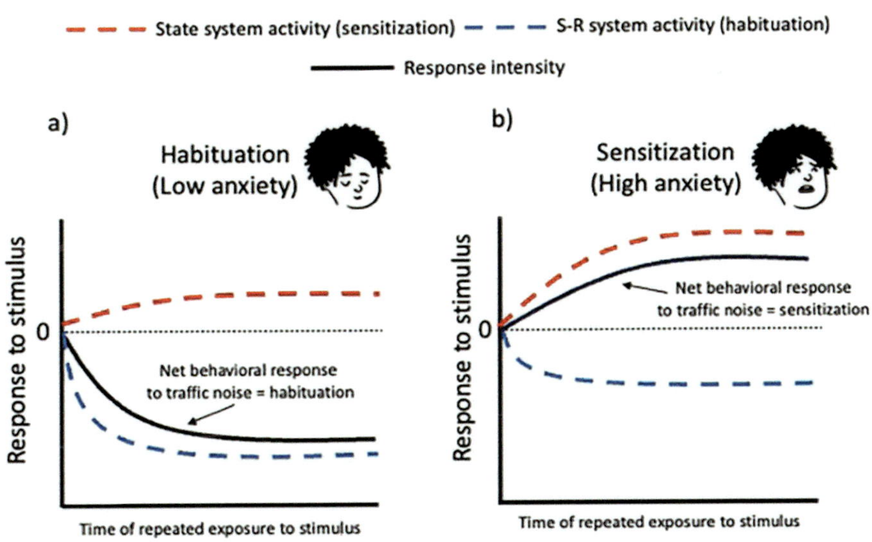

Figure 4.6 The activation of the state and S-R systems, which reflect the sensitization (red) and habituation (blue) processes, respectively, are added together to produce a net behavioral response curve (black). Deflections from zero (blacked dotted line) indicate the extent to which the sensitization (state) and habituation (S-R) responses are pronounced. The greater the deflection from the baseline, the greater the system activity. a) With low anxiety, the habituation process is pronounced relative to the sensitization system. b) With high anxiety, it is the sensitization process that is pronounced relative to the habituation system.

As shown in Figure 4.6a, the student is habituated to traffic noise (the stimulus) when not anxious. In contrast, the student is sensitized to the traffic noise when anxious (Figure 4.6b). The student's anxiety levels might be caused by an upcoming exam or the loudness of the traffic noise itself, with low traffic noise leading to habituation and loud traffic noise leading to sensitization.

What in the Brain?

Habituation and Sensitization in the Sea Slug

In an elegant set of experiments using sea slugs (also known as *Aplysia californica*) conducted in the 1960s, neuroscientist and Nobel Prize laureate Eric Kandel and colleagues discovered the neural mechanisms of habituation and sensitization (Kandel, 2001; Pinsker et al., 1970). The sea slug is a simple marine organism. It has a gill reflexively withdrawn under the mantle for some time as a defense mechanism when another part called the siphon is touched. This is known as the gill-withdrawal reflex. It also has an abdominal ganglion that contains the connections between the sensory neuron of the siphon and the motor neuron that connects to the gill muscles.

Figure 4.7 illustrates how Kandel and colleagues elicited the sea slug's gill-withdrawal reflex. The reflexive withdrawal of the gill was evoked by stimulation of the siphon with a jet of water. This caused a neurotransmitter called glutamate to be released from a siphon's sensory neuron onto receptors of a motor neuron. In turn, this causes the motor neuron to release a neurotransmitter on the gill muscles, causing it to retract for a brief period.

Habituation

Next, Kandel and colleagues wanted to find out whether repeatedly stimulating the sea slug's siphon would result in the habituation of the reflex. This is precisely what happened. They found that repeatedly stimulating the siphon resulted in its sensory

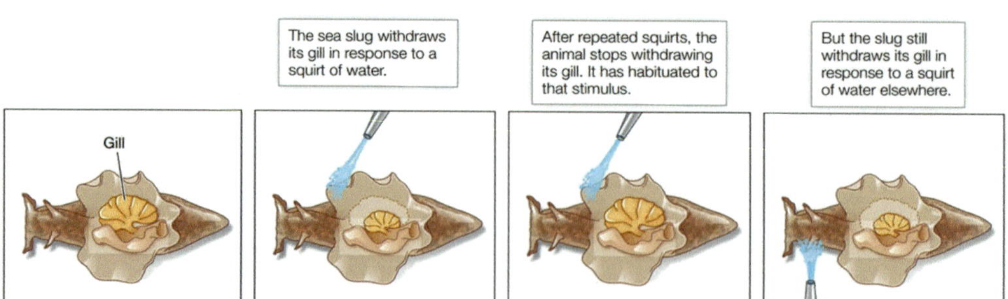

Figure 4.7 The method used to induce habituation in the aplysia.

Source: Breedlove, S. M. (2015). *Principles of psychology*. Sunderland, MA: Sinauer Associates/Oxford University Press, Figure 8.2b.

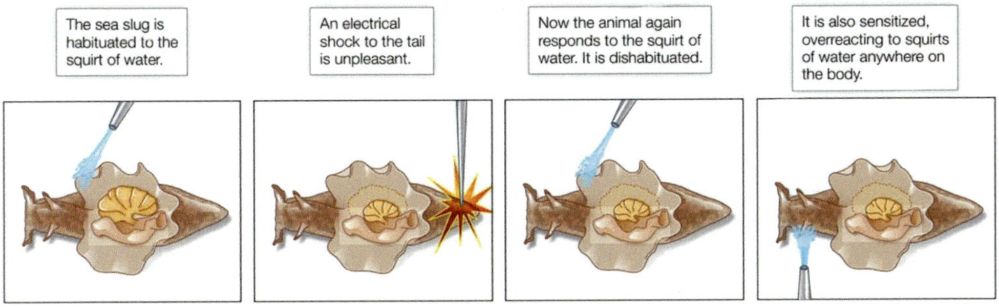

Figure 4.8 Method used to induce dishabituation and sensitization in the aplysia.

Source: Breedlove, S. M. (2015). *Principles of psychology*. Sunderland, MA: Sinauer Associates/Oxford University Press, Figure 8.3b.

neuron progressively releasing fewer neurotransmitters onto the receptors of the motor neuron. This, in turn, caused the motor neuron to release less neurotransmitter on the gill's muscles, reducing the duration for which the gill remained withdrawn.

Dishabituation and Sensitization

After habituating the gill-withdrawal reflex in *Aplysia*, Kandel and colleagues investigated dishabituation and sensitization. As shown in Figure 4.8, they applied a strong, noxious stimulus (an electric shock) to the sea slug's tail, which served as the dishabituating stimulus. When they reapplied the weak stimulus to the siphon, they observed that the gill-withdrawal reflex had returned to its original strength and often exceeded it, demonstrating successful dishabituation. Moreover, this weak siphon stimulus now elicited a stronger gill-withdrawal reflex than initially, with the gill remaining withdrawn longer than before the tail shock. This enhanced response exemplified sensitization, a form of nonassociative learning where the response to a stimulus is amplified following exposure to a strong or noxious stimulus.

Kandel's team further explored the phenomenon by applying multiple tail shocks. They discovered that repeated noxious stimuli led to increasingly stronger and longer-lasting gill-withdrawal reflexes. This finding demonstrated that sensitization could be intensified through repetition, revealing a cumulative effect in this form of learning. These experiments were groundbreaking in elucidating the neural mechanisms underlying simple forms of learning and memory, showcasing how a single reflex circuit could be modified by experience in various ways.

Are You Thinking Critically?

1. Why did Kandel and colleagues decide to use such a simple organism (i.e., *Aplysia californica*) to conduct their experiments?
2. What did Kandel and colleagues find in follow-up experiments on habituation?
3. What do Kandel and colleagues' results mean about the innateness of reflexes?

Critical Thinking Spot Check 4.1

1. Differentiate between habituation and sensitization by offering real-life examples. How do these processes manifest in everyday scenarios?
2. Explain the concept of stimulus specificity in habituation. How does it differ from sensory adaptation? Provide an example to illustrate.
3. Summarize the key principles of the comparator model of habituation. How does this model explain the brain's response to repeated stimuli?
4. Critically assess the dual-process theory of habituation and sensitization. How well does it explain the variations in responses to stimuli based on the organism's state?

4.2 Habituation and Emotions

So far you have learned about the adaptive value of habituation that permits organisms to ignore irrelevant elements of their environments and sensitization that permits organisms to increase the frequency or intensity of response to a stimulus, which might normally habituate, in the presence of stimuli that might signal danger. However, we have not discussed how these processes might be involved in motivation and the regulation of emotions.

Hedonic Adaptation

Philosophers and psychologists have been interested in the regulation of emotions for centuries. One of the main questions concerns the extent to which people can increase their levels of happiness, also known as **subjective well-being.** Psychologists have proposed several theories which question whether a long-term increase in subjective well-being is even possible. For example, it has been proposed that a new stimulus increases well-being if it provides more happiness than the average happiness provided by all stimuli previously experienced (Helson, 1948).

According to the **hedonic adaptation theory** (Brickman and Campbell, 1971), habituation to both positive stimuli result in one's return to a baseline mood state (a minimum level used as a basis for comparison) known as the **emotional set point**. This leaves people constantly seeking novel experiences to enhance their moods in what is known as the **hedonic treadmill.** The authors of this theory found evidence for it in a study in which lottery winners rated their levels of happiness. Interestingly, they found that the lottery winners did not report significantly higher levels of happiness than control participants or participants who had recently become paraplegic in an accident. The explanation was that although winning the lottery provided the participants with an initial boost of happiness, they eventually habituated to the experience of having more money, which became a new set point against which all other positive events were judged. This resulted in a reduced ability to derive pleasure from everyday events (Brickman, Coates and Janoff-Bulman, 1978).

Before going on, it is important that you realize that people differ in their emotional set point and that a single person may have set points that vary across experiences (Diener, Lucas and Scollon, 2009; Mancini, Bonanno and Clark, 2011). However, according to a more recent theory known as the **hedonic adaptation prevention model**, the hedonic treadmill can be avoided by appreciating positive life changes and by continuing to vary positive experiences (Sheldon and Lyubomirsky, 2012). The hedonic adaptation model is the subject of this module's application box.

Opponent Process Theory

The **opponent process theory**, proposed by psychologist Richard Solomon (1918–1995), defines a process aimed at keeping emotions at stable equilibrium by counteracting deviations in the intensity of an emotion from a baseline (Solomon, 1980; Solomon and Corbit, 1974). In other words, when we feel something very strongly, an opposite reaction is produced to bring our feelings back to normal. This theory provided a mechanism for the hedonic adaptations described previously. It states that emotions exist in opponent pairs such as pleasure/pain, joy/sadness, elation/depression, fear/relief, and so on. When the intensity of an emotion in the pair is activated above baseline, it is counteracted by the simultaneous activation of the opponent emotion. This causes the intensity of the original emotion to be pulled back towards baseline to the point at which only the opponent emotion is experienced.

Solomon (1980) suggested that people's motivations for sensation seeking, social attachments, love, food, and so on were regulated by opponent processes in a way similar to how drug addiction is maintained. That is, the initial pleasant rush produced by a drug is counteracted by the opponent process consisting of unpleasant withdrawal symptoms and tolerance, in which progressively larger doses of the drug are needed to have the same effects. For example, new lovers often go through a honeymoon period in which they may experience intense feelings of infatuation, which eventually subside. This is sometimes followed by the opponent emotions of dissatisfaction, frustration, and resentment that may lead to arguments and fights, which may ultimately lead to a breakup.

The opponent process also explains how positive emotions can counteract negative emotions. For example, an intense workout can be a painful experience. However, the pain is counteracted by elation after exercising for an extended period. This is especially the case of marathon runners, who report experiencing what is known as *runner's high* due to the release of endorphins, one of the brain's chemicals associated with pleasure and pain-killing properties. Once habituated to these activities, pleasurable feelings can be derived from them.

Solomon (1980) called the process by which the intensity of an emotional state rises above the baseline the **A-process**. He called the process by which that emotion is pulled back towards the baseline the **B-process**. How these processes oppose each other to determine the emotional response to a stimulus is illustrated in Figure 4.9, and how it applies to the emotional reactions to a real-life situation, such as parachute jumping, in Figure 4.10.

Unhabituated Stimulus (Left Column)

As shown in Figure 4.9, a surge in the A-process coincides with the onset of the experience and is unopposed by the B-process (middle). This surge in the A-process coincides with a peak in the intensity of the emotional experience elicited by the stimulus (bottom). The onset of the B-process, which lags behind that of the A-process, reduces the intensity of the emotional experience, bringing it down towards the baseline, or resting state, for the duration of the stimulus. The offset of the A-process coincides with the termination of the stimulus. At this point, the B-process, which lags the A-process, continues unopposed. This results in the experience of an emotion opposite from that initially elicited by the stimulus (bottom). The B-process and its effects on emotional experience then subsides, resulting in a return to baseline.

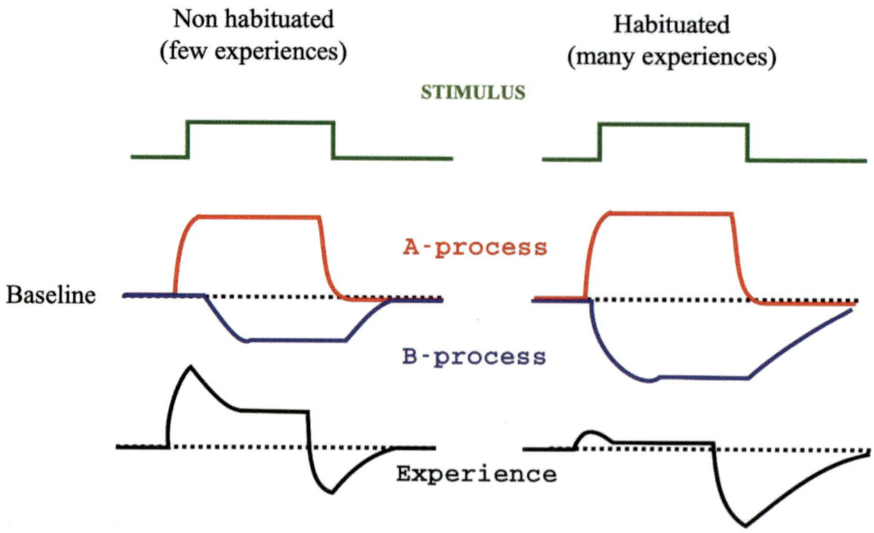

Figure 4.9 The opponent process theory. See text for details.

Source: Creative Commons (https://commons.wikimedia.org/wiki/File:Opponent_process_theory_of_drug_addiction.svg).

First skydiving experience
(Unhabituated)

1. During the first skydive, the experience is dominated by terror. The sudden exposure to the novel, dangerous situation triggers a strong A-process (fear response) that initially surges unopposed, creating intense terror as the person exits the plane.

2. As the jump continues and the parachute opens, the B-process begins to develop and oppose the A-process. The terror diminishes somewhat, though the experience remains frightening throughout the descent.

3. After landing safely and the stimulus ends, the A-process terminates quickly. However, the B-process continues unopposed for a brief period, producing a mild sense of relief and perhaps slight euphoria, the opposite of the initial terror.

4. The relief is relatively short-lived, and the person quickly returns to their baseline emotional state.

After several skydiving experiences
(Habituated)

1.During the jump, the experienced skydiver no longer feels intense terror. The A-process (fear response) is immediately opposed by a well-developed B-process that has strengthened through repeated exposure. This prevents any significant fear from arising. The person may feel calm, focused, or only mildly aroused during the jump itself.

2. Throughout the descent, the emotional experience remains relatively flat, staying at or near baseline. The jump itself has lost its capacity to produce strong emotional responses.

3. After landing and the stimulus ends, the strong B-process continues unopposed. This produces an intense feeling of exhilaration, euphoria, or a "rush", the opposite of fear.

4. This euphoric state is much stronger and lasts considerably longer than the mild relief experienced after the first jump. The effects persist for an extended period before gradually returning to baseline.

Figure 4.10 The opponent-process theory of emotion demonstrated through first-time versus experienced skydivers. Initially (left), the A-process produces intense terror that is only weakly opposed by the B-process relief upon landing. With repeated exposure (right), the A-process habituates and diminishes while the B-process strengthens, resulting in minimal fear during the jump but intense euphoria afterward—the 'rush' that experienced skydivers seek.

Source: Top: IStock photo ID:467638220, Bottom: Stock photo ID:954842178.

Habituated Stimulus (Right Column)

As occurs with the unhabituated stimulus, a surge in the A-process coincides with the onset of the experience. However, the B-process no longer lags and exerts a more significant influence on the A-process than it did on the unhabituated stimulus (middle). Hence, no surge in the A-process with the onset of the stimulus is observed (middle). This coincides with a reduction in the intensity of the emotional experience compared to the baseline, or resting state, throughout the stimulus (bottom). As with the unhabituated stimulus, the offset of the A-process coincides with the termination of the stimulus. The B-process, which lags the A-process, continues unopposed. However, with the habituated stimulus, the contrasts between the emotion experienced after the offset of the unhabituated and habituated stimulus are more drastic (bottom). The effects of the B-process also persist for a more extended period than after offsetting the unhabituated response.

The Brain and the Opponent Process Theory

The A-process in the opponent process theory (Figure 4.9 [red line]) is believed to be caused by an excessive surge of activity, driven by the neurotransmitter dopamine, in the brain's reward system (i.e., ventral tegmental area, nucleus accumbens, and striatum) in response to appetitive stimuli such as the initial rush experienced when taking a drug. This surge of activity disrupts emotional equilibrium, forming the theory's basis. The B-process (Figure 4.9 [blue line]), which is associated with the aversive experience related to the removal of a pleasant stimulus (e.g., withdrawal symptoms), is believed to be a result of the activation of an emotional stabilization system that counteracts emotional deviations from equilibrium (Koob, 2021). One of the ways by which this is achieved is by shutting down activity in the brain's reward system through the inhibition of dopamine neurons that involve other brain areas (e.g., the habenula). Another way in which this is achieved is through the activation of regions outside the brain reward system, such as the amygdala, which is involved in processing pain signals, and the brain's stress system centered around the hypothalamic-pituitary-adrenal axis (Koob and Le Moal, 2008).

Critical Thinking Spot Check 4.2

1. Analyze the hedonic adaptation theory and its implications on subjective well-being. How does habituation contribute to the concept of the emotional set point? Provide examples to support your analysis.
2. Synthesize the opponent process theory and its application to various emotions, such as pleasure/pain or joy/sadness. How does this theory explain the dynamics of emotional experiences in situations like new relationships or intense workouts?
3. Evaluate the hedonic adaptation prevention model. Can appreciating positive life changes and varying positive experiences truly prevent the hedonic treadmill, as proposed by this model? Support your evaluation with critical analysis.
4. Apply the opponent process theory to real-life scenarios. Choose an example from your life or popular culture and explain how the opponent process theory could elucidate the emotional experiences in that situation.

Chapter Summary

Each bullet point aligns directly with the learning objectives outlined at the beginning of the chapter.

- Nonassociative learning refers to the process by which changes in behavior in response to the environment do not include forming links between one stimulus and another or between an action and its consequence. Nonassociative learning includes habituation and sensitization.
- Habituation refers to a reduction in the frequency or intensity of a response with repeated stimulation. It is essential to distinguish between habituation and sensory adaptation, which is also a reduction in the frequency or intensity of a response but because of a reduction in the response to a stimulus by sensory receptors.
- Habituation has several characteristics: spontaneous recovery, which refers to the return of a response after habituation; short-term habituation, which is habituation with short intervals between presentations of a stimulus; and long-term habituation, which is habituation with relatively long intervals between stimulus presentations. Short-term habituation results in a rapid response decrement but is associated with quicker spontaneous recovery. Long-term habituation is associated with a relatively longer time to habituation but is associated with less rapid spontaneous recovery.
- Habituation is stimulus specific, which means that being habituated to one stimulus does not widely generalize to other stimuli. In dishabituation, exposure to another stimulus may cause a habituated response to return. In contrast to habituation, dishabituation is not stimulus specific.
- Sensitization is an increase in responding to repeated presentations of a stimulus due to the presentation of another stimulus known as a sensitizing stimulus. Sensitization is not stimulus specific; any stimulus can act as a sensitizing stimulus.
- Several theories have been proposed to explain habituation and sensitization. The comparator model states that the brain forms a model of the frequently presented stimulus and generates a response to stimuli that do not match it. However, when a stimulus matches the model, no response is generated. According to the dual-process theory, whether habituation or sensitization occurs depends on the simultaneous and relative activation of a stimulus-response system and a state system. If activation of the stimulus-response system predominates, then habituation occurs. If activation of the state system predominates, then sensitization occurs.
- The opponent process theory is a process that keeps emotions in a state of equilibrium by counteracting emotional reactions that deviate from the baseline. The opponent processes theory proposes that motives are regulated by the same process that underlies drug addiction in which the pleasant feelings provided by a drug are counteracted by the opposing unpleasant experience that constitutes withdrawal symptoms.

Glossary

A-process The initial emotional reaction to a stimulus, typically strong and immediate.

B-process The delayed, opposing response that helps regulate emotional balance after the initial reaction.

Behavioral sensitization The process in which repeated exposure to a stimulus leads to progressively stronger behavioral reactions.

Comparator model A theory suggesting that habituation occurs by comparing incoming stimuli with stored memories of prior experiences.

Dishabituation The renewal of a habituated response when a new stimulus is introduced.
Dual-process theory A model explaining both habituation and sensitization as occurring through separate neural processes.
Emotional set point A baseline level of happiness or emotional stability that individuals tend to return to over time.
Habituation A decrease in response to a repeated, non-threatening stimulus over time.
Hedonic adaptation prevention model A framework suggesting strategies to slow down adaptation and sustain happiness over time.
Hedonic adaptation theory The concept that people return to a stable level of happiness despite positive or negative life changes.
Hedonic treadmill The idea that individuals continuously adapt to changes in life circumstances, maintaining a consistent level of happiness.
Long-term habituation A lasting reduction in response to a stimulus even after periods of non-exposure.
Non-associative learning Learning that occurs through repeated exposure to a stimulus without forming associations between different stimuli.
Opponent process theory A theory stating that emotional experiences trigger opposing physiological responses to maintain balance.
S-R system The stimulus-response system responsible for direct, automatic reactions to environmental cues.
Sensitization An increased response to a repeated stimulus, often due to its intensity or emotional significance.
Sensitizing stimulus A stimulus that increases reactivity to future stimuli by heightening responsiveness.
Sensory adaptation The process where sensory receptors reduce their response to constant stimuli over time.
Short-term habituation A temporary reduction in response to a stimulus that recovers after a brief absence.
Spontaneous recovery The reappearance of a previously diminished response after a period of non-exposure.
Startle response A reflexive reaction to a sudden, unexpected stimulus, often involving a physical jump or flinch.
State system The broader neural system that modulates sensitivity to stimuli based on factors like arousal and attention.
Subjective well-being An individual's perceived quality of life, including emotional satisfaction and happiness.

Module Summary

In Chapter 3, you learned that although many behaviors can be characterized as innate, most scientists believe that they can be modified by learning. You also learned that innate behaviors comprise reflexes and instincts and can be subdivided into appetitive and consummatory behaviors. In addition, you are now aware that the general process approach is an inadequate theory to explain learning. Instead, you have learned that learning can better be explained by what is known as the behavior systems approach.

In Chapter 4, you learned about nonassociative learning, which does not involve associations between stimuli or between a stimulus and a response. This is in contrast with associative learning, which occurs through associations between stimuli or between responses and stimuli. Nonassociative learning includes habituation and sensitization, which several theories can explain. Several theories have been proposed to explain habituation and sensitization. The comparator model states that the brain forms a model of the frequently presented stimulus and generates a response to stimuli that do not match it. Finally, you have learned about the opponent process theory, which keeps emotions in equilibrium.

Module 2

Application

The Hedonic Adaptation Prevention Model: A Way to Sustain Well-Being After Positive Experiences

According to the hedonic adaptation theory, a positive life change results in bursts of positive emotions followed by a period during which people habituate to the change and experience a return to their previous levels of well-being. The theory also states that, because of this, people constantly seek new experiences to achieve greater levels of well-being, in what became known as the hedonic treadmill (Brickman and Campbell, 1971). This would suggest that creating lasting changes in one's well-being is impossible. However, according to the hedonic adaptation prevention model (HAP), the hedonic treadmill can be avoided (Sheldon and Lyubomirsky, 2012).

According to the theory, adaptation to positive life changes occurs because a lack in the number and variety of positive events that can be derived from the positive life change prevents people from experiencing a continuity of positive emotions brought upon by the positive life change. In addition, a positive life change may result in a rise in one's aspiration level, meaning that ever better experiences are desired, leaving the person dissatisfied with their current happiness levels. Hence, two solutions to the hedonic treadmill are proposed, each following its distinct path (Figure 1-M2 App).

Path 1 (top): A positive life change creates long-lasting changes in happiness and well-being when the variety of experiences it generates is appreciated. Both variety and appreciation work together to prevent rising aspirations, that is, when one recognizes and is grateful for the diverse ways the change has improved one's life, aspirations are less likely to increase, leading to greater satisfaction and happiness. For example, learning to ski provides the opportunity to ski on various mountains and with various people (variety). When you appreciate these diverse experiences—being grateful that you are healthy enough to practice skiing, that you have the talent to do so, that you are physically able to do so, and that you have the financial means to afford the equipment—you prevent your aspirations from rising and maintain sustained well-being.

Path 2 (bottom): A positive life change can also increase one's long-term happiness and well-being when it generates an increased number of positive events combined with variety in those experiences. This combination increases the variety of positive emotions one experiences. For example, learning to ski may include going on multiple ski trips during which many pleasurable events occur. The variety in these experiences—skiing different mountains, trying different runs, skiing in different weather conditions, and skiing with various people—generates a diverse range of positive emotions such as excitement, accomplishment, social connection, and tranquility, all contributing to sustained well-being.

DOI: 10.4324/9781003491828-8

Figure 1-M2 App Two solutions to the hedonic treadmill (see text for details).
IStock photo ID:1185792622.

Try It Yourself

Now that you have learned about the hedonic adaptation model, think and write about how to prevent yourself from adapting to new positive events along the two pathways illustrated in Figure 1-M2 App.

1. Describe a positive life change that you have experienced.
2. What emotions did you feel at the time?
3. Did the experience produce long-lasting changes in your happiness and well-being?
4. If the emotions and sense of heightened well-being derived from the experience were short lived, what could you have done to create a lasting change along both paths of the HAP model?
5. Pick and describe a recent or upcoming positive life change that you hope will produce long-term changes in your happiness and well-being.
6. Describe how the initial burst of happiness and well-being will be transformed into sustained well-being.

Are You Thinking Critically?

1. Why is it essential to understand hedonic adaptation?
2. Describe the hedonic adaptation model.
3. How would your levels of well-being change if you were more appreciative of the positive events in your life?

Module 3

The ABCs of Classical Conditioning

Introduction

Many of an animal's behaviors are automatically triggered by environmental events. These behaviors are known as reflexes. In newborn humans, reflexes are the most basic form of organized behavior. The most obvious of these are known as newborn reflexes. These include the rooting, sucking, palmar grasp, stepping, and eyeblink reflexes. These reflexes are present at birth and have essential survival value. However, newborn reflexes disappear as a child's nervous system develops with age. Other reflexes form the basis for complex motor skills. Most of our reflexes are taken for granted but create a significant subset of our behavioral repertoire. This is because they prevent us from having to plan and consciously carry out every movement. In the 1920s, an experimental procedure was developed by which reflexes could be conditioned. By using this procedure, a reflex could be triggered by a stimulus that never triggered it in the past. This was done by associating that stimulus with one that usually triggered the reflex. This procedure became known as classical conditioning. This demonstration that reflexes could be conditioned paved the way for researchers to investigate the possibility that behaviors other than reflexes could also be conditioned. Chapter 5 explores the context of the discovery of classical conditioning and methodological considerations. In Chapter 6, you will learn about the various experimental situations in which classical conditioning can be studied, some of the brain areas involved, and its contributions to understanding neurological disorders and drug addiction.

DOI: 10.4324/9781003491828-9

5 Foundations and Basic Concepts of Classical Conditioning

Learning Objectives

- Describe Pavlov's discovery of classical conditioning and its independent discovery by Twitmyer in the United States.
- Explain the different types of conditioning procedures explored by Pavlov.
- Design a hypothetical experiment that ensures that the observed conditioned responses are not due to pseudoconditioning.
- Compare the various methods for measuring conditioned responses.
- Explain stimulus generalization and discrimination in classical conditioning experiments by using everyday examples.
- Consider the applications of extinction, spontaneous recovery, and conditioned inhibition for modifying behavior.
- Explain how US devaluation experiments supported the S-S theory of classical conditioning proposed by Pavlov and not the S-R theory proposed by Hull regarding the mechanisms underlying classical conditioning.

Salman and Coconut

IStock photo ID:1158324623

DOI: 10.4324/9781003491828-10

Salman's dog, Coconut, constantly barked at the neighbor's dog immediately after leaving the house for a walk. He also barked at dogs encountered on the sidewalk. Salman's friend, Deepika, a certified dog trainer, told Salman that Coconut's behavior was typical of fear aggression, a self-defense reaction aimed at driving threats away. She told Salman that as long as Coconut perceived other dogs as threats, he would continue to react that way. "I will show you how to deal with it," she said confidently. The next day, Deepika met with Salman as he was about to take Coconut for a walk and discreetly handed him a small bag of dog treats. "What am I supposed to do with these?" he asked. Deepika replied that he was to give Coconut several treats every time another dog was encountered. "What is that going do?" he asked with a puzzled look. "The goal is for Coconut to associate the sight of other dogs with getting treats," she answered. She further explained that Coconut would eventually learn to expect treats and get excited instead of expressing a fear response when seeing other dogs.

"Awesome!" exclaimed Salman. She then gave Salman simple instructions, which he carried out over the next few days. Coconut loved the treats and drooled profusely whenever he ate them. Soon enough, Salman noticed that Coconut had stopped barking at other dogs and that he now drooled upon seeing them. A few days later, he discovered Coconut also drooled when he jingled his keys before taking him for a walk. Salman realized that Coconut must have learned an indirect association between the sound of the jingling keys and getting treats because no other dog was in Coconut's presence when he heard that sound. When he told Deepika about this, she looked at him and said: "Of course, it is all a part of classical conditioning, one of the most basic forms of learning."

5.1 Foundations of Classical Conditioning

Vul'fson and Snarskii's experiments

As you read in Chapter 2, Russian physiologist Ivan Petrovitch Pavlov showed that understanding behavior requires understanding reflexes. While working in his laboratory, some of his students noticed that the **salivary reflex** of dogs (i.e., the automatic production of saliva), typically elicited when food was placed in their mouths, also occurred when their mouths were empty. To explain this phenomenon, they hypothesized that the salivary reflex might be elicited by stimuli associated with food delivery. This could have included different objects in the room or the sight of the experimenters preparing the food. They called this saliva production (i.e., the salivary reflex) "psychic secretion" because it indicated that the dogs could predict food delivery. However, Pavlov disliked the term because of its esoteric and unscientific overtones. He renamed the phenomenon "anticipatory salivation" to convey the idea that the dogs learned to anticipate the delivery of food from cues that had become associated with it. Pavlov found this accidental finding interesting and worthy of further study.

The initial studies in which these findings were investigated were not performed by Pavlov himself but by S. G. Vul'fson and A. T. Snarskii, two of his students (Pavlov, 1927). They conducted experiments that consisted of placing a variety of stimuli, such as sand, dry food, wet food, and sour water, in the mouths of dogs and measuring how much they salivated. They found that these stimuli triggered the dogs to salivate when placed in their mouths. They also found that the dogs salivated at the sight of the stimuli. For example, in one experiment, Snarskii gave dogs sour water that was colored black and found that the dogs eventually salivated at the sight of a bottle that contained a black liquid.

Pavlov's Famous Experiment

To better study the phenomenon, Pavlov (1927) set up an apparatus in a soundproof room where the dogs were placed to make sure that stimuli other than the ones he intended to present them, such as sounds coming from outside the room, could not be heard. He also set up a partition between the dogs and the experimenter. He did so to ensure that neither outside sounds nor the sight of the experimenter would not influence the dogs' behaviors. Any saliva produced by the dogs was collected in a bottle to be used as a measure of the salivary reflex. A tube connected to the bottle conveyed the saliva to a registering apparatus, which recorded the dogs' salivation. He then found neutral stimuli (i.e., that had never been associated with food) that could easily be paired with food and described in physical terms (e.g., a sound). This is because he wanted to find out if the dogs could learn to salivate to these neutral stimuli after being associated with food. It was also important that the stimuli were not part of the food, as in Vul'fson and Snarskii's experiments (e.g., sour water colored black). This is because if the stimuli were part of the food, they could not be independently manipulated. However, stimuli that were not part of the food, such as tones and lights, could be independently associated with the food.

Pavlov then established precise schedules that determined the timing and order in which the stimuli and the food were paired. In a typical experiment (Figure 5.1), Pavlov first presented dogs with a **neutral stimulus (NS)**, which did not elicit any particular response in the dogs except for an investigatory reflex (i.e., an animal's natural response to explore new things in their environment, such as turning their head towards the stimulus). The NS consisted of various stimuli, such as sounds, light flashes, or skin stimulation. He then exposed the dogs to trials (called conditioning trials) in which he repeatedly paired the NS with food, which he called unconditional stimulus (US). The dog's natural response to the food was the production of the salivary reflex, which he called the unconditional response (UR).

After several conditioning trials, he found that the dogs salivated to the NS when presented without the food. Pavlov concluded that the NS elicited the salivation reflex through its association with the food (US) during the conditioning trials and thus became what he called a conditional stimulus (CS). He called the salivation that occurred in response to the CS a conditional response (CR). Pavlov's procedure became known as **classical conditioning** but is often referred to as Pavlovian conditioning. Note the similarities between how Pavlov trained his dogs and Salman trained Coconut. The CS was another dog for Coconut, and the US was the treats. The UR was Coconut's drooling upon receiving the treats, and the CR was drooling in response to seeing other dogs. In contemporary literature, the terms

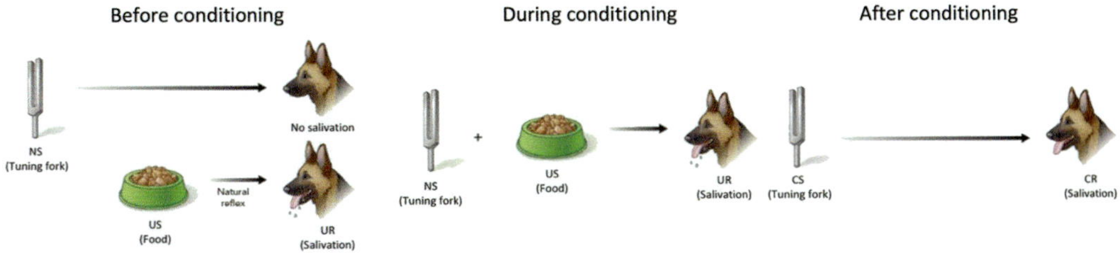

Figure 5.1 Classical conditioning procedure designed by Pavlov in which the sound of a tuning fork, which was initially a neutral stimulus (NS), became a CS that elicited salivation (CR) through its association with food (US).

Source: Modified from Okami, P. (2017). *Psychology*. Oxford University Press Academic US (page 335, Figure 7.3).

conditional stimulus, unconditional stimulus, conditional response, and unconditional response used by Pavlov have been mistranslated to **conditioned stimulus, unconditioned stimulus, conditioned response,** and **unconditioned response** (Clark, 2004). To avoid confusion, I use these latter terms throughout this textbook.

Classical Conditioning in the United States

Many students are familiar with Pavlov's original experiment on classical conditioning in Russia. However, a lesser-known fact is that, at about the same time, classical conditioning was independently discovered in the United States by psychologist Edwin Burket Twitmyer (1873–1943) while studying the patellar reflex, more commonly known as the "knee-jerk" reflex (Twitmyer, 1974). This reflex is elicited by tapping a rubber mallet just below the kneecap, performed during routine medical examinations. Twitmyer wanted to determine whether the patellar reflex could be facilitated by having subjects clench their fists before their patellar tendon was struck. As part of the experimental procedure, Twitmyer signaled when the subjects were to perform these actions by sounding a bell. While doing so, he accidentally discovered that the subjects responded to the sound of the bell before their patellar tendon was struck. In terms of classical conditioning, the sound of the bell was initially an NS, the tapping of the rubber mallet was the US, and the reflex was the UR. After several repetitions of the procedure, the bell became a CS that triggered the reflex as a CR. As interesting as this finding was, Twitmyer did not conduct further experiments to investigate it, possibly because the study of reflexive responses was not of primary interest to American psychologists, who were more interested in studying consciousness at the time.

Critical Thinking Spot Check 5.1

1. Explain the concept of "anticipatory salivation" and how Pavlov renamed it to convey that dogs learned to anticipate food delivery from associated cues.
2. How did Vul'fson and Snarskii's experiments contribute to understanding classical conditioning, especially regarding stimuli triggering salivation?
3. Compare Pavlov's classical conditioning experiment with Salman's training of Coconut, highlighting similarities and differences in CS, US, UR, and CR.
4. Evaluate the significance of Twitmyer's accidental discovery of classical conditioning in the United States and the potential impact on the field of psychology.

5.2 Methodological Aspects of Classical Conditioning

CTA: Conditioned Taste Aversion

Pavlov and his colleagues wondered whether the effectiveness of conditioning depended on the timing between CS and US presentations (Pavlov, 1927). They sought to answer this question with five different classical conditioning procedures: delay conditioning (also known as forward conditioning), trace conditioning, simultaneous conditioning, backward conditioning, and temporal conditioning. Each procedure, described subsequently and summarized in Table 5.1, differs in its effectiveness in learning an association between the CS and the US (Fitzwater and Reisman, 1952).

Table 5.1 Temporal arrangements in classical conditioning.

Delay conditioning	The CS precedes and ends with the overlapping onset of the US.	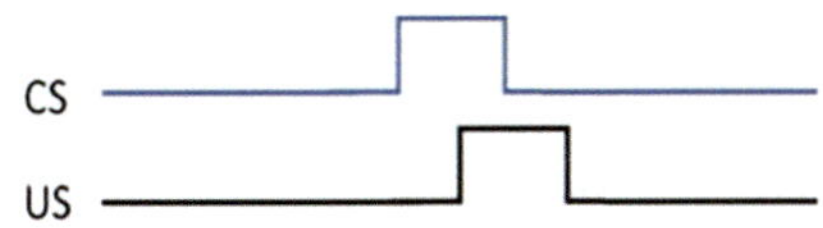
Trace conditioning	The offset of the CS and the onset of the US are separated by an interval known as a trace interval.	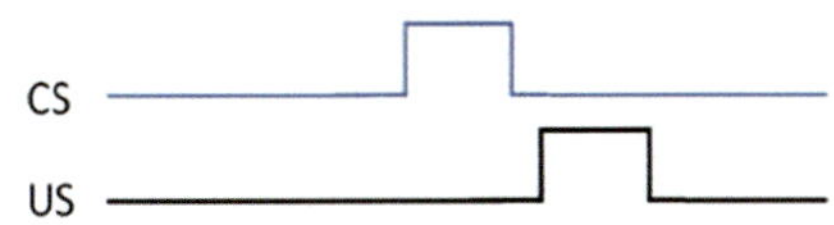
Simultaneous conditioning	The onset and offset of the CS and the US occur at the same time.	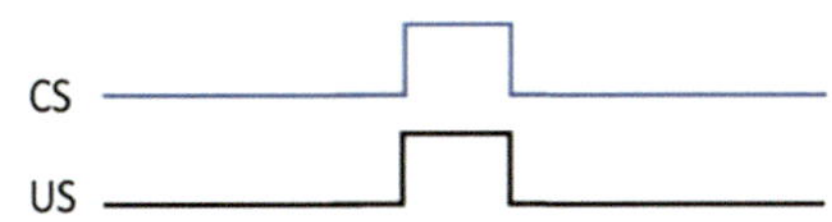
Backward conditioning	Presentation of the US precedes that of the CS.	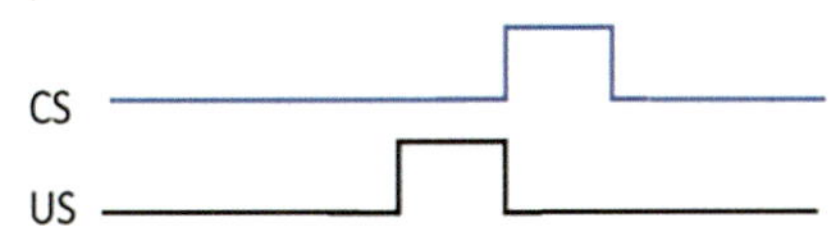
Temporal conditioning	The US is presented at regular intervals without a CS.	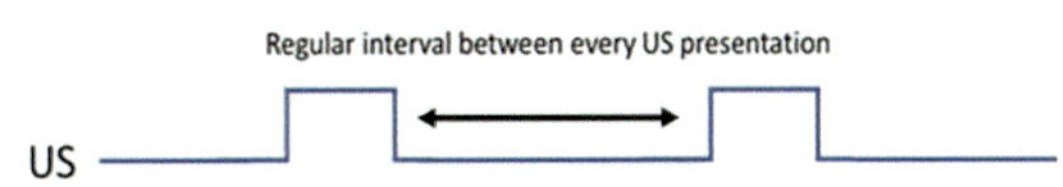

1. **Delay conditioning** (forward conditioning) occurs when the CS begins before administering the US. The US continues after the CS ends. Depending on how long the CS precedes the US, short- and long-delay conditioning types exist. For example, if Salman gave Coconut a treat (US) shortly after encountering another dog (CS) and kept giving treats until after the other dog left, he used short delay conditioning, which is the most effective method.
2. **Trace conditioning** occurs when the CS ends before the US begins. Hence, the CS and the US are separated by an interval called a *trace interval*. Successful trace conditioning requires animals to remember the CS for later association with the US. Hence, it can be successful if a short delay is interposed between the CS and US during training. With long delays, trace conditioning is less likely and was found to involve the hippocampus, a brain area crucial for memory (Clark, Manns and Squire, 2001; Clark and Zola, 1998).

   Conditioned taste aversion (CTA): an exception to the rule

   One exception to this rule is how a phenomenon known as **conditioned taste aversion (CTA)** occurs. In CTA, a person who becomes ill (US) after experiencing the gastrointestinal effects of spoiled food (UR) may experience nausea (CR) when again tasting or even smelling that food (CS). You may have experienced this yourself or know someone who has experienced it. The particularity of CTA, regarding trace conditioning, is that contrary to that description, the CS (taste of the food) and the US (feeling ill) are separated by an extended period. This is because, as you know, the illness experienced with eating spoiled food (US) only comes hours after eating it or tasting it (CS). This is believed to be a response developed by animals to increase their probability of survival after eating food that may be poisonous. If a poisonous food is consumed and the animal survives, it will never eat that food again. CTA and its various implications for behavior are discussed in detail in Chapter 7.

3. **Simultaneous conditioning**: Occurs when the CS and US start and end at the same time. It is less effective than delay or trace conditioning because animals need more time to process the CS before the US.
4. **Backward conditioning:** Occurs when the unconditioned stimulus (US) precedes the conditioned stimulus (CS). This method is considered the least effective form of conditioning in terms of CS signaling the US. Instead, in backward conditioning, the CS signifies the absence or removal of a US. For example, imagine that Salman (in the opening vignette) misunderstood the instructions given to him by his friend Deepika and gave Coconut treats (US) before he saw another dog (CS). As a result, Coconut would have learned that encountering another dog (CS) signaled that he would no longer receive treats (US). However, he would continue to bark when seeing another dog, perhaps more than ever, because he may have also associated barking with getting the treats. Similarly, when presented after the US, the CS indicates the end of an aversive stimulus, such as when a recess bell (CS) signals the end of the class (US). Finally, in backward conditioning, a CS, such as a buzzer, when presented after a series of electric shocks (US), can become a safety signal that indicates a period of safety during which an animal will no longer be subjected to the shocks (Moscovitch and LoLordo, 1968).
5. **Temporal conditioning**: Occurs when an unconditioned stimulus (US) is presented at regular intervals without a conventional CS, such as lights or sounds. In temporal conditioning, an association is formed between the US and the time it occurs. For example, people often feel hungry at particular times of the day, leading them to have breakfast at around 9:00 a.m., lunch at about noon, and dinner at approximately 5:00 p.m. Indeed, it was found that time of day plays a role in determining whether a person feels hungry (Weingarten, 1985; Franja et al. 2020) and that hunger is not only triggered by internal signals related to low energy levels (Louis-Sylvestre and Le Magnen, 1980; Mayer, 1955).

In another example of temporal conditioning, you may notice that you start waking up just before your alarm goes off if you consistently set it for the same time every morning. This happens because your alarm follows a regular schedule, ringing simultaneously every morning. As a result, the specific time of day when the alarm goes off (CS) becomes associated with the sound of the alarm (US), which triggers you to wake up (UR). Over time, the time of day transforms into a cue (CS) that signals your wake-up response (CR).

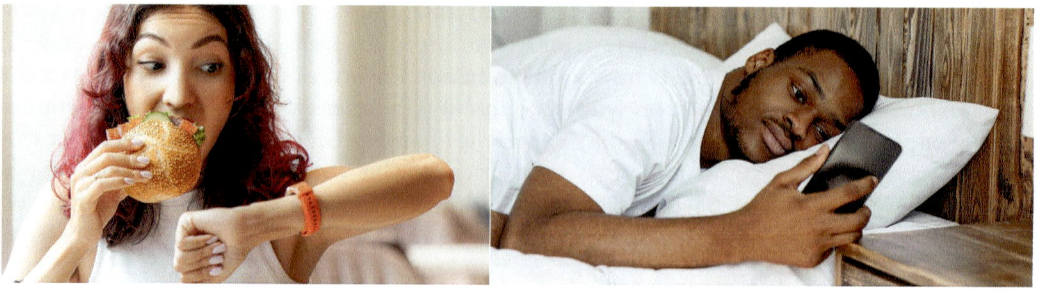

Due to temporal conditioning, people may tend to become hungry at the same times every day and may begin waking up before their alarm rings.

Source: Food and time: IStock photo ID:1441312667 Man with phone alarm: IStock photo ID:1286472865.

Control Groups

Adequately designed experiments include control groups. A control group consists of subjects not exposed to the treatment conditions to which experimental groups are subjected. For example, in a study investigating the effects of sleep deprivation on the ability to memorize lists of words, experimental groups would be subjected to different amounts of sleep deprivation. The results obtained in a subsequent memorization test by individuals in those groups would be compared to the performance of the control group who were not sleep deprived. This ensures that impairments observed in the memorizing of the lists are due to the sleep deprivation. This is because if individuals in the control group perform as poorly as the individuals in the experimental groups, then the observed impairment must be due to factors other than sleep deprivation.

What does the control group in a classical conditioning experiment comprise? It is agreed that for a conditioning procedure to succeed, an association between the presentation of a CS and the occurrence of a US must exist (Escobar and Miller, 2004; Rescorla, 1967). The association between the CS and the US is known as a **CS-US contingency** and typically grows stronger with the number of CS-US pairings.

To ensure that responding to the CS is genuinely due to learning the association between a CS and the US, the results of control procedures in which the CS-US contingency is absent or weak are compared to those of the experimental procedure in which a CS-US contingency exists. Hence, if what appears to be a CR in the control group is observed, what seems to be a CR in the experimental group might be caused by factors other than a learned association between the CS and US.

The Truly Random Control Procedure and the Explicitly Unpaired Control Procedure

Two control procedures are used in classical conditioning experiments (Rescorla, 1967). In one of these procedures, known as the truly **random control procedure**, the CS and the US are presented in random order with respect to each other, eliminating the possibility that a contingency could be detected between the orderly presentation of the CS followed by the occurrence of the US. However, this method has been criticized because it can still develop an association between the CS and the US (Papini and Bitterman, 1990). In the **explicitly unpaired control procedure**, the CS and the US are presented on separate trials. The trials are sufficiently spaced apart in time, rendering the development of an association between the CS and the US unlikely.

Pseudoconditioning

The inclusion of control groups addresses the possibility of **pseudoconditioning**, which refers to the elicitation of response to a neutral stimulus following repeated presentations of a CS. For example, exposure to a light (CS) followed by a shock (US) in a previous experiment may make a subject "jumpy" so that the presentation of any untrained stimulus could elicit a response (Smith, McFarland and Taylor, 1961). Therefore, if what seems to be a CR occurs in a group where the CS and US are presented in random order with respect to each other or widely spaced in time, pseudoconditioning is suspected.

What Is Measured in Classical Conditioning?

Throughout this textbook you will read about many experiments that involve classical conditioning. A variety of conditioned responses can be elicited and measured in classical conditioning experiments (Ayers and Powell, 2002). Therefore, you must familiarize yourself with the measures used to assess the effectiveness of conditioning in these experiments.

1. **Response Frequency:** Measures the percentage or number of trials in which the subject performs the CR. The more frequent the response, the stronger we assume the association between the CS and the US has become.
2. **Latency of Response:** Measures the time it takes for an animal to respond to a CS. A short latency indicates that a CS-US association is well learned. Longer latencies suggest the association is in the course of being learned or has not been learned.
3. **Response Magnitude:** Measures the intensity or amount of behavior the CS triggers. In Pavlov's famous experiment, this meant measuring salivation in response to the CS. With an unpleasant US like an electric shock, the measure could be the period during which an animal remains immobile (freezing), which is taken as a sign of fear.
4. **Physiological Measures:** Measures bodily responses to the CS, such as changes in heart rate, blood pressure, and the galvanic skin response (GSR). GSR measures the tiny amounts of sweat on the skin in an anxiety-provoking situation. Experimenters can also measure muscle tension and the secretions of hormones.
5. **Resistance to Extinction:** Measures the number of times an animal keeps responding to a CS when repeatedly presented without the US. The stronger the association between the CS and US, the longer an animal keeps responding. We focus on **extinction** in the next section.

Critical Thinking Spot Check 5.2

1. Explain the differences between delay conditioning and trace conditioning, highlighting the role of the trace interval in successful trace conditioning.
2. Why is simultaneous conditioning considered less effective than delay or trace conditioning, and how does the timing influence the learning process?
3. If you were designing an experiment to study classical conditioning, which of the five procedures (delay, trace, simultaneous, backward, temporal) would you choose, and why?
4. How might you apply the principles of temporal conditioning to understand habitual behaviors in daily life?
5. Propose an experimental design that investigates the effectiveness of classical conditioning in real-world scenarios, considering the principles of CS-US contingency.

5.3 Basic Observations in Classical Conditioning

Extinction

If you ever made the mistake of feeding your dog while at the table, you may now realize that you became a CS that predicts the delivery of food (US) and that your dog has acquired the annoying CR of coming up to you every time you sit at the table "begging" for food. This may be especially embarrassing when you have guests over to your house. How to eliminate such an annoying response? One solution to this problem is **extinction.** Extinction refers to the reduction of the frequency or intensity of a response due to repeated presentations of the CS without the US. The extinction of this response would consist of you sitting at the table, never again feeding it no matter how much it "begs." In the opening vignette, it was important for Salman to make sure that he consistently gave Coconut treats when encountering other dogs to prevent his more desirable behavior from undergoing extinction. Note that, as described, resistance to extinction is the extent to which an animal keeps responding during extinction trials and is a measure of the strength of association between a CS and a US.

Spontaneous Recovery

Pavlov (1927) observed that CRs spontaneously returned after extinction. He called this phenomenon **spontaneous recovery**. For example, the conditioned salivary reflex of a dog was extinguished by presenting it with the CS without the US every 10 minutes. By the end of these extinction trials, the amount of saliva secreted by the dog was reduced to zero. Spontaneous recovery occurred when the CS was presented after a 20-minute pause that followed the last extinction trial. Therefore, your dog's behavior is likely to recur after you thought it extinguished. The solution is to not give in and to keep subjecting it to further extinction trials. The existence of spontaneous recovery shows that extinction cannot be attributed to forgetting the CS-US association or unlearning. The curves representing the acquisition, extinction, and spontaneous recovery of a conditioned response are illustrated in Figure 5.2a. However, keep in mind that you still have much to learn about extinction. Its mechanisms, efficacy, and various behavioral effects are discussed more fully in Chapter 12.

Stimulus Generalization

Stimulus **generalization** refers to a phenomenon by which stimuli similar enough to a CS paired with the US elicit the same CR despite never having been paired with the US. Pavlov (1927) demonstrated this phenomenon in an experiment where vibrations on dogs' thigh areas (CS) were associated with food (US). He found that not only did the thigh vibrations (CS) produce salivation (CR) when administered on their own but that the dogs also salivated when the vibrations were administered to adjacent areas which were never paired with the US, such as the hind paw, pelvis, trunk, shoulder, foreleg, and forepaw. He also found that his procedure resulted in a **stimulus generation gradient**, in which the amount of salivation produced depended on the distance between the area stimulated and the thigh, which was the area stimulated during conditioning. The results of this experiment are illustrated in Figure 5.2b.

Stimulus generalization is an adaptive response because it permits responding similarly to stimuli associated with the same outcome, preventing people and animals from constantly learning redundant associations. For example, you likely react similarly to stimuli similar to CSs you first learned to associate with various USs. These include the sound of fire alarms, cell phone ringtones, traffic lights, and emergency vehicle sirens. Similarly, Salman did not have to train Coconut to associate food with every variety of dog because when it comes to generalization, "close enough" is the rule.(Roesmann et al., 2020).

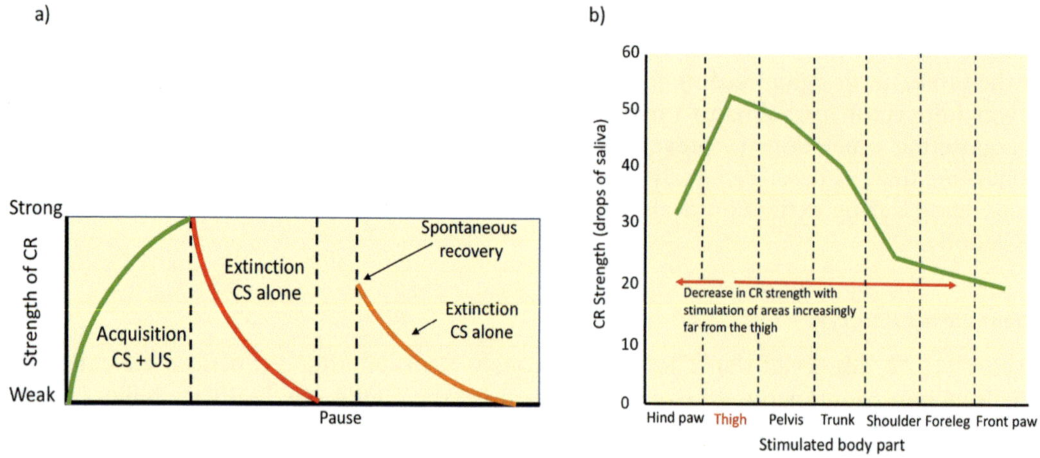

Figure 5.2 a) Left: The acquisition curve during hypothetical CS + US conditioning trials was followed by the extinction curve produced by presentations of the CS alone. Right: Spontaneous recovery and further extinction observed after a pause that followed the last extinction trial. b) The results of Pavlov's stimulus discrimination experiment show a decrease in CR strength with stimulation at increasing distance from the thigh.

Stimulus Discrimination

Stimulus discrimination refers to a phenomenon by which animals learn to respond differently to different stimuli. For example, an animal may learn that the sound of a bell (CS) signals the delivery of food (US) and therefore salivate (CR) when it hears it, while also learning that the sound of a buzzer (CS) signals a foot shock (US) and flex its leg (CR) upon hearing it.

Humans must also learn to discriminate between CSs. For example, you learned long ago to cross the street when the traffic light turns green and to refrain from doing so when it turns yellow or red. You have also learned to discriminate between cell phone rings, such as when assigning one to different friends and family members, each of which may elicit a different emotional reaction. Hence, learning to generalize in some situations and discriminate in others is essential.

Conditioned Inhibition

Conditioned inhibition is a procedure in which a CR elicited by a CS is inhibited when another concurrently trained CS signals the absence of a US. Pavlov (1927) developed a conditioned inhibition procedure comprising two trial types (trial type A and trial type B), illustrated in Figure 5.3.

In trial type A (left), CS-US pairings are repeated until a reliable CR is observed. The CS in this trial type is CS^+ and reflects the standard classical conditioning procedure you already learned about. In trial type B (right), administered periodically, a new CS, referred to as CS^-, is presented simultaneously with the CS^+, but the US is omitted. As a result of this training, an animal will produce a CR when presented with the CS^+ but will withhold

Figure 5.3 Conditioned inhibition procedure. An animal learns a CS-US association in trial type A (left). In the present example, the association is between the sound of a whistle (CS^+) and food (US). The dog eventually produces a CR (in this case, the salivation reflex) upon the sound of the whistle (CS^+). In trial type B (right), a new stimulus, which in the present example is a flash of light (designated as CS^-), is presented along with the whistle (CS^+). No US is presented when the CS^+/CS^- combination is presented. The animal eventually produces the CR only when the CS^+ is presented by itself but withholds responding when the CS^+/CS^- combination is presented.

response when the CS^+ is presented along with the CS^-. Similarly, a child may have associated an abusive father (CS) with harsh punishment (US) and experience intense fear (CR) whenever the father is around. However, because the father never punishes the child in the mother's presence (CS^-), the child's fear response may be inhibited when the mother is also present.

Critical Thinking Spot Check 5.3

1. Define extinction and describe its role in classical conditioning.
2. Analyze the Pavlovian experiment on spontaneous recovery. What does this phenomenon reveal about the nature of extinction and the persistence of conditioned responses?
3. How might stimulus generalization be advantageous for survival in the natural environment? Provide examples to support your answer.
4. Evaluate the adaptive value of stimulus discrimination in various real-life situations. When would it be advantageous for an organism to respond differently to different stimuli?
5. How might condition inhibition contribute to adaptive behavior in humans? Provide examples of situations where the inhibition of a conditioned response is beneficial.

5.4 What Is Learned in Classical Conditioning: SS and SR Theory

Stimulus-Stimulus or Stimulus-Response Associations?

Although it was evident to Pavlov that his dogs learned to associate a CS with the US, which resulted in a CR when the CS was presented by itself, the question remained about the nature of these associations in the brain. Pavlov hypothesized that, in classical conditioning, a brain center represented the CS, another center represented the US, and another represented the UR. He also believed that with repeated CS-US pairings, connections developed between the neurons across these centers and that they eventually became so intense that activation of the neurons in the US center was activated by activation of the neurons in the CS center, resulting in the activation of the UR center which elicited the CR when the CS was presented by itself. In the case where the US was food, as in his original experiment, the presentation of the CS activated the food center (US center), which in turn elicited salivation (UR center) through its pre-existing connections with the salivary glands. Hence, Pavlov believed that conditioning occurred through stimulus-stimulus (S-S) connections (i.e., CS to the US) in the brain, resulting in the CS eliciting the same response as the US. Therefore, Pavlov's idea of how conditioning occurs in the brain is known as the **S-S theory**.

However, psychologist Clark Hull (1884–1952) believed that once the connections between the CS and the US centers were strengthened, activation of the CS center directly activated the UR center, without the intermediary step of activating the US center, in stimulus-response connections (S-R) (Hull, 1943). Therefore, Hull's theory is known as **S-R theory**. The difference between S-S and S-R theory is illustrated in Figure 5.4.

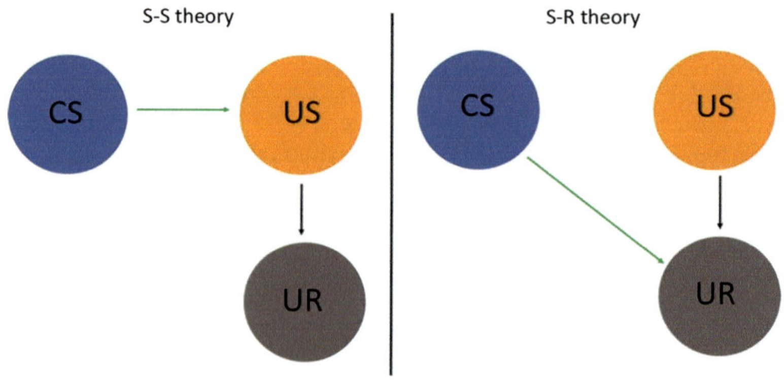

Figure 5.4 The S-S and S-R theories proposed by Pavlov and Hull, respectively (see text for details).

US Devaluation: Evidence for S-S Theory

At this point, you might wonder which of the two classical conditioning theories is correct, S-S or S-R. Fortunately, researchers designed experiments to try to answer this question (Holland and Rescorla, 1975; Holland and Straub, 1979). They hypothesized that if, as Pavlov suggested, the CS elicited the CR through strengthening connections between a CS and US center in the brain, then devaluating the US (i.e., making it less appealing) should weaken these connections, resulting in a weaker CR. On the other hand, if a direct association between the CS and the UR developed during conditioning, then devaluating the US should have no effect on the strength of the CR when the CS was presented by itself.

Holland and Straub (1979) tested this hypothesis using a procedure known as **US devaluation**, in which the US was deliberately made unappealing. As illustrated in Figure 5.5, the experiment consisted of three phases. In Phase 1, two groups of rats were placed in an experimental chamber that contained a food magazine. The rats were exposed to a 10-second noise (CS) followed by food delivery in the magazine (US) until they reliably

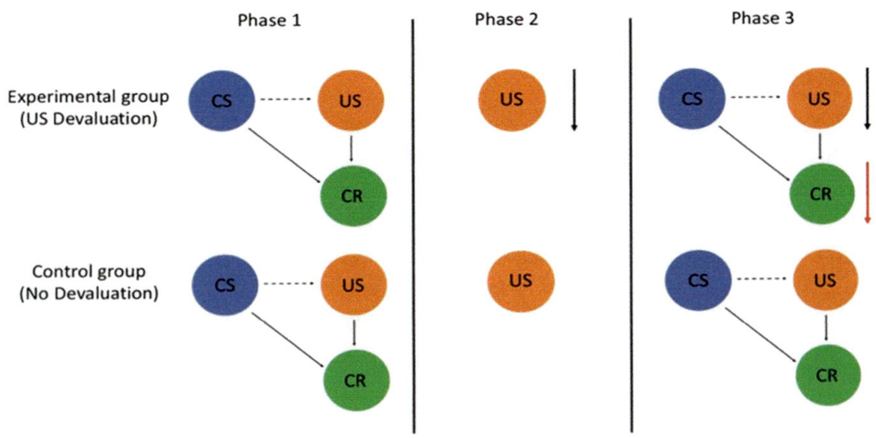

Figure 5.5 US devaluation procedure used by Holland and Straub (1979) (black arrows in Phase 2 and Phase 3 indicate that the US has been devaluated; the red arrow in Phase 3 indicates the weakened conditioned response).

performed the CR, which consisted of increased general motor activity, head movements, and the time spent in front of the food magazine.

In Phase 2, one group of rats, the experimental group, was permitted to eat the food freely. Afterward, they were placed on a phonograph turntable (record player) and spun at 120 revolutions per minute for 10 minutes. This manipulation devalued the US because the illness produced by being spun became associated with the food (US). Think about how you may have felt sick from going on an amusement park ride after eating. The rats in the control group were spun around similarly but were not given free access to the food (US) beforehand. Hence, for that group, the illness produced by being spun was not associated with the food (US), resulting in no US devaluation.

In Phase 3, Holland and Straub (1979) assessed how the rats responded to the CS by measuring their degree of motor activity, head movements, and orientation toward the food magazine (CR). They found that the rats in the experimental group, for which the US was devalued, showed a significant decrement in the CR compared to the rats in the control group. These results supported the S-S theory of conditioning. This is because if activating the association between the CS and the US had not been necessary for conditioning, devaluating the US in an attempt to weaken this connection would have had no effect.

Critical Thinking Spot Check 5.4

1. Describe Clark Hull's stimulus-response (S-R) theory and highlight the critical difference between S-S and S-R theories.
2. Discuss how the experimental design of US devaluation, as conducted by Holland and Straub, provides insights into the nature of classical conditioning theories.
3. Apply S-S and S-R theories to analyze a real-world scenario, explaining how each would predict the observed conditioning outcomes.

5.5 Indirect CS-US Associations

Higher-Order Conditioning

Higher-order conditioning refers to procedures in which a CS (let us call it CS_1), which has never been paired with the US, elicits a CR because of its association with another CS (let us call this one CS_2), which was directly paired with the US. In other words, in higher-order conditioning, a CS is "guilty by association." For example, if your friend has been caught cheating, you may be accused of being a cheater, even if you have never cheated. Higher-order conditioning can occur in two ways, each of which has been demonstrated by a specific procedure. These are known as **sensory preconditioning** and **second-order conditioning** (Figure 5.6).

Sensory Preconditioning

The sensory preconditioning procedure, illustrated in Figure 5.6 (top), was first used in an experiment conducted by psychologist Wilfred Brogden (1912–1973). It consisted of three phases. In Phase 1, the preconditioning phase, he repeatedly simultaneously exposed dogs to the sound of a doorbell (CS_1) and a flash of light (CS_2 [the preconditioned stimulus]).

In Phase 2, the conditioning phase, one group of dogs received pairings of the doorbell sound (CS_1) with a foot shock (US) until it reliably elicited a CR, which consisted of a flexion of the corresponding foreleg. In Phase 3, the test phase, the flash of light (CS_2) was presented by itself and elicited the same CR (flexion of foreleg) even if it was never directly associated with the US (foot shock). The result of Brogden's (1939) experiment supported

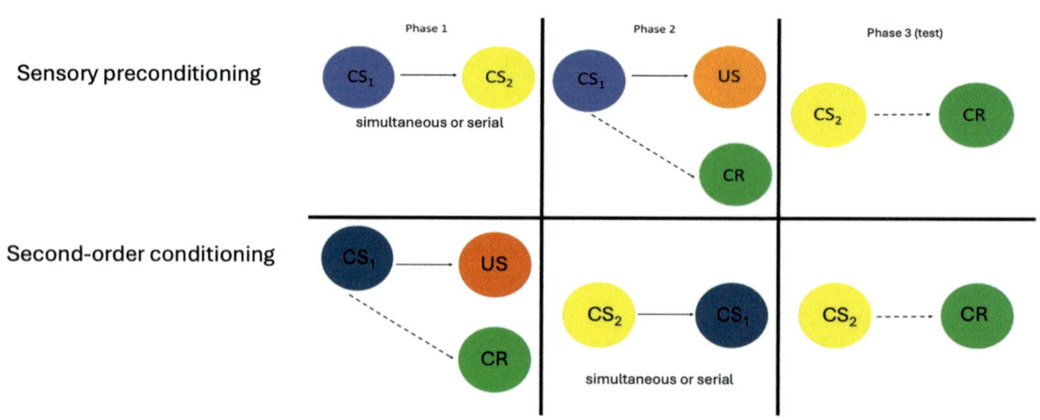

Figure 5.6 Higher-order conditioning. Top: Sensory preconditioning. In Phase 1, CS_1 and CS_2 are repeatedly presented simultaneously or serially. In Phase 2, CS_1 is paired with the US until it reliably elicits the CR. In Phase 3 (test), CS_2 elicits the CR despite never being directly paired with the US. Bottom: Second-order conditioning. In Phase 1, CS_1 is paired with the US until it elicits a CR. In Phase 2, a new stimulus (CS_2) is paired with CS_1 (simultaneous or serial). In Phase 3 (test), the presentation of CS_2 elicits the CR despite having never been directly paired with the US.

the idea that classical conditioning could occur through S-S associations, as predicted by Pavlov and consistent with the US devaluation experiment by Holland and Straub (1979) described previously. It showed that a CS could elicit a CR through its association with another CS, bypassing a direct association with the US.

Sensory preconditioning can be made more explicit by considering a real-life example. Imagine frequently hearing a specific song (CS_1) while studying in a coffee shop (CS_2). One day, after studying, you attend a gathering with your friends. All is fun and games (US), and the song (CS_1) you frequently hear in the coffee shop (CS_2) is played. The next day, your mood is elevated (CR) as soon as you enter the coffee shop (i.e., before hearing the song again). Hence, entering the coffee shop (CS_2), which has never been associated with fun and games, elevates your mood (CR) through its association with the song (CS_1), which has been associated with fun and games at the gathering.

Second-Order Conditioning

Pavlov developed the second-order conditioning procedure, illustrated in Figure 5.6 (bottom) (Pavlov, 1927). In Phase 1, CS_1, the first-order CS, is associated with the US until it reliably elicits a CR. In Phase 2, CS_2, the second-order CS, which has never been associated with the US, is associated with CS_1. In Phase 3 (test), CS_2 is presented by itself and elicits the same CR as CS_1, even if it was never directly associated with the US. You may have noticed that Phases 1 and 2 of second-order conditioning and sensory preconditioning are presented in reverse order.

Remember from the opening vignette that after Coconut was conditioned to anticipate a snack (US), as shown by his conditioned drooling (CR) when he saw other dogs (CS_1), he also drooled when hearing the jingling of Salman's keys (CS_2) just before going for a walk, even if the jingling of keys was never directly associated with other dogs. This is a clear example of second-order conditioning (i.e., CS_1 [other dogs], CS_2 [jingling of keys], CR [drooling]).

Further experiments showed that the CS_2 continues to elicit a CR despite the US devaluation and extinction of the CS_1. For these reasons, second-order conditioning provides evidence that classical conditioning can result in the development of an S-R association. Note that in Phase 2, the CSs can be presented simultaneously or serially (one after the other).

Second-order conditioning has been shown in many animal species, including humans (see Lee, 2021 for review). In humans, second-order conditioning is believed to play a role in phobias, in which people develop fears of objects or situations through their association with a traumatic event (Reynolds, Field and Askew, 2017) and in posttraumatic stress disorder (PTSD) (Wessa and Flor, 2007), in which people may relive a traumatic event when exposed to environmental cues associated with it. For example, a person who developed a phobia of dogs (CS_1) after having been bitten may now avoid malls (CS_2) after seeing a blind person with a guide dog in a mall. Similarly, a person who has PTSD who "relives" a traumatic event when hearing sirens (CS_1), which were associated with being in a horrible accident, may now avoid busy streets (CS_2) where sirens are often heard (phobias and a type of therapy used to treat them are discussed in the next chapter).

Focus On

Classical Conditioning in Advertising

In classical conditioning, a neutral stimulus, such as a buzzer or a bell, which does not produce a significant response, is paired with a biologically relevant stimulus called an unconditioned stimulus (US), such as food. On its own, this stimulus produces an unconditioned response (UR), such as salivation. After a few pairings, the initially neutral stimulus becomes a conditioned stimulus (CS) that elicits the response, now referred to as conditioned response (CR), when presented by itself.

Evaluative Conditioning

Advertisers aim to influence people's attitudes (i.e., how they feel or think) about their products. Advertisers can achieve this goal by taking advantage of a particular case of classical conditioning known as **evaluative conditioning.** In evaluative conditioning, a neutral stimulus is paired with an emotionally significant US, which causes the initially neutral stimulus to become a CS that elicits an affective or emotional response. Hence, advertisers aim for consumers to associate a brand name (CS) with a US charged with positive emotions to become a CS that evokes the same positive emotions (CR) when encountered, increasing the probability that their brand is selected over another (Schachtman, Walker and Fowler, 2011).

Applying classical conditioning to advertising has been the focus of study for many years (Allen and Janiszewski, 1989; Razran, 1954; Staats and Staats, 1958). In a classic study, researchers asked participants to evaluate musical segments as pleasant or unpleasant, each of which subsequently served as the US. The participants in one group then viewed the image of a blue or beige-colored pen, one of which was paired with the music they had rated as pleasant (CS). For the other group, the image of one of the colored pens was paired with the music they had rated as unpleasant. They found that when given a free choice, 79% of the participants for whom one of the colored pens was paired with the pleasant music chose that pen over the unpaired colored pen (CR). In contrast, only 30% of the participants, for whom one of the colored pens was paired with music and rated as unpleasant, chose the pen over the unpaired pen (Gorn, 1982).

In their use of evaluative conditioning, sports apparel companies often associate their brand with famous athletes. For example, in a television ad, the company's highly recognizable logo is seen at the top of the screen against the background of a city. Seconds later, a famous athlete who instills inspiration and feelings of admiration due to his support of an important cause is seen silently walking down a street. In this example, the company has chosen an inspirational and admired athlete (US) who elicits strong positive emotions as a UR. By pairing its logo with the athlete's sight, the company hopes it will become an effective CS at eliciting the same positive emotions in consumers as a CR.

Second-Order Conditioning

Second-order conditioning occurs when a CS (CS_1) is paired with a US until it elicits a CR. A second CS (CS_2) is then paired with the CS_1, eliciting the same CR as CS_1

without ever having been directly paired with the US. In addition to evaluative conditioning, second-order conditioning is another tool advertisers use to influence consumers' attitudes toward their products. For example, in a television ad for a caffeinated energy drink, happy-looking teens (CS_1) are seen enjoying themselves while gaming (US) and looking very excited (UR). Near the end of the ad, the teens are shown downing a can of the drink with the logo and brand name of the company (CS_2) visible. The advertisers' goal is for consumers to first pair the image of happy teens (CS_1) with the enjoyment induced by gaming (US) and then show the happy teens (CS_1) with the brand's logo (CS_2). They hope that the sight of their brand (CS_2) will produce the same excitement experienced while gaming (CR) when seen on store shelves.

Companies often show people enjoying themselves while consuming their product in commercials, hoping it will become a CS associated with positive emotions (US).

Source: IStock photo ID:92190732.

Are You Thinking Critically?

1. Advertisers aim to associate a brand with a positive emotional response in evaluative conditioning. Can you provide examples of successful brands that have achieved this through evaluative conditioning?
2. Using either evaluative conditioning or second-order conditioning, how would you create a public message discouraging people from drinking and driving?
3. What is the value of knowing about classical conditioning for advertisers?

Critical Thinking Spot Check 5.5

1. What is sensory preconditioning, and how does it differ from second-order conditioning?
2. Explain the concept of higher-order conditioning with an example from the text.
3. Analyze the results of Brogden's sensory preconditioning experiment. How do the findings support the idea of classical conditioning through stimulus-stimulus (S-S) associations?
4. Evaluate the role of second-order conditioning in real-life scenarios, such as the development of phobias or symptoms of posttraumatic stress disorder (PTSD).
5. Apply the concept of second-order conditioning to analyze a specific advertising campaign. How is a secondary stimulus (CS2) associated with the primary stimulus (CS1) to influence consumer attitudes?

Chapter Summary

Each bullet point aligns with the learning objectives outlined at the beginning of the chapter.

- Two of Pavlov's students, Vul'fson and Snarskii, discovered that dogs salivated when exposed to cues associated with food that had been placed in their mouths. To study this phenomenon, Pavlov invented a procedure known as classical conditioning, in which a neutral stimulus (NS) becomes a conditioned stimulus (CS) that elicits a conditioned response (CR) after being paired with an unconditioned stimulus (US). Classical conditioning was independently discovered in the United States by Edwin Burket Twitmyer as Pavlov was conducting his experiments in Russia. However, Twitmyer never pursued his studies of the phenomenon.
- Pavlov investigated the effects of manipulating the temporal order of the CS and US presentation, which gave rise to short-delay conditioning, long-delay conditioning, trace conditioning, simultaneous conditioning, backward conditioning, and temporal conditioning. Pavlov found the most effective procedure to be short-delay conditioning and the least effective procedure to backward conditioning. Classical conditioning experiments must include appropriate control groups to ensure that the CR is genuinely due to the association between the CS and the US and not to pseudoconditioning. Control procedures include the truly random control procedure and the explicitly unpaired control group.
- Conditioned responses can be measured in several ways, including frequency, latency of response, response magnitude, resistance to extinction, and physiological measures.
- Stimulus generalization refers to the spread of conditioning to stimuli that resemble the stimulus used during conditioning. Stimulus discrimination refers to differentially responding to stimuli that differ from the stimulus used in conditioning.
- Extinction refers to the reduction in the frequency or intensity of a CR with repeated presentations of the CS by itself. Spontaneous recovery refers to the phenomenon by which an extinguished CR recurs following the last extinction trial. Spontaneous recovery is taken as evidence that extinction is not the same as forgetting but a form of learning.
- In conditioned inhibition, a CR elicited by a CS is inhibited when another concurrently trained CS signals the absence of a US. The conditioned inhibition procedure consists of two types of trials. In Type A trials, animals are exposed to pairings between a CS (CS^+) and the US, resulting in the CS eliciting a CR when presented by itself. In Type B trials, a second CS (CS^-) is presented concurrently with the CS^+ and the US is omitted.

- Pavlov believed that, in classical conditioning, a brain center representing the CS activated another representing the US, which activated the salivary glands to produce conditioned salivation CR. This became known as the S-S theory. However, Clark Hull believed that the CS directly activated the CR after conditioning. This became known as the S-R theory. To find out which of the two theories was correct, Holland and Straub performed a US devaluation experiment, which showed that the CR depended on the activation of the US representation by the CS, consistent with the S-S theory.

Glossary

Backward conditioning A conditioning method where the unconditioned stimulus appears before the conditioned stimulus, often resulting in weak learning.

Classical conditioning A learning process where a neutral stimulus becomes associated with a meaningful stimulus, producing a conditioned response.

Conditioned inhibition A learned suppression of a conditioned response due to specific signals indicating the absence of the unconditioned stimulus.

Conditioned response (CR) A learned reaction to a conditioned stimulus due to previous association.

Conditioned stimulus (CS) A previously neutral stimulus that, after association with an unconditioned stimulus, elicits a learned response.

Conditioned taste aversion (CTA) A learned avoidance of a specific food due to a negative experience, such as illness.

CS-US contingency The degree to which the conditioned stimulus reliably predicts the presence of the unconditioned stimulus.

Delay conditioning A form of classical conditioning where the conditioned stimulus appears before and overlaps with the unconditioned stimulus.

Evaluative conditioning A learning process where a stimulus gains positive or negative associations based on prior pairings with emotional experiences.

Explicitly unpaired control procedure A technique ensuring that the conditioned stimulus and unconditioned stimulus are presented separately to rule out conditioning effects.

Extinction The gradual weakening of a conditioned response when the conditioned stimulus is repeatedly presented without the unconditioned stimulus.

Generalization The tendency to respond similarly to stimuli resembling the conditioned stimulus.

Latency of response The time delay between stimulus presentation and behavioral reaction.

Neutral stimulus (NS) A stimulus that initially does not elicit a response but can acquire significance through conditioning.

Physiological measures Biological responses used to assess learning, such as heart rate or neural activity.

Pseudoconditioning An increase in response to a stimulus due to prior exposure, not true conditioning.

Random control procedure A method where the conditioned stimulus and unconditioned stimulus are presented randomly, preventing strong associations.

Resistance to extinction The persistence of a conditioned response despite repeated exposure to the conditioned stimulus without reinforcement.

Response frequency The number of times a behavior occurs within a given time frame.

Response magnitude The intensity or strength of a behavioral reaction to a stimulus.

Salivary reflex An automatic physiological response where saliva is produced in reaction to food-related stimuli.

Second-order conditioning A method where a conditioned stimulus is used to condition a new stimulus, creating a chain of learned associations.

Sensory preconditioning A process where two neutral stimuli are associated before one becomes a conditioned stimulus, influencing later responses.

Simultaneous conditioning A procedure where the conditioned stimulus and unconditioned stimulus occur at the same time.

Spontaneous recovery The sudden reappearance of an extinguished conditioned response after a rest period.

S–S theory (Stimulus–Stimulus theory) A learning theory proposing that organisms learn an association between two stimuli, such that one stimulus comes to predict or represent another (e.g., a conditioned stimulus predicts an unconditioned stimulus).

S–R theory (Stimulus–Response theory) A learning theory proposing that learning consists of forming a direct association between a stimulus and a behavioral response, strengthened through reinforcement or repetition.

Stimulus discrimination The ability to distinguish between different stimuli, responding only to the conditioned stimulus.

Stimulus generalization gradient A pattern showing how response strength varies as stimuli become less similar to the conditioned stimulus.

Temporal conditioning A process where an unconditioned stimulus is presented at regular time intervals, leading to an association with time itself.

Trace conditioning A conditioning method where the conditioned stimulus stops before the unconditioned stimulus appears, creating a gap in time.

Unconditioned response (UR) A natural, automatic reaction to an unconditioned stimulus.

Unconditioned stimulus (US) A stimulus that naturally triggers an automatic response without prior learning.

US devaluation A reduction in the effectiveness of the unconditioned stimulus, weakening conditioned responses.

6 Classical Conditioning Beyond Pavlov

From Little Albert to Peter and the Rabbit

Learning Objectives

- Explain fear conditioning using Pavlov's and Watson's experiments, detailing how neutral stimuli can elicit fear responses through associative learning in humans and animals.
- Describe the conditioning of the eyeblink reflex and its neural mechanisms involving the cerebellum.
- Analyze autoshaping as a form of conditioning in which animals exhibit either sign-tracking or goal-tracking responses to conditioned stimuli, exploring its implications for understanding addictive behaviors in humans.
- Discuss counterconditioning as a technique for reversing conditioned responses by pairing a conditioned stimulus with a new, incompatible, unconditioned stimulus and highlight its application in behavioral therapy, such as systematic desensitization for phobias.

Giuseppina's Needle Phobia

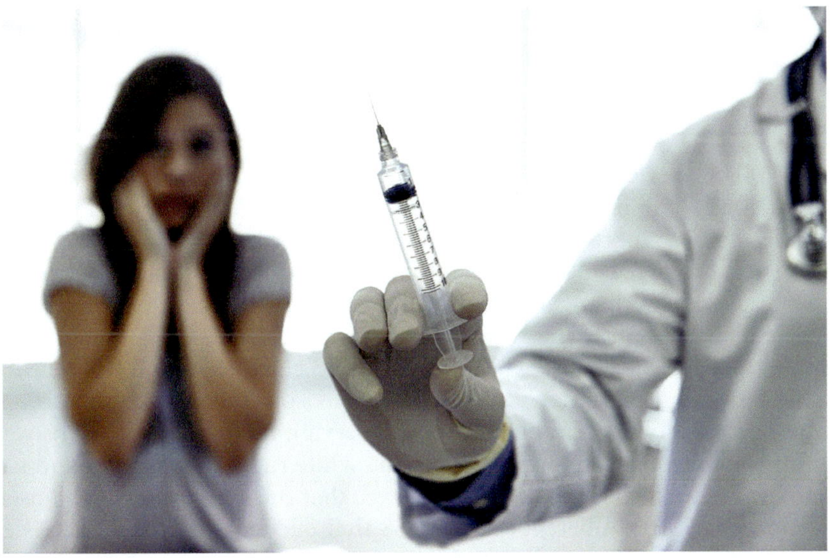

Istock photo ID:487998

DOI: 10.4324/9781003491828-11

Giuseppina was a psychology student during the COVID-19 pandemic. She was happy to hear that a vaccine became available at the time. However, even though she knew vaccines were safe, she was extremely anxious about getting one. This is because she suffered from needle phobia, defined as an extreme fear of undergoing a medical procedure that involves an injection. When asked about the source of her phobia, she recounts suffering anaphylaxis, a rare but severe allergic reaction which can occur after getting allergy shots. This happened after undergoing immunotherapy, during which a small amount of allergen was injected under her skin to reduce her severe bee-sting allergy. Her reaction included a narrowing of her airways, which impeded her breathing and led her to feel dizzy and nauseous. It was Giuseppina's most traumatizing event of her life, which left her with an extreme fear of needles. Her fear was so intense that just imagining getting an injection triggered in her a wave of intense anxiety and a feeling that she was about to faint. However, for Giuseppina, contracting COVID-19 and possibly infecting those around her was out of the question. She finally decided that it was time to cope with her fear. She underwent exposure therapy, during which she learned to relax while being exposed to progressively more threatening situations that involved needles. The least threatening situation consisted of imagining a needle, and the most threatening consisted of being in the presence of one. A few weeks later, she felt ready for the vaccine and mustered the courage to get the jab. Still apprehensive, she asked her best friend to accompany her for comfort. There are several causes for injection phobia. One of them may be that an injection (CS), like for Giuseppina, was associated with an aversive medical experience (US) and now triggers a conditioned fear response (CR) at the sight of needles or whenever the possibility of getting an injection presents itself. If you, like Giuseppina, suffer from injection phobia, know that you are not alone. It was found that 20% to 30% of young adults suffer from needle phobia, which in turn may account for 16% of adults not getting vaccinated (McLenon and Rogers, 2019).

6.1 Fear Conditioning

Little Albert

In the early 1900s, American psychologist John B. Watson (1878–1958) hypothesized that emotional reactions could be conditioned similarly to how Pavlov conditioned dogs to salivate. Watson tested his hypothesis in an experiment where he conditioned fear reactions in a baby (Watson and Rayner, 1920).[1] The subject was a nine-month-old infant who famously became known as Little Albert. The CS in the experiment was a white rat, which Little Albert initially enjoyed—observing Little Albert's excitement and joy whenever the white rat was around made this obvious. The US was a loud clanging sound produced by striking a steel bar with a hammer. Little Albert's UR to this sound consisted of raising his arms, puckering his lips, trembling, and breaking into a crying fit, all of which consisted of a fear response. Conditioning trials involved pairing the white rat (CS) with the loud sound of the hammer striking the metal bar (US). The result was that the white rat, which initially elicited a joyous response in Little Albert, became a CS that elicited a fear response (CR) in Little Albert, which Watson called a **conditioned emotional response** (Watson and Morgan, 1917).

After the experiment, Watson wondered whether Albert's conditioned emotional response would generalize (see Chapter 5 for an explanation) to other animals or objects resembling the white rat. Indeed, it did. Watson found that Little Albert displayed the same fear response when presented with a white fur coat, rabbit, and a Santa Claus mask (which included the white beard). Watson and Rayner (1920) suggested that the results of the Little Albert experiment could explain the development of phobias in which an initially neutral stimulus, such as an innocuous object or situation, becomes a CS that triggers a fear reaction (CR) through its association with an aversive stimulus (US). Other psychologists later expanded this idea (e.g., Mowrer, 1939).

You can now understand how Giuseppina, in the opening vignette, might have acquired her needle phobia. Before suffering from anaphylaxis induced by the injections she received as part of her immunotherapy, needles did not cause her to experience any fear. Needles became CSs that triggered fear as a CR only after she experienced the symptoms of anaphylaxis as a result (US). She eventually overcame her phobia by undergoing a type of behavioral therapy known as **systematic desensitization,** which is described in this module's application.

Phobias and Vicarious Classical Conditioning

It is essential to understand that phobias can be acquired in ways that differ from how Giuseppina acquired her needle phobia. Phobias can also be learned in what is known as **vicarious classical conditioning** (Ost and Hugdahl, 1985). The term "vicarious" comes from the Latin "vicarius," meaning "to take the place of" or "second-hand." Therefore, vicarious classical conditioning involves learning a CS-US association by observing others. For instance, a fear of the dentist (CS) may be acquired by witnessing another person experiencing pain (US) during a dental procedure.

An Animal Model of Fear Conditioning

Fear conditioning, such as that experienced by people suffering from phobias, can be studied in the laboratory using animal models. For example, animal models of fear conditioning are often used in studies aiming to uncover the neurobiological processes involved in fear (Yau and McNally, 2018), the various factors involved in the expression of fear (Poulos et al., 2016), and the factors involved in the development of anxiety and stress-related disorders (Campos et al., 2013).

A typical fear-conditioning experiment in animals, known as **auditory fear-conditioning** (Johansen et al., 2011) is illustrated in Figure 6.1. A rat is given a mild foot shock (US) shortly after the onset of a tone (CS) played through a speaker. The shock causes the rat to display a startle response (UR), which involves a sudden contraction of the muscles, causing it to jump. Hence, the tone, originally an NS (left), becomes a CS that predicts the shock. Subsequently, the presentation of the tone (CS) without the foot shock causes the rat to freeze in place (CR), a response taken to be an expression of fear.

As shown in Figure 6.1, CRs can also be observed in physiological processes, such as increased blood pressure. Before conditioning, the tone alone results in a slight rise in blood pressure, and the time the rat spends freezing is minimal. During conditioning, the rat's blood pressure and the time it spends freezing rises significantly. After conditioning, presenting the tone (CS) increases the rat's blood pressure to the levels observed during conditioning, during which the shock was administered.

Similar physiological changes are observed in people with phobias when thinking about or confronted with a feared object or situation; for people with needle phobia, such as

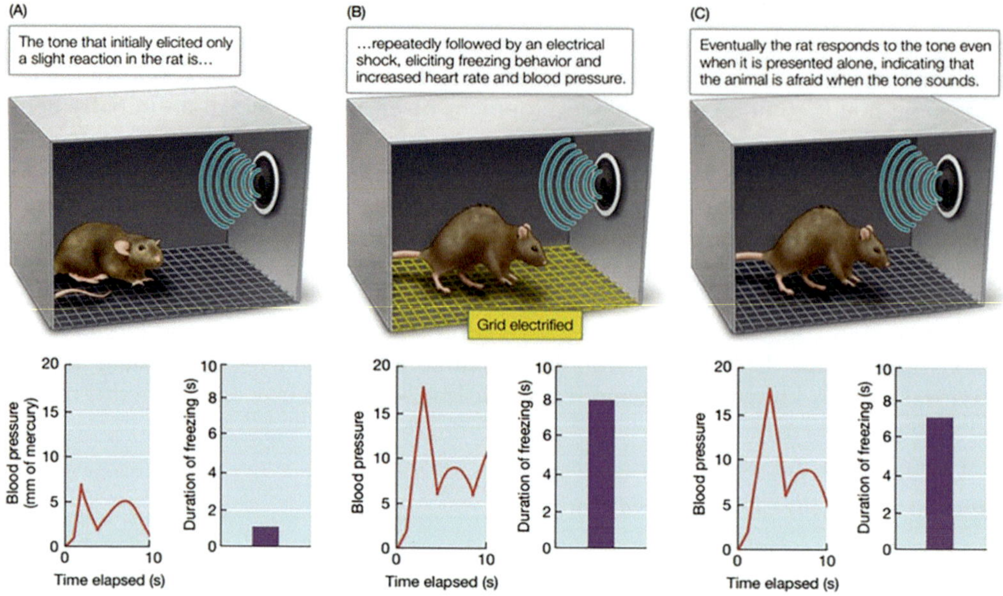

Figure 6.1 Fear conditioning procedure (see text for details).

Source: Breedlove, M. (2015). *Principles of psychology*. Oxford University Press Academic US. Page 320, Figure 8.15.

Giuseppina, an increase in heart rate and blood pressure is counteracted by an opposite reaction that results in feeling faint (Ritz, Meuret and Ayala, 2010).

Fear Conditioning Experiments Show the UR Can Differ From the CR

While reading about the typical fear conditioning experiment results, you may have noticed that the UR that occurs during the CS-US pairings differs from the CR. That is, during the pairings, the rat's UR in response to the shock (US) is to jump (which is part of the startle response). However, after conditioning, its response to the CS is to freeze in place.

This finding and many others provide support for the behavior systems approach to learning, discussed in Chapter 1, in which responses to stimuli reflect the functional requirements of animals, as opposed to the general systems approach in which general theories of behavior apply to all situations regardless of the nature of stimuli. The results of fear conditioning experiments show that learning about the relationship between a CS and a US may alter how an animal responds to a CS. That is, it may be adaptive for rats to try to escape (UR) a harmful stimulus (US) when it occurs (i.e., escaping the shock by jumping, which is part of its startle response). However, when in its natural environment, it may be more adaptive for a rat to freeze (CR) in response to a stimulus (CS) that signals a potential threat (US). For example, if the danger is a predator, it is less likely to be detected if it remains immobile (Blanchard and Blanchard, 1969; Fanselow, 1980). I will return to this issue in Chapter 7.

The Amygdala: A Brain Area Involved in Fear Conditioning

The study of animals and people has provided substantial evidence that the amygdala, a structure buried deep in the brain's temporal lobes, is essential for processing emotions. The amygdala's role in processing fear has often been studied in rats that received experimental damage to the amygdala before being subjected to the auditory fear conditioning procedure shown in Figure 6.1. The rats in these studies often failed to show responses attributed to fear, such as freezing, after being presented with a tone paired with shock (LeDoux, 2000).

Interestingly, fear conditioning (where the CS was a tone and the US was an aversive white noise) was also found to be impaired in college students who regularly indulge in binge drinking versus those who do not (Stephens et al., 2005). It was also found that fear conditioning (where the CS was a tone and the US was a mild shock to the arm) was impaired in men who do not have alcohol use disorder but who have a family history of alcoholism (Finn, Kessler and Hussong, 1994). This led researchers to wonder whether the functioning of the amygdala was altered in individuals who abuse alcohol. For example, in one study, researchers compared the activity in the amygdala of participants who suffered from alcohol use disorder with those of healthy participants through functional magnetic resonance imaging (fMRI). They found that the amygdala of the participants who suffered from alcohol use disorder was significantly less activated during fear conditioning (where a lampshade of a certain color was the CS and the US was a mild shock to the palm) than the amygdala of healthy participants (Muench et al., 2021).

Critical Thinking Spot Check 6.1

1. Describe John B. Watson's choice of a white rat as the conditioned stimulus (CS) in the Little Albert experiment and the initial reaction of Little Albert to the rat.
2. Summarize the conditioned emotional response (CR) Little Albert developed and explain how it was generalized to other stimuli.
3. Relate Giuseppina's needle phobia to the principles of fear conditioning discussed, emphasizing the role of conditioned stimuli (CS) and unconditioned stimuli (US).
4. Examine the ethical implications of Watson's Little Albert experiment, considering contemporary ethical standards and the impact on psychological research practices.

6.2 Eyeblink Conditioning

Following Pavlov's experiments, researchers wondered whether motor reflexes could be conditioned using the same basic conditioning procedure Pavlov used. One motor reflex that became the focus of the study was the eyeblink reflex. The eyeblink reflex refers to a defensive response in which involuntary blinking occurs in response to stimulation of the cornea (i.e., the transparent layer that covers the front of the eye). The first eyeblink reflex conditioning experiments were conducted in the 1930s on dogs and human participants (Hilgard, 1931; Hilgard and Marquis, 1935). In **eyeblink conditioning** experiments, the US is an air puff to the cornea. The eyeblink reflex triggered by the air puff is the UR. The CS is typically a tone. After several pairings of the tone (CS) and the puff of air (US), the tone elicits the blinking CR when presented by itself (i.e., without the air puff).

In the 1960s, it was discovered that an inner translucent eyelid in albino rabbits called the nictitating membrane (which they have in addition to a regular eyelid) can be made to reflexively extend to cover the eye in response to an air puff to the cornea. Researchers set out to test whether the **nictitating-membrane reflex** in rabbits could also be conditioned. In a

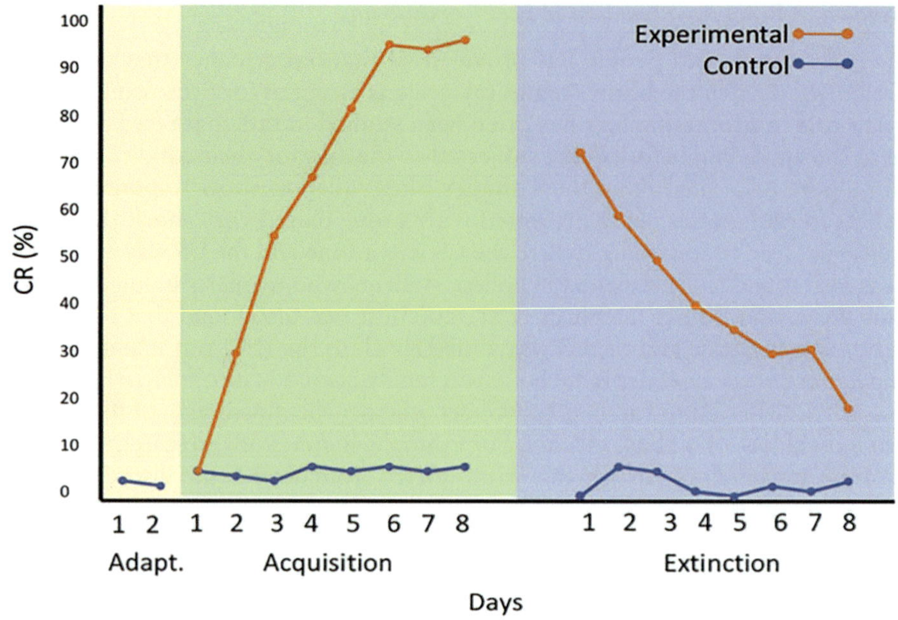

Figure 6.2 The results of the Gormezano et al. (1962) experiment (see text for details).

Source: Modified from Nictitating Membrane: Classical Conditioning and Extinction in the Albino Rabbit. *Science, 138* (3536), 33–36. https://doi.org/10.1126/science.138.3536.33).

landmark experiment (Gormezano et al., 1962), the right upper and lower eyelids of albino rabbits were taped open to observe the nictitating membrane. The rabbits were divided into a control and an experimental group. The rabbits in the experimental group were exposed to 70 pairings per day of a tone (CS) with air puff to the cornea (US) on eight consecutive days. The rabbits in the control group received 70 presentations of the CS alone and 70 presentations of the US alone per day randomly (see an explanation of control procedures for classical conditioning experiments in Chapter 5). An eyeblink reflex (CR) was considered to have occurred when a 1-mm deflection from spontaneous membrane movements was detected.

The results of the experiment are shown in Figure 6.2. The dependent measure was the percentage of trials where a CR was observed. During adaptation, spontaneous responses were approximately 1.5% for the experimental and control groups. However, during acquisition, a gradual increase in the percentage of CRs was observed in the experimental group until it reached its asymptote level of 92%. In contrast, the rate of CRs in the control group never exceeded 6% during extinction trials (where resistance to extinction, as explained in Chapter 5, is the measure), in which the CS was presented by itself; the experimental group continued to respond on 70% of the trials after which the percentage of CRs gradually dropped to about 20%.

Eyeblink Conditioning, the Brain, and Neurological Disorders

Eyeblink Conditioning and the Brain

As you will learn in this chapter's "What in the Brain?" box, scientists have discovered how different brain areas (e.g., in the cerebellum) affect the interconnection between the brain areas that produce eyeblink conditioning (McCormick and Thompson, 1984). They have also found that specific regions may be recruited depending on the timing between the CS and the US. For example, studies have shown that trace eyeblink conditioning, in which a memory of the CS has to be retained throughout the CS-US interval, requires an intact hippocampus and prefrontal cortex, both of which are important for memory (Moyer, Deyo and Disterhoft, 1990; Solomon et al., 1986).

Eyeblink Conditioning and Neurological Disorders

The study of eyeblink conditioning plays a vital role in *translational research* (i.e., applying basic research findings to address human needs). This is because eyeblink conditioning deficits have been observed in people suffering from various neurological disorders. For example, a deficit in eyeblink conditioning might indicate memory loss is due to brain damage (e.g., the hippocampus) associated with Alzheimer's disease rather than to normal aging (Woodruff-Pak, 2001). An eyeblink conditioning deficit can also be observed in people who have schizophrenia, which might be due to damage to the cerebellum, which is essential for regulating and coordinating movements (Kent et al., 2020). Eyeblink conditioning deficits were also found to be a predisposing factor for autism spectrum disorder (Welsh and Oristaglio, 2016). Hence, eyeblink conditioning deficits might be a neurodevelopmental disorder marker (i.e., an indicator) (Reeb-Sutherland and Fox, 2015).

What in the Brain? Eyeblink Conditioning and the Cerebellum

Eyeblink conditioning was extensively studied in albino rabbits, which possess a translucent membrane known as the nictitating membrane. This membrane is drawn across the eye (UR) as a reflex response to an aversive stimulus, such as an air puff to the cornea (US). Following many pairings between a tone (CS) and the US, the tone triggers the nictitating membrane reflex when presented by itself (CR).

In the 1980s, neuroscientist Richard F. Thompson discovered that the cerebellum, a part of the brain involved in motor functions such as regulating and coordinating movements, was the main structure involved in eyeblink conditioning. He experimentally destroyed a group of neurons within the cerebellum called the *interpositus nucleus* (Thompson, 1986). Through extensive research involving various experimental methods, the neural pathways involved in eyeblink conditioning have since been identified (Christian and Thompson, 2003; Thompson and Steinmetz, 2009).

Figure 6.3 shows the three main pathways of connections between neurons involved. These are the CS pathway (green), activated by the tone (CS); the US pathway (purple), activated by the air puff (US); and a pathway along which information from the CS and US is combined (red). The figure also shows how different areas of the brainstem and cerebellum are connected along these various pathways.

The tone triggers activity in the CS pathway, whereas the airpuff triggers activity in the US pathway. Information from the tone (CS) and air puff (US) converge onto a group of neurons in the CR pathway known as the *interpositus nucleus*. As the number of CS-US (tone-airpuff) pairings increases, stimulation of the *interpositus nucleus* from the CS pathway causes the *interpositus nucleus* to gradually acquire the capacity to produce the CR, independent from stimulation of the US pathway.

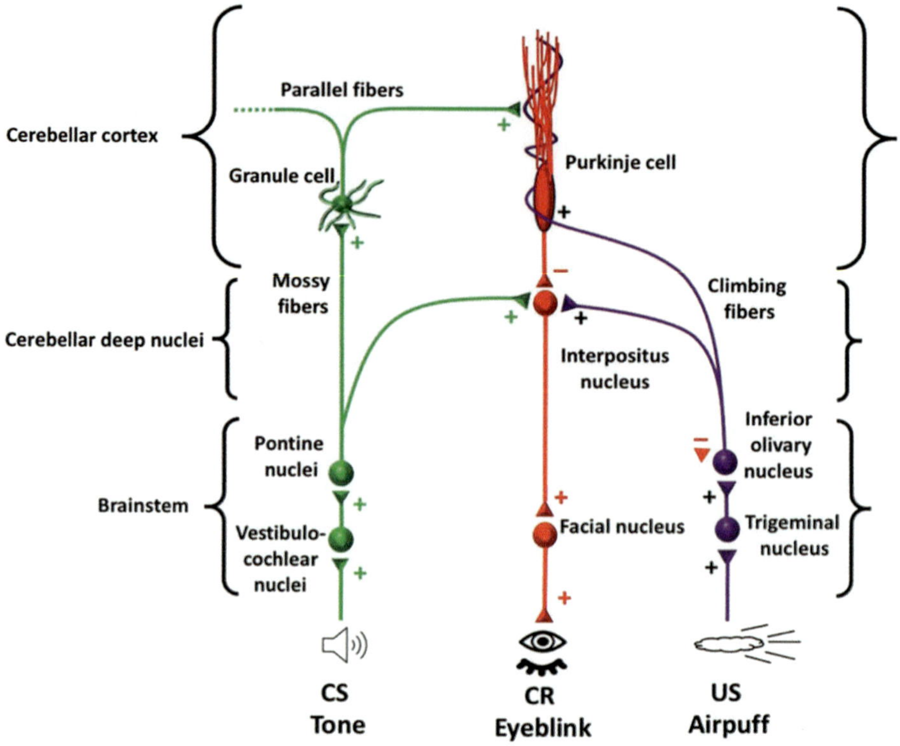

Figure 6.3 Neural pathways are involved in eyeblink conditioning within the cerebellum (see text for details).

Are You Thinking Critically?

1. What role did neuroscientist Richard F. Thompson play in understanding eyeblink conditioning?
2. Explain the importance of the interpositus nucleus in eyeblink conditioning.
3. How do the three main pathways of connections between neurons (CS pathway, US pathway, and CR pathway) contribute to developing the conditioned response in eyeblink conditioning?

Critical Thinking Spot Check 6.2

1. Describe a typical eyeblink conditioning experiment.
2. Explain how deficits in eyeblink conditioning contribute to our understanding of neurological disorders and their relevance in translational research.
3. Illustrate the involvement of specific brain areas, such as the amygdala and cerebellum, in different types of eyeblink conditioning and their importance in neurological processes.
4. Evaluate the role of eyeblink conditioning as a potential marker for various neurological disorders, considering its manifestations in different experimental conditions.

6.3 Stimulus-Substitution Theory

Autoshaping and Sign Tracking

The **stimulus-substitution theory**, proposed by Pavlov (1927), states that the CS becomes a substitute for the US during classical conditioning. Pavlov proposed this theory after observing that dogs exposed to CS-US pairings performed responses directed toward the CS when freed from their restraints. For example, if a light was used as a CS, the dogs would approach the light and lick it as if it were the food (US).

Brown and Jenkins (1968) provided evidence for stimulus substitution by conducting an experiment in which they exposed pigeons to pairings of the onset of a critical light (CS) (i.e., a translucent disc that could be illuminated) with the delivery of food (US). In their experiment, the key light was turned on every 30–90 seconds and remained on for 8 seconds. Food was available in a tray directly under the key light for four seconds after being turned off. Hence, the key light became a CS that signaled food delivery (US), just as the light in Pavlov's experiment mentioned previously became a CS that signaled food delivery (US) to his dogs. Brown and Jenkins (1968) discovered that, after several such pairings, the pigeons persisted in pecking the key light (CR) despite the food being delivered at regular intervals whether or not they pecked at it (Brown and Jenkins, 1968). This suggested that the pigeons conditioned themselves to persistently perform a response directed at a CS (i.e., the key light). The process and procedure by which this occurs became known as **autoshaping**. The CR directed toward the CS became known as sign-tracking because the pigeons seemed to be tracking the CS (Hearst and Jenkins, 1974). This is similar to when you continuously tap an application icon on your smartphone because it has been associated with sought-after information or the delivery of a message.

Jenkins and Moore (1973) provided further support for the stimulus-substitution theory by conducting an experiment in which they subjected pigeons to 30 trials in which a key light was paired with food delivery and 30 trials in which the key light was paired with water in random order. They hypothesized that if the CS became a substitute for the US (as proposed by the stimulus substitution theory), the response directed at the key should resemble the consummatory response generally directed at the US. This is precisely what they found. When the key light was paired with food, the pigeons approached the key and responded with brief, hard pecks, which they perform when they eat. When the key light was paired with water, the pigeons responded with soft sipping-like pecks performed when they drink (Jenkins and Moore, 1973).

A Challenge to Stimulus-Substitution Theory: Evidence for the Behavior Systems Approach

Despite the evidence provided for the stimulus substitution theory described previously, it did not remain unchallenged. For example, Timberlake and Grant (1975) found that the CR of rats (test rats) to a CS that signaled food delivery differed depending on the nature of the CS, that is, whether the CS was another rat (stimulus rat) or an inanimate object (i.e., a wooden block). If stimulus substitution were correct, rats exposed to pairings of a CS with food (US) should exhibit feeding behaviors such as gnawing and biting (CR) at the stimulus rat (CS). However, because rats feed in groups and follow each other to food in nature, the researchers hypothesized that rats subjected to CS-US pairings where the CS was another rat (stimulus rat) would display social behaviors related to feeding (CR) towards the stimulus rat (CS). They would not gnaw and bite the stimulus rat (CS) as predicted by the stimulus-substitution theory.

Their findings supported their hypothesis. They found that the test rats did not display feeding behaviors towards the stimulus rat, as predicted by stimulus substitution theory. Instead, they displayed a greater frequency of orienting, approaching, sniffing, and social behaviors (CR) in response to the stimulus rat (CS) than before conditioning. In contrast, test rats exposed to pairings of a wooden block (CS) with food (US) oriented towards the CS more often than before conditioning. However, they showed no increase in their frequency of approaching, sniffing, or social behaviors towards it.

Timberlake and Grant's (1975) results were another demonstration, in addition to the results of the fear conditioning experiment described previously, that the CR elicited by a CS depends on the nature of the CS and US. These findings support the behavior systems approach to learning (in contrast to the general process approach), which states that the CS elicits the most adaptive responses (Timberlake, 2001). Sometimes, this response is most compatible with obtaining a reward, as in the previous Timberlake and Grant (1975) experiment, and at other times with escaping or avoiding danger, as in fear conditioning.

Sign Tracking and Goal Tracking

As mentioned, sign-tracking refers to a CR directed towards a CS during autoshaping. Sign tracking is an **expectancy-mediated behavior**, meaning that animal and people's behaviors are influenced by expectations of the outcomes of their actions. It is adaptive because biologically important stimuli such as the availability of food (e.g., prey) or of potential mates are often preceded by stimuli that signal their occurrence. In terms of classical conditioning, this means that an animal may develop the expectancy (CR) of an outcome (US) based on the presence of specific environmental cues (CS).

However, laboratory experiments have shown that sign tracking only sometimes occurs. For example, Boakes (1977) subjected rats to an auto-shaping procedure in which a lever was illuminated before food delivery in a cup. Food delivery occurred irrespective of what the rats were doing, meaning they did not have to press the lever to receive it. Boakes (1977) measured the extent to which the rats' responses were directed toward the lever and the food cup (Figure 6.4). They found that about one-third of the rats displayed behavior directed towards the food cup, such as placing their snouts in it (Figure 6.4a). Boakes (1977) coined the term **goal tracking** to refer to this response. However, another third of the rats displayed a sign-tracking response in that they directed their behavior towards the lever, the sign-tracking response you learned about previously (Figure 6.4b). The other third of the rats showed a mixture of both goal tracking and sign tracking. These findings suggested that animals' inclination to respond to an autoshaping procedure differs.

Interestingly, sign-tracking and goal-tracking rats were found to differ in their susceptibility to engage in addictive-like behaviors (Saunders, Yager and Robinson, 2013; Yager and Robinson, 2013). In one study, food-restricted rats (i.e., presumably made hungry), some identified as sign-trackers and others as goal-trackers in an autoshaping experiment, were trained to press a bar to receive infusions of cocaine. They were also trained to press

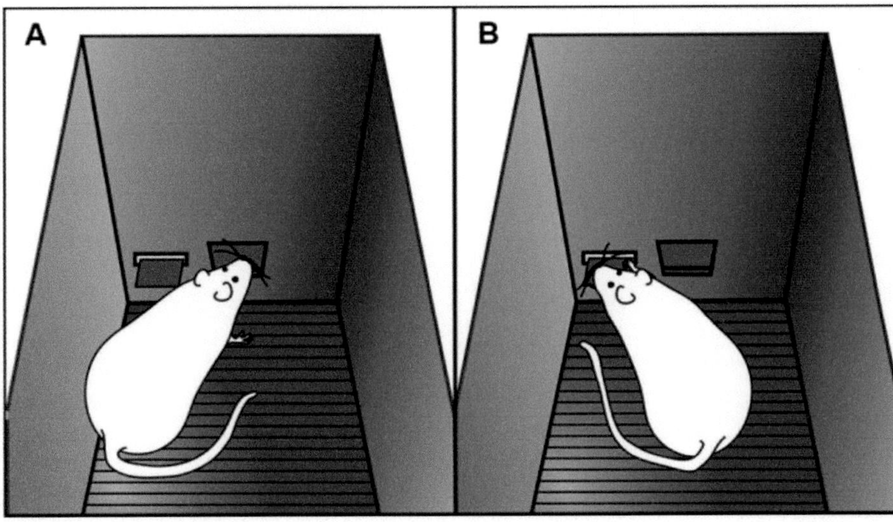

Figure 6.4 a) Goal tracking: the rat directs its behavior towards the food cup. b) Sign tracking: the rat directs its behavior towards the lever.

Source: Haight, J., & Flagel, S. (2014). A potential role for the paraventricular nucleus of the thalamus in mediating individual variation in Pavlovian conditioned responses. *Front Behav Neurosci, 8*, 79. https://doi.org/10.3389/fnbeh.2014.00079.

a bar that gave them access to food (remember that they are food restricted). When given a choice between pushing a bar for cocaine and pressing a bar for food, sign-trackers pressed the bar for cocaine in a higher percentage of trials than goal-tracking rats (Tunstall and Kearns, 2015).

These findings suggest that understanding how sign-tracking and goal-tracking can also occur in humans may provide essential insights into the mechanisms of drug addiction (Colaizzi et al., 2020). For example, in what is known as **incentive salience theory** (Robinson and Berridge, 1993, 2000), cues associated with taking drugs become significantly more noticeable (salient). They become potent CSs that elicit approach responses in a process similar to sign tracking in animals. As an analogy, you can think of conditioned cues as powerful magnets pulling the addicted person towards them, increasing the probability of drug-taking behavior by producing a state described as "wanting," which translates into intense cravings, which may precipitate recovering people with an addiction into relapse.

It was also found that similarly to how people who suffer from substance use disorder attribute high levels of salience to drug-related cues, people suffering from anxiety disorders, such as post-traumatic stress disorder and phobia, may attribute high levels of salience to cues related to feared stimuli (Morrow, Maren and Robinson, 2011). Hence, it is possible that Giuseppina, in the opening vignette, quickly notices any cue in her environment related to needles or injections, such as a road sign promoting vaccinations.

According to the incentive salience theory, environmental cues associated with taking drugs become conditioned stimuli (CS) that elicit approach responses (CR), similar to sign tracking in animals.

Source: IStock photo ID:164640831.

Critical Thinking Spot Check 6.3

1. Provide examples of experiments supporting the stimulus-substitution theory, such as autoshaping experiments in pigeons.
2. Differentiate between sign-tracking and goal-tracking behaviors and discuss their implications for understanding addictive-like behaviors.
3. Relate the stimulus-substitution theory to real-life scenarios, explaining how it may apply to behaviors observed in individuals with phobias or substance use disorders.
4. Compare and contrast the findings of experiments challenging the stimulus-substitution theory, such as Timberlake and Grant's study, highlighting the importance of the nature of the conditioned stimulus (CS) and unconditioned stimulus (US).

6.4 Counterconditioning

Associating a New US to a CS

After the conditioning of fear response in Little Albert, Watson proposed that such a conditioned fear could be removed by associating the original CS with a new US to elicit a new and incompatible CR, a procedure known as **counterconditioning**. Pavlov (1927) demonstrated a similar procedure with dogs. He associated a CS with a painful US, such as an electrical shock, which produced a solid unconditioned defensive reflex (UR). He then associated the same CS with food (US). The result was that the dogs that displayed CRs geared towards removing the aversive stimulus now displayed salivation and lip-smacking (CR).

It is important to understand that in certain cases, counterconditioning may not function as intended. For example, suppose a dog has learned to associate a tone (CS) with an aversive shock (US), leading to a defensive response (UR) such as freezing or withdrawing in response to the tone (CS). Now, counterconditioning is attempted by pairing the same tone (CS) with food (a new US). Ideally, the dog should learn to associate the tone with food and exhibit salivation instead of fear. However, in some instances, the dog may experience conflict because the tone has both a history of predicting pain and a history of predicting food, which can result in ambivalent behavior, negative transfer, or resurgence, as described subsequently.

Ambivalent Behavior: The dog may exhibit both defensive responses (e.g., freezing, withdrawal) and appetitive responses (e.g., salivation, lip-smacking) simultaneously, leading to signs of distress or hesitation.

Negative Transfer: The presence of food may not eliminate the defensive response but may instead cause the food to become associated with anxiety, making the dog reluctant to eat in specific contexts.

Resurgence of Fear: If the new positive association (food) is weak or inconsistent, the original defensive reaction may still emerge when the CS is presented, particularly in high-stress situations.

Peter and the Rabbit

The kind of experiment described above was first conducted on a human subject by Mary Cover Jones (1897–1987), one of Watson's students (Jones, 1991), who later became known as the mother of behavior therapy (Rutherford, 2000). The only subject in her experiment was a three-year-old boy named Peter, whom she described as Little Albert having grown older. Peter had an intense fear of a rabbit (CS). To rid Peter of this fear (UR), Jones brought him the rabbit while he enjoyed milk and cookies (US). After several occasions on which this occurred (CS-US pairings), the rabbit, which initially elicited fear in Peter (UR), became a CS that signaled milk and cookies (US), which resulted in Peter feeling happy in the presence of the rabbit (CR). Counterconditioning forms the basis of a type of behavior therapy known as systematic desensitization, discussed in this module's application box.

Critical Thinking Spot Check 6.4

1. Define counterconditioning as proposed by Watson and demonstrated by Pavlov, emphasizing the role of associating a new unconditioned stimulus (US) with an existing conditioned stimulus (CS).
2. Summarize Mary Cover Jones's application of counterconditioning in the case of Peter and his fear of a rabbit, highlighting the procedure's success.

Chapter Summary

Each bullet point aligns with the learning objectives outlined at the beginning of the chapter.

- After Pavlov published his results on the conditioning of the salivary reflex, psychologist John B. Watson successfully conditioned fear in a child known as Little Albert. This was achieved by presenting Albert with a white rat, which he initially enjoyed. Watson then paired the white rat with the sound of a hammer striking a metal bar, which elicited a fear response in Little Albert. Eventually, the same fear response was elicited in Little Albert when the white rat was presented to him by itself. Fear conditioning is also used in animal studies. In a typical experiment, a rat is placed in a chamber where the floor can be electrified. Then, a tone is paired with a foot shock and behavioral measures, taken as an indication of fear, are recorded. In the test phase, the rat is exposed to the tone without the foot shock. Upon hearing the tone, a conditioned fear response is typically elicited in the rat.

- It was found that reflexes other than the salivary reflex can be conditioned. One of the best-known examples is the eyeblink reflex. The eyeblink reflex can be elicited by a US, such as a puff of air in the eye. It was found that a neutral stimulus, such as a tone, elicits an eyeblink when it is repeatedly paired with a puff of air to the cornea. Conditioning of the eyeblink reflex was found in both humans and animals. In rabbits, it is known as the nictitating membrane reflex. It also depends on the cerebellum and, in certain circumstances, the prefrontal cortex, hippocampus, and amygdala.
- Autoshaping is a type of conditioning in which an animal conditions itself to respond to a CS that predicts the delivery of a reward. It was observed that if a CS is paired with the US at regular intervals, regardless of what the animal does, it will produce an irrelevant response directed toward the CS. This is known as sign tracking and was taken as evidence for stimulus substitution. In addition, the animal response seemed to correspond to the nature of the CS. However, it was shown that this was only sometimes the case and that animals responded to the CS in a way that reflected species-specific behavior. It was also demonstrated that not all animals showed sign-tracking responses. It was found that the reaction of some animals was directed towards the area where food was delivered. This type of response is known as goal tracking. Other animals showed a mixture of both types of responses. It was suggested that sign tracking may be a characteristic of people who are addicted to drugs.
- In counterconditioning, a CS that elicits a specific CR through its association with a US is paired with a new US that elicits an incompatible CR. Mary Cover Jones used this procedure to reverse a child's fear of a rabbit by pairing it with pleasant stimuli. Counterconditioning is the basis for a type of behavioral therapy known as systematic desensitization.

Note

1 Note that Watson's experiment would be judged unethical by today's standards.

Glossary

Ambivalent behavior Behavior marked by conflicting or mixed responses to a stimulus due to competing motivations or emotions.

Auditory fear-conditioning A form of classical conditioning where a sound becomes associated with a fear-inducing stimulus, leading to a learned fear response.

Autoshaping A learning process where animals instinctively develop responses to a stimulus without direct reinforcement.

Conditioned emotional response A learned emotional reaction to a previously neutral stimulus, often linked to fear or anxiety.

Counterconditioning A method of altering conditioned responses by pairing the stimulus with a new, opposing association.

Expectancy-mediated behavior A response guided by expectations rather than automatic conditioning processes.

Eyeblink conditioning A classical conditioning procedure where a neutral stimulus is paired with an air puff or other stimulus to elicit a blink response.

Goal tracking A learned behavior in which an organism approaches and interacts with cues associated with a desired outcome.

Negative transfer A situation where prior learning interferes with the acquisition of new skills or behaviors.

Nictitating-membrane reflex A protective, involuntary blinking movement of the third eyelid in some animals, often studied in conditioning research.

Resurgence of fear The return of a previously extinguished fear response after a period without exposure to the feared stimulus.

Stimulus-substitution theory A theory of classical conditioning stating that the conditioned stimulus functions as a substitute for the unconditioned stimulus in triggering a response.

Systematic desensitization A therapeutic technique used to reduce fear or anxiety by gradually exposing an individual to the feared stimulus while practicing relaxation.

Vicarious classical conditioning Learning through observing others' experiences with classical conditioning rather than experiencing it directly.

Module Summary

In the first chapter, you learned that the study of classical conditioning began with Pavlov, who conditioned dogs to salivate to a neutral stimulus (NS) after having been paired with food (US). American psychologist Edwin Burket Twitmyer concurrently discovered classical conditioning. Contrary to Twitmyer, Pavlov pursued his studies and extensively described the details of his experiments and findings. He found that a CR could be elicited by stimuli that differed from but closely resembled the original CS, a phenomenon known as stimulus generalization. In contrast, he showed that a CR was not elicited by stimuli that differed too much from the original CS, a phenomenon known as discrimination. Pavlov also discovered that the intensity or frequency of a response is reduced by repeated presentation of the CS by itself, a phenomenon known as extinction, and the spontaneous recovery of the response after a period during which it had been extinguished. He also discovered that a CR can be attenuated by a CS that signaled the absence of a US, in what is known as conditioned inhibition. To Pavlov, a CR occurred because a brain center representing the US came to be activated by a brain center representing the CS. This became known as the S-S theory.

Contrary to Pavlov, Clark Hull believed that classical conditioning involved the direct activation of the CR by the CS. This became known as the S-R theory. Evidence for Pavlov's S-S theory was provided by an experiment by Holland and Straub known as a US devaluation experiment.

In the second chapter, you learned that several classical conditioning procedures have been developed. For example, in fear conditioning, a tone elicits a fear response when paired with a shock. In eyeblink conditioning, a tone elicits an eyeblink after being paired with a puff of air to the cornea. In autoshaping, animals condition themselves to respond to a CS paired with a US delivered at regular intervals, irrespective of their behavior, by directing their responses toward the CS. This response, known as sign tracking, is taken as evidence for stimulus substitution, which is thought to be characteristic of people who are addicted to drugs. Finally, in a procedure known as counterconditioning, the same CS that previously elicited an undesired CR is paired with a new US that elicits a response incompatible with the original CR. Over time, the CS comes to elicit the new, incompatible CR.

Module 3

Application

Behavior Therapy: Flooding and Systematic Desensitization

People who suffer from phobias have excessive and persistent fears of specific objects or situations and go to great lengths to avoid them (American Psychiatric Association, 2013). Phobias can be acquired through classical conditioning (White and Cheung, 2021). For example, someone who has experienced high levels of fear (UR) while trapped in an elevator may subsequently avoid elevators at all costs. In a classical conditioning account of this example, elevators, which were initially neutral stimuli, have become conditioned stimuli (CS) that elicit anxiety (CR) through their association with being trapped (US).

The Treatment of Phobias

Behavior therapy involves applying learning principles to treat various psychological disorders, including phobias. Two types of behavioral therapies are briefly discussed: flooding and systematic desensitization.

Flooding

Flooding is based on extinction, in which repeated presentations of a CS reduce the frequency or intensity of a CR. A person with a phobia constantly avoids the anxiety-provoking stimulus (CS), so they are rarely exposed to it alone for periods long enough for their fear responses (CR) to undergo extinction. Flooding aims to extinguish a patient's conditioned fear response by exposing them to the feared CS without the possibility of escaping.

In a typical flooding procedure, a man who developed a phobia of bridges (CS) after being trapped on one during a severe winter storm (US) is asked by a therapist to visualize the worst possible situation involving bridges. The therapists may then enhance the visualization by having him imagine the most noticeable features of the experience. Maintaining the visualization usually produces extreme anxiety. However, the exercise is only terminated once the fear has subsided, permitting the response to undergo extinction. Flooding can also be performed "in favor," in which a patient is put in the actual presence of the feared object or the feared situation while being prevented from escaping. Flooding is effective in treating some types of phobias. However, it is also highly traumatic, discouraging some patients from continuing their treatments. This has prompted many therapists to employ less traumatic forms of behavioral therapy, such as systematic desensitization, as discussed subsequently.

DOI: 10.4324/9781003491828-12

Systematic Desensitization

Psychiatrist Joseph Wolpe (1915–1997) developed a treatment for phobias based on counterconditioning known as systematic desensitization (Wolpe, 1961, 1982). Systematic desensitization involves three stages:

1. The client is trained in deep-muscle relaxation.
2. The client is asked to rate the amount of anxiety provoked by instances in which a feared object or situation is involved, from instances that evoke the lowest amount of fear to those that evoke the highest amount of anxiety (e.g., on a scale of 1 to 10).
3. The client is asked to imagine or confront these instances in reality (in vivo) while practicing the deep relaxation method learned in stage 1. This is done hierarchically, beginning with the instance that elicits the least anxiety and ending with the instance that elicits the most anxiety.

Counterconditioning results when the CS, which is the feared object or situation, becomes associated with deep relaxation, a response incompatible with anxiety. Systematic desensitization can also be applied in a virtual reality environment. For example, in a recent study, participants with driving phobia were gradually immersed in the scenarios they described in a hierarchy of fears that involved driving (Trappey et al., 2021).

Are You Thinking Critically?

1. Which features of classical conditioning (discovered by Pavlov) could prevent flooding and systematic desensitization from eliminating a phobia?
2. In what ways, other than classical conditioning, can phobias can be acquired?
3. What are the benefits of knowing how phobias can be acquired?

Module 4

Behavioral Adaptations, Determinants, and Modeling of Classical Conditioning

Introduction

Animals evolved adaptations that make them well suited to survive in their environment. These adaptations include both biological processes and behavioral responses. Evolved behavioral responses that increase an animal's survival in its environment are known as behavioral adaptations. These adaptations permit animals to avoid potentially dangerous stimuli and recognize signals, leading to their reproductive success. In Chapter 7, you will learn about some behavioral adaptations related to classical conditioning. Understanding these adaptations requires abandoning the general process approach to learning, which is the idea that learning occurs through general processes that apply across situations, species, and types of stimuli that can be associated. Instead, they must be viewed as resulting from the activity of what often are species-specific behavioral systems that contribute to an animal's survival in specific circumstances. In Chapter 8, you will learn about some of the variables that determine the efficacy of classical conditioning, which include the extent to which previous experience with stimuli affects their associability (i.e., how well they can be associated with each other). Finally, in Chapter 9, you will learn how some learning theorists sought to explain the change in the strength of association between stimuli (e.g., the progression of how well a CS elicits a CR) as animals learn by devising two models of classical conditioning, one of which is mathematical.

Chapter 7: Behavioral Adaptions of Classical Conditioning
Chapter 8: Determinants and Modeling of Classical Conditioning
Chapter 9: Models of Classical Conditioning

DOI: 10.4324/9781003491828-13

7 The Power and Adaptive Functions of Classical Conditioning

Learning Objectives

- Recognize the role of CS-US relevance in classical conditioning and its challenge to the general process approach of learning.
- Analyze conditioned taste aversion (CTA) as a challenge to the general process approach, considering its rapid learning after a single trial, specificity to taste or smell, and conditioning with long CS-US intervals.
- Understand the significance of fear learning in survival and its implications for phobia development, highlighting the role of the fear module in the brain.
- Identify sexual conditioning as a challenge to the general process approach, emphasizing the importance of species-typical localized stimuli in eliciting conditioned responses.
- Explain the phenomenon of conditioned compensatory responses, illustrating how they contribute to drug tolerance and homeostasis maintenance in autonomic conditioning.

Joshua's Scare

(Source: Istock photo ID:1169727806)

DOI: 10.4324/9781003491828-14

Joshua had just finished studying for his final examinations when he received a text from his best friend Mario, asking him to visit. Upon arriving at Mario's apartment, Joshua noticed several cans of drink on the kitchen table. The cans were colorful and appealing. "What are those?" asked Joshua. "It's a new drink," answered Mario. Joshua picked up one of the cans, read the list of ingredients, and asked. "Taurine and guarana, aren't those sources of caffeine?" "Yes," answered Mario, "and, as you can see, it's also 12% alcohol." After almost downing the whole can, Joshua turned to Mario and said, "It tastes and smells very fruity; you would never know it contains alcohol."

Before too long, Joshua had downed three cans, after which Mario noticed that Joshua seemed confused and had trouble speaking. Not feeling well, Joshua lay on Mario's couch, passed out, and remained unresponsive to Mario's efforts to wake him. In a panicked state, Mario called 9–1–1 (a phone line for emergency assistance). Later, Mario was told that Joshua was suffering from alcohol intoxication. After making a full recovery, Joshua sought help for his drinking problem. One day, he read an article about the company that makes the drink that almost killed him. The article was about several young people who found themselves in the emergency room after having the drink. However, being an experienced drinker who had built up a tolerance to alcohol, he wondered why he reacted that way. Some blamed the mix of alcohol and caffeine for the beverage's ill effects. However, in an interview, an expert stated that caffeine had nothing to do with it. He explained that when a drug is repeatedly taken, cues, such as its presentation, taste, and smell, become associated with the effects of the drug through classical conditioning, which is known as the situational specificity of tolerance. This means that these specific cues eventually become conditioned stimuli that elicit compensatory responses in the body to counteract the effects of the drug. According to the expert, the new drink was dangerous because its presentation, taste, and smell were so different from how alcoholic beverages usually taste and are presented, preventing these compensatory responses from taking effect.

7.1 Belongingness and Biological Preparedness in Classical Conditioning

Abandoning the General Process Approach

Classical conditioning serves adaptive functions, which means that it is essential for the reproductive success of animals. Many examples of classical conditioning show that the ways it fulfills these adaptive functions cannot be explained by the general process approach to learning (Macphail and Bolhuis, 2001), according to which learning can be accounted for by a set of laws that apply across species and situations (Revusky, 1977). Pavlov espoused the general process approach to learning by thinking that all stimuli could equally be associated with producing a response. This idea became known as the **equivalence of associativity** (Seligman, 1970). However, in nature, survival often depends on **selective associations**, meaning that not all stimuli could as easily be associated. For example, feeling nauseated is more readily associated with the taste of food or drinks than with sights or sounds, which are more easily associated with physical pain, such as that inflicted by predators (see conditioned taste aversion [CTA] subsequently). Indeed, certain stimuli seem to belong with one another. Psychologists use the term **belongingness** to refer to this phenomenon (Thorndike, 1932). In classical conditioning, the relevance of certain CS-US combinations leads to facilitated learning, a phenomenon known as **CS-US relevance** (LoLordo, 2014). Belongingness and CS-US relevance are a challenge to the general process approach to learning.

Selective associations are better explained by the operations of behavior systems (introduced in Chapter 3), which are species-specific learning mechanisms. When activated, these behavior systems permit animals to fulfill their needs, such as feeding, reproduction, and defense (Shettleworth, 2009b; Timberlake, 2000). Consistent with this idea, psychologist Martin Seligman (1971) proposed that animals are biologically prepared to fear stimuli that threaten their evolutionary ancestors' survival. Seligman's theory is known as **biological preparedness.** The situational specificity of tolerance, explained in detail in its own section below, responsible for Joshua's ordeal in the opening vignette, may have evolved to increase the probability of survival of an animal that has ingested a poisonous substance found in its environment by preparing its body to counteract its effects. In the remainder of this chapter, you will learn about cases of classical conditioning that reflect behavioral adaptations that can best be explained by the behavior systems approach and biological preparedness rather than the general process approach.

Critical Thinking Spot Check 7.1

1. Explain the concept of CS-US relevance in classical conditioning and its implications for learning.
2. Compare and contrast the general process approach to learning with the concept of biological preparedness in classical conditioning.

7.2 Behavioral Adaptations in Classical Conditioning

Conditioned Taste Aversion

Animals can learn to discriminate between safe and poisonous foods through a form of classical conditioning known as conditioned taste aversion, which was alluded to previously and briefly discussed in Chapter 5. Superficially, the mechanisms of CTA appear to be the same as for other instances of classical conditioning. That is, a food's taste (CS) is associated with post-ingestion consequences (US) that provoke nausea (UR). On subsequent exposures to the taste or smell of the food (CS), the animal experiences nausea (CR), causing it to avoid the food. This is especially important for rats because they do not have a gag reflex, meaning they cannot regurgitate (vomit) potentially poisonous foods (Horn et al., 2013). An interesting feature of CTA is that it more readily develops when an animal becomes ill after eating food it has never tasted. This is because, in that case, the animal has never tasted the food without getting sick. Note that this differs from what happens in the situational specificity of tolerance. Remember that in Joshua's case, the novelty of the stimulus (CS), that is, the novel presentation of an alcoholic beverage and the fruity taste of the drink, led to a reduction of the CR as opposed to the facilitation of the CR as observed in CTA.

Conditioned taste aversion can develop to drinks and foods. Some researchers have suggested that conditioned flavor aversion (CFA) may be more appropriate than CTA because aversions can also develop to the smell of a food or drink. However, for the sake of simplicity, I will continue using CTA throughout the text.

The Study of CTA

During World War II, scientists tried to find ways to protect England's food supply from rodents (Elton, 1954; Keiner, 2005). Using poisons seemed to be an obvious way to start. However, while investigating the effects of various poisons, the scientists noted two phenomena that could hinder their efforts. First, they noticed that rats often did not ingest the poison because they were reluctant to approach new elements in their environments, such as food containing it. They called this behavior a *new object reaction*. Second, if the rats ingested a sub-lethal dose of the food that contained the poison, they showed an aversion to the food and never ingested it again. They called this behavior *refusal response* or *bait shyness*, which is the one relevant to the subject at hand and, from now on, is referred to as CTA.

However, most of what we know about CTA comes from the pioneering studies conducted by psychologists John Garcia (1917–2012) and colleagues while studying the effects of ionizing radiation on physiological processes while working at the U.S. Naval Radiological Defense Lab in San Francisco, California (which was closed in 1969). His studies were motivated by the observation that rats reduced their food and water consumption during radiation exposure, which induces nausea. Garcia and some of his colleagues hypothesized that the reduction of food and water consumption by the rats exposed to radiation was due to a conditioned association acquired between the nausea (UR/CR) induced by the radiation and the taste of the food and plastic taste of the water (CS), due to its storage in plastic bottles (Garcia, Kimeldorf and Koelling, 1955).

They tested this hypothesis by first assessing rats' preference for a saccharine solution over plain tap water. When given a choice between drinking from a tube that contained the saccharine solution and one that contained tap water, the rats preferred the saccharine solution. The rats were then separated into three groups and given six hours of access to the saccharine solution while exposed to radiation. One group of rats was exposed to a low dose of radiation, while the other group was exposed to a relatively high dose of radiation. The third group of rats, which served as control, also had access to the saccharine solution but was not exposed to radiation. Forty-eight hours later, the rats in all three groups were tested for their preference of the saccharine solution over the tap water while not exposed to radiation.

They found that the groups of rats exposed to radiation developed a dose-dependent aversion to the saccharine solution. That is, while the preference for the saccharine solution

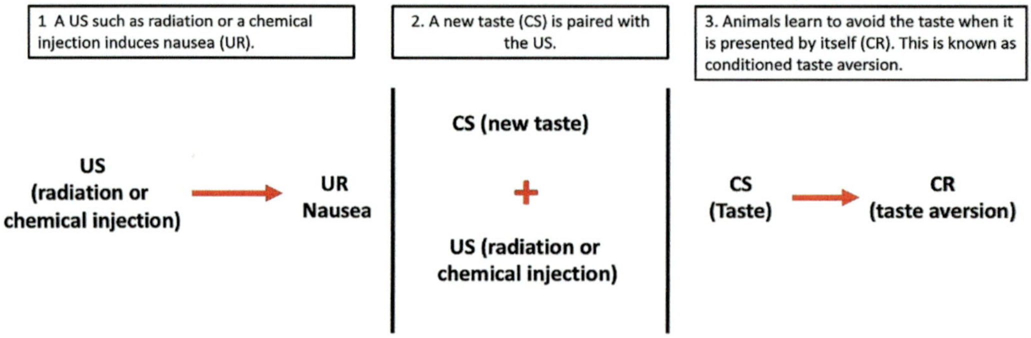

Figure 7.1 General procedure for inducing CTA.

was significantly reduced for the groups exposed to the low radiation dose, it was eliminated in the group that received the relatively higher dose. They also found that the aversion to the saccharine solution in both groups persisted for more than four weeks, showing that the aversion was resistant to extinction. No aversion to the saccharine solution was found in the control group, which was never exposed to radiation. Since Garcia and colleagues (1955) pioneered this procedure, other means of inducing CTA (besides radiation) have been used in the laboratory. These include the injection of agents that cause nausea, such as lithium chloride (Chambers, 2018; Kunin et al., 2001; Kunin et al., 2000). The general procedure for inducing a CTA is illustrated in Figure 7.1.

CTA: A Challenge to the General Process Approach

One-Trial Learning

Garcia and colleagues showed that CTA learning did not conform to the general process approach. For example, according to the general process approach, several CS-US pairings are required for animals to acquire a classically conditioned response. However, Garcia and colleagues (1955) showed that rats subjected to a single pairing trial between a sweetened water solution and radiation-induced illness developed a CTA to the sweetened water solution. These results make sense from the biological preparedness perspective proposed by Seligman (1971) because, in nature, animals that survive ingesting a poison might not have a second chance of survival should they ingest the poison again.

Selectivity of Associations

Remember that according to the general process approach, animals should show an equivalence of associativity between all stimuli. However, in nature, survival depends on an animal's ability to form selective associations between stimuli. These associations may depend on the activation of specific behavior systems. Consistent with this idea, Garcia and Koelling (1966) hypothesized that a system selectively associates taste to sickness and another that selectively associates audiovisual stimuli to physical pain existed (because, in nature, audiovisual stimuli such as the sight or sounds of a predator might signal an imminent attack). To test their hypothesis, they conducted an experiment known as the "bright, noisy water" experiment (Garcia and Koelling, 1966). The results of their experiment supported their hypothesis. Rats readily associated an audiovisual stimulus (CS) with an electric shock but not radiation-induced sickness. In contrast, rats readily associated the taste of sweetened water with the illness induced by radiation but not with an electric shock. The design of the experiment is described in Figure 7.2.

Long CS-US Interval

According to the general process approach, successful conditioning requires the CS and US to occur in close temporal contiguity. However, a CTA can be acquired despite long delays between the CS and the US. For example, it was found that rats acquired a CTA to a saccharine solution when access to the solution was followed by an injection of lithium chloride (an illness-producing agent) 3 hours later (Garcia, Ervin and Koelling, 1966) and 24 hours later (Etscorn and Stephens, 1973). Note that this is an important adaptation because nausea is often experienced several hours following the ingestion of poisons or spoiled food.

Suppressed drinking = learned avoidance
Normal drinking = no avoidance learned

Group	Training	AV Test (plain water triggers AV)	Taste test (sweetened water does not trigger AV)
Shock	Sweetened water + Light and sound (AV)	Suppressed drinking Shock associated with AV.	Normal drinking Shock not associated with sweetened water.
Radiation	Sweetened water + Light and sound (AV)	Normal drinking Radiation sickness not associated with AV.	Suppressed drinking Radiation sickness associated with sweetened water.

Figure 7.2 Biological constraints on classical conditioning demonstrated by Garcia and Koelling (1966). Rats were trained with sweetened water paired with audiovisual stimuli (light and sound), followed by either electric shock or radiation-induced illness. Testing revealed selective associations: rats avoided the taste when paired with illness but not shock (bottom row), while avoiding the audiovisual cues when paired with shock but not illness (top row). This demonstrates that organisms are biologically prepared to associate certain stimuli with specific consequences.

CTA in Humans

Conditioned taste aversion is part of the human experience. A study showed that 65% of college students out of a sample of 517 reported having experienced taste aversions (Logue, Ophir and Strauss, 1981). As found in rats and other animals, CTA in humans can occur with long delays between consuming food or drink (CS) and illness (US) (Logue, Ophir and Strauss, 1981). The propensity to assign the ingestion of a food to sickness is so powerful that a CTA to a particular food can develop even if a person knows that the food was not responsible for the illness. For example, knowing that nausea is caused by the stomach flu or resulting from a wild rollercoaster ride does not prevent the development of a CTA to food eaten before these events (Arwas, Rolnick and Lubow, 1989; Kirsch et al., 2004; Seligman, 1971). This feature of CTA shows that CTA learning is non-cognitive.

Pregnant women often experience conditioned taste aversion. One study found that although many pregnant women experience food cravings, 51% reported developing conditioned taste aversions (Bayley et al., 2002). It is also believed that CTA may play a role in the development of anorexia in some women. It is also thought that nausea induced by increased secretion of estrogens (a group of hormones) during puberty in girls may become associated with the foods consumed during that period. Support for this hypothesis comes from the observation that anorexia is ten times more prevalent in women than in men (American Psychiatric Association, 2013). Conditioned taste aversion is also sometimes experienced by people undergoing chemotherapy as a treatment for cancer (Chopra et al., 2016), a topic discussed in this chapter's "Focus On" box.

Focus On

CTA Induced by Chemotherapy

Nausea is a common side effect of the drugs used in chemotherapy for the treatment of cancer (Chopra et al., 2016). It was also observed that many chemotherapy patients experience a loss of appetite (Barajas Galindo et al., 2017). This continues to be a problem despite the development of *anti-emetic medications* commonly used to prevent vomiting and nausea (Crowder et al., 2022). It was hypothesized that one of the reasons for the loss of appetite in these patients is the development of CTAs to the taste of certain foods (CS) because of their association with the nausea (UR) induced by the drugs used in chemotherapy (US). This hypothesis was first tested in the 1970s. In one study, children treated for cancer with chemotherapy were divided into three groups (Bernstein, 1978). The children in Group 1 were given an unusually flavored ice cream before chemotherapy (Group 1). Group 2 received the same drug treatment but was not given the ice cream. Group 3 received the ice cream before either receiving either a drug not associated with nausea or no drug. Several weeks later, the children in each group were given a choice between eating the ice cream or playing a game. It was found that only 21% of the children in Group 1 chose to eat the ice cream over playing the game. However, 67% of the children in Group 2 and 73% in Group 3 chose the ice cream. These results were later replicated in adults (Bernstein and Webster, 1980; Jacobsen et al., 1993).

The Scapegoat-Food Effect

Fortunately, it was found that CTAs induced by chemotherapy can be alleviated by having patients consume a "scapegoat food" after their meals. In one study, children undergoing chemotherapy were offered a choice of various flavored Life Savers candies, which they were instructed to eat after every meal during an intervention phase. During the control phase, the same children were not offered the candies. The experimenters found that the children were more willing to ingest the foods that were part of their regular meals during the intervention phase than during the control phase (Broberg and Bernstein, 1987). This "scapegoat-food" effect has been demonstrated in several other studies (Mattes, 1994; Mattes, Arnold and Boraas, 1987).

The critical element in the success of this method of alleviating CTA in cancer patients undergoing chemotherapy is that the scapegoat food must be new to the patient (Bernstein, 1985). The use of a novel and salient stimulus is believed to be effective in blocking CTAs induced by the tastes of foods included in a patient's regular meals through the phenomenon of overshadowing (Geiger and Wolfgram, 2013), which occurs when the more salient of two CSs, in this case, the Life Savers, paired with the same US acquires more conditioning strength.

Are You Thinking Critically?

1. What might happen if the food aversions developed by chemotherapy patients were left untreated?
2. What is the meaning of the term "scapegoat food"?
3. How would you develop a treatment program to prevent the development of CTA in cancer patients undergoing chemotherapy?

Fear Learning

In Chapter 6, you learned about the fear conditioning procedure used for laboratory animals. In this section, you will learn that, similarly to CTA, fear learning cannot be explained by the general process approach.

Selectivity of Associations

It is worth repeating that according to the general process approach, any arbitrarily chosen stimulus can become an effective CS when paired with any US. This means that people should acquire phobias through classical conditioning by associating any object or event with any kind of aversive situation (note that classical conditioning is only one of several ways phobias can be acquired; see Chapter 6). However, this is not the case. People are more likely to develop phobias of animals, potentially dangerous environmental events (such as heights, enclosed spaces or crowds), and blood/injection injuries than harmless stimuli such as coffee cups, cell phones, or chairs (Mallan, Lipp and Cochrane, 2013; Polák et al., 2020; Samra and Abdijadid, 2022). This is consistent with Seligman's (1971) biological preparedness theory, which states that humans are biologically prepared to fear some stimuli more than others.

Resistance to Extinction

As you learned in Chapter 5, extinction refers to the process by which the response to a CS diminishes in strength or frequency with repeated presentations of the CS without the US. Resistance to extinction refers to the persistence in responding to a CS with repeated exposures. It is often used to measure the strength of conditioning (also see Chapter 5). The greater the resistance to extinction, the stronger the conditioning. Seligman (1971) proposed that phobias are more resistant to extinction than fears conditioned to the arbitrary, fear-irrelevant stimuli used in laboratory experiments (e.g., buzzers, tones, and lights).

Greater resistance to extinction has repeatedly been found when fear-relevant stimuli (such as those that potentially represent real dangers) are used as CSs in laboratory experiments. Psychologist Arne Öhman (1943–2020) and colleagues conducted several of these experiments (Fredrikson, Hugdahl and Öhman, 1976; Öhman, Eriksson and Olofsson, 1975; Öhman, Erixon and Lofberg, 1975; Öhman et al., 1976).

For example, Öhman and colleagues (1976) showed human participants a picture (CS) of either fear-relevant stimuli (spider or snake [fear-relevant group]), fear-irrelevant stimuli (mushroom or flower [fear-irrelevant group]), or a standard laboratory stimulus, often used in these kinds of experiments (circle or square [control group]). As shown in Figure 7.3, the experiment consisted of an acquisition phase and an extinction phase. During the acquisition phase, all pictures were paired with an uncomfortable, but not painful, electric shock (US) to a finger (CS-US pairing). The conditioned response (CR) measured by the experimenters was the skin conduction response (SCR), which is a physiological measure taken to detect emotional reactivity (e.g., fear) through the amount of sweat released to the surface of the skin. The extinction phase consisted of presentations of the CS (i.e., a picture) by itself (i.e., without the electric shock [US]).

They hypothesized that the fear-relevant group would show greater resistance to extinction, as measured by the continued high level of SCR when the fear-relevant CS (i.e., spider or snake) was repeatedly presented without the shock (US), than the fear-irrelevant group, for which the CS was a mushroom or a flower, and the control group, for which the CS was

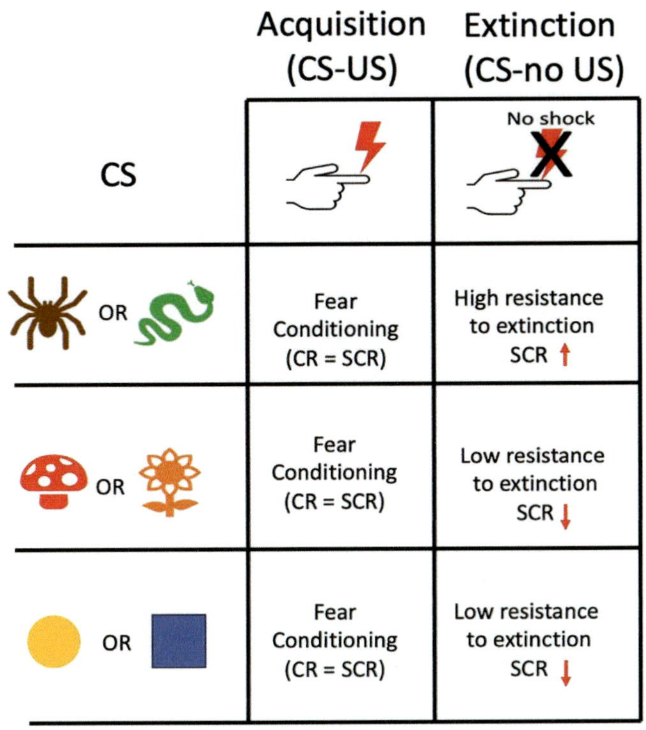

Figure 7.3 Depiction of the experiment conducted by Öhman and colleagues (1976). The first column shows the type of CS presented. The second column shows the results of acquisition trials during which a CS was paired with a US (shock). The third column shows the results of extinction trials during which the CS was not followed by a US (see text for details).

a standard laboratory stimulus (i.e., circle or square). This is precisely what they found. The result of their experiment supported their hypothesis and provided evidence that humans are biologically prepared to fear potentially dangerous stimuli (fear relevant) as proposed by Seligman (1971).

A Fear Module Imperviousness to Cognition

Öhman and Mineka (2001) proposed that biological preparedness for potentially threatening stimuli could be explained by the existence of a fear module in the brain, centered on the amygdala, a brain structure known to be involved in processing emotion (Figure 7.4), that evolved to respond to fear-relevant stimuli. According to Öhman and Mineka (2001), this fear module is impervious to cognition, meaning that a fear response continues to occur during extinction even if a subject knows that an aversive stimulus no longer follows the CS. This phenomenon is observed in people with phobias who say that, even if they know that an object or situation no longer poses a threat, they cannot help feeling anxious and fearful when it is encountered.

This idea was tested by an experiment in which participants were told that the US would no longer occur before being given extinction trials. They found that informing the subjects that the US would not be delivered significantly reduced the number of trials needed

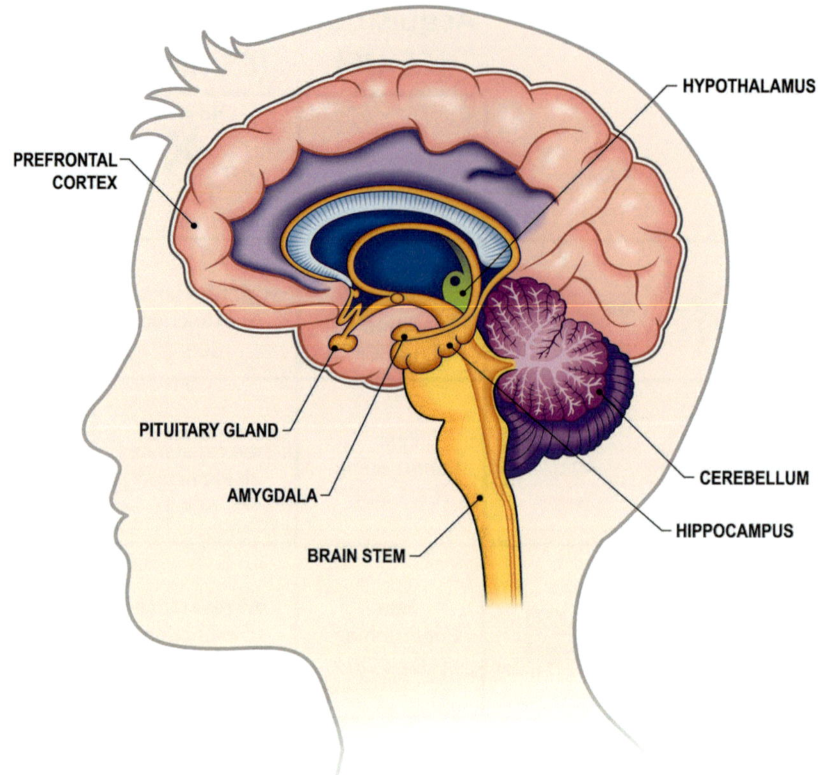

Figure 7.4 According to Öhman and Mineka (2001), the amygdala (shown in the figure among other brain structures) constitutes the center of a fear module, impervious to cognition that evolved to respond to fear-relevant stimuli.

Source: IStock illustration ID:502041209.

to extinguish the fear response in participants for which the CSs were fear-irrelevant but failed to reduce the number of trials to extinguish the fear responses in subjects for which the CSs were fear-relevant (Hugdahl and Ohman, 1977). More recently, it was found that informing participants that the US would no longer be delivered enhanced extinction of a fear response to a fear-relevant CS but did not affect the return of the fear response when the fear-relevant CS was represented to them 24 hrs after the last extinction trial (Wendt et al., 2020).

Unconscious Fear Response

In another experiment (illustrated in Figure 7.5), Öhman and colleagues also showed that, in addition to an increase in SCR, which was used as a measure of fear in the studies described previously, the amygdala was found to respond to potential threats without conscious awareness of the stimuli provoking the response (Morris et al. 1998). In Phase 1 of the experiment, participants were shown pictures of expressionless and angry faces. Some

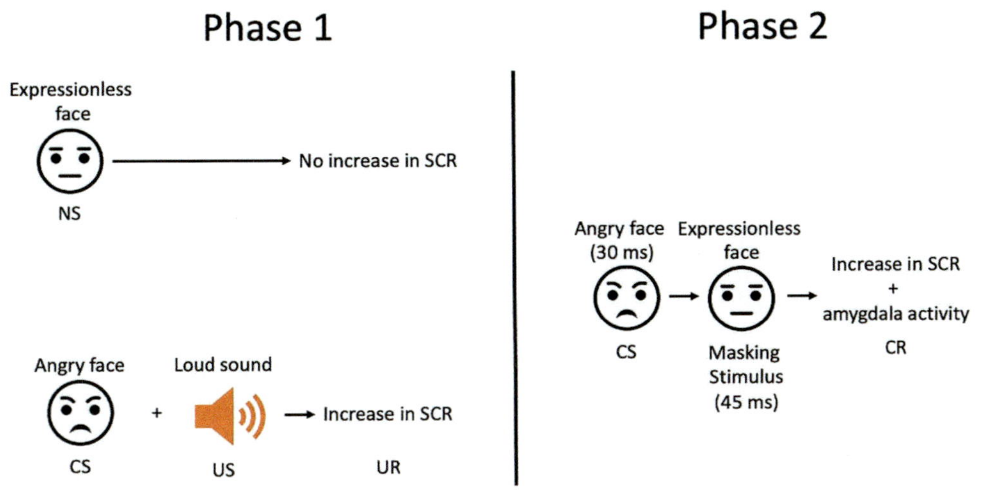

Figure 7.5 Experiment conducted by Morris, Öhman, and Dolan (1998) (see text for details).

angry faces were presented along with an unpleasant sound, while others were not. Photos of an expressionless face did not increase autonomic activity in participants as measured by SCR (neutral stimulus [NS]). However, pictures of an angry face (CS) presented along with an unpleasant sound (US) did increase autonomic activity (UR).

In Phase 2, the angry faces (CS) were presented for a very brief period (30 milliseconds [ms]) followed by a 45-ms masking stimulus, which consisted of an expressionless face (the masking stimulus ensured that no visual trace remained of the angry face). The participants indicated that they saw the expressionless face but not the angry face. The participants previously exposed to angry faces followed by the aversive sound (US) showed a significantly higher degree of skin conduction than participants whose presentations of the angry faces were not followed by the aversive sound (CR). In addition, the same participants also showed increased activity in the amygdala. Remember that this is even though the participants reported not having consciously perceived the angry faces.

Sexual Conditioning

Another challenge to the general process approach to learning comes from the study of the sexual behavior of quails. Psychologist Michael Domjan proposed that sexual behavior relies on a behavior system composed of three major stimulus categories (see Chapter 3 for a general description of behavior systems). Figure 7.6 shows these consist of 1) **spatially distributed contextual stimuli**, 2) **arbitrary localized stimuli** and 3) **species-typical localized stimuli** (Domjan and Gutierrez, 2019). Spatially distributed contextual stimuli such as illumination levels, temperature, and sounds compose the animal's general environment. Arbitrary localized stimuli consist of objects present within the animal's general context. In classical conditioning experiments, these can be a variety of neutral stimuli that are not part of an animal's sexual behavior system but that can nevertheless be conditioned to the US. Spatially distributed contextual and arbitrary localized stimuli elicit general search behavior as URs. A potential mate provides species-typical localized stimuli. These may be visual, gestural, chemical, or auditory. Species-typical localized stimuli are the only stimuli that directly trigger approach and copulatory behaviors as URs.

All three types of stimuli (i.e., spatially distributed contextual stimuli, arbitrary localized stimuli, and species-typical localized stimuli) make effective CSs in laboratory experiments. It was found that, when used as CSs, spatially distributed contextual stimuli and arbitrary localized stimuli elicited approach behavior in male quails when the US was an opportunity to copulate with a female (US) (Crawford and Domjan, 1996; Tzschentke, 2007). However, out of the three stimulus categories, species-typical localized stimuli are the only ones that can be used as CSs to produce both approach responses and copulatory behavior as CRs.

It was demonstrated that approach and copulatory behavior can be elicited in male quails even if a rough model of a female is used as a CS. For example, in one experiment, male quails were exposed to a model female with a taxidermic head and a terrycloth body. For one group of males, exposure to the model (CS) was paired with the opportunity to copulate with a live female (US). Another group of males were exposed to unpaired presentations in which the US preceded the presentation of the CS. The males were then given a series of trials, some of which consisted of test trials during which the CS was presented by itself. The dependent measure was the time the quails spent near the female model as a CR. The results were that the quails receiving the paired CS/US presentations spent significantly more time near the CS than those receiving unpaired CS/US presentations (Köksal, Domjan and Weisman, 1994).

In a similar experiment (Cusato and Domjan, 1998), male quails were also exposed to pairings of a model female with copulation. However, this time, the dependent measure was the extent to which the male quails attempted to copulate with the model when presented

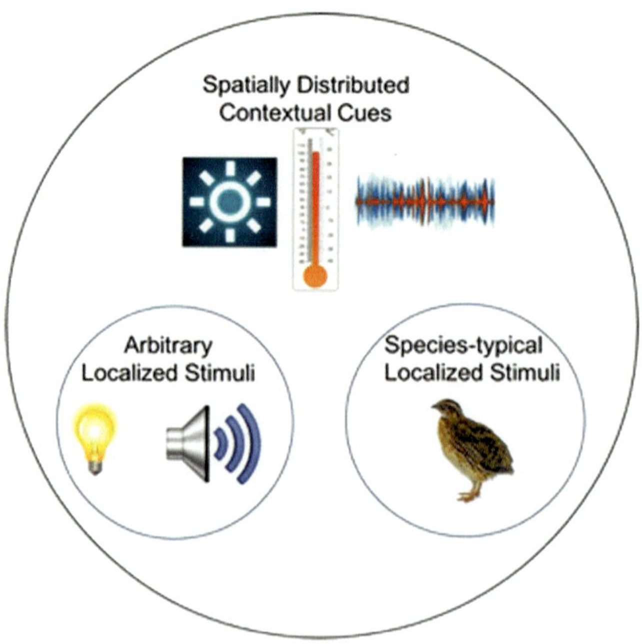

Figure 7.6 Three major stimulus categories of the sexual behavior system proposed by Domjan and Gutierrez, 2019.

by itself. When later presented with the model female, the males approached, grabbed, and mounted the model as if copulating with it. It was shown that these behaviors toward the CS only occurred with a female quail model. Such copulatory CRs did not happen when the CSs were arbitrary localized stimuli such as a block of wood, a piece of rigid foam, or a stuffed toy. Also, the behaviors did not occur if the female model lacked a critical species-typical cue, such as the head, or when the CSs were spatially distributed contextual cues.

Conditioned Modification of Responses to the Unconditioned Stimulus

Autonomic Conditioning

According to the general process approach, the CR should always be the same as the UR. However, classical conditioning includes instances where the UR differs from the CR. In other words, the response to the US when it is present (UR) can differ from the response it elicits when the US is not present. Such is the case of fear conditioning, discussed in Chapter 6, in which the UR consists of jumping (when a shock [US] is administered), and the CR consists of freezing when the shock is predicted by the CS (e.g., a tone). A similar situation exists in what is known as **autonomic conditioning**.

The autonomic nervous system regulates involuntary bodily functions such as heart rate, blood pressure, respiration, and body temperature. It is regulated by the activity of the hypothalamus (shown in Figure 7.4) and is critical for maintaining **homeostasis** (Yoon and Diano, 2021). Homeostasis is the process by which bodily conditions are maintained, such as when your body is cooled by sweating when it gets too warm or warmed by shivering when its temperature gets too low. When blood glucose levels get too high, they are regulated by a hormone called insulin, released by the pancreas.

It was discovered that the functions of the autonomic nervous system, thus homeostatic processes, can be controlled through classical conditioning. This was demonstrated in a landmark experiment (Figure 7.7) by psychologist Sheppard Siegel (1975). In Phase 1 (baseline) of the experiment, he measured a group of rats' baseline blood glucose levels. In Phase 2 (training), he injected some of the rats with either insulin (experimental rats) or saline, which consisted of salted water (control rats) on four occasions. In Phase 3 (testing), he injected both the experimental rats (i.e., who received insulin injections in Phase 2) and the control rats (i.e., who received saline in Phase 2) with a single saline injection.

The insulin injections in Phase 2 decreased the experimental rats' blood glucose levels relative to the baseline in Phase 1. The saline injections did not cause such an decrease in blood glucose levels relative to the baseline in the control rats. In Phase 3, the experimental rats that received insulin injections in Phase 2 showed increased blood glucose levels in response to a single saline injection. In contrast, the control rats that received saline injections in Phase 2 did not show such an increase in blood glucose levels.

Why did the saline injections in Phase 3 cause an increase (instead of a decrease) in blood glucose levels in the experimental rats which previously received insulin injections? The authors proposed that, as expected in Phase 2, the insulin injections (US) caused blood glucose levels to drop (UR). In response, the autonomic nervous system orchestrated an increase in blood glucose levels to compensate for the drop in blood glucose levels caused by the insulin to restore homeostasis. After repeated insulin injections, the environmental context in which the insulin injections were given became a CS that predicted the insulin injections (US). In response to the context of the injections (CS), which were associated with

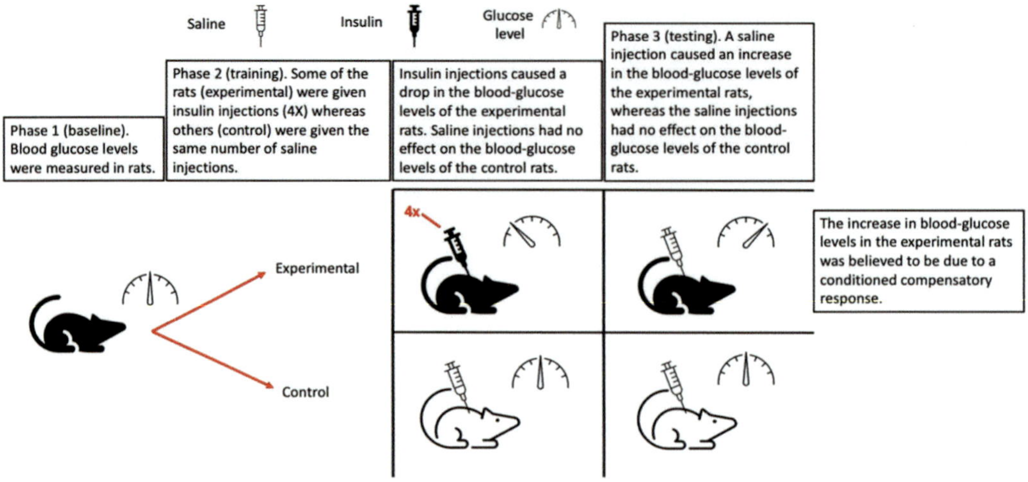

Figure 7.7 Depiction of the procedure used by Siegel (1975).

a drop in blood glucose levels in Phase 2, the autonomic system engaged in a homeostatic response to compensate for the drop in blood glucose levels by raising them (CR). Such a response is known as a **conditioned compensatory response**, which refers to a preparatory response aimed at restoring homeostasis disrupted by the administration of a drug. Such a conditioned compensatory response is well documented (Siegel et al., 2000).

Situational Specificity of Tolerance

One of the hallmarks of drug addiction is the development of tolerance. Tolerance is expressed in two ways: 1) metabolic tolerance, in which the body's ability to metabolize a drug is enhanced, and 2) functional tolerance, in which brain functions adapt to compensate for the effects of a drug. Tolerance explains why addicted individuals require progressively larger doses of a drug to experience the same effects. It also explains why addicted individuals can survive the ingestion of high doses of a drug that would result in an overdose in a person taking the drug for the first time.

However, it was found that people can suffer what seems to be a drug overdose with a dose they have tolerated. This led researchers to believe that, in those cases, what initially appeared to be a drug overdose was, in reality, the person's temporary inability to tolerate the drug (Beecher, 1953). It was then found that in a significant number of cases in which a person seemingly suffered a heroin overdose, the drug was taken in a context that differed from the one in which the person was accustomed to taking it (Gerevich et al., 2005; Siegel et al., 1982). This raised the possibility that the physiological processes involved in the compensatory mechanisms of tolerance (UR) become conditioned responses (CRs) to the environmental cues (CS) in which the drug (US) is usually taken. This allows the compensatory responses to be engaged when an individual enters the context in which the drug is generally taken.

More specifically, exposure to environmental cues, such as those that characterize the specific locations, people, objects, and drug paraphernalia, which are often present at the times a drug is usually taken, become CSs that predict the intake of the drug (US). Many of these environmental cues may be absent when a person takes the drug in a context that differs from the one in which the drug is usually taken, resulting in the failure of the individual's body to engage the CRs that usually account for the body's ability to begin compensating for the drug's effects before it is taken.

This process is the same as the conditioned compensatory response you learned about in the previous section. When applied to tolerance, it is known as the **situational specificity of tolerance.** It is also thought to explain the emergency room visits by people who consumed a novel alcoholic beverage that differs significantly in the taste and container in which it is presented from to what drinkers are accustomed (Siegel, 2011). Such was the case of Joshua in the opening vignette of the chapter.

Critical Thinking Spot Check 7.2

1. What is the importance of the selectivity of associations in both fear learning and conditioned taste aversion?
2. What contribution does resistance to extinction make to the adaptability of fear learning?
3. Compare the effectiveness of three types of stimuli in sexual conditioning.
4. What is the importance of autonomic conditioning in the maintenance of homeostasis?
5. Briefly describe a study in which autonomic conditioning was demonstrated.
6. Describe a situation in which the situational specificity of tolerance would lead to potentially deadly consequences.

Chapter Summary

Each bullet point aligns with the learning objectives outlined at the beginning of the chapter.

- The general process approach of learning states that all learning can be explained by a set of rules regardless of the associated stimuli, sometimes referred to as the equivalence of associativity. However, survival depends on forming associations between specific kinds of stimuli. In classical conditioning, this is known as CS-US relevance. Behavioral systems theory posits that learning can be explained by activating behavioral systems. In his biological preparedness theory, psychologist Martin Seligman proposed that animals are biologically prepared to fear stimuli that potentially threatened a species in the evolutionary past.
- The most often cited example of CS-US relevance is conditioned taste aversion (CTA). CTA challenges the general process approach because it needs to conform to its laws in the following ways. For example, 1) CTA can be learned after a single training trial; 2) illness can only readily be associated with taste or smell; and 3) conditioning occurs with long CS-US intervals.
- Fear learning has important survival value in alerting animals of potential threats. However, fear can also be maladaptive, as in people who have phobias. Fear learning challenges the general process approach because animals are biologically prepared to form selective associations. For example, phobias mainly develop into potentially threatening stimuli. Psychologist Arne Öhman proposed that the brain contains a fear module, organized around the amygdala, that operates independently from cognition. Once learned, conditioned fears are resistant to extinction and impervious to cognition. A conditioned fear response can also occur without being conscious that the CS is being presented.

- Another challenge to the general process approach of learning is sexual conditioning. It is proposed that sexual behavior depends on activating a specific behavioral system containing three stimulus categories: spatially distributed contextual stimuli, arbitrary localized stimuli, and species-typical localized stimuli. Only species-typical localized stimuli can effectively be used as a CS to elicit copulatory behavior as a conditioned response.
- Yet another phenomenon that the general process cannot explain is the condition modification of the unconditioned response to the US. Such modification occurs through autonomic conditioning and maintains the body's homeostasis. Examples of such changes include insulin-induced hypoglycemia, in which insulin injections increase blood glucose levels as the CR, as opposed to a decrease in blood glucose levels before conditioning. This phenomenon is known as a conditioned compensatory response. It was also shown that tolerance to drugs of abuse can be attributed to the compensatory responses to the effects of the medications elicited by exposure to the environmental cues that have been associated with the intake of the drug.

Glossary

Arbitrary localized stimuli Specific stimuli that are positioned in a particular location but have no inherent relevance to an organism's natural behavior.

Autonomic conditioning A learning process that affects involuntary physiological responses, such as heart rate or blood pressure regulation.

Belongingness The idea that organisms are predisposed to form certain associations more easily than others because those associations are biologically adaptive.

Biological preparedness The concept that organisms are naturally inclined to form certain associations more readily than others, such as fear of predators.

Conditioned compensatory response A learned physiological reaction that counteracts the effects of an expected stimulus, often seen in drug tolerance.

CS–US relevance The degree to which a conditioned stimulus (CS) is meaningfully related to an unconditioned stimulus (US), with more relevant pairings producing stronger and faster learning.

Equivalence of associativity The idea that all stimuli have an equal potential to form associations in classical conditioning, though exceptions exist based on biological factors.

Homeostasis The body's ability to maintain a stable internal environment despite external changes.

Selective associations The tendency for certain stimuli to be more easily linked with specific responses due to evolutionary or biological predispositions.

Situational specificity of tolerance The observation that tolerance to a stimulus, such as a drug, can vary depending on the environment in which it is repeatedly experienced.

Situational specificity The idea that learned behaviors or responses can be highly dependent on the specific context in which they were acquired.

Spatially distributed contextual stimuli Environmental cues spread out across a space that influence learning or memory retrieval.

Species-typical localized stimuli Stimuli that are naturally relevant to a species and positioned in ways that align with their evolutionary adaptations.

8 Unraveling the Building Blocks of Classical Conditioning

Learning Objectives

- Describe latent inhibition and the US preexposure effect.
- Differentiate between the attentional and switching models for latent inhibition and the associative and nonassociative theories for the US preexposure effect.
- Define compound CS, blocking, and overshadowing, including Kamin's memory search hypothesis and the role of stimulus salience.
- Analyze the mechanisms of blocking and overshadowing, including the impact of stimulus salience and Kamin's memory search hypothesis on learning associations.

The Machine Operator

Source: IStock photo ID:175212866.

DOI: 10.4324/9781003491828-15

Massimo was the newest member of the production team at Sweet Treats Cookie Factory. He stood before an intimidating packaging machine with buttons, lights, levers, and conveyor belts. He was waiting for Ajeet, an experienced operator, to train him on how to use it. "Don't worry, it looks complicated, but you will get the hang of it in no time," she said as she arrived. "I hope she's right," Massimo thought to himself. She showed him how to load cookies on the conveyor belt and to set the parameters to package them. She turned on the machine and went through a cycle so Massimo could see it in operation. As the cookies whizzed by, she pointed out the possible problems. For example, plastic wrappers sometimes got stuck in the machine, and at other times, cookies stayed stuck. Arjeet called these wrapper jams and cookie jams, respectively. She showed Massimo how to resolve each of these issues. When a wrapper jam occurred, a musical tone sounded with a blue light, whereas a cookie jam triggered a different tone without a light. In either case, Massimo learned that he had to stop the machine, follow instructions on how to clear the jam, and restart the machine. It took Massimo some time to learn this. At first, he failed to react quickly to the musical tone that signaled the cookie jam. He figured this was because it sounded like an application notification on his phone, which he learned to ignore. He had no trouble associating the other musical tone with the wrapper jam. Since wrapper jams could damage the machine, its manufacturers added a flashing blue light to the musical tone to make the problem more evident to the operator whenever a jam occurred. This addition was made after Massimo experienced many wrapper jams. Hence, Massimo had already associated the tone with the wrapper jam when the flashing blue light was added. One day, a manager noticed that having two tones (one for the cookie jams and another for the wrapper jams) sounding at the factory was too distracting and decided that the wrapper jams would only be signaled by the flashing blue light. This resulted in many wrapper jams that were not resolved quickly enough to prevent damaging the machine. A few weeks later, the manager reinstated the musical tone that signaled wrapper jams.

8.1 Associability of the CS and US: Preexposure Effects

Latent Inhibition (CS-Preexposure Effect)

Latent inhibition, also known as the CS-preexposure effect, is the phenomenon by which repeated exposure to a stimulus without any meaningful event makes it difficult for that stimulus later to become an effective conditioned stimulus (CS). Indeed, researchers have shown that preexposure to a stimulus can retard its association with the US in CS-US conditioning trials. Thus, latent inhibition may have been responsible for Massimo's difficulty associating the musical tone with cookie jams in the opening vignette.

Psychologist Robert Lubow conducted the first experiment on latent inhibition (Lubow and Moore, 1959). The experiment consisted of the three phases illustrated in Figure 8.1. In Phase 1 (preexposure phase), goats and sheep were preexposed to either a flashing light or a moving rotor. Half of the animals were preexposed to the flashing light and the other half to the moving rotor. In Phase 2 (conditioning phase), half of the animals were given conditioning trials in which the CS was the stimulus to which they were preexposed in Phase 1. For the other half of the trials, the CS was the stimulus they were not preexposed in Phase 1. The US was a shock to the foreleg. In Phase 3, the animals were tested for how

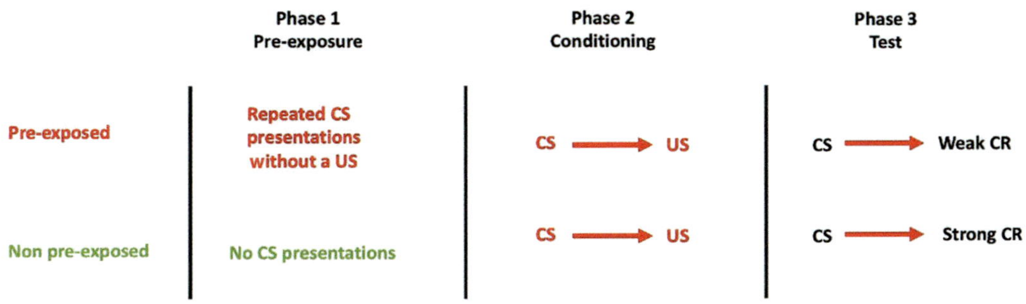

Figure 8.1 The latent inhibition procedure.

much they associated the CS with the shock. The CR consisted of a flexion of the foreleg. The conditioning strength was measured by the number of trials for the animals to perform ten CRs. Two mechanisms by which the latent inhibition effect occurs have been proposed. These are described in the sections subsequently.

Figure 8.2 shows the experiment's results. The animals took significantly more trials to perform ten CRs when the CS was the stimulus to which they were preexposed during Phase 1 (preexposed) than with the CS to which they were not preexposed during Phase 1 (novel).

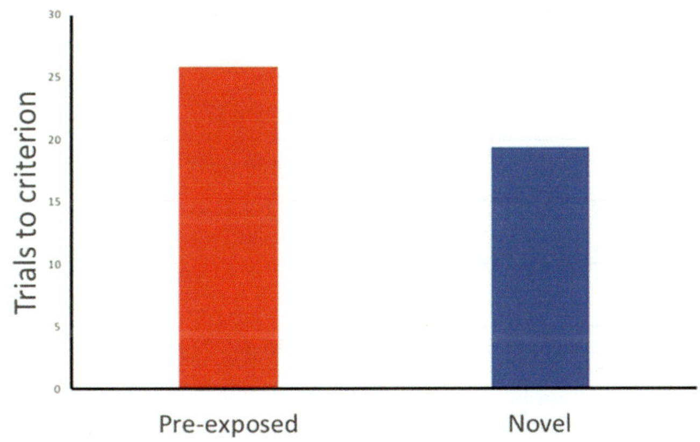

Figure 8.2 Results from the Lubow and Moore (1959) experiment. Animals required significantly more trials to reach the learning criterion when the CS was a stimulus they were pre-exposed to than when the CS was novel.

Source: Adapted from Lubow, R. E., & Moore, A. U. (1959). Latent inhibition: the effect of nonreinforced preexposure to the conditional stimulus. *J Comp Physiol Psychol, 52*, 415–419 (Page 416, Table 1).

Mechanisms of Latent Inhibition

The Attentional Model of Latent Inhibition

In what is known as the **attentional model of latent inhibition**, preexposure to a stimulus reduces its saliency or the extent to which it is surprising. Hence, according to this model, the acquisition of a conditioned association between the CS and the US is inhibited by preexposure trials to the CS because, during those trials, animals learned not to pay any attention to it (Lubow, 1989). According to the attention model, Massimo would have had trouble associating the sound signaling a cookie jam because he had previously learned to ignore it.

The Switching Model of Latent Inhibition

According to the **switching model of latent inhibition**, illustrated in Figure 8.3, latent inhibition occurs because of a conflict involving learning that the CS signals nothing during preexposure trials and that it signals the US during training trials (Weiner and Feldon, 1997). Thus, this explanation of latent inhibition is based on the phenomenon known as proactive interference, which occurs when previously learned information interferes with learning new information (Bouton, 1993). According to the switching model, Massimo would have had trouble associating the sound signaling a cookie jam because he had previously learned it to be a social media notification.

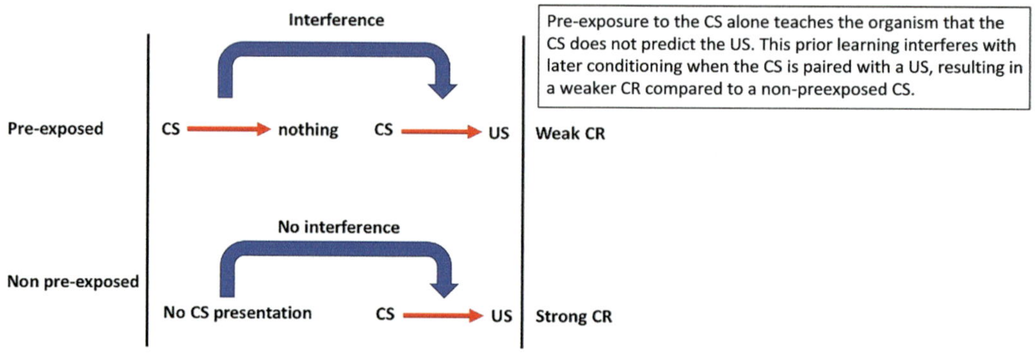

Figure 8.3 The switching model of latent inhibition.

CS-Preexposure Does Not Always Lead to Latent Inhibition

Although latent inhibition has been repeatedly demonstrated, you may wonder if preexposure trials always inhibit the acquisition of CS-US associations. The answer is that it does not. In a phenomenon known as latent learning (see Chapter 19), the ability of rats to find food in a maze is enhanced by preexposure trials (Gaskin, Chai and White, 2005; Tolman, 1948). Indeed, it was found that whether preexposure trials inhibit or facilitate the acquisition of associations depends on several factors. For example, it was shown that preexposure to the context in which rats will be exposed to shocks can facilitate the formation of an association between the context and the shocks. That is, an animal will more readily show a fear response when later placed into that context than animals that were not preexposed (Fanselow, 1990). This indicates that preexposure to the general context of an event may have a different effect than preexposure to individual cues that are part of a context. It was also shown that whether facilitation or inhibition of conditioning is found may depend on the type of stimulus used, the timing of the test, or even the measure of behavior recorded by the experimenters (Holland, 2018).

Focus On

Latent Inhibition in Humans

Latent inhibition is an adaptive process that limits the time spent paying attention to irrelevant stimuli. In the first test of latent inhibition in humans, two groups of participants were asked to count the frequency of nonsense syllables played in an audio recording. For one group (the preexposed group), bursts of white noise were also played throughout the recording. Bursts of white noise never occurred for the participants in the other group (the non-preexposed group). All participants then learned that the white noise burst was associated with a one-point increase on a scoreboard. The experimenters found that the preexposed group participants were significantly slower at learning this association than those not exposed to the bursts of white noise. This indicated that the participants in the preexposed group failed to pay attention to the white noise, deeming it irrelevant to the task (Ginton, Urca and Lubow, 1975).

Low Latent Inhibition

Schizophrenia

Low levels of latent inhibition are believed to contribute to schizophrenia, a brain disorder which may include delusions, hallucinations, disorganized speech, cognitive problems, and a lack of motivation. It is believed that the altered perceptions of the world experienced by people with schizophrenia are at least partly due to their inability to filter out unimportant environmental stimuli. In addition, it was found that schizophrenia and low latent inhibition have in common that they both involve disruptions in the brain's dopamine system. In fact, it was found that injections of amphetamine, a drug that is known to increase dopamine levels in the brain, block the latent inhibition of CTA learning (Meyer et al., 2004). Therefore, it is believed that deficits in latent inhibition can be used as a marker for schizophrenia (Dawes et al., 2022; Granger, Talwar and Barnett, 2020; Lubow and Gewirtz, 1995; Yogev et al., 2004).

Creativity

Interestingly, it was also found that low levels of latent inhibition were related to high levels of creativity. Creativity can be defined as the amount of originality in how people solve problems. This includes personal, scientific, and mathematical problems. It also refers to originality in arts and language. In one study, psychologist Shelley Carson and colleagues found that creative achievers were seven times more likely to have low latent inhibition than high latent inhibition (Carson, Peterson and Higgins, 2003). However, Carson believes that low latent inhibition increases creativity only in people with a high intelligence quotient (IQ) who have better than normal working memory and exhibit heightened cognitive flexibility. She believes that in these people, the large number of stimuli that enter their consciousness is combined and manipulated to form original ideas. In contrast, in people with schizophrenia, this increased exposure to irrelevant stimuli is associated with cognitive problems (Carson, 2011).

The US Preexposure Effect

The **US preexposure effect** refers to the phenomenon by which preexposure to the US before being used in CS-US pairings retards the acquisition of a CR (Randich and LoLordo, 1979). The US preexposure effect has often been demonstrated in CTA learning (de Brugada et al., 2021; Revillo, Arias and Spear, 2013). The typical experiment consists of three phases. In Phase 1 (preexposure), animals are given preexposure trials to the US, consisting of an illness-producing agent. This usually consists of injections of lithium chloride (LiCl), which is known to produce nausea. In Phase 2 (conditioning), the animals are exposed to conditioning trials in which consumption of a flavored solution is followed by the US (the illness-producing agent). In Phase 3, the amount of flavored solution consumed is compared to that of a group that received conditioning trials but was not preexposed to the US. It is typically found that the animals preexposed to the US before conditioning trials show an attenuated CTA compared to the animals not preexposed to the US. Three theories have been put forward to explain this phenomenon. One of the theories is associative, whereas the other two are nonassociative. These are described in the next sections.

Mechanisms of the US Preexposure Effect

The Associative Theory of the US Preexposure Effect

According to the associative theory, an association is created between the context in which preexposure occurs and the US. Thus, the context-US association blocks the formation of any other conditioned association between a new stimulus subsequently added to this context and the same US. The reason is that adding a new stimulus to the context is redundant in predicting the US and does not elicit a CR (de Brugada et al., 2021; Mackintosh and Turner, 1971).

Nonassociative Theories of the US Preexposure Effect

According to one nonassociative theory, US preexposure reduces the animal's reactivity to the US through habituation. As a result, little attention is paid to it during conditioning trials, which reduces its associability (Konorski, 1967). According to another nonassociative theory, preexposure to the US reduces the extent to which it is surprising to the animal, which impedes its ability to become associated with a CS (Domjan and Best, 1980).

Critical Thinking Spot Check 8.1

1. Describe latent inhibition and the classic experiment in which it was first demonstrated.
2. Give two everyday life examples of latent inhibition.
3. Distinguish latent inhibition from latent learning by describing a situation where preexposure to the CS does not result in latent learning.
4. Name and explain two proposed mechanisms of latent inhibition.
5. How might your levels of creativity be augmented if your capacity for latent inhibition was diminished?

8.2 Associability of the CS and US: Conditioning With Stimulus Compounds

Blocking

Imagine that you have felt refreshed and satisfied for many years after drinking your favorite soft drink, Brand-X. You feel happy when seeing the brand on store shelves and in advertisements. One day, when thirsty at a friend's backyard party, you reach out for a can of your favorite Brand-X soft drink in a cooler. However, you notice that cans of a soft drink called Sugar-Bluff, which you have never seen before, are scattered among the Brand-X cans. You decide to try Sugar-Bluff and notice that it leaves you just as refreshed and satisfied as the Brand-X drink. However, given the option between Sugar-Bluff and Brand-X in the future, Brand-X will likely still be your choice. This shows that changing your preference for a brand once you have associated it with positive emotions is difficult. This is why first impressions are important for marketers (Oxoby and Finnigan, 2007). The same could be said about Massimo in the opening vignette when he could not associate the new flashing blue light with a wrapper jam that was added to the tone.

This example demonstrates a phenomenon called **blocking.** Blocking occurs when learning an association between a CS and a US blocks learning an association between a new CS and the same US when both CSs are presented together. The original CS is often referred to as $CS_{1,}$ whereas the new CS is referred to as CS_2. If this sounds familiar, it is because it forms the basis for the associative learning hypothesis of the US preexposure effect described previously. Blocking was first demonstrated in a landmark experiment by psychologist Leon Kamin (1927–2017) in the late 1960s (Kamin, 1968, 1969a, 1969b). The experiment, consisting of three phases, is described in Figure 8.4.

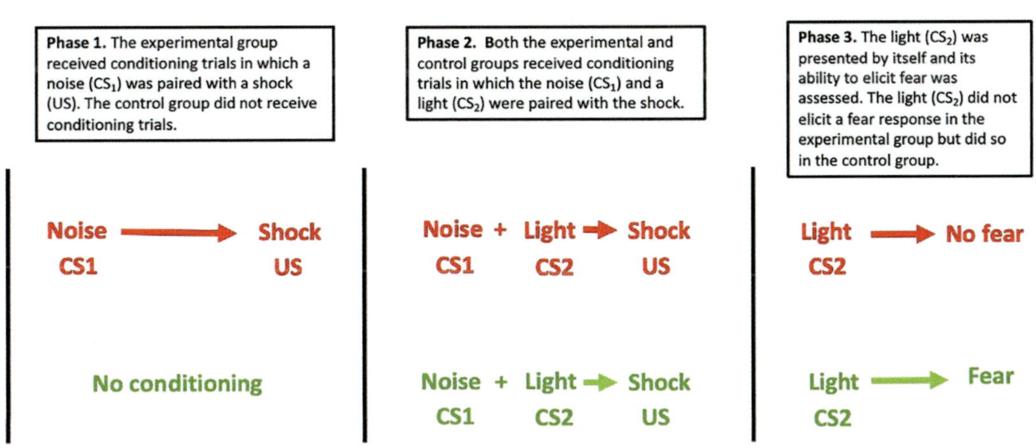

Figure 8.4 The blocking procedure.

Blocking Shows That Temporal Contiguity Is Not Sufficient for Learning

Remember that according to the general process theory, stimuli that occur in temporal contiguity should easily be associated. However, the blocking effect presents a serious challenge to this assumption. This is because in Phase 2 of a blocking experiment, CS_2 and the US are presented in close temporal contiguity, but no association is created between them. Hence, the results of blocking experiments show that contiguity between stimuli is insufficient for learning to occur. They show that the effectiveness of a CS depends on whether another CS has already been established as a reliable predictor of the US.

Why Blocking Occurs: Kamin's Memory Scan Hypothesis

According to **Kamin's memory scan hypothesis** (1968), when the US is surprising to an animal, a scan of its memory is performed. Kamin believed that the purpose of this scan was to learn about the cause of the US. A memory scan is unnecessary if the US is expected, and no new learning occurs. In the blocking experiment described in Figure 8.4, the rats in the experimental group are not surprised by the occurrence of the foot shock during Phase 2 of the experiment. This is because they have already learned to predict its occurrence by being conditioned to the noise in Phase 1. Hence, the light was redundant, and no learning about its association with the shock was necessary. Therefore, no memory search was triggered for the cause of the foot shock during Phase 2.

Overshadowing

Imagine that one of your friends insists you taste his peanut butter and banana smoothie. You gladly accept and quickly gulp down a large glass of the concoction. Later that day, you feel pretty nauseous and run to the restroom, where you throw it up. Ever since that day, you become nauseated at the taste or smell of peanut butter but have no problem eating bananas. I am sure you recognize this as a clear case of conditioned taste aversion (CTA) to peanut butter due to the earlier ingestion of the smoothie.

However, since the smoothie also contained bananas, why did you not also develop CTA to bananas? One reason might be that the taste of peanut butter and banana in the smoothie formed a compound CS, making peanut butter taste more intense than the taste of banana. Hence, the taste of banana was overshadowed by the taste of peanut butter in its ability to be associated with nausea.

This phenomenon is known as **overshadowing.** Overshadowing occurs when the CR elicited by one of two CSs (CS1) conditioned to the US in a compound (CS_1+CS_2) is weaker than the CR elicited by the other CS (CS_2) of the compound, in which case we would say that CS_2 overshadowed CS_1. Pavlov first demonstrated this phenomenon in the experiment described in Figure 8.5, where thermal stimulation was overshadowed by tactile stimulation in eliciting salivation in dogs (Pavlov, 1927).

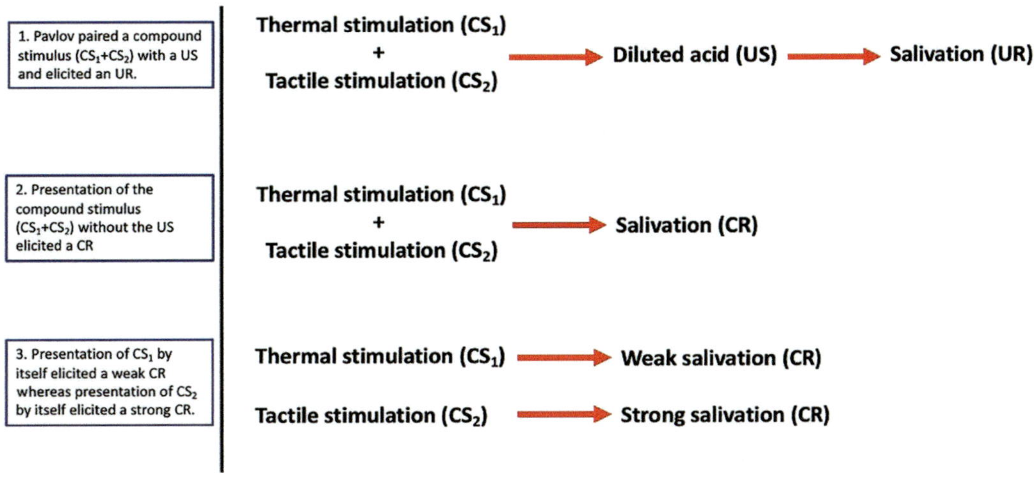

Figure 8.5 The overshadowing procedure developed by Pavlov.

Why Does Overshadowing Occur?

Overshadowing may occur because the US only has a certain amount of associative strength to be allotted to a CS. Therefore, each stimulus of the compound acquires less associative strength to the US than if each had been conditioned by themselves (Rescorla and Wagner, 1972). Hence, if one stimulus of the compound is less salient than the other, it may be overshadowed by the more salient stimulus in its ability to elicit a CR (Mackintosh, 1976).

Critical Thinking Spot Check 8.2

1. Compare blocking and overshadowing by outlining their similarities and differences.
2. How does the blocking phenomenon show that temporal contiguity is insufficient for learning?
3. How does Kamin's memory scan hypothesis explain blocking?

Chapter Summary

Each bullet point aligns with the learning objectives outlined at the beginning of the chapter.

- Many variables can interfere with how much a stimulus can become an effective CS or the US. One of these variables is how animals have experienced the CS or the US before conditioning trials occur. Latent inhibition, or the CS-preexposure effect, refers to the reduction in the ability of a stimulus to become an effective CS when preexposed to an animal before conditioning trials.

- Two explanations for latent inhibition have been proposed: the attentional and switching models. The US preexposure effect refers to the reduction in a stimulus's ability to become an effective US when preexposed to an animal before conditioning trials. Three theories of the US preexposure effect have been proposed: an associative theory and two nonassociative theories.
- A CS may be composed of more than one stimulus. Such a CS is known as a compound CS. Conditioning with a compound CS gives rise to a series of interesting phenomena. These include blocking and overshadowing. In blocking, a CS (CS_A) conditioned to the US blocks another CS (CS_B) from being conditioned to the same US when both CSs are presented as a compound during conditioning trials. Blocking is believed to occur during compound conditioning trials because the presence of CSA can already predict the US; CSB is redundant, and therefore, no attention is paid to it.
- According to Kamin's memory search hypothesis, conditioning can only occur if the US is surprising. The surprisingness of the US causes the animal to search its memory for what caused the US, and learning happens. During compound conditioning trials, the US is not surprising due to the presence of $CS_{A.}$ Hence, no memory search for the cause of the US is triggered, and no association between CS_B and the US is learned. In overshadowing, one of the stimuli that is part of a compound CS gains greater associative strength than the other and elicits a stronger CR due to higher levels of salience.

Glossary

Attentional model of latent inhibition A theory suggesting that latent inhibition occurs because attention to a stimulus decreases when it is repeatedly presented without meaningful consequences.

Blocking A process where prior learning about one stimulus prevents the formation of an association with a second stimulus presented simultaneously.

Kamin's memory scan hypothesis The idea that blocking occurs because organisms selectively process information about surprising events and disregard predictable ones.

Latent inhibition A phenomenon where prior exposure to a stimulus without reinforcement slows down later conditioning to that stimulus.

Overshadowing A phenomenon where a stronger or more salient stimulus overshadows a weaker stimulus, reducing the weaker stimulus's ability to be conditioned.

Switching model A model of learning proposing that organisms switch between different attentional states based on how relevant a stimulus is to a given situation.

US preexposure effect A reduction in conditioning effectiveness caused by prior exposure to the unconditioned stimulus before pairing it with a conditioned stimulus.

9 Cracking the Code

Modeling Classical Conditioning

Learning Objectives

- Identify and describe specific limitations or shortcomings of the Rescorla-Wagner Model in explaining certain aspects of classical conditioning.
- Evaluate the relevance and importance of addressing the Rescorla-Wagner Model's shortcomings in advancing our understanding of classical conditioning.
- Define the comparator hypothesis and its role in explaining classical conditioning processes.

Wing Night

Source: IStock photo ID:1471867854.

Benjamin could not wait to get home from school. As soon as he walked into the house, a wave of joy overtook him because his mom often surprised him with one of his favorite meals. "Smells amazing!" exclaimed Benjamin as the smell of chicken wings smothered in his favorite BBQ sauce filled the air. He loved his mom's home-cooked meals, but there was something special about his mom's chicken wings. Seeing how Benjamin appreciated her wings, she secretly decided to make Fridays "wing night."

DOI: 10.4324/9781003491828-16

Fridays were nothing special to Benjamin except for being the last day of the week. However, after a few "wing nights," his anticipation grew with every passing day of the week, culminating in a wave of excitement on Friday morning. Being a psychology student, Benjamin believed this excitement to be a conditioned response (CR). His explanation for it went something like this. At first, no connection existed in his mind between Fridays and chicken wings. Therefore, he did not expect chicken wings on Fridays. However, as the weeks went by, Fridays gradually became a reliable predictor (CS) of chicken wings (US) until they predicted the wings 100% (or just about) of the time. From his learning class, he remembered that some theorists developed a model for how this happened. He thought, "At first, a large difference exists between what is predicted and what occurs. Classical conditioning reduces that difference until what occurs aligns with what is expected."

9.1 The Rescorla-Wagner Model

Kamin's Influence

Remember from the discussion on the blocking phenomenon that, for Kamin, surprise was an essential prerequisite for learning. No surprise, no learning. In other words, learning depends on the extent to which what occurs differs from what is expected, as seemed to be understood by Benjamin in the opening vignette. For example, finding your notebook in your schoolbag when reaching for it would not be surprising. You expected it to be there, and it was there.

In contrast, it would surprise you if you reached into your bag and did not find it. You expected it to be there, but it was not. Consistent with Kamin's memory search hypothesis, this surprising event would likely trigger you to search your memory for the cause for it not being there. For Benjamin, in the opening vignette, a memory search for what caused him to be treated with chicken wings must have been initiated to connect the event with Friday nights.

The Model

In a model of Kamin's hypothesis, which states that surprise is an essential learning component (Rescorla and Wagner, 1972), Robert Rescorla (1940–2020) and Allan Wagner (1934–2018) explained how what can be learned from an experience diminishes as it becomes progressively more predictable. This model became known as the **Rescorla-Wagner model** (RW model). The RW model is a mathematical model that seeks to explain the changes in associative strength between a CS and the US resulting from conditioning. If you are like many of my students, the mere thought of having to learn anything related to mathematics in a psychology class might have been enough to make you think twice before taking it. However, mathematical models of behavior are mainstream in behavior analysis (Mazur, 2006). They began to emerge as groups of psychologists sought to render the study of behavior more scientific by deriving general rules and behavior theories that can be expressed mathematically as in other sciences such as physics, chemistry, and biology (Baum, 2012). However, you can rest assured that I will do my best to simplify the model to retain its essence without you having to learn any complex math. The following equation expresses the Rescorla-Wagner model:

$$\Delta V = c\ (V_{max} - V)$$

This formula is a simplified version of the original but sufficient for understanding the model's fundamental ideas. On the left side of the formula (before the equal sign), ΔV (pronounced "delta-V") represents the change in associative strength of the CS. The Greek letter Δ (delta) means "change," and V stands for the associative strength of the CS and any other stimuli present during conditioning that have been paired with the US.

On the right side of the equation *c* stands for a constant that represents the learning rate and salience of the CS and US. You need not worry about this constant to understand the model since the learning rate and salience of the CS and US are assumed to stay the same throughout conditioning trials.

The term V_{max} stands for the maximum associative strength that can be supported by the US. This value remains the same throughout conditioning trials. We have already stated the significance of the second term between the parentheses (V). It is the same as on the right side of the equation. That is the associative strength of the CS as a result of being paired with the US during each of the conditioning trials.

We can now express the formula in words in the following way: The change in the associative strength of the CS on each conditioning trial is equal to the difference between the maximal associative strength that can be supported by the US and the associative strength of the CS. Hence, the Rescorla-Wagner model views classical conditioning as an error correction mechanism. In every trial, prediction errors are reduced. A prediction error occurs when there is a difference between what is expected and what happens. Thus, prediction error is essential in shaping expectancies to guide appropriate actions. A prediction error also serves as a signal that our expectations need to be updated to fall in line with what occurs. Let us walk through a simple example where an experimenter pairs a light (CS) with food (US) across multiple conditioning trials.

1. On the first trial, the US closely follows the CS. However, after being presented with the CS, the animal has no reason to expect the US, so the food is highly surprising. Hence, the CS has no associative strength on the first conditioning trial, so the difference between V_{max} and V on the right side of the equation (V_{max} – V) is large (Figure 9.1a). Thus, the prediction error is large.
2. As conditioning trials are added, the associative strength of the CS (V) increases, and the animal gradually develops a greater expectancy of the US in response to the CS. In other words, the difference between what is expected to occur in the presence of the CS and what happens in the US on every successive trial (V_{max} – V) becomes smaller.
3. Eventually (V_{max} – V) is reduced to 0. At this point, the animal fully expects the US upon presentation of the CS. Since the US is no longer surprising and no more associative strength is acquired by the CS, the prediction error is 0.
4. Note that, as shown in Figure 9.1b, the increase in associative strength acquired by the CS diminishes on every trial until it no longer acquires any associative strength at V_{max} .

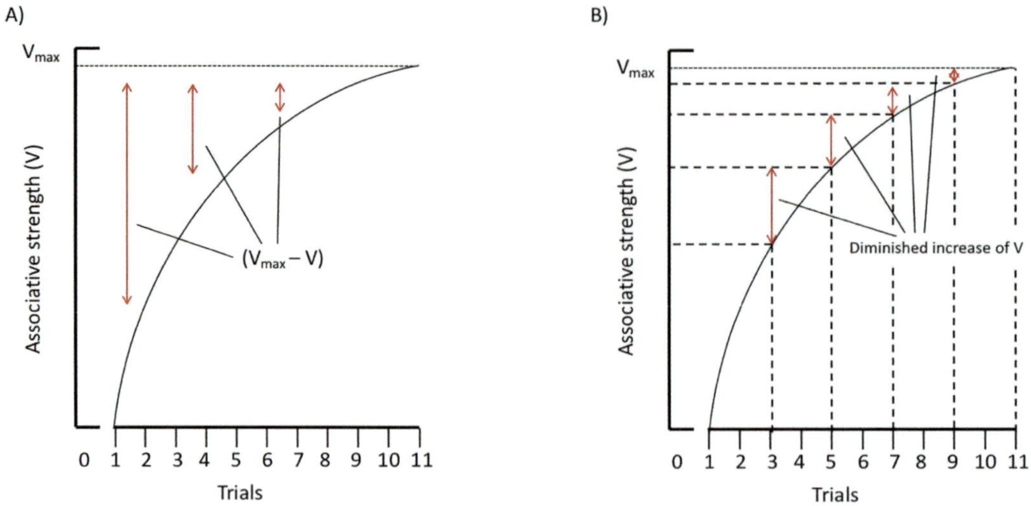

Figure 9.1 Graphical representations of the Rescorla-Wagner model. a) The difference between V_{max} and V (V_{max} – V) is large during the first conditioning trials, as indicated by the longest of the three arrows. Thus, a large prediction error exists. However, prediction error diminishes with repeated trials, as the medium-length and short arrows indicate. At V_{max}, the prediction error is reduced to 0. b) Increases in associative strength (V) diminish over successive trials until no associative strength is added to the CS at V_{max}.

Let us look at how the formula applies to how Benjamin eventually connected Fridays to chicken wings.

1. The first time Benjamin's mom cooked wings (US) on Friday (CS), he had no reason to expect the wings on that Friday (remember she planned this in secret). Therefore, the wings came as a surprise. Hence, on the first "wing night," Friday (CS) had no associative strength, so the difference between V_{max} and V on the right side of the equation (V_{max} – V) was large. Thus, the prediction error was large.
2. On each successive Friday (CS), its associative strength (V) increased, and Benjamin gradually developed a greater expectancy of the wings (US) in response to it being a Friday. In other words, the difference between what was expected to occur on Fridays and what occurred (the wings [US]) on every successive trial (V_{max} – V) became smaller.
3. Eventually (V_{max} – V) was reduced to 0. At this point, Benjamin fully expected the wings (US) on Fridays (CS). Since the wings (US) were no longer surprising on Fridays, no more associative strength was acquired by the Fridays. Thus, the prediction error became 0.

The Rescorla-Wagner model is undoubtedly the most famous mathematical model of classical conditioning and has generated much research. In addition, neurobiological findings showing dopamine neurons' involvement in prediction error support the Rescorla-Wagner model (see this chapter's "What in the Brain?" box).

Shortcomings of the Rescorla-Wagner Model

Although the Rescorla-Wagner model explains several classical conditioning phenomena, it fails to explain others. For example, extinction is the reverse of acquisition within the

Rescorla-Wagner model. However, the spontaneous recovery of a previously extinguished response and other phenomena show that extinction is not simply the reverse of acquisition or due to unlearning. Instead, it is thought that extinction involves new learning in which the CS now accumulates negative prediction errors in predicting the absence of the US. We will return to this topic in Chapter 11.

The Rescorla-Wagner model also fails to explain latent inhibition (described in the previous chapter), in which animals are given preexposure trials to a CS and show impaired conditioning compared to those not preexposed to the CS. The Rescorla-Wagner model predicts that the CS would not acquire associative strength in either group. The CS would not acquire any associative strength in the preexposed group because no US is present. Therefore, both V_{max} and V would equal 0, resulting in $\Delta V = c\ (0 - 0) = 0$. The problem is that V_{max} and V would also be 0 in the control group since they receive no preexposure trials to the CS and no US is present. Therefore, according to the Rescorla-Wagner model, conditioning should occur equally well in both groups, but this does not happen.

What in the Brain?

The Rescorla-Wagner Model, Blocking, and Prediction Error

Dopamine neurons of the mesolimbic dopamine system, including the ventral tegmental area (VTA) and the nucleus accumbens (NAc), are known to process reward information (Wise and Hoffman, 1992). In the 1980s, neuroscientist Wolfram Schultz and colleagues recorded the electrical activity of dopamine neurons in the VTA of monkeys as they were subjected to classical conditioning trials. During these trials, pressing a lever when a lightbulb was illuminated (CS) resulted in the delivery of a juice reward (US). As a result of these conditioning trials, the CS eventually became a reliable predictor of the US, and the monkeys learned to press the lever in the presence of the CS (Schultz et al. 1997). They found that dopamine neurons increased their electrical activity shortly after the delivery of the US. However, as conditioning trials progressed, the same dopamine neurons shifted their peak of electrical activity from occurring after the delivery of the US to happening with the presentation of the CS. As a result of this experiment, they proposed that dopamine neurons encode the discrepancy between what is predicted and what occurs—in other words, the extent to which the CS accurately predicts the delivery of the US.

Dopamine Neurons and the Rescorla-Wagner Model

The encoding of prediction error by dopamine neurons provides a neurobiological framework for the Rescorla-Wagner model. The model holds that, in classical conditioning, most of the associative strength acquired by the CS occurs early in a series of conditioning trials, when the US is most surprising and the prediction error is large. However, as conditioning trials progress, the US becomes less surprising and prediction error eventually drops to 0. This process mirrors the results of Schultz, Dayan, and Montague (1997), who found that peak electrical activity of dopamine neurons occurs after the delivery of a US at the beginning of conditioning trials and then switches peak activity to presentations of the CS in later trials.

Dopamine Neurons and Blocking

Blocking refers to the phenomenon by which a CS (CS_A) that has already been conditioned to the US blocks the conditioning of another CS (CS_B) to the same US when both CSs are presented together as a CS_A-CS_B compound. Psychologist Leo Kamin (1968) proposed that blocking occurs because CS_A in the CS_A-CS_B compound already predicts the delivery of the US due to prior conditioning. Therefore, in compound trials, the US is not surprising; the prediction error is small, and no learning about the association between CS_B and the US is possible (Kamin, 1968). More recently, neuroscientists have uncovered at least some of the neurobiological mechanisms of blocking. In one study (Aggarwal et al., 2020), it was hypothesized that blocking occurs because of the inhibition of dopamine neurons in the mesolimbic dopamine system after the delivery of the US during compound trials. Inhibition of dopamine neurons at that moment would result in their failure to encode a prediction error between the presentation of CS_B and the delivery of the US, resulting in no conditioning of CS_B to the US. They tested this hypothesis by removing the inhibition on dopamine neurons in the VTA by pharmacological means. The researchers thought this would result in increased activity after the delivery of the US and restore their ability to encode prediction errors, permitting CS_B to become associated with the US. This is precisely what they found. Removing the inhibition on dopamine neurons during compound conditioning trials prevented blocking from happening. The researchers claimed that removing the inhibition on dopamine neurons permitted them to encode prediction errors between CS_B and the US, thus resulting in their successful association.

Are You Thinking Critically?

1. What evidence is there that dopamine neurons signal prediction error?
2. How do the findings on the involvement of dopamine neurons in prediction error relate to the Rescorla-Wagner model?
3. How would you explain the activity of dopamine neurons during classical conditioning?
4. Can you think of another way to test the role of dopamine neurons in blocking other than removing their inhibitory effects?

How the Rescorla-Wagner Model Explains Blocking

In addition to providing a mathematical explanation for the acquisition of a conditioned response, the Rescorla-Wagner model accurately describes many other classical conditioning phenomena, including overshadowing, conditioned inhibition, and blocking (Miller,

Barnet and Grahame, 1995; Rescorla and Wagner, 1972). I will focus on blocking, which you learned about in the previous chapter. Let us take it step by step.

1. In Phase 1 of a blocking procedure, a conditioned stimulus (CS_A), such as a light, is paired with an unconditioned stimulus (US), such as a shock, until it reliably elicits a conditioned response (CR), such as freezing. The light (CS_A), represented by V_A, achieves maximum associative strength (V_{max}). Hence, at the end of Phase 1, $V_A = V_{max}$.
2. In Phase 2, a second conditioned stimulus (CS_B), for example, a tone, is introduced, creating a compound CS (light + tone) associated with the same US. This requires us to modify the equation to $V_A + V_B$, where V_B is the associative strength of CS_B.
3. As CS_A achieved maximal associative strength in Phase 1, $V_A = V_{max}$. Substituting V_{max} for V_A results in $V_{max} + V_B$.
4. We can now simplify the equation because $V_{max} + V_B = V_{max}$, which means $V_B = 0$.
5. At the beginning of Phase 2, the associative strength of the tone (CS_B) is 0, as it has never been paired with the US. Since $V_B = 0$, no change in associative strength occurs for CS_B.

In conclusion, the tone (CS_B) is blocked from gaining any associative strength because the light (CS_A) has already reached the maximum available associative strength from the US, leaving none for the tone to acquire.

9.2 The Comparator Hypothesis

The Rescorla-Wagner model focuses on the acquisition phase of classical conditioning, during which the CS-US association is formed. It specifies how the associative strength between a CS and a US gradually increases as conditioning trials progress up to a point when no additional associative strength can be added. Although the Rescorla-Wagner model does this exceptionally well, no attention is paid to the retrieval processes that give rise to the CR when the CS is presented after CS-US pairings.

In contrast to the Rescorla-Wagner model, the **comparator hypothesis**, illustrated in Figure 9.2, proposed by psychologist Ralph Miller (Kasprow, Schachtman and Miller, 1987; Miller and Matzel, 1988), focuses on the retrieval processes that result in a CS eliciting a CR after CS-US pairings. It proposes a *response rule*. That is, the strength of the CR to an intended or purposely trained CS (i.e., a CS chosen by the experimenter) depends both on the strength of association between the intended CS and the US and on the strengths of association created between the US and other elements of the environment that have become unintended CSs.

During testing (i.e., when the trained CS is presented by itself), the associative strength between the trained CS and US is compared to the associative strengths acquired between unintended CSs and the US. If the associative strengths of the unintended CSs with the US are stronger than that of the trained CS and US, responding to the trained CS is inhibited.

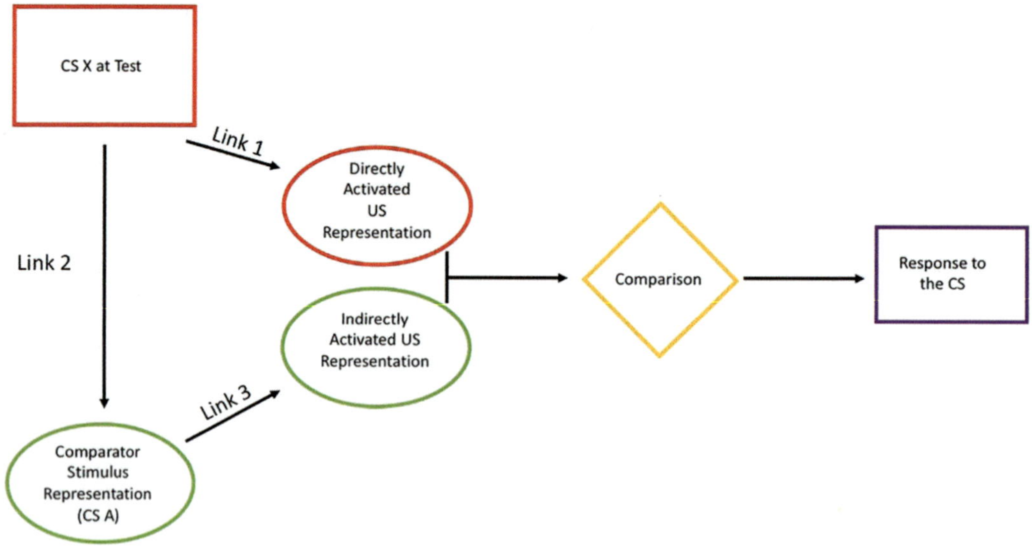

Figure 9.2 The comparator hypothesis (see text and steps 1–10 for details).

The details of the comparator hypothesis can better be understood by breaking it down into the following steps.

1. According to the comparator hypothesis, three distinct associations (CS-US pairings) are formed in classical conditioning's acquisition phase.
2. During testing, these associations are retrieved and compared.
3. These associations are referred to as "links."
4. The three types of links are referred to as Link 1, Link 2, and Link 3.
5. Link 1 connects the intended CS, known as the target CS (CS X), directly to the US.
6. Link 2 connects the target CS and unintended CSs, referred to as comparator stimuli (CS A).
7. Link 3 connects the comparator stimuli (CS A) with the US. This link indirectly connects the target stimulus to the US through its associations with the comparator stimuli.
8. The comparison involves evaluating the strength of association between the US directly activated through Link 1 and the indirect associations between the target stimulus and the US through Link 3.
9. The strength of the conditioned response (CR) upon the presentation of the target CS (CS X) hinges on the relative associative strengths of Link 1 and Link 3.
10. If the associative strength of Link 1 surpasses that of Link 3, a response to the target CS (CS X) occurs. Conversely, inhibition of the response to the target CS occurs when the associative strength of Link 3 outweighs that of Link 1.

How the Comparator Hypothesis Explains Blocking

According to the Rescorla-Wagner model, blocking occurs because all the associative strength that can be supported by the US was taken up by its association with CS_A during Phase 1 of the experiment. This interpretation of blocking is based on what occurs during the acquisition phase of conditioning. After learning about the comparator hypothesis, you may wonder how it explains blocking by focusing on retrieval processes during the test phase. According to the comparator hypothesis, blocking occurs due to a retrieval deficit during the test phase of a blocking experiment rather than an acquisition deficit (i.e., the inability to associate CS_B with the US) in Phase 2 of the blocking experiment. This can better be understood by re-examining Figure 9.2 and the following steps.

1. In Phase 1 of a blocking experiment, a CS (call it CS X, to be consistent with Figure 9.2) is paired with the US until it has acquired maximal associative strength (Link 1).
2. In Phase 2 of a blocking experiment, another CS (CS A) is presented along with CS X to form a compound stimulus (Link 2).
3. Consequently, CS X establishes an indirect association with the US through its association with CS A.
4. CS A becomes directly associated with the US (Link 3).
5. Given that CS X achieved maximum conditioning to the US in Phase 1, its associative strength with the US surpasses the associative strength acquired by CS A to the US in Phase 2.
6. During the test phase, the associative strength between CS X and the US is compared to that of CS A's association with the US.
7. CS X "wins" control over the CR, as its pre-established association with the US is stronger than the association between CS A and the US.

Testing the Comparator Hypothesis Explanation of Blocking

Suppose the comparator hypothesis's explanation for blocking is correct. In that case, it stands to reason that weakening the associative strength between CS X and the US formed during Phase 1 of a blocking experiment should remove its ability to block CS A's association with the US. Aaron Blaisdell and colleagues tested this hypothesis (Blaisdell, Gunther and Miller, 1999). To do so, they trained rats in a conditioned lick suppression test.

In Phase 1 of the experiment, rats received four conditioning trials per day over three days, in which a tone (CS X) was followed by a foot shock (US). In Phase 2, the blocking phase, the rats received four training trials in which a new CS, consisting of white noise (CS A), was presented in a compound along with CS X and followed by the same US. The responses of all rats to CS X were then tested in Phase 3. The dependent measure was how long the rats took to accumulate 5 seconds of licking. The more time they took, the more their licking was taken to have been suppressed by CS X. Another group of rats was subjected to the same blocking procedure with the exception that they were given an extinction trial to CS X following Phase 2 (that is, CS X was repeatedly presented without the foot shock [US]).

They found that the rats in the blocking group took significantly less time to accumulate 5 seconds of licking (CR) during the presentation of CS A in the test phase than the rats that did not receive extinction trials to CS X after Phase 2. This indicated that extinction trials, during which CS X was repeatedly presented by itself, were effective in attenuating the blocking effects of CS X. This suggested that the group of rats who were not subjected to extinction trials after Phase 2 did, in fact, associate CS A to the US during the conditioning trials when it was presented with CS X. However, the expression of this learning was blocked during the test due to the high strength of association acquired between CS X and the US during Phase 1. Once extinction trials reduced this associative strength, the ability of CS A to elicit the CR was uncovered.

Critical Thinking Spot Check 9.3

1. What influence did Kamin have on developing the Rescorla-Wagner model?
2. Why is the Rescorla-Wagner model important to understand classical conditioning?
3. Summarize the basic principles of the Rescorla-Wagner model. What are its main assumptions and components?
4. Identify and discuss at least two shortcomings or limitations of the Rescorla-Wagner model in explaining certain aspects of classical conditioning.
5. Propose a hypothetical experiment that explicitly tests one of the limitations of the Rescorla-Wagner model. What predictions would the model make, and how might the results either support or challenge the model?
6. Explain the fundamental principles of the comparator hypothesis in the context of classical conditioning. How does it differ from the Rescorla-Wagner Model?
7. Analyze an everyday example of classical conditioning from the point of view of both the Rescorla-Wagner model and the comparator hypothesis.

Chapter Summary

Each bullet point aligns with the learning objectives outlined at the beginning of the chapter.

- Mathematical models of classical conditioning have been developed, the Rescorla-Wagner model being the most influential of these models. It holds that the change in the associative strength of a CS during conditioning trials is equal to the maximal associative value of the US minus the associative strength of the CS. It states that learning is greatest at the beginning of a sequence of conditioning trials when the US is surprising or the prediction is significant. As conditioning trials progress, the US becomes progressively less surprising until prediction error eventually falls to 0 when learning no longer occurs. The Rescorla-Wagner model has successfully predicted the results of many classical conditioning experiments, including blocking and overshadowing.
- Most theories of conditioning have focused on the acquisition of information during training. However, a theory known as the comparator hypothesis focuses on retrieving information acquired during conditioning trials. It holds that, during the test phase of a classical conditioning experiment, the conditioning strength of the trained CS (target) is compared to the conditioning strength acquired by other stimuli present during training (comparator stimuli). The stimuli that acquired the greatest condition strength will more likely elicit a response. According to the comparator hypothesis, blocking occurs at the time of retrieval as opposed to during training, as posited by the Rescorla-Wagner model. Because CSA has acquired more conditioning strength than CSB, CSA is more likely to elicit a CR than CSB when their conditioning strengths are compared. Evidence for this comes from a study in which extinction trials to CS_A removed its block on CS_B, indicating that CSB had acquired an association with the US during training but could not be expressed during testing.

Glossary

Comparator hypothesis A theory proposing that conditioned responding depends on comparisons between the conditioned stimulus and other stimuli present during learning. It suggests that the strength of a conditioned response is not just influenced by direct stimulus pairing but also by the organism's ability to contrast the conditioned stimulus with other potential predictors of the unconditioned stimulus.

Rescorla–Wagner model A mathematical model of classical conditioning that explains how the strength of an association between a conditioned stimulus and an unconditioned stimulus is influenced by prediction errors. The model suggests that learning occurs when an organism is surprised by an outcome, leading to adjustments in associative strength.

Module Summary

In this module, you have learned that studying classical conditioning goes far beyond simply knowing about and understanding the basic associations that Pavlov created between arbitrary stimuli in his laboratory. In the first chapter, you learned that the general process approach to learning does not explain all types of classical conditioning. For example, you learned that the existence of behavioral systems more readily explains CTA, sexual conditioning, and fear learning. In all of these examples, the assumptions of the general process approach are violated by factors such as the specificity of associations, resistance to extinction, and findings that close temporal contiguity between stimuli is not always required for learning. Instead, these examples show that those that belong together are more readily associated. This is, in turn, consistent with the idea that animals are biologically prepared to form certain types of associations more readily than others. In the second chapter, you learned about the variables that influence classical conditioning and the mechanisms by which this influence is exerted. You learned that preexposure to a CS or a US results in poor conditioning when subsequently presented during conditioning trials in a phenomenon known as latent inhibition and US preexposure effects, respectively. You also learned that conditioning trials in which CSs are presented in a compound with the US can give rise to two different outcomes. In overshadowing, one of the CSs acquires less conditioning strength than the other and produces comparatively weak CR. In blocking, a new CS acquires no conditioning strength to the US when presented along with a CS that has already been conditioned to the same US. Finally, you learned about a mathematical model of classical conditioning known as the Rescorla-Wagner model, which explains that conditioning occurs through a reduction of prediction error across training trials and that in another model, known as the comparator hypothesis, the emphasis is placed on retrieval rather than acquisition processes. You also learned how each model provides an explanation for blocking.

Module 4

Application

The Connection Between "Diet Drinks" And Learning

There is a notable increase in sugar consumption across the world. Much of it is due to the widespread consumption of sugar-sweetened beverages, which is contributing to an increased risk of type 2 diabetes, cardiovascular disease, hypertension, and stroke (Cheungpasitporn et al., 2015). An obvious way to reduce those risks is to reduce sugar intake. For many people, reducing sugar intake includes replacing sugar-sweetened beverages with their artificially sweetened counterparts, the so-called diet drinks (Bleich et al., 2014). However, there is evidence that consuming artificially sweetened beverages may lead to the same adverse health outcomes that come with consuming excessive amounts of natural sugar. For example, several studies have found that consuming artificially sweetened beverages was related to an increased risk of developing type 2 diabetes (Imamura et al., 2015). In addition, animal studies have shown that artificial sweeteners can potentiate weight gain when combined with a high-fat and sugar diet (Feijó et al., 2013). It has also been found that artificial sweeteners may also interfere with regulating glucose levels (Swithers et al., 2012).

These findings may seem illogical to you. How can diet soft drinks be related to the same adverse health outcomes associated with excess caloric intake? In autonomic conditioning, environmental stimuli can be conditioned to elicit compensatory responses to substances that disrupt homeostasis (Swithers et al., 2012). As shown in Figure 1-M4 App, when one ingests sugar (US), unconditioned compensatory responses (UR) involved in glucose metabolism are engaged to restore glucose homeostasis. The sweet taste of sugar thus becomes a conditioned stimulus (CS) that elicits the same compensatory responses (CR). The taste of artificially sweetened beverages elicits the same conditioned compensatory reactions. However, the sweet taste is never followed by the ingestion of sugar, which results in the extinction of the conditioned compensatory responses that regulate glucose levels. This impairs the body's ability to regulate glucose levels when natural sugar is ingested.

DOI: 10.4324/9781003491828-17

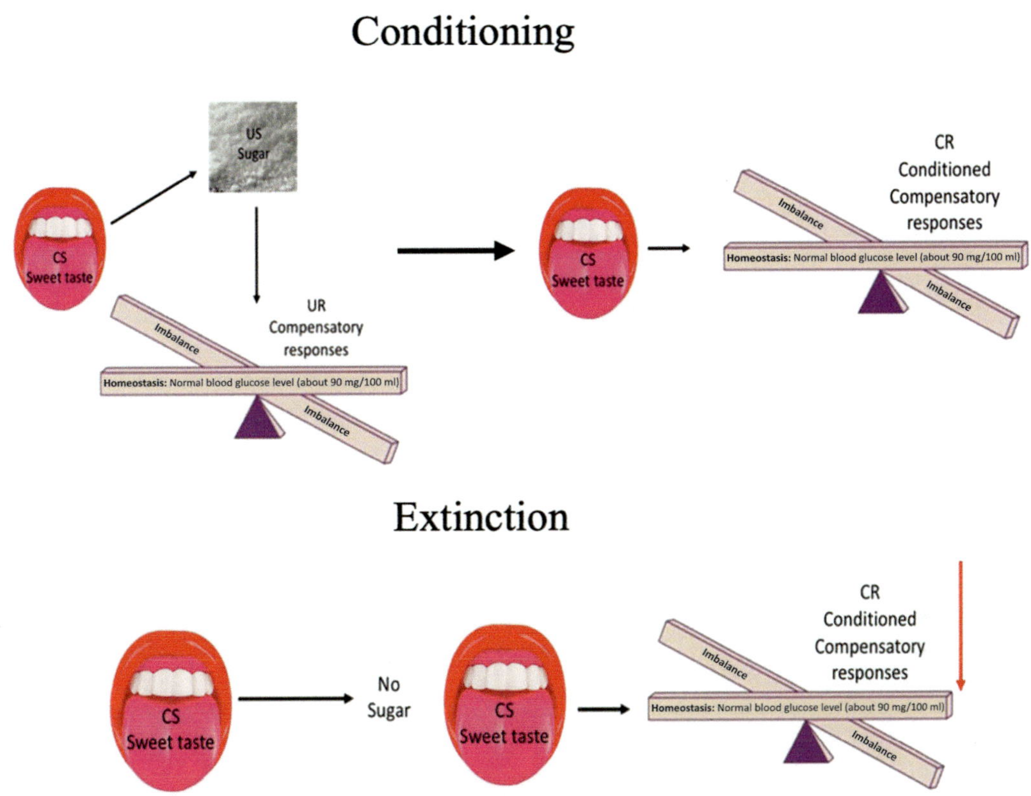

Figure 1-M4 App Top: The sweet taste of natural sugar becomes a CS, repeatedly paired with sugar ingestion. The body then uses compensatory mechanisms that metabolize sugar to maintain glucose homeostasis. Hence, the sweet taste of sugar by itself elicits these mechanisms, which have become conditioned compensatory responses. Bottom: The conditioned compensatory responses are weakened when the sweet taste is experienced without ingesting sugar, as it occurs with artificially sweetened beverages.

Are You Thinking Critically?

1. Distinguish between an unconditioned and conditioned compensatory response.
2. What other examples of conditioned compensatory responses can you think about?
3. What are the benefits of knowing your body can produce conditioned compensatory responses?

Module 5

The Fundamentals of Operant Conditioning and Types of Reinforcers

Introduction

Why do we behave the way that we do? This is arguably the most fundamental question in the study of psychology. However, an answer to this question has been sought within various belief systems and fields of study. Philosophers from Aristotle to the British associationists proposed principles of association which determined learning and behavior. Freud and his followers attributed the determination of behavior to deeply rooted unconscious processes. Today, behavioral neuroscientists seek explanations for behavior in the functioning of the nervous system and their interactions with the environment. This is also the question that ultimately drives research in all schools of thought in psychology. For example, cognitive psychologists focus on the influence of various mental processes, including attention, decision-making, perception, learning, and emotions. Developmental psychologists are interested in explaining behavior by studying how experiences throughout life interact with physical, emotional, and cognitive maturation. Social psychologists seek to describe people's behaviors in the actual, imagined, or implied presence of others. Behaviorists hold that behavior can be explained by the consequences of one's actions on the environment without recourse to mentalistic concepts. The process by which this occurs is known as operant conditioning. The principles of operant conditioning have been applied to education, psychotherapy, and personal growth. In Chapter 10, we will explore the roots of operant conditioning and the principal mechanisms by which it occurs. In Chapter 11, we will explore the factors involved in the effectiveness of reinforcers.

Chapter 10: The Fundamentals of Operant Conditioning
Chapter 11: Types of Reinforcers

DOI: 10.4324/9781003491828-18

10 From Puzzle Boxes to Skinner Boxes

The Fundamentals of Operant Conditioning

Learning Objectives

- Discuss the historical roots of operant conditioning.
- Be able to explain operant conditioning.
- Understand how operant conditioning can be used to control behavior and acquire new skills.

First Lesson

IStock photo ID:501064029

It was Yaëlle's first tennis lesson with Coach Garcia, who greeted her at the neighborhood courts, after which he handed her a racket and said: "Let me see your stance." She stood in the best way she knew from watching countless tennis matches on television.

DOI: 10.4324/9781003491828-19

"Not bad," said Coach Garcia, "But right now, I want you to assume a closed stance." After a few adjustments, Coach Garcia remarked, "That's awesome! Just like a pro." He then asked Yaëlle to grip the racket. Coach Garcia showed her an appropriate grip, and when Yaëlle finally got it, he said, "Hey! You got this fast." Feeling proud of herself, Yaëlle couldn't wait for what was coming next. Coach Garcia then asked her to assume the proper stance, but this time, he also asked to see her grip. He then waited until Yaëlle successfully performed these two actions to praise her. Next, he looked at Yaëlle's backswing, made a few adjustments, and let her practice it. When Yaëlle performed an acceptable backswing, Coach Garcia said, "Wow! I have never seen anyone learn so fast." He next taught Yaëlle the forehand stroke and praised her again as she improved. He then asked Yaëlle to sequence all the movements she had learned: the stance, grip, backswing, and forehand stroke.

Coach Garcia praised Yaëlle only once she successfully performed the entire sequence. Coach Garcia then stood on the other side of the net, gently hitting a ball toward Yaëlle and letting her go at it. "Awesome!" Coach Garcia yelled out after Yaëlle hit the ball back over the net. Coach Garcia's instructional style was far from random. He had a precise goal in mind for Yaëlle: successfully hit the ball over the net with proper form by the end of the session. To get Yaëlle there, he praised her every time she got one of the skills right, and then only once she performed them in progressively longer chains. This procedure, known as shaping, is used by sports coaches, teachers, animal trainers, and parents to teach people and animals complex behaviors.

10.1 Historical Roots of Operant Conditioning

The Anecdotal Method

Charles Darwin (1809–1892) believed that intelligence, like physical characteristics, evolved by natural selection; hence, he thought that humans' intelligence level was continuous with that of other species. This idea was embodied in his book *The Descent of Man* (Darwin, 1871), where he states that "the difference in mind between man and the higher animals, great as it is, certainly is one of degree but not of kind" (p. 126). Darwin's idea about the evolution of intelligence greatly impressed evolutionary biologist George Romanes (1848–1894), one of his most ardent supporters. Consistent with Darwin's point of view, Romanes described animal behavior with the assumption that animals and humans have similar mental processes, such as problem-solving, decision-making abilities, insight (i.e., to gain an intuitive understanding of the situation), and the ability to learn from the consequences of their actions. Romanes recorded **anecdotal reports**, which consisted of snapshots of animal behaviors made by casual observers, and attributed the causes of these behaviors to human-like mental abilities (Romanes, 1882). By doing so, Romanes committed what is known as the **anthropomorphic error** in which human characteristics are attributed to animals, a topic discussed in more detail in Chapter 21. An example of such an anecdote is quoted subsequently.

> One day, watching a small column of these ants (*Eciton hamata*), I placed a little stone on one of them to secure it. The next that approached, as soon as it discovered its situation, ran backwards in an agitated manner and soon communicated the intelligence to the others. They rushed to the rescue; some bit at the stone and tried to move it, others seized the prisoner by the legs and tugged with such force that I thought the legs would

be pulled off, but they persevered until they got the captive free. I next covered one up with a piece of clay, leaving only the ends of its antennae projecting. It was soon discovered by its fellows, which set to work immediately, and by biting off pieces of the clay soon liberated it.

(p. 48)

Thorndike's Cat in a Box

Psychologist Edward Lee Thorndike (1874–1949) rejected the idea of continuity between the intelligence of animals and that of humans, as proposed by Darwin. He was also opposed to the anecdotal method used by Romanes. Thorndike conducted experiments with dogs, chicks, and, most famously, cats. The results of his experiments led him to conclude that animal learning could be explained without reference to human-like mental abilities such as problem-solving, decision-making, and insight (i.e., reasoning abilities) or to the ability to learn from the consequences of their actions, as Romanes believed (Thorndike, 1898).

In some of his experiments, Thorndike tested the ability of hungry cats to escape a **puzzle box** similar to the one shown in Figure 10.1. A puzzle box looked like a wooded crate from which animals could escape by performing a series of actions that eventually triggered a mechanism that opened a door that gave the cats access to food outside the box. Thorndike built several versions of the puzzle box. One of the puzzle boxes had a weight attached to the end of a string, which ran over a pulley before being connected to the door. The cats could open the door by releasing the weight from a bolt that secured it to gain access to the food. Another puzzle box required the cats to perform three separate acts to open the door: pressing a pedal, pulling on a string, and pushing a bar up or down. In addition, Thorndike built a puzzle box with a compartment attached so that a cat could observe another cat trying to escape. He did so to determine whether the cats could learn to escape the puzzle box by imitation.

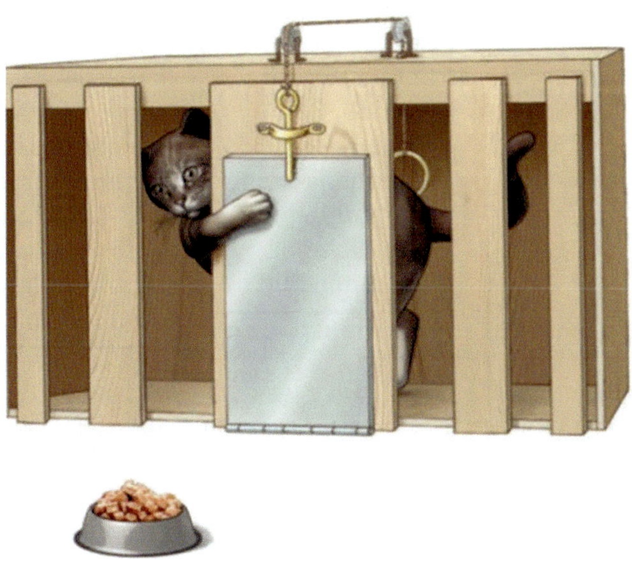

Figure 10.1 A cat in one of Thorndike's puzzle boxes.

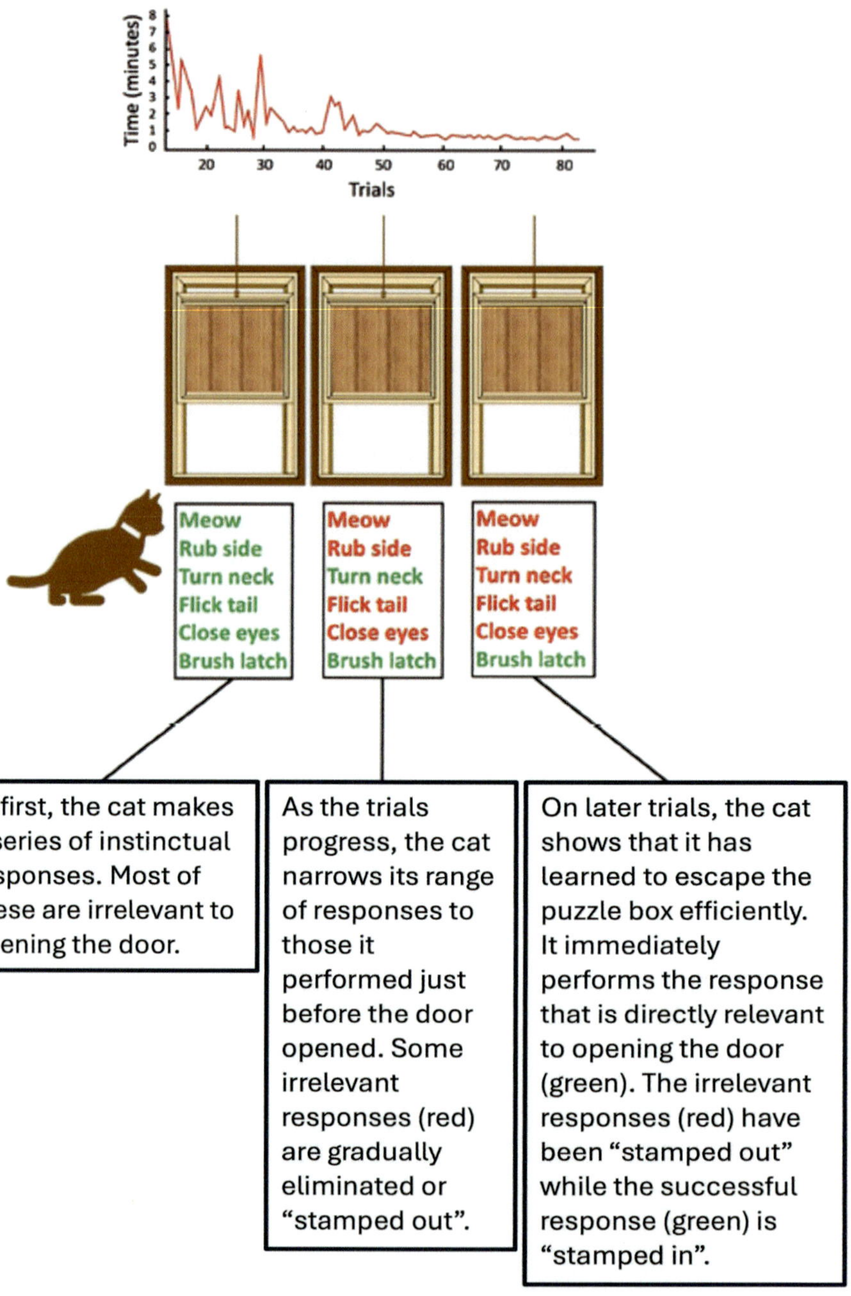

Figure 10.2 Top: Graph showing that the cat took progressively less time to escape a puzzle box (Data from Thorndike, E. L. (1911). *Animal intelligence*. New York, NY: Macmillan). Bottom: A cat's behavior as the trials progressed (see text for details).

The Behavior of Thorndike's Cats

When first placed in a puzzle box, Thorndike's cats reacted with instinctual behaviors aimed at escaping confinement. Eventually, the cats accidentally produced behaviors that triggered the mechanism that opened the door and gained access to the food. Thorndike observed that, over successive trials, the cats only repeated the behaviors they performed just before the door opened. Thorndike referred to these behaviors as being "*stamped in.*" In contrast, behaviors that did not result in the door opening were gradually eliminated. Thorndike referred to these behaviors as being "*stamped out.*" This process, which resulted in the cats taking less time to escape the box as the number of trials progressed, eventually led the cats only to perform the behavior that directly opened the door. Thorndike called this process **instrumental learning** because the cats learned that certain actions were instrumental in escaping the box and reaching the food. The results of one of Thorndike's experiments with the puzzle box are shown in Figure 10.2.

Thorndike's Conclusions About His Cats' Behavior in the Puzzle Box

Thorndike (1898) drew several conclusions from his experiments' results, each consistent with the idea that cats did not find the solution to escape the boxes using human-like mental abilities (Chance, 1999). He found no evidence of reasoning or insight, but that learning to escape the puzzle box gradually took place through trial and error. He also did not find evidence that his cats learned to escape the puzzle boxes by forming associations between their actions and their consequence or that they could learn to escape the puzzle boxes by imitation (Table 10.1).

What Did Thorndike's Cats Learn?

An anthropomorphic explanation for how the cats learned to escape the puzzle boxes would have been that when placed in the puzzle box, they remembered the necessary actions that led them to open the door and associated this behavior with the pleasant experience of getting food. Thorndike believed that no such association of ideas occurred in his cats. Instead, he thought that a sensory impression of the puzzle box and its environment was created in the cats' brains, and these impressions became associated with impulses to act. In other words, Thorndike thought that his cats formed an association between a stimulus (S) (the puzzle box) and the response necessary to escape it. Thus, his cats learned to escape the puzzle box through stimulus-response learning (S-R).

Table 10.1 Conclusions drawn by Thorndike from his experiments with cats.

1. No evidence of reasoning or insight.	No evidence that the cats could reason or have insight into how the door could be opened during the first trials was found.
2. Learning to escape was gradual.	The observation that the cats learned gradually, by trial and error, further supported the idea that they did not reason their way out of the box; if they did, their learning curve would have been steeper.
3. No understanding of an association between actions and consequences.	The cats kept pawing the empty space where a loop which had to be pulled to open the door had been before it was removed.
4. The cats could not learn by imitation.	The rate at which the cats learned to escape the box could not be increased by letting them observe a model.

Both people and animals can learn by trial and error. However, humans are exceptionally good at learning by insight, in that they can spontaneously come up with the solution to a problem (insight) and understand the consequences of their actions.

Source: IStock photo ID:596348736.

The Law of Effect

Thorndike's (1898) findings with the puzzle box led him to formulate the **law of effect**. This law states that an association between a stimulus and a response is strengthened if the response is followed by a satisfying outcome, making it likely that an animal will perform the response again when in the presence of the same stimulus. Conversely, an association between a stimulus and a response is weakened if the response is followed by discomfort, making it less likely that an animal will repeat the response when in the presence of the stimulus.

The law of effect is perhaps best expressed in Thorndike's own words:

> Of several responses made to the same situation, those which are accompanied or closely followed by satisfaction to the animal will, other things being equal, be more firmly connected with the situation, so that, when it recurs, they will be more likely to recur; those which are accompanied or closely followed by discomfort to the animal will, other things being equal, have their connections with that situation weakened, so that, when it recurs, they will be less likely to occur. The greater the satisfaction or discomfort, the greater the strengthening or weakening of the bond.
>
> (p. 244)

The steps outlined subsequently show how Thorndike's law of effect can explain how the law of effect applies to how his cats learned to escape his puzzle boxes.

1. When Thorndike first placed a cat in a puzzle box, it acted instinctually to escape confinement.
2. Eventually, the cat performed the response that led to the opening of the door, giving it access to the food.
3. According to the law of effect, the sensory stimuli (S) that composed the puzzle box became associated with the action necessary to open the door (R) so that the cat could access the food, which was a satisfying outcome.
4. Thorndike believed that on each trial, having access to food gradually strengthened the association between the puzzle box's environment and the responses required to open the door.
5. Thorndike did not believe that the food was part of this association but only served to strengthen it or "stamp in" the association between the stimulus and the response in the first few trials. He believed that after several trials, the association between the stimuli and the responses grew so strong (in Thorndike's words, "stamped in") that it became independent of the outcome (the food). Thorndike's explanation does not include a mentalistic process, such as consciously remembering the association between performing a specific response and getting food, as an anthropomorphic explanation would have it.

Operant Conditioning

Operant conditioning is a process by which an animal's behavior is controlled by its consequences. The term operant conditioning was coined by one of the most influential figures in the history of psychology, B.F. Skinner (1904–1990), who described its principles in a book entitled *The Organization of Behavior* (1938).

Contrary to Thorndike, Skinner believed that outcomes strengthened the association between a stimulus and a response (S-R) and reinforced the responses they followed. For this reason, an outcome that increases the probability of the response it follows became known as a **reinforcer**. Skinner coined the term operant conditioning to identify this type of learning because he believed that responses (which he also called operants) operated on the environment to produce outcomes (1969). He also believed that operant conditioning connected the environmental stimulus present when a response occurs to the response and the outcome. For this reason, operant conditioning became known as S(R-O) learning instead of Thorndike's S-R learning (Skinner, 1938). This distinction explains why you may have also heard the term **instrumental conditioning**. Although the terms operant conditioning and instrumental conditioning are often used interchangeably, instrumental conditioning is a more inclusive term that includes S-(R-O) learning, S-R learning, associations between the stimulus and the outcome (S-O learning), and associations between the response and the outcome (R-O) learning. Each of these are discussed in Chapter 13, where we will explore the associative structure of instrumental conditioning.

Operant Conditioning Procedures

At about the same time as Thorndike was conducting his cat experiment with puzzle boxes, psychologist Willard Small (1870–1943) was developing the first mazes used in the

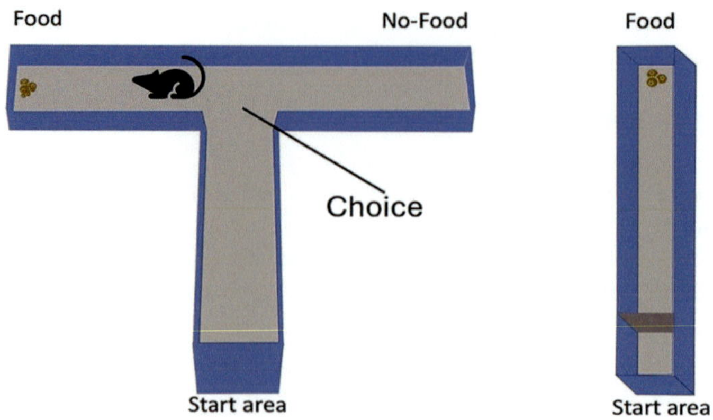

Figure 10.3 a) A T-maze. b) A straight-alley maze (see text for details).

experimental study of animal behavior. Because rats dig underground pathways and tunnels from their nests, he believed that mazes would provide a way to study the learning abilities of rats in relatively naturalistic conditions (Small, 1901).

However, the types of mazes that Small built were overly complex. Hence, over the years, researchers built simpler mazes. One such maze is the T-maze shown in Figure 10.3a. In a typical T-maze procedure food (the reinforcer) is placed at the end of the left or right arm of the T. An animal, typically a rat, is released from a start area and permitted to explore the maze. Eventually, the rat discovers the food at the end of one of the arms. Once the rat has eaten the food, the experimenter picks it up and places it into the start box to begin the next trial. After several trials, the rat shows that it has learned the food's location by making the correct turn at the choice point. Another type of maze is known as the straight-alley maze and is shown in Figure 10.3b. A straight-alley maze procedure consists of placing food at the end of an alley. The animal is released from the start area and the time taken to reach the food is recorded. Rats show that they have learned the food's location by taking progressively less time to reach the goal box over successive trials. Note that, in both procedures, animals have a single opportunity to receive the food reinforcer on each trial after which they are removed from the maze until their next trial. Such a procedure is known as a **discrete-trial procedure.** Many other mazes and apparatuses have since been devised to study animal learning, some of which are discussed in Chapter 20.

Skinner's Disenchantment With Discrete Trial Procedures

Skinner experimented with discrete trial procedures in his early studies. However, he eventually became annoyed with manually baiting mazes with food and removing the rats from them after every trial. This led him to devise the apparatus illustrated in Figure 10.4. A rat was permitted to run through a tunnel, which caused it to tilt. The tilt triggered a mechanism that caused a wooden disc to turn and release a food pellet from one of several holes located along its periphery. After retrieving the food, the rat returned to the start of the runway. All Skinner had to do was ensure the food supply did not run out (Skinner, 1956).

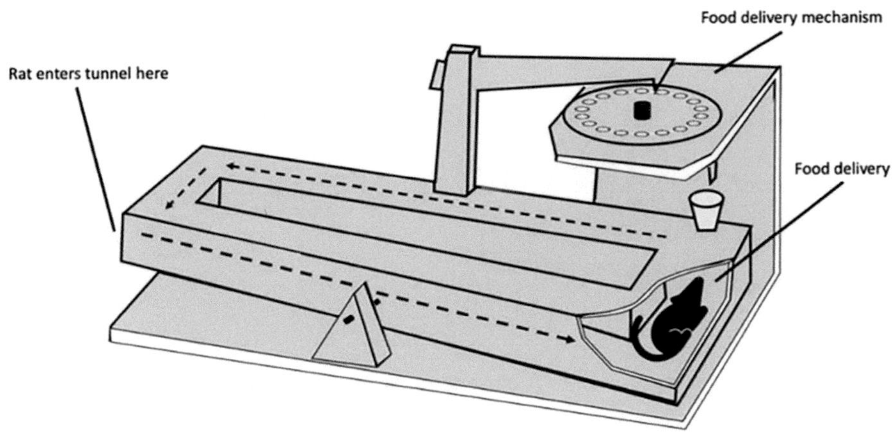

Figure 10.4 Apparatus invented by Skinner (1956) to automate a learning task. The weight of the rat causes the tunnel to tilt, which triggers the food delivery mechanism; the cut-away portion to the right shows a rat in the food delivery area inside the tunnel (see text for details).

Source: Redrawn from Skinner, B. F. (1956). A case history in scientific method. *Am Psychol, 11*(5), 221–233, Figure 4.

The Skinner Box

Skinner realized that the runway he incorporated in the apparatus shown in Figure 10.4 was unnecessary and that rats could be trained to press a lever to obtain the food. This realization led him to build soundproofed boxes containing a lever and a food magazine where the rats received food when they pressed the lever. This type of box became known as a Skinner box; a modern conception is shown in Figure 10.5a.

The Skinner box has since been used in thousands of behavioral experiments. It can include lights, sounds delivered through a loudspeaker, and an electrified gridded floor that can be used depending on the purpose of the experiment. For example, a rat can learn that pressing the lever will result in the delivery of food only when the red or green light is on. Rats can also learn that pressing the bar permits them to avoid electric shocks delivered through the gridded floor, an example of negative reinforcement (Bolles and Warren, 2014). The loudspeaker can be used to determine whether rats can learn that pressing the bar will only result in avoiding the shocks during a tone signal (Blankenship, Finn and Steinmetz, 2000).

WHAT DID SKINNER MEASURE IN THE SKINNER BOX?

Skinner was interested in the rate at which the rats pressed the lever, that is, the number of responses per minute. This is known as the response frequency (ratio). Another way to measure responding used by Skinner was the average amount of time that elapses between each response. This is known as the **inter-response time (IRT).**

Response Topography and Function

Skinner believed that operant conditioning could not be defined only by the physical movements involved in the response, its **topography**, but also by its function. For example, it

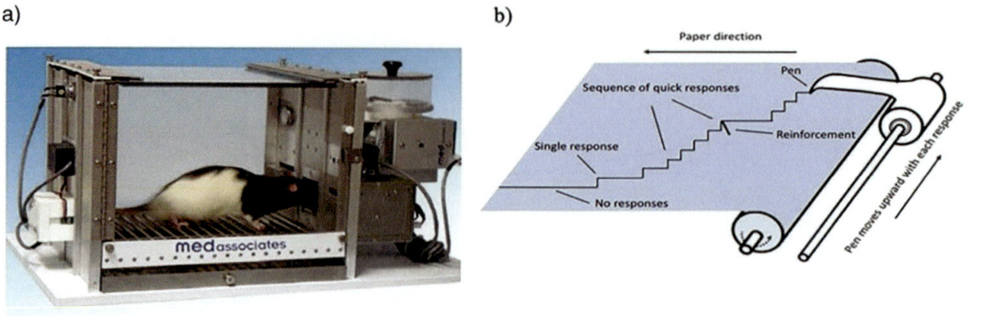

Figure 10.5 a) A modern Skinner box. b) A cumulative recorder. Deflections of pen represent patterns of responses.

Source: a) Breedlove, M. (2015). *Principles of psychology*. Oxford University Press Academic US. Page 325, Figure 8.16.

did not matter to Skinner whether the rat pressed the lever with its paws or with its snout because both topographies served the same function. Contrary to the discrete-trial procedure, the Skinner box permitted the rats to respond freely with no intervention from the experimenter in what became known as the **free operant procedure**.

THE CUMULATIVE RECORDER

To automatically record the number and pattern of lever presses performed by a rat in a Skinner box, Skinner invented the **cumulative recorder** illustrated in Figure 10.5b, which consisted of an apparatus from which a paper was released by a roller at a constant speed. Each time the rat pressed the lever, a pen marked the paper in one-step increments and drew a downward deflection each time a reinforcement was delivered. The pen reset to the bottom of the paper once it reached the top. The record of responses thus received is known as a **cumulative record** (Heron and Skinner, 1939).

Learning to Respond in Operant Conditioning

Pressing a lever while confined in a Skinner box is not a high-probability response for a rat. To facilitate the rats' learning process, Skinner devised two methods by which the rats could more easily learn to associate pressing the lever with food delivery. These methods are described in the subsequent sections.

Magazine Training

With **magazine training,** Skinner familiarized animals with the mechanisms by which a reinforcer was delivered. To train the rats to press a lever, he first dropped a food pellet in the magazine at random intervals with the lever locked downward. When the rat ate the pellets as soon as they were dropped into the magazine, he freed the lever and rewarded the rat with a pellet each time it pressed it.

Shaping

A more efficient method used by Skinner was **shaping**. Shaping involves determining a target behavior and reinforcing successive responses that lead to its behavior in incremental steps. Once an animal has learned a response, the reinforcer is withheld until it also performs a response closer to the target behavior. Figure 10.6 describes an example of shaping for the succession of steps that can be followed to get a rat to press a lever in a Skinner box.

With successive approximations, Skinner taught animals many complex behaviors. For example, he taught a rat named Pliny to 1) cause a marble to fall to the floor of its cage by pulling on a chain; 2) pick up the marble, take it to the location of a slot; and 3) drop the marble into the slot to obtain food. Two of Skinner's graduate students, Keller Breland (1915–1965) and Marian Breland (1920–2001), started a successful business (Animal Behavior Enterprises) in which they trained a wide variety of animals for the military, television shows, commercials, trade shows, and their theme park called the I.Q. Zoo. Their training methods, based on successive approximations, proved more humane than the methods used by animal trainers of the day, which often included harsh punishments for undesired behaviors. Even today, many techniques used to train marine animals at marine parks, such as SeaWorld and Marine Land, can be traced back to the Brelands (Gillaspy, Brinegar and Bailey, 2014).

Successive approximations are part of many instruction programs for learning new skills. For example, when learning to play tennis, such as in Yaëlle's case in the opening vignette, a good instructor does not expect a perfect forehand the first time you step onto a court.

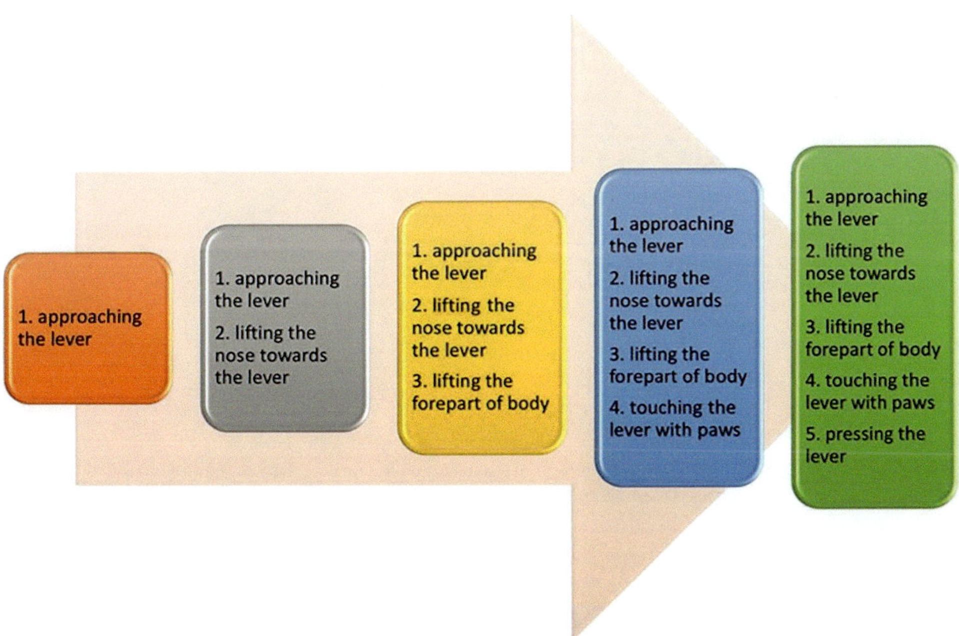

Figure 10.6 Shaping a rat to perform an operant response in a Skinner box using successive approximations.

As you read in the vignette, the instructor may first reinforce proper stance, grip, backswing, forehand stroke, and hitting the ball with praise, such as "Good job" or "Now you got it." Eventually, each step towards the final desired behavior is no longer reinforced by the instructor, and only the proper execution of the entire sequence of responses, such as adequately gripping the racket, assuming the appropriate stance, generating the backswing, performing a forehand stroke, hitting the ball, is reinforced.

A response chain is the sequence of responses required to deliver a reinforcer. There are two methods by which response chains can be taught. In **forward chaining**, responses are reinforced in the same order as desired in the goal behavior. In **backward chaining**, responses are reinforced in reverse order as they are desired to occur in the goal behavior. That is, it consists of first reinforcing the last response in the chain. Next, the previous response is reinforced only when performed after the second-to-last response, the third and second-to-last response, and so on, is executed. Backward chaining is used when the last step in a chain is easily executable. For example, teaching a child to make pancakes from scratch may be challenging, but it is easy for the child to transfer one from a pan to a plate when it's ready. The child's behavior would immediately be reinforced for this final step by getting praised by the parent and having the opportunity to eat the pancake. The child may be highly motivated to learn the previous steps in reverse order, such as flipping the pancake, pouring the mixture into the pan, and so on.

Humans can acquire complex skills through shaping.
Source: IStock photo ID:472139065.

Superstitious Behavior

A superstition is the belief that unrelated prior events can predict future events. Superstitions abound in all cultures the world over. **Superstitious behavior** can be defined as the attribution of a non-existent causal relationship between a behavior and an outcome, resulting in repeated behavior (Foster and Kokko, 2009). Superstitious behaviors are pervasive in sports. In fact, four out of five professional athletes perform some type of superstitious behavior (Schippers and Van Lange, 2006). For example, some athletes have been known to wear their "lucky" underwear for important games, others will grow a beard during the playoffs, and some goaltenders in hockey talk to their goalposts. You may also perform superstitious behaviors or have observed them in some of your classmates. For example, it is not uncommon to see students place a "lucky" object on their desk while taking an exam. It is believed that superstitious behavior stems from the desire to control elements of chance (Brevers et al., 2011).

Superstitious Behavior in Pigeons

Remember that contingency refers to the relationship between a response and an outcome. One of the ways of looking at contingency is by assessing the extent to which a behavior produces the outcome it follows. This differs from contiguity, which refers to how closely a response and an outcome follow a response in time or place. Superstitious behaviors are contiguous with the outcomes they follow. However, the outcomes are not contingent upon superstitious behavior, which means that the behavior does not produce the outcome but co-occurs. That is, an event may be an effective reinforcer if it is contiguous to a response without having to be contingent upon it. For example, wearing lucky socks did not make the baseball player hit a home run, but it happened that she did so while wearing them, which increased the probability that she would wear them again.

Skinner tested this idea (1948) in a famous experiment in which he presented hungry pigeons with a food hopper, giving them 5 seconds of access to food at 15-second intervals, irrespective of the behavior they might be engaged in at the time. He found that the pigeons not only learned to eat from the hopper but repeated the behaviors they happened to be performing before the presentation of the hopper, even if those behaviors had nothing to do with the delivery of the food. For example, one pigeon learned to turn counter-clockwise, another repeatedly made head movements towards a corner of the cage, and another developed a pendulum motion of the head and body. He also found that lengthening the interval between subsequent reinforcements increased the number of responses emitted by the pigeons from the beginning of the interval to the delivery of food. This led Skinner to believe that contiguity between a response and a reinforcer is sufficient for operant conditioning to occur.

WAS THE BEHAVIOR OF SKINNER'S PIGEONS SUPERSTITIOUS? INTERIM AND TERMINAL RESPONSES

A closer analysis of Skinner's superstition experiment revealed that his pigeons' behavior may not have been superstitious after all. It was proposed that what Skinner called superstitious behaviors were actually instinctive preparatory responses that naturally occur in anticipation of food, rather than behaviors accidentally reinforced by reinforcement. These responses were observed during the waiting period between the last food delivery and the next. It was also found that these responses could be divided into interim responses, which appear immediately and at intermediate times after food delivery, and terminal responses, which appear at the end of the delay interval just before the next food delivery. This reinterpretation suggests that the pigeons' behaviors were not the result of accidental reinforcement (contiguity) but rather species-typical responses triggered by periodic food delivery (Staddon and Simmelhag, 1971).

Contingencies of Reinforcement

The **contingencies of reinforcement** refer to the relationships between a response and its outcome in terms of whether the response results in an outcome that increases or decreases the probability of the response that produced it. There are four types of contingencies of reinforcement, which are described subsequently and summarized in Table 10.2.

Positive Reinforcement

Positive reinforcement occurs when the delivery of an **appetitive stimulus** increases the probability of the response it follows. Many examples of positive reinforcement exist in everyday life. For example, a mother gives her son extra video game playing time after he takes out the garbage, a boss gives her employees a bonus after completing an important task, and a friend gives you $200 for having taken care of her dog while she was on vacation.

Negative Reinforcement

Negative reinforcement occurs when a response results in the removal or avoidance of an aversive stimulus, increasing the probability of the response when the aversive stimulus is again encountered. For example, you take an aspirin to relieve your headache, you put on sunglasses to avoid the glare of the sun, or a teacher expels an overly disruptive student

Table 10.2 Contingencies of reinforcement.

Contingency Type	*Definition*	*Examples*
Positive Reinforcement	An appetitive stimulus increases the probability of the response it follows.	A child receives extra video game playing time after taking out the trash.
Negative Reinforcement	The removal of an aversive stimulus following a response increases the probability of that response.	Putting on sunglasses to remove the glare from the sun while driving.
Positive Punishment (punishment)	An aversive stimulus decreases the probability of the response it follows.	A child is spanked by a parent for misbehaving.
Negative Punishment (omission training and response cost)	**Omission training:** A response leads to the withholding of a reinforcer. **Response cost:** Taking away something a subject already possesses as a result of their response.	A parent forbids her child to play video games after hitting his sister. A person caught drinking and driving has his license suspended.

from class. Negative reinforcement is associated with escape and avoidance behaviors, a topic that we will discuss at greater length in Chapter 17.

Positive Punishment

Positive punishment, or simply punishment, occurs when the delivery of an aversive stimulus decreases the probability of the response it follows—for example, if a child is spanked for misbehaving or a person is given a ticket for speeding or a student a failing grade for partying instead of studying.

Negative Punishment

There are two forms of **negative punishment: omission training** and **response cost.** Omission training occurs when a response leads to the withholding of a reinforcer. For instance, a parent might prohibit her child from playing video games after he hits his sister. Response cost involves taking away something a subject already possesses as a result of their response. For example, a man caught drinking and driving might have his license suspended.

Now that you have learned about the various contingencies of reinforcement, it may have become apparent to you that in certain situations, the increased probability of the occurrence of a response may be due to both positive and negative reinforcement. For example, you can explain that wearing a sweater on a cold day is reinforced by the pleasant feeling of warmth, which provides an example of positive reinforcement. However, you can also say that wearing the sweater is reinforced by no longer feeling cold, an example of negative reinforcement. In fact, some researchers believe that situations in which positive reinforcement is observed always involve negative reinforcement (Michael, 1975). However, psychologist Murray Sidman (1923–2019) pointed out that positive and negative reinforcement often occur alone (Sidman, 2006).

> Would the production of an aspirin suffice to reinforce the opening of the bottle if the pill did not turn off the headache? I think we know what would happen to aspirin consumption if we filled aspirin bottles with falsely labeled placebo tablets. Might a child turn on a TV program even if it took her away from a favorite game or a much-wanted dessert? Such an event is certainly possible, and when it happens, it would be difficult to identify the reinforcement as escape from boredom. Do spouses usually seek divorces independently of their marital experiences? Surely, we do not need experimental data to classify many, if not most, divorces as escape behavior.
>
> (p. 137)

Critical Thinking Spot Check 10.1

1. Compare Darwin's idea of intelligence in animals with Thorndike's.
2. What three conclusions did Thorndike come to from his experiments?
3. Explain the learning mechanism by which Thorndike's cats gradually learned to escape the puzzle boxes.
4. How valuable was the law of effect in developing learning theory?
5. Distinguish reward from reinforcement by giving an everyday example of each.

6. Describe the differences that exist between operant and classical conditioning.
7. Why would understanding the contingencies of reinforcement be important for controlling undesirable behaviors?
8. Describe how you would use the shaping method to teach a child the sequence of movements necessary for performing a sport of your choice.

10.2 Schedules of Reinforcement

What Are Schedules of Reinforcement?

It may be evident that not every particular instance of an animal's or person's behaviors is necessarily reinforced. For example, most people get paid weekly or bi-weekly, regardless of how much work they perform leading up to payday. People do not receive praise from their bosses, teachers, or parents every time they do something right. However, it does happen that every instance of response is reinforced, such as when you press an icon on your smartphone to open an application or when a rat is reinforced for every lever press it performs.

Schedules of reinforcement are rules that determine which particular instance of a response will be reinforced. If every instance of a response is reinforced for every instance of a behavior, it is called a **continuous reinforcement schedule**.

When Skinner first trained rats in his conditioning chambers, he worried that their high response rates would soon deplete food pellets. This made him wonder whether he could save on food by not reinforcing every response (Skinner, 1956). He found that the rats would keep responding if food was delivered intermittently following a response, which led Skinner to the discovery of **partial reinforcement schedules**.

There are two types of partial reinforcement schedules: ratio schedules and interval schedules. Ratio schedules include the fixed-ratio schedule (FR) and the variable-ratio schedule (VR). Interval schedules include the fixed (FI) and variable (VI) schedules. We will now discuss each of these schedules. In addition, Table 10.3 summarizes the response requirements for each schedule and provides an example for each.

Ratio Schedules

THE FIXED-RATIO SCHEDULE

On an FR schedule, the number of responses required for an animal to obtain the reinforcer is fixed. For example, on an FR-10 schedule, a rat in a Skinner box has to press the lever 10 times before it receives the reinforcer, 15 times on an FR-15 schedule, 20 times on an FR-20 schedule and so on. An FR-1 schedule, or a continuous reinforcement schedule (CRF), is one in which every response is reinforced.

THE VARIABLE-RATIO SCHEDULE

On a VR schedule, a reinforcer is delivered after a random number of responses are performed. For example, on a VR-10 schedule, a rat in a Skinner box has to perform an average of ten responses for a reinforcer to be delivered. This means that sometimes a reinforcer may be delivered after 10 responses and a random number of responses, such as 12, 8, 9, 13, or 7 responses.

Interval Schedules

FIXED-INTERVAL SCHEDULE

On an FI schedule, a response is reinforced only if a fixed amount of time has elapsed since the last time a response was reinforced. For example, on an FI-60 seconds schedule, a response is only reinforced if at least 60 seconds have elapsed since the last time a response was reinforced. Any response made by the rat during that interval is not reinforced.

VARIABLE-INTERVAL SCHEDULE

On a VI schedule, a random amount of time has to elapse since the last time a response was reinforced. For example, on a VI-60 seconds schedule, an average of 60 seconds has to elapse since the last time a response was reinforced. For example, a reinforcer may become available not only after 60 but also randomly after 55, 65, 61, and 62 seconds.

RESPONSE PATTERNS (PERIODICITY)

Skinner also discovered that animals developed different response patterns depending on the schedule of reinforcement. He recorded these patterns using the cumulative recorder depicted in Figure 10.5b. The pattern of responses under each schedule is illustrated in Figure 10.7. The slopes of the lines indicate the response rate, and the black notches represent the delivery of a reinforcer. Ratio schedules (FR and VR) are characterized by a high response rate, as indicated by the steep slope of their lines (blue and green).

Under the FR schedule, an increase in the response rate is often observed as the animal approaches the number of responses required to fulfill the ratio. This is known as a **ratio run**. A significant reduction in the number of responses is often observed once an animal's response is reinforced. This is known as the **post-reinforcement pause**. The length of the pause was found to be related to the ratio requirement. In other words, higher requirements are associated with longer pauses. If a significant increase in the ratio requirement is imposed, an animal may reduce its response rate in what is known as a **ratio strain**. Under a

Table 10.3 Schedules of reinforcement.

Schedules	*Definitions*	*Examples*
Fixed-ratio schedule	Reinforcement is delivered after a fixed number of responses are performed.	A carpenter gets paid for a specific number of cabinets she builds.
Variable-ratio schedule	Reinforcement is delivered after a random number of responses are performed.	Playing a slot machine.
Fixed-interval schedule	Reinforcement is delivered after a fixed amount of time has elapsed since the last response.	You get paid every Thursday regardless of how much work you perform.
Variable-interval schedule	Reinforcement is delivered after a random amount of time has elapsed since the last response.	Your boss praises your work at random times during the week.

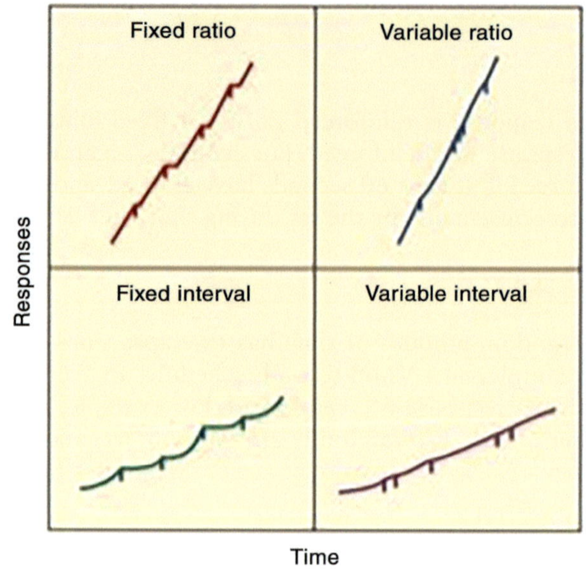

Figure 10.7 The patterns of responses recorded under fixed ratio, variable ratio, fixed interval, and variable interval schedules (see text for details).

Source: b) Bouton, M. E. (2016). *Learning and behavior* (2nd ed.). Oxford University Press Academic US. Page 258, Figure 7.8.

VR schedule, animals respond steadily because the number of responses required to obtain the reinforcer is unpredictable. Under an FI schedule, animals learn not to respond throughout much of the interval but begin to respond near the end of the interval in what is known as a **fixed interval scallop**. Finally, animals respond consistently throughout the interval under VI schedules since the reinforcer is delivered randomly.

Focus On ABA

Differential Reinforcement Schedules

Differential reinforcement schedules refer to a set of procedures by which reinforcement is delivered when an individual performs a specific target behavior but withheld when the same individual performs a behavior other than the target without recourse to punishment (Deitz, Repp and Deitz, 1976). For example, if the target behavior is for a child to ask for access to a toy politely, the child is only reinforced when politely asking for a toy. The child is not reinforced for screaming, hitting, or trying to take the toy without asking. There are four ways in which a differential reinforcement schedule can be implemented. These are differential reinforcement of incompatible behavior (DRI), differential reinforcement of alternative behavior (DRA), differential reinforcement of other behaviors (DRO), and differential reinforcement of low/high rates (DRL/DRH). Each one of these implementations is described subsequently.

Differential Reinforcement of Incompatible Behavior (DRI)

DRI consists of only reinforcing behavior that is incompatible with an undesired behavior (Luiselli et al., 1980). This means reinforced behavior cannot be done simultaneously with the undesired behavior. For example, a child cannot simultaneously shout and quietly read a book. Therefore, a teacher or parent may implement a schedule where quietly reading a book is reinforced but not shouting. Also, a child cannot remain seated while walking around in the classroom at the same time. Therefore, a teacher may reinforce sitting but not walking around.

Differential Reinforcement of Alternative Behavior (DRA)

DRA consists of reinforcing an alternative behavior that is not necessarily incompatible with the problem behavior (Vollmer et al., 1992). For example, a child who blurts out answers to the teacher's questions without raising her hand only receives the teacher's attention when she raises her hand. Note that blurting out answers and raising a hand are not incompatible behaviors in that they can be performed simultaneously. DRA can also be used to increase response variability. For example, reinforcing response variability is essential in martial arts training, where one's success depends on the ability to perform a variety of defensive and offensive behaviors (Harding et al., 2004).

Differential Reinforcement of Other Behaviors (DRO)

DRO consists of delivering a reinforcer only when an undesired behavior has not occurred for a specific amount of time. For example, while watching television, a parent may only praise a child if she sits quietly until commercials, or a teacher may place a timer on a child's desk and praise the child only if she has remained quiet for a specified period.

Differential Reinforcement of High/Low Rates (DRL/DRH)

DRH/DRL consists of delivering a reinforcer if a behavior occurs above or below a specified rate (Austin and Bevan, 2011). As an example of DRH, a child may only be reinforced if she studied for at least one hour, or a hockey player may receive praise only if she obtained a certain number of shots on goal during a game. As an example of DRL, a basketball coach may want to curtail a player's aggressive behavior due to receiving a high number of fouls. However, the coach may, at the same time, not want to eliminate the player's aggressive behavior. Therefore, she may praise the player if the instances of aggressive behavior are limited to a certain number during the game.

Are You Thinking Critically?

1. Can you think of an unwanted behavior that could not be controlled using a differential reinforcement method?
2. Distinguish the different types of differential reinforcement methods and imagine situations where each can be applied.

Critical Thinking Spot Check 10.2

1. Define the concept of schedules of reinforcement and provide examples from everyday life.
2. Explain the difference between continuous reinforcement (CRF) and partial reinforcement, highlighting how Skinner's experiments contributed to the discovery of partial reinforcement schedules.
3. Consider a scenario where an employer reinforces employee behavior using a fixed-interval schedule. What might be the potential advantages and disadvantages of such a reinforcement strategy?
4. Compare and contrast the response patterns under fixed-ratio (FR) and variable-ratio (VR) schedules. How do animals' behaviors differ under these two types of schedules, and what factors contribute to these differences?
5. Devise a hypothetical situation where a variable interval (VI) schedule is implemented to shape a specific behavior in a classroom setting. Describe the expected patterns of responding and potential challenges associated with this reinforcement schedule.

Chapter Summary

Each bullet point aligns with the learning objectives outlined at the beginning of the chapter.

- Thorndike performed experiments in which cats gradually learned to escape "puzzle boxes" by trial and error, showing no evidence of reasoning or understanding of the mechanism involved in escaping the boxes. Thorndike proposed that the cats learned to escape the boxes by associating sense impressions and an impulse to act. He believed that the food was not part of this association but served to stamp in the association. This became known as S-R learning. Thorndike also proposed the law of effect, which states that the association between a stimulus and a response is strengthened when followed by a pleasant outcome and weakened when followed by an unpleasant outcome.
- Operant conditioning is a learning process by which the consequences of its actions control an animal's behavior. It is associated with B.F. Skinner. Thorndike proposed a difference between operant conditioning and S-R learning: In operant conditioning, an association is learned between the response and its outcome, which is known as R-O learning. A distinction must be drawn between reinforcement and reward. A reinforcer increases the probability of the response, whereas a reward does not necessarily do so.
- The use of mazes involves removing the animal from it after every trial to place it back at the beginning of the maze for the subsequent trial. This is known as a discrete-trial procedure. Skinner designed a chamber in which animals could perform continuous responses (continuous reinforcement) without needing to be removed after every trial. He was interested in rates of responding and interresponse times and invented the cumulative recorder with which the pattern and number of responses performed by an animal could be recorded. Because Skinner's procedure permitted the animals to respond freely with no intervention from the experimenter, it became known as a free-operant procedure.
- Skinner used magazine training and shaping to facilitate the acquisition of lever-pressing responses. Magazine training refers to a process by which animals are familiarized with the mechanism that delivers the reinforcer. Shaping refers to a method by which each successive step towards performing a response is reinforced. This includes forward chaining and backward chaining. However, he found that operant responses can be conditioned in

pigeons even if no contingency existed between their responses and food delivery. Skinner called this superstitious behavior. He believed this showed that operant conditioning can occur as long as a response and reinforcer are contiguous. However, it was later revealed that the pigeons displayed instinctual responses in anticipation of food delivery, known as interim and terminal responses.

- Reinforcement contingencies include positive reinforcement, negative reinforcement, positive punishment, and negative punishment. Differential reinforcement is a procedure in which a reinforcer is withheld following an unwanted response and only delivered following a desired response.
- Animals can be reinforced under different schedules of reinforcement. Under partial schedules of reinforcement, animals may be reinforced only after they have performed a fixed or average number of responses. These are known as fixed ratio and variable ratio schedules, respectively. Animals may only be reinforced after a fixed or average period has elapsed since performing the last response. These are known as fixed-interval and variable-interval schedules, respectively. Different schedules of reinforcement give rise to different response patterns or periodicity. Fixed-ratio schedules typically give rise to a ratio run, post-reinforcement pauses, and ratio strain. Fixed-interval schedules usually give rise to a fixed-interval scallop.

Glossary

Anecdotal reports Informal observations or personal accounts of behavior that lack systematic scientific validation.

Anthropomorphic error Attributing human-like traits, emotions, or motivations to non-human animals in behavioral analysis.

Appetitive stimulus A stimulus perceived as rewarding or desirable, often used to reinforce behaviors.

Backward chaining A training method where the last step in a behavioral sequence is taught first, progressing backward toward the first step.

Contingencies of reinforcement The relationships between a behavior and its consequence, determining whether reinforcement or punishment strengthens or weakens the behavior.

Cumulative record A graphical representation of behavioral responses over time, displaying patterns of reinforcement and response rates.

Cumulative recorder A device used in behavioral experiments to record response rates over time as a continuous graphical output.

Discrete-trial procedure A conditioning method in which learning occurs through separate, controlled trials, with distinct start and end points.

Fixed interval scallop A characteristic pattern of responding where activity increases toward the end of a fixed-interval reinforcement period.

Forward chaining A training technique where a complex behavior is taught step by step, beginning with the first action in a sequence.

Free operant procedure A conditioning method where organisms can respond freely and repeatedly without distinct trial separations.

Instrumental conditioning Another term for operant conditioning, emphasizing that behavior is modified through reinforcement or punishment.

Magazine training The initial step in operant conditioning where an animal learns to associate a dispenser (magazine) with food reinforcement.

Negative punishment The removal of a desirable stimulus to reduce the occurrence of a behavior.

Negative reinforcement The removal of an aversive stimulus following a behavior to strengthen its occurrence.

Omission training A form of negative punishment where access to a reinforcer is withheld following a behavior to discourage its repetition.

Operant conditioning A learning process where behaviors are strengthened or weakened based on consequences such as rewards or punishments.

Partial reinforcement schedules Reinforcement patterns where a behavior is not reinforced every time, influencing persistence and resistance to extinction.

Positive punishment The introduction of an aversive stimulus to decrease the likelihood of a behavior.

Positive reinforcement The addition of a desirable stimulus following a behavior to increase its occurrence.

Post-reinforcement pause A temporary reduction in responding that occurs after receiving reinforcement in fixed-ratio schedules.

Ratio run A burst of rapid responses occurring when reinforcement is contingent on completing a set number of actions.

Ratio strain A disruption in responding caused by overly demanding reinforcement schedules, leading to avoidance or breakdown of learned behavior.

Response cost A behavioral reduction method where something valued is taken away as a consequence of undesired behavior.

Schedules of reinforcement Rules governing how and when reinforcements are delivered to shape behavior.

Shaping A process in operant conditioning where successive approximations toward a desired behavior are reinforced.

Superstitious behavior A behavior that arises when an organism mistakenly associates a response with reinforcement, even when there is no actual causal connection.

Topography The physical form or movement pattern of a behavior, including its structure and execution.

11 Reinforcers

How They Work and What Makes Them Effective

Learning Objectives

- Know about the different types of reinforcers and learn how they are used.
- Be able to explain the factors that determine the effectiveness of reinforcers.
- Understand secondary reinforcement and how it can be used to control behavior.

Hakem's Disappointing New Job

IStock photo ID:1194668332

Hakem recently lost his job as a data analyst. What upset him most was that, for once, he had a job he immensely enjoyed, where his skills were highly valued and where he developed positive relationships with his coworkers. In addition, everyone's efforts were always met with words of encouragement such as "good job" and "keep going, you're

DOI: 10.4324/9781003491828-20

doing well." The job also offered many opportunities for training and promotions. In addition, the salary was excellent, and he was allowed to work from home three days per week. Hakem had no trouble finding another job because of his high skill level and the connections he had formed. Within six weeks, he was already working at a similar company. However, Hakem found that the new job was not as promising as it looked when he applied. He realized that there were no opportunities for training or any chance for advancement. His coworkers mostly kept to themselves, and employees were never congratulated on their excellent work. He also missed working from home, which was not an option at his new job. "The job also pays less," he told his friend Annisa. She answered that she had also switched jobs but had gone from one horrible job to another. While having dinner one evening, their mutual friend Bao boasted that he was ecstatic about finding his dream job after accepting less-than-ideal work conditions for many years. Hakem's, Annisa's and Bao's experiences reflect the idea that the effectiveness of reinforcers must be examined in relative terms. For example, if Hakem had never experienced having such a great job, he may not have lacked the motivation to work at his new one.

In contrast, Annisa's motivation to work was not reduced when she changed because she did not experience a change in the quality or magnitude of reinforcement she received at her previous job. On the other hand, Bao was ecstatic about his new job because it was significantly more fulfilling than his last job. These types of contrasts in reinforcement from one situation to another for the same behavior are known as incentive contrasts.

11.1 There Are Several Types of Reinforcers

Primary Reinforcers

Primary reinforcers are stimuli animals do not have to learn about to be effective. These include food, water, sex, sleep, shelter, sensory stimulation, warmth, and coolness. Pleasure is also a primary reinforcer. For example, it was found that rats will press a lever to receive direct electrical stimulation of brain areas believed to be involved in feeling pleasure (Olds and Milner, 1954) and being administered various psychoactive drugs such as cocaine, morphine, and alcohol (Barrett et al., 2006; Holstein, Barkell and Young, 2021; Suto, Wise and Vezina, 2011; Wise, Murray and Bozarth, 1990). The joy Hakem felt working at his first job was an important source of primary reinforcement.

Secondary Reinforcers

Secondary reinforcers are stimuli that derive their reinforcing properties by being associated with primary reinforcers. Money is a secondary reinforcer, which can be used to acquire a wide range of primary reinforcers. However, for some people the accumulation of wealth itself may be reinforcing. Good grades are also secondary reinforcers because they lead to greater access to college or university programs, which may ultimately lead to better career prospects. Hence, for Hakem, in the opening vignette, the opportunity for training and his excellent salary were important sources of secondary reinforcement.

Tokens

Tokens are secondary reinforcers that can be exchanged for goods or services. They include coins, poker chips, fake money, and points, which can be exchanged for primary or other secondary reinforcers. The value of a token is established strictly through its relationship with other reinforcers. The token itself has no value. Money is a token because the coins and strips of paper themselves are virtually worthless. The value is in what can be acquired with them.

Tokens can be used as a behavior modification tool in various settings. For example, teachers can use tokens as classroom management strategies by setting up a **token economy** (Ackerman, Samudre and Allday, 2020; Cavalier, Ferretti and Hodges, 1997). In a classroom setting, a token economy may reinforce children's good behavior with tokens such as colored plastic chips or stickers, which can be exchanged for toys or snacks. The list of reinforcers in a classroom setting may also include access to video games or operating the laptop to change the slides during a presentation.

Tokens have also successfully been used to reinforce animal behavior. In a classic study, psychologist John Bascom Wolfe (1904–1988) trained chimpanzees to put white but not brass-colored plastic chips through a slot to obtain food. Through their association with food, the white plastic chips were as effective as the food in reinforcing another behavior: raising a lever from the horizontal to the vertical position (Wolfe, 1936).

Social Reinforcers

Social reinforcers derive their value from the behavior of other individuals in response to approved behaviors. They include praise, affection, attention, smiles, thumbs ups, and high-fives. They can also include verbal encouragements such as "great job," "good girl/boy," or "awesome." These can also act as secondary reinforcers. For example, candy or other goodies may follow a thumbs up. These are the types of reinforcers Hakim, in the opening vignette, had gotten used to at his previous job.

Critical Thinking Spot Check 11.1

1. List and define examples of primary reinforcers mentioned in the text. Provide real-life examples of how these primary reinforcers can influence behavior.
2. Explain the concept of secondary reinforcers and provide examples from the text. How do secondary reinforcers differ from primary reinforcers, and how are they related?
3. Imagine a scenario where a child is reluctant to study. How might a teacher use tokens as secondary reinforcers in a token economy to encourage studying habits?
4. Compare and contrast social reinforcers with primary and secondary reinforcers. How do social reinforcers derive their value, and how can they act as secondary reinforcers in different contexts?

11.2 Determinants of Reinforcer Effectiveness

What Determines the Effectiveness of a Reinforcer?

In the previous section, you learned that several forms of reinforcers exist. However, you have not yet learned about the factors related to the effectiveness of reinforcers. In this section, you will learn that the effectiveness of reinforcers depends on reinforcer magnitude, reinforcer quality, and delay in the reinforcement (Hoch et al., 2002; Trosclair-Lasserre et al., 2008).

Reinforcer Magnitude

The magnitude of a reinforcer may refer to its quantity, intensity, or duration. For example, a researcher wanting to use access to toys to reinforce appropriate behaviors in children may have to systematically vary the number of toys used as reinforcers to determine which is most effective (variations in quantity). Wanting to reinforce appropriate behaviors with music might require experimenting with different volumes (variations in intensity). Finally, the researcher also has to consider whether the effectiveness of a reinforcer depends on the amount of time to which it is exposed (variations in duration).

Shifts in Reinforcer Magnitude: Incentive Contrast

Incentive contrast occurs when the effectiveness of a reinforcer is affected by a shift in its magnitude. **Positive incentive contrast** occurs when increased reinforcer magnitude results in increased response rates. For example, Bao , in this chapters opening vignette, experienced positive incentive contrast when he moved from years of less-than-ideal work conditions to his dream job. The dramatic improvement in his work environment made the reinforcers at his new job highly effective, leaving him ecstatic and highly motivated. **Negative incentive contrast** occurs when decreased reinforcer magnitude results in decreased rates of responding. Hakem experienced this when he moved from his highly satisfying previous job to his new position with fewer opportunities and benefits. The contrast made his current job feel less reinforcing than it might have seemed if he had never experienced such excellent work conditions before. As noted in the vignette, if Hakem had never experienced having such a great job, he may not have lacked motivation at his new one. The previous high-quality reinforcement created a comparison that diminished his current job's reinforcing value.

Contrast effects were first demonstrated by psychologist Leo Crespi (1916–2008). Crespi (1942) reinforced rats to run down a straight-alley maze. He found that rats reinforced with a relatively large amount of food at the end of the alley ran faster than those reinforced with less food. He then reduced the amount of food reinforcement for some of the rats in the group that received the larger reinforcer and increased the amount for some of the rats that received the smaller reinforcer. He found that the rats who experienced a downward shift in reinforcement magnitude took longer to reach the goal box than in previous trials when the reinforcer was larger. This is an example of negative contrast. Crespi also called this a *depression effect* because the rats also took more time to reach the goal box than rats for which the smaller reinforcer remained the same.

Conversely, the rats who experienced an increase in the amount of food they received took significantly less time to reach the goal box than when the reinforcer they received was smaller. This is an example of positive contrast. Crespi called this an *elation effect* because the rats also took less time to reach the goal box than the rats for which the larger reinforcer remained the same.

ANTICIPATORY NEGATIVE CONTRAST EFFECT

Another type of contrast effect is known as **anticipatory negative contrast**. This effect occurs when an organism responds less vigorously for a low-value reinforcer if it knows a high-value reinforcer is coming next. In other words, responding to a low-value reinforcer decreases when it is immediately followed by a high-value reinforcer, compared to when the same low-value reinforcer is followed by another low-value reinforcer. For example, researchers gave rats access to two drinking tubes in succession. In one condition, rats first drank from a tube containing 15% saccharin solution, immediately followed by access to a tube with 32% sucrose solution (a more preferred, sweeter option). In another condition, rats first drank from a 15% saccharin tube, followed by access to another 15% saccharin tube.

The rats drank significantly less from the first 15% saccharin tube when they knew the highly preferred 32% sucrose was coming next, compared to when another 15% saccharin tube would follow. In other words, anticipating the better reinforcer reduced their consumption of the lesser one (Flaherty and Checke, 1982).

Why did the rats decrease their intake of saccharin? The rats learned to anticipate the preferred sucrose solution through repeated pairings when presented with the least preferred solution. It is suggested that this anticipation led to the progressive devaluation of the least preferred stimulus to the point at which it was avoided (Flaherty, Turovsky and Krauss, 1994). A proposed process for this effect is known as *reward comparison* (Grigson, 1997). That is when a highly preferred reward follows one that is least preferred, the intensity of their effects is compared. If the difference is significant enough, the first reward is further devalued (Feltmann et al., 2018; Grigson, 1997; Parylak et al., 2012).

Anticipatory negative contrast is believed to play an essential role in drug addiction. For example, it is often observed that addicted individuals have lost their interest in natural reinforcers after experiencing the effects of the drug. For example, an addicted person may no longer enjoy activities they loved to engage in. This may be because the reward value of primary reinforcers pales in comparison to that offered by the drug, thus resulting in their avoidance (Grigson, 2008).

Anticipatory negative contrast may occur when an addicted person may no longer enjoy activities they loved to engage in through the process of reward comparison. This may be because the reward value of primary reinforcers pales in comparison to that offered by the drug.

Source: Soccer: IStock photo ID:636267430. Addiction: IStock photo ID:1154734877.

Reinforcer Quality

The quality of reinforcers refers to the extent to which one type of reinforcer is preferred over another. For example, a researcher may compare children's responses to one stimulus versus several others in the initial stage of a study to choose the one that elicits the highest response rate. Stimuli that elicit a high response rate are called high-quality reinforcers, and the stimuli that elicit a relatively low response rate are often called *low-quality reinforcers*. For example, in an early study, pigeons were given a choice between pressing a lever to receive food and another to receive electrical brain stimulation. It was found that the pigeons responded on the lever associated with food at a significantly higher rate than on the lever associated with brain stimulation (Hollard and

Davison, 1971). This showed that, for the pigeons, food was a higher-quality reinforcer than brain stimulation.

Response Reinforcer Relations: Contingency and Contiguity

In operant conditioning, **contingency** refers to how a response produces a reinforcer. For example, flicking a light switch is highly contingent on a light being turned on. In contrast, contingency is low if one is flicking the switch because it is defective and only sometimes turns on the light. Contiguity could either be temporal or spatial. Temporal contiguity refers to the extent to which a reinforcer closely follows a response. For example, raising your hand is highly contiguous, with the teacher paying attention to you if she promptly does so. In contrast, contiguity is low if you need to keep your hand up for an extended period before you get her attention.

As illustrated in Figure 11.1, contiguity and contingency are independent. For example, your friend might answer your texts every time (high contingency) with little delay (high contiguity). It may also be that she always answers your texts (high contingency) but takes a long time to do so (low contiguity). A third possibility is that she only sometimes answers your texts (low contingency) but answers quickly when she does (high contiguity). Finally, it might also be that she rarely answers your texts (low contingency) and takes a long time to answer when she does (low contiguity).

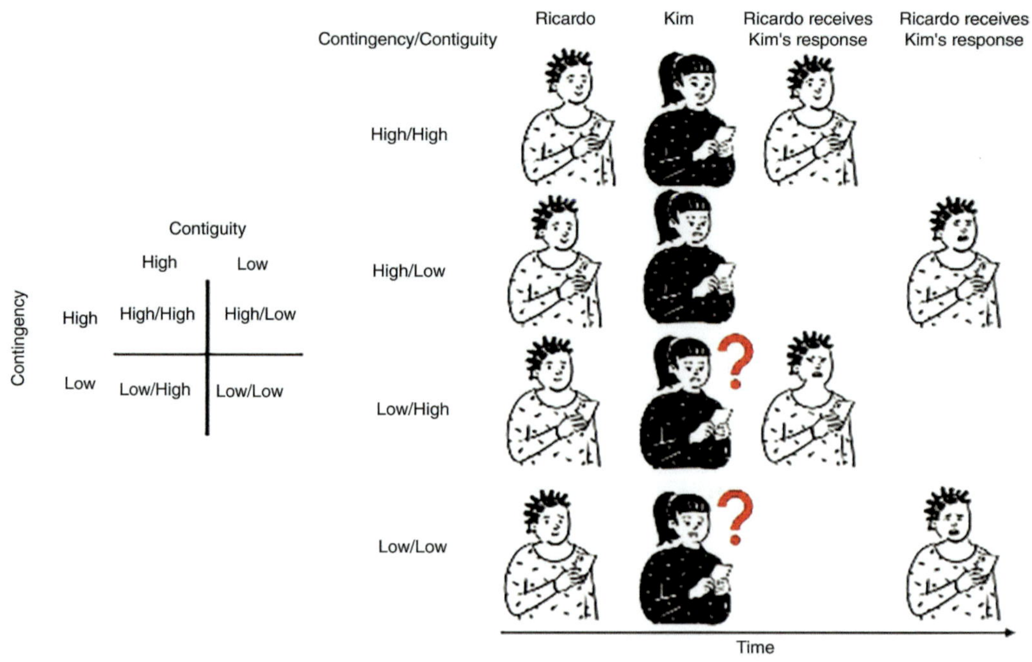

Figure 11.1 The independence of contingency and contiguity. Top row: Kim always answers Ricardo's texts (high contingency). She does so within minutes of receiving them (high contiguity). Second row: Kim always answers Ricardo's texts (high contingency) but takes hours to respond (low contiguity). Third row: Kim only answers Ricardo's texts on some occasions (low contingency), but when she does respond, she does so within minutes (high contiguity). Bottom row: Kim only answers Ricardo's texts on some occasions (low contingency) and takes hours to respond when she does (low contiguity).

Delay to Reinforcement

As you just learned in the last section, contiguity (temporal) refers to the extent to which a reinforcer closely follows the response that preceded it. However, researchers questioned how much a delay between a response and an outcome in an instrumental task would impair performance. The search for an answer to this question has a long history (Renner, 1964). It was found early on that performance in an instrumental task is inversely related to the time to reinforcement after a response. For example, psychologist John Wolfe (1904–1988) trained rats to obtain food from a goal box at the end of the arms of a T-maze (Wolfe, 1934). The particularity of Wolfe's experiment is that the rats were delayed for a predetermined length of time by being confined in a box at the entry of an arm after having made their choice before gaining access to the food. He found that the rats made progressively more errors as the delay was increased from 0 to 60 seconds. The effect of delay on learning was also found in rats bar pressing for food in a Skinner box. As shown in Figure 11.2, rats performed progressively fewer responses as the delay between responses and the delivery of the reinforcer was increased from 2 to 64 seconds (Dickinson, Watt and Griffiths, 1992).

The reason for imposing a delay between a response and its outcome may seem obvious. After all, forgetting seems to be a function of the time that has elapsed since information was acquired. However, for a behavioral scientist, the mere passage of time is an observation, not an explanation. It was hypothesized that lack of contiguity makes it difficult for animals to detect the contingency between a response and the following reinforcement. That is the extent to which the response will produce the reinforcer.

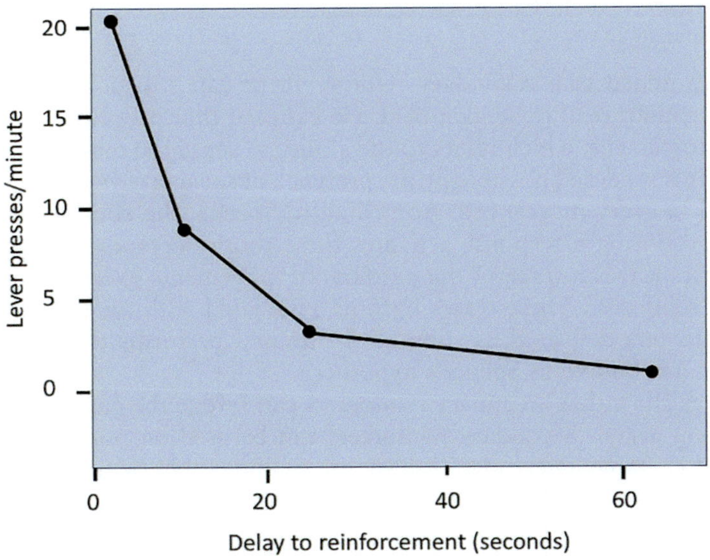

Figure 11.2 Effects of delay of reinforcement on operant conditioning (from Dickinson, Watt and Griffiths, 1992).

Source: Modified from Dickinson, A., Watt, A., & Griffiths. (1992). Free-operant acquisition with delayed reinforcement. *Q J Exp Psychol, 45*, 241–258. https://doi.org/10.1080/14640749208401019.

Critical Thinking Spot Check 11.2

1. What is the importance of knowing the determinants of reinforcer effectiveness in controlling behavior?
2. Explain how reinforcer magnitude differs from reinforcer quality.
3. How might an employee's productivity change if she went from having a manager who praises a job well done to a manager who never praises employees?
4. People who become addicted to drugs often give up activities they used to love. Which of the contrast effects might explain this change in behavior?
5. Why does a long delay to reinforcement affect the effectiveness of a reinforcer?

11.3 Secondary Reinforcement

Bridging the Gap

As you read, Wolfe (1934) found that delays of 0 to 60 seconds impaired the learning of rats in a T-maze. However, he also found that imposing delays of more than 60 seconds did not impair the rats' learning. He even found evidence for learning in some rats with delays of up to 20 minutes. This raised the question of how learning was still possible with such a long delay. Why was the learning that Wolfe observed not affected by the credit assignment problem mentioned in the previous section?

Clark Hull (1930) believed that secondary reinforcers can bridge a delay between a response and a reinforcer. Remember that secondary reinforcers are stimuli that derive their reinforcing properties by being associated with primary reinforcers. Hence, in Wolfe's experiment, the stimuli that composed the delay box, such as its odor, shape, and color, provided immediate reinforcement through its association with the primary reinforcer.

Spence's Hypothesis

Kenneth Spence added that secondary reinforcement can still occur even when secondary reinforcers cannot readily be identified. He believed that proprioception could provide secondary reinforcement, which refers to the ability to sense the movement and location of body parts. This is rendered possible by the presence of specialized receptors called *proprioceptors* located in every muscle cell. According to Spence, the contraction of the muscles necessary for producing a response activates these proprioceptors. In turn, the activation of proprioceptors leaves a trace of the patterns of movements executed shortly before the delivery of the reinforcer. These traces become associated with the primary reinforcer and secondary reinforcers delivered as soon as the animal performs the movements (Spence, 1947). This became known as **Spence's hypothesis.**

These findings show that secondary reinforcers can bridge the gap between response and reinforcer at long delays. Secondary reinforcers can be used on purpose when delivering a primary reinforcer immediately after a response is impossible or inconvenient. The use of secondary reinforcers is well known by animal trainers and was described by Skinner (1951). The method is illustrated in Figure 11.3a. It consists of repeatedly pairing a stimulus with a primary reinforcer, such as a noise or a flash of light through classical conditioning. After several pairings, these stimuli can become effective conditioned reinforcers and reinforce desired behaviors until a primary reinforcer is delivered. In a procedure known as **clicker training** (introduced by the Brelands), the secondary reinforcer is a clicking sound produced by what is known as a box clicker. It has been used extensively ever since (Gilchrist et al., 2021; Paredes-Ramos et al., 2020).

Memory Interference

Psychologist Sam Revusky (1971) proposed that impairments in learning associations between events when a significant delay exists between them are not due to the delay itself but to other events' interference in forming these associations. Longer delays increase the probability that more interfering events will occur. The delay also increases the likelihood that chance associations between responses other than for which the animal was reinforced also increases.

The Credit Assignment Problem

Remember Kamin's memory search hypothesis, discussed in the context of the blocking phenomenon in Chapter 8, according to which when an unexpected event, such as the delivery of a US, occurs, the animal searches its memory for what has caused it. With a long delay between the response and the reinforcer, it may be difficult for an animal to identify, in its memory, which of the many behaviors it performed during the delay that was responsible for producing the reinforcer. This is known as the **credit assignment problem.** Psychologist David Lieberman and colleagues (1979) hypothesized that the credit assignment problem could be solved by making an animal's correct response "stick out" from other behaviors by associating it with a highly noticeable or salient event.

Marking

Lieberman and colleagues (1979) hypothesized that the credit assignment problem could be solved by having an animal experience a highly noticeable stimulus, such as a bright light, sound, or tactile stimulus, immediately after it performed the response that produces the reinforcer. This procedure, illustrated in Figure 11.3b, became known as **marking** because the correct response (i.e., that which directly results in the delivery of the reinforcer) is "marked" by a stimulus (i.e, a "marker stimulus") so that the animal can more easily identify it.

They tested their hypothesis (the marking hypothesis) in an experiment where two groups of rats, designated as Marked and Unmarked, were trained to enter one of two arms to obtain a food reinforcer. The marking stimulus in the Marked group consisted of being picked up by the experimenter immediately after making their choice and placed in a delay box for 1 minute. They were then placed in a goal box where they obtained the food reinforcer only if they made the correct arm choice. When the rats in the Unmarked group made their choice, they were permitted to walk through doors that led to the delay box. At the end of the 1-minute delay, they were picked up and placed in the goal box, where they were given food if they previously chose the correct arm.

The results showed that the Marked group showed more correct choices over several trials than the Unmarked group. These results indicated that the correct responses performed by the Marked group increased in salience so that it was more easily identified when they searched their memory for what produced the reinforcer. In contrast, no such increase in saliency of the correct response occurred in the Unmarked group of rats. A follow-up experiment found that a burst of white noise and a flash of light presented when the correct response was made were also effective at marking stimuli (Lieberman, McIntosh and Thomas, 1979). It was also found that a marking stimulus administered just before the response is as effective as when administered immediately after (Thomas et al., 1983).

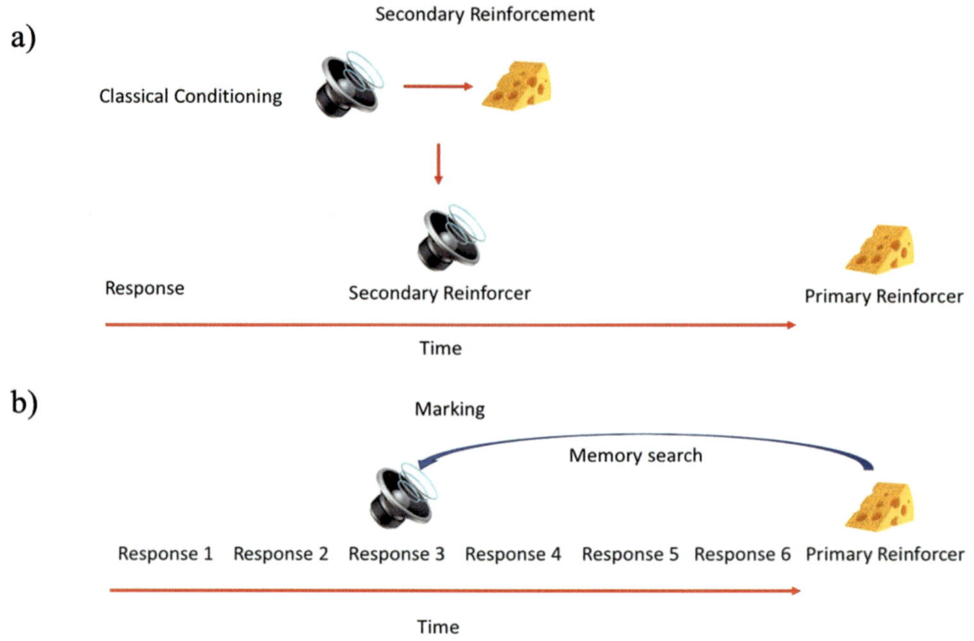

Figure 11.3 **Secondary reinforcement and marking procedures.** a) In secondary reinforcement, a neutral stimulus (e.g., a sound) acquires reinforcing properties through classical conditioning by being paired with a primary reinforcer (food). Once established, the sound becomes a secondary reinforcer that can strengthen behavior when presented immediately following a response. b) In marking, a "marker stimulus" (e.g., a sound) is presented immediately after a target response occurs, "marking" that specific response in a sequence of behaviors. This facilitates the identification of the target response during the memory search triggered by the reinforcer.

Consistent with Kamin's hypothesis, a salient event prompts a memory search for its antecedents. During the marking process, when a salient stimulus (such as being picked up, a flash of light, or sound) occurs immediately after a response, it emphasizes that response in memory. Subsequently, when the food delivery in the goal box triggers a memory search for the response that led to reinforcement, the previously marked response is more readily identified. A similar highlighting effect happens if the marking stimulus is presented just

What in the Brain?

The credit assignment problem and prefrontal cortex

The prefrontal cortex is essential for executive functions, which include planning, attention, inhibition, cognitive flexibility, and working memory. It consists of the orbitofrontal cortex and the dorsolateral prefrontal cortex (dlPFC), shown at the top left of Figure 11.4. The dlPFC is essential for working memory, which manipulates and keeps information in mind briefly. Neurons in the dlPFC are active in tasks that require working memory. In a classic experiment, monkeys were subjected to what is known as an oculomotor delayed response task while the electrical activity of neurons in their dlPFC was recorded (Goldman-Rakic, 1995). In this task, monkeys stare at a fixation point at the center of a screen. About half a second later, a visual cue appears in one of the corners of the screen and remains visible for about two seconds. The cue then disappears for a few seconds, during which the center fixation point remains visible. The monkeys are reinforced to move their eyes to the location of the screen where the cue was previously located.

Some of the monkeys' dlPFC neurons responded both when the cue first appeared and when the monkeys later responded by moving their eyes. Other neurons were active during the delay when the cue was not visible. These findings showed that the dlPFC is involved in attending to relevant environmental information and maintaining this information in working memory during a delay.

However, the dlPFC seems to have functions beyond working memory. For example, damage to the dlPFC impairs the ability to use the outcome of choices to guide future behaviors. Those properties of the dlPFC may provide neuroscientists with clues to how the brain might solve the credit assignment problem. Neuroscientist Wael Asaad and colleagues investigated this possibility by testing monkeys in the task described in Figure 11.4 while measuring the patterns of electrical activity in groups

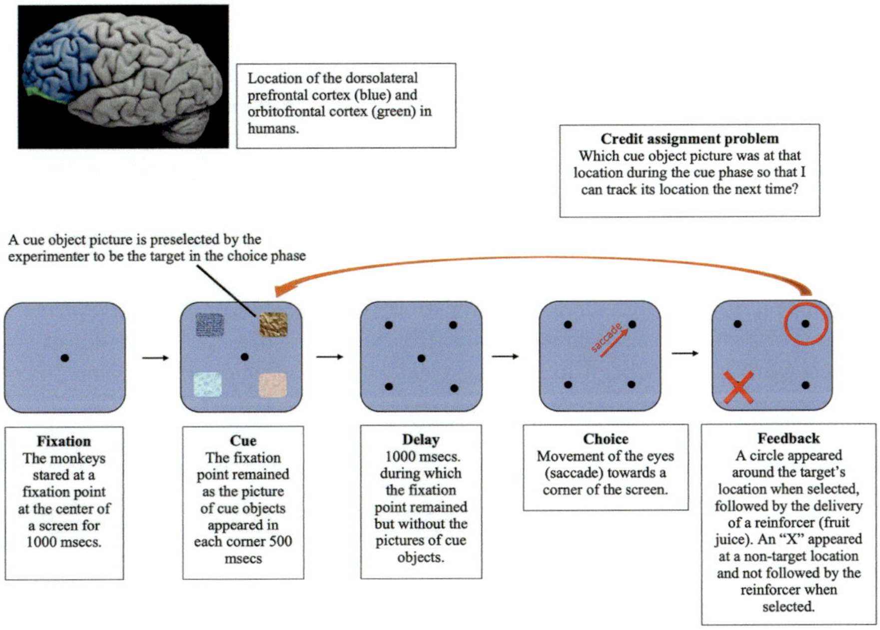

Figure 11.4 The task was used to test the dlPFC's involvement in the credit assignment problem by Assad and colleagues (2017).

Source: Brain picture (Watson, Neil V. *The Mind's Machine*. 3rd Edition). Oxford University Press Academic US, 2020 (Figure 11.20).

Rest of figure: Based on Prefrontal Neurons Encode a Solution to the Credit-Assignment Problem. Wael F. Asaad, Peter M. Lauro, János A. Perge and Emad N. Eskandar Journal of Neuroscience 19 July 2017, 37 (29) 6995–7007; doi: https://doi.org/10.1523/JNEUROSCI.3311-16.2017) (Figure 11.1).

of dlPFC neurons (Asaad et al., 2017). In this task, monkeys were required to solve the credit assignment problem by remembering the location of a target object picture they previously saw in one of the corners of a screen to subsequently move their eyes to that location when it was no longer visible to receive a reinforcer. The monkeys eventually learned to track the target object's location to move their eyes to the correct location during the choice phase during subsequent trials.

The results of the study found evidence of involvement of the dlPFC in the credit assignment problem for the following reasons:

- Neurons that represented the relevant cues fired during the feedback phase when the cues were no longer visible. They also fired simultaneously with the delivery of the reinforcer.
- The pattern of neuronal firing in the dlPFC during feedback resembled the representation of the relevant cues when they were visible during the cue phase, indicating that the identity of the correct cue was decoded.
- The pattern of neuronal firing in the dlPFC during feedback resembled the pattern activated during the presentation of the cues, mainly at the beginning of trials when learning credit assignment was most crucial.

Are You Thinking Critically?

1. Explain the logic of using a delayed oculomotor response task to test the role of the dorsolateral prefrontal cortex in solving the credit assignment problem.
2. How would you create a different task serving the same purpose?
3. What could be the consequence of damage to the prefrontal cortex in determining the behavior that led to a reinforcer?

before the response, in which case it draws attention to the upcoming response and aids its encoding. The procedure for making is illustrated in Figure 11.3b. Evidence shows that the prefrontal cortex is essential in solving credit assignment problems (see "What in the Brain?" box).

Critical Thinking Spot Check 11.3

1. Distinguish between primary and secondary reinforcement by giving an example of each.
2. Why would knowing about the credit assignment problem when raising children be important?
3. Name and describe two methods by which the credit assignment problem can be solved.
4. Explain the relationship between Kamin's memory scan hypothesis and the credit assignment problem.

Chapter Summary

Each bullet point aligns with the learning objectives outlined at the beginning of the chapter.

- Different types of reinforcers exist. Primary reinforcers such as food, water, sex, sleep, shelter, sensory stimulation, warmth, and coolness are stimuli that do not have to be learned about to be effective. Secondary reinforcers are stimuli that derive their reinforcing properties by being associated with primary reinforcers. Tokens such as coins, poker chips, fake money, and points are secondary reinforcers that can be exchanged for goods or services. Social reinforcers such as praise, affection, attention, smiles, thumbs ups, and high-fives derive their value from the behavior of other individuals in response to approved behaviors.

- Many factors affect the effectiveness of reinforcers. These factors may include the magnitude of a reinforcer, such as its quantity, intensity, or duration. The quality of the reinforcer refers to the extent to which one type of reinforcer is preferred over another.
- Another factor that influences a reinforcer's effectiveness is whether its value changes for the same behavior. This is known as incentive contrast, which includes positive incentive contrast, which occurs when an increased reinforcer magnitude results in increased rates of responding; negative incentive contrast, which occurs when a decrease in reinforcer magnitude results in decreased rates of responding; and anticipatory contrasts, in which responding to a reinforcer of low value is reduced when immediately followed by responding to a reinforcer of higher value.
- The effectiveness of a reinforcer also depends on the delay between it and a response. When too long a delay exists between a response and a reinforcer, it may be challenging to determine which of many responses was responsible for delivering the reinforcer. This is known as the credit assignment problem.
- Secondary reinforcers can bridge the gap between the response and the reinforcer, solving the credit assignment problem. Another method, marking, can make the correct response more obvious by associating it with a salient stimulus.

Glossary

Anticipatory negative contrast A reduction in responding to a current reward due to the expectation of a better reward in the future.

Clicker training A form of operant conditioning using a clicker sound as a secondary reinforcer to mark correct behaviors in animals and humans.

Contingency The relationship between a behavior and its consequences, determining whether reinforcement or punishment will occur.

Credit assignment problem The challenge in learning where an organism must determine which specific action led to reinforcement.

Incentive contrast A phenomenon where the perceived value of a reward changes based on prior experiences with different reward magnitudes.

Marking A technique in operant conditioning where a distinct stimulus is used to highlight the correct behavior, helping improve learning outcomes.

Negative incentive contrast When a reward appears less valuable after exposure to a larger, more rewarding stimulus.

Positive incentive contrast When a reward appears more valuable after experiencing a smaller, less rewarding stimulus.

Primary reinforcers Naturally rewarding stimuli that fulfill basic biological needs, such as food, water, and warmth.

Secondary reinforcers Learned reinforcers that acquire their value through association with primary reinforcers, like money or praise.

Social reinforcers Rewards that come from social interactions, such as approval, recognition, or affection, which strengthen behaviors.

Spence's hypothesis A theory suggesting that reinforcement strength depends on the difference between the expected and received reward magnitude.

Tokens Secondary reinforcers that can be exchanged for goods or services.

Token economy A reinforcement system where tokens or symbolic rewards are given for desirable behavior and can later be exchanged for meaningful reinforcers.

Module Summary

In this module, you were introduced to operant conditioning. In the first chapter, you learned that the historical roots of classical conditioning are grounded in Thorndike's rejection of Darwin's idea that the intelligence of animals and humans differs only in degree but not in kind. To prove his point, Thorndike designed experiments using puzzle boxes, showing that, unlike humans, cats and other animals do not learn to solve problems by rational decision processes, insight, or imitation of humans. Instead, the results of his experiments suggested that animals learn by trial and error, resulting in environmental stimuli becoming associated with responses that lead to desirable outcomes. This became known as stimulus-response learning (S-R). This formed the basis for the law effect, which states that behaviors that lead to desirable consequences will tend to be repeated.

In contrast, behaviors that result in undesirable consequences will not. You also learned about B.F. Skinner, who was influenced by Thorndike's law of effect and invented the free-operant procedure, in which animals learn to press a bar or peck at a key to obtain a food reward. Skinner coined the term operant conditioning because he believed that animals operate on their environments through responses that produce reinforcers that increase or decrease the probability that those responses will be repeated.

You learned that operant conditioning differs from the S-R learning proposed by Thorndike in that it involves R-O, or the association learned between a response and its outcome. In addition, Skinner explored different contingencies of reinforcement, laying the conditions under which the result of a response increased or decreased the probability of the reaction it followed. Skinner also found that reinforcing animals under different schedules led to varying patterns of responses.

In the second chapter of the module, you learned that different types of reinforcers exist. These are primary reinforcers, secondary reinforcers, tokens, and social reinforcers. You also learned that factors such as a reinforcer's magnitude and quality affect its effectiveness at increasing the probability that the response it follows will be repeated. Incentive contrast affects the effectiveness of a reinforcer through its relative value to a reinforcer already received. The effectiveness of a reinforcer also depends on the delay between the response and the delivery of the reinforcer. A reinforcer delivered after too long of a delay may be ineffective due to the credit assignment problem, which makes identifying the behavior that produced the reinforcer difficult. The credit assignment problem may be solved by secondary reinforcement and marking.

Module 5

Application

Reinforcement and Self-Monitoring: Decreasing Undesired Behaviors and Increasing Desired Behaviors

You likely engage in behaviors you wish you didn't or wish you engaged in less often. These may include overeating, nail-biting, procrastination, overspending, excessive use of social media, and smoking. You may also want to increase the frequency at which you perform other behaviors, such as the time you spend studying, exercising, paying your bills on time, and saving your money. There are many reasons people engage in undesired and unwanted behaviors. In her book entitled *The Healthy Mind Toolkit: Simple Strategies to Get Out of Your Way and Enjoy Your Life,* psychologist Alice Boyes lists and explains four reasons we do (Boyes, 2018). These are emotion payoffs, thought payoffs, physical payoffs, and situation payoffs.

- **Emotion payoffs** are reinforcers that provide immediate pleasure or relaxation. Unwanted behaviors may riddle you with guilt. However, other feelings associated with them can act as powerful. The behavior may also be maintained through negative reinforcement, for example, by alleviating the intensity of a range of negative emotions such as anxiety, anger, or loneliness.
- **Thought payoffs** refers to thoughts that serve as favorable reinforcement. For example, overspending may be reinforced by the thought that others view you as rich or generous. Thoughts can also serve as negative reinforcers in that unwanted behavior, such as spending too much time on social media can distract you from thinking about your problems.
- **Physical payoffs** are the reinforcing effects of the behavior felt within your body. For example, you experience increased energy after eating a sugary snack. The physical payoff can also be negative reinforcers, such as the decreased tension a smoker experiences after smoking a cigarette.
- **Situation payoffs** are reinforcements that perpetuate a behavior by effecting some desired change. For example, procrastination is negatively reinforced by permitting one to avoid performing what is perceived as a painful task, often in exchange for doing something pleasant, such as when one decides to go to a movie instead of studying.

According to Boyes (2018), eliminating undesired behaviors involves identifying the payoffs perpetuating them. Understanding why we engage in these behaviors makes it easier to devise alternative behaviors that provide similar payoffs but are not associated with guilt or long-term negative consequences.

DOI: 10.4324/9781003491828-21

Self-Monitoring and Reinforcement for Increasing Study Time

Self-reinforcement is an effective way to increase your time studying per week. To do this, set a goal for the hours you want to study daily and plot the hours studied on a graph. Figure 1-M5 App shows graphs drawn by a hypothetical student based on a seven-day schedule.

The student set a goal to study for two hours daily. She achieved her goal on the first day of the week and surpassed it on the following days. She rewarded herself with an activity of her choice (two hours spent on social media) every time she achieved her goal but did not engage in the activity on days her goal was not achieved. Whenever she did not reach her goal, she found the reason(s) why and made the necessary adjustments.

The graph on the right, in Figure 1-M5 App, shows the total time she spent studying the four subjects she is taking during the week. In this way, she can more easily adjust the time she spends studying each subject depending on how difficult they are or the amount of material to study.

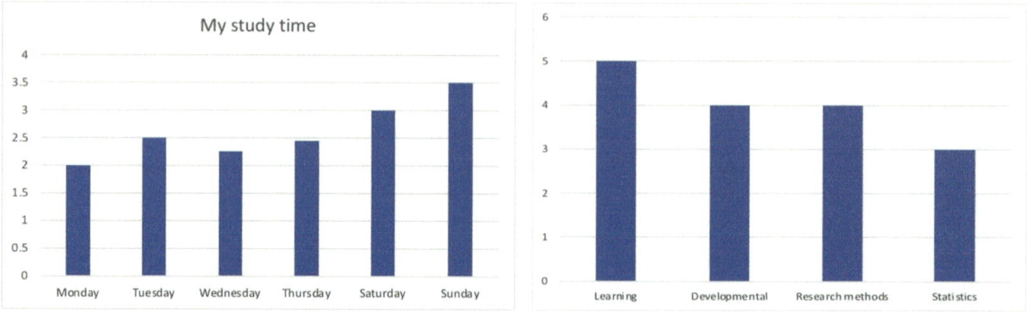

Figure 1-M5 App Graphs drawn by a hypothetical student of the number of hours spent studying each day (left) and the breakdown of the total number of hours spent researching each of the four subjects during the week (right).

Are You Thinking Critically?

1. Show your understanding of each type of payoff by distinguishing between them.
2. Describe a desired behavior that would substitute for an undesired behavior for each type of payoff.
3. Explain how self-monitoring and self-reinforcement can help you achieve your goals.
4. Create your own self-monitoring and self-reinforcement schedule to achieve a goal.

Module 6

Reinforcement and Extinction

Introduction

So far, you have learned that reinforcers are appetitive stimuli that increase the probability of the responses they follow. However, you have yet to learn about the properties of reinforcers that increase this probability. That is, what makes reinforcers reinforcing? It is precisely this question that will be addressed in Chapter 12. You will learn to think about reinforcers in different ways. For example, having the opportunity to eat following a response may be the reinforcer that increases the probability of that response rather than the food itself. In Chapter 13, you will also learn how the outcomes of their actions do not always control people's behaviors. This is apparent when certain behaviors partially performed by habit are repeated despite leading to undesirable consequences, such as what occurs in drug abuse and overeating. At the same time, many behaviors are goal directed and repeated when followed by a desirable outcome. Finally, in Chapter 14, you will learn about the effects and theories of extinction. In operant conditioning, extinction (more precisely, operant extinction) refers to a reduction in the intensity or frequency of a response when a reinforcer no longer follows it. Extinction may lead to various behavioral effects. These effects include variations in how a response is performed, frustration and aggressive behavior. You will also learn about multiple lines of evidence showing that extinction is a form of learning and not forgetting.

Chapter 12: Theories of Reinforcement
Chapter 13: The Associative Structure of Instrumental Conditioning
Chapter 14: Theories of Extinction

DOI: 10.4324/9781003491828-22

12 Theories of Reinforcement

Learning Objectives

- Analyze Paul Meehl's defense of the law of effect through the hypothetical Martian scientist analogy and its implications for understanding reinforcement laws.
- Evaluate the validity of the transsituational hypothesis proposed by Meehl about the law of effect and the limitations of testing reinforcers in similar situations.
- Examine the Premack principle's perspective on reinforcers as opportunities for high-probability responses and the importance of relative rather than absolute reinforcement terms.
- Differentiate contingent activities, instrumental activities, and the unconstrained baseline in the response deprivation hypothesis and explain how higher-probability responses can reinforce low-probability responses.
- Apply the concepts of set point and bliss point in designing a reinforcement schedule based on the deprivation of preferred activities to increase the probability of least preferred responses.

Balancing Gaming and Studying

IStock photo ID: 863476764

DOI: 10.4324/9781003491828-23

Like many of her generation, Seo-Jun's preferred activity is playing video games, closely followed by listening to music and engaging on social media. She did not spend much time watching movies or going out with friends, and certainly not enough time studying. She knew that to improve her grades, she needed to study more in proportion to her preferred activities. She also found that many of the stimuli in her study space led her to engage in more pleasant activities than studying. For example, seeing the computer screen at the desk where she usually studies prompted her to check her social media and spend hours on it. When she finally began studying, it was almost time for bed. However, things changed for Seo-Jun when she learned to allocate the time she spent on her activities in a way that increased the time she spent studying. She recorded the hours she spent playing video games in a day versus the hours she spent studying. She calculated that in one day, she spent an average of seven hours playing video games for less than one hour studying. She resolved that to have access to three hours of gaming, she would have to study for two hours. She understood that depriving herself of her preferred activity would make it a powerful reinforcer for studying. She also learned that the stimuli in her study space triggered her preferred activities by becoming associated with the pleasurable outcomes that these activities produced. She reorganized her study space so that none of these stimuli were present. Seo-Jun's newfound knowledge worked wonders for her grades, and she successfully applied the same principles to various areas of her life.

12.1 The Law of Effect Revisited

In Chapter 10, you learned about Thorndike's law of effect, which states that when responses are followed by something satisfying (or, as he put it, a satisfying state of affairs), it's more likely that the response will be repeated in the future when in a similar situation. On the other hand, if the response leads to discomfort, it will be less likely to be repeated in the future. Thorndike's law of effect served as the foundation for instrumental conditioning.

Later, learning theorists added that the probability that an animal (or a person) would perform an instrumental response, such as a cat pulling on a lever in one of Thorndike's puzzle boxes or a rat pressing a lever in a Skinner box, depended on the consequence of the response. They meant that some consequences increase the probability that an instrumental response will be made in the future, whereas others will not. Notably, they called a consequence a reinforcer only if it increased the likelihood of the response it followed.

The Circularity of the Law of Effect

Some researchers believed that learning theorists such as Skinner (1953) did not sufficiently explain the properties of reinforcers that account for their reinforcing effects (Catania, 1973; Sidman, 2006). They asserted that the definition of a reinforcer is circular because it states that the likelihood of a response increases when followed by a reinforcer and that a reinforcer increases the probability of a response. This means that a reinforcer is something that reinforces, which doesn't clarify anything. In other words, it lacks explanatory power.

The Martian Analogy

In response to the criticism that the definition of the law of effect is circular, psychologist Paul Meehl (1950) explained that, despite its circularity, the law of effect is scientifically sound and that careful observations can reveal the principles governing reinforcement. To illustrate his point, Meehl (1950) presented an analogy involving a hypothetical Martian scientist observing the behavior of a rat in a maze without any prior knowledge that food can fulfill the physiological needs of animals. Initially, the Martian notices that the rat makes right and left turns in the maze with roughly equal frequency. However, after spending time in the maze, the rat consistently turns to the right. Curious about what caused this change, the Martian looks for something to explain the rat's right turns. He discovers that various stimuli have begun to follow the right turns. One such stimulus is the presence of sunflower seeds. Through systematic experimentation, the Martian finds that the presentation of sunflower seeds significantly enhances the preference for right turns in the rats. He concludes that sunflower seeds are reinforcers.

The Transsituational Hypothesis

Meehl (1950) also introduced the **transsituational hypothesis** to define reinforcers further. This hypothesis posits that certain stimuli can reinforce behaviors across different situations. However, it has been noted that reinforcers may appear transsituational only because they are consistently tested in similar contexts, such as hungry rats pressing a bar or pigeons pecking a key for food. Additionally, the fact that animals only engage in these responses when hungry is often overlooked (Timberlake and Allison, 1974).

Criticisms of the law of effect motivated learning theorists to propose alternative theories. The **Premack principle** and the **response deprivation hypothesis** are two of these theories, which are discussed in the unit below.

Critical Thinking Spot Check 12.1

- Explain why the definition of the law of effect was seen to be circular.
- Describe Paul Meehl's Martian scientist analogy in his defense of the definition of the law of effect.
- Explain the transsituationality hypothesis and why reinforcers might only seem to be transsituational.

12.2 The Premack Principle and Response Deprivation Hypothesis

The Premack Principle

The Premack principle, also known as the differential-probability hypothesis, was proposed by psychologist David Premack (1925–2015) in the 1950s. According to Premack, reinforcers are not discrete stimuli, such as food, but the opportunity to respond to stimuli (1959). According to him, the opportunity to eat is a reinforcer, not food. Premack subdivided responses into **high-probability responses** and **low-probability responses** according to the rate at which an animal produces a response when a response is available. For example, eating is a high-probability response to a rat when food is available. However, pressing the lever is a low-probability response. He called the response rate when a response is available the **independent rate** of that response. Hence, in our example, eating when food is available is the independent rate of eating, and lever-pressing, when a lever is available, is the independent rate of lever pressing.

According to the Premack principle, the opportunity to perform a high-probability response reinforces the performance of a low-probability response. Thus, eating, a high-probability response, can reinforce lever pressing, a low-probability response. Premack referred to the low-probability response, which must be performed to gain the opportunity to engage in the high-probability response as the **instrumental response**, also referred to as the instrumental activity (which, in our example, is lever pressing). He designated the high-probability response, which reinforces the instrumental response, as the **contingent response**, also called the contingent activity (which, in our example, is the opportunity to eat).

A well-known human example of the Premack principle in action is exemplified by "grandma's rule," which states, "First eat your vegetables; then you can have dessert." Eating vegetables (especially for a child) is a low-probability response, while eating dessert is a high-probability response. Therefore, the opportunity to eat dessert can reinforce eating vegetables. In the case of Seo-Jun, from the opening vignette, she applied the Premack principle to regulate her gaming behavior (a high-probability response [contingent]) to reinforce studying (a low-probability response [instrumental]).

The Premack principle showed that reinforcers must be defined in relative rather than absolute terms. This is because, contrary to what is proposed by the transsituational hypothesis described in the previous section, the opportunity to respond may be reinforcing in one situation but not in another. To show this, Premack suggested that if the independent rates of several responses could be determined in advance, the response could be ranked from being of high-probability response to low-probability. Then, their ability to reinforce each other could be determined by varying the contingencies (how one response reinforces another) between pairs.

For example, consider three different responses: A, B, and C. A has the highest probability, B has a lower probability, and C has a lower probability than B. Which of these responses can serve as a reinforcer for another? The answer is that A (highest probability) can reinforce B and C, both lower probability responses. B can reinforce C, which is of lower probability than B, but B cannot reinforce A, which is of higher probability.

A concrete example of this is shown in Figure 12.1, where the responses of (A) gaming, (B) writing, and (C) doing the laundry are ranked in order from high to low probability.

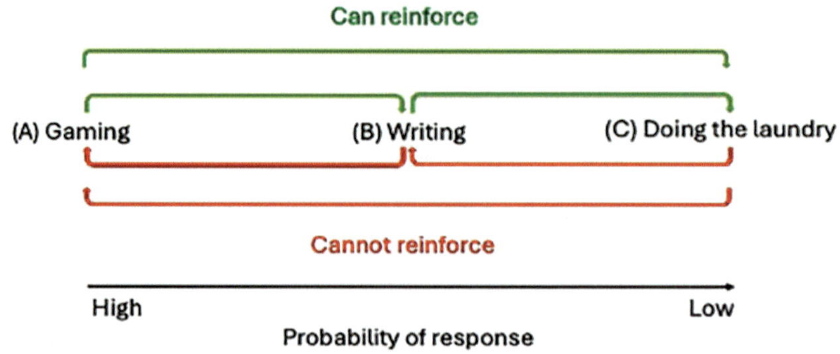

Figure 12.1 Illustration of the Premack principle. Because it is the highest-probability response, A can reinforce both B and C. Because it is of intermediate probability, B can reinforce C but cannot reinforce A. Because it is of the lowest probability, C cannot reinforce A or B.

You can see that B can both be and not be a reinforcer, depending on whether it follows response A or C. Think about how you can use the Premack principle to regulate your behavior. Remember, "first this, then that."

Reversibility of the Reinforcer Relation

Remember that Premack believed that reinforcers had relative but not absolute value and that high-probability responses could reinforce low-probability responses but not vice versa. Hence, Premack (1962) hypothesized that conditions could be set up in the laboratory so that the experimenter could control the probabilities of engaging in one response versus another. Premack tested his hypothesis by doing just that. In the first part of an experiment, he purposely allowed rats less access to food than wheel running. This turned the high-probability response of eating into a low-probability response and wheel running into a high-probability response. The results supported his hypothesis: the rats engaged in a significant amount of eating to obtain the opportunity to run in the wheel.

The Response-Deprivation Hypothesis

Psychologist William Timberlake (1942–2019) proposed what is known as the response deprivation hypothesis, which states that, in nature, an equilibrium exists between an animal's contingent responses (or activities) and instrumental responses (or activities) (1980). You should be familiar with these two terms after reading the previous section on the Premack principle. To recap, contingent activities are behaviors an animal tries to gain access to. In the example given, the contingent response was eating. However, animals and people engage in a wide range of contingent responses; these include drinking, receiving attention, sexual intercourse, and playing with toys. Instrumental responses are behaviors by which animals gain access to contingent responses. In the example, the instrumental response was pressing a lever for the opportunity to eat. As for contingent responses, animals and people perform various instrumental responses, including yelling to receive attention and performing courtship behaviors for the chance to mate. In the case of Seo-Jun, in the opening vignette, the contingent response was playing video games, and studying was the instrumental activity that gave her access to video games.

The equilibrium between contingent and instrumental responses can be measured when an animal's activities are performed without restrictions and simultaneously available. This period is known as the **unconstrained baseline**, or what Premack called an independent response rate. For example, Seo-Jun's unconstrained baseline was seven hours of gaming for every hour of studying daily.

In their response deprivation hypothesis, Timberlake and Allison (1974) proposed that the schedules of reinforcement employed in an operant conditioning experiment increase the rate of a low-probability response (e.g., pressing a lever, the instrumental response) because the demands of the schedules deprive the animal of performing a high-probability response at levels that match its **unconstrained baseline** (this is the "response deprivation" from which the hypothesis gets its name). It used to eat the amount of food it wanted without having to produce an instrumental response, but now it must do work to receive a limited amount of it at a time. Thus, an animal's performance (instrumental responding) under a schedule of reinforcement reflects an animal's regulatory efforts to restore this equilibrium, that is, trying to eat as much food as it did before being put on a schedule (Timberlake and

Allison, 1974). For Seo-Jun, the time spent studying she imposed on herself prevented her from playing video games at their unconstrained baseline level.

Evidence for the Response Deprivation Hypothesis

The results of several studies supported the response deprivation hypothesis. In one of these studies (Eisenberger, Karpman and Trattner, 1967), participants (college students) were first allowed to turn a wheel or press a bar. They were also instructed to engage in both behaviors simultaneously or do nothing (unconstrained baseline or operant period). They were then divided into two groups: High and Low bar pressers. Both groups were then exposed to a contingency period, in which the wheel was locked but could be unlocked for 10 seconds with a single bar press. Pressing the bar 30 times unlocked the wheel for five minutes. The results of the experiment were that the Low bar pressers significantly increased their rate of bar pressing in the contingency period (during which they had to bar press to earn the opportunity to turn the wheel) compared to their rate of bar pressing during the operant period (during which they could bar press at will). This supported the Premack principle, which states that the opportunity to engage in a high-probability response (in this experiment, the wheel turning) reinforces the performance of a low-probability response (in this experiment, the bar pressing).

In a second experiment, the experimenters wanted to see if depriving the participants of the low-probability response (bar pressing) would reverse the first experiment's results. Could the low-probability response (bar pressing) now be used to reinforce the high-probability response (wheel turning)? In the operant period, the participants were told to turn the wheel several times before performing a bar press. This resulted in a deprivation of the opportunity to bar press. Remember that bar pressing is the low-probability response. In the contingency period, the participants had to execute ten turns of the wheel to earn a single bar press. This resulted in most participants executing more wheel turns in the contingency period than in the operant period.

In another study (Allison and Timberlake, 1974), rats were first allowed to alternately drink from a drinking tube (by licking it) containing a 4% sucrose solution and another containing a 3% sucrose solution (operant period). The time the rats spent licking both tubes was recorded. As you can guess, the rats spent less time licking the 3% drinking tube than the 4%. Hence, licking the 3% drinking tube was the lower-probability response and licking the 4% drinking tube was the higher-probability response.

During the contingency period, the rats were then required to lick the 4% drinking tube for 80 seconds to have the opportunity to lick the 3% drinking tube for 10 seconds. This schedule established the deprivation from licking the 3% drinking tube. The results were that the rats significantly increased the amount of time they licked the 4% compared to the time they spent licking it during the operant period.

The results of these experiments are in line with the predictions made by the response deprivation hypothesis. They showed that a low-probability response can reinforce a high-probability response, providing the deprivation of the low-probability response.

Behavior Allocation and the Response Deprivation Hypothesis

Life is full of behavioral choices. As shown in Figure 12.2, students perform various activities during a typical day. Since there are only 24 hours in one day, time must be allocated to each of these behaviors. The **behavior allocation approach** states that the time spent

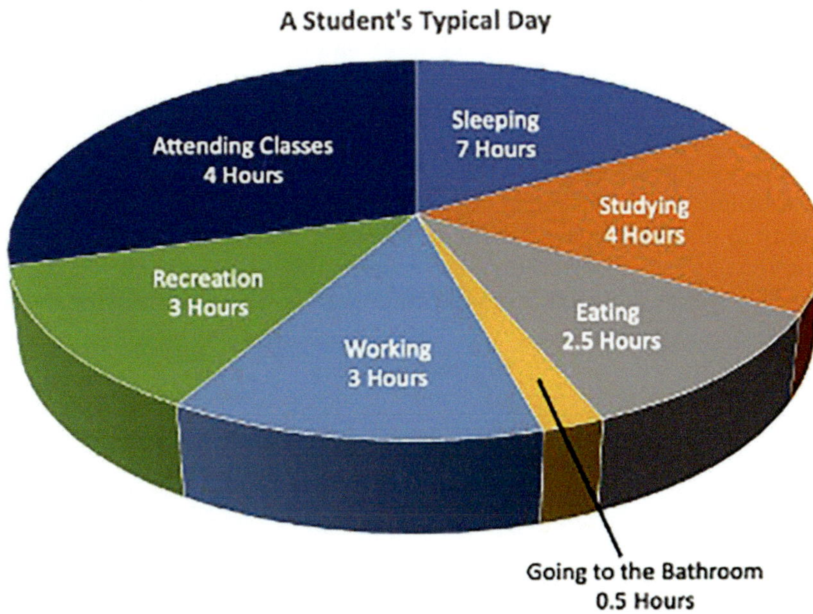

Figure 12.2 Pie chart showing how time could be allocated to various behaviors in a typical day.

performing one activity comes at the expense of the time that could be spent performing another. Put another way, the time we allocate to one activity is constrained by the time spent performing another.

With your recently acquired understanding of the response deprivation hypothesis and what you just learned about behavior allocation, you should better understand how Seo-Jun, in the opening vignette, got her video game playing time under control so that she could spend more time studying. From a behavior allocation standpoint, Seo-Jun's problem was that the number of hours she allocated to playing video games came at the expense of being unable to study for a suitable number of hours.

She solved her problem by employing the response deprivation approach. That is, she trained herself to spend a certain number of hours playing video games, a high-probability response (contingent), only after she spent a certain number of hours studying, a low-probability response (instrumental). Hence, she deprived herself of video game playing to its unconstrained baseline. This motivated her to study a greater number of hours because it was the only way to approach her unconstrained baseline of gaming.

It is not always the case that a person wants to modify her behavior, as Seo-Jun did in the opening vignette. Sometimes, people want to alter the behaviors of others. For example, imagine that this time, a parent wants to increase her child's motivation to spend more time studying relative to the time she spends gaming. Figure 12.3a shows that the child spends about six hours playing video games for every three hours studying (what the child does). Also shown is the **bliss point** (or unconstrained baseline [green dot]), which is the time ratio spent performing the instrumental and contingent responses. The time spent performing each activity when unconstrained is known as that activity's **set point**. Figure 12.3 shows that six hours is the set point for the child's video game playing time (O_i), and three hours is the child's set point for studying (O_C). The child's bliss point is represented by the ratio O_i/O_C, which is the number of hours spent studying divided by the number of hours spent playing video games. Hence, the child's bliss point is $O_i/O_C = 3/6 = .5$.

The parent's goal is to make a video game playing the contingent response to studying (an instrumental response). According to the response deprivation hypothesis, this goal can be achieved by constraining the amount of time the child spends playing video games by imposing on her a schedule of reinforcement in which three hours of studying are required to have the opportunity to play video games for two hours. This schedule of reinforcement is represented by the red dot in Figure 12.3b. What is known as a **schedule line** can also be seen in Figure 12.3b. The schedule line indicates the number of hours spent studying the child would

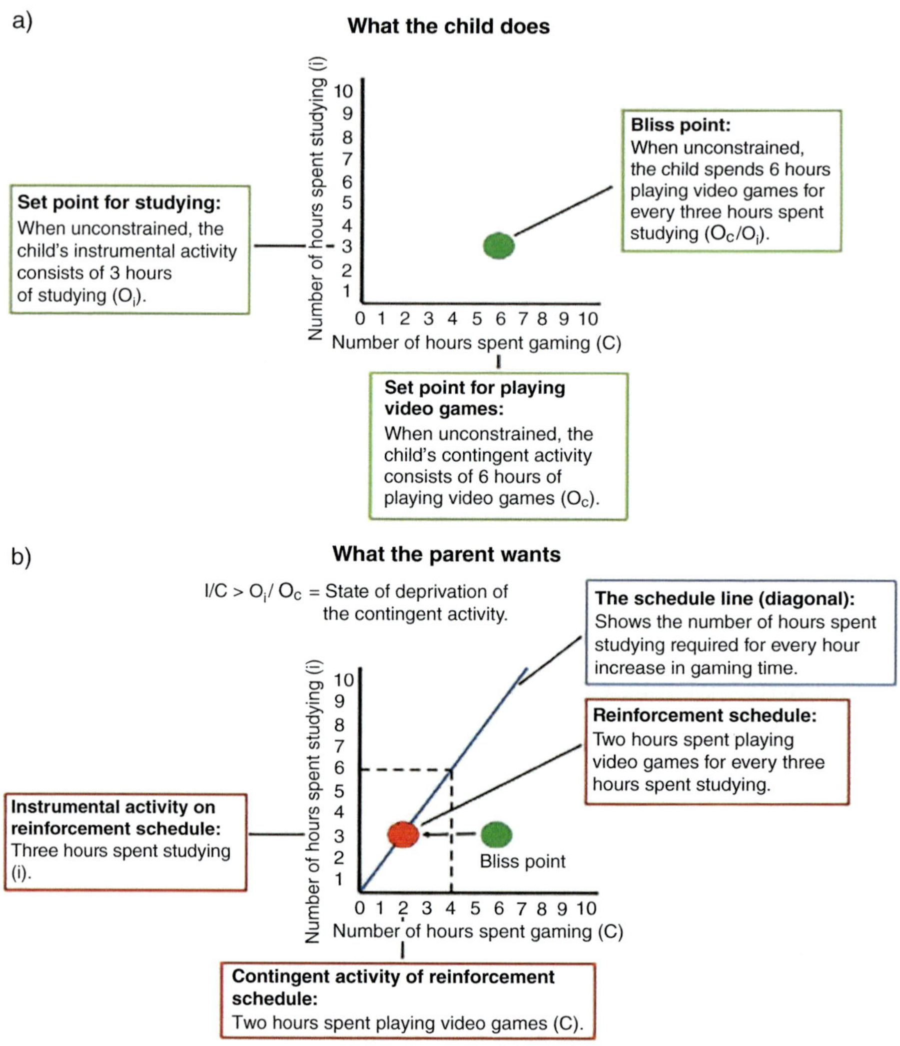

Figure 12.3 a) The time a child spends studying and playing video games when unconstrained (set points), as well as the child's bliss point (green dot). b) The reinforcement schedule imposed by the parent (red dot). See text for details.

have to perform to have the opportunity to play video games for various amounts of time. For example, to be allowed to play video games for four hours, you would have to spend six hours studying, eight hours studying to play video games for six hours, and so on.

Response deprivation occurs when an imposed ratio of instrumental activity (I) to contingent activity (C) or (I/C) exceeds the ratio of unconstrained instrumental responses to unconstrained contingent responses, which is the bliss point represented by the ratio Oi/OC described previously. A state of response deprivation occurs when the ratio of instrumental activity to contingent activity is greater than the ratio of the set points for the same activities or when $I / C > O_i / O_C$.

The simple calculations subsequently show that this would be the case if the parent succeeded in implementing the intended schedule:

I / C ratio
3 hours of studying (I)/2 hours of video game playing (C) = 1.5
O_i / $O_C$ratio
3 hours spent studying (O_i)/6 hours of video game playing (O_C) = 0.5
$I / C > O_i / O_C$

Focus On

Self-Determination Theory: Intrinsic Motivation

Self-determination theory proposes that people have a greater sense of well-being when they feel competent to meet life's challenges, feel in control of their fate, and connect with others. Another component of the theory proposes that behavior can be extrinsically or intrinsically motivated. Extrinsically motivated behaviors are activities performed for external rewards such as money, grades, praise, or approval. Intrinsically motivated activities are performed for the sense of enjoyment, exploration, and interest inherent to the activity.

Controlled and Autonomous Motivation

In extrinsic motivation, the delivery of rewards is controlled by others. For example, getting a paycheck at the end of the week depends on the company you work for, the grade you get for writing a paper comes from your professor, the praise you receive for cleaning up your room comes from your parents, and the approval you receive for choosing to apply to university may come from family and friends. According to the theory, activities performed to obtain extrinsic rewards are said to be externally controlled.

In contrast, it is possible that you find your job enjoyable, that studying provides you with a satisfying sense of exploration and discovery, that you feel accomplished when cleaning up your room, or that applying to university gives you a sense of confidence and direction. In these cases, your behaviors would be intrinsically motivated and said to be autonomously controlled. The theory states that people derive greater well-being when performing autonomously controlled activities.

Undermining Intrinsic Motivation

There is evidence that receiving an external reward for an intrinsically motivated activity may reduce the value of the rewards provided by the activity itself. This is known as the overjustification effect (Lepper, Greene and Nisbett, 1973). For example, if you enjoy painting for the calm and serenity it gives you, you might enjoy it less if asked to paint for money. Reasons for this effect may be the perceived loss of control over the activity, feeling bribed, or the pressure derived from having to please the one(s) providing the reward. The overjustification effect may also explain why some professional athletes reduce their performances once they net a big contract. In this case, their dwindling performance may also be due to the feeling that continued efforts to perform well no longer matter. However, more recent research shows that motivation for an intrinsically motivated task may not occur if an external reward is given at the initiation of the task rather than at task completion (Woolley and Fishbach, 2018). The reason may be that getting a reward at the beginning of a task increases interest and the amount of enjoyment derived from performing it. Hence, whether extrinsic rewards undermine intrinsic motivation may be a question of timing.

The Self-Determination Continuum

As mentioned, intrinsic motivation is generally related to greater well-being than extrinsic motivation. However, some conditions under which extrinsically motivated activities can provide a sense of well-being, provided that others approve the activity, are valued and are ones to which the person performing it can identify. This is despite the lack of intrinsic motivation for the activity. For example, you may not be intrinsically motivated at your work. However, you may still derive a sense of well-being from it if you recognize how valuable your job is, if people tell you how good you are at it, or if you feel your work is congruent or fits well with who you are.

Are You Thinking Critically?

1. Distinguish between extrinsic and intrinsic motivation.
2. How can someone's intrinsic motivation for an activity be undermined?
3. How would you help someone not intrinsically motivated by their work derive a sense of well-being from performing it?

Critical Thinking Spot Check 12.2

1. How does the Premack principle provide a distinct perspective on the nature of reinforcers?
2. Provide an example for contingent and instrumental activities and explain how they differ.
3. What constitutes an unconstrained baseline, and why must it be considered in behavioral analysis?
4. Compare and contrast the Premack principle and the response deprivation hypothesis, highlighting their key differences and similarities.
5. Explain how the behavior allocation approach can be combined with the response deprivation hypothesis to modify behavior.

Chapter Summary

Each bullet point aligns directly with the learning objectives outlined at the beginning of the chapter.

- Some learning theorists circularly defined reinforcers by stating that the probability of a response is increased when followed by a reinforcer and that a reinforcer increases the probability of a response. Psychologist Paul Meehl explained that, despite its circularity, the definition of the law of effect was scientifically sound and that careful observations could derive the laws governing reinforcement. To make his point, Meehl (1950) presented the analogy of a hypothetical Martian scientist observing the behavior of a rat in a maze.
- In further defense of the law of effect, Meehl proposed the transsituational hypothesis, which is the idea that certain stimuli can reinforce behaviors across situations, which he believed underscored the value and usefulness of the law of effect. However, reinforcers may have only seemed transsituational because they were constantly tested in similar situations, ignoring that animals only perform operant responses when hungry.
- The Premack principle, also known as the differential probability hypothesis, proposes that reinforcers are not discrete objects but opportunities to perform high-probability responses. According to this principle, reinforcers must be viewed in relative rather than absolute terms.
- Contingent activities are those which an animal tries to gain access to. Instrumental activities are those by which an animal gains access to contingent activities. The unconstrained baseline consists of a period during which these activities are performed without restrictions. According to the response deprivation hypothesis, schedules of reinforcement deprive the animal of engaging in these activities at their unconstrained baseline level. In this way, a low-probability response, such as bar pressing, can reinforce a higher-probability response, such as eating when deprived of bar pressing.
- The time spent performing contingent and instrumental activities performed by an animal when unconstrained is known as the set point, and the combined time spent performing contingent and instrumental activities when unconstrained is known as the bliss point. Knowledge of the set point and bliss point can be used to set up a schedule of reinforcement in which a state of deprivation of the preferred activity can be used to increase the probability of a least preferred response.

Glossary

Behavior allocation approach A model explaining how individuals distribute behaviors to maximize reinforcement while minimizing effort.

Bliss point The optimal distribution of behaviors that an individual would engage in freely, without external constraints or reinforcements.

Contingent response A behavior that occurs as a direct result of reinforcement or punishment conditions.

High-probability responses Behaviors that an individual is more likely to perform naturally due to preference or habit.

Independent In learning theory, a term referring to responses or events that occur without direct influence from another variable.

Instrumental response A behavior performed to produce a specific consequence or outcome, as seen in operant conditioning.

Low-probability responses Behaviors that are less preferred and occur infrequently but can be reinforced through association with high-probability behaviors.

Premack principle A theory stating that high-probability behaviors (preferred activities) can reinforce low-probability behaviors (less preferred activities).

Response deprivation hypothesis A model suggesting that when access to a normally frequent behavior is restricted, the opportunity to perform that behavior becomes more reinforcing.

Schedule line A graphical representation of how reinforcement contingencies shape behavior under different schedules.

Set point A theoretical balance point for a behavior or physiological state, which an organism strives to maintain.

Transsituational hypothesis The idea that a reinforcer in one situation will also function as a reinforcer in other situations, regardless of context.

Unconstrained baseline The natural frequency of behavior when no restrictions or reinforcement schedules are applied.

13 How Does It Come Together? The Associative Structure of Instrumental Conditioning

Learning Objectives

- Explain the concepts of S-R and R-O learning.
- Compare and contrast the habit system (S-R learning) and goal-directed system (R-O learning) within the dual systems model of instrumental learning, emphasizing their changing influence with extensive training.
- Evaluate the importance of balancing S-R and R-O learning for adaptive behavior, distinguishing between repetitive tasks and thoughtful, goal-directed actions.
- Analyze the process of S-O learning and its impact on R-O responding, including the influence of classical conditioning and emotional responses as motivators, as evidenced in Pavlovian-instrumental transfer experiments.
- Describe Skinner's concept of S-R-O learning within the three-term contingency framework, emphasizing the role of discriminative stimuli in signaling when a response will be reinforced.

Massamba Gets a Lesson in Learning

Source: IStock photo ID:1356750609

DOI: 10.4324/9781003491828-24

Massamba is a marketing director for a major corporation. His job requires him to provide solutions to problems daily. Fortunately, many of the issues he must solve tend to recur, so over the years, he learned which solutions he proposes will result in the best outcomes. His friend Olivia recently decided to return to school to complete a degree in psychology. Her favorite course is "Learning." One day, Massamba told her that when asked to solve a problem, he would come up with the correct solution every time. Olivia, who had just finished a class on instrumental conditioning, exclaimed, "This makes me think of response-outcome learning, also known as R-O learning!" "What was that?" replied Massamba. Olivia explained that she learned that responses that lead to desirable outcomes tend to be repeated. "Not only that, the fact that recurring problems lead you to propose the same solution makes me think of stimulus-response-outcome learning or S-R-O learning." "Stop it," he answered, "you're confusing me."

"It's simple," she replied, "The problem you are asked to solve serves as a stimulus for you to propose a specific solution." The next day, Olivia invited Massamba for dinner at her house. When he got there, he explained to her that her neighborhood was still a little new to him and that he got worried on his way there because he forgot his cell phone, so he couldn't use its Global Positioning System (GPS) receiver function to guide him to her house. He explained that he still made it there because different landmarks directed him to turn right or left as if it were automatic. "That's stimulus-response learning or S-R learning. You have been here enough times for it to have kicked in," she answered. Massamba let out a loud sigh and told Olivia, "I think you are getting carried away with your learning course," as they went on to enjoy their dinner.

13.1 What Is Instrumental Conditioning?

As mentioned in Chapter 10, the term instrumental conditioning is often used interchangeably with operant conditioning. In this chapter, you will learn that instrumental conditioning is a more inclusive concept linking three elements. These elements are the stimuli present when a response occurs (the stimulus context), the behavioral response, and the outcome of the response. These elements form what is known as *the associative structure of instrumental conditioning*. As shown in Figure 13.1, four types of relationships, or associations, emerge between these elements:

1. Between the stimulus context and the response (S-R or habit learning).
2. Between the response and the outcome (R-O or operant conditioning).
3. Between the stimulus context and the outcome (S-O or classical conditioning).
4. Between stimulus context and the relationship between the response and the outcome (S-R-O or occasion setting).

In the following sections, you will learn about the types of learning that result from each of these associations.

S-R Learning (stimulus-response) or habit learning

Recall Thorndike's cats from Chapter 9. When initially placed in a puzzle box, they exhibited frantic behavior, which Thorndike characterized as instinctual escape responses. However, over successive trials, the cats' actions became less random. Only a subset of their behaviors triggered the mechanism that opened the door, granting them access to the food outside the box. Thorndike proposed that the behaviors leading to the door opening were "stamped in," while those that did not were "stamped out." For Thorndike, the food accessed by the cats

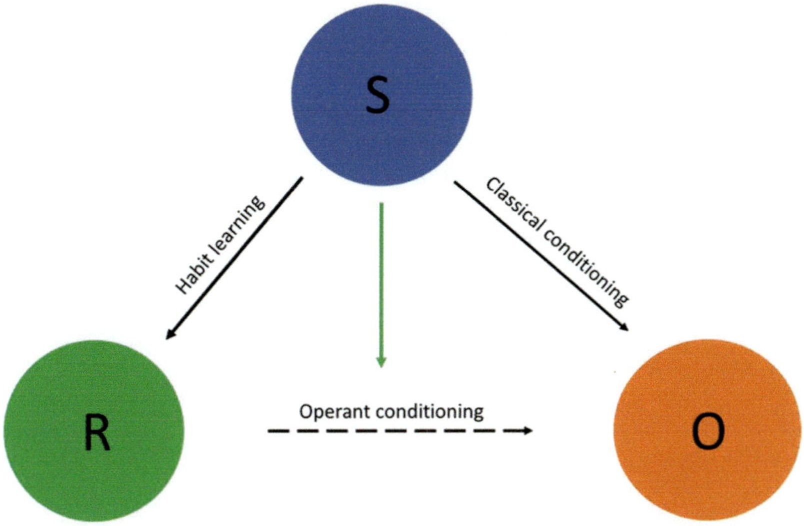

Figure 13.1 Associations between stimulus context (S), response (R), and outcome (O).

due to their actions reinforced the association between the stimuli in the puzzle-box environment and the behavioral response to open the door. However, it was not part of this association. He believed that after several trials, exposure to the box's environment automatically elicited the cats' responses, rendering the outcome irrelevant in maintaining these responses. Thorndike referred to S-R learning as **habit learning**, as illustrated in Figure 13.1.

Habits are acquired gradually. However, once ingrained, behaviors that form habits are not the product of thoughtful reflection but are elicited by environmental stimuli that have repeatedly been paired with a response. This is known as **direct context cueing** (Neal, Wood and Quinn, 2006), which is consistent with what is known as the **mechanistic model of behavioral control** (Dickinson, 1985).

Habits permit people to act quickly and automatically in situations where the same response to a stimulus has repeatedly been required to achieve a particular outcome. People perform many behaviors by habit. It was found that habits account for up to 45% of our behavioral repertoire (Wood, Quinn and Kashy, 2002). Habits are important because they free up cognitive resources for thoughtful activities such as decision-making and planning for the future. Think of all the behaviors you perform by habit, from those you routinely perform upon waking to automatically turning left or right in the corridor after exiting a classroom. This kind of learning permitted Massamba, in the chapter's opening vignette, to find his way to Olivia's even though he forgot his GPS. However, note that excessive S-R or responding by habit can also be maladaptive (see this chapter's "What in the Brain?" box).

In one study, researchers found that eating habits developed through their association with contextual cues despite one's attitude toward food (Neal et al., 2011). In that study, researchers gave college students popcorn before they entered a movie theatre, where they were shown previews of upcoming movies. Unbeknownst to them, the participants received either fresh or stale popcorn. The fresh popcorn was popped one hour before the experiment, whereas the stale popcorn was popped seven days before. After the viewing, the participants were asked to rate their liking of the popcorn and the frequency at which they ate it in the movie theatre on a seven-point scale. The latter result was the basis for separating the participants into three groups: low, moderate, or high-habit popcorn eaters. Another group of participants was treated similarly, except that they viewed clips of music videos in a meeting room.

They found that, in the cinema context, the participants in all three groups gave higher ratings to the fresh popcorn than to the stale popcorn. The amount of popcorn the participants ate in each of these contexts is shown in Figure 13.2. Participants in the low and moderate-habit groups ate significantly more popcorn when fresh than when it was stale. However, the participants in the high-habit group ate about the same amount of popcorn regardless of whether it was fresh or stale. In the meeting room context, the three groups' participants ate more fresh than stale popcorn. These results indicate that habitual responses towards food can be elicited regardless of one's preference or attitude towards the food when consumed in a context associated with eating in the past.

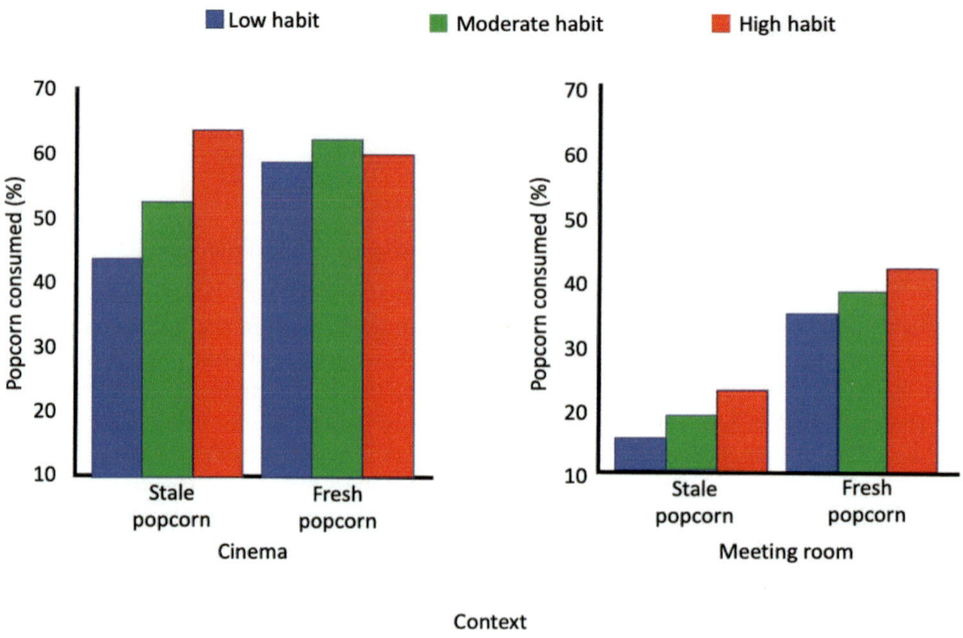

Figure 13.2 High-habit participants ate stale popcorn at similar rates to fresh popcorn when in their habitual context (cinema), but strongly preferred fresh popcorn in a novel context (meeting room). Low- and moderate-habit participants preferred fresh popcorn in both contexts, showing less context-dependent eating behavior (Neal et al., 2011).

R-O Learning (Operant Conditioning)

Thorndike's idea that the outcome of a behavior is irrelevant to the maintenance of the behavior might have been surprising to you. After all, many of our behaviors are goal directed, with the expectation that they will result in a particular outcome. For example, studying (response) for an exam is usually expected to result in a good grade (outcome). Massamba's responses to problems in the vignette were reinforced by their positive outcomes, and he learned to expect those outcomes. This is consistent with what is known as the **teleological model of behavioral control** (Dickinson, 1985).

Evidence for R-O learning (or operant conditioning), in which responses were associated with a particular outcome, was found in what are known as *outcome devaluation experiments*. For example, rats could press a lever or pull a chain to receive food in one study. The food associated with one of the behaviors was devalued by giving the rats an injection that made them sick after consuming it. They found that the rats later avoided pressing the lever or pulling the chain when these responses were associated with the devalued food (Colwill and Rescorla, 1985). In another study, rats learned to push a rod to the left to obtain food pellets and to push the same lever to the right to receive a starchy mixture. Then, either the food pellets or starchy mixture was devalued by giving the rats free access to them. The rats then avoided pushing the lever in the direction associated with the devalued food (Dickinson et al., 1996).

Remember that the outcome might only strengthen the association between the stimulus and the response in S-R learning. Once this association is sufficiently strengthened, the outcome no longer influences behavior. Hence, devaluing the outcome should not affect the rats' response. Thus, the results of these studies demonstrated the rats' capacity for R-O learning. If they had only learned an S-R association between the stimuli and the response, they would have had difficulty withholding their responses after the outcome had been devalued. See this chapter's "What in the Brain?" box for such an outcome devaluation experiment with humans.

What in the Brain?

Dissociation Between S-R and R-O Learning in the Brain

Evidence shows that the brain contains a stimulus-response system (S-R) and a response-outcome system (R-O). The S-R system includes a neuronal pathway between the posterior putamen and the premotor cortex, and the R-O system consists of a neuronal pathway between the caudate nucleus and the ventromedial prefrontal cortex (Balleine and O'Doherty, 2010) (Figure 13.3).

Adaptive behavior depends on a balance between S-R- and R-O-driven responses. Excessive S-R responding is associated with maladaptive behaviors such as those observed in obsessive-compulsive disorder (OCD) (Gillan et al., 2011) and substance use disorder (Everitt, Dickinson and Robbins, 2001). Psychologist Sanne de Wit and colleagues (2012) investigated whether people's amount of connectivity in these systems related to the extent to which they were engaged in S-R or R-O responding. They did so by first measuring the amount of connectivity between the areas of the S-R and R-O systems in the brains of university students using a form of magnetic resonance imaging (MRI) called diffusion tensor imaging (DTI).

They then assessed the university students on tasks that measured how they responded by habit (S-R) or goal-directed (R-O) behavior. In the first part of the

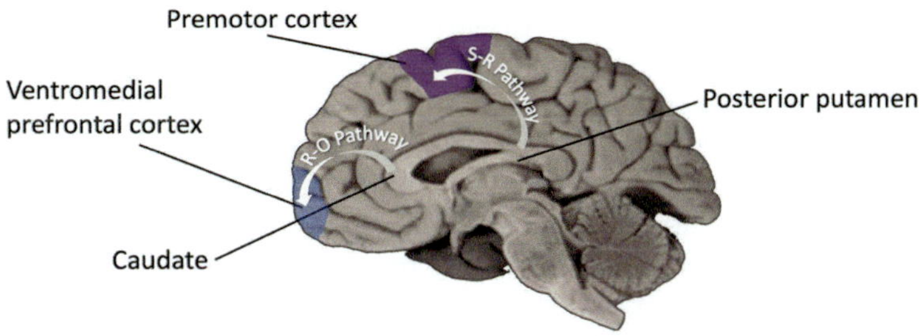

Figure 13.3 There is evidence that the brain contains a stimulus-response system (S-R) and a response-outcome system (R-O).

Source: Modified from Breedlove, S. M. (2015). *Principles of psychology*. Sunderland, MA: Sinauer Associates/Oxford University Press, Figure 3.17b.

experiment, the participants were subjected to an instrumental task in which they were to learn, by trial and error, which picture of fruit outside a box (stimulus), shown on a computer screen, signaled which of a left or right key press was rewarded by a picture of fruit inside the box and a card indicating that they earned course credits, versus the picture of an empty box with a picture of a card indicating that no course credits were earned (outcome) (Figure 13.4a). The participants were subjected to three discrimination trials: standard, congruent, and incongruent. These trials differed in the extent to which the stimulus and outcome they contained could be confounded (Figure 13.4b).

Discrimination Trial Types

Standard: One fruit served as the stimulus, and another served as the outcome (e.g., if the stimulus picture is of grapes, press the right key to receive an orange + credits (outcome); if the stimulus picture is of bananas, press the left key to receive a pineapple + credits (outcome).

Congruent: The stimulus fruit was always the same as the outcome (e.g., if the stimulus picture is of a strawberry, press the right key to receive a strawberry + credits (outcome); if the stimulus picture is of a coconut, press the left key to receive a coconut + credits (outcome).

Incongruent: Each fruit served as a stimulus and outcome for opposite responses (e.g., if the stimulus picture is of cherries, press the right key to receive a pear + credits (outcome); if the stimulus picture is of a pear, press the left key to receive cherries + credits (outcome).

It was found that the participants chose the wrong key press more often in the incongruent condition than in either the standard or congruent condition, indicating that they preferentially engaged in S-R responding. The participants were then subjected to a slips-of-action test (Figure 13.4c). The slip-of-action test was designed to assess the extent to which participants showed S-R or R-O learning to obtain the outcome. This was achieved by devaluating the outcome of a subset of responses they performed in the previous experiment. S-R learning was assumed to be if participants had difficulty withholding their responses to stimuli, which was associated with a devalued outcome. R-O learning was assumed if a participant could withhold responding to a stimulus associated with a devalued outcome. The participants were subjected to the same discrimination conditions as the previous experiment.

A superimposed red X indicated the subset of devalued outcomes. The test's success was measured by the subjects' ability to withhold responding to a stimulus that signaled devalued outcomes (the "no-go" trial) and respond to a stimulus that signaled a non-devalued outcome (the "go trials"), indicating R-O learning.

A difference score was calculated for each participant by subtracting the number of responses during the "no-go" trials from the number of responses during the "go" trials. This meant that their difference scores increased with the frequency at which the participants successfully used an R-O strategy to withhold responses to devalued outcomes. The difference scores were compared to those obtained in a control condition (baseline) in which the outcome was not devalued.

As illustrated in panel d of Figure 13.4, the two systems make contrasting predictions: an R-O goal-directed system should enable participants to withhold responses when outcomes are devalued (high difference scores), while an S-R habit system should produce automatic responding regardless of outcome value (low difference scores). The participants' difference scores in the standard and congruent conditions were not significantly different from those in the control condition, indicating successful R-O learning in these conditions.

However, the study's main findings, shown in panels e and f, revealed a significant correlation between the difference scores and the amount of connectivity in the participants' R-O and S-R brain systems. The higher the difference score, the

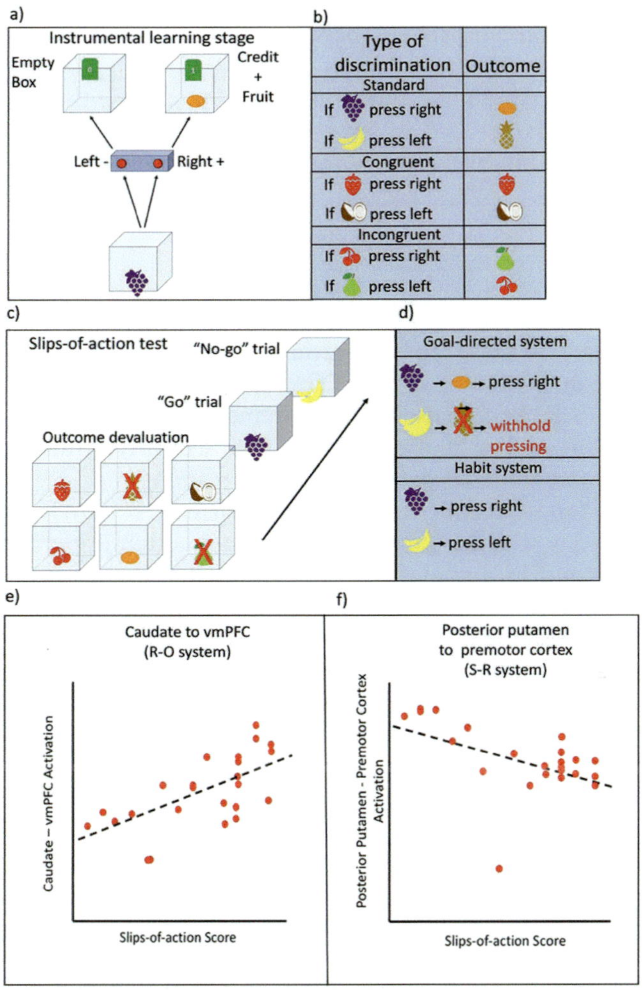

Figure 13.4 Illustration of the de Wit and colleagues (2012) study. a) The instrumental learning stage. b) The types of discrimination. c) The slips of action test. d) Responses expected when driven by an R-O goal-directed system and an S-R habit system. e) Correlation between the amount of connectivity in the R-O system and difference scores (a higher score indicates better performance). f) Correlation between the amount of connectivity in the S-R system and difference scores (a higher score indicates better performance). See text for details.

Source: Modified from de Wit, S., Watson, P., Harsay, H. A., Cohen, M. X., van de Vijver, I., & Ridderinkhof, K. R. (2012). Corticostriatal connectivity underlies individual differences in the balance between habitual and goal-directed action control. *J Neurosci, 32*(35), 12066–12075. https://doi.org/10.1523/jneurosci.1088-13.2012.

higher the connectivity in the R-O system (Figure 13.4e). Conversely, the higher the connectivity in the S-R system, the lower the difference scores (Figure 13.4f). These results indicated that some individuals tend to perform S-R or habit-driven responses even in situations where R-O-driven or goal-directed actions may be more appropriate.

Are You Thinking Critically?

1. Distinguish between the connectivity between the brain areas involved in S-R learning and those engaged in R-O learning.
2. What assumptions permitted de Wit et al. (2012) to choose the slips-of-action test to test their hypothesis?
3. What are the practical implications of the study by de Wit et al. (2012)?

S-R and R-O Learning?

Animals and people exhibit both S-R and R-O learning. In fact, it was found that the brain contains a system for each of these types of learning (see this chapter's "What in the Brain?" box). According to the dual systems model (Dickinson, 1985), instrumental learning develops through the habit (S-R) and goal-directed systems (R-O) simultaneously. However, the influence of the goal-directed system diminishes with extensive training. In contrast, the influence of the habit system increases with extensive training.

However, it is important to balance both types of learning. It is often adaptive to respond by habit (S-R) in everyday mundane tasks. Still, it is also often important to inhibit habitual responses and respond in a goal-directed fashion (R-O) when thoughtful actions are required.

A lack of balance between the influence of these systems can lead to maladaptive behaviors such as those observed in some psychological disorders (see this chapter's "What in the Brain?" box). Impairments in response inhibition that result in excessive S-R responding are also found in people with brain damage, such as those who have Parkinson's disease (Manza et al., 2017).

S-O (Classical Conditioning) and S-R-O (the Three-Term Contingency)

In the previous section, you learned that, in S-R learning, environmental stimuli elicit responses to which they were repeatedly associated. Remember also that Thorndike believed that the outcome strengthened the association between the stimulus and the response but that it was not part of the association. Nevertheless, the outcome occurs in the presence of the same environmental stimuli that elicit the response. Hence, it would be reasonable for an association to develop between these stimuli and the outcome, with a subset of the stimuli becoming CSs that predict the outcome (US) through classical conditioning.

Skinner proposed that the stimuli present when a response produces an outcome become discriminative stimuli that predict whether performing a specific response in the presence of such discriminative stimuli will lead to reinforcer or punishment. For this reason, Skinner also called such discriminative stimuli *occasion setters* because they set the occasion for when a response will produce a specific outcome (Skinner, 1938). For example, a worker might learn to ask (response) to leave work early only when her boss looks like she is in a good mood (discriminative stimulus), which is likely to be met with a positive response (outcome). Skinner named the association between stimulus, response, and outcome (S-R-O) the *three-term contingency*.

Critical Thinking Spot Check 13.1

1. What are the four types of relationships (associations) between stimulus, response, and outcome in operant conditioning, as illustrated in Figure 13.1?
2. How does the concept of S-R learning, as exemplified by Thorndike's experiments with cats, contribute to the development of habits, and what is the significance of habits in daily life?
3. Provide examples of situations where S-R learning (stimulus-response) and R-O learning (response-outcome) are evident in human behavior. How do these types of learning influence daily actions and decision-making?
4. Explain the dual systems model of instrumental learning (S-R and R-O systems) and discuss the potential consequences of an imbalance between these systems. How might imbalances contribute to maladaptive behaviors or psychological disorders?
5. In what ways can S-O learning (stimulus-outcome) influence instrumental responding, considering the conditioned association between stimuli and outcomes? How might this type of learning impact goal-directed behaviors and decision-making in various contexts?

13.2 Two-Process Theories of Instrumental Responding

According to what are known as **two-process theories**, instrumental responding is influenced by both S-R learning and classical conditioning. In the 1930s, Harold Schlosberg (1904–1964) differentiated between two processes in rats confronted with an aversive situation (US). The first process was the pairing of environmental stimuli (CS) that composed the context in which the aversive situation occurred (US). The second process was the emotional and attentional conditioned reactions (CR) elicited by the CS to prepare the animal to deal with the US (Schlosberg, 1937).

Psychologists Clark Hull (1930) and Kenneth Spence (1956) proposed that the context (CS) in which an event (US) occurred elicited *internal drives* such as hunger or thirst (CR). For example, in the case of an appetitive outcome, such as food (US), the context in which it repeatedly occurred (CS) elicited hunger that pushed organisms towards it. Spence (1956) believed that exposure to the context energized responses towards the outcome not only because of internal drives but through its reinforcing properties, which acquired *incentive value*.

In the 1960s, psychologists Robert Rescorla and Richard Solomon (1918–1995) proposed what became known as the **two-process theory of instrumental conditioning,** in which: 1) repeated pairings of the stimulus context (S) with the outcome elicit an emotionally conditioned response, and 2) the emotional response acts as a motivator that influences operant responding (Rescorla and Solomon, 1967). This may explain how Seo-Jun was compelled to engage in her preferred activities instead of studying when in her study space.

Pavlovian-Instrumental Transfer

The effects of an S-O association on instrumental conditioning can be tested in a procedure known as **Pavlovian-instrumental transfer.** This test of the two-process theory of instrumental conditioning is thus Pavlovian-instrumental transfer. Three different paradigms of the

Pavlovian-instrumental transfer procedure have been developed for animals: the single lever paradigm, the specific transfer paradigm, and the general transfer paradigm. As shown in Figure 13.5, all three paradigms involve three phases: Pavlovian training (classical conditioning), instrumental training (operant conditioning), and a transfer test.

The Single Lever Paradigm

In Phase 1 of the single lever paradigm (Pavlovian training) (Figure 13.5a), an animal learns to associate a CS^{+}, such as a tone, to the delivery of dry food and a CS^{-}, such as a burst of white noise, to the absence of dry food. In Phase 2 (instrumental training), the animal is trained in an instrumental conditioning procedure, such as learning to press a lever to obtain the dry food without the CSs (sounds) of Phase 1. In Phase 3 (transfer test), the animal is allowed to press a bar to obtain the food in the presence of the tone (CS^{+}) and the burst of white noise (CS^{-}). Lever pressing is usually enhanced in the presence of the CS^{+}, which was associated with food in Phase 1, but not in the presence of the CS^{-}, which was not associated with food. Because the animal only learns to respond on one lever during Phase 2, this procedure is known as the single lever paradigm.

Specific Transfer Paradigm

Although the single lever paradigm is effective at producing Pavlovian instrumental transfer, it does not tell researchers if the CS associated with the outcome in Phase 1 elicited a motivational state that specifically enhanced responding for the same outcome during the test phase, known as specific transfer.

Testing whether a specific transfer occurred requires the specific transfer paradigm. An example of this paradigm is illustrated in Figure 13.5b. In Phase 1, two different CS^{+}s are associated with a different outcome: a tone (CS^{+}_{1}) is associated with receiving dry food, and a burst of white noise (CS^{+}_{2}) is associated with receiving wet food. In Phase 2, the animal is trained to press a bar illuminated by a green light when dry food is the outcome and illuminated with a red light when wet food is the outcome. In Phase 3, the *transfer test*, the animal is only exposed to the lever illuminated by the green light, which was associated with the dry food outcome in Phase 2. The animal's instrumental responses are recorded in the presence of CS^{+}_{1}, associated with the dry food in Phase 1, and CS^{+}_{2}, associated with the wet food in Phase 1. Evidence for specific transfer is obtained if the animal's responses to the lever illuminated by the green light are enhanced in the presence of CS^{+}_{1} but not in the presence of CS^{+}_{2}.

General Transfer Paradigm

General transfer occurs when a CS enhances instrumental responding even if it was never associated with the response outcome. Evidence for both specific and general transfer can be obtained using a third version of the paradigm, illustrated in Figure 13.5c. In this version, three CSs, for example, a tone (CS^{+}_{1}), a burst of white noise (CS^{+}_{2}), and a clicking sound (CS^{+}_{3}), are each associated with a different outcome, for example, dry food, wet food, and sucrose pellets, respectively. In Phase 2, the animal is trained to press a bar illuminated by a green light when dry food is the outcome and illuminated with a red light when wet food is the outcome. In Phase 3, the animal is only exposed to the lever illuminated by the green light, which was associated with the dry food outcome in Phase 2. The animal's responses on the lever are recorded in the presence of each of the CSs associated with food in Phase 1. CS^{+}_{1} was associated with dry food, CS^{+}_{2} was associated with wet food, and CS^{+}_{3} was associated with sucrose pellets.

The results show that responding to the lever illuminated with a green light was only enhanced when responding occurred in the presence of CS^+_1 but not in the presence of CS^+_2. This is an example of specific transfer. This happened because responding to the lever illuminated by the green light was associated with the same outcome as CS^+_1 in Phase 1. In contrast, CS^+_2 was associated with a different outcome in Phase 1, related to pressing the lever illuminated by the red light in Phase 2.

However, CS^+_3 enhanced responses to the lever illuminated by the green light even if it was paired with an outcome (sucrose pellets) in Phase 1 for which the animals never learned to perform an instrumental response in Phase 2, an example of general transfer. This means that a CS, in this case through its association with something as appetitive as sucrose pellets, can enhance instrumental responding for an outcome to which it was never associated.

The results obtained from these paradigms are consistent with the idea that CSs associated with an outcome elicit an emotional state that can enhance instrumental responding in their presence (Rescorla and Solomon, 1967). Another interpretation is that the CS elicits a preparatory, appetitive, or consummatory response that enhances instrumental responding (Dickinson and Balleine, 2002). It was also suggested that the enhancement of instrumental responding occurs through eliciting specific or general motivational states. For example, it was found that a CS associated with sugar enhanced instrumental responding in either thirsty or hungry rats, an example of general transfer. However, a CS associated with food only enhanced instrumental response when rats were hungry (Dickinson and Dawson, 1987).

Pavlovian-instrumental transfer learning is essential in guiding our behaviors towards appropriate actions in everyday life. For example, you may have a job where your boss rewards you for your efforts with large amounts of praise (instrumental conditioning), which

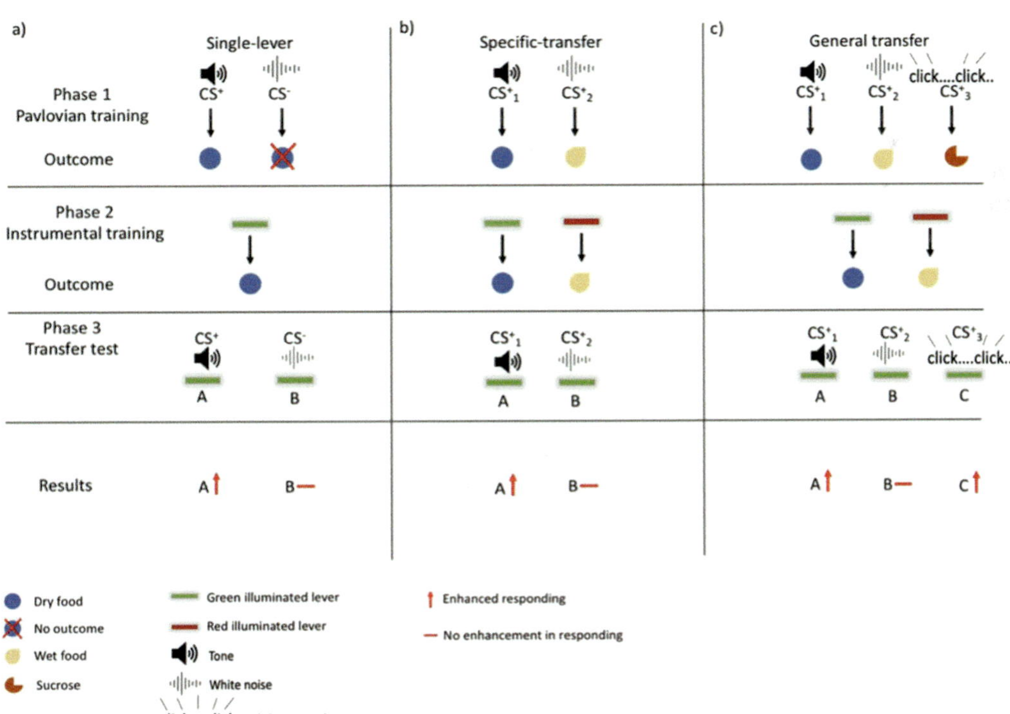

Figure 13.5 Pavlovian-instrumental transfer paradigms. See text for details.

has been associated with your workplace (classical conditioning). Hence, walking into your workplace elicits a positive, conditioned emotional response that energizes your work efforts.

Pavlovian-instrumental transfer learning also has important implications for the development and maintenance of substance use disorder and other addictions, as well as for understanding the factors related to relapse in people recovering from these disorders. For example, exposure to environmental cues that have been associated with drugs can create intense cravings in the drug-addicted individual, which in turn engages in more vigorous drug-seeking and intake behavior (Creswell and Skrzynski, 2021; Perry et al., 2014). People struggling to control their weight may have difficulty resisting food-related cues, leading to overeating (Deweese et al., 2021; Schag et al., 2013). Exposure to gambling-related cues may precipitate bouts of gambling in pathological gamblers (Vizcaino et al., 2013). You may recognize this as a component of the incentive salience theory discussed in Chapter 6.

Critical Thinking Spot Check 13.2

1. According to two-process theories, what are the two processes that Harold Schlosberg identified in rats when confronted with an aversive situation? Briefly explain each process.
2. How did psychologists Clark Hull and Kenneth Spence contribute to the two-process theory, particularly about the context and internal drives? How did Spence propose that exposure to the context energizes responses toward the outcome?
3. Explain the Pavlovian-instrumental transfer procedure and its three paradigms (single lever, specific transfer, general transfer). How do these paradigms test the influence of stimuli on instrumental conditioning? Provide a real-life example where Pavlovian-instrumental transfer might occur.
4. Evaluate the results obtained from the specific transfer paradigm and general transfer paradigm. How do these results support the idea that conditioned stimuli associated with an outcome elicit emotional states or enhance instrumental responding? Discuss the potential implications of these findings.
5. Consider the practical implications of Pavlovian-instrumental transfer learning in everyday life. Provide examples where this learning might influence behaviors, such as in the workplace or the development and maintenance of substance use disorders. How might understanding Pavlovian-instrumental transfer contribute to interventions or treatments for such behaviors?

Chapter Summary

Each bullet point aligns with the learning objectives outlined at the beginning of the chapter.

- In S-R learning, also known as habit learning, a response is eventually performed without the influence of the outcome. The response comes to be elicited by contextual cues. This is known as context cueing and is consistent with the mechanistic model of behavioral control. R-O learning is goal directed; hence, the outcome is essential. Hence, R-O learning is consistent with the teleological model of behavioral control.
- The dual systems model proposes that instrumental learning develops through both a habit system (S-R) and a goal-directed system (R-O) simultaneously. However, the influence of the goal-directed system diminishes with extensive training, whereas the influence of the habit system increases with extensive training.

- Adaptive behavior requires a balance between S-R and R-O learning. S-R learning involves adaptive, repetitive tasks, whereas R-O learning requires thoughtful, goal-directed actions.
- In S-O learning, the contextual stimuli present when a response is performed become a CS that predicts the outcome of the response, which consists of the US. According to the two-process theory, R-O responding is influenced by both S-R learning and classical conditioning. It was also proposed that repeated pairings of the stimuli that compose the context with the outcome of the response elicit an emotional response that acts as a motivator for the response. This idea has been tested and confirmed in a type of experiment known as Pavlovian-instrumental transfer.
- Skinner proposed that the environmental stimuli present when an animal learns the association between a response and its outcome serve as discriminative stimuli that specifies the occasion for when a response will be reinforced (S-R-O learning). The relationships between the stimuli, response, and outcome is known as the three-term contingency.

Glossary

Direct context cueing The process by which environmental cues directly trigger learned behaviors without requiring conscious thought.

Habit learning A form of learning where behaviors become automatic and less dependent on external rewards or conscious decision-making.

Mechanistic model of behavioral control A theory suggesting that behavior is governed by automatic processes, such as stimulus-response associations, rather than cognitive reasoning.

Pavlovian-instrumental transfer A phenomenon where a conditioned stimulus (learned through classical conditioning) influences an operant (instrumental) response, often enhancing or modulating the behavior.

Teleological model of behavioral control A perspective on learning that emphasizes goal-directed behavior based on expectations and cognitive processing.

Two-process theories Theories proposing that learning involves both Pavlovian (classical conditioning) and operant (instrumental conditioning) mechanisms.

Two-process theory of instrumental conditioning A theory proposing that learning involves two steps: first, the repeated pairing of a stimulus context (S) with an outcome produces a conditioned emotional response, and second, this emotional response motivates and influences the organism's operant behavior.

14 Exploring the Dynamics of Extinction

Learning Objectives

- Explain operant extinction's role in exposure therapy and behavior modification.
- Analyze the significance of extinction burst, extinction-induced response variability, and extinction-induced aggression in behavior modification.
- Compare resistance to extinction under partial reinforcement with continuous reinforcement, considering the discrimination hypothesis, Capaldi's sequential theory, and the frustration hypothesis.
- Evaluate the evidence supporting the non-erasure theory of extinction using phenomena such as spontaneous recovery, renewal, reinstatement, and resurgence in behavior modification.

Cameron's Addiction

Source: IStock photo ID:961900320

DOI: 10.4324/9781003491828-25

Cameron got his first taste of alcohol when he was seven years old when one of his dad's friends let him sip from his glass of wine at a family gathering. Growing up in a small town lacking community resources, he and his friends often drank in a park. When he turned eighteen, Cameron joined his older brother in going to bars, where he first tried cocaine, which he went on using in conjunction with alcohol. He eventually found a job and moved out of his parents' house into an apartment. Cameron was soon confronted with a multitude of problems, including having trouble paying the rent due to spending much of his money on drugs. Cameron eventually realized that he had hit rock bottom and decided to enter a drug rehabilitation program, which included exposure therapy. Part of the therapy consisted of a therapist driving him down the streets where many of the bars in which he drank and consumed cocaine were located. The purpose of these drives was to expose him to the cues he associated with drugs so that the cravings induced by them would eventually undergo extinction. Initially, the drives induced intense cravings, but these became progressively less intense on subsequent drives. Coming out of the program, Cameron felt he had conquered his addictions and began thinking he could "just have a drink" at social occasions. This led him to go back to the bars in which he used to drink and take cocaine. One night, he even did a little bit of cocaine at a party. Unsurprisingly, Cameron suffered a relapse. This made him realize that remaining sober would require him to make significant changes to his environment, away from the temptations that he felt were about to retake control of his life. He moved to a neighboring town where he landed a good-paying job, resumed the drug rehabilitation program he was in, and has remained sober ever since.

14.1 What Is Extinction?

Operant Extinction

As briefly discussed in the context of classical conditioning in Chapter 5, extinction refers to the process by which the frequency or intensity of a CR diminishes with repeated exposures to the CS without the US. For Cameron, in the opening vignette, the places in which he used to drink and consume cocaine became powerful CSs that induced irresistible cravings as CRs. However, the extinction of conditioned responses is not limited to those acquired through classical conditioning but also to those acquired through operant conditioning. In what is known as **operant extinction**, a decrease in the frequency of an operant response occurs when it is no longer reinforced. This phenomenon was accidentally observed by Skinner (1956), who recounts that, from time to time, the food magazine mechanism he had invented for his operant chambers jammed, resulting in the rats' lever presses no longer being reinforced.

Operant extinction has since been demonstrated in many studies with various reinforcers. In one study, rats were trained to press one of two levers to obtain intravenous infusions of nicotine (active lever). Pressing the other lever was of no consequence (inactive lever). Once the response was acquired, the experimenters discontinued the delivery of nicotine when the active lever was pressed. As shown in Figure 14.1, the number of responses performed by the rats across extinction sessions was reduced to the point that they nearly matched the number of responses performed on the inactive lever (Liu, 2016).

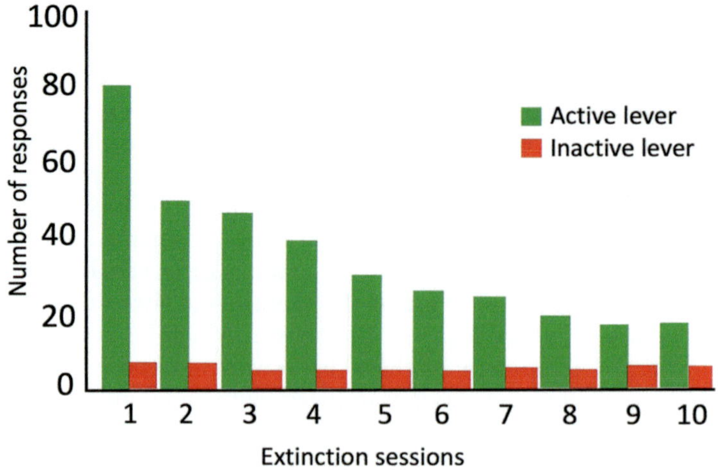

Figure 14.1 Results from the Liu (2016) experiment in which rats that learned to press a lever for nicotine infusions were given extinction trials (see text for details).

Theories of Extinction

Several theories of extinction have been proposed. Pavlov (1927) believed that continued presentations of the CS lead to a buildup of fatigue in neural cells. During extinction trials, he thought this fatigue buildup led to response inhibition. However, he believed that fatigue did not lead to such inhibition during acquisition because the association between the CS and the reinforcer counteracted it.

According to another theory, extinction trials may also lead to inhibition by reducing the amount of attention to the CS when it is no longer followed by the US (Robbins, 1990). It is also believed that extinction occurs because animals learn that the outcome of their behavior is ineffective during extinction trials (Kehoe and White, 2002).

Neurophysiologist Jerzy Konorski (1903–1973) proposed that animals learn that food no longer follows the CS during extinction. He believed this to represent the learning of a new CS-US association that competes with the original association in which the CS was paired with food (Konorski, 1948). Note that this is very different than saying that extinction trials result in memory erasure. Evidence for the idea that extinction is a form of new learning is evidenced by the response recovery effects discussed below.

The Effects of Extinction

As you read in the application box for Module 3, extinction forms the basis of exposure therapy for people suffering from psychopathologies such as post-traumatic stress disorder (PTSD) and phobia. Extinction also forms the basis of behavioral modification programs used in applied behavior analysis for children in which unwanted behaviors have been accidentally reinforced (see Chapter 1 to review the goals of applied behavior analysis). For example, a child may have learned she gets her mother's attention by throwing her toys. Although the mother does not intend to reinforce the child's behavior, it is reinforced by the attention given to the child when she throws her toys.

In another example, a child throws a tantrum when his father asks him to make his bed. When the tantrum occurs, the father punishes the child by sending him to a corner of the room where he must remain for some time. Meanwhile, the father makes the child's bed himself.

In the first example, the child's behavior is maintained through positive reinforcement, whereas in the second case, the behavior is maintained through negative reinforcement. The solution for the parent in the first example is that she ignore the child when she throws her toys. In the second example, the parent should insist that the child makes his bed despite the tantrums. Because the children's unwanted behaviors go unreinforced, they will likely undergo extinction, and the parents will likely observe a gradual decrease in their children's undesirable behaviors.

EXTINCTION BURST

In the examples given previously, it is possible that the intensity and frequency of the children's unwanted behavior will temporarily increase at the beginning of the extinction process, that is, more toy-throwing and more intense tantrums. This phenomenon is known as **extinction burst**, which can be defined as a temporary and immediate increase in the frequency or intensity of a response following the onset of extinction. You can imagine that extinction bursts are problematic because they may make parents more likely to "give in" to a child's unwanted behavior. However, parents must know that this is a normal part of the process. They must learn that the increased unwanted behavior is only temporary, and they must "stay the course."

Extinction bursts have been demonstrated in laboratory experiments with both animals (Pushparaj et al., 2012; Skinner, 1938; Ward, Walker and Dykstra, 2007) and people (Alessandri and Lattal, 2021). Figure 14.2 shows the typical response pattern, which includes reinforced trials (i.e., pre-extinction-level responses), extinction bursts, extinction, and spontaneous recovery. However, it is important to note that the factors that give rise to extinction bursts are not fully understood and that several laboratory experiments have failed

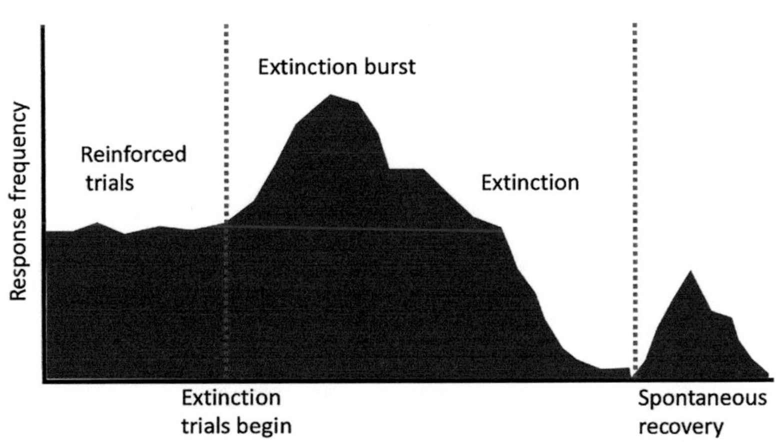

Figure 14.2 The behavioral changes induced by extinction (see text for details).

to demonstrate them consistently (Katz and Lattal, 2020; Lattal, Kuroda and Cook, 2020; Nist and Shahan, 2021).

Extinction-Induced Response Variability

As you already learned, a reinforcer increases the probability of the response it follows. This led some researchers to believe that operant conditioning procedures inevitably lead to the performance of repetitive, identical responses as well as a lack of behavioral flexibility and creativity. However, the results of several studies have shown that this assumption is not entirely correct. It was demonstrated that both animals and people can learn to produce a variety of responses if the response requirement to be reinforced varies from trial to trial or needs to differ from responses performed in previous trials (Neuringer and Jensen, 2010; Ross and Neuringer, 2002).

Interestingly, response variability was also shown to increase during extinction. For example, imagine that pressing the power button on your laptop, a behavior you have performed countless times, does not result in the usual outcome of turning on. Before giving up on it, you may think it might be out of charge, plug it into an electrical outlet, and press the power button again. If this does not solve the problem, you might repeatedly press the button and may even apply more pressure to it than usual. You might then check whether the charging cable is damaged, and so on. This is known as **extinction-induced response variability**, which can be defined as an increase in the variability of a response following the onset of extinction.

This effect was demonstrated by an experiment in which rats received the reinforcer to perform a sequence of three responses (Morgan and Lee, 1996). This included pressing the left or right lever on one chamber wall and a response key on the opposing wall. However, the requirement to receive the reinforcer was to vary the sequence in which they performed these responses from trial to trial. For example, if a rat received a reinforcer for pressing the right lever twice before pressing the response key once (RRK) during one trial, it only received the reinforcer on the subsequent trial if it performed a different sequence of responses (e.g., LRK).

Another group of rats received the reinforcer for performing a sequence of three responses but were not required to vary the sequence in which they did so. As expected, the group of rats that received the reinforcer for varying their responses showed a significantly greater amount of variability in their responses than the rats whose variety of responses was not reinforced. Both groups of rats were then subjected to extinction trials, meaning they no longer received the reinforcer for performing the sequence of responses. As expected, a decrease in the response rate for both groups of rats was observed. However, both groups showed an increase in the extent to which their sequence of responses varied.

Interestingly, applied behavior analysts can use extinction-induced variability to increase the frequency of socially appropriate behaviors in children. For example, studies have shown that if the frequency of socially inappropriate behaviors to gain access to a reinforcer such as toys is higher than that of socially appropriate behaviors, the socially inappropriate behaviors can first be put under extinction. Then, the greater variability of responses that emerges during early extinction trials may include a variety of socially appropriate responses that can subsequently be reinforced (Cengher, Ramazon and Strohmeier, 2020; Grow et al., 2008).

Parents can use extinction-induced response variability to elicit socially acceptable behaviors in children.

Source: Istockphoto I.D. 639403466.

EXTINCTION-INDUCED AGGRESSION

In addition to extinction bursts and extinction-induced response variability, extinction can also induce frustration. The frustration induced by extinction may, in turn, lead to aggressive behavior. For example, imagine that your next-door neighbor often plays loud music while you are trying to study. When this happens, you get him to turn his music down by gently knocking on the wall your apartment shares with his. However, one day, your neighbor has friends over for a party and ignores your knocks. As your frustration builds, your knocks get progressively louder, becoming loud thumps executed with the side of your fists. This is an example of **extinction-induced aggression**, defined as aggressive behavior following the onset of extinction.

Extinction-induced aggression has been demonstrated in several studies. In a classic study, Azrin, Hutchinson and Hake (1966) trained pigeons, referred to as the experimental pigeons, to peck a response key located on one side of a Skinner-box-type apparatus to obtain food. Another pigeon, the target, was restrained in a box on the opposite side of the apparatus. The experimental pigeons were subjected to alternating reinforced trials and extinction trials. The experimenters wanted to determine whether the experimental pigeons would attack the target during extinction trials. They found that shortly after the onset of extinction, the experimental pigeons pecked at the key at a higher rate than usual, which is characteristic of an extinction burst, as described earlier. However, this was followed by periods during which the experimental pigeons walked over to the target pigeon and attacked it by pecking at its throat and head around the eyes and pulling out its feathers.

Extinction-induced aggression was also found in experiments with human participants. For example, in one study (Kelly and Hake, 1970), participants were trained to pull a knob to get the opportunity to put a coin through a slot located on the front of a machine, resulting in the delivery of a monetary reward. The reinforced trials were followed by extinction trials, during which putting a coin in the slot did not result in the delivery of the reinforcer. During the experiment, the machine emitted an annoying tone. The participants were told that the tone could be avoided or terminated by pressing a button on the machine or punching a cushion beside the machine. Punching the cushion was considered more aggressive than simply pressing a button. The experimenters hypothesized that if extinction leads to aggressive behavior, the participants would punch the cushion more often than push the button during extinction trials. This is precisely what happened.

What in the Brain?

Extinction

Extinction refers to the decrease in the intensity or frequency of a conditioned response (CR) due to the repeated presentation of a conditioned stimulus (CS). For instance, repeated exposure to a CS, such as a tone, associated with an aversive unconditioned stimulus (US), such as a shock, ultimately diminishes the intensity of the conditioned fear response (CFR) triggered by the tone. However, extinction is not the sole means by which a decline in the intensity or frequency of a conditioned response can occur. One of these alternative methods is known as the overexpectation effect.

The Overexpectation Effect

When individual CSs are presented together as a compound, animals expect the intensity of the associated US to increase proportionally. For example, if two CSs have each been conditioned to predict the same US, then presenting them together should theoretically signal a US of doubled intensity. However, in the overexpectation procedure, this expectation is violated because the compound CS is paired with a US of the same intensity as the one previously associated with each CS. In other words, animals overexpect the intensity of the US—twice the CS is assumed to produce twice the US. When this does not happen, the mismatch between expectation and reality may lead animals to adjust their expectations. This adjustment is often reflected in a reduced CR to the individual CSs that make up the compound. To reconcile the fact that the US does not summate as anticipated, animals may scale down their CRs to the individual CSs accordingly. Figure 14.3 illustrates and describes the overexpectation procedure.

Brain Areas Involved in Extinction and the Overexpectation Effect

Neuroscientists have investigated the brain areas involved in extinction and the overexpectation effect (Figure 14.4) through various methods.

They have found that the infralimbic cortex, an area of the ventromedial prefrontal cortex, is important for the extinction of conditioned fear responses (CFRs). However, the question remains whether the infralimbic cortex is also important for reducing the intensity of CFRs observed in the overexpectation procedure.

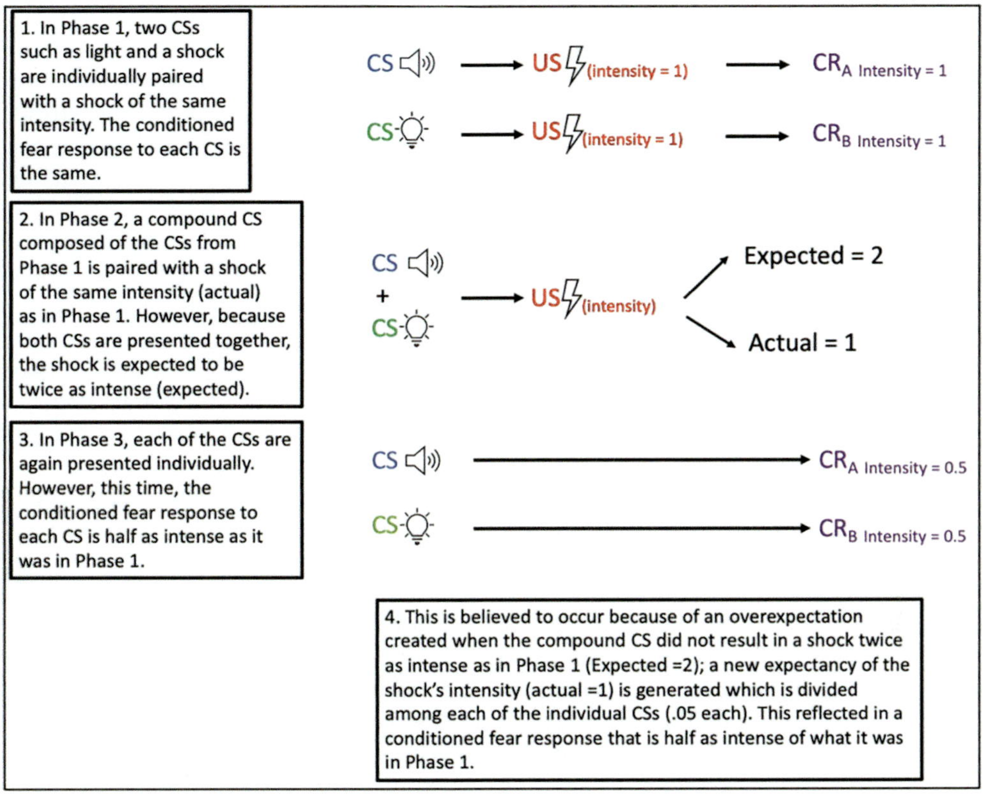

Figure 14.3 The overexpectation procedure.

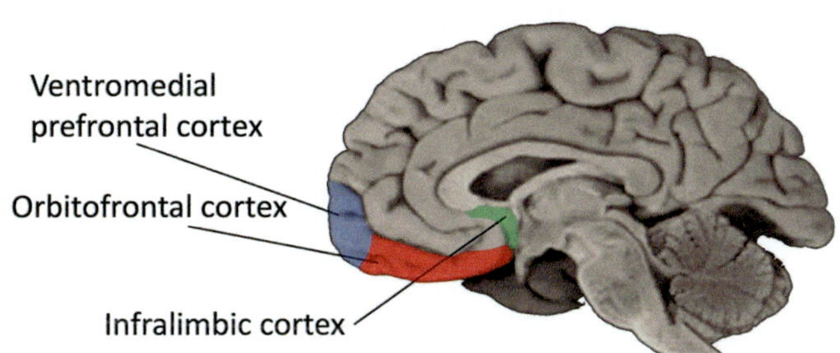

Figure 14.4 Brain areas involved in extinction and the overexpectation effect.

Neuroscientist Mihaela Iordanova and her colleagues at Concordia University in Montréal investigated this question. They began by examining the infralimbic cortex's role in an extinction and overexpectation procedure. This was achieved by comparing groups of rats whose infralimbic cortex was inactivated through the infusion of a drug combination, focusing on the intensity of conditioned fear responses (CFRs) following each procedure. Consistent with previous studies, they found that inactivation of the infralimbic cortex prevented the normal reduction of CFRs that typically occurs during the extinction procedure, indicating that IL inactivation disrupted the extinction process. Meanwhile, the inactivation of the infralimbic cortex did not reduce the intensity of CFRs during the over-expect procedure. These findings suggest that the infralimbic cortex is essential for extinction but not overexpectation learning.

This raised the question of which brain area is necessary for the overexpectation effect, if not the IL. The researchers hypothesized that the orbitofrontal cortex, which encompasses the ventral region of the frontal lobes, would be essential for overexpectation learning. Their hypothesis rested on three lines of evidence: first, the orbitofrontal cortex has reciprocal connections with the amygdala, which is known to play a role in conditioned fear learning and extinction; second, the orbitofrontal cortex is involved in the expression of fear and anxiety; third, it is involved in the expectation of rewards.

To test their hypothesis, they conducted another experiment in which they replicated the procedure of the first experiment, except they compared the effects of inactivating the orbitofrontal cortex instead of the infralimbic cortex in the extinction and overexpectation procedures. The results were contrary to those of the first experiment. Inactivation of the orbitofrontal cortex did not eliminate the reduction in the intensity of the conditioned fear response (CFR) during the extinction procedure. Still, it significantly impaired the CFR in the overexpectation procedure.

Overall, the study's findings indicated that the extinction and overexpectation procedures, both of which reduce a conditioned fear response, rely on different brain areas. The infralimbic cortex is crucial for the extinction of a CFR, while the orbitofrontal cortex is vital for reducing a CFR in the overexpectation procedure.

Are You Thinking Critically?

1. Distinguish between the extinction procedure and the overexpectation procedure.
2. Discuss how the overexpectation procedure is thought to result in the overexpectation effect.
3. Why might it be essential to know that extinction and the overexpectation effect depend on different brain areas?

Resistance to Extinction

Extinction is an essential form of learning. On the one hand, it permits animals and people not to waste time and energy performing a response that no longer results in the delivery of a reinforcer. Extinction is also essential in behavior modification and is the basis for exposure therapy. On the other hand, **resistance to extinction**, which refers to the persistence of a response when it is no longer reinforced, plays an important role because it can cause a person to persist in a wide range of behaviors despite repeated failures. This includes persistently turning a key into a defective lock until it opens and the persistence of behaviors important to achieving life goals despite setbacks. As the old saying goes, "If at first you don't succeed, try, try again."

Achieving goals, such as those associated with health and fitness, after repeated failures requires resistance to extinction.

Source: IStock photo ID:1188769924.

The Partial Reinforcement Extinction Effect

The partial reinforcement extinction effect (**PREE**) is the phenomenon by which behavior learned under a partial reinforcement schedule is more resistant to extinction than behavior learned under continuous reinforcement. Next, you will learn about three concepts proposed to explain the PREE. These are the discrimination hypothesis, Capaldi's sequential theory, and the frustration hypothesis.

THE DISCRIMINATION HYPOTHESIS

One explanation for the PREE is known as the **discrimination hypothesis**. The discrimination hypothesis, proposed by Mowrer and Jones (1945), states that the resistance to extinction observed after training under a partial reinforcement schedule is due to the similarity between the schedule of reinforcement during training and extinction trials.

For example, behavior is under a variable ratio schedule (VR) when playing a slot machine. That is, only a random number of responses are reinforced. Therefore, the person gambling is not surprised when no money is won after a response and keeps playing. She would keep playing for a long time, even if the machine were secretly made never to pay off again. According to the discrimination hypothesis, she keeps gambling because she has difficulty determining whether the machine is no longer paying off or if a long period of non-reinforcement is simply part of the schedule. In contrast, if each response had previously been followed by a payoff (a CRF schedule), she would quickly realize that the machine is no longer delivering and stop playing.

However, remember that the finding has challenged the discrimination hypothesis that a lack of ability to discriminate between a training schedule of reinforcement and an extinction schedule does not explain the PREE. For example, Jenkins (1962) exposed one group of rats to a VI schedule of reinforcement and another group to a CRF schedule (in which every response was reinforced). In the second phase, he exposed both groups to a CRF schedule. In the third phase, the rats in both groups were given extinction trials. He found that only the rats that had been exposed to the VI schedule showed significant resistance to extinction relative to the rats who had only been exposed to CRF schedules. Jenkins (1962) reasoned that the PREE could not be due to a failure to discriminate between the schedule of reinforcement they were exposed to during training and the schedule to which they were exposed during extinction. This is because the reinforcement schedule to which they were exposed during extinction radically differed from the one to which they were previously exposed. They went from a CRF schedule to an extinction schedule, where none of the responses were reinforced. Instead, Jenkins (1962) proposed that the rats learned to persist in responding during the initial VI schedule.

CAPALDI'S SEQUENTIAL THEORY

In the 1960s, psychologist E.J. Capaldi proposed a more precise version of the discrimination hypothesis to explain the PREE (Capaldi, 1966). For Capaldi, two important sequential factors present during training trials were essential to consider in determining the extent to which an animal will keep responding during extinction trials. These are the number of transitions between nonreinforced (N) and reinforced trials (R), called NR-transitions, and the number of consecutive nonreinforced trials before a rewarded trial, called N-length.

To help you understand this, imagine a simplified hypothetical experiment with two rats trained to run down a straight alley maze to obtain a food reward, as illustrated in Figure 14.5. As you can see in the figure, each rat is under a different fixed ratio schedule of reinforcement (FR). Rat 1 is on an FR 2 schedule of reinforcement (NRNR), whereas Rat 2 is on an FR 3 schedule of reinforcement (NNRNNR). As a reminder, an FR 2 schedule means that the rat must respond twice before it receives a reinforcer, and an FR 3 schedule means that the rat must respond three times before receiving a reinforcer. You can also see that both rats experience two NR transitions. However, Rat 1 experiences an N-length of 1, whereas Rat 2 experiences an N-length of 2.

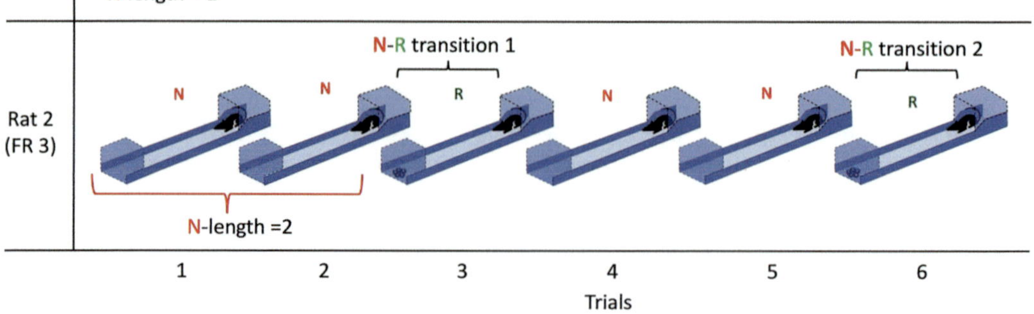

Figure 14.5 Hypothetical experiment describing Capaldi's sequential theory.

Having this knowledge in mind, how can we predict which of the two rats will show greater resistance to extinction during extinction trials? Figure 14.6 illustrates the cognitive process by which this occurs, using Rat 2 as an example. According to Capaldi (1966), rats record what happens in each trial, including whether or not they receive a reinforcer. When a rat is placed into the start box to begin a new trial, its memory of what happened in previous trials is activated. In addition, an association between running down the alley and finding no food on nonreinforced trials is formed and strengthened by the food reward the rat receives on reinforced trials (R). This is similar to running for the bus and just making it (R), which might remind you of the previous day or days when you ran for the bus and it left without you (N).

Capaldi proposed that the degree to which a rat will resist extinction depends on two sequential factors: the number of NR transitions and the N-length. In our hypothetical experiment, both rats experience two NR transitions. This means both rats were reinforced

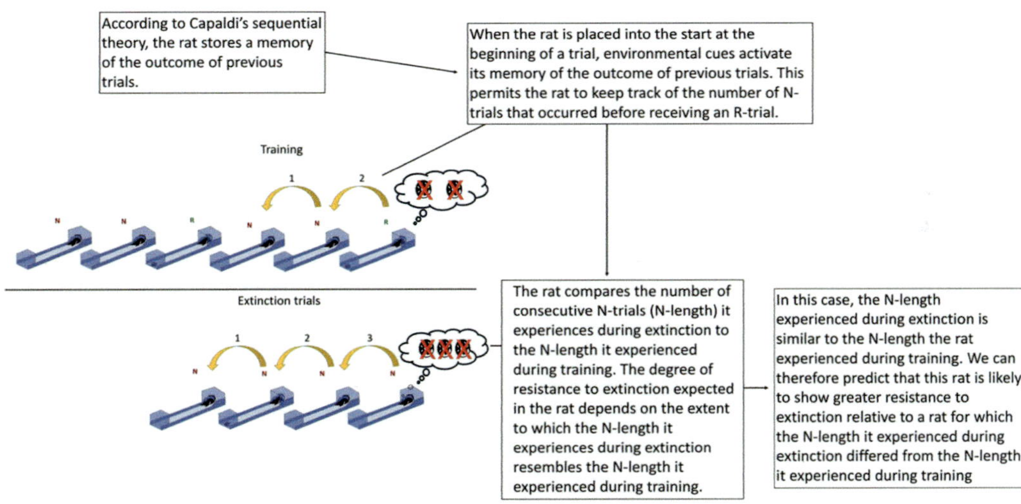

Figure 14.6 The process by which resistance to extinction can be explained by the similarity between the schedule of extinction and that of training according to Capaldi (1966).

twice after experiencing trials in which they did not receive food. Therefore, by only considering the number of NR transitions, both rats would be predicted to show the same degree of resistance to extinction. However, the schedules experienced by the rats differed in terms of the other sequential factor, N-length. Rat 1 experiences an N-length of 1, whereas Rat 2 experiences an N-length of 2.

According to Capaldi, a rat compares its experience of the number of consecutive nonreinforced trials during extinction to its memory of the N-lengths experienced during training. As illustrated in Figure 14.6 for Rat 2, during the extinction phase, the rat experiences three consecutive N-trials. The rat searches its memory of training trials and compares this extinction N-length to the N-lengths it experienced during training. For Rat 2, the N-length during extinction (N-length = 3) is similar to the N-length it experienced during training (N-length = 2). In contrast, for Rat 1, the N-length during extinction (N-length = 3) is quite different from what it experienced during training (N-length = 1). Although Figure 14.6 illustrates this process for Rat 2, the same memory-matching process would occur for Rat 1. When the N-length experienced during extinction closely resembles the

N-lengths experienced during training, the rat generalizes from its training experience and continues responding, leading to greater resistance to extinction.

This explains why the slot machine gambler from our earlier example keeps playing even when the machine stops paying. On a variable ratio schedule, she experiences many different N-lengths during training, sometimes winning immediately, sometimes after many losses. When the machine stops paying altogether, the long losing streak matches N-lengths she experienced during training, so she continues playing.

Therefore, even though the rats in our hypothetical experiment experienced the same number of NR transitions, Rat 2 would likely continue responding through more extinction trials than Rat 1. This is because Rat 2 experienced an N-length during training (N-length = 2) that more closely resembled the N-length during extinction (N-length = 3), whereas Rat 1's training N-length (N-length = 1) differed more greatly from its extinction N-length (N-length = 3).

THE FRUSTRATION HYPOTHESIS

Psychologist Abram Amsel (1922–2006) proposed that under a partial reinforcement schedule, the frustration induced by not obtaining a reinforcer after a response had motivational effects. To show this, Amsel (1958) trained rats to run down a runway (Runway A) from a start box to a goal box (Goal Box 1) and then down another runway (Runway B) to another goal box (Goal Box 2). In early reward trials, food was available in both goal boxes. Then, on some frustrated trials, food ceased to be available in Goal Box 1 but remained available in Goal Box 2. Amsel hypothesized that finding no food in Goal Box 1 after learning it contained food on reward trials would increase the rats' motivation to run to Goal Box 2. To test this hypothesis, he measured the rats' running speed down the runway to Goal Box 2 and the time it took them to leave Goal Box 1 (latency) on frustration trials. He found that the rats ran significantly faster down Runway B to Goal Box 2 after leaving Goal Box 1 and displayed a shorter latency to leave Goal Box 1 on frustration trials than on reward trials. This supported his hypothesis that frustration had motivational effects. In addition, Amsel proposed that responding on unrewarded trials became associated with frustration and that responding in the face of frustration was reinforced by the reward, which was always available in Goal Box 2. Hence, during extinction trials, rats subjected to a partial reinforcement schedule persist in responding during extinction trials because they have been reinforced to respond on non-rewarded trials during training.

Critical Thinking Spot Check 14.1

1. Define operant extinction.
2. Distinguish between the different behavioral effects of extinction.
3. Why is it important to know about the behavioral effects of extinction when attempting to modify a child's behavior?
4. What is the partial reinforcement effect?
5. Distinguish between three theories that explain the partial reinforcement effect.

14.2 Response Recovery Effects

Extinction Is Not Memory Erasure

As mentioned in Chapter 5, in the context of classical conditioning, extinction does not involve the complete erasure of a CS-US association from memory but instead learning a new CS-noUS association that competes with the established CS-US association (Bouton, 1993). A similar process occurs in operant conditioning, whereby a new association, which consists of a response-no reinforcer association, competes with the existing memory in which a reinforcer follows a response.

Evidence that associations learned through classical and operant conditioning are not erased by extinction was found in response recovery effects, in which a return to responding occurs following extinction. Four types of response recovery effects have been identified: **spontaneous recovery**, **renewal**, **reinstatement**, and **resurgence**.

Spontaneous Recovery

Spontaneous recovery refers to the spontaneous return of an extinguished response. Pavlov himself (1927) observed this phenomenon. He found that conditioned salivation, extinguished by presentations of the CS by itself, spontaneously returned with time after the last extinction trial. In a more recent experiment, rats were trained to associate food delivery with a light (S1) and a sound (S2). Once the rats learned these associations, they approached the food delivery (CR) location in response to both conditioned stimuli (CSs).

The rats were then subjected to extinction trials and tested for spontaneous recovery by being re-exposed to the CSs (S1 and S2) eight days (S1) or immediately (S2) after the last extinction trial (Rescorla, 1997). The results are shown in Figure 14.7; spontaneous recovery was only observed in the group tested to S1, which occurred eight days after the last extinction trial. No spontaneous recovery was found in the group tested for S2, which occurred immediately after the previous extinction trial.

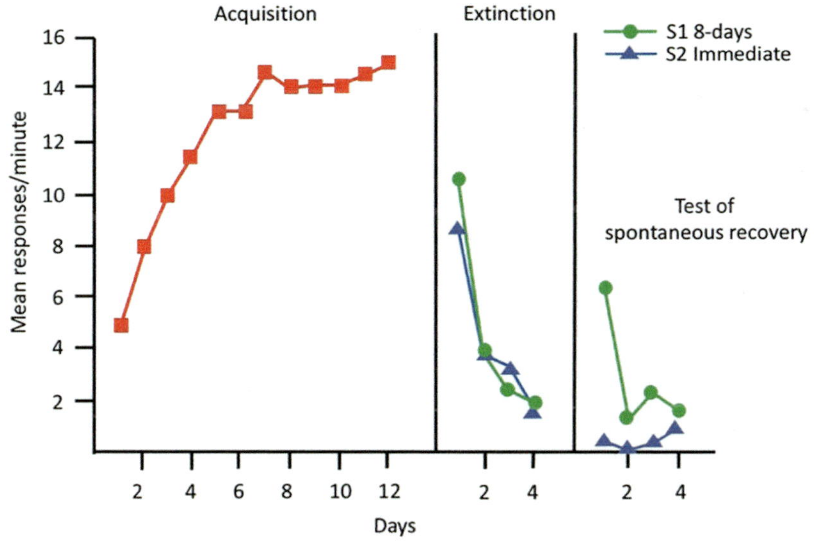

Figure 14.7 Results of the Rescorla (1997) experiment. (left) Combined responses to the S1 and S2 CSs during acquisition. (middle) Responses to S1 (green) and S2 (blue) CSs during extinction trials. (right) Responses to S1 (green) and S2 (blue) CSs during a test for spontaneous recovery.

Source: Modified from Rescorla, R. A. (1997). Spontaneous recovery after Pavlovian conditioning with multiple outcomes. *Anim Learn Behav, 25*(1), 99–107. https://doi.org/10.3758/BF03199028.

CHARACTERISTICS OF SPONTANEOUS RECOVERY

There are four main characteristics of spontaneous recovery (Rescorla, 2004). First, the probability of spontaneous recovery increases with time between the end of the last extinction trial and testing. Second, spontaneous recovery is incomplete. Third, spontaneous recovery diminishes with repeated extinction sessions (Rescorla, 2004), and fourth, spontaneous recovery can be brought under stimulus control. For example, it was found that a tone played during extinction trials reduced the extent to which spontaneous recovery occurred when it was also played during the test (Brooks, 2000). The first three characteristics can be observed in the Rescorla (1997) experiment described previously (Figure 14.7). Can you identify them in the graph?

THEORIES OF SPONTANEOUS RECOVERY

As was the case for extinction theories, several spontaneous recovery theories were also proposed. Pavlov believed spontaneous recovery occurred because response fatigue accumulated during responding and dissipated with time (Pavlov, 1927). Robbins (1990), consistent with the idea that extinction was due to a loss of attention to the CS, believed that attention recovered over time. Another idea is that the frustration that builds when a response no longer gives rise to an appetitive outcome inhibits some learning during extinction—responding returns once the effects of frustration have subsided (Amsel, 1958).

According to William Keyes Estes (1919–2011), one of Skinner's students, stimuli are composed of many elements. An element is fully conditioned once associated with a reinforcer. Some of these elements become unconditioned during extinction trials since the reinforcer is no longer available. However, a few elements remain conditioned. The few elements that have remained conditioned are not likely to drive spontaneous recovery immediately following extinction trials, but the likelihood is that they will increase with time.

It was also suggested that a temporal weighing rule can explain spontaneous recovery (Devenport, 1998). According to this idea, how animals respond during a test depends on weighing what they experienced before the test according to the time between these experiences and the test. Hence, animals tested immediately after extinction trials place a lot of weight on the recent training-extinction experience. However, over time, the influence of this experience of responding diminishes.

As may have been the case for theories of extinction discussed previously, you may wonder which of these theories of spontaneous recovery is correct. The answer is that spontaneous recovery possibly occurs through a combination of these mechanisms.

Renewal

Renewal refers to the phenomenon by which an operant response returns when an animal is tested in a context other than the one in which extinction trials occurred. Hence, the renewal effect shows that extinction is context dependent and that it does not constitute an erasure or forgetting about the association between an operant response and its outcome acquired during training. Renewal can be observed in three experimental procedures: ABA, AAB, and ABC renewal. All three procedures involve three phases: acquisition, extinction, and test.

In the acquisition phase of ABA renewal, animals learn to perform an operant response in an apparatus designated as Context A. The animals are then subjected to extinction trials in a different apparatus, designated as Context B. In the test phase, the animals are further subjected to extinction trials in Context A, where they were initially trained. In AAB renewal, both the acquisition and extinction phases occur in Context A. However, they are tested in Context B. In ABC renewal, the acquisition phase occurs in Context A, the extinction phase in Context B, and the test phase in Context C. A study in which ABA and AAB renewal were found (Bouton et al., 2011) is summarized in Figure 14.8. The findings show that each of these procedures results in renewal.

Notice that in each renewal procedure, the test occurs in a context that either differs from the context of extinction, as in the ABA procedure, or in a context where the animal has never been, such as in the AAB and the ABC procedures. Only in the ABA procedure is the animal returned to the acquisition context for the renewal test. AAB and ABC renewal shows that the context in which extinction occurred is inhibitory and that switching the animal out of it for testing is enough to produce renewal. However, as you can see, the number of responses during renewal is significantly greater in the ABA

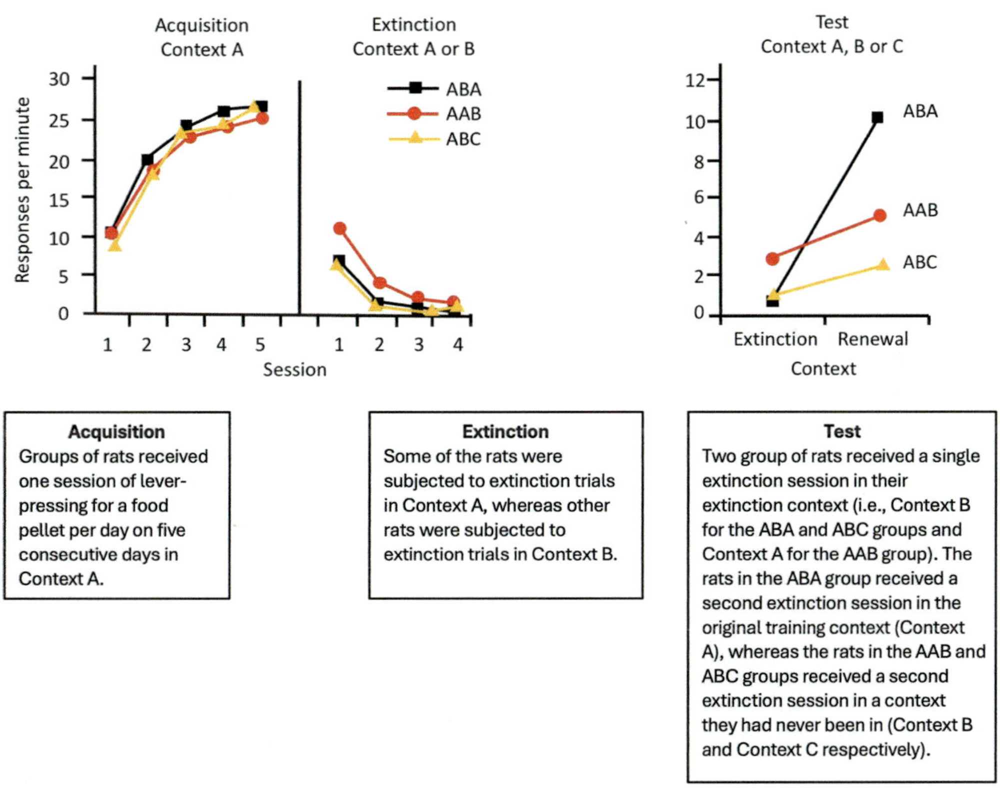

Figure 14.8 ABA, AAB, and ABC renewal effects found by Bouton et al. (2011).

Source: Modified from Bouton et al. (2011), Figures 14.1 and 14.3.

procedure than in the AAB or ABC procedures. This might be because Context A serves as an occasion setter by which the animals learned that responding in this context results in the reinforcer. Since the animals are not returned to the acquisition context for renewal testing in the AAB and ABC procedures, no such occasion setting occurs. In addition, the animal's responses might be somewhat inhibited by seeing the lever in a new context (Contexts B or C).

Reinstatement

Reinstatement refers to the resumption of reinforced behavior by *non-contingent* exposure to the reinforcer after extinction. This phenomenon was documented by Skinner (1938), who found that rats having undergone extinction of lever pressing for food were reinstated by *non-contingent* food presentation. Reinstatement is considered to be a valid model of drug relapse in humans (Bossert et al., 2013; Farrell et al., 2022; Kuhn, Kalivas and Bobadilla, 2019; Shaham et al., 2003). For example, drug relapse is often precipitated by *re-exposure* to the drug or *drug-associated* cues after a period of abstinence. This is the phenomenon that resulted in Cameron's relapse in the opening vignette when he thought he could have just a drink and did a little bit of cocaine at a party after the cravings induced by the *drug-related* cues were *extinguished*.

In an early demonstration of reinstatement, psychologist Jane Stewart and colleague Harriet de Wit trained rats to press a lever to receive cocaine infusions into the jugular vein (de Wit and Stewart, 1981). Once the rats responded consistently, the power to the syringe pump by which the infusions were administered was disconnected. After extinction, the rats were given an injection of either 0.0, 0.5, 1.0, or 2.0 mg/kg of cocaine (priming), which reinstated responding. The mean number response was initially the highest for the rats receiving the lowest dose (0.5 mg/kg) but did not persist through the post-prime period. The mean number of responses by the rats that received the highest (2.0 mg/kg) was initially lower but persisted at the highest level throughout the post-prime period. The mean number of responses by the rats that received the intermediate dose (1.0 mg/kg) was intermediate to the two other groups in their initial level of responding and persistence. Finally, no response increase was found in the rats not receiving a priming injection. The details of the experiment are illustrated in Figure 14.9. In other experiments, they discovered that priming injections of amphetamine and morphine also reinstated responding, even if these were not drugs the rats were trained to press a bar for. They also found that exposure to a tone, which the rats heard during training, also reinstated responding.

Stress-Induced Reinstatement Studies have shown that drug relapse in humans can be precipitated by stress (Khantzian, 1985). Thus, scientists have developed animal models of *stress-induced* reinstatement. Animals can be subjected to various stressors in the laboratory, including footshocks, food deprivation, tail pinch, and restraint. Each of these stressors has been found to reinstate extinguished operant responses for one drug or another, including heroin, cocaine, methamphetamine, nicotine, alcohol, and morphine (Karimi et al., 2014; Shalev et al., 2000).

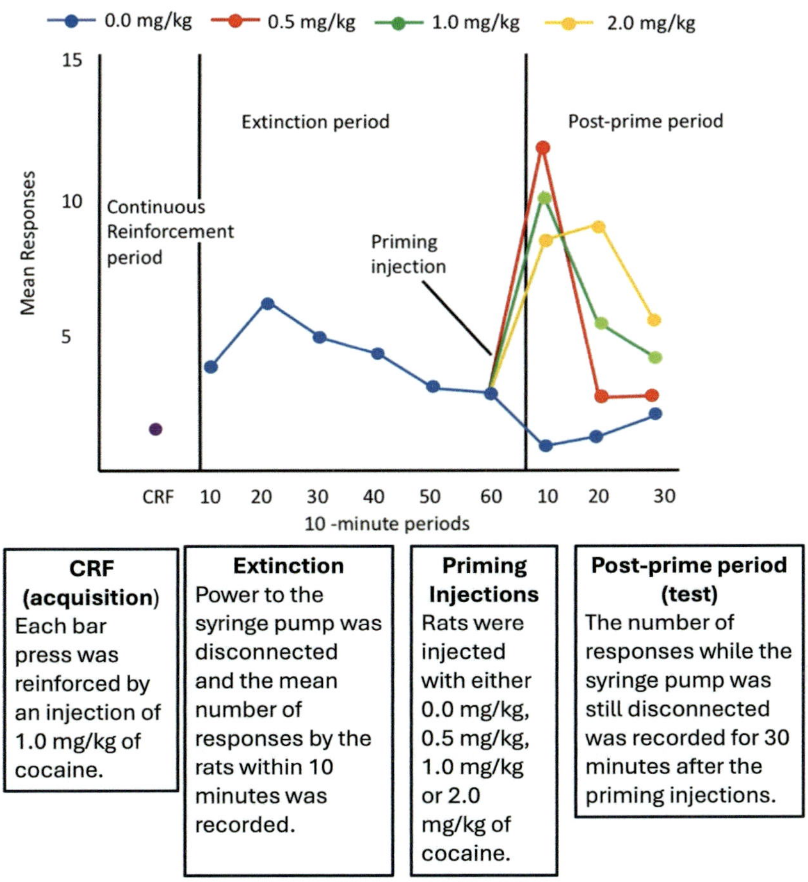

Figure 14.9 Reinstatement effects found by de Wit and Stewart (1981).

Source: Modified from de Wit and Stewart, 1981 (Figure 1).

Focus On

A Model of Drug Relapse

What Is a Model?

The word model may make you think of the kits that contained the parts and instructions to build more or less sophisticated scaled replicas of objects such as cars, ships, buildings, and robots featured in movies. You may also be familiar with the computer modeling responsible for the realistic experiences computer games provide. However, too many people think that models are nothing more than representations of real-world objects and they only make superficial comparisons. The term model has a different meaning in science. In addition to being representations of real-world events or situations, models are used to test the validity of ideas in ways that would be impossible in the real world. However, scientists recognize that models are not exact replicas of the real world. Models are often revised and improved to be more consistent with observation and increase researchers' ability to make predictions.

The Reinstatement Model of Drug Relapse

The reinstatement model of drug relapse describes both a laboratory model and a behavioral phenomenon (Epstein et al., 2006; Shaham et al., 2003). Relapse refers to the return of drug-taking behavior after a period of abstinence. Reinstatement describes both the model and a phenomenon. The phenomenon is observed in laboratory animals when an operant behavior that has been extinguished, such as lever pressing for drug injection, returns when animals are re-exposed to the drug.

For the reinstatement model of drug relapse to be valid, it must be shown to match the drug relapse process in humans closely. Epstein et al. (2006) tested the validity of the reinstatement model in three ways. First, they examined the similarities and differences between the laboratory conditions of reinstatement in animals and those present in human relapse cases. Second, they compared the results of laboratory studies conducted on animals with relapse in people. Third, they studied clinical reports of human cases of relapse. Table 14.1 summarizes the results of their comparative analysis based on the extent to which any of the six measurable factors were present in the reinstatement of drug relapse in animals and humans.

As shown in Table 14.1, four factors are present in both animals and humans. These shared factors provide strong support for the validity of the reinstatement model: both animals and people have a history of drug use and self-administration, are drug-free before reinstatement, show drug-seeking behavior after re-exposure to drugs or drug-related cues, and demonstrate drug-seeking behavior following stressful events.

The remaining three factors differ between species. One factor applies exclusively to the animal model: the period of extinction during which drug-seeking responses are performed but not reinforced by drugs. This is because experimenters control the delivery of drugs during reinstatement procedures, making extinction periods easily implemented. In contrast, drug-seeking behaviors in people usually do not cease due to extinction alone but due to personal decisions to minimize or eliminate the negative consequences that result from their drug taking.

Two factors apply exclusively to humans. First, drug self-administration is not associated with negative consequences for animals, whereas in humans it is often associated with family problems, job loss, and social disapproval. Second, only humans can report on the expectancies and subjective feelings related to drug use, which presents the most significant challenge to an animal model of relapse.

Despite these differences, researchers believe there are enough similarities to make the reinstatement model a valuable tool in studying relapse in people.

Table 14.1 Results of comparative analyses conducted by Epstein et al. (2006).

Factors	*Animals*	*People*
History of drug use and self-administration is available.	✓	✓
Drug-free and not actively seeking drugs before reinstatement.	✓	✓
Drug seeking returns after the administration of a drug or drug-related cue.	✓	✓
Drug-seeking returns following a stressful event.	✓	✓
Controlled experimental extinction period during which drug-seeking responses are performed but not reinforced by drugs.	✓	✗
Negative consequences of drug self-administration.	✗	✓
Ability to communicate expectancies and subjective feelings related to drug use.	✗	✓

Are You Thinking Critically?

1. How does reinstatement qualify as a model of drug relapse?
2. What are the shortcomings of the reinstatement model?
3. If you were asked to do so, how would you contest the validity of the reinstatement model?

Resurgence

Resurgence refers to the phenomenon by which a previously extinguished behavior re-emerges after a more recent alternative behavior has been extinguished. Understanding resurgence is essential for managing problem behaviors (Lattal and St. Peter Pipkin, 2009). For example, imagine a teacher ignoring a child's negative attention-seeking attempts but praising the child's good behavior. It may be observed that the child's misbehavior diminishes due to extinction and that the frequency of her good behaviors increases. However, if the teacher stops reinforcing the child's good behaviors, the misbehavior may re-emerge (resurge).

Resurgence can also account for drug relapse in people undergoing contingency management as part of their treatment approach in which alternative behaviors are reinforced. For example, in contingency management, patients' proven abstinence by drug-negative tests may be reinforced by money or vouchers exchangeable for goods or services (Petry, 2011). As you can imagine, ending the reinforcement of abstinence may result in the resurgence of drug taking.

Resurgence has been studied in laboratory experiments that typically consist of three phases. In the first phase, animals are trained to press one of two levers present for reinforcement (R1). In the second phase, the animals are trained to press a second lever (R2) while the first (R1) is extinguished. In the third phase, R2 is extinguished. What is typically observed is that, after R2 extinction, R1 resurges (Sweeney and Shahan, 2013; Winterbauer and Bouton, 2010). Resurgence has also been found in laboratory studies with human participants. In one study, participants learned to press a button to receive snacks (R1). Participants learned to press another button in the second phase to receive virtual coins (R2). Pressing the first button (R1), associated with getting snacks, was extinguished. In the third phase, R2 was extinguished, which resulted in the resurgence of R1 (Thrailkill, Ameden and Bouton, 2019).

Resurgence is thought to occur through a mechanism similar to the renewal effect. Similarly to what happens in a renewal experiment, the test occurs in a context that differs from extinctions. That is, extinction trials to R1 are conducted simultaneously with the reinforcement of R2. However, this is not the case during the test when responding to R1 is measured after R2 has been extinguished. In other words, a resurgence experiment is similar to the ABC version of renewal where R1 is acquired by itself, extinguished concurrently to R2 reinforcement, and tested while responses to R2 are extinguished (Winterbauer and Bouton, 2010).

Critical Thinking Spot Check 14.2

1. Distinguish between the different response recovery effects.
2. Why is it important to know about response recovery effects to understand:

- The efficacy of psychotherapy?
- Relapse in drug addiction?
- The misbehavior of children?

Justify your answers by providing an example for each.

Chapter Summary

Each bullet point aligns with the learning objectives outlined at the beginning of the chapter.

- Operant extinction refers to a decrease in the frequency or intensity of a response when it is no longer reinforced. Extinction forms the basis of exposure therapy and behavior modification programs, often used in applied behavior analysis.
- Extinction is associated with several behavioral phenomena: extinction burst, which refers to an immediate but temporary increase in the frequency or intensity of a response following the onset of extinction; extinction-induced response variability, which refers to an increase in the variability of a response following the onset of extinction; and extinction-induced aggression, which refers to aggressive behaviors observed after the onset of extinction.
- Resistance to extinction refers to the extent to which an animal keeps responding after the onset of extinction. In what is known as the partial reinforcement extinction effect (PREE), behavior learned under a partial reinforcement schedule is more resistant to

extinction than behavior learned under a continuous schedule of reinforcement. Several theories have been proposed to explain the PREE. According to the discrimination hypothesis, resistance to extinction after exposure to a partial reinforcement schedule is due to the similarity between the schedule of reinforcement and extinction trials. According to Capaldi's sequential theory, two factors account for the PREE. These are sequential factors, which refer to 1) the number of transitions between reinforced and nonreinforced trials and 2) the number of consecutive nonreinforced trials before a reinforced trial. According to the frustration hypothesis, the PREE is due to the motivational effects of frustration experienced during nonreinforced trials.

- Four phenomena prove that extinction is not the result of an erasure of the original memory of reinforcement. These are spontaneous recovery, in which a response returns at some point following the end of extinction trials; renewal, in which a response returns when in a context that differs from the one in which extinction trials occurred; reinstatement, in which an extinguished response returns upon presentation of the US; and resurgence, in which an extinguished response returns after a reinforced response that replaced it is extinguished.

Glossary

Discrimination hypothesis The idea that extinction is slower following partial reinforcement because organisms struggle to distinguish between reinforcement and non-reinforcement periods.

Extinction burst A temporary increase in the frequency or intensity of a behavior when reinforcement is first removed, before the behavior declines.

Extinction-induced response variability The phenomenon where an organism exhibits new or varied behaviors during extinction as it searches for reinforcement.

Operant extinction The process in which a previously reinforced behavior decreases and eventually stops when reinforcement is no longer provided.

Partial reinforcement extinction effect (PREE) The observation that behaviors reinforced intermittently take longer to extinguish than those reinforced continuously.

Reinstatement The resurgence of an extinguished behavior after exposure to the unconditioned stimulus or reinforcement again.

Renewal The return of an extinguished response when the organism is placed in a different context from where extinction occurred.

Resistance to extinction The persistence of a learned behavior despite the removal of reinforcement, influenced by reinforcement history and schedule type.

Resurgence The reappearance of a previously reinforced behavior when a more recently reinforced behavior is extinguished.

Spontaneous recovery The reappearance of an extinguished behavior after a rest period without additional reinforcement.

Module Summary

In Chapter 12, you learned that the opportunity to perform a high-probability response can be used to reinforce a low-probability response. This is known as the Premack principle. However, according to the response deprivation hypothesis, operant reinforcement procedures deprive animals of performing a high-probability response at their unconstrained baseline level. In Chapter 13, you also learned about the associative structure of operant conditioning, which consists of a set of associations between the context in which a response occurs, the response itself, and the outcome of the response. These associations simultaneously give rise to S-R, R-O, and S-O learning. Skinner proposed S-(R-O) learning in which the stimuli present when the response gives rise to an outcome sets the occasion for the outcome to occur if the response is performed. In what is known as the dual systems approach, instrumental learning develops through both the S-R and R-O systems simultaneously. Still, the influence of the R-O system diminishes with extensive training. In contrast, the influence of the S-R system persists; you have learned that S-O learning may elicit an emotional response that acts as a motivator for the response the contextual stimuli present when a response is performed. Hence, according to the two-process theory, the R-O response is influenced by both S-R learning and classical conditioning.

Finally, in Chapter 14, you learned about operant extinction, which refers to a decrease in the frequency or intensity of a response when it is no longer reinforced. You also learned that extinction gives rise to extinction bursts, extinction-induced response variability, and extinction-induced aggression. The extent to which extinction effectively suppresses a response is known as resistance to extinction. Resistance to extinction was found to be stronger in animals trained under a partial schedule of reinforcement rather than under a continuous schedule. This is known as the partial reinforcement extinction effect (PREE). Several theories have been put forward to explain the PREE. These are the discrimination hypothesis, Capaldi's sequential theory, and the frustration hypothesis; the PREE is due to the motivational effects of frustration experienced during nonreinforced trials. Finally, you learned that four phenomena are taken as evidence for the idea that extinction is not an erasure of the memory of reinforcement but a form of learning. These are spontaneous recovery, renewal, reinstatement, and resurgence.

Module 6

Application

A Method for Breaking Bad Habits

Habits are well-ingrained behavioral patterns that are resistant to change and inflexible—they permit us to perform highly practiced and routine actions in response to cues. Habits sometimes include patterns of behaviors that lead to undesired outcomes. People generally refer to those as bad habits, which can negatively impact your life. People spend a significant amount of time trying to break bad habits. Several books dedicated to helping people break bad habits and develop good ones, such as *The Power of Habit: Why We Do What We Do in Life and Business* (Duhigg, 2014) and *Atomic Habits: An Easy & Proven Way to Build Good Habits & Break Bad Ones* (Clear, 2018), have been written.

Duhigg (2014) states that habits comprise four elements: cues, cravings, responses, and rewards. He believes that these four elements form what he calls "habit loops." The cue is the external or internal stimuli that signal that a reward will be obtained if a specific response is performed. The cue does not directly lead to the reaction but induces a craving for the reward. For example, a person recovering from drug addiction is at risk for relapse when exposed to the environment in which she used to take the drug. This is because the environment has become a cue, which induces a craving that may lead to a pattern of responses aimed at obtaining the drug, which constitutes the reward.

Understanding Your Patterns of Responses

Understanding how the pattern of responses, or routine, constitutes your bad habit can be broken down into four steps: 1) identify the routine, 2) experiment with reward, 3) isolate the cues, and 4) take action.

I used an example from my experience to illustrate those steps, which you can apply to your bad habits. When I started writing this book, I always did so at a café. I would get up in the morning, worry about how much work I would get done during that day, get dressed, and go off to the café. I would then sit down and write for hours. I have done a lot of work but have spent much money in the process. A coffee and a muffin was costing me $7.50 per day. Something had to change.

The following table reproduces the notes I took to break my habit and implement a new one. I first identified my routine's components (1. Identify the Routine). I then identified the rewards I believed reinforced my routine (Table 1-M6 App.). Over four days, I experimented with these rewards by a process of elimination. The outcome of this process was that the feeling of getting work done, coffee, and the café's atmosphere were the rewards that reinforced my habit (2. Rewards). The next step was to identify the cue that triggered my habit, which turned out to be feeling anxious about getting work done. By placing the

DOI: 10.4324/9781003491828-26

context in which my habit was triggered, waking in the morning, I could predict when I would get the urge to go to the café (3. Cues). Finally, I formulated an implementation intention, an "if-then" plan that can lead to achieving your goals. The implementation intention was "If I feel anxious about getting work done, then I will brew my coffee, play lounge music, sit at my desk, and write" (4. Planning).

1.Identify the Routine

1) Wake up 2) Get up 3) Get dressed 4) Go to café 5) Order coffee 5) Set up laptop 6) Work 7) Go home

2.Rewards

Identify Rewards	**Experiment with rewards**	**Process of elimination**	**Results**
1) The feeling of getting work done **2) Getting out of the house** **3) Coffee** **4) Café atmosphere**	Day 1: Get up and start working. Day 2: Instead of going to the café, go for a walk. Day 3: Go to the café, buy a coffee, bring it home, and have it there. Day 4: Get up, stay home, brew own coffee, and try to recreate the café's atmosphere by playing lounge music.	1) If the reward is the feeling of getting work done, then staying home and working should be just as satisfying. 2) If the reward is getting out of the house, then going out for a walk should work just as well. 3) If the reward is coffee, then bringing the coffee home should work just as well. 4) If the reward is the café's atmosphere, then reproducing it at home should work just as well.	*I found that getting out the house was not what rewarded going to the café.* *However, I found that the feeling of getting work done, coffee, and the café's atmosphere all served as rewards for going to the café.*

3. Cues

Five categories of habitual cues	**Identify cues that trigger the habit**	**Results**
1) Location **2) Time** **3) Emotional state** **4) Other people** **5) Immediately preceding action**	1) Where are you? *Answer: Sometimes at home, sometimes driving around.* 2) What time is it? *Answer: Often in the morning after waking.* 3) What is your emotional state? Answer: *Anxious about getting work done on time.* 4) What other people are around you? *Answer: Usually no one.* 5) What did you do just before? Answer: *Nothing in particular.*	*After a few days of observation, I found that the cue that triggered my habit was the emotional state of feeling anxious about getting work done on time.*

4. Plan for the cue		
Implementation intention	**Attention**	**Response**
Next time I feel anxious about getting something done on time, I will brew my own coffee, play lounge music, sit at my desk, and write.	Be attentive to the cue(s). *Am I feeling anxious about getting something done on time? Yes!*	*Brew my own coffee when feeling anxious about getting work done on time after waking up, play lounge music, sit at my desk, and write.*

Are You Thinking Critically?

1. Identify the areas of your life where habits play an essential role.
2. Distinguish between habits that bring you closer to your goals and those that make achieving your goals more difficult.
3. What other methods, besides developing good habits, can you use to help you reach your goals?

Module 7

The Principles of Stimulus Control and Behavioral Effects of Stimulus Discrimination

Introduction

Consider the following situations. You chit-chat with a classmate before class and quiet down when the teacher enters the classroom. You feel compelled to take notes when the first presentation slide goes up. You find it difficult not to eat snacks while watching a movie. You step on the accelerator when the traffic light turns green. In each of these situations, your behavior is controlled by environmental stimuli. The teacher walking into the classroom causes you to quiet down, the presentation slides compel you to take notes, the movie incites you to eat snacks, and the green traffic light drives you to step on the accelerator. The reason why these behaviors tend to recur in those situations is that desirable outcomes follow them. Knowing that environmental stimuli exert control over behavior can help people set up their environment in ways that increase the probability that they will behave in desirable ways. Behaving appropriately requires that you learn to discriminate between various environmental stimuli. For example, standing up, cheering, and high-fiving perfect strangers is normal when your favorite team scores a touchdown at a football game. However, the same behavior is not appropriate in the library. It is also noteworthy that environmental stimuli play an important role in the causes and maintenance of psychological disorders such as drug abuse or gambling disorders.

In a type of behavior therapy called applied behavior analysis (ABA), understanding and changing behavior involves carefully observing the situations in which behavior occurs and its consequences. This form of therapy is used to help improve communication skills, social skills, and self-care in children with autism spectrum disorders. In this module, you will learn how environmental stimuli control behavior. In Chapter 15, you will learn about the principles of stimulus control. In Chapter 16, you will learn how the ability to discriminate among environmental stimuli plays an important role in eliciting behaviors appropriate for given situations.

DOI: 10.4324/9781003491828-27

15 Under Stimulus Control

The Environment's Influence on Behavior

Learning Objectives

- Define stimulus control and explain how environmental stimuli influence the behavior of people and animals.
- Demonstrate an understanding of Skinner's three-term contingency model.
- Analyze stimulus generalization and discrimination phenomena in animal behavior training.
- Evaluate stimulus generalization gradients based on their properties (area, height, slope, and form).

Hassan's Struggle

IStock photo ID: 106594115.8

DOI: 10.4324/9781003491828-28

Hassan has been struggling with his weight for several years. Coming from a family where many suffer from obesity, he worries that he is destined to be overweight. Recently, he became discouraged when he read that heritability accounts for 40% to 70% of an individual's weight (Herrera and Lindgren, 2010). However, he recalled learning in one of his psychology classes that the expression of traits occurs through complex interactions between genetics and environmental factors. He reasoned that he could change his environment, even if he couldn't do anything about his genes. "After all," he thought, "environmental influences account for 30% to 60% of an individual's weight." He began monitoring his eating habits and observed that he tended to eat more in certain situations than others.

For example, he often ate potato chips mindlessly while studying or checking his social media posts. One day, he realized that this habit was due to associating being at the computer while eating. In other words, simply being at the computer eventually led him to reach for the snacks in the cupboard. Knowing this, he now includes healthy snacks on his grocery list. He also noticed that he tended to consume more snacks when a greater variety was available in the cupboard and bought more snacks while shopping on an empty stomach. "The snack aisle is so much more appealing when I'm hungry," he told himself. However, even when he wasn't hungry, the variety on the shelves and the aroma of sweet foods compelled him to purchase several packages of tasty snacks. Since making this connection, he ensures he is not hungry when grocery shopping and avoids the snack aisle altogether. He also keeps only one or two snack foods in his cupboard. By gradually adapting to his environment, Hassan achieved a comfortable weight. Now, he feels he has experienced first-hand the influence of the environment on behavior.

15.1 What Is Stimulus Control?

The Three-Term Contingency

Stimulus control refers to the extent to which various stimuli influence behavior. For example, Hassan's eating behavior in the opening vignette was influenced by being at his computer and seeing the variety of foods in his well-stocked cupboard. Hassan's example shows that behavior is controlled not only by its consequences but also by the stimuli present when it is reinforced. This led Skinner (1969) to propose the **three-term contingency** (Figure 15.1). The three-term contingency refers to the relationship between behaviors and the environmental events that precede them. According to Skinner, any behavioral act can be broken down into three components: *discriminative stimuli* (S^D), *response (R)*, and *reinforcer* ($S^{+/-}$), which are often referred to as the *antecedent*, *behavior*, and *consequence*, respectively, or the *ABCs of behavior*.

The antecedent is the discriminative stimulus that precedes a behavioral response. It influences the behavior by signaling when a response will be reinforced ($S^{r+/r-}$) or punished ($S^{P+/P-}$). For example, an illuminated green traffic light is an antecedent to stepping on the

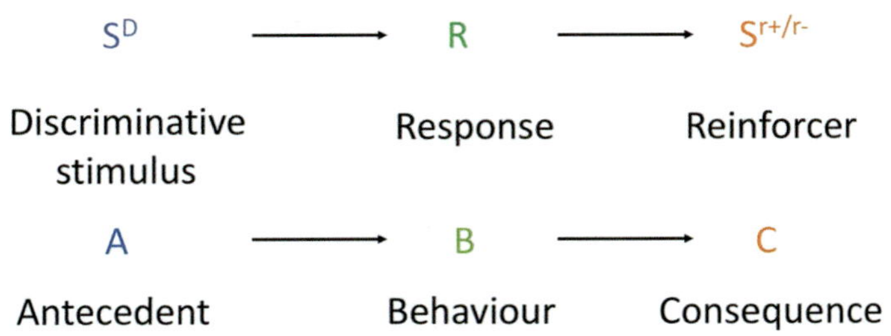

Figure 15.1 Skinner's three-term contingency (top) is often called the ABCs of behavior (bottom). The antecedent signals the occasion during which a response will be positively (S^{r+}), negatively reinforced (S^{r-}), positively (S^{P+}), positively punished (S^{P+}), or negatively punished (S^{P-}) (S^{P+} and S^{P-} are not shown).

accelerator (behavior), which is positively reinforced by the vehicle advancing through the intersection (consequence).

Identifying the antecedents and consequences of behavior is essential for eliminating undesired behaviors. For example, in the opening vignette, Hassan's behavior of eating potato chips while at the computer can be broken down into the components of the three-term contingency. Sitting at the computer is an antecedent to his behavior of eating potato chips, which has a consequence: weight gain. Knowing the antecedents of his unhealthy eating, Hassan could better control his eating behavior and make better food choices. For example, he made sure to purchase only healthy snacks while working at his computer. He also avoids the snack aisle at the grocery store, which was antecedent to buying unhealthy foods. Awareness of the antecedents and consequences of behavior can also help eliminate undesired behaviors such as knuckle cracking and nail-biting. Once the antecedent is identified, the undesired behavior can be predicted, and measures can be taken to prevent it. The three-term contingency is also the cornerstone of applied behavior analysis (ABA), in which trained therapists help children with problem behaviors.

Critical Thinking Spot Check 15.1

1. Describe stimulus control and give an everyday example of how environmental stimulus can influence behavior.
2. Explain what Skinner meant by the three-term contingency.
3. Describe an undesired behavior and explain how it can be eliminated using the three-term contingency.

15.2 Identifying Controlling Stimuli

An Early Analysis of Stimulus Control

Identifying which of several environmental stimuli is the antecedent to any given behavior is not always as obvious. For instance, a student's note-taking may be elicited by information

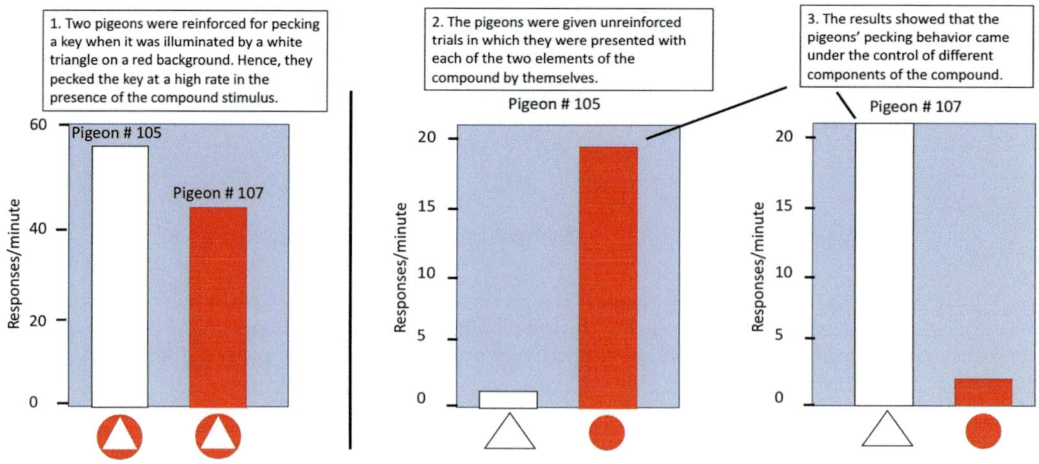

Figure 15.2 Results of the Reynolds (1961) experiment.

Source: Modified from Reynolds, G. S. (1961). Attention to the pigeon. *J Exp Anal Behav, 4*, 203–208. https://doi.org/10.1901/jeab.1961.4-203.

written on a presentation slide or by the teacher telling everyone to pay attention. That is, different stimuli may control the same behavior. The same can be said about the stimuli that control the behavior of animals in laboratory experiments. This was demonstrated by psychologist George Reynolds (1936–1987) in the classic experiment described in Figure 15.2.

These results showed that, similarly to students' note-taking behavior, different environmental stimuli can control the same behavior in other individuals. The results also showed that, out of the large variety of environmental stimuli, it may be difficult to pinpoint the stimulus or combination of stimuli that control behavior.

An interesting aspect of how environmental stimuli exert control over behavior is that they can do so even if they have never been associated with a response. This was demonstrated in an experiment by Morse and Skinner (1958). The experiment is described in Figure 15.3.

The Morse and Skinner (1958) findings were significant for two reasons: 1) They showed that operant responding can come under the control of environmental stimuli. 2) It showed that a stimulus can exert control over operant behavior by being associated with the reinforcer even if an animal is not trained to respond in its presence. Remember that, in Phase 1 of the experiment, the pigeons received food while the chamber was illuminated with colored light (red or green) regardless of their behavior. They were then trained to associate key pecks with the reinforcer but did so under a white light. Note that this procedure also involves classical conditioning in that, during Stage 1, the colored lights became CSs that predicted the presence of food. You are correct if you guessed this is an example of Pavlovian-instrumental transfer, as discussed in Chapter 11.

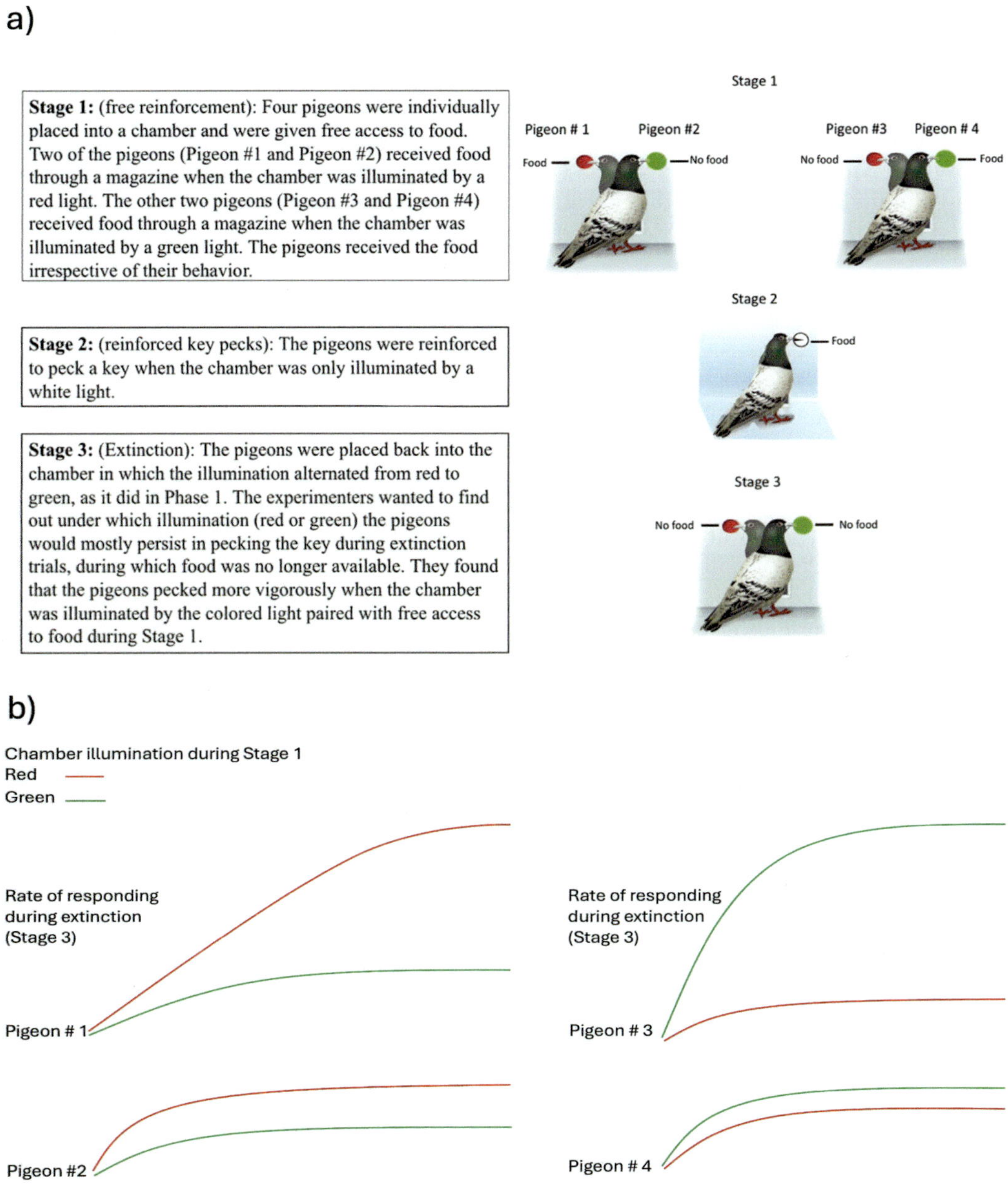

Figure 15.3 a) Procedure followed in the Morse and Skinner (1958) experiment. b) Pigeons pecked at a significantly higher rate during extinction trials when the colored light that was paired with food during Stage 1 was on.

Source: a) Modified from Bouton, M. E. (2016). *Learning and behavior* (2nd ed.). Oxford University Press Academic US. Page 261 Figure 7.9. b) Modified from Morse, W. H., & Skinner, B. F. (1958). Some factors are involved in the stimulus control of operant behavior. *J Exp Anal Behav, 1*, 103–107. https://doi.org/10.1901/jeab.1958.1-103.

Critical Thinking Spot Check 15.2

1. Explain why it might be challenging to determine which of several stimuli exert control over one's behavior.
2. Describe Reynolds's (1961) experiment on stimulus control in pigeons. a) What did Reynolds want to find out? b) What did he find? c) What did the results mean?
3. How did Morse and Skinner's (1958) experiment show stimulus control in pigeons? How did their methodology differ from that of Reynolds (1961)?
4. What were the two reasons Morse and Skinner's (1958) findings were important?

15.3 Generalization and Discrimination

Same or Different?

Generalization

Generalization refers to the ability to respond in the same way to similar but different stimuli. For example, traffic lights exert control over the behaviors of stepping on the brake or accelerator pedal depending on whether a red or green light is illuminated. However, the shades of color and the type of casing in which the lights are housed may vary across street corners, neighborhoods, and cities. Nevertheless, your behavior does not vary across these different situations. Similarly, I am easily triggered to write while sitting in a coffee shop where I have never been because most are similar. This was also true for Hassan in the opening vignette of the chapter. Because the snack aisles of grocery stores differ slightly from each other, they all serve as antecedent conditions for his eating behavior. Generalization has significant adaptive value. For example, as you can read about in the "What in the Brain?" box, it was found that humans learn to trust people with faces similar to those of people who have proven trustworthy (FeldmanHall et al., 2018).

Discrimination

Discrimination refers to the ability to respond in one way in the presence of one stimulus and in a different way in the presence of another. For a behavior to come under the control of one stimulus but not of another, one must be able to discriminate between them. For example, differentially responding to a red, yellow, and green traffic light implies that one can discriminate between red, yellow, and green. In the 1950s, psychologists Norman Guttman and Harry Kalish sought to understand the relationship between generalization and discrimination (Guttman and Kalish, 1956). In a landmark study, Guttman and Kalish (1956) trained four groups of pigeons to peck at an illuminated key to obtain food on a variable interval schedule of reinforcement (VI-1). Each group was trained to peck a key illuminated by one of four colors (i.e., wavelengths of 530, 550, 580, and 600 nanometers [nm]) to obtain food. These were the discriminative stimuli (S^D) for each group. Once the pigeons learned to peck at the key associated with the S^D for their respective group, they were given extinction trials in which 11 different wavelengths of light illuminated the key in random order. They were never reinforced during training (S^D), and one was the S^D.

The experiment aimed to determine the extent to which the pigeons would keep pecking the key as the wavelengths of light illuminating it differed from the training stimulus. The average number of key pecks across the different wavelengths of light by which the key was illuminated is shown in the **stimulus generalization gradients** presented in Figure 15.4. A stimulus generalization gradient is a graphical representation of the number of responses across a range of S progressively dissimilar to the S^D. As you can see in the figure, each group of pigeons responded most in the presence of the S^D. However, you can also see that the number of responses gradually declined as the wavelengths illuminating the key progressively differed from the S^D. Studying stimulus generalization gradients such as the ones in Figure 15.4 provides researchers with the differences required between stimuli for animals to respond to them differently. A stimulus generalization gradient also tells us how powerfully a stimulus controls a behavior. This is because it measures the change in response probability with a change in the value of a stimulus.

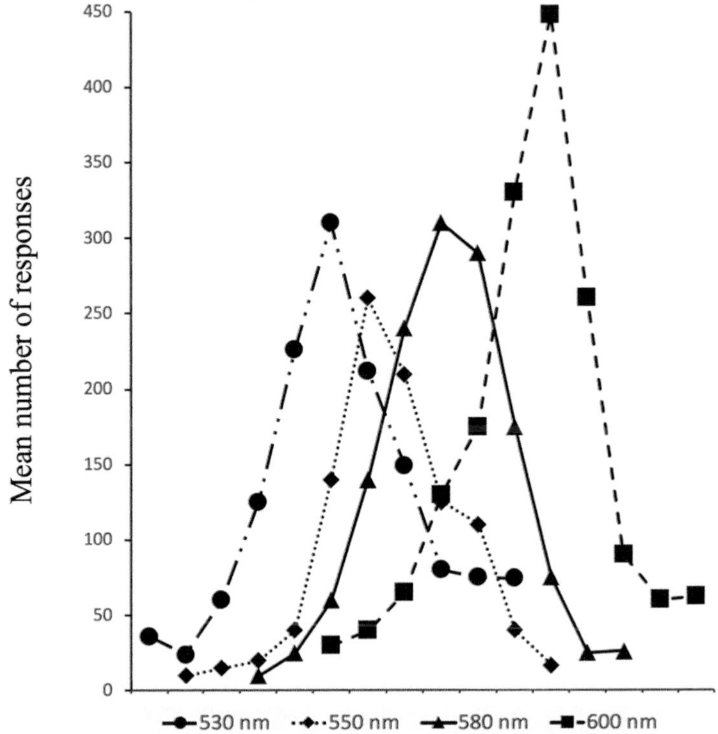

Figure 15.4 Stimulus generalization gradients for four groups of pigeons reinforced for pecking a key when illuminated by lights of various wavelengths (see text for details).

Source: Modified from: Guttman, N., & Kalish, H. I. (1956). Discriminability and stimulus generalization. *J Exp Psychol, 51*(1), 79–88. https://doi.org/10.1037/h0046219.

What in the Brain?

Stimulus Generalization, Trust, and the Brain

Psychologist Oriel FeldmanHall and colleagues hypothesized that learning to assign social value to unfamiliar people occurs through stimulus generalization (Feldman-Hall et al., 2018). That is, unfamiliar people may acquire positive or negative social values based on their degree of resemblance to familiar people who have already been assigned social values. Hence, the decision to trust a stranger may be influenced by how much she resembles someone we have learned to trust.

They tested their hypothesis via an experiment consisting of two phases (conditioning and generalization), during which participants played a computerized trust game in which they were made to believe they were real playing partners. In fact, these were virtual partners whose computer-generated facial images were displayed on a screen.

Conditioning Phase

The participants were given $10 and acted as investors in a trust game. They were asked to entrust their money to three players designated as trustees. The sum of money invested was multiplied by a factor of four. The trustees decided to either "reciprocate" by sharing back the money or to "defect" by keeping it all. The trustees were considered highly trustworthy, moderately trustworthy, or untrustworthy based on the percentage of money they reciprocated (93%, highly trustworthy; 60%, moderately trustworthy; 7%, untrustworthy). Thus, the subjects learned which of the three players could be trusted to reciprocate with the most money.

Generalization Phase

The participants were given the choice of new partners with whom to play another round of the game. Pictures of new potential partners were shown on the screen with the written question, "Who do you want to play with?" Unbeknownst to the participants, the pictures of the faces from which they chose were morphs of the faces they saw in the conditioning phase with never-before-seen faces. The morphed faces gradually more closely resembled the original faces in 11% increments. Notably, the participants did not consciously recognize the new partners as derivatives of the faces they saw in the conditioning phase.

Results

The degree of resemblance of the morphs to the highly trustworthy trustee in the conditioning phase predicted which morphs the participants chose to play with. In contrast, the degree of resemblance of the morphs to the untrustworthy trustee predicted which of the morphs the participants decided not to play with. These results showed that the decision to trust or not to trust unfamiliar people may result from an unconscious generalization process of the facial features of people we have learned to trust or mistrust.

Brain Mechanisms

In a second experiment, the brain areas involved in trust and mistrust were investigated in participants who played the same trust game while having their brains scanned by fMRI. The areas of interest included the amygdala and the caudate nucleus (Figure 15.5).

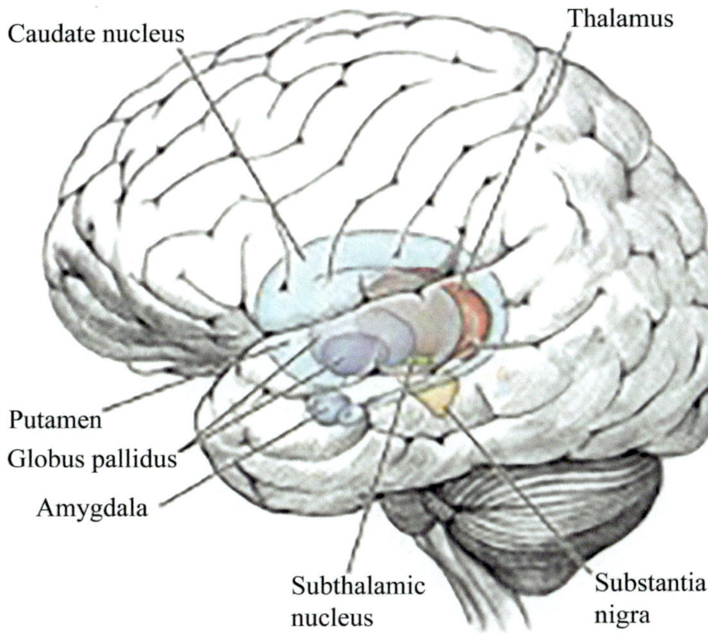

Figure 15.5 Location of the caudate nucleus and amygdala among various other brain areas.

Source: Watson, N. V. (2020). *The mind's machine* (3rd ed.). Oxford University Press Academic. Page 43, Figure 2.14 (left).

The Amygdala

Activity in the amygdala, previously found to process information about aversive and socially threatening stimuli (Baron et al., 2011), increased as the similarity between the morphs in the generalization phase and the pictures of not-at-all-trustworthy trustees in the conditioning phase also increased. However, amygdala activity remained stable across the degrees of resemblance of the morphs with the somewhat trustworthy trustees in the conditioning phase.

The Caudate Nucleus

Activity in the caudate nucleus, previously found to process socially rewarding stimuli (Fareri, Chang and Delgado, 2012), increased as the similarity between the morphs in the generalization phase and the pictures of the highly trustworthy trustees in the conditioning phase increased.

Are You Thinking Critically?

1. Can you think of another process that might be involved in the decision to trust strangers?
2. For what other reasons could these brain areas have become activated?
3. Have you ever been in a situation where you trusted or mistrusted a stranger but could not explain why?

Properties of Stimulus Generalization Gradients

As shown in Figure 15.4, stimulus generalization gradients can vary widely in shape. By studying how they differ along four dimensions—area, height, slope, and form—stimulus generalization gradients can be analyzed and compared (Honig and Urcuioli, 1981). In the following, they are briefly described without a detailed discussion of each dimension.

- **Area:** The area of a stimulus generalization gradient is the total space it takes up on a graph. It represents the extent to which responses are distributed and the range of values used during the generalization test.
- **Height:** The height of a stimulus generalization gradient is the stimulus value at which the maximal amount of responding occurred during the generalization test. This is usually the value at which responses were reinforced during training.
- **Slope:** The slope of a stimulus generalization gradient is the rate of change in responses from the training value (S^D) to the values of generalized responses (S^Δ).
- **Form:** The form of a stimulus discrimination gradient refers to the extent to which the slopes on each side of S^D are symmetrical. The form of the gradient depends on how the change in the values of a stimulus presented during the test is similar on each side of the S^D. For example, if the values below S^D consistently change by units of 5, but change by units of 10 above S^D, then the gradient form will be asymmetrical.

Figure 15.4 also shows that the stimulus generalization gradients for the four groups of pigeons are similar in area, slope, and form but differ in height, as well as the properties of the training stimulus for each group.

Critical Thinking Spot Check 15.3

1. Distinguish between stimulus generalization and stimulus discrimination.
2. What is important to know about stimulus generalization and stimulus discrimination in understanding behavior?
3. Provide an everyday example in which you learned to generalize a stimulus.
4. Provide an everyday example in which you learned to discriminate between environmental stimuli.
5. Describe a classic experiment in which stimulus generalization gradients were shown in pigeons.
6. Identify and explain each of the components of a stimulus generalization gradient.

Chapter Summary

Each bullet point aligns directly with the learning objectives outlined at the beginning of the chapter.

- People's and animals' behavior is often controlled by environmental stimuli, a process known as stimulus control. For example, Skinner believed that behavior was controlled by its consequences and the stimuli present when it was reinforced. In what he called the three-term contingency, he proposed that any behavioral act could be broken down into discriminative stimuli (S^D), response (R), and reinforcer ($S^{+/-}$). These are often referred to as antecedent, behavior, and consequence, or the ABCs of behavior.
- It is not always obvious which of many different stimuli that precede a behavior is exerting its influence on it. Experiments designed to identify controlling stimuli out of several others have been conducted. In one experiment, psychologist George Reynolds (1961) demonstrated that different pigeons produced the same response due to various aspects of the same stimulus. In another experiment, Morse and Skinner (1958) showed that environmental stimuli can control the occurrence of an operant response even if it was never associated with that response.
- Two interesting phenomena occur when animals are trained to respond to obtain a reinforcer: generalization and discrimination. Norman Guttman and Harry Kalish (1956) showed that animals will respond to the training stimulus and other stimuli that vary along the same dimension during testing. This is known as a stimulus generalization gradient, which can be graphically represented.
- A stimulus generalization gradient shows how much a stimulus must differ from a training stimulus to respond differently to it. In certain situations, an animal's survival depends on its ability to generalize, but in other situations, it depends on its ability to discriminate. Stimulus generalization gradients can be distinguished by four properties: area, height, slope, and form.

Glossary

Discrimination The ability to differentiate between similar stimuli and respond only to the specific stimulus associated with reinforcement or punishment.

Generalization The tendency for a learned response to extend to similar stimuli rather than being restricted to the exact stimulus present during training.

Stimulus control The process by which behavior is influenced by environmental cues, meaning responses occur more frequently in the presence of certain stimuli.

Stimulus generalization gradients A graphical representation of how response strength varies depending on the similarity between new stimuli and the original conditioned stimulus.

Three-term contingency The foundational principle of operant conditioning, consisting of an antecedent (stimulus), a behavior (response), and a consequence (reinforcement or punishment).

16 Fine-Tuning Behavior

The Behavioral Effects of Stimulus Discrimination

Learning Objectives

1. Define stimulus generalization according to Pavlov's and Spence's theories and explain Reynolds's development of stimulus discrimination training to address discrimination challenges in animal behavior.
2. Demonstrate understanding of the peak-shift effect of stimulus discrimination training, including explanations based on generalization gradients and signal detection theory.
3. Analyze how conditioned stimuli elicit different behaviors when presented alone versus as compounds, reflecting natural conditioning processes.
4. Evaluate the concept of derived relations and stimulus equivalences proposed by Murray Sidman (1971), including reflexivity, symmetry, and transitivity.

Armand's Amazement at Sports Judges

Source: IStock photo ID 43373832.

DOI: 10.4324/9781003491828-29

While watching the Olympic Games with his friend Travis, Armand expressed his amazement at how he found it difficult to differentiate between the gold, silver, and bronze medal performances in judged sports such as figure skating, freestyle skiing, and diving. "I don't know how they do it," he told Travis during the freestyle aerial skiing finals. In the second year of his psychology degree, Travis replied, "They're experts." "I know," said Armand, "but still." In Armand's opinion, except in cases when a competitor fell or made an obvious blunder, he found the performances of all the athletes to be just as good. "You see," said Travis, "over many years of observing a sport, expert judges learned to make fine discriminations between the components that compose the performance of one athlete from those that compose the performance of another." Noticing that he piqued Armand's interest, Travis continued, "You must understand that if you have not watched the sport or practiced it for many years, a much larger difference between performances must exist for you to notice. In addition," said Travis, "sports judges learned to assign different scores to athletes depending on how well or whether they performed certain required components of their routines." Travis told Armand that his difficulty in discriminating the quality of performances stemmed from his lack of experience with the sport, which led him to generalize his appreciation across performances. At Travis's urging, Armand later read about experts' fundamental qualities. He learned that one of the criteria by which an expert is defined is the ability to discriminate between closely related stimuli along the same dimension. This fits well with Travis's explanation for why sports judges were so good at discriminating between slight differences in athletes' performances.

16.1 Stimulus Discrimination Training

What Causes a Generalization Gradient?

Irradiation of Excitation

In what he called **irradiation of excitation**, Pavlov (1927) proposed that the training stimulus used in stimulus discrimination training activated neurons in a particular brain area. He believed that his activation irradiated (or spread) to neurons located in the neighboring regions. He also thought that the strength of this activation decreased as a function of its distance from the area activated by the training stimulus. Therefore, stimuli other than the training stimulus elicited the same response at intensities proportional to their degree of similarity. Hence, Pavlov believed that generalization gradients were due to the animal's inability to discriminate closely related stimuli.

The Lashley-Wade Hypothesis

Alternative explanations that challenged Pavlov's view of stimulus generalization were proposed. For example, in what is known as the **Lashley-Wade hypothesis**, psychologists Karl Lashley (1890–1958) and Marjorie Wade (1946) hypothesized that animals fail to

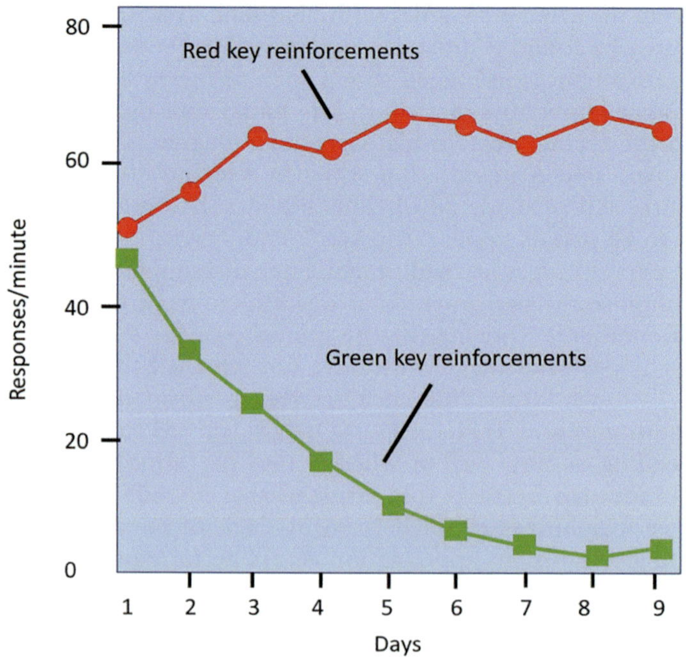

Figure 16.1 The results of stimulus discrimination training in pigeons (see text for details).

Source: Modified from: Reynolds, G. S. (1975). *A primer of operant conditioning*. Glenview, IL: Scott, Foresman.

distinguish stimuli by their more subtle characteristics, not because of their inability to do so but because they have never been trained to do so. This should make you think of Armand, in the chapter's opening vignette, who could not discriminate between a gold, silver, and bronze medal performance in the Olympics. This was possibly not due to his lack of ability to do so but to his lack of experience with the sport.

The **Lashley-Wade hypothesis** was tested using a procedure known as **stimulus discrimination training**, in which animals are reinforced for responding in the presence of one stimulus value and not reinforced for responding in the presence of another stimulus value. For example, in one experiment, pigeons were reinforced for pecking a key when in the presence of a red light (S^+), but not reinforced for pecking the key when in the presence of a green light (S^-). As shown in Figure 16.1, the difference in response rates per minute was slight at the beginning of training but became progressively more significant as training progressed across daily sessions (Reynolds, 1975).

Sharpening the Stimulus Discrimination Gradient

Psychologists H.M. Jenkins and R.H. Harrison tested the Lashley-Wade hypothesis in an experiment that examined the effects of stimulus discrimination training on a stimulus generalization gradient (1962). In that experiment, pigeons obtained a food reinforcer when they pecked a key in the presence of a 1000 CPS tone (S^+) but not when no tone was

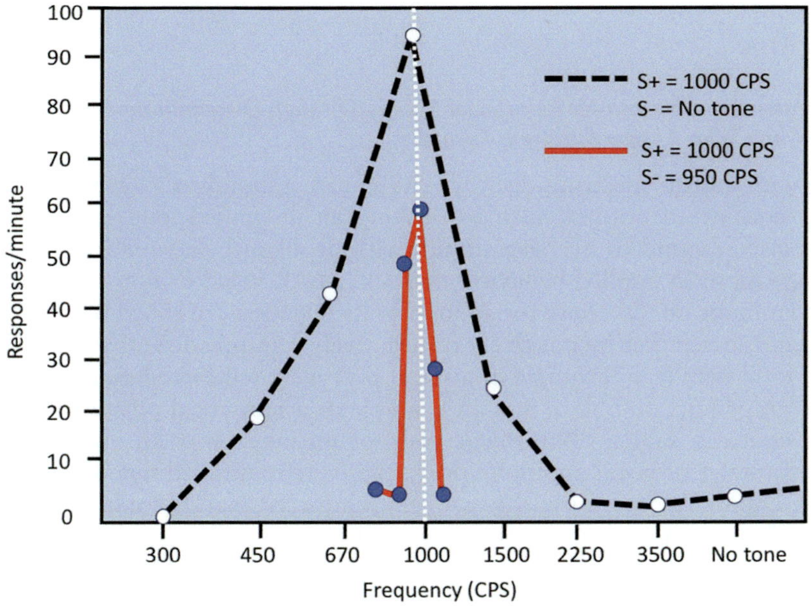

Figure 16.2 Sharpening of a stimulus generalization gradient obtained in pigeons by Jenkins and Harrison (1962) (see text for details).

Source: Modified from Jenkins, H. M., & Harrison, R. H. (1962). Generalization gradients of inhibition following auditory discrimination learning. *J Exp Anal Behav, 5*, 435–441. https://doi.org/10.1901/jeab.1962.5-435.

presented (S^-). The pigeons were then given extinction trials in which a range of tones, including the training frequency of 1000 CPS, were presented. The number of responses observed at each of these frequencies was recorded. The resulting generalization gradient for a single pigeon is shown in Figure 16.2 (broken line). They then conducted stimulus discrimination training with the same pigeons, with an S^+, which also consisted of a 1000 CPS tone, and an S^-, which consisted of a 950 CPS tone.

The resulting post-discrimination generalization gradient (solid line) and the generalization gradient obtained without discrimination training are shown. In support of the Lashley-Wade hypothesis, the generalization gradient was sharpened, suggesting that discrimination training resulted in the pigeon improvement in discriminating closely related frequencies. In the case of sports judges, so admired by Armand in the opening vignette, one might say that their discrimination gradient when judging between performances was sharpened by the years of experience with the sport, permitting them to differentiate between gold, silver, and bronze medal performances successfully.

The results of this study also point to the role of stimulus-discrimination training in developing human expertise. This is obvious in wine or beer tasters, who, after several years of training, can discriminate between wines or beers by detecting subtle differences that are difficult to detect by untrained individuals. Similarly, it is difficult for an amateur to distinguish a gold, silver, or bronze medal performance in sports judged by experts, such as figure skating, diving, or gymnastics.

Focus on ABA

Teaching Alternative Negatively Reinforced Mands Through Discrimination Training in Children With Autism Spectrum Disorder

Children with autism spectrum disorder (ASD) can respond to aversive stimuli with behaviors considered normal, such as pushing an unwanted item away. However, they may also respond to aversive stimuli with problem behaviors such as screaming or aggression. In applied behavior analysis (ABA), vocal or non-vocal behaviors used to communicate the desire for an item or its rejection are called mands (Skinner, 1957). Mands can either be positively or negatively reinforced. Verbally asking for a preferred food item is an example of a vocal positively reinforced mand. Pointing to a glass of grape juice to obtain it is an example of a non-vocal positively reinforced mand. In contrast, saying "No, thank you" or pushing away an unpreferred food item are examples of vocal and non-vocal negatively reinforced mands, respectively. Increasing children's repertoire of negatively reinforced mands could allow them to avoid aversive stimuli by emitting a greater variety of socially acceptable behaviors.

Special education professor Laura Chezan and colleagues (2019) investigated this possibility in an experiment with three children (Adrian, Julian, and Justin) diagnosed with ASD. The researchers first observed the negatively reinforced mands used by each of these children to reject unpreferred items and activities in their homes and institutional environments. These included pushing away, dropping, giving back, squeezing, whining, covering the eyes, running away, and turning away. They then taught the children alternative negatively reinforced mands, chosen in conjunction with their parents and teachers, through stimulus discrimination training. The new mands taught to each of the children are described subsequently.

Adrian: Picking up a rejection card (laminated square with an X in the middle) and extending the arm with the card facing the trainer.

Julian: Picking up a rejection card and extending his arm with the card facing the trainer, paired with vocally stating, "No, thank you."

Justin: Signing "no" by extending his index and middle finger and tapping his thumb with both fingers.

Training

The children were given two types of training trials: non-example and example trials. In non-example trials, the children were presented with preferred food items, which elicited positively reinforced mands. In example trials, the children were presented with non-preferred food items, which elicited negatively reinforced mands. All the positively reinforced mands were considered correct and reinforced on non-example trials. However, in the example trials, only the alternative negatively reinforced mands were considered correct and reinforced.

Generalization

The children were then given generalization trials to see whether their emission of new, alternative, negatively reinforced mands generalized to untrained stimuli by presenting them with items not used in training.

Discriminated Maintenance

The researchers also wanted to see whether the emission of new, alternative, negatively reinforced mands would persist beyond training by testing the children three and four weeks after training.

Results

All three children successfully learned the alternative nonreinforced minds. The emission of the alternative nonreinforced mands also generalized to untrained stimuli. During the discriminated maintenance phase, the children also persisted in their emission of the alternative nonreinforced minds. These results show that teaching children alternative negatively reinforced mands is possible, thus improving their repertoire of socially acceptable responses to reject non-preferred items and activities.

Are You Thinking Critically?

1. Distinguish between positively reinforced and negatively reinforced mands.
2. Describe real-life situations in which children might need to learn new mands.
3. Can you think of other ways children can be taught mands?

The Peak-Shift Effect

The **peak-shift effect** refers to the phenomenon in which the peak of generalization gradients of animals trained to discriminate between a S^+ and S^- along the same dimension (i.e., between two frequencies of light or sound), shifts from the S^+ in the direction opposite to the S^-. The peak-shift effect was first reported in a study investigating the impact of stimulus discrimination training on generalization gradients (Hanson, 1957). In one experiment, different groups of pigeons were subjected to stimulus discrimination training. All the pigeons were trained to peck a key illuminated by a 550 nm light (S^+) to receive food reinforcement. The S^- was of a different wavelength for each group of pigeons ($S^-_{555\ nm}$, $S^-_{560\ nm}$, $S^-_{570\ nm}$, and $S^-_{590\ nm}$). Another group of pigeons (the control group) was trained to peck the key when illuminated by a 550-nm wavelength light but was never trained with an S^-. All groups were then given post-discrimination extinction tests, during which they were randomly presented with a range of wavelengths that included the training stimulus along with wavelengths that they had never experienced during training (480, 500, 510, 520, 530, 540, 550 [training stimulus], 560, 570, 580, 590, 600, 610, and 620 nm).

The results of this experiment are shown in Figure 16.3. The generalization gradient for one of the groups subjected to stimulus discrimination training showed a significant sharpening of the range of wavelengths of light to which they responded. This finding was consistent with the Lashley-Wade hypothesis and the findings of Jenkins and Harrison (1962) described previously. The second observation is that a shift in the response peak away from the S^+ in the direction opposite the S^- was found for each group subjected to stimulus discrimination training. That is, the $S^-_{555\ nm}$, $S^-_{560\ nm}$, $S^-_{570\ nm}$, and $S^-_{590\ nm}$ groups shifted the peak of their response from 550 nm during training to about 530, 540, 540, and 540 nm during the post-discrimination generalization test, respectively. In contrast, no shift in the response peak occurred in the control group, which was not subjected to stimulus discrimination

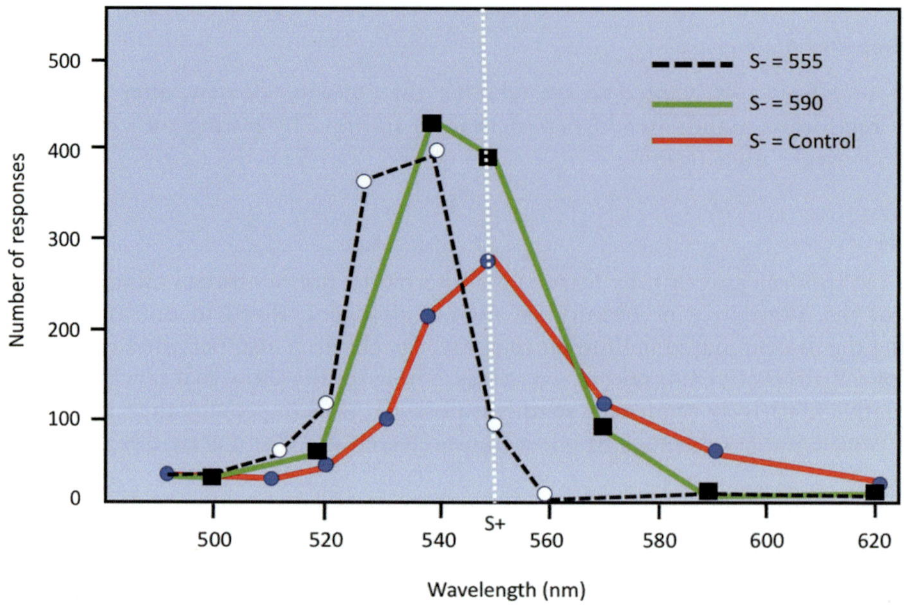

Figure 16.3 The peak-shift effect. Postdiscrimination generalization gradients of pigeons subject to stimulus discrimination training in which the S^+ was 550 nm and the S^- was either 555 nm or 590 nm (in Hanson, 1957) (see text for details).

Source: Hanson, H. M. (1957). Discrimination training effect on stimulus generalization gradient for spectrum stimuli. *Science, 125*(3253), 888–889. https://doi.org/10.1126/science.125.3253.888.

training. A third observation is that the closer the CS^- frequency is to the frequency used as a CS^+, the greater the shift in the peak of responses away from the CS^+.

Explaining the Peak-Shift Effect

SPENCE'S EXPLANATION

How can the peak-shift effect be explained? Psychologist Kenneth Spence (1907–1967) proposed that during stimulus discrimination training, an excitatory generalization gradient builds around the S^+, and an inhibitory generalization gradient builds around the S^-. What is observed in the post-discrimination test is the sum of these two gradients, which determines the amount of responding that occurs in the presence of generalized stimuli (Spence, 1937). To put this more simply, the resulting shift in the peak of responses can be calculated by subtracting the level of inhibition from the level of excitation at each point along the stimulus dimension. This results in a net excitatory gradient shown in Figure 16.4, with its peak of responding shifted from the S^+ in the direction opposite the S^-.

SIGNAL DETECTION THEORY

An alternative to Spence's explanation for the peak-shift effect is based on **signal-detection theory (SDT)**. SDT helps us understand how animals (and people) make decisions when

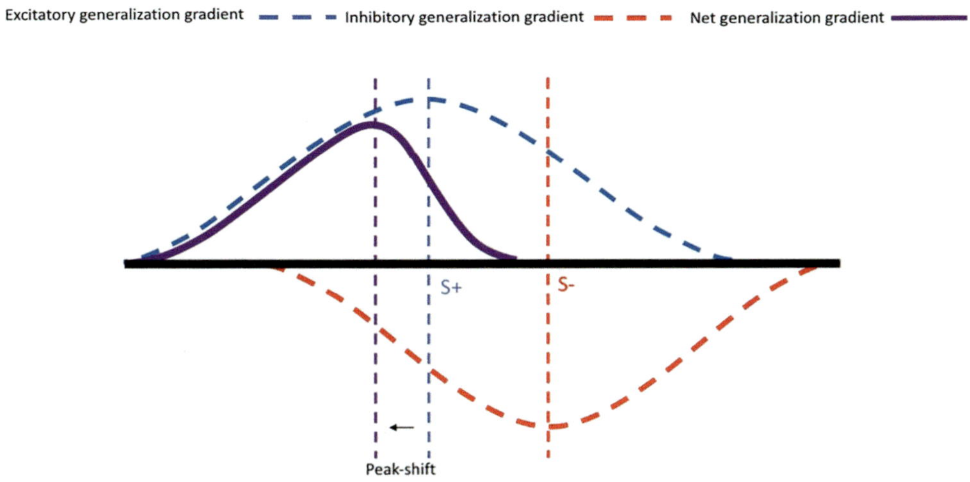

Figure 16.4 Spence's (1937) explanation for the peak-shift effect (see text for details).

things are unclear or uncertain. In SDT experiments, researchers measure how often subjects correctly identify when something is present (hits) versus how often they mistakenly think something is there when it's not (false alarms).

SDT can explain the peak-shift effect in the following way. Imagine an animal has learned that one stimulus (S+) means food is coming, while a similar but slightly different stimulus (S–) means no food. Now imagine testing the animal with a whole range of stimuli that gradually change from looking like the S+ to looking like the S–. Some of these test stimuli fall right in the middle—they're sort of like both the S+ and the S–. This creates a problem: How does the animal decide which ones to respond to?

If the animal responds to stimuli that are too close to the S–, it wastes energy responding when there's no food (a false alarm). But if it's too cautious and only responds to stimuli exactly like the S+, it might miss out on food opportunities. The solution? Shift its responding away from the S+ in the opposite direction from the S–. This creates a safety margin. By doing this, the animal can be more confident that when it responds, food will actually be there. It's like the animal is saying, "I'll only respond to stimuli that are clearly on the S+ side, not the ambiguous middle ones."

This strategy maximizes correct responses while minimizing mistakes. In nature, this is incredibly useful. It helps animals distinguish safe, nutritious food from dangerous, toxic food. Animals that can make this distinction reliably have a survival advantage (Lynn et al. 2005). Many toxic prey advertise their danger through bright colors, foul odors, or warning sounds—these are called aposematic signals, including chromatic aposematism (Seymoure et al. 2018), odor aposematism (Eisner and Grant, 1981), and acoustic aposematism (Barber et al. 2009). The peak-shift effect may also play a role in mate selection, helping animals choose the best possible partners (Andersson and Simmons, 2006).

THE PEAK-SHIFT EFFECT AND HUMAN BEHAVIOR

The peak-shift effect plays an essential role in human behavior. Neuroscientist V.S. Ramachandran and painter William Hirstein suggested that the peak-shift effect is one

Once you have identified a section of the road as a speed trap, you may reduce your speed below the limit, shifting your peak response downwards to avoid a fine.

Source: I Stock photo ID:15.32501559.

of eight laws constituting the artistic experience (1999). For example, they believe that, when painting a scene, the artist tries to convey the essence of a scene and amplify it to trigger the same neurobiological response elicited by the actual scene. The peak-shift effect is evident in caricatures, where a person's noticeable trait is amplified. This results in the shift of the peak of the response to the feature from the actual trait to the one caricatured.

The peak-shift effect also explains why people are drawn to extreme versions of stimuli they already like. Advertisers exploit this propensity. For example, the hamburgers in fast-food commercials always look bigger and juicer than ordinary food. The peak-shift effect is also highly relevant to social media, where clicking behavior is controlled by more attractive stimuli, bigger or better versions of stimuli we are accustomed to or already like. The peak-shift effect is also important for avoiding aversive situations. For example, after getting a speeding ticket at a speed trap on the highway, you may reduce your speed to lower than the allowable limit when driving through that location again, maximizing the probability that you will not get a ticket. In another example, feeling that your parents are disappointed by the unripe apples you brought home may lead you to choose exceptionally red apples without a tinge of green the next time you shop for them.

Critical Thinking Spot Check 16.1

1. Distinguish between Pavlov's irradiation of excitation theory and the Lashley-Wade hypothesis.
2. Describe the peak-shift effect.

3. Provide two explanations for the peak-shift effect.
4. Provide an everyday life example of the peak-shift effect.

16.2 Patterning

Positive and Negative Patterning

So far, we have discussed experiments and situations in which discrimination between discrete stimuli has been emphasized. However, life is more complex. Both people and animals are confronted with situations in which stimuli signal one outcome when encountered by themselves but signal another when presented as a compound. This is achieved through what is known as patterning. Two types of patterning exist. These are positive patterning and negative patterning. **Positive patterning** occurs when individual stimuli are associated with an adverse outcome but with a positive outcome when presented as a compound stimulus. Positive patterning is therefore referred to as A^-B^-/AB^+.

In contrast, **negative patterning** occurs when individual stimuli are associated with a positive outcome but with a negative outcome when presented as a compound stimulus. Negative patterning is referred to as A^+B^+/AB^-. To illustrate, consider the following situations. You have learned that you seldom have a good time when going out with either two of your friends (A^-B^-) when they are by themselves. However, you have also learned that you have a blast when going out with them together (AB^+), an example of positive patterning. The opposite situation is also true. Imagine that you have a great time with either of two friends when they are alone (A^+B^+). However, when they are together, they always argue with each other and ruin the evening (AB^-), an example of negative patterning. Negative patterning is how we may have learned not to drink and drive. Social drinking is pleasant when done responsibly (A^+), and driving can be fun (B^+). However, drinking and driving can have devastating consequences (AB^-).

Experimental Evidence of Patterning

Positive and negative patterning has been demonstrated in a variety of species. For example, researchers tested whether positive and negative patterning in the classical conditioning of the **proboscis extension reflex (PER)** can be achieved in harnessed honeybees (Mansur, Rodrigues and Mota, 2018). The PER is the extension of an insect's proboscis, a tubular mouthpart used for feeding and sucking, which is triggered when a sweet solution touches its antennae, mouthparts or feet.

The researcher used a visual CS and an olfactory CS in that study. Note that the discrimination was bimodal because the CSs stimulated two senses (i.e., taste and smell). The visual CS (A) consisted of an illuminated blue or green screen presented to one of the bee's eyes. The olfactory CS (B) consisted of either hexanol (the smell of freshly mown grass) or nonanol (a citrus smell), which was delivered to the bee's antennae through a syringe that contained a filtered paper to which the odorants were applied. The unconditioned stimulus was a 30% sugar solution. The experiments in the study consisted of ten training trials and a test trial in which each CS was presented without the delivery of the US one hour later. During both the training trials and the test, the percentage of time the PER was observed was recorded when the bees were exposed to each CS (A and B) and the compound stimulus composed of a visual and an olfactory stimulus (AB).

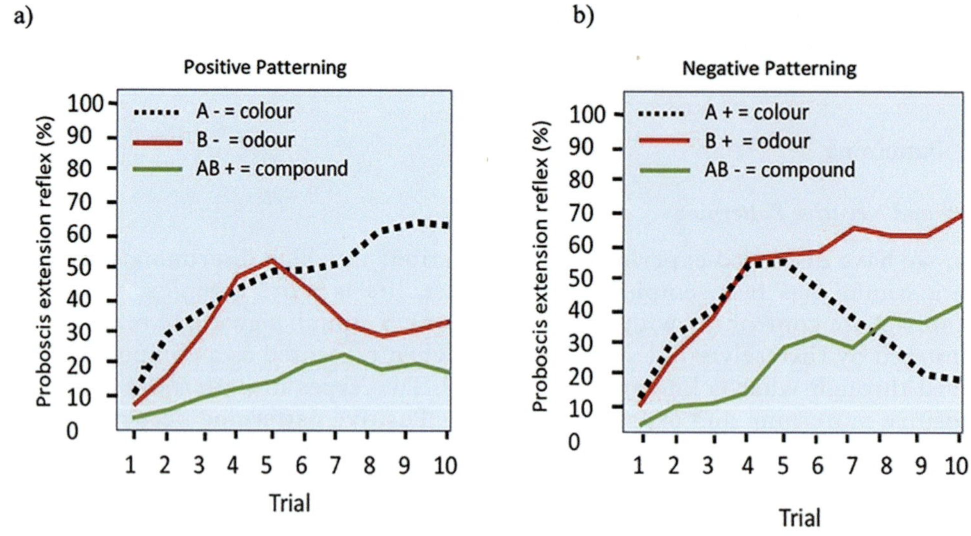

Figure 16.5 a) Positive patterning. A significantly higher percentage of proboscis extension reflex (PER) was observed when the bees were exposed to the AB⁺ than each of the A⁻ and B⁻ by themselves by the end of the ten training trials and during a single test trial in which the US (30% sugar solution) was not presented. b) Negative patterning. A significantly lower percentage of proboscis extension reflex (PER) was observed when the bees were exposed to the AB⁻ than each of the A⁺ and B⁺ by themselves by the end of the ten training trials and during a single-test trials in which the US (30% sugar solution) was not presented (Mansur, Rodrigues and Mota, 2018).

Source: Modified from Mansur, B. E., Rodrigues, J. R. V., & Mota, T. (2018). Bimodal patterning discrimination in harnessed honey bees. *Front Psychol*, *9*, 1529. https://doi.org/10.3389/fpsyg.2018.01529.

Figure 16.5 shows the results of two of these experiments. As you can see in Figure 16.5a (left) (positive patterning), the bees successfully discriminated between the individual CSs (A^- and B^- [no US]) and the compound (AB^+ [US]) by the end of the training trials. The bees showed a significantly higher percentage of the PER when presented with the AB^+ compound than the A^- or B^- by themselves. This is positive patterning because they learned that either CS by itself led to no US but that they were associated with the US when presented together.

The results for the negative patterning condition are shown in Figure 16.5b. As you may have expected, the bees discriminated between the CSs (A^+ and B^+ [US]) and the compound (AB^- [no US]) by the end of the training trials. The bees showed a significantly lower percentage of the PER when presented with the AB compound than the A^+ or B^+ by themselves. This is negative patterning because they learned that either CS by itself led to the US but that they were associated with no US when presented together.

16.3 Conditional Discrimination

What Is a Conditional Discrimination?

In many situations, stimuli control behavior and signal whether a behavior will result in reinforcement. For example, when planning your weekend, you may decide to go to the beach if it is sunny, but you will go to a movie if a cloudy day is forecast. In other words, whether you go to the beach or a movie depends on the weather. This is known as **conditional discrimination,** in which a behavior is reinforced only when performed in a specific

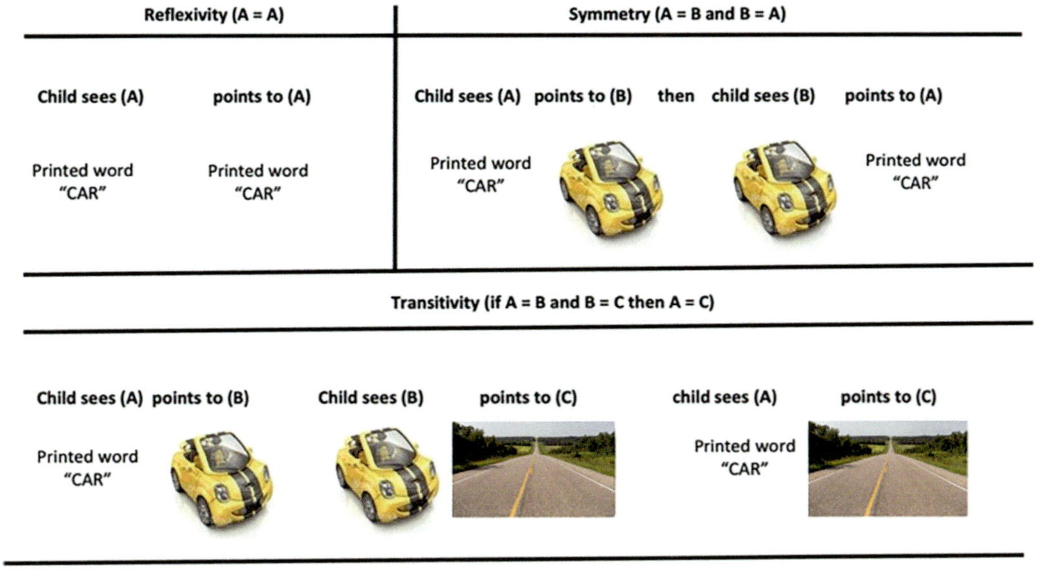

Figure 16.6 The equivalence relations of reflexivity, symmetry, and transitivity (see text for details).
Source: Road picture: Istock photo: Stock photo ID:586726296.

context or the presence of a particular stimulus. In the previous example, going to the beach is only rewarding if it is sunny. The following rule can also define conditional discrimination. If A1 is present, select B1; if A2 is present, choose B2. In our example, A1 represents a clear sky, and B1 represents the beach. A2 represents a cloudy sky, and B2 represents a movie. The sports judges alluded to in the opening vignette also perform conditional discriminations in the course of their work, in the form of allotting athletes a different number of points depending on the quality of the skills that are part of their routines.

Stimulus Equivalence

Stimulus equivalence refers to the phenomenon by which individual stimuli become related in new ways during a series of conditional discriminations with no additional training (Hayes, 1989; Sidman, 1971). Relationships between stimuli that developed without explicit training are known as **derived relations**. Sidman (1971) initially found evidence for derived relations while children were trained on conditional discrimination. These derived relations are known as stimulus equivalences. Sidman (1971) identified three types of stimulus equivalences: **reflexivity**, **symmetry**, and **transitivity**, each described subsequently and illustrated in Figure 16.6.

- **Reflexivity** refers to the ability to relate the sample stimulus in a conditional discrimination to itself. That is "A = A." For example, if a child is shown the printed word "car" as the sample stimulus, it should be able to point to the printed word "car" shown as a comparison stimulus (Figure 16.6 [top left]).
- **Symmetry** refers to the ability to derive that "B = A" after being taught that "A = B." For example, after having been taught to associate the printed word "car" with the picture of a car, a child can point to the printed word "car" without explicitly having been trained to do so (Figure 16.6 [top right]).

- **Transitivity** refers to the ability to relate a new stimulus to the original sample stimulus, even if they have never explicitly been paired. That is, if "A = B" and "B = C," then "A = C." For example, if a child learns that the printed word "car" is the equivalent of the picture of a car and that the picture of the car is equivalent to the picture of a road, a child learns that the printed word "car" is equivalent to the picture of the road even if it was never explicitly taught to do so (Figure 16.6 [bottom row]).

Critical Thinking Spot Check 16.2

1. Distinguish between the different types of patterning.
2. Why is it important to know about patterning in understanding stimulus control?
3. Define conditional discrimination.
4. How would you use conditional discrimination training to teach a child appropriate behavior?
5. Explain stimulus equivalence and the meaning of derived relations.
6. Distinguish between the three derived relations of stimulus equivalence by giving an example of each.

Chapter Summary

Each bullet point aligns with the learning objectives outlined at the beginning of the chapter.

- Pavlov believed that a stimulus generalization occurred because animals could not discriminate between closely related stimuli. He thought this happened because of the irradiation of excitation from the brain area activated by a training stimulus. However, Lashley and Wade believed that generalization occurred when animals were not trained to discriminate between stimuli. To address this problem, Reynolds developed a procedure known as stimulus discrimination training in which pigeons were reinforced for pecking a key in the presence of one stimulus but were not reinforced for pecking the key in the presence of another stimulus. Jenkins and Harrisson tested Spence's hypothesis. They found better stimulus discrimination by pigeons that underwent stimulus discrimination training than by pigeons that did not undergo such training.
- Another consequence of stimulus discrimination training is that the peak of responding is shifted from the S^+ in a direction away from the S^-. This is known as the peak-shift effect. According to one explanation, the peak-shift effect occurs because a generalization gradient develops around the S^+ and the S^-. The stimulus to which an animal responds is determined by the net result of subtracting the inhibitory gradient from the excitatory gradient. Another explanation is based on signal detection theory. This explains that animals respond to a utility function by resolving ambiguity between stimuli.
- In nature, stimuli can be conditioned to elicit a specific behavior when presented alone but elicit another behavior when conditioned as a compound.
- Conditional discrimination training can produce derived relations, which produce functionally related or equivalent classes of objects. Derived relations between objects of a functional class are made without explicit training and are known as stimulus equivalences. Psychologist Murray Sidman (1971) identified three equivalences: reflexivity, symmetry, and transitivity.

Glossary

Conditional discrimination A type of learning where responses depend on the presence of a specific context or additional stimulus cues.

Derived relation A learned connection between stimuli that emerges without direct training, based on prior associations.
Irradiation of excitation The spread of neural activation from a conditioned stimulus to nearby areas in the brain, influencing responses to similar stimuli.
Lashley–Wade hypothesis A theory suggesting that stimulus generalization occurs due to prior experiences with similar stimuli, rather than an innate tendency.
Negative patterning A conditioning process where reinforcement is given when stimuli are presented separately but not when presented together.
Peak–shift effect A phenomenon in discrimination learning where the strongest response shifts away from the reinforced stimulus toward a more extreme version due to previous training with a similar but non-reinforced stimulus.
Positive patterning A conditioning process where reinforcement is given when two stimuli are presented together, but not when presented individually.
Proboscis extension reflex (PER) An automatic response in insects, particularly honeybees, where the proboscis extends in response to food-related stimuli.
Reflexivity The ability to recognize that a stimulus is identical to itself in stimulus equivalence learning.
Signal-detection theory (SDT) A framework for understanding how organisms differentiate between relevant signals and background noise, particularly in perceptual decision-making.
Stimulus discrimination training A learning process where an organism is taught to respond differently to two or more stimuli by reinforcing responses to one and not the others.
Stimulus equivalence A learning phenomenon where different stimuli become interchangeable in meaning due to learned associations.
Symmetry A property in stimulus equivalence where if an organism learns that A is related to B, it also recognizes that B is related to A.
Transitivity A principle in stimulus equivalence where if an organism learns that A is related to B and B is related to C, it deduces that A is related to C.
Utility function A mathematical representation of how choices are valued based on potential outcomes, often used in decision-making theories.

Module Summary

In this module, you learned about stimulus control of behavior. We began by explaining that the factors that elicit operant responses are not always apparent and how Skinner proposed the three-term contingency model of operant conditioning. The three terms in the contingency are 1) discriminative stimuli (S^D) (antecedent), 2) response (behavior), and 3) reinforcer ($S^{r+/r-}$) (consequence). You then learned that discriminating among the stimuli that serve as stimulus control for behavior is not always obvious. However, experiments by which the antecedent or discriminative stimuli to behavior could be identified were designed. Two phenomena associated with stimulus control are generalization, in which animals respond to the stimuli they were trained to respond to, and discrimination, in which animals can differentiate between stimuli they were trained to respond to and stimuli they were not trained to respond to. Both discrimination and generalization are adaptive responses. Pavlov believed that generalization occurred because animals were unable to discriminate. However, it was later shown that animals could learn to discriminate through discrimination training. Discrimination training also revealed that animals will learn to respond to an untrained stimulus that is more extreme than the trained stimulus. This is known as the peak-shift effect. The peak-shift effect can be explained by subtracting a generalization gradient that develops around the S^- from a generalization gradient that develops around the S^+ or by signal detection theory. In what is known as patterning, stimuli signal different consequences to behavior when presented by themselves than when presented in a compound. In conditional discrimination, one learns to respond only when one stimulus is present but not when another is present. For example, you may respond to a sunny day by going to the beach but to the movies on a rainy day. Finally, you learned that relationships between stimuli can develop without explicit training in what is known as stimulus equivalence.

Module 7
Application

Stimulus Control to Increase Desirable Behavior or Decrease Undesirable Behavior

Stimulus control refers to how environmental stimuli exert control over behavior. These stimuli can serve as discriminative stimuli, also known as occasion setters, that signal the occurrence of reinforcement (Watson et al., 2017). For example, suppose one always eats while watching television. In that case, the television may become a stimulus that signals food, increasing the probability that the person will eat again. This may present a problem for people struggling to lose weight, especially if the food includes high-calorie snacks.

Knowing that environmental stimuli can exert control over one's behavior by setting the occasion for reinforcement can be a powerful tool to increase desirable behavior or reduce undesirable behavior. It was found that setting up one's environment in ways that set the occasion for desirable behaviors effectively controls overeating, increases study time, and treats insomnia (Bootzin and Perlis, 2010; Edinger et al., 2021). Examples of "stimulus control plans" in which you set up your environment to increase or decrease undesirable behavior are outlined subsequently.

Stimulus Control to Increase Studying Time

1. Designate a limited number of areas as "study areas" (e.g., this could be one at home and one at school, such as the library). If you can, dedicate an area for studying each subject.
2. Study areas should be reserved for studying only. Do not eat, use social media, or do anything else in those areas.
3. Plan the order in which you will study your subjects and stick to that order.
4. Make sure that your study areas are free of distractions.
5. Don't study in places associated with being too comfortable, such as your bed or the couch on which you watch TV. Remember, the area needs to be exclusively dedicated to studying.
6. Only keep what you need for studying on your desk. Ensure you have everything before you start so you don't have to interrupt your study time to get something.

Stimulus Control to Decrease Overeating

1. Designate one place to eat all meals and snacks.
2. Decide in advance on the meals and snacks you will have, schedule the times you will eat them, and only eat at those times.

DOI: 10.4324/9781003491828-30

3. Be in the kitchen to prepare meals only.
4. Avoid all other activities, such as reading or watching television, while eating.
5. Rearrange the refrigerator and cupboards so that snack foods are not visible.
6. Shop for food only when you are not hungry and avoid snack aisles.
7. Make portions appear larger by using small plates and bowls.

Stimulus Control for Insomnia

1. Plan to rise at the same time every morning regardless of sleep time.
2. Go to bed only when sleepy.
3. Reserve your bed for only two activities: sleep and sex (i.e., do not use your cell phone or laptop, study, or engage in any other activity while in bed).
4. If unable to fall asleep, get out of bed and return to bed only when feeling sleepy.

Are You Thinking Critically?

1. Explain the rationale behind each step of the previous stimulus control plans.
2. Think of a desirable behavior that you would like to increase in frequency or an undesirable behavior you would like to decrease in frequency. How would you devise a stimulus control plan to help you reach your goals?
3. What other methods, besides stimulus control, can you use to help you increase or decrease undesirable behaviors?

Module 8

Choice Behavior and Self-Control

Introduction

From when you wake up in the morning to when you go to bed at night, you are confronted with various behaviors to choose from. You may choose to either get out of bed or to sleep in. Choosing to sleep in might be due to your choice of partying late into the night instead of going to bed early. Getting up early may be due to your choice of early morning classes over afternoon classes. You may be confronted with a choice of breakfast cereal, a bowl of oats, or pancakes. You may also choose to skip breakfast. Some of the choices you make are of little consequence. However, your choice of career paths, of whether to purchase a home or start a family, can profoundly affect your life. Chapter 17 explores how animals and people distribute their choices and behaviors among alternatives in a way proportional to the reinforcement they receive from them. For example, you may sleep in because it feels much better than getting up to class. You may go out partying instead of studying because the reinforcement you get from studying does not compare to the fun you have going out with your friends. In Chapter 18, you will learn how people do not always choose most advantageously. This is partly due to our limited ability to delay gratification. Indeed, when confronted with being instantly gratified and receiving a delayed reward, it is often difficult not to choose instant gratification. This occurs even if the later reward is larger or of better quality than a smaller immediate reward.

Chapter 17: Choice Behavior
Chapter 18: Self-Control

DOI: 10.4324/9781003491828-31

17 Choices, Choices, Choices

Choice Behavior Unveiled

Learning Objectives

- Define the matching law and explain its shift from proportion-based to ratio-based formulations.
- Differentiate between strict matching, undermatching, overmatching, and bias within the context of the matching law.
- Apply concurrent reinforcement schedules, specifically concurrent chain schedules, to assess matching behavior with primary and secondary reinforcers.
- Analyze and compare molar and molecular matching theories in terms of their explanations for matching behavior.

Gaming Through the Pandemic

Source Istock photo: Stock photo ID:1302987967.

DOI: 10.4324/9781003491828-32

Arash, a 19-year-old college student, has been an avid gamer for several years. His favorite games are massive multiplayer online role-playing games (MMORPG). Arash always managed his gaming time so as not to interfere with his studies and the time he spent socializing in person. He also spent much of his weekends playing basketball and engaging in other outdoor activities with his friends. However, when the pandemic hit, the lockdown curtailed the range of activities he loved to engage in. Arash thought the situation would only be temporary and that he and his friends would soon return to regular activities. As the lockdown was extended, Arash took up jogging and went to shoot hoops by himself in a nearby schoolyard. However, he eventually immersed himself in an MMORPG called Cave Dwellers. He became so absorbed by the game that he only occasionally stopped playing when his mom called him out of his room for meals. Arash's gaming time eventually got out of hand, and it was a regular occurrence for Arash to engage in marathon sessions that lasted well over ten hours. For Arash, immersion into the MMORPG provided him with reinforcers that the remaining choice of activities he perceived as available during the lockdown could not offer. These included admiration from other gamers due to skillful playing, social acceptance, making new friends, and escaping real-life problems. These reinforcers were significantly more potent at controlling his gaming behavior than any reinforcement he got from jogging and throwing hoops by himself. Arash realized that his gaming had started taking over his life. He started worrying that he may have internet gaming disorder, in which people lose interest in and give up activities they previously enjoyed in favor of gaming. He also read that people who experience the loneliness he experienced when deprived of habitual everyday interactions with others were especially vulnerable. Fortunately, Arash resolved to replace much of his gaming time with calisthenic exercises and going out for jogs. He also started having a more positive outlook and thinking about other activities he could do with the extra time spent out of school.

17.1 The Matching Law

Concurrent Schedules of Reinforcement and Matching

In this chapter's opening vignette, Arash was subjected to a simple rule of learning proposed by psychologist Aubrey Daniels in his book *Other People's Habits* (2005), which states that "behavior goes where reinforcement flows." That is, Arash had difficulty pulling himself away from gaming because the rate and intensity of reinforcement he received far surpassed the rate and intensity of reinforcement he received from any other activity. This chapter focuses on choice behavior and a simple formula that can account for it.

Richard Herrnstein (1930–1994), one of Skinner's students, investigated choice behavior in pigeons. To do so, he conducted an operant conditioning experiment in which animals were exposed to **concurrent schedules of reinforcement**. In this procedure, two separate reinforcement schedules are in effect simultaneously (Herrnstein, 1961). The pigeons were exposed to two response keys, each activated when pecked by the pigeons. Each response key (one situated to the left and one located to the right of the pigeons) was associated with a different variable interval (VI) schedule of food reinforcement. Pecking the left response key may have been related to a VI-30-second schedule, and pecking the right response key with a VI-60-second schedule. If you don't remember the reinforcement schedules, you may want to revise the relevant section in Chapter 10 (unit 10.2). However, the table in which they are summarized is replicated below for convenience.

The Schedules of Reinforcement (replicated from Chapter 10).

Schedules	*Definitions*	*Examples*
Fixed-ratio schedule	Reinforcement is delivered after a fixed number of responses are performed.	A carpenter gets paid for a specific number of cabinets she builds.
Variable-ratio schedule	Reinforcement is delivered after a random number of responses are performed.	Playing a slot machine.
Fixed-interval schedule	Reinforcement is delivered after a fixed amount of time has elapsed since the last response.	You get paid every Thursday regardless of how much work you perform.
Variable-interval schedule	Reinforcement is delivered after a random amount of time has elapsed since the last response.	Your boss praises your work at random times during the week.

This arrangement is illustrated in Figure 17.1. Remember that animals only receive a reinforcer under a VI schedule if a specified average amount of time elapses from when they received their last reinforcer. Therefore, under a VI-30 second schedule, an average of 30 seconds since the previous reinforcer must have elapsed before another response is reinforced, an average of 60 seconds under a VI-60 second schedule, 120 seconds under a VI-120 second schedule, and so on.

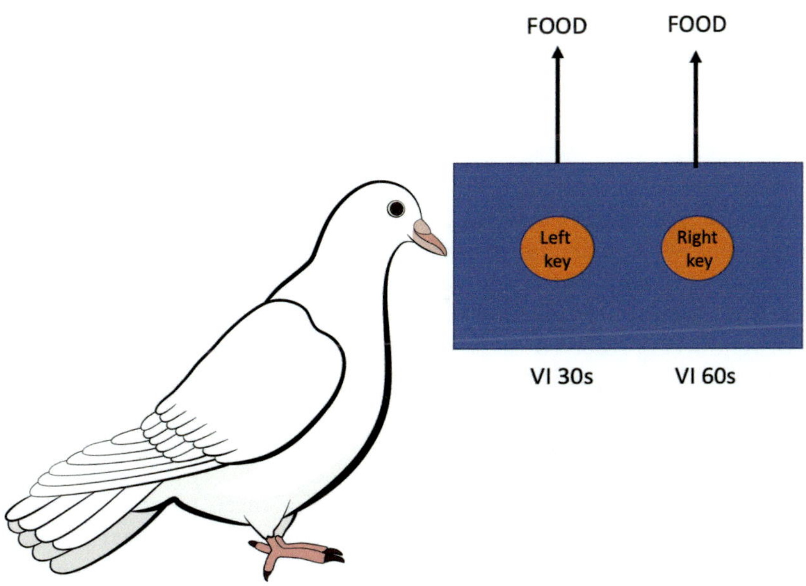

Figure 17.1 Concurrent schedule of reinforcement (see text for details).

Source: Pigeon stock illustration ID:1302627660.

Herrnstein (1961) also imposed a 1.5-second delay before the pigeons' responses were reinforced after switching from responding on the left key to responding on the right key and vice versa. This is known as a **changeover delay (COD)**. The COD prevented the pigeons from being reinforced for constantly switching from one key to the other, regardless of the difference in the reinforcement schedules, by getting food upon their very first peck on the other key.

Herrnstein (1961) wanted to determine how the pigeons would allocate their responses between the two keys. Would the pigeons respond at a higher proportional rate on the key associated with the schedule that offered a higher proportional rate of reinforcement? Hypothetically, if the schedules associated with each response key were VI-60 seconds (left) and VI-120 seconds (right), a pigeon might respond on the left key at 2500 times per hour versus 1250 times per hour on the right response key. As calculated by dividing the number of responses to the key associated with the VI-60 second key by the total number of responses to both keys, the proportion of responses allocated to the left response key is 66%.

$$\frac{\text{VI-60 responses}}{\text{V-60 responses + VI-120 responses}} = \frac{2500}{2500 + 1250} = .66$$

However, these responses were not all reinforced because they were performed under a VI schedule. For example, if the responses on the left key resulted in 55 reinforcements and responses on the right response key resulted in 28 reinforcements, the proportion of reinforcers received after one hour would also be 66%, the same as the responses to the left key.

$$\frac{\text{VI-60 reinforcement}}{\text{VI-60 reinforcement + VI-120 reinforcement}} = \frac{55}{55 + 28} = .66$$

As you can see, the proportion of responses to the left response key matches the proportion of reinforcers our hypothetical pigeon received by responding on the left response key, that is, 66. In other words, the relative rate of responses matched the relative rate of reinforcement they produced. This pattern of results is consistent with what is known as the **matching law**. The matching law was expressed by Herrnstein (1961) in the following formula:

$$\frac{R_1}{R_1 + R_2} = \frac{r_1}{r_1 + r_2}$$

The numerator, R_1, represents the number of responses allocated to alternative 1 (which in our previous example was the left response key, associated with the VI-60 second schedule), R_2 is the number of responses allocated to alternative 2 (which in our example was the right response key, associated with the VI-120 second schedule). In the denominator, r_1 is the number of reinforcers received by responding to alternative one, and r2 is the number of reinforcers received by responding to alternative 2.

An Example of Nearly Strict Matching

Figure 17.2 shows Herrnstein's (1961) results for the three pigeons in the experiment described at the beginning of the chapter. The pigeons displayed nearly strict matching. The vertical axis (or y-axis) shows the ratio of responses to key A relative to the total of responses to keys A and B (R_1/R_1+R_2) across a range of concurrent schedules of reinforcement for Pigeons 055, 231, and 641. The horizontal axis (or x-axis) shows the relative rates of reinforcements obtained from the ratio of responses to key A (r_1/r_1+r_2). Each data

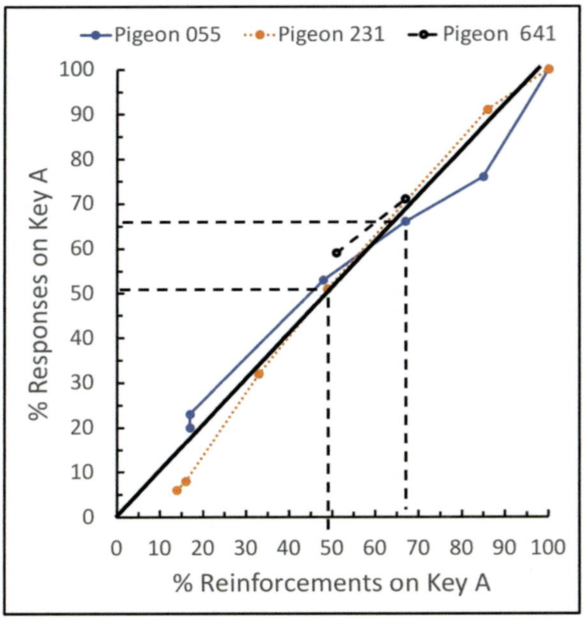

Figure 17.2 Results of the Herrnstein (1961) experiment (adapted from Herrnstein (1961); see text for details).

Source: Modified from: Herrnstein, R. J. (1961). Relative and absolute strength of response as a function of frequency of reinforcement. *J Exp Anal Behav, 4*, 267–272. https://doi.org/10.1901/jeab.1961.4-267.

point represents the average proportion of responses (%) and reinforcements for the last five sessions of the experiment when responding to different concurrent VI schedules. The regression line (black solid line) that runs across the graph has a slope of 1, meaning that the pigeons strictly matched their response rate to the left response key to the reinforcement they received from pecking it. As you can see, pigeons 231 and 055 responded to Key A at just above 50% and 65%, respectively, matching their ratio of reinforcements of 50% and just above 60%, respectively.

John Staddon, one of Herrnstein's students, found that using proportions of responses and reinforcers as calculated with Herrnstein's equation could not appropriately show the regularity of his data (Staddon, 1968). Therefore, as shown, he chose to represent his data as a function of the ratio of reinforcement obtained from responding to each of the alternatives. Using percentages instead of proportions, he found that the data points relating to his pigeons were spaced more equally. The matching equation thus adjusted is shown here.

$$\frac{R_1}{R_2} = \frac{r_1}{r_2}$$

It is important to remember that the study of choice in the laboratory is most often conducted with two choice alternatives. However, studies in which animals were presented with more than two choice alternatives have also been conducted. In these studies, the matching equation was adapted by expressing the ratio of responses allocated to one alternative versus several others compared to the ratio of reinforcements obtained by responding to that alternative versus the others in the way indicated subsequently (Davison and Hunter, 1976; Pliskoff and Brown, 1976).

Deviations From Strict Matching

Strict matching, which occurs when the proportion of responses to an alternative exactly matches the proportion of reinforcers it receives from selecting that alternative, does not always occur. Three types of deviations from strict matching may occur. These are **undermatching, overmatching**, and **bias**.

UNDERMATCHING

Undermatching occurs when an animal allocates a higher proportion of its responses to the alternative associated with the lowest rate of reinforcement. Why does undermatching occur? Several factors were found to account for undermatching. One possible reason for undermatching may be that an animal is not sensitive enough to the rate of reinforcement associated with one of the alternative schedules of reinforcement. In extreme undermatching, the animal is insensitive to the difference between the two schedules, resulting in the inability to differentiate between them and leaving the animal indifferent in its choices.

Undermatching may also occur if the COD is too short (Baum, 1974). Remember that a COD is a delay imposed by the experimenter when an animal begins to be reinforced after switching its responses from one alternative to the other. A short COD may cause the animal to be reinforced for switching from one alternative to the other, resulting in rapid switching between alternatives despite their different schedules of reinforcement.

A lack of sensitivity to the differences in the reinforcement rates of all alternatives may be why a person consistently makes terrible choices. For example, in alternating between cardiovascular exercise and weight training to lose weight, one may engage in a smaller ratio of cardiovascular exercise to weight training than has made them lose weight in the past because they were not aware that it was the amount of cardiovascular exercise they engaged in that accounted for most of the weight loss.

Undermatching may also occur when one is not well informed about all options. For example, it was found that low-income, high-achieving students apply to highly selective colleges versus less selective colleges at a rate that is below the rate at which they would get accepted if they did apply. This phenomenon, known as academic undermatching, is thought to deprive society of the contribution of a large pool of highly achieving individuals. It is believed to be partly due to the lack of information disseminated to low-income students about their college options, including the availability of financial aid and admission policies of highly selective colleges (Hoxby and Avery, 2013; Kelchen, Goldrick-Rab and Hosch, 2017).

OVERMATCHING

Overmatching occurs when an animal responds at a higher rate to the alternative associated with the largest rate of reinforcement in a way that is more extreme than matching. Why does overmatching occur? It has been found that overmatching may occur if the cost of moving from one alternative to the other is high or requires effort. For example, overmatching was found in a study where pigeons were required to run from one alternative to the other (Baum and Aparicio, 1999) and rats were required to jump over a barrier to move from one alternative to the other (Aparicio, 2001). In contrast to undermatching, overmatching may occur if one is overly sensitive to the reinforcement schedule of one of the alternatives (Reed and Kaplan, 2011).

An example of overmatching, where the cost of switching from one alternative to the other is relevant, can be drawn from computer gaming. When playing a first-person shooter game, one often has the choice of different weapons. Some weapons may be more effective in certain situations than in others. For example, a player may learn to match her use of her most potent weapon with her success rate for killing a highly threatening monster. She may also know that her least powerful weapon is as effective for killing the least threatening monsters. However, she may keep using her most powerful weapon, at the cost of wasting ammunition, to destroy the least threatening monsters if switching weapons is arduous and entails a break in concentration or a significant delay.

Using an overly powerful favored weapon to kill monsters in gaming instead of a weaker, less favored weapon that is just as effective is an example of overmatching, if switching to the weaker weapon entails a cost, such as a break in concentration or wasted time.

Source: IStock photo ID:1157159136.

BIAS

A bias occurs when the preference for one alternative is consistently higher or lower than predicted by matching, regardless of the difference in reinforcement contingencies between alternatives. This includes situations in which the reinforcement contingencies for the alternatives are equal. Why are animals sometimes biased towards one alternative? Bias occurs when some variable in the experimental procedure is left unaccounted for by the experimenter. For example, when a rat chooses between two levers, one may be more difficult to depress, causing the rat to choose the more accessible lever to depress more often. In another example, a child who is equally reinforced for choosing cards from two decks, one positioned to the right and the other to the left, may more often choose from one of the decks due to handedness.

Bias towards one of the alternatives may also be due to a difference in the quality of the reinforcers. For example, in one study, children with learning difficulties completed more math problems to obtain nickels, a high-quality reinforcer, than program money, a lower-quality reinforcer. This occurred even if more program money than nickels was earned by doing the problems (Neef et al., 1992). Think about how bias might influence your choices in everyday life. For example, you may choose to eat at a restaurant serving small portions of high-quality food rather than at one serving large portions of low-quality food.

The Generalized Matching Equation

It became apparent that the original matching equation proposed by Herrnstein (1961) was inadequate to describe choice in situations where deviations from strict matching (undermatching, overmatching, and bias) occurred. For this reason, William Baum, another one of Herrnstein's students, proposed what is known as the **generalized matching equation (GME)** (Baum, 1974).

$$\frac{B_1}{B_2} = b\left(\frac{r_1}{r_2}\right)^S$$

The generalized matching equation, shown previously, has the same basic structure as the original matching equation with the addition of two free parameters where b indicates the extent to which a bias is present and s indicates sensitivity. When no bias exists, b is equal to 0. Bias can either be greater or smaller than 0, depending on the alternative for which a bias exists. When neither undermatching nor overmatching is present, s is equal to 1. Undermatching results in a value of s less than 1, and overmatching results in a value of s greater than 1. Hence, when strict matching occurs, bias is 0, and sensitivity is equal to 1.

The Matching Law in the Study of Human Behavior

Social Behavior

In the previous sections, the matching law was mainly explained in the context of animal studies. Hence, you may wonder whether the matching law can help explain human behavior. Indeed, it can. In one study, psychologist J.C. Borrero and colleagues tested the applicability of the matching law to the verbal behavior of adults during social interactions (2007). As part of the study, the participants were asked for their opinions on the factors influencing juvenile delinquency. To get a conversation going, the experimenters suggested a list of discussion topics (i.e., drug and alcohol use, peers and cliques, school system quality, unfavorable home environment, and subculture populations).

Two confederates reinforced the participants for participating in the discussion with statements of approval such as "you are right" on concurrent VI schedules of reinforcement. The experimenters measured the time and frequency at which the participants attended to each of the confederates by recording eye contact between the participants and confederates as well as orientation of the participants' bodies toward either confederate. They found that the relative rate at which the participants attended either confederate was proportional to the time and frequency of approval they received from them.

Sports

Researchers have found that allocating behavioral responses in sports is an excellent way to study the application of the GME to human behavior (Falligant et al., 2021). This is because 1) similarly to everyday life, many response options are available during the practice of a sport; 2) more than one response option can give rise to the same reinforcer(s); 3) different response options may also give rise to different reinforcers, in terms of the quality and quantity; and 4) the allocation of behavior, as well as reinforcement contingencies, may differ depending on the situational context or antecedent conditions.

An advantage of studying the allocation of behavior in sports is that, for most sports practiced at a high skill level, statistics about a variety of behaviors and their outcomes are tabulated and made available on a particular league's or organization's website. Recording and analyzing the allocation of various behaviors and contexts in a naturalistic setting, outside sports, in numbers great enough to produce reliable data would be extremely difficult.

In addition, the study of response allocation in sports is important to sports psychologists. Applying the concepts of applied behavior analysis, such as the GME, can help athletes maximize their performances by improving their skills and helping predict opponents' moves. The GME has been applied in studies that examined response allocation in football (Critchfield and Stilling, 2015; Falligant, Boomhower and Pence, 2016), basketball (Alferink et al., 2009; Vollmer and Bourret, 2000), baseball (Cox, Sosine and Dallery, 2017; Poling et al., 2011), hockey (Seniuk et al., 2015), mixed martial arts (MMA) (Seniuk, Vu and Nosik, 2020), and volleyball (Rotta, Kranak and Poling, 2021).

BASKETBALL

In one of the studies cited previously, Vollmer and Bourret (2000) compared the allocation of 3-point versus 2-point shots by players on NCAA college basketball teams during the 1998–1999 season. For those unfamiliar with basketball rules, the distance from which a shot is made dictates the number of points scored by the shot. Three points are scored for a successful shot in the basket when made from outside an arc delineated on the court floor, and 2 points are scored when a shot is made from inside that arc. Taking a shot is an operant behavior, and making the shot is the reinforcer. This is a naturalistic model of a concurrent schedule of reinforcement, with one behavioral option, the 3-point shot, resulting in a greater quantity of reinforcement than a 2-point shot.

Considering the differential reinforcement for the two responses, the authors adjusted the GME to account that the reinforcer for 3-point shots was 1.5 times greater than for the 2-point shots. Hence, throughout an entire season, if a player scored 30 times on 3-point shots and 55 times on 2-point shots, it was predicted that 45% of the player's shots would be 3-point shots. The study's findings were that the players' allocation of 3- and 2-point shots during the season was consistent with what was predicted by the GME.

MIXED MARTIAL ARTS

In another study, Seniuk, Vu and Nosik (2020) examined whether the GME could describe the strike selection of 37 mixed martial arts fighters (MMA) in fights that took place between 2011 and 2015. The alternatives were strikes to either the head, body, or legs. Successfully landing a strike was considered a reinforcer for these behaviors. The main measure was the extent to which the proportion of head-directed strikes to all other strikes matched the proportion of reinforcers the fighters obtained from them.

The results of the study showed that the GME described strike selection for 78% of the fighters. The findings also showed that many of the fighters showed overmatching. That is, their proportions of strikes to the head to the other parts of the body were higher than the proportion of reinforcers they obtained from them. They also showed a bias toward strikes to the head. The experimenters could not explain the overmatching and bias observed across fighters. However, they suggested these may have occurred due to fighting strategy and the changing situational context across the fight.

Focus On

Graphical Representations: Matching, Undermatching, Overmatching, and Bias

Imagine an experiment in which three pigeons were consistently reinforced for pecking a left key under a VI-60 second schedule of reinforcement but exposed to four conditions (i.e., concurrent schedules) under which they were reinforced under a VI-60 second, VI-120 second, VI-30 second, and VI-240 second schedule of reinforcement for pecking a right key, as shown in Table 17.1.

Table 17.1 Four VI concurrent schedules under which pigeons were reinforced.

Condition	*Left key*	*Right key*
1	VI-60	VI-60
2	VI-60	VI-120
3	VI-60	VI-30
4	VI-60	VI-240

Imagine also that the experimenter tabulated the ratio of responses to the right key versus the left key (R_1/R_2) and the ratio of reinforcers the three pigeons received for pecking the right key versus the left key (r_1/r_2) per the general matching equation, shown subsequently, and that she plotted these ratios on a graph.

$$\frac{B_1}{B_2} = b\left(\frac{r_1}{r_2}\right)^S$$

Figure 17.3 represents hypothetical results in which either matching, undermatching, overmatching, or a bias was observed. The data clusters define the conditions in Table 17.1 in order from the bottom left to the top right of the graphs.

Matching

In our hypothetical example of matching (Figure 17.3a), you can see that the ratios of responses (R_1/R_2) performed by the pigeons match the ratios of reinforcers they received (r_1/r_2). For example, in one condition, Pigeon 3 responded to the right key in a 2:1 ratio, which matched the 2:1 ratio it received from distributing its responses in this way. As you can see, when matching occurs, every change in the response ratio is accompanied by a corresponding change in the ratio of reinforcers received. There is no bias (b) and sensitivity (s) is equal to 1.

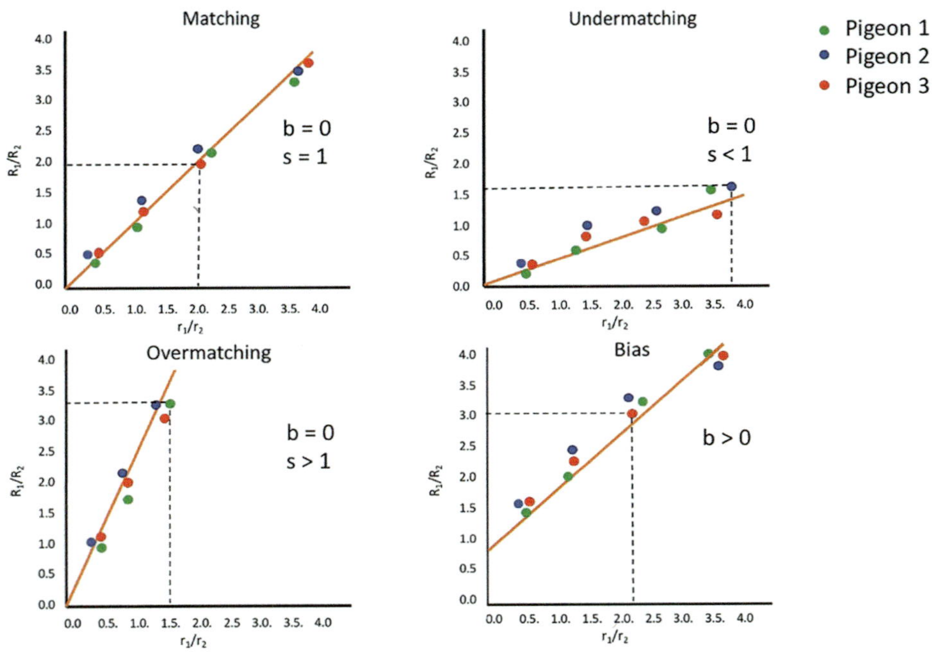

Figure 17.3 Scatterplots represent matching, undermatching, overmatching, and bias (see text for details).

Undermatching

Figure 17.3b represents a hypothetical case of undermatching. In this case, every change in the ratio of responses (R_1/R_2) is not accompanied by a corresponding change in the ratio of reinforcers the pigeons received (r_1/r_2). As you can see, a higher ratio of reinforcements for responding to the right key did not result in a corresponding increase in their response rate. For example, in one condition, Pigeon 2 was reinforced at a ratio of almost 4:1 for responding to the right key but did not respond correspondingly by only pecking the right key at a ratio of just over 1.5:1. There is no bias (b) and sensitivity (s) is less than 1.

Overmatching

Figure 17.3c represents a hypothetical case of overmatching. In this case, the ratio of responses (R_1/R_2) is accompanied by a smaller than corresponding change in the ratio of reinforcers the pigeons received (r_1/r_2). As you can see, the increased ratios of the pigeons' responses to the right key surpassed the ratios of reinforcement they received from responding to it. For example, in one condition, Pigeon 1 was reinforced at a ratio of 1.5:1 for pecking the right key but responded by pecking the right key at a ratio of almost 3.5:1. There is no bias (b) and sensitivity (s) is greater than 1.

Bias

Figure 17.3d represents a hypothetical case of bias. In this case, the pigeons responded more to the right key even when the schedule of reinforcement was the same for pecking both keys. This is why the line in the graph starts at a response level that is more than 0. Because of this, the pigeons did not distribute their responses on the keys in a manner consistent with the schedules of reinforcement. For example, in one condition, Pigeon 3 was reinforced at a ratio of just over 2:1 but responded to the right key at a ratio of 3:1. Bias (b) is greater than one. Sensitivity (not shown) can be either lower, greater or equal to 1.

Are You Thinking Critically?

1. What are the advantages of graphically representing matching, undermatching, overmatching, and bias?
2. What would a graph representing no relationship between the choice of lever and reinforcement look like?
3. Create a graph of bias towards the left instead of the right lever.

Critical Thinking Spot Check 17.1

1. Explain the matching law.
2. What is the significance of each one of the components in the generalized matching equation?
3. Name and describe how choice behavior can deviate from matching.
4. Give an everyday example of where a) matching, b) overmatching, and c) undermatching can occur.
5. Under what circumstances can an animal or person show a bias towards one option versus another?

17.2 Theories of Matching

Molar and Molecular Theories

Although matching has been observed across many experiments and involving different species of animals, considerable debate exists as to the mechanisms by which matching occurs. This debate affects the proponents of two major perspectives, each claiming to explain how animals distribute their choices. These perspectives are embodied by what are known as **molar** and **molecular theories** of matching.

Molar Theories

According to molar theories, matching occurs because animals distribute their responses among alternatives to maximize the reinforcers they receive in the long run. This is known as **molar maximizing.** What is the long run? The long run refers to the reinforcers received as the result of an aggregate number of responses within an entire experimental session rather than from the reinforcers an animal gets from moment to moment responding to the alternatives. The term "molar" comes from the Latin word "mole," which means mass, which, as far we are concerned, has come to signify a "mass" of responses.

This perspective is also known as optimization theory (or maximization). Evidence supporting this perspective comes from ecology, which studies how animals distribute their choices to maximize the benefits of their environment, and economics, which studies how people use their income to maximize the perceived benefits they can get from it (Rachlin et al., 1981).

Based on the observation that animals match their ratio of responding to the alternative that provides the highest ratio of reinforcers, the matching law is also a molar explanation. This is because ratios are calculated based on the relative number of responses to the choice alternatives across an entire session.

In many situations, optimization and matching theories predict that animals exposed to the VI schedule of reinforcement will distribute their responses between alternatives in the same way. However, in some situations, the maximal number of reinforcers that can be obtained from each alternative is not received by responding to each alternative in proportions predicted by the matching law (Mazur, 1981). For example, a sports bettor may do reasonably well by betting on teams according to their records of wins and losses but can miss out on potential gains or lose money if one or more teams go on an unexpected winning or losing streak.

Molecular Theories

According to molecular theories, matching occurs due to the immediate consequences of an animal's choice behavior. This is known as **momentary maximizing**. Therefore, the proponents of these theories are interested in a moment-to-moment analysis of an animal's responses. The term "molecular" comes from the Latin term "molecular," meaning tiny particle. Therefore, contrary to molar theories, in which aggregates of responses are analyzed, molecular theorists are interested in the units of behavior.

Proponents of momentary maximizing believe an animal will select the alternative with the highest reinforcement value when a choice is made. Therefore, they think that matching is achieved from the moment-to-moment switching between alternatives induced by tracking the probability of reinforcement for responding to each. Molar and molecular theories are often in opposition. This is because, although both types of theories seek to explain how animals try to maximize the value obtained by their choices, what is of high value in the short term is not always of high value in the long run. For example, having a drink to relieve stress may feel good in the short term (molecular) but may have devastating consequences if this behavior is repeated in the long run (molar).

Critical Thinking Spot Check 17.2

1. Distinguish between the molar and molecular theories of matching.
2. Give an everyday example of molar maximizing.
3. Give an everyday example of molecular maximizing.

17.3 Concurrent-Chains Schedules of Reinforcement

Reinforcement Schedules Maintained by Secondary Reinforcement

Behavior is often controlled by secondary reinforcers associated with primary reinforcers. For example, money is a secondary reinforcer because it provides access to primary reinforcers such as food and shelter.

Autor (1960) developed a procedure to determine whether the matching law could describe reinforcement schedules maintained by secondary reinforcers rather than primary reinforcers. This procedure is known as **concurrent-chains schedules**. In a concurrent chain schedule experiment, an animal is first exposed to concurrent schedules of reinforcement in what is known as the *initial links*. However, instead of receiving a primary reinforcer, such as food, to respond to the alternatives, each alternative grants the animal access to two other concurrent schedules in what is known as the *terminal links*. Responding in the terminal links is associated with delivering a primary reinforcer, typically a food reward. Once a primary reinforcer is obtained from a terminal link, another trial begins, during which the animal chooses from the initial link. In other words, during the initial link period, the animal chooses the reinforcement schedule it will be exposed to in the terminal links. This means that once the animal has made its choice in the initial-link period it is committed to it and must face the consequences of that choice in the terminal-link period. For this reason, concurrent chain schedules are sometimes referred to as *choice with commitment*.

The concurrent-chains schedules procedure is illustrated in Figure 17.4. The initial links consist of a choice between two equal schedules of reinforcement. For example, a pigeon chooses to peck either of two response keys illuminated by the same color light (e.g., white), each associated with the same schedule of reinforcement (e.g., VI 20s–VI 20s).

Completing the schedule on one of the keys gives the pigeon access to the corresponding terminal link. Within each terminal link, the animal chooses between a colored key and a dark key. Each colored key (e.g., RED or GREEN) is associated with a schedule of reinforcement, which is determined by the experimenter (e.g., RED = VI-5s and GREEN = VI-10s). Pecking on the colored key is associated with food delivery according to the corresponding schedule, whereas pecking on the dark key is not associated with food. Once the animal has completed the schedule and received the food reward, a new trial begins, in which it chooses between the initial links.

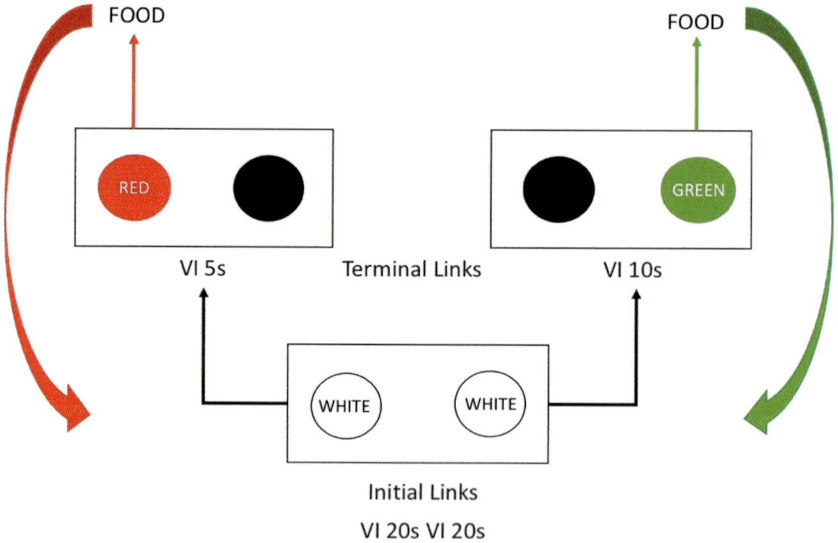

Figure 17.4 The concurrent chains schedule procedure. Choice during the initial link period does not lead to the delivery of a primary reinforcer but to the opportunity to respond to one of two schedules of reinforcement in the terminal link period. The stimuli (red or green key) in the terminal links are secondary reinforcers because they are associated with a primary reinforcer (see text for details).

Animals typically more often choose the initial link associated with the schedule of reinforcement that gives access to the higher rate of reinforcement in the terminal links. In Figure 17.4, this is the schedule illuminated by the red light. Hence, the colored light associated with the schedule, which provides the highest rate of reinforcement, acts as a secondary reinforcer because it reinforces responding in the initial link without itself being a primary reinforcer.

Is it possible to predict which of the two initial links an animal will choose more often? The answer is that, in a concurrent chain schedule, the response pattern in the initial links period conforms to the matching law. Herrnstein (1964) showed that, in concurrent chain schedules, animals would distribute their responses among the initial-link alternatives in a ratio that matches the ratio of primary reinforcement between the terminal-link alternatives. Figure 17.4 illustrates a situation where the initial links consist of two VI-20s alternatives. Responding to the left key provides access to a VI-5s schedule of reinforcement compared to a VI-10 schedule of reinforcement for responding on the right key in the terminal-link period. Hence, responding to the left key in the initial link period leads to a greater rate of reinforcement in its associated terminal link than responding to the right key. If responding to the red key is associated with delivering twice as many reinforcers, the animal will perform twice the number of responses on the left alternative as it does on the right.

Human Choices With Commitment

Concurrent chain schedules are integral to human decision-making processes in that people are often confronted with the consequences of the choices they make once committed (i.e., choice with commitment). For example, when deciding between two classes, say class A and class B, you might first evaluate the amount of work required for each class (the initial links). However, you might also consider the perceived ease of the final exam (the terminal links). Drawing from this information, you may choose to take class A, even if it demands more work but offers an easier final exam compared to class B, which requires less work but has a more difficult final exam. You might regret your choice because of the overwhelming work the class requires. However, you still might go through with it because you have already committed to it.

In another example, one might choose between driving to work or taking public transit (initial links). While driving may be more costly, it offers greater flexibility than public transit, which could be more economical in the long run (terminal links). Based on this information, one might decide to drive to work because they value the flexibility that driving provides. Committing to that choice means facing the consequence of a higher financial cost over time.

In yet another example, consider the commitment people make when getting married. The choice of lifelong partners forms the initial link, while the terminal links consist of the level of happiness provided by the spouse.

Critical Thinking Spot Check 17.3

1. Describe how a concurrent chain schedule maintains responding using secondary reinforcers.
2. What parallels can you draw between the behavior of animals responding under a concurrent chain schedule and the choices made by humans?

Chapter Summary

Each bullet point aligns directly with the learning objectives outlined at the beginning of the chapter.

- The matching law states that the relative rate of responses between choice alternatives tends to equal the relative rate of reinforcements obtained between these alternatives. The matching law was initially expressed as an equation in which the proportion of the responses to one option equaled the proportion of reinforcement obtained from responding to that alternative. However, it was then found that this formula needed to be revised to show the regularity of the data in some experiments appropriately. Therefore, the relative rate of responding to choice alternatives compared to the reinforcements obtained from those choice alternatives began to be expressed as ratios.
- In certain situations, strict matching does not occur. Undermatching occurs when an animal's relative rate of responding to an alternative is less than the rate of reinforcement it can receive from that alternative. In contrast, overmatching occurs when an animal's response rate is higher than the rate at which it can be reinforced by responding to that alternative. Finally, bias occurs when an animal shows a preference for one alternative over another, even if the schedules of reinforcement for responding to either alternative are the same. The generalized matching equation was proposed to account for situations where strict matching does not occur. This equation accounts for deviations from strict matching by adding two free parameters, sensitivity and bias, with sensitivity accounting for undermatching and overmatching.
- Different theories of matching exist. In molar theories, matching occurs because animals distribute their responses among alternatives to maximize the number of reinforcements they receive in the long run. In molecular theories, matching occurs due to the immediate consequences of an animal's choice of behavior.

Concurrent reinforcement schedules can also be utilized to assess matching with secondary reinforcers, employing a procedure referred to as concurrent chain schedules. In concurrent chain schedules, animals select between two reinforcement schedules during initial links to access a primary reinforcer via terminal links. This results in a choice with commitment. Concurrent chain schedules play a crucial role in the human decision-making process.

Glossary

Bias A systematic preference for one reinforcement alternative over another, independent of reinforcement rates.

Changeover delay (COD) A brief time delay imposed when switching between two concurrent reinforcement schedules, preventing rapid alternation and ensuring commitment to one schedule.

Concurrent-chains schedules A reinforcement paradigm where an organism first selects between different reinforcement schedules and then completes a sequence of responses to obtain reinforcement within the chosen schedule.

Concurrent schedules of reinforcement A situation where two or more reinforcement schedules are available simultaneously, allowing an organism to choose between different behaviors.

Molar maximizing A decision-making strategy where an organism distributes responses to maximize overall reinforcement over time.

Molar theories of matching Explanations of behavior that focus on overall reinforcement distributions over extended time periods rather than individual responses.

Molecular theories of matching Explanations of behavior that examine moment-to-moment interactions and reinforcement contingencies affecting individual responses.

Momentary maximizing A behavior-selection strategy where an organism chooses responses based on the highest immediate reinforcement probability rather than long-term outcomes.

Overmatching A deviation from strict matching where response allocation is more extreme than predicted, typically occurring when switching between alternatives is difficult or costly.

Strict matching A principle stating that response allocation between concurrent schedules is directly proportional to the reinforcement rates of each schedule.

Undermatching A deviation from strict matching where response allocation is less extreme than predicted, often due to lack of sensitivity to reinforcement differences.

18 Do Good Things Come to Those Who Wait? Unraveling the Mechanisms of Self-Control

Learning Objectives

1. Define delaying gratification, delay discounting, hyperbolic discounting function, indifference point, and point of preference reversal in intertemporal choice scenarios.
2. Analyze research findings demonstrating age-related differences in delay discounting behaviors among children, adolescents, and adults.
3. Compare how different rewards (e.g., alcohol, money, food) are discounted and consider the role of primary reinforcers, secondary reinforcers, consumables, and satiability.
4. Evaluate the impact of excessive delay discounting as a trans-disease process on psychological disorders such as compulsive overeating, substance use disorder, pathological gambling, Internet gaming disorder, and attention deficit hyperactivity disorder (ADHD).

Manan's Credit Card Ordeal

Source: IStock photo: Stock photo ID:1064958502.

DOI: 10.4324/9781003491828-33

Manan is in the first year of her undergraduate program. One day, while walking through the mall near her college, she was approached by a sales representative from a credit card company. The representative asked Manan if she was a student at the nearby college and if she had a couple of minutes to spare. When Manan said yes, the representative introduced himself as a popular credit card company representative. The representative told Manan that his company offered financial assistance to help students like Manan tend to their needs. Manan confided to the representative that she had trouble making ends meet, having only a part-time job to pay her share of the rent and some bills. The representative told Manan that he could indeed help and asked Manan to show him her student ID. Manan filled out and signed a form and received a credit card a few days later in the mail. Armed with her credit card, Manan was amazed that she did not have to wait to get the things she wanted. However, by the time Manan graduated, she owed the credit card company over $7,000, and her financial situation had worsened. Manan was now ridden with anxiety and depression about having added to her financial burden, often barely being able to make the minimum payment on her card. Manan eventually got a good-paying job and regretted having built up such a large debt because now, even if she was making a good salary, all of it went to paying it off, and she couldn't put any money aside. Although this is not where most students acquiring early credit find themselves, it is many's plight. You may wonder why some students who obtain a credit card early in life use it responsibly and others, like Manan, drown themselves in debt. One factor is that credit card companies take advantage of many people's difficulty in delaying gratification.

18.1 Delay of Gratification and Delay Discounting

Intertemporal Choice and Delay of Gratification

Manan's credit card ordeal in the opening vignette illustrates how choices are not always between behavioral options that are concurrently available. Manan's choice alternatives were intertemporal. **Intertemporal choice** is an economics term that describes how decisions made at one point affect the availability of choice alternatives later. Hence, what Manan decided to do at one point (i.e., getting into debt) affected the range of options she would have in the future (not being able to put money aside). In another example, choosing between a juicy hamburger and a salad may satisfy a craving and feel good. However, if giving in to such immediate cravings occurs frequently, a person's long-term commitment to lose weight will be in jeopardy.

Why do people so often make bad choices? People sometimes make bad choices because they fail to see or acknowledge the long-term consequences of their behaviors. For example, a person may choose to take an addictive drug to feel good in the short term but fail to acknowledge the possibility of getting addicted, with all the destructive consequences this may eventually entail. People also often struggle with forgoing a small immediate reward at the expense of obtaining a later but larger reward. When this occurs, it is usually said that the person cannot delay gratification.

Delay of gratification refers to the act of forgoing a soon but small reward (SSR) to obtain a later but large reward (LLR). The degree to which one can delay gratification is associated with better academic performance (Morisano et al., 2010), higher intelligence (Basile and Toplak, 2015), healthier social relationships (Hirsh, Morisano and Peterson, 2008), better mental health, less criminal behavior, and more adaptive social functioning (Shamosh and

Gray, 2008). A lack of the ability to delay gratification often reflects a propensity towards *impulsive behavior* and a lack of *self-control*. Impulsive behavior is characterized by acting without thinking, unplanned and risky behavior, difficulty withholding responses, insensitivity to the consequences of one's actions, and inadequate attention (Dickman, 1990, 1993; Eysenck, 1993). A lack of self-control refers to the inability to control one's thoughts, emotions, and impulses (Baumeister, Heatherton and Tice, 1994).

Another factor associated with the inability to delay gratification is *time orientation*. Time orientation refers to the perspective from which a person has an outlook on life to guide their behavior. Some people rely primarily on the past, others on the present, and others on the future, with most people having a balanced outlook (D'Alessio et al., 2003). However, it was found that people who have difficulty delaying gratification are caught up in the present. They tend to look for immediately available rewards and feel pessimistic about the future (Kim, Kim and Kim, 2020).

However, knowing that people's financial situations can influence how they handle immediate versus future rewards is important. Studies across different countries show that people who've faced economic hardships or grew up in relative poverty tend to choose immediate, smaller rewards over the possibility of larger future rewards. This may be because those with less tend to focus more on the present, while those from more financially stable backgrounds can afford to be more patient with rewards (Griskevicius et al., 2011; Haushofer and Fehr, 2014; Yu et al., 2023).

Delay Discounting

Why is delaying gratification often difficult? The delay in gratification is related to a phenomenon known as **delay discounting** (Reynolds and Schiffbauer, 2005). Delay discounting refers to the process by which a reward's present value declines with the delay to its receipt (Odum, 2011). This may explain the difficulty experienced by dieters when choosing between a healthy, low-calorie meal and a delicious, calorie-rich meal. This difficulty stems from the fact that the reward of eating healthy, such as weight loss, will only be experienced at some future point, resulting in significant discounting of its value when the choice is made. In contrast, the value of the immediate reward provided by the delicious calorie-rich meal has not been discounted by a delay. Delay discounting is expressed in an equation known as the **hyperbolic discounting function** (shown subsequently), which describes the relationship between a reward's value and its time of receipt (Mazur, 1987).

$$V = \frac{A}{1 + K(D)}$$

The present value of the reward (V) is a function of its undiscounted value (A) divided by the rate at which the value of the reward is discounted (k) and multiplied by the delay to the reward (D). The greater the value of (k), the quicker the reward will be devalued. The constant 1 in the denominator prevents (V) from approaching infinity as (D) approaches 0.

Figure 18.1 illustrates a graphic, hypothetical situation to which the hyperbolic discounting function can be applied. The vertical axis (y-axis) represents the present value of rewards (V). The horizontal axis (x-axis) represents the delay to the rewards. The green bar represents the SSRs, and the red bar represents the LLRs with their respective undiscounted values (A). The green and red curves originating from the top of each bar represent the rate at which each reward (SSR and LLR) is discounted (k). Note that the discounting rate is the same for both.

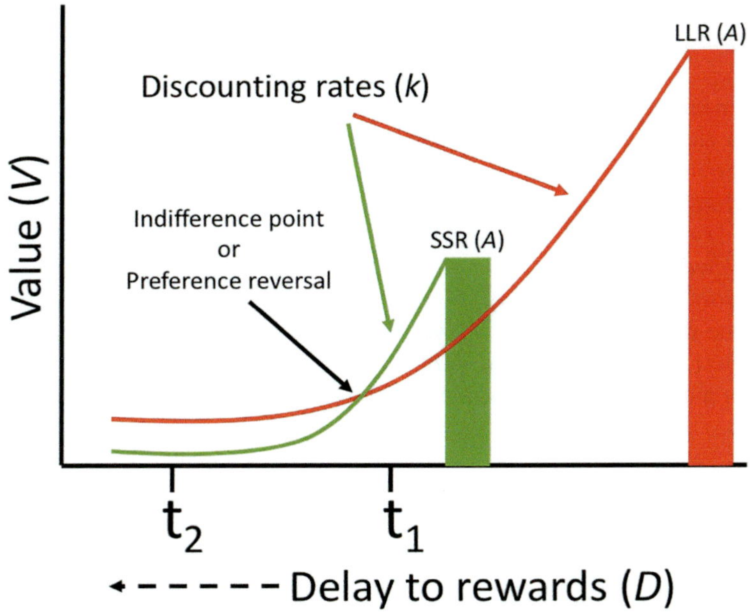

Figure 18.1 Hyperbolic discounting function to which a hypothetical situation is applied (see text for details).

Along the horizontal axis, t_1 and t_2 represent the discounted SSR and LLR rewards at two time points. At t_1, the LLR accrued a more significant discount than the SSR, resulting in less value. Therefore, the SSR is likely to be preferred.

A hypothetical situation will help clarify what you see in Figure 18.1. Suppose that one of your friends asks to help her move. The moving date is set to be on the following day. She promises that she will pay you $100 immediately after the move. However, she feels terrible about paying you so little and tells you that if you can wait until her next payday, which is in one week, she will give you $150. In the graph, the day of the move corresponds to t_1, and the delay in the SSR reward ($100) is only one day. Therefore, you would likely decline your friend's offer of getting $150 two weeks later (the LLR) and take the $100 on the day of the move (the SSR). This is because when deciding, the value of $150 (the LLR) declined due to delay discounting to the point where it is worth less than $100, whose value has been discounted by less.

THE INDIFFERENCE POINT

If you shift your attention to t_2 of Figure 18.1, which represents a more remote period to the SSR than t_1, you will notice that the discounted value of the LLR is higher than that of the SSR. Therefore, at t_2, a preference for the LLR would be expected. How is this happening? As you can see in the figure, the discounting lines cross over at a time point about three-quarters of the way to t_1, moving from left to right. This point of crossover is known as the **indifference point**. The indifference point is the point at which the SSR and LLR have the same subjective value. It is also the point beyond which subjects switch from choosing the LLR to selecting the SSR. This well-documented phenomenon is known as **preference**

reversal (Ainslie and Herrnstein, 1981; Beeby and White, 2013; Rachlin and Green, 1972; Yi, Matusiewicz and Tyson, 2016).

A slight change in the hypothetical situation described previously may help you understand both the meaning of the indifference point and preference reversal. Imagine that her moving day has changed to one week from today and that she will either give you $100 on the day of the move or $150 one week later. What would you choose then? Again, the prediction of what you are likely to answer is obtained by looking at Figure 18.1. In this situation, the delay to the SSR begins at t_2. This results in the SSR and LLR being delayed by an additional week.

In that situation, you would likely prefer receiving $150 one week after the move rather than $100 on the day of the move. Why? Because at t_2, the discounted value of the LLR is higher than that of the discounted value of the SSR. However, as the day of the move approaches, you may regret choosing the LLR as the $100 on the day of the move becomes more attractive.

A TYPICAL DELAY DISCOUNTING EXPERIMENT

In delay discounting studies, participants are typically tested for their preference for a soon but small monetary reward (SSR) and a later but larger monetary reward (LLR). The choices are presented as a series of gradually increasing SSR alternatives versus a constant LLR. Figure 18.2 illustrates a hypothetical experiment where participants choose between an SSR and an LLR in three conditions. As shown in Figure 18.2, the SSRs range from $1.00–$9.00 in each condition, and the LLR is always $10. What changes across the conditions is the delay to the LLR: 1) $10 in one week, 2) $10 in two weeks, and 3) $10 in one month. In condition 1), the participants are asked if they would prefer to receive $1 now and $10 in one week, $2 now and $10 in one week, and so on. In condition 2), the participants are asked if they would prefer to receive $1 now and $10 in two weeks, $2 now and $10 in two weeks, and so on. In condition 3), the participants are asked if they would prefer to receive $1 now and $10 in one month, $2 now and $10 in one month, and so on.

SSR		LLR	SSR		LLR	SSR		LLR
1$ now	or	10$ in one week	1$ now	or	10$ in two weeks	1$ now	or	10$ in one month
2$ now	or	10$ in one week	2$ now	or	10$ in two weeks	2$ now	or	10$ in one month
3$ now	or	10$ in one week	3$ now	or	10$ in two weeks	3$ now	or	10$ in one month
4$ now	or	10$ in one week	4$ now	or	10$ in two weeks	4$ now	or	10$ in one month
5$ now	or	10$ in one week	5$ now	or	10$ in two weeks	5$ now	or	10$ in one month
6$ now	or	10$ in one week	6$ now	or	10$ in two weeks	6$ now	or	10$ in one month
7$ now	or	10$ in one week	7$ now	or	10$ in two weeks	7$ now	or	10$ in one month
8$ now	or	10$ in one week	8$ now	or	10$ in two weeks	8$ now	or	10$ in one month
9$ now	or	10$ in one week	9$ now	or	10$ in two weeks	9$ now	or	10$ in one month

Figure 18.2 A hypothetical experiment in which the extent to which participants select an SSR over an LLR in three conditions was investigated (see text for explanation).

What is typically found in this type of experiment is that the participants prefer the LLR up to a point where they show a preference reversal for the SSR. The preference reversal for one participant occurred at $6.00 when the delay to the LLR was one week (left column), $3.00 when the delay to the LLR was two weeks (middle column), and $2.00 when the delay to the LLR was one month (right column). In other words, the longer she waits for the LLR, the less money she will accept as the SSR.

The indifference point for each condition is calculated by averaging the value of the SSR at preference reversal and the value of the SSR immediately below it. Figure 18.3 shows how the indifference points across all three delay conditions for the participant can be plotted as a hyperbolic function. The x-axis represents the value of $10 across delay conditions. You can see on the graph that with a delay of one week, the value of the $10 LLR is $5.50, $2.50 with a two-week delay, and $1.50 with a one-month delay.

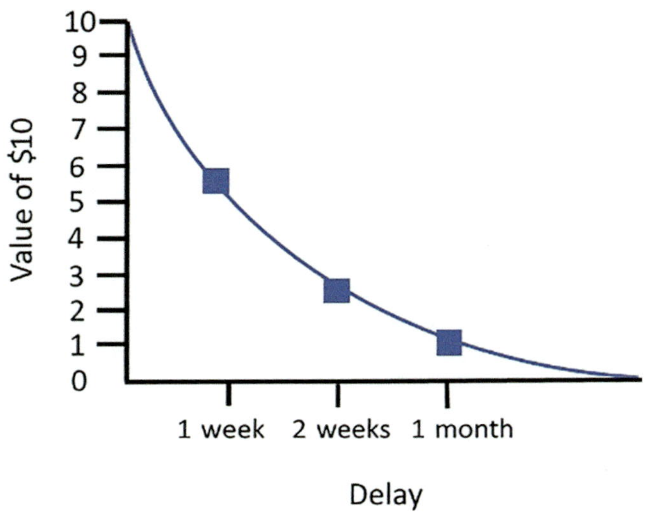

Figure 18.3 Hyperbolic function onto which hypothetical indifference points (squares) are plotted.

Critical Thinking Spot Check 18.1

1. Explain how delay discounting accounts for difficulties in delaying gratification.
2. Name and describe each of the components of the hyperbolic decay function.
3. Why would the timing of choosing between a sooner but smaller reward or a later larger reward matter?
4. Why might it be important to know about the hyperbolic discounting function in pursuing your goals?
5. Describe a typical delay discounting experiment.

18.2 Individual Difference in Delay Discounting

Differences Across the Lifespan

Psychologist Walter Mischel (1930–2018) discovered a connection between the ability to delay gratification and children's personal characteristics, such as their capacity to concentrate and plan, scores on scholastic aptitude tests (SATs), and their ability to manage stress. Others have revealed that children's ability to delay gratification may also depend on intelligence and mindset. Yet other researchers focused on the variation in individuals' ability to delay gratification throughout their lifespan. For example, in one study (Green, Myerson and Ostaszewski, 1999), researchers examined whether the rate at which delayed rewards were discounted (i.e., the value of k in the hyperbolic decay function) differed among children (sixth graders), young adults (college students), and older adults (approximately 68 years and older). The steps involved in the experiment's procedure are outlined subsequently:

1. Participants were asked to choose between hypothetical amounts of money, printed on index cards attached to a two-ring binder.
2. For both college students and sixth graders, each participant received two sets of index cards—one set positioned on their right and the other on their left. They were instructed to flip through the left-side stack of index cards (with immediate reward amounts) and compare each one to the fixed delayed reward card on the right to make a decision.
3. The set placed to the right contained fixed delayed rewards of $1,000 and $10,000 for college students and $100 and $1,000 for older adults. The left-side set featured immediate rewards ranging from 0.1% to 100% of the delayed reward value on the right.
4. These fixed-amount delayed rewards could hypothetically be obtained after delays of one week, one month, six months, 1 year, 3 years, 5 years, 10 years, and 25 years (the delays are represented by D in the equation). The fixed-amount delayed rewards are indicated by A in the hyperbolic decay function, as they represent the undiscounted values.

The results, shown in Figure 18.4, indicated that:

1. For sixth graders, an immediate $1,000 reward is equivalent to about $225 if the reward is delayed by four years.
2. For college students, an immediate $1,000 reward is equivalent to about $350 for a four-year delay.
3. For older adults, an immediate $1,000 reward is equivalent to about $750 for the same four-year delay.

These equivalence points correspond to V in the hyperbolic discounting equation, representing the discounted value of the delayed reward at a specific time point. The results indicate that the same delayed reward amount is discounted at a steeper rate for sixth graders than for college students and at a steeper rate for college students than for older adults. This means that younger individuals are more likely to prefer an immediate reward over a delayed one, reflecting a higher degree of impulsivity.

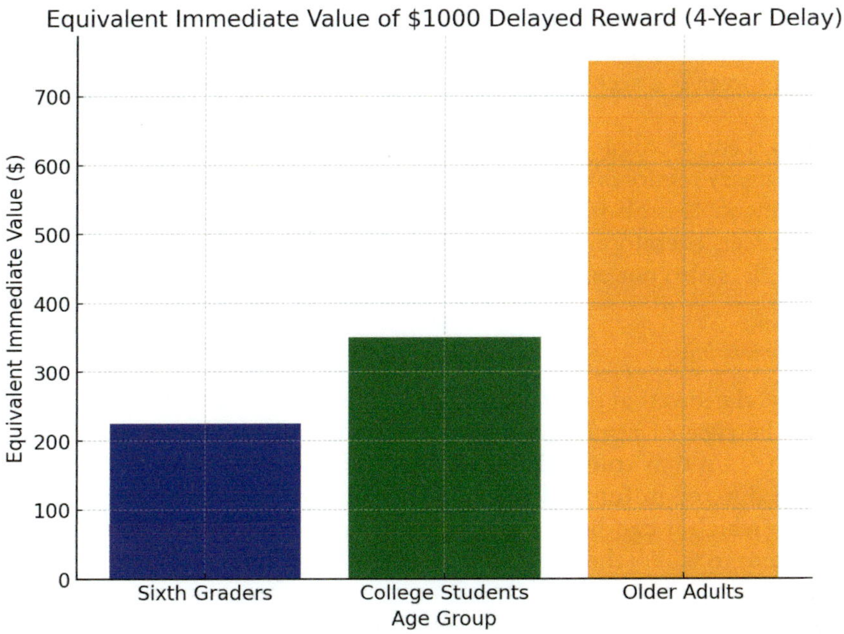

Figure 18.4 Results of the Green, Myerson, and Ostaszewski (1999) study (see text for details).

Critical Thinking Spot Check 18.2

1. Why would you expect differences in the degree of delay discounting across the lifespan?
2. a) Describe a study in which those differences were shown. b) What was found? c) What did the findings suggest?

18.3 Delay Discounting Across Different Types of Rewards

The Domain Effect

Most studies of delay discounting in humans use different amounts of money as immediate and delayed rewards. However, in everyday life, people receive many kinds of rewards, other than money, as a consequence of their behavior. These include food, good health, marital satisfaction, praise, recognition, awards, sex, gifts, drugs, and so on. This raises the question of whether the delay discounting rate differs across different types of rewards in what is known as the **domain effect**.

In one study, the rate of discounting for delayed monetary, alcohol, and food rewards was compared in individuals without gambling problems, alcoholism, or eating disorders (Odum and Rainaud, 2003). The experimenters found that money was less steeply discounted than alcohol and food but that no difference existed in the rate at which alcohol and food were discounted. The results of this study led the authors to propose that the differences in the discounting rate of delayed rewards may be related to whether the reward is a primary reinforcer, is a secondary reinforcer, is consumable, serves a direct function, or is satiable.

According to them, alcohol and food are more steeply discounted than money because they are both primary reinforcers and consumables. In addition, food serves the direct function of nourishment. It is also satiable in that it satisfies hunger. In contrast, money is a secondary reinforcer. Therefore, it serves an indirect function in that its value is based on its exchangeability. It is also not consumable.

Fungibility and Perishability

In another study, the idea that differences in the discounting rate between different rewards depending on the type of reinforcers (the domain effect) was more deeply investigated (Holt et al., 2016). In that study, the experimenters tested the rates of delay discounting to rewards that differed in **fungibility** and **perishability**. The fungibility of a good refers to the extent to which it can be exchanged for other goods. The perishability of a good refers to the extent to which the good will no longer be consumable after a certain amount of time has passed.

Figure 18.5 shows the items used in the study are plotted as a function of their fungibility and perishability. Pizza slices and candies were considered non-fungible and perishable items. On the other hand, pizza gift cards and jeans were considered non-perishable but of low fungibility. Clothing gift cards, grocery gift cards, Visa gift cards, and money were all considered fungible and non-perishable.

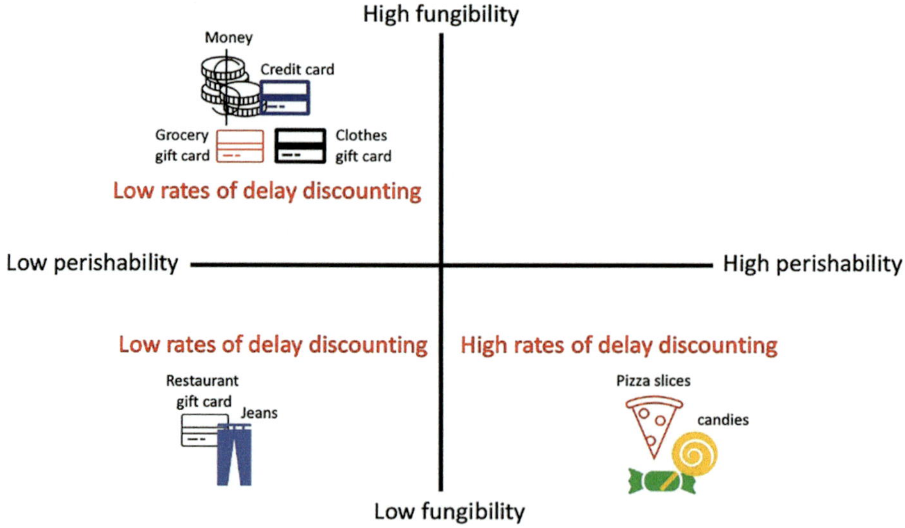

Figure 18.5 The relative rates of delay discounting for the items used in Holt et al. (2016) as a function of perishability and fungibility. Perishable items had the most significant rate of delay discounting (modified from Holt et al., 2016).

Source: Holt, D. D., Glodowski, K., Smits-Seemann, R. R., & Tiry, A. M. (2016). The domain effect in delay discounting: The roles of fungibility and perishability. *Behav Process, 131*, 47–52. https://doi.org/10.1016/j.beproc.2015.08.006.

They found that the most perishable items, pizza slices and candy, also had greater delay discounting rates. In contrast, the most fungible items, clothing gift cards, grocery cards, Visa gift cards, and money, were the least discounted items. The importance of perishability in the discounting rate is shown by the finding that pizza, rendered less perishable by being presented as gift cards, was associated with a lower rate of discounting than pizza slices, even if the degree of fungibility of the gift cards was low. Jeans, which are also not perishable, are associated with low delay discounting despite their lack of fungibility. However, the high value of jeans may have accounted for their relatively low delay discounting rate.

What in the Brain?

Stages of Delay Discounting

The delay discounting processes is believed to comprise three stages. These are the valuation, imagery/prospection, and cognitive control stages (Peters and Büchel, 2011).

1. *Valuation* refers to the subjective value of available options. In the case of delay discounting, this refers to the relative values of the immediate small rewards and the later larger reward.
2. *Cognitive control* refers to the ability to inhibit choosing the immediate but smaller reward for the later but larger reward.
3. *Imagery/prospection* refers to the ability to imagine future outcomes.

Cognitive neuroscientists (scientists who study the neurobiological basis of cognitive processes) have identified different networks of brain areas associated with each delay-stage discounting using neuroimaging methods (Figure 18.6).

The Valuation Network

The valuation network includes the substantia nigra (SN) and ventral tegmental area (VTA), which play an important role in reinforcement learning and processing rewards (Schultz, Dayan and Montague, 1997). These areas are connected to the ventral striatum (VS) and ventromedial prefrontal cortex (VMPFC), which are known to process subjective value during reward-based decision making (Peters and Buchel, 2010).

Immediate rewards more strongly activate the valuation network than delayed rewards. Studies have also shown that higher delay discounting rates are associated with lower VS activity in healthy populations (Sripada et al., 2011). Higher rates of delay discounting were also found in addicted versus non-addicted individuals (Madden et al., 1997), which may be due to a lack of sensitivity of their VS to delayed rewards.

The Cognitive Control Network

The cognitive control network comprises the anterior cingulate cortex (ACC) and the lateral prefrontal cortex (PFC) (Cole and Schneider, 2007). The ACC, thought to be involved in conflict monitoring, is highly active in delay discounting tasks when the value of the immediate reward is similar to the value of the delayed reward (Marco-Pallarés et al., 2010). The lPFC is believed to mediate the cognitive control that must be exerted to inhibit choosing the immediate small reward over the larger delayed reward (McClure et al., 2004).

Higher delay discounting rates are also associated with reduced activation of the lPFC and ACC. Greater activity of the lPFC is also associated with reduced impulsivity in healthy populations (Miller and Cohen, 2001). Reduced activity in the lPFC was found in individuals addicted to methamphetamine (Ipser et al., 2018).

The Medial Temporal Lobe Network: Imagery and Prospecting

The medial temporal lobe network plays a role in delay discounting by mediating imagery and prospection. It includes the hippocampus (HPC) and amygdala (AMG). The HPC is believed to be important for representing and enabling the use of experience to guide decisions (Biderman, Bakkour and Shohamy, 2020). At the same time, the AMG is considered important for activating emotional states related to rewards (Langenecker et al., 2020).

Some neurons in the HPC, known as delay-active neurons, encode the delay associated with a reward by increasing their firing rates at more prolonged delays. Other neurons, known as delay-suppressed neurons, decrease their firing rates with increasing delay length. Both types of neurons also respond to the location and value of rewards. However, delay-active neurons decrease their firing rates with diminishing reward value, whereas delay-suppressed neurons increase their firing rates with diminishing reward value.

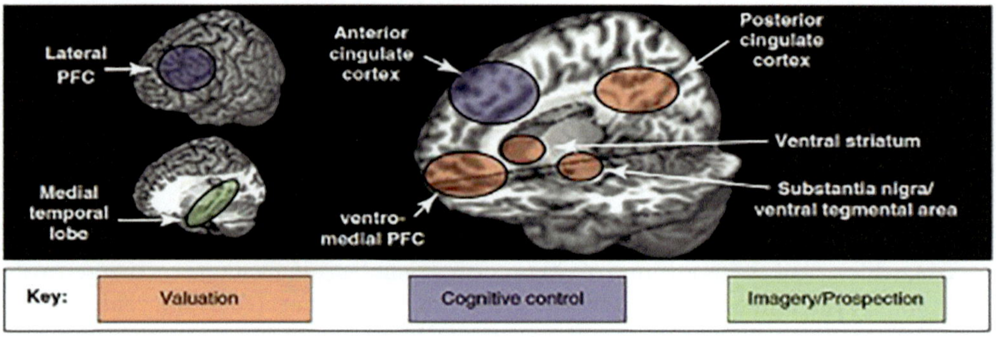

Figure 18.6 Brain networks associated with each stage of delay discounting.

Source: Peters, J., & Büchel, C. (2011). The neural mechanisms of intertemporal decision-making: understanding variability. *Trends Cogn Sci, 15*(5), 227–239. https://doi.org/10.1016/j.tics.2011.03.002.

Are You Thinking Critically?

1. Distinguish between the functions of the brain areas involved in the stages of delay discounting.
2. How does knowing about the brain areas involved in delay discounting contribute to our understanding of drug addiction?
3. Apply your knowledge of the stages of delay discounting to personal experiences in which it was difficult to delay gratification.

Critical Thinking Spot Check 18.3

1. Distinguish between objects of different levels of fungibility and perishability by their respective rates of delay discounting.
2. Name and describe a method by which the ability to delay gratification can be increased.
3. Give an example of how domains of rewards interact with different reward categories to predict the rate of delay discounting.

18.4 Delay Discounting: A Trans-Disease Process

Excessive rates of delay discounting are part of several psychological disorders. For this reason, they are believed to be part of a trans-disease process (Bickel et al., 2019). Psychological disorders that include excessive rates of delay discounting include compulsive overeating (Kekic et al., 2020; Stojek and MacKillop, 2017), substance use disorder (Kräplin et al., 2020; MacKillop et al., 2011; Naudé et al., 2021), pathological gambling (Kyonka and Schutte, 2018), Internet gaming disorder (Yan et al., 2021), and attention deficit hyperactivity disorder (ADHD) (Marx et al., 2018).

In one study, opioid-dependent and non-dependent participants were compared on the degree to which they discounted future monetary rewards (Madden et al., 1997). In addition, the opioid-dependent participants were tested on the extent to which they discounted future monetary rewards versus heroin. The monetary rewards ranged from \$1000 to \$1. The heroin rewards were expressed as the amount of heroin that could be purchased with the equivalent monetary amount (e.g., \$1000 worth of heroin), based on the street price of approximately \$35 per bag. The delays were one week, two weeks, two months, six months, 1 year, 5 years, and 25 years. The results of the experiment are shown in Figure 18.7. The y-axis shows the median indifference point as the percentage of the value of the large reward, and the x-axis shows the delays in months.

Figure 18.7a compares monetary reward discounting between opioid-dependent and control participants. Control participants discounted money gradually, with the value remaining at approximately 45% after 100 months (about 8 years) and dropping to approximately 10% only after 300 months (25 years). In contrast, opioid-dependent participants discounted monetary rewards much more steeply, with the value dropping to approximately 35% after 50 months and to nearly 0% after 300 months. This demonstrates that opioid-dependent individuals discount delayed monetary rewards significantly more than non-dependent control participants.

Figure 18.7b compares how opioid-dependent participants discounted heroin versus money. The heroin reward was discounted extremely steeply, dropping to approximately 40% of its value after less than 50 months and to nearly 0% after 100 months. In comparison, the monetary reward for opioid-dependent participants was discounted less steeply, maintaining approximately 35% of its value at 50 months. These results show that opioid-dependent participants discounted delayed heroin rewards at a significantly greater rate than delayed monetary rewards, suggesting that drug rewards are discounted even more steeply than non-drug rewards in individuals with substance use disorders.

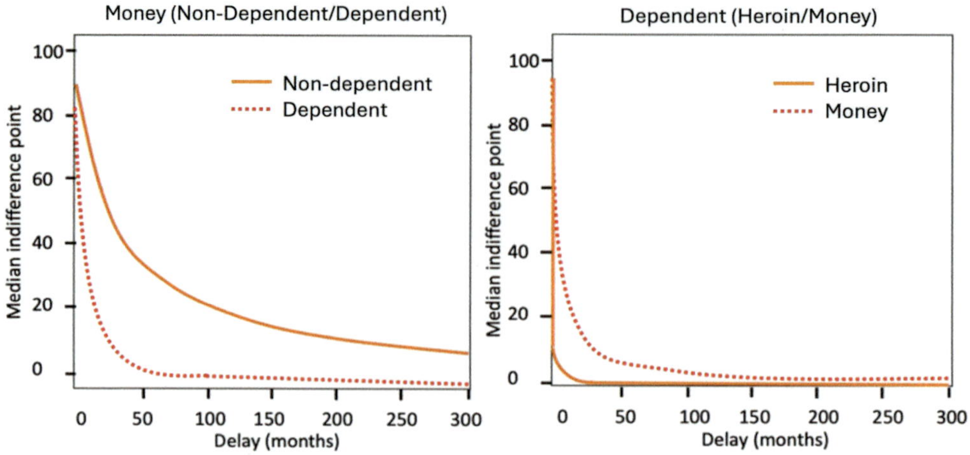

Figure 18.7 Delay discounting in opioid-dependent and control participants (Madden et al., 1997). (a) Comparison of monetary reward discounting between non-dependent control participants (orange solid line) and opioid-dependent participants (red dotted line). Opioid-dependent participants showed significantly steeper discounting of monetary rewards than controls. (b) Comparison of heroin reward discounting (orange solid line) versus monetary reward discounting (red dotted line) in opioid-dependent participants only. Heroin was discounted more steeply than money within the opioid-dependent group. The y-axis shows median indifference point as a percentage of the delayed reward value; the x-axis shows delay in months.

Source: Madden, G. J., Petry, N. M., Badger, G. J., & Bickel, W. K. (1997). Impulsive and self-control choices in opioid-dependent patients and non-drug-using control patients: drug and monetary rewards. *Exp Clin Psychopharmacol, 5*(3), 256–262. https://doi.org/10.1037/1064-1297.5.3.256.

Internet Gaming Disorder

Internet gaming disorder has only recently been identified as a psychological disorder in comparison to other addictive disorders (American Psychiatric Association, 2013). It is characterized by a preoccupation with gaming, tolerance, giving up other activities, and continuing to play despite experiencing problems. I want to stress that nothing is inherently wrong with gaming as long as it does not cause significant distress or impairments to your life.

Individuals who are addicted to gaming were found to discount the value of future rewards at higher rates than people in the general population. In one study, researchers divided gamers into three groups (Low, Medium, and High) based on their weekly gaming hours (Buono et al., 2017). Participants in the Low group reported playing 0–5 hours per week, the Medium group reported playing 6–17 hours per week, and the High group reported that they played over 18 hours per week.

The participants were tested for how much they discounted monetary rewards. The time delays included in the experiment were one week, two weeks, one month, six months, one year, three years, and ten years, and the rewards ranged from $1000 to $10. The indifference point was determined at each delay, which represents the proportion of the immediate reward equivalent to the delayed reward.

The results of the experiment are shown in Figure 18.8. The y-axis shows the subjective value as a proportion of the maximum reward the participants could receive, and the x-axis shows the delay in weeks. As shown in the figure, all three groups started at approximately 0.9 (90% of maximum value) at the shortest delay. However, the groups diverged as delays increased. The High video game group (red dotted line) showed the steepest discounting,

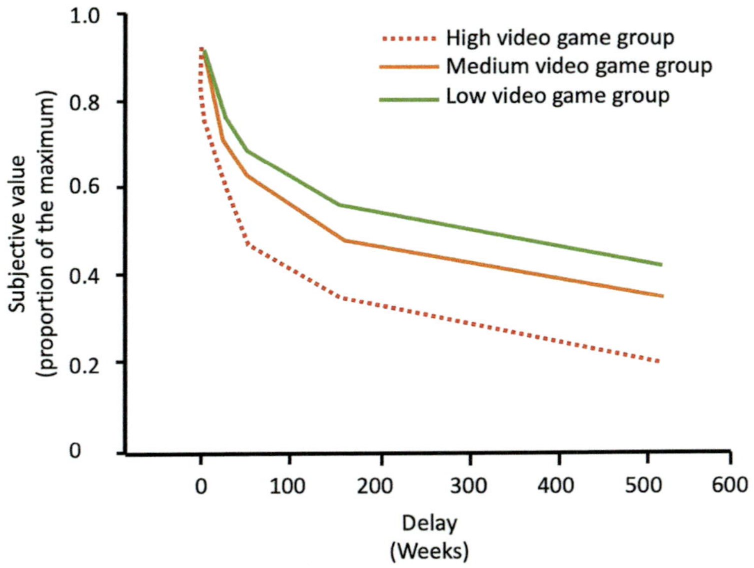

Figure 18.8 Delay discounting curves for gamers grouped by weekly gaming hours (Buono et al., 2017). The y-axis shows subjective value as proportion of the maximum reward; the x-axis shows delay in weeks. The High video game group (red dotted line, 18+ hours/week) showed the steepest discounting, followed by the Medium group (orange solid line, 6–17 hours/week), and the Low group (green solid line, 0–5 hours/week) showed the shallowest discounting.

Source: Buono, F., Sprong, M., Lloyd, D., Cutter, C., Printz Pereira, D., Sullivan, R., & Moore, B. (2017). Delay discounting of video game players: comparison of time duration among gamers. *Cyberpsychol Behav Soc Netw, 20*. https://doi.org/10.1089/cyber.2015.0451.

with subjective value dropping to approximately 0.45 at 100 weeks, 0.30 at 300 weeks, and 0.20 at 500 weeks. The Medium video game group (orange solid line) showed intermediate discounting, with subjective value dropping to approximately 0.60 at 100 weeks, 0.45 at 300 weeks, and 0.35 at 500 weeks. The Low video game group (green solid line) showed the shallowest discounting, with subjective value dropping to approximately 0.70 at 100 weeks, 0.50 at 300 weeks, and 0.42 at 500 weeks. These results demonstrate that individuals who play video games more hours per week discount delayed monetary rewards more steeply, suggesting that problematic gaming is associated with increased impulsivity and steeper temporal discounting.

Critical Thinking Spot Check 18.4

1. Discuss what is meant by the trans-disease process.
2. Describe studies in which delay discounting was a factor in psychological disorders.
3. How is delay discounting thought to differ across different psychological disorders?

Chapter Summary

Each bullet point aligns directly with the learning objectives outlined at the beginning of the chapter.

- Delaying gratification refers to forgoing a soon but small reward to obtain a later but large reward. It is a form of intertemporal choice, meaning that a decision made at one point affects the availability of alternatives later. The difficulties often experienced in delaying gratification are believed to occur due to a phenomenon known as delay discounting, which is the process by which the present value of a reward declines with the length of delay to its receipt. Delay discounting is often illustrated by a mathematical expression known as the hyperbolic discounting function. The hyperbolic discounting function demonstrates the rate at which the value of a commodity is discounted over time. When the discounting rates of the soon but small and large but later rewards are plotted, the indifference point, which is the point at which both rewards have the same subjective value, and the point of preference reversal, the point at which subjects switch their preference from a large but later reward to a soon but small reward, can also be observed.

- In a typical laboratory experiment of delay discounting, participants are typically tested for their preference for soon but small monetary rewards and a later but larger monetary reward across different conditions. The value of the soon but small reward varies across conditions. The delay to the larger but later reward is systematically varied, while its value remains constant. Typically, participants prefer the large but later reward but eventually switch their preference for the larger but later reward to the soon but small reward at the point of preference reversal. The point of preference reversal for different subjects can be plotted along the hyperbolic decay function.
- Researchers found that the rate at which delayed rewards are discounted differs across different age groups. In an experiment, they found the indifference point between the value of a delayed reward and its equivalent immediate reward for each age group. Children discounted delayed rewards more steeply than adolescents, and adolescents discounted delayed rewards more steeply than adults.
- Researchers have found that the rate at which delay discounting occurs depends on the type of reward. This is known as the domain effect. Alcohol was discounted at a higher rate than money but at the same rate as food. It was also proposed that the rate at which rewards are discounted depends on whether the reward is a primary reinforcer, is a secondary reinforcer, is consumable, serves a direct function, or is satiable.
- It was also proposed that the degree to which delayed rewards are discounted depends on the extent to which they can be exchanged for other goods (fungibility) and the extent to which goods will no longer be consumable after a certain amount of time (perishability).
- Excessive delay discounting is believed to be a trans-disease process, which means that it is shared across several psychological disorders, which include compulsive overeating, substance use disorder, pathological gambling, Internet gaming disorder, and attention deficit hyperactivity disorder.

Glossary

Delay discounting The tendency to devalue rewards as the delay to receiving them increases, leading to preferences for immediate gratification.

Delay of gratification The ability to resist an immediate reward in favor of a larger or more valuable reward in the future.

Domain effect The tendency for individuals to make different types of choices depending on the specific context or category of decisions, such as financial or health-related choices.

Fungibility The property of an asset or resource being interchangeable with others of the same kind, such as money or commodities.

Hyperbolic discounting function A mathematical model describing how people disproportionately discount future rewards, making short-term choices seem more appealing than long-term benefits.

Indifference point The moment in decision-making where an individual perceives two options as equally valuable.

Internet gaming disorder A condition characterized by excessive and compulsive engagement in online gaming, leading to negative consequences in daily life, such as impaired social functioning or academic performance.

Intertemporal choice Decision-making involving trade-offs between rewards received at different points in time, balancing immediate versus delayed gratification.

Perishability The characteristic of goods or resources that degrade or lose value over time if not used, often applied to food, tickets, or time-sensitive products.

Preference reversal A shift in preference depending on how choices are framed or when decision-making occurs, often observed in time-sensitive rewards.

Trans-disease process A concept describing psychological or behavioral mechanisms that contribute to multiple disorders, rather than being specific to one condition.

Module Summary

In this module, you learned about choice and self-control. The first chapter explored how behavioral decisions are distributed according to the matching law, expressed in a simple mathematical equation. The matching law states that the distribution of behavioral choices is dictated by the relative extent to which each behavior is reinforced. However, you also learned that behavior is not always distributed according to the strict matching law, for example, undermatching, in which not enough time is spent responding to the most advantageous option, and overmatching, in which more time than necessary is spent responding to the most beneficial option. You also learned that a bias is when one of the options is preferred over another, even if they are both equally advantageous. This led to the adjustment of the matching equation to include a measure of sensitivity and bias. You also learned about different theories of matching. These are molar and molecular theories. In the second chapter, you learned about self-control by exploring the ability to delay gratification and discounting. You also learned that delay discounting can be expressed mathematically in what is known as the hyperbolic decay function. It was found that delay discounting occurs across the lifespan but at a greater rate in children, followed by college students and adults. It was also found that the delay discounting rate differs across different types of rewards, depending on whether they are primary or secondary reinforcers, consumable, have a direct function, or are satiable. It was also found that the delay discounting rate also depends on the degree to which rewards are perishable and fungible. This is known as domain specificity. Finally, you learned that excessive delay discounting is a trans-disease process, meaning it is part of several psychological disorders.

Module 8

Application

Stop Delaying Gratification: The Hidden Zero Effect

It was found that the extent to which people discount the value of large but late rewards (LLR) in delay discounting experiments depends on how choice alternatives are described. *Framing* consists of reformulating how the other options are presented while preserving their economic value. One way to do this is to make explicit the outcome of the participant's choice. In a typical delay-discounting task, a participant's choice alternatives are presented in the following way:

"Would you like to receive $100 now or $150 in one week?"

When framed this way, participants often overlook their *opportunity cost and* the potential benefits they missed by choosing one alternative over the other because the $0 outcome is hidden. More precisely, choosing $100 now means getting $0 in one week, and choosing $150 in one week means getting $0 now. It was found that delay discounting is reduced when choice alternatives are framed so that the zero, in this case $0, is made explicit. This is known as the *hidden-zero effect* (Dang et al., 2020; Magen, Dweck and Gross, 2008; Read, Olivola and Hardisty, 2017). This is a puzzling phenomenon because both ways of presenting the alternatives lead to the same outcome.

In one study (Magen, Dweck and Gross, 2008), participants were asked to indicate their preference for receiving a soon but small (SSR) and an LLR. The rewards were real money for some participants and hypothetical cash for others. The participants in both groups were assigned to the implicit-zero condition and the explicit-zero condition. In the implicit-zero condition, the choice alternatives were presented in the typical way.

"Would you like to receive $5 now or $6.20 in 26 days?"

However, in the explicit zero condition, the hidden zero was made explicit in the following way:

"Would you like to receive $5 now and $0 in 26 days or $6.20 in 26 days and $0 now?"

Which of these two conditions do you think participants chose the SSR more often? The experiment results for both hypothetical and real money are shown in Figure 1-M8 App.

The number of impulsive choices (SSR) was lower in the explicit zero condition than in the hidden zero condition for the participants, in which the choice alternatives involved

DOI: 10.4324/9781003491828-34

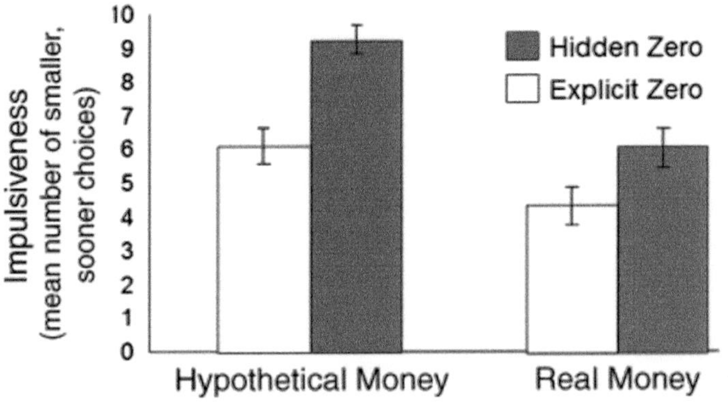

Figure 1-M8 App The hidden-zero effect (Magen, Dweck and Gross, 2008).

Source: Magen, E., Dweck, C. S., & Gross, J. J. (2008). The hidden-zero effect: representing a single choice as an extended sequence reduces impulsive choice. *Psychol Sci, 19*(7), 648–649. https://doi.org/10.1111/j.1467-9280.2008.02137.x.

hypothetical money or real money. These results support the idea that how alternatives are framed in a delay discounting task influences the extent to which SSRs are chosen over LLR and that making obvious the cost of selecting one choice alternative over the other, the opportunity cost, resulted in fewer impulsive choices. Can you find a way to try this for yourself the next time you find yourself having trouble delaying gratification?

Are You Thinking Critically?

1. Explain the hidden zero effect.
2. Describe a situation that does not involve money in which the hidden zero effect can be applied.
3. How can you apply your knowledge of the hidden zero effect to prevent delay discounting in your everyday life?

Module 9

Avoidance Behavior and Punishment

Introduction

So far, we have primarily focused on how behavior can come under the control of appetitive stimuli. However, responses frequently give rise to aversive outcomes. Both people and animals generally learn to escape or avoid environments in which responses have led to these aversive outcomes. Avoidance and escape behaviors are adaptive in that they increase one's chances of survival when facing threatening situations. We tend to escape dangerous situations and tend to avoid them in response to environmental cues that have been associated with them. Avoidance and escape also keep us from mundane everyday situations we do not want to find ourselves in. However, when exaggerated, avoidance and escape behaviors are maladaptive. This is the case for people who suffer from anxiety disorders such as phobias or post-traumatic stress disorder. Aversive outcomes can also suppress behavior. The suppression of behavior can occur in an adventitious manner, such as when a child is burned when touching a hot stove, or in an intentional manner, such as when a child is given time out to correct an unwanted behavior. This is known as punishment. In Chapter 19, we will explore the mechanisms and theories that underlie avoidance and escape behavior. In Chapter 20, we will discuss the suppressing effects of punishment on behavior and its adverse consequences.

Chapter 19: Avoidance Behavior
Chapter 20: Punishment

DOI: 10.4324/9781003491828-35

19 Surviving in a Potentially Dangerous Environment

Understanding Avoidance Behavior

Learning Objectives

1. Differentiate between active and passive avoidance behaviors, explaining their prerequisites for avoiding aversive stimuli effectively.
2. Explain the concept of discriminated avoidance and its reliance on conditioned stimuli and target responses, as outlined in Mowrer's two-process theory.
3. Discuss Seligman and Maier's findings on learned helplessness following exposure to inescapable shocks and its relevance to understanding avoidance behaviors.
4. Explore unsignaled or free operant avoidance, highlighting how animals can learn avoidance responses without explicit warning cues.
5. Describe Michael Fanselow's predatory imminence continuum and its impact on species-specific defense reactions (SSDRs) and defensive behaviors based on perceived predator threat levels.

Dawei's Greatest Fear

IStock photo ID:1095047118

DOI: 10.4324/9781003491828-36

Dawei is a 21-year-old university student who does well in all his courses. He is only one year away from graduating. This, despite the bouts of anxiety he experienced at the beginning of every semester, terrified that one of his classes would require an oral presentation. He carefully skimmed every class syllabus for any sign that an oral presentation was required. If an oral presentation was required, he quickly dropped the class and chose another. Eventually, Dawei learned that a particular teacher always required an oral presentation, leading him to avoid her classes. However, this did not always shield him from situations where he might have to express himself in front of other students. For example, in one of his classes, the teacher asked the students to introduce themselves to the group. The situation took Dawei by surprise. He panicked and quickly escaped the classroom before his turn came. Dawei's fears were not limited to public speaking. He also avoided any social interaction in which he could be evaluated, embarrassed, or humiliated, even if that possibility was slight. Dawei suffered from social phobia, which began in high school, where he was often bullied and picked on. His classmates once laughed at and mocked him as he stumbled through an oral presentation. Fortunately, Dawei sought the advice of a counselor who referred him to a therapist. Through cognitive-behavioral therapy, Dawei learned to deal with his fears by changing the way he thought about feared situations, which in turn increased his ability to cope with his anxiety. He also learned to change his behaviors by being taught to relax during gradual exposure to feared situations. Dawei now feels that he is conquering his fears. He eventually became confident enough to register for a class in which he had to present orally and successfully pulled it off.

19.1 What Is Avoidance Behavior?

Avoidance behavior permits animals and people to avoid aversive (unpleasant) and potentially dangerous stimuli. Avoidance behavior is common in everyday life experiences, such as when one avoids walking through a dark alleyway. People may also engage in avoidance behaviors for more benign reasons, such as avoiding a party when they know a person they dislike will be attending. You may also avoid registering for classes you believe will be uninteresting to you. People who are lactose intolerant avoid milk products unless they are lactose-free to avoid gastrointestinal discomfort. As you will read, there are two types of avoidance behaviors: active and passive.

Active Avoidance

In **active avoidance**, animals and people learn to actively perform a response (or action) that permits them to avoid or postpone an aversive stimulus (Boeke et al., 2017). In other words, they learn to do something to avoid the aversive stimulus. For example, steering a car away from incoming traffic to avoid an accident, turning off a stove to avoid burning food, and putting on suntan lotion to avoid a sunburn are all examples of active avoidance. Active avoidance is typically studied in the laboratory using a procedure in which animals are exposed to a stimulus such as a light or a sound (CS), triggered by the experimenter, that signals the delivery of the aversive stimulus (e.g., a footshock) (US) and learn to perform a specific action, such as pressing a lever, that prevents them from having to experience the aversive stimulus in response to the CS (Figure 19.1a). To put it more simply, the tone or the light is a sign that something bad is coming (footshocks), and pressing the lever prevents that.

Active avoidance learning involves both classical and instrumental conditioning (Diehl, Bravo-Rivera and Quirk, 2019; Mowrer, 1951). That is, the animal learns to expect the aversive stimulus through classical conditioning (i.e., CS paired with the US) and learns to avoid it through negative reinforcement (i.e., its response prevents it from experiencing the aversive stimulus). In Dawei's case, he learned to drop any class (instrumental response) at any sign (CS) that an oral presentation (US) would be required.

Passive Avoidance

In **passive avoidance**, animals and people refrain from performing a response due to its association with an aversive stimulus (Krypotos et al., 2015). For example, refraining from eating spicy food to avoid heartburn and not getting a worrisome symptom checked out for fear that it indicates a serious medical condition are all examples of passive avoidance. Passive avoidance is typically studied in the laboratory using procedures in which animals are placed in an environment (CS) that contains an aversive stimulus (e.g., a footshock or the odor of a predator) (US). After experiencing the aversive stimulus, the animal learns to refrain from producing the response that led to its experience (Figure 19.1b). Passive avoidance is also known as inhibitory avoidance because it inhibits the approach towards an aversive stimulus.

As for active avoidance, passive avoidance involves both classical and operant conditioning. However, two important differences exist between active and passive avoidance. The first is that in active avoidance experiments, the experimenter produces a discrete CS (e.g., tone or light) that predicts the aversive stimulus. In contrast, in passive avoidance, the CS consists of the context in which the aversive stimulus was experienced (e.g., the inside of the apparatus). The second difference is that the instrumental response is the omission of the response that brought the animal to the context of or in contact with the aversive stimulus. Remember that another way by which Dawei avoided oral presentations (US) was by

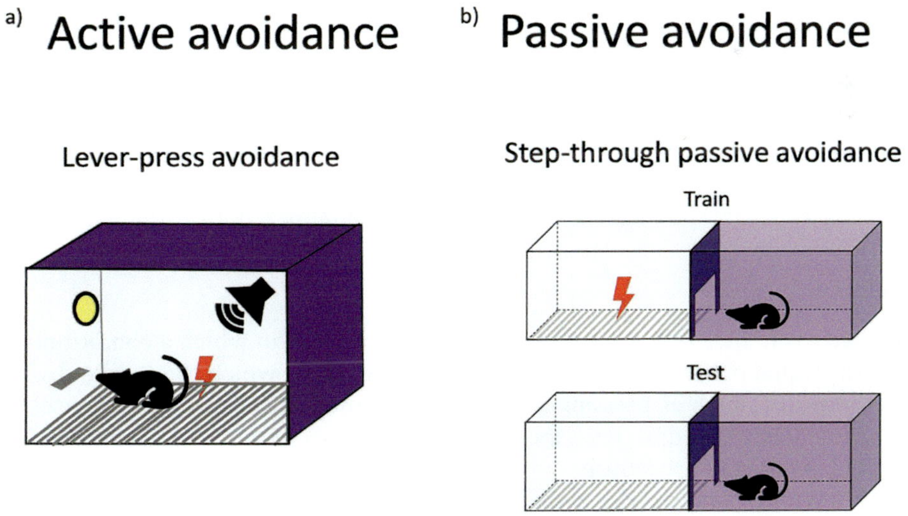

Figure 19.1 Active and passive avoidance. a) A type of active avoidance procedure known as lever-press avoidance in which animals learn to avoid footshocks (US) by pressing a lever (instrumental response) in response to a tone or a light (CS) that signals that footshocks are about to be delivered. b) A type of passive avoidance procedure known as step-through passive avoidance, in which animals avoid stepping through (instrumental response) to the side of a two-chamber apparatus (CS) in which they receive an aversive stimulus such as a footshock (US).

Examples of active and passive avoidance are stopping at the nearest gas station to fill up when the fuel gauge indicates low fuel (left) and avoiding going to a party because of shyness (right).

Source: Fuel gauge IStock illustration ID:1026199170, party IStock photo ID:1181396290.

simply not registering (instrumental response) for a class (CS) for which he knew one was required, a clear case of passive avoidance.

Escape Behavior

Animals and people are often confronted with aversive stimuli. **Escape behavior** refers to responses aimed at getting away from aversive stimuli when in their presence. Animals can escape prey once they have entered their territory; people can escape the site of accidents and make excuses to leave boring classes or work meetings. In the chapter's opening vignette, Dawei escapes from the classroom where the teacher surprisingly asked everyone to introduce themselves at the beginning of the semester.

Avoidance and escape behaviors are adaptive. However, when they are excessive, they may be part of the maladaptive behaviors observed in people with anxiety disorders. For example, a person with a phobia of germs (mysophobia) constantly avoids situations which they believe will put them in contact with germs. For example, such a person might avoid walking down certain streets on the days she knows people will have their garbage out for collection, an example of passive avoidance. However, if the same person accidentally turns onto one of those streets on a garbage collection day, she might immediately escape the situation by turning back out of it.

Discriminated Avoidance

Discriminated avoidance refers to an experimental procedure in which a conditioned stimulus, a **warning signal** (CS), signals the onset of an aversive US, which can be avoided if a specific **target response**, such as pressing a lever, is performed (instrumental response). Hence, the active avoidance procedure described in the opening section of this chapter is, in fact, a discriminated avoidance procedure.

Escape behavior often precedes avoidance behavior. This is because associations between environmental cues and the aversive events they precede are usually learned while experiencing them. For example, you may only now realize that you always argue with a friend when she is in a bad mood. Before realizing this, you kept arguing with her and stormed out of her house, an escape behavior. But since you have been able to predict an argument by noticing her bad mood (CS), you leave her house before an argument starts (instrumental response), which is an example of active avoidance.

Discriminated Avoidance Procedures Include Both Escape and Avoidance Trials

Escape responses often precede avoidance responses, which is evident in discriminative avoidance procedures, which include both escape trials and avoidance trials (Figure 19.2).

The animals' response determines the trial type. Escape responses occur during early training trials. This is because, during early trials, animals have yet to learn the association between the warning stimulus (CS) and the aversive stimulus (US), which they must avoid. Avoidance trials involve training animals to perform a response (CR), such as pressing a lever that turns off an aversive stimulus, such as footshocks (US), in response to a warning stimulus, such as a tone or a light (CS). A prototypical discriminated avoidance procedure in which escape and avoidance response trials can be differentiated is **two-way discriminated avoidance procedure** (Warner, 1932), illustrated and explained in Figure 19.3.

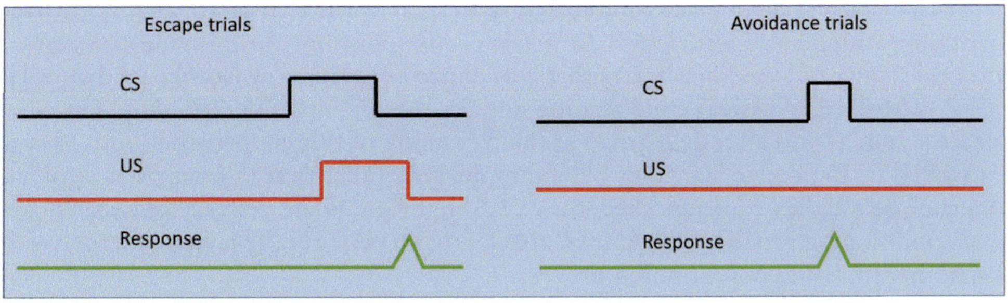

Figure 19.2 The discriminative avoidance procedure comprises escape and avoidance trials (see text for details).

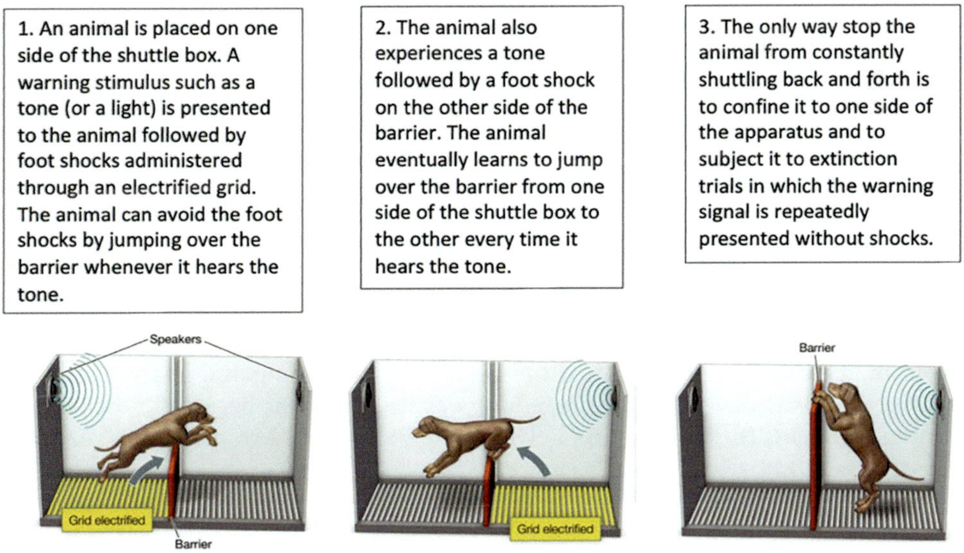

Figure 19.3 The two-way discriminated avoidance procedure (note that dogs are no longer used in these types of experiments).

Source: Modified from Breedlove, M. (2015). *Principles of psychology*. Oxford University Press Academic US. Page 331 Figure 19.21.

The One-Way Discriminated Avoidance Procedure

In a variant of the discriminated avoidance procedure, the experimenter removes the animals from the safe side of the shuttled box after performing the instrumental escape response. They are then placed back into the shocked side of the box for the subsequent trial. This is known as the *one-way discriminated avoidance procedure*. The advantage of this procedure is that it does not require the animals to cross back over to the side of the apparatus where they receive shocks, thus accelerating their learning rate.

What Is Learned in Discriminated Avoidance

The Two-Process Theory of Avoidance

What is learned in discriminated avoidance? Psychologist O.H. Mowrer (1907–1982) proposed the **two-process theory of avoidance** (also known as the two-factor theory) (Mowrer, 1951; Rescorla and Solomon, 1967) to answer this question. As its name suggests, the two-process theory of avoidance states that avoidance behavior consists of two distinct processes (or factors): 1) classical conditioning and 2) instrumental conditioning. This should not surprise you, as you already learned at the beginning of this chapter that both processes were involved in avoidance learning. For example, remember that in lever-press avoidance, a signal such as a light or a sound becomes a CS that signals the delivery of shocks (US), a classical conditioning process. The animal also learns to perform the lever press to avoid the shocks, an instrumental conditioning process.

Although these two processes were identified, a question remained. What aversive stimulus is escaped or avoided by performing the instrumental response? If you believe this question has an easy answer (i.e., "the shock, of course"), read on. In the two-way discriminated avoidance procedure (shuttle box), the first process in Mowrer's theory, classical conditioning, consists of the association between the warning CS and the shock through classical conditioning. The second process is instrumental behavior (negative reinforcement), which consists of moving to the side of the box opposite to the one where a shock is about to be delivered (safe side). Mowrer hypothesized that what the animals learned in the procedure was not that the instrumental response permitted them to avoid the shocks but rather the fear induced by the CS due to its association with shocks because the CS was turned off when the animals moved to the safe side of the shuttle box.

ESCAPE FROM FEAR EXPERIMENTS

The two-process theory proved challenging because classical and instrumental conditioning occurred within the same trial, making it difficult to disentangle the two processes. To solve this problem, a procedure that isolated the classical conditioning and instrumental conditioning processes was devised. This procedure was used in what became known as **escape from fear experiments (EFF)** (Cain and LeDoux, 2007; Esmorís-Arranz, Pardo-Vazquez and Vázquez-García, 2003).

In the first phase of the experiment, only one of the compartments of the shuttle box is used (shock side). An animal is placed in the compartment, and a warning CS (e.g., tone or light) is followed by shocks (US). During that phase, no escape is possible, as the archway leading to the safe compartment of the apparatus is blocked. The typical response of animals in this situation is to display a fear response or "freeze" upon hearing the warning signal. Next, the archway leading to the safe side of the apparatus is opened and escape to the safe side of the apparatus is possible. The animal is then given several trials in which the CS is presented without shocks. During the first trials, animals tend to "freeze," as in the first phase. However, the freezing response ceased after a few trials due to extinction, and the animals moved to the safe side of the apparatus in response to the CS, which remained on until they arrived there and turned off.

Using this procedure, it was found that rats took progressively less time to cross over to the safe side of the apparatus at the onset of the CS. This indicated that the rats learned to escape from the fear induced by the CS because moving to the safe side of the shuttle box terminated the CS. The rats could not have moved to the safe side because they wanted to avoid the shock because the fear response (freezing) initially elicited by the CS was extinguished; hence, the CS no longer predicted a shock (Esmorís-Arranz, Pardo-Vazquez and Vázquez-García, 2003). This result provided evidence in favor of Mowrer's (1951) theory that in a discriminated avoidance procedure, animals learn to escape the fear induced by the CS, which has been paired with the aversive US by performing an instrumental response and that it does not do so to avoid the aversive US.

Critical Thinking Spot Check 19.1

1. Distinguish between active and passive avoidance by giving an everyday life example.
2. Distinguish between avoidance and escape responses by showing how they consist of different trial types within the same procedure.
3. Define discriminated avoidance and give an example demonstrating its importance to everyday life.
4. Describe the two-process theory of avoidance.
5. Explain what motivated the development of the escape from fear experiment.

19.2 Fear and the Controllability of Painful Experiences

In 1948, Mowrer, the author of the two-process theory, whom you read about in the previous section, wondered if the level of anticipatory fear of shocks (experiencing fear ahead of getting shocked) depended on whether the shocks were escapable (or controllable) by the performance of an operant response or inescapable (or uncontrollable). To answer this question, he conducted an experiment in which rats were placed in a rectangular chamber with a gridded floor through which they received foot shocks ten seconds after having been fed food pellets. For one group of rats, leaping into the air put an end to the shocks. Hence, the rats in that group eventually learned to jump into the air to escape the shocks (instrumental response). Thus, for those rats, the shocks were escapable. Another group of rats was treated identically, except that the shocks continued for a predetermined period no matter what the rats did (i.e., no instrumental response could be made that turned off the shocks). Thus, for this group of rats, the shocks were inescapable (Mowrer and Viek, 1948).

The results of the experiment are shown in Figure 19.4. The rats' level of anticipatory fear was measured by the amount of food they ate before the end of each trial on successive days of testing. Rats were taken to experience anticipatory fear if their food consumption was significantly inhibited (number of response inhibitions). Food consumption was substantially more inhibited across days of testing in the rats exposed to inescapable shocks (S-UnC [red line]) than in the rats that received escapable shocks (S-C [black line]). Mowrer concluded that, as in humans, the ability to control painful experiences results in less anticipatory fear than uncontrollable ones.

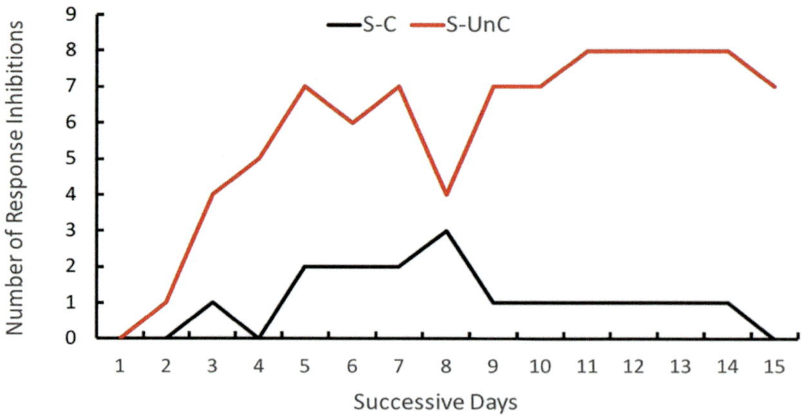

Figure 19.4 Results from the Mowrer and Viek (1948) experiment compared the number of response inhibitions of rats subjected to escapable shocks (S-C) versus rats subjected to unescapable shocks (S-UnC).

Source: Converted from the table in Mowrer, O. H., & Viek, P. (1948). An experimental analogue of fear from a sense of helplessness. *J Abnorm Psychol*, *43*(2), 193–200. https://doi.org/10.1037/h0057165.

Learned Helplessness

The effect of being exposed to unavoidable shocks was further explored by psychologists Martin Seligman and Steven Maier in the 1960s. They tested the effects of exposure to inescapable shocks on the ability of dogs to learn the escape response (instrumental) in a discriminated avoidance procedure (Seligman and Maier, 1967). The design of this experiment, known as the **triadic design**, is illustrated in Table 19.1.

The experiment consisted of exposure (Phase 1) and conditioning (Phase 2). The dogs were subdivided into Escape, Yoked, and Normal control. In Phase 1, the Escape group was restrained in a type of restraint similar to a "hammock" and subjected to a series of escapable shocks. The shocks were escapable because they could be terminated by pressing a panel with their noses (instrumental response). Each dog in the Escape group was yoked (matched) to a dog in a group and treated the same way, except they received inescapable shocks. That is, they received them regardless of their responses (Yoked). The dogs in a third group, the Normal control group, were also restrained and were never shocked.

In Phase 2, which occurred the day after Phase 1, all dogs were trained in the one-way discrimination avoidance procedure described previously (escape/avoidance). Table 19.1 shows the results of the experiment. One hundred percent of the dogs in the Escape group who learned the instrumental response to terminate the shocks in Phase 1 rapidly learned the instrumental escape/avoidance response in Phase 2. In contrast, only 25% of the dogs in the Yoked group, for which the shock was inescapable in Phase 1, learned the instrumental escape/avoidance response in Phase 2 and did so at a slow rate. Almost all the dogs (87%) in the Normal control group quickly learned the instrumental escape/avoidance response. Seligman and Maier (1967) suggested that the Yoked group failed to learn the escape/avoidance response in Phase 2 due to learning that there was nothing they could do to avoid getting shocked in Phase 1. Seligman and Maier referred to this phenomenon as **learned helplessness**.

Table 19.1 The triadic design (Seligman and Maier, 1967).

Group	*Phase 1 Exposure*	*Phase 2 Conditioning*	*Test results*
Escape	Escapable shock (pressing a panel terminated the shock)	Escape/avoidance (shuttle box)	Rapid avoidance learning (100%)
Yoked	Yoked inescapable shock (shocks administered regardless of response)	Escape/avoidance (shuttle box)	Slow avoidance learning (25%)
Normal Control	Restricted to the apparatus (no shocks administered)	Escape/avoidance (shuttle box)	Rapid avoidance learning (87.5%)

Objective Helplessness and Subjective Helplessness

They also proposed that helplessness can be subdivided into **objective and subjective helplessness.** Objective helplessness occurs when no response to avoid an aversive outcome is possible. In contrast, subjective helplessness occurs when a response to avoid an aversive stimulus is possible but not performed (Maier and Seligman, 2016). In Seligman and Maier's (1967) experiment, the objective helplessness they experienced in Phase 1 caused their subjective helplessness in Phase 2.

Focus On

The Learned Helplessness Theory of Depression

Cognitive theories emphasize the role of thoughts and beliefs in the development and maintenance of depression. For example, in what is known as the unfavorable triad of depression, psychologist Aaron Beck proposed that depressed individuals have a pessimistic view of the self, the world, and the future. Depressed individuals also have cognitive biases that act to maintain their depression. These include overgeneralization, in which individuals draw general conclusions, sometimes based on a single event (Beck, 1976). For example, a man may believe he is a terrible father because he was late picking up his daughter from school, or a student may think herself worthless for failing an exam. In another cognitive bias, a person may exaggerate the importance of the adverse outcomes of their behavior while minimizing the positive outcomes. For example, a student may feel she is an idiot for ruining her laptop when she notices a tiny dent on one of its sides, whereas she attributes getting an A+ on a midterm to luck.

Having a sense of control over one's life is associated with psychological well-being. In contrast, a perceived lack of control over one's life is associated with depression and anxiety. In the learned helplessness theory of depression, proposed by psychologist Martin Seligman (1975), people become depressed after experiencing adverse life events which they feel they cannot control. For this reason, subsequent adverse events are met with the passivity that often characterizes individuals who suffer from depression. The theory originated from the findings that dogs exposed to inescapable shocks were subsequently impaired at learning a response permitting them to avoid a shock compared to dogs not exposed to inescapable shocks.

The learned helplessness theory was revised to include the reasons to which people suffering from depression attribute their failures (Abramson, Seligman and Teasdale, 1978; Seligman, 2002). According to this revision, people feel helpless when attributing their failures to global factors, stable factors, and internal characteristics. Global attributions refer to an individual's perceived general ability to succeed. For example, a non-depressed person who fails at a specific task may feel incompetent but retain an intact sense of competency for other tasks. In contrast, the depressed person failing at a particular task may take failing at one task as a sign of generalized incompetence encompassing all other tasks. Stable attributions refer to an individual's perception of the extent to which failures are likely to continue. For example, after a failure, the non-depressed person may think, "I will do better next time."

In contrast, the depressed individual is more likely to think, "I will always fail at this." Finally, a non-depressed person is likelier to attribute failures to a balance of external and internal characteristics. However, the depressed person is more likely to attribute failures to internal factors. For example, following a failure, the depressed person is more likely to think, "Here I go again, messing things up because of my stupidity."

The second revision of the learned helplessness theory is known as the learned *hopelessness theory* (Abramson, Metalsky and Alloy, 1989). This theory includes the attributions of the first revision but also adds low self-esteem and the extent to which life events are perceived as unfavorable. Another addition is the extent to which individuals expect that desired outcomes will ever occur in certain situations.

Are You Thinking Critically?

1. Identify the differences and similarities between Beck's negative triad of depression and learned helplessness.
2. How would a therapist who strictly adheres to the learned helplessness theory of depression treat depressed patients?
3. Describe a hypothetical experiment by which you would test the learned helplessness theory of depression.

Critical Thinking Spot Check 19.2

1. Describe the triadic design and what was learned from its use.
2. Distinguish between learned helplessness, objective helplessness, and subjective helplessness.
3. What did the learned helplessness theory contribute to our understanding of psychopathology?

19.3 Unsignaled (Free Operant) Avoidance

In the previous sections, you learned how aversive stimuli can be avoided by performing a behavior in response to an external warning stimulus. However, aversive stimuli are not always preceded by an external warning stimulus so we can take the appropriate action to avoid it. For example, you may periodically check whether a police car is in the vicinity when waiting for your friend while illegally parked. In that situation, your checking behavior is not controlled by an external warning signal but by whether you feel it is time to check. Once you have checked and reassured yourself that no police cars are in sight, you focus on your friend's possible arrival until you feel it is time to check again. We also avoid burning food on the stove by periodically checking on it. These are examples of **unsignaled (free operant) avoidance.** An experimental procedure in which unsignaled avoidance is used is illustrated in Figure 19.5.

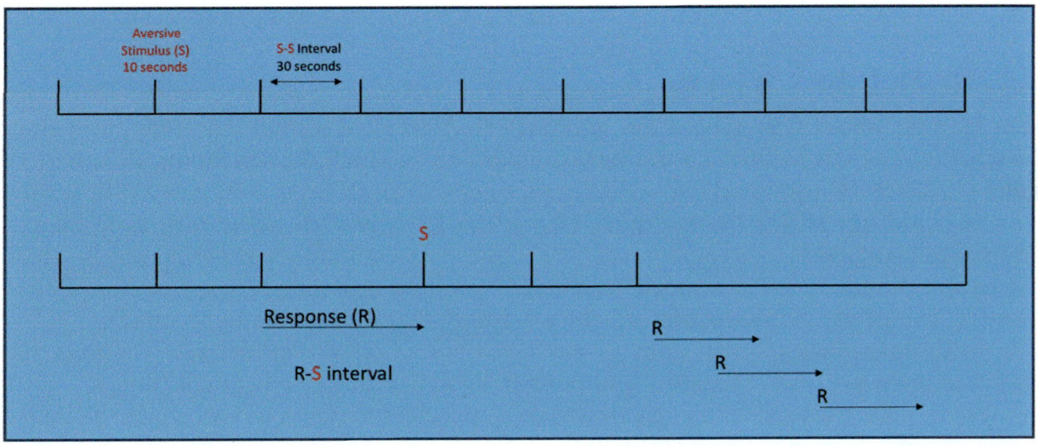

Figure 19.5 A hypothetical unsignaled-avoidance experiment (see text for details).

The top line represents a schedule under which an aversive stimulus (S) is presented and remains for 10 seconds. A period of 30 seconds elapses between each stimulus presentation. This is known as the stimulus-stimulus interval (S-S). The bottom line shows what happens when a target instrumental response (R) (i.e., the response that terminates (S) is performed. In the current example, performing the target response delays the onset of the next shock by 10 seconds (R-S interval). At the far right of the bottom row, you can see that an individual can learn to permanently avoid S by repeatedly performing the response within the R-S interval.

The Safety-Signal Hypothesis

As you just learned, in unsignaled avoidance, no stimulus external to the animal serves as a warning signal for the following aversive stimulus. This led researchers to wonder about the basis by which animals learn to avoid the aversive stimulus. According to the **safety-signal hypothesis**, the proprioceptive feedback cues from the movements involved in the performance of an avoidance response, such as pressing a bar, become associated with the absence of an aversive stimulus, known as a safe period. These feedback cues thus become conditioned inhibitors of the fear response. In addition, the same cues are negative reinforcers of the avoidance response (Fernando et al., 2014; Konorski, 1967). So, to recap, the proprioceptive feedback cues act as both conditioned inhibitors of fear and as negative reinforcers of the avoidance response. However, this explanation still leaves out the warning signal. If no external signal exists, how does the animal learn a conditioned avoidance response? The answer is that the animals may be sensitive to the time elapsed since they performed their last response and have a sense of when the next aversive stimulation may come.

Critical Thinking Spot Check 19.3

1. Describe the (unsignaled) free-avoidance procedure.
2. Give an example of unsignaled avoidance in everyday life.
3. Explain the safety signal hypothesis.

19.4 Specific Defense Reactions

After learning about how laboratory animals avoid aversive stimuli, you may now wonder whether animals in their natural environment do so similarly. Psychologist Robert C. Bolles (1928–1994) proposed two main reasons he believes this is not the case. 1) In nature, animals could not afford the multiple learning trials, typical of laboratory experiments, required to learn avoidance responses, and 2) contrary to laboratory experiments, in which an aversive stimulus such as a shock is signaled by a light or a tone (CSs), predators do not always conveniently give their prey advance warning that they are going to attack.

Instead, Bolles believed that animals possessed innate behavioral defense reactions that permitted them to escape predators and potentially dangerous novel stimuli (Bolles, 1970). He also thought these defense reactions were specific to each species, which he called **species-specific defense reactions (SSDRs)**.

The Predatory Imminence Continuum

According to the **predatory imminence continuum theory**, proposed by psychologist Michael Fanslow, the form and intensity of SSDRs performed by animals depend on the threat posed by predators (Fanselow and Lester, 1988).

Figure 19.6 illustrates the predatory imminence continuum. The arrow at the bottom of the figure represents the growing imminence or likelihood of a predator attack. With *no predator potential*, the animal engages in its *preferred activity pattern, such as foraging* (i.e., searching for food). However, if environmental cues signal *predatory potential* (the potential presence of a predator), the animal engages in **pre-encounter defensive behavior**. This includes a change in eating patterns, such as a reduction in the number of eating bouts but an increase in the amount of food it eats during those bouts. This change in eating patterns was also found in rats under a high threat of shocks in the laboratory (Fanselow, Lester and Helmstetter, 1988).

However, when a predator is *detected*, the animal engages in **post-encounter defense behavior**, such as freezing. Flight can also occur if a well-practiced escape route is available. However, freezing (remaining immobile) is a more efficient means of avoiding predators. Animals are generally selective about the location where they freeze, showing that

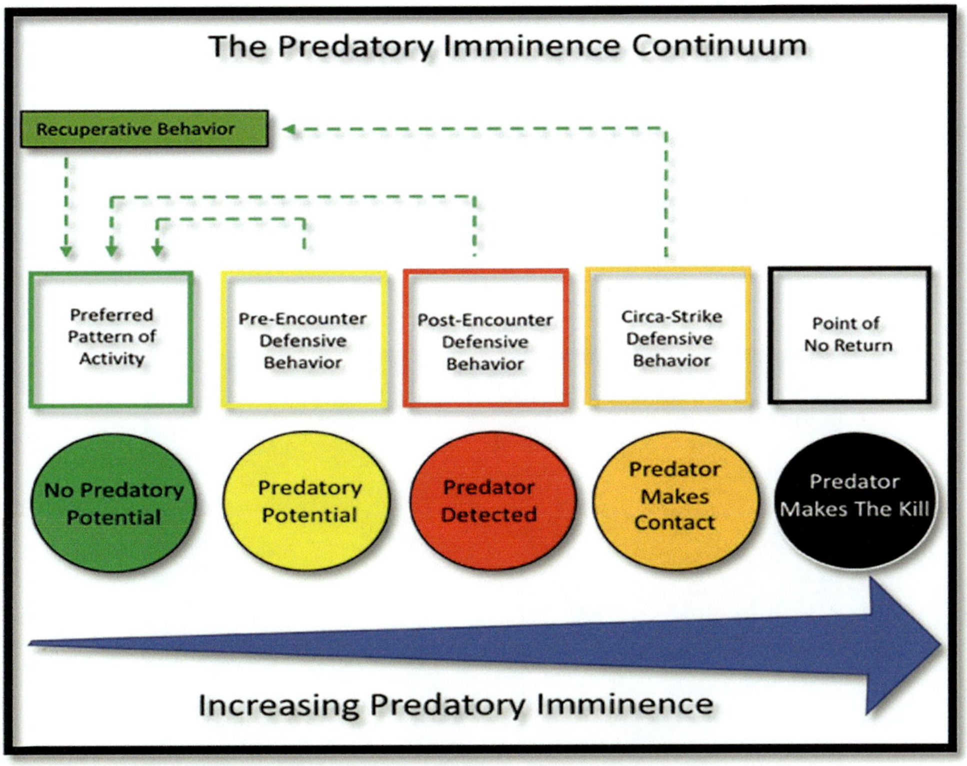

Figure 19.6 The predatory imminence continuum (see text for details).

it is an active process. For example, rats often freeze in the darker of two areas, making detecting them more difficult for predators. If a *predator makes contact*, the prey engages in **circa strike defensive behaviors**. These behaviors, which include leaping up in the air, biting, fighting, or struggling, might permit the prey to escape once caught by the predator (Fanselow and Lester, 1988). If no defensive behavior results in escape or avoidance, it is killed by the predator at the *point of no return*.

However, suppose the prey successfully avoids or escapes the predator in the early stages of the continuum. In that case, it will return to its preferred pattern of activity (green hashed lines). However, notice that following a circa-strike defense, the prey does not directly return to its preferred pattern of activity but first engages in recuperative behavior for a period of resting and healing (Fanselow and Sigmundi, 1982).

Predatory Imminence Continuum Theory in Humans

After learning about the predatory imminence continuum in animals, you might wonder if it also applies to humans. Fanselow, the author of the theory, believes it does so by being involved in people's ability to deal with potentially threatening life events that induce fear (an emotional reaction to a present threat) and anxiety (a sense of apprehension about a possible upcoming threat). For example, at the beginning of the COVID-19 crisis, many people became anxious, interrupted their standard patterns of activity, and engaged in hoarding behavior, such as stocking up on food and household supplies such as toilet paper, in a way similar to pre-encounter defense behaviors displayed by animals (Fanselow, 2022).

It can also be added that as the COVID-19 threat became more imminent, many people's fear and anxiety actively suppressed normal behaviors, such as going out in public, for fear of getting infected. This is similar to the post-encounter defense behavior of animals, in which they freeze to avoid being detected. Finally, as the threat intensified, some experienced panic, characterized by intense fear and frantic ways to deal with the danger. This is similar to the circa-strike defense behaviors displayed by animals caught by predators.

The COVID-19 crisis caused people to interrupt their regular patterns of behavior, similar to what occurs in the pre-encounter defense stage of the predatory imminence continuum—some hoarded household supplies.

Source: iStockphoto: ID:1215276732.

A Distorted Predatory Imminence Continuum

Fanselow (2022) proposed that a distorted predatory imminence continuum can partly explain the exaggerated anxiety and fear experienced by people suffering from anxiety disorders. He suggested that anxiety disorders are partly due to a lowering of the adaptive defense activation threshold for the activation of the behaviors along the continuum. As shown in Figure 19.7, in people not suffering from an anxiety disorder (top), preferred patterns of activity, such as the ones people in which people engage in their daily lives, dominate within a wide range of experiences. Anxiety, fear, and panic are only experienced once the imminence of a threat crosses a reasonable threshold (i.e., in the face of a real danger). In contrast, in people suffering from anxiety disorders, the threshold for triggering anxiety, fear, and panic might be lowered, leading them to engage in these responses when they are not warranted by the level of threat (middle). In a specific anxiety disorder, known as generalized anxiety disorder, people experience sustained levels of anxiety unwarranted by any immediate danger, which may be due to a selectively prolonged pre-encounter defense stage (bottom).

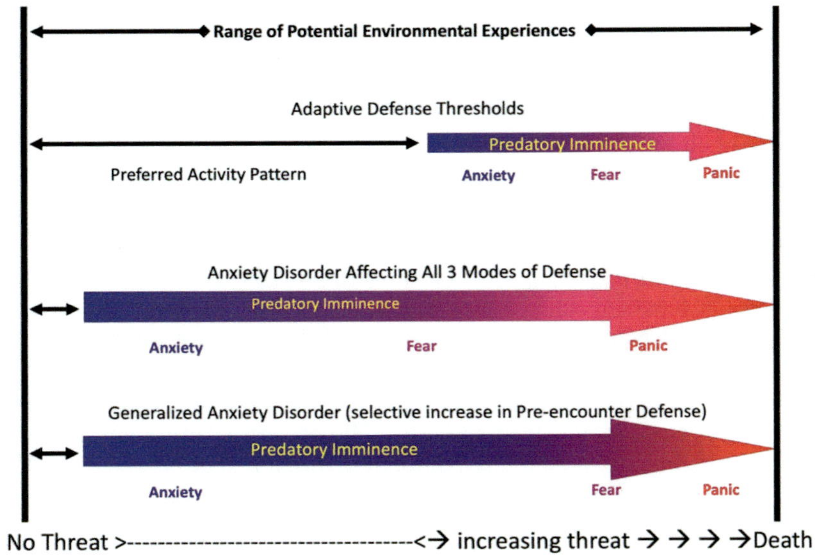

Figure 19.7 Normal and distorted predatory imminence continuums (see text for details).

Source: Fanselow, M. S. (2022). Negative valence systems: sustained threat and the predatory imminence continuum. *Emerg Top Life Sci*, *6*(5), 467–477.

Critical Thinking Spot Check 19.4

1. Explain how specific defense reactions (SSDRs) contribute to the survival of animals.
2. Give an example of how the predatory imminence continuum applies to human behaviors.
3. How can distortions in the predatory imminence continuum contribute to the development of anxiety disorders?

Chapter Summary

Each bullet point aligns directly with the learning objectives outlined at the beginning of the chapter.

- Avoidance behavior permits organisms to stay away from aversive stimuli. Several theories have been proposed to explain avoidance behavior. Two types of avoidance behaviors exist: active avoidance and passive avoidance. Active avoidance refers to behavior that prevents or postpones the delivery of an aversive stimulus. In passive avoidance, a behavior is suppressed due to its association with an aversive stimulus. Not all aversive stimuli can be avoided. It must be predictable, and a way to avoid it must be available. Escape behavior occurs when an aversive stimulus that is already present is not signaled, and a way to get away from it is available.
- Discriminated avoidance refers to an experimental procedure in which a conditioned stimulus signals the onset of an aversive stimulus, and a target response permits the avoidance of that stimulus. To explain avoidance, psychologist Mowrer proposed the two-process theory of avoidance, which states that avoidance behavior depends on classical and instrumental conditioning.

- In the 1960s, psychologists Martin Seligman and Steven Maier studied the effects of exposure to inescapable shocks in what became known as the triadic design. They found that dogs that learned that nothing they could do would permit them to avoid a shock failed to learn an avoidance response later. Seligman and Maier referred to this phenomenon as learned helplessness.
- An external warning stimulus that signals an avoidance stimulus is not always present. However, an avoidance response can still be learned. Avoidance behavior learned without an explicit signal is unsignaled or free-operant avoidance.
- Animals are believed to possess innate behavioral defense reactions that evolved to permit them to escape predators. These are known as species-specific defense reactions (SSDRs). Psychologist Michael Fanselow proposed the predatory imminence continuum in which an SSDR depends on the imminent encounter with a predator, leading to three types of defensive behaviors: pre-encounter defensive behavior, post-encounter defense behavior, and circa strike defensive behaviors. The predatory imminence continuum also applies to humans facing varying environmental threats, such as the COVID-19 crisis. A distorted predatory imminence continuum may also play a role in the development and maintenance of anxiety disorders.

Glossary

Active avoidance A learned response where an organism actively performs a behavior to prevent encountering an aversive event.

Avoidance behavior Actions taken to prevent exposure to an aversive stimulus, often learned through conditioning.

Circa-strike defensive behaviors Immediate and intense defensive reactions that occur at the moment of a direct threat or attack.

Discriminated avoidance A type of avoidance learning where an organism responds to a specific warning signal to prevent an aversive event.

Escape behavior Actions that immediately terminate exposure to an aversive stimulus once it is encountered.

Escape from fear (EFF) experiments Studies investigating how organisms learn to escape from conditioned fear responses through avoidance behaviors.

Learned helplessness A psychological condition in which an organism fails to escape or avoid aversive stimuli due to previous experiences of uncontrollable events.

Objective helplessness A condition in which an organism or individual is genuinely unable to escape or alter an aversive situation, independent of subjective perception.

Passive avoidance Learning to refrain from certain behaviors to avoid an aversive stimulus.

Post-encounter defensive behavior Protective responses occurring after encountering a threat to minimize harm.

Pre-encounter defensive behavior Actions taken before an actual threat is encountered, aimed at reducing the likelihood of danger.

Safety-signal hypothesis The idea that cues signaling the absence of an aversive event can reinforce avoidance behavior and reduce fear responses.

Subjective helplessness The perceived inability to control or change aversive situations, leading to passivity and decreased motivation.

Target response The specific behavior required to prevent or escape from an aversive stimulus in an avoidance learning task.

Triadic design An experimental setup used in learned helplessness research, involving three groups: one with control over aversive events, one without control, and one unexposed to aversive stimuli.

Two-process theory of avoidance A theory proposing that avoidance learning involves both classical conditioning (fear of a warning signal) and operant conditioning (behavior to reduce fear).

Two-way discriminated avoidance procedure A prototypical discriminated avoidance procedure in which escape and avoidance response trials can be differentiated.

Unsignaled (free operant) avoidance Avoidance learning that occurs without explicit warning signals, where the organism responds at regular intervals to prevent aversive consequences.

Warning signal A stimulus that indicates the impending occurrence of an aversive event, triggering avoidance responses.

20 Punishment

Learning Objectives

1. Define positive and negative punishment and its effects on behavior, emphasizing passive avoidance and stimulus removal.
2. Discuss the subjective nature of punishment severity and its impact on behavior reduction, considering individual differences and the role of extinction and habituation.
3. Examine Skinner and Thorndike's doubts about long-term punishment effectiveness, highlighting Skinner's compensatory recovery theory.
4. Evaluate factors influencing punishment effectiveness, such as intensity, delay, schedule, and stimulus control in behavior suppression.
5. Explore adverse effects of physical punishment in children, including fear generalization, normalization of violence, mental health issues, and the cultural impact on perceptions of force usage.

To Punish or Not to Punish

Source: IStock photo ID:469612008.

DOI: 10.4324/9781003491828-37

Sofia sometimes squeezes the cheeks or pinches the skin on the forearms of her four-year-old boy, Julio, when he misbehaves. She feels terrible about doing so, especially since she found out that physical punishment is detrimental to a child's self-esteem and is associated with higher rates of mental health problems such as anxiety and depression. She confided in her friend Levi that she sometimes physically punished Julio. He commended her for being aware of her behavior and having the courage to make such an admission. He explained that, in his developmental psychology class, he learned that parents should focus on teaching their children to act kindly toward others. "How do you do that?" asked Sofia. Levi explained that children learn to treat others as they have been treated. He suggested that she use reasoning while being warm and understanding to get Julio to comply. "Easier said than done," she replied. "This does not mean you should never yell at him," he said. "Yelling might be necessary to stop Julio from engaging in dangerous behaviors." Upon hearing Levi mention this, she let out a sigh of relief and confessed that, on the previous day, Julio was going to run across a busy intersection at the stop light. She explained that she panicked, yelled at him, and tightened her grip on his hand to the point at which he screamed in pain. Later that evening, Sofia looked up everything Levi had told her online. She came across many parenting websites citing studies supporting everything Levi told her. She read that physical punishment was associated with many harmful effects on children's development. For example, she learned that physical punishment could lead to aggression and poor academic performance in adolescence and that children subjected to physical punishment are more likely to engage in criminal behavior, commit spousal and child abuse, and become addicted to drugs. Realizing the harm she might be causing Julio, she immediately joined a virtual parenting support group for help.

20.1 What Is Punishment?

Learning Not to Respond

Punishment refers to procedures in which the frequency of a response is reduced by its consequence. Thus, in addition to extinction, which you learned about in Chapters 5 and 12; conditioned inhibition, which you learned about in Chapter 5; and passive avoidance learning (Chapter 19), punishment is another way animals learn not to respond (Bouton and Broomer, 2023).

Learning not to respond is essential. It permits animals to conserve energy when a stimulus does not signal anything dangerous, as in extinction; to concentrate on stimuli that signal appetitive outcomes versus those that do not, as in conditioned inhibition; and to avoid responding to environmental cues which have been associated with an aversive stimulus, as in passive avoidance learning. Punishment helps prevent further response when the outcome of a response becomes potentially dangerous. It also plays a vital role in adapting one's responses to environmental changes. That is, the same response may be appropriate at one point in time or place when or where it is reinforced but inappropriate at another time or place when or where it is punished.

Positive and Negative Punishment

Punishment can be subdivided into positive punishment and negative punishment. Positive punishment occurs when a response leads to the delivery of an aversive stimulus, such as when a child gets reprimanded for misbehaving. Negative punishment occurs when a response leads to the removal or deprivation of a stimulus that has positive hedonic value (i.e., that provides pleasure). For example, the suspension of one's driver's license for drunk driving is a form of negative punishment—a type of negative punishment known as response cost discussed in Chapter 9.

Time Out

You are undoubtedly familiar with a form of negative punishment called **time out**. Time out is used by applied behavior analysts, teachers, and parents (Poling et al., 2002). There are two types of time-out procedures: exclusionary time-out and nonexclusionary time-out. In what is known as *exclusionary time out*, the type you are probably most familiar with, a misbehaving individual (usually a child) is removed from an environment that provides many positive reinforcers and placed into an area with few or no positive reinforcers. Four *nonexclusionary time-out* procedures have been developed:

Time-out ribbons: This method involves giving a child an accessory, such as a ribbon or wristband, to wear upon entering an environment where good behavior is encouraged. The wearing of an accessory indicates that the child can receive positive reinforcers. If the child misbehaves, the accessory is removed for a predetermined period.

Planned ignoring: Planned ignoring is used in environments where attention from an individual, such as a therapist or a teacher, is highly valued. It involves ignoring an individual when she engages in inappropriate target behaviors, such as aggressive remarks. Planned ignoring requires sound judgment, as certain aggressive behaviors (e.g., hitting another child) cannot be ignored.

Contingent observation: Contingent observation involves removing a misbehaving individual from a group to an area where she can observe the group interacting and receiving social reinforcers for a predetermined period. This method serves the dual purpose of depriving the individual of the social reinforcers and observing the behaviors required to obtain them.

Prevention of preferred activities: In this form of negative punishment, a misbehaving individual is deprived of a preferred activity whenever a target undesired behavior is performed. For example, a teacher may turn off the computer used by the individual to play video games.

Laboratory Procedures for Positive and Negative Punishment

Figure 20.1 illustrates a typical laboratory procedure for positive punishment. Animals (often rats) are placed in a chamber and trained to press a lever (instrumental response acquisition) to receive a food reinforcer (US) (Figure 20.1a). Once the rats acquire the lever-press response, they are subjected to trials during which the lever-press results in an aversive stimulus such as a foot shock and the food reinforcer (punishment) (Figure 20.1b). Figure 20.1c–d shows the results of a hypothetical experiment using this procedure. In the acquisition phase, two groups of rats (Punishment and No-punishment) were reinforced for pressing a lever for food. In the punishment phase, the Punishment group received a foot shock in addition to the food as a consequence of pressing the lever. The No-punishment group only received food, as they did in the acquisition phase. As shown in the figure, both groups of rats acquired the lever press response at equal rates during acquisition. However, the Punishment group's responses were significantly suppressed compared to those of the No-punishment group, which kept increasing their response rate.

Figure 20.2 illustrates a laboratory procedure for negative punishment called lick-contingent (or dependent) delay. A hungry animal is placed in a chamber where

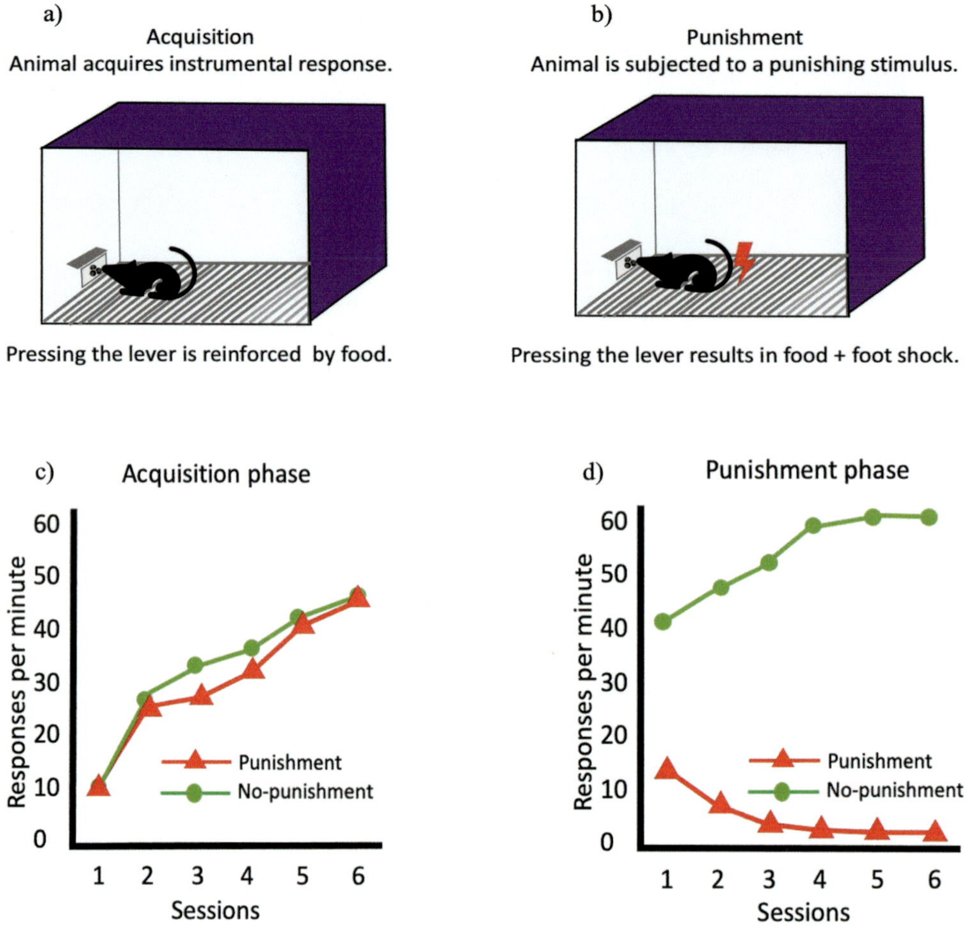

Figure 20.1 a) Acquisition phase and b) punishment phase of a positive punishment procedure. c) Results of the acquisition phase of a hypothetical positive punishment experiment. Rats in the Punishment (Red) and No-punishment group (Green) acquired the lever response reinforced by food at similar rates across sessions. d) During the punishment phase, the Punishment group's responses were suppressed across sessions, whereas the No-punishment group continued to rise.

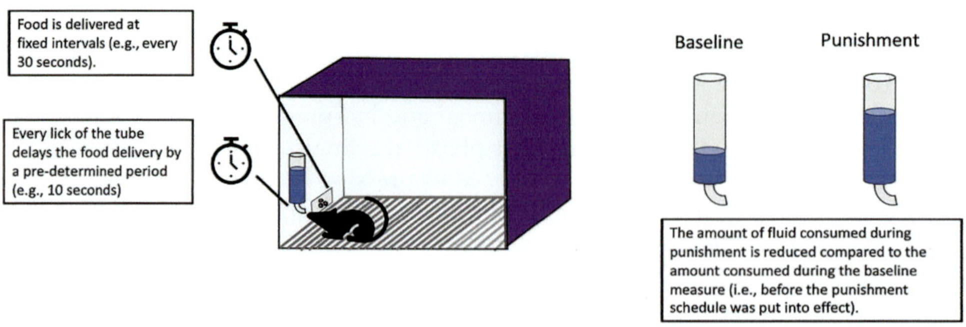

Figure 20.2 The lick-contingent delay procedure for negative punishment.

food is delivered in a receptacle at a fixed interval (i.e., every 30 seconds). The animal can also drink from a water bottle by licking a spout. In the first phase of the experiment (baseline condition), the food continues to be delivered at the predetermined interval regardless of whether the animal licks the spout, and a baseline measure of the amount of fluid consumed is recorded. In the second phase of the experiment (punishment), every lick of the spout results in a delay in the food delivery by the predetermined interval. This reduces the amount of fluid consumed compared to the amount consumed in the baseline condition.

The Effectiveness of Punishment

Thorndike (1898) initially viewed punishment as the opposite of reinforcement. That is, he believed that punishers were just as effective at weakening the connection between a stimulus and a response as reinforcers were effective at strengthening this connection. However, Thorndike later revised his formulation after conducting an experiment in which human participants were required to match uncommon English or Spanish words to a synonym presented among a list of five words. Correct answers were reinforced by the phrase "Right," uttered by the experimenter, and incorrect answers were punished by "Wrong." He found that hearing the word "Right" was an effective reinforcer of the correct response but that "Wrong" was not an effective punisher. It did not significantly decrease the probability that an incorrect response was produced (Thorndike, 1932). Instead, he believed that the aversive stimulation of punishment only temporarily suppressed behavior by competing with the effects of reinforcers.

Skinner (1938) also found punishment ineffective at suppressing responses. In one experiment, he reinforced rats to press the lever. He then gave the rats extinction trials for 120 minutes on two consecutive days. On the first day of extinction trials, some rats received an aversive slap on the paw for pressing the lever during the first ten minutes of each extinction trial. As was expected, the rate at which the rats responded decreased until they no longer responded. However, the suppression of responses lasted only as long as the slaps were administered, and the rats made the same overall number of responses.

Skinner concluded from these results that punishment only led to temporary suppression of behavior. He believed that punishment temporarily put the behavior in "reserve" to re-emerge without reinforcement once the suppressing effect of the punisher was taken away. He thought this explained why the rats' response rate caught up with the response rate of the unpunished rats. This "catching up" phenomenon has been termed **compensatory recovery** (Boe and Church, 1967). These results also showed that punishment was not simply the opposite of reinforcement. You may wonder, then, what resulted in the initial suppression of the behavior, if not punishment. Skinner answers that the slaps triggered an emotional state incompatible with the rats' feeding behavior. To Skinner, this was akin to a mother pinching her child as a punishment for laughing in church. Similarly, the pinching only indirectly suppresses the child's laughing behavior because it elicits a response incompatible with laughing (Skinner, 1953).

The idea that punishment only temporarily suppressed behavior was also supported by W.K. Estes (1919–2011), one of Skinner's students. In a classic study, he compared the effectiveness of extinction when accompanied by punishment with electric shocks to extinction without shocks in rats after they were trained to press a lever for food reinforcement without shocks. He found that adding electric shocks to extinction trials enhanced the suppression of the rats' responses. However, he also found that the number of responses during extinction trials for rats that were also punished returned to those of rats that were not punished during extinction. This suggested that punishment did not have lasting effects in suppressing behavior (Estes, 1944).

However, Estes's (1944) findings were challenged by psychologist Nathan Azrin (1930–2013). Azrin (1966) replicated Estes's findings but used non-punishing flashes of light during extinction instead of electric shocks. The rats who received light flashes during extinction responded similarly to those who never received light flashes. This suggested that Estes's results may not have been due to the punishing effects of electric shocks but that the shocks provided a discriminative stimulus (stimulus control) for reinforcement. That is, they signaled when food was or was not available.

In other words, both the results of Estes's (1944) and Azrin's (1966) experiments may have been because the rats did not receive any shocks (Estes, 1944) or light flashes (Azrin, 1966) during either training or testing but they did so during extinction trials. This means that testing occurred in a context that differed from that of extinction, which contained shocks or light flashes, but in the same context as training, which did not include them. Therefore, as shown in Figure 20.3, both experiments may have been cases of ABA renewal, as you learned in Chapter 12. However, this is not the end of the story.

Psychologist Timothy Shahan and colleagues replicated Estes's (1944) experiment in a more recent study. They included groups of rats to test whether the effects of the shocks in Estes (1944) could have been due to ABA renewal. They found only limited evidence that it could have been so. In summary, they concluded that shocks may have had a temporary effect in suppressing behavior and, to some extent, served as a discriminative stimulus (Shahan et al., 2023).

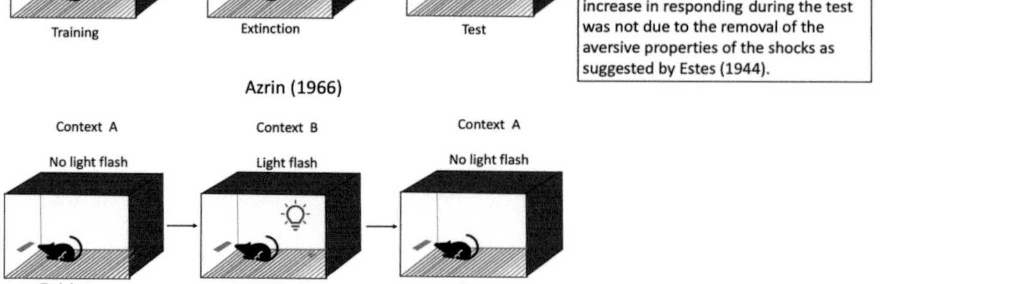

Figure 20.3 Experimental design used by Estes (1944) and Azrin (1966), which may have led to ABA renewal (see accompanying text for details).

What in the Brain?

Neurotransmitters and Sensitivity to Punishment

Neuroscientists have identified some of the neurobiological mechanisms involved in sensitivity to punishment. Studying the role of neurotransmitter systems in sensitivity to punishment has provided important insights into the understanding of psychological disorders in which changes to punishment sensitivity are observed. These include risk-taking behaviors, pathological gambling, obsessive-compulsive disorder (OCD), conduct disorders, and depression.

Sensitivity to punishment is often assessed in experiments in which the same response leads to reinforcer and punishment. These experiments are known as conflict protocols (Campos et al., 2013; Geller and Seifter, 1960; Vogel, Beer and Clody, 1971). In some experiments, rats are trained to press a lever to obtain a reinforcer, such as a sweetened water solution. During subsequent training trials, a light or a sound signals that an electric shock will be administered along with the delivery of the reinforcer. This creates a conflict between the opportunity to drink the sweet solution and getting a shock. In this situation, rats typically reduce their bar-pressing behavior compared to the level at which they bar-pressed during training, showing that they are sensitive to the punishing effects of the shock.

Gamma-Aminobutyric Acid

Rats given anxiolytic drugs, which reduce anxiety in humans, do not decrease their levels of response in conflict situations compared to rats that did not receive the drug. These results show that anxiolytic drugs have anti-punishment effects by reducing sensitivity to punishment (Geller and Seifter, 1960). The anti-punishment effect of anxiolytic medications has since been replicated across species (Illescas-Huerta et al., 2021; Rowlett et al., 2006). Gamma-aminobutyric acid (GABA) is the most common inhibitory neurotransmitter in the brain, meaning that it reduces the probability that neurons will fire action potentials. Anxiolytic drugs decrease anxiety by binding to GABA receptors in the brain. This suggests that the anti-punishment effects induced by anxiolytic medications are due to increased GABA activity. Alcohol, which also increases GABA activity, was also found to have anti-punishment effects in humans (Domi et al., 2021; Rasmussen and Newland, 2009).

Norepinephrine and Serotonin

The role of neurotransmitters in sensitivity to punishment is not limited to GABA. The role of other neurotransmitters in sensitivity to punishment has been discovered using a variety of behavioral procedures. For example, norepinephrine, an excitatory neurotransmitter known to regulate wakefulness and the activity of the sympathetic nervous system (fight or flight), has also been shown to produce anti-punishment effects (Tornatzky and Miczek, 1994). It has been shown to increase the effects of reinforcers while decreasing the impact of punishment. Serotonin, involved in mood, sleep, and appetite, has also been involved in sensitivity to punishment (Gleeson et al.,

1989). For example, it was found that inhibiting neurons from releasing serotonin or blocking serotonin receptors also has anti-punishment effects. In contrast, drugs that increase levels of serotonin, such as selective serotonin inhibitors (SSRIs), widely used as antidepressants, increase sensitivity to punishment (Pelloux et al., 2012).

Are You Thinking Critically?

1. Can you think of other reasons why it might be important to elucidate the role of neurotransmitter systems in sensitivity to punishment?
2. What are the effects of increasing or decreasing the activity of neurotransmitters on sensitivity to punishment?
3. What other approaches can you think about that would permit the assessment of sensitivity to punishment?

Critical Thinking Spot Check 20.1

1. Describe what you understand by the term punishment.
2. Explain why an aversive stimulus may not necessarily be considered a punisher.
3. Discuss what made Skinner believe the punishment was ineffective at controlling behavior.
4. Give an example from your everyday life in which punishment was ineffective.

20.2 Factors Related to the Effectiveness of Punishment

Despite the findings that punishers may only temporarily affect behavior (Estes, 1944; Shahan et al., 2023; Skinner, 1938; Thorndike, 1932), it was found that punishers were effective at permanently suppressing behavior when they met four criteria. These are intensity, delay, schedule, and stimulus control (Azrin and Holz, 1966). Also, as explained in the "What in the Brain?" box previously, drugs can decrease or increase sensitivity to punishment.

Intensity of Punishment

One study found that the degree of response suppression was related to the intensity of the punishing stimulus. Azrin (1960) investigated the effects of various shock intensities on key-pecking behavior in pigeons. The pigeons were first trained to peck a response key, consisting of an illuminated disk, to obtain a food reinforcer. The pigeons were then subjected to mild, moderate, or severe punishment, contingent upon a key peck. This continued until the pigeons showed a stable level of responding for at least ten sessions at the given intensity. The pigeons decreased their response rate at the beginning of each punished period at all shock intensities. However, the degree to which the pigeons' response rate was suppressed depended on the intensity of the shock. That is, higher shock intensities produced greater response suppression. The experimenters also measured the rate of recovery of the pigeons' responses. At mild shock intensity, the pigeons quickly recovered their unpunished response rate. At moderate shock intensity, recovery was incomplete, and no recovery occurred in the pigeons that received severe punishment.

In another study, Boe and Church (1967) trained six groups of rats to press a lever to obtain a food reinforcer. They were then subjected to a series of extinction trials. For the first 5 to 20 minutes of the first extinction session, the rats in the five groups (experimental groups) received an electric shock of either 35, 50, 75, 120, or 220 volts contingent upon a lever press. The sixth group (control group) received no shocks.

They found a negative relationship between the degree to which the rats in each group recovered by responding over the extinction trials and the shock intensity. The more intense the shock, the less response recovery was observed.

Delay

Another factor that influences the efficacy of punishment is the delay between the response and the punishing stimulus. Long delays between response and punishment were less effective at suppressing responses than short delays. For example, Solomon, Turner, and Lessac (1968) gave dogs a free choice between eating a preferred food (canned meat) and a non-preferred food (dried dog chow) in an experimental chamber (Figure 20.4 top).

Each food type was presented in a separate dish on each experimenter's side. All the dogs were permitted to eat the dry dog chow. However, one group of dogs (Group 1 [0-second delay]) received a hard swat on the snout with a rolled-up newspaper administered by the experimenter immediately after touching the canned meat with the mouth or tongue. The dogs in another group (Group 2) were punished similarly after eating the canned meat for five seconds. The dogs in another group (Group 3) were punished after eating the canned meat for 15 seconds. This treatment continued until the dogs reached the learning criterion of 20 consecutive days without touching the canned meat.

The dogs were then given daily ten-minute sessions in the experimental chamber where they were given a free choice between eating from a dish that contained 500 grams (g) of canned meat, which they had been punished for touching, and from a dish that contained only 20 g of the dry dog chow, which they were always permitted to eat. The experimenters called these sessions "temptation testing" because they wanted to see how many days it would take for the dogs in the different groups to give in to the temptation of touching the canned meat.

Figure 20.4 (bottom) shows the experiment's primary results. The dogs in Group 1 resisted the temptation according to resistance criterion 1 (just touching the meat) for 16.3 days, whereas the dogs in Group 2 resisted for 8.2 days and those in Group 3 for 0.3 days. The study's results were clear: the shorter the delay between the response and the punishment, the longer it took for the dogs to break the taboo of touching canned meat.

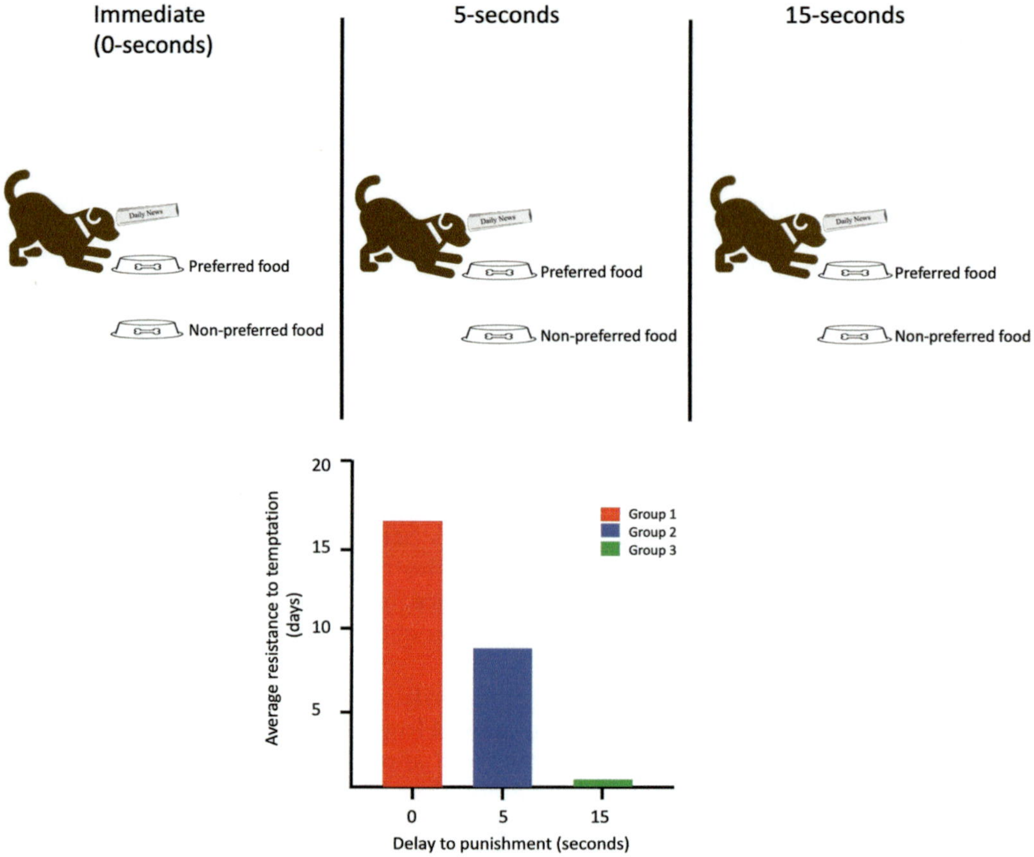

Figure 20.4 Effect of punishment delay on behavioral suppression (Solomon, Turner, & Lessac, 1968). The top panel shows the experimental procedure in which dogs were punished for touching preferred food (canned meat) at three different delays: 0 seconds (Group 1), 5 seconds (Group 2), or 15 seconds (Group 3). The bottom panel shows the average number of days dogs resisted touching the canned meat during temptation testing. Immediate punishment (0-second delay) was most effective, with resistance decreasing as punishment delay increased.

Shock-Delay Interaction

It was also found that a relationship exists between the intensity of punishment and the delay between response and punishment. That is, with a longer delay between response and punishment, a more intense punisher was found to be necessary to suppress the response effectively. For example, one study found that a shock of at least .50 milliamperes was required to increase the latency to press the lever when the rats received the shock 7, 14, or 28 seconds following a response. In contrast, a shock of only .20 milliamperes effectively increased the latency to press the lever when it immediately followed the response (Cohen, 1968).

Schedule

A third factor that affects the efficacy of punishment is the schedule under which it is administered. In one study, Azrin, Holz, and Hake (1963) tested whether different fixed-ratio schedules of punishment were associated with differences in the efficacy of punishment in suppressing an instrumental response. They hypothesized that the frequency at which punishment was administered would be related to the degree to which the punisher effectively suppressed the response.

They trained pigeons to peck a response key to obtain a food reward. Once they acquired the response, the pigeons received a shock contingent upon the key pecks. The experimenters compared the efficacy of punishment when presented at different frequencies determined by a range of fixed-ratio punishment schedules. The fixed-ratio schedule used for comparison in the experiment ranged between FR-1 and FR-1000. They found thicker schedules (i.e., those requiring fewer responses before punishment) were more effective at suppressing responses than thinner schedules (i.e., those requiring more responses before punishment).

Stimulus Control

In Chapter 13, you read that animals could learn that a response is reinforced when performed in certain environmental stimuli but not in the presence of other stimuli (i.e., stimulus control). You also learned that the control exerted by a stimulus on a response can generalize stimuli that are too closely related. Honig and Slivka (1964) tested whether this effect extended to punishment. To do so, they first trained pigeons to peck a response key illuminated by a green light to obtain food. Next, the pigeons were trained to peck a key randomly illuminated by each of the seven colors. Finally, the pigeons were punished for pecking the response key when illuminated by the green light under which they were previously trained. The experimenters wanted to determine the extent to which the green light took control over the pigeon's key-pecking behavior and whether the effect of punishment when the green light illuminated the key generalized to lights of different colors. They found a generalization gradient of response decrement as the color of the response key became progressively similar to the green light.

Critical Thinking Spot Check 20.2

1. Name the criteria that need to be met for punishment to be effective.
2. Describe experiments that showed that punishment can be effective.
3. Think of a situation in which punishment was effective. Which factor(s) related to the effectiveness of punishment rendered it effective?

20.2 Adverse Effects of Punishment on Children

We now turn our attention to the adverse effects that punishment may have on children. Punishment can have a wide range of adverse, long-lasting impacts on children. This is especially true if punishment includes physical harm (Durrant and Ensom, 2012). Learning about the adverse effects of physical punishment on children made Sofia realize that she needed to stop punishing her son Julio. Indeed, current and future parents must learn about alternatives to physical punishment to correct their children's misbehavior. Such alternatives to physical punishment are discussed in the application box at the end of this module.

Generalization of Fear-Eliciting Stimuli

One possibility is that the fear elicited by punishment becomes associated with the punishing stimulus and other elements of the situation or context in which the punishment occurred. Hence, these elements may become conditioned stimuli that elicit a fear response.

For example, a child punished by severe reprimands for not doing well on homework may avoid doing homework and, through generalization, avoid studying, or even find reasons to miss school (Martin, 1977).

The stimuli with which fear of punishment becomes associated can also generalize to the person who administered the punishment. For example, a parent who frequently administers punishments may become a conditioned stimulus that elicits fear as a conditioned response, causing a child to avoid the punishing parent. A child often punished by a teacher may avoid the teacher by skipping classes. Because of the avoidance of situations to which a conditioned stimulus has generalized, a child might be found to be socially isolated, thus potentially interfering with the child's emotional and social development.

Legitimizing Violence and the Modeling of Aggression

Another possible effect of physical punishment is the legitimization of violence. Loved ones most often administer punishment, and people who command respect, such as those in positions of authority. The punishment may also be perceived as being administered to correct a moral transgression. Hence, a physically punished child may develop the belief that deciding to administer physical punishment is a morally correct choice. A major concern is that what a child learns about punishment might spill over into the child's future relationships as an adult in the form of child or spousal abuse.

Another concern is that violence in one sphere of life spills over to other spheres. According to the **cultural spillover theory**, punishment may blur the boundaries between the legitimate and criminal use of force. This means that a person or a group may resort to violence to achieve their ends, pointing to the legitimate use of force by authorities to justify their actions (Straus, 1991).

In addition, it was found that children who witness parents' aggressive behavior while administering punishment can model it. For example, children who watched a video of parents punishing children for misbehaving by spanking, shaking, or yelling displayed more aggressive acts when later playing with dolls than children who had not watched the video (Fairchild and Erwin, 1977).

Physical Punishment, Mental Health, and Brain Development

Studies in both the United States and Canada have found that 80% to 90% of adults reported being spanked as a child (Hemenway, Solnick and Carter, 1994; MacMillan et al., 1999). This has raised concern as to whether a connection exists between physical punishment during childhood and mental health problems in adulthood. Indeed, in one study, it was found that an association existed between slapping and spanking during childhood and psychiatric disorders such as anxiety, depression, and drug abuse in adulthood (Afifi et al., 2006; Turner and Muller, 2004). It was also found that physical punishment is associated with childhood depression and anxiety (Rodriguez, 2003).

Other studies have focused on the effects of physical punishment on brain development. A history of physical punishment was found to be associated with a reduction of gray matter in the prefrontal cortex and the anterior cingulate cortex. This reduction in gray matter may be related to addiction, depression, posttraumatic stress disorder, and reduced intelligence quotient (IQ) (Tomoda et al., 2009).

Critical Thinking Spot Check 20.3

1. Name and describe each of the adverse effects of punishment on children.
2. Why is it important to know about the adverse effects of punishment?

Chapter Summary

Each bullet point aligns directly with the learning objectives outlined at the beginning of the chapter.

- Positive punishment refers to a behavioral procedure in which an aversive stimulus reduces the probability of the response it follows. The aversive stimulus used in such a procedure is known as a punisher. After a response has been punished, the aversive stimulus is avoided by not performing the punished response. Punishment, therefore, leads to passive avoidance. In negative punishment, a loss of privilege or of an appetitive stimulus reduces the probability of the response it follows.
- Punishment can range from mild to severe. However, these are relative terms in that what is considered mild to one individual may be considered severe to another. The consequence of a response can only be considered a punisher if it reduces the probability of the response it follows. Also, the extent to which a punisher suppresses a response may depend on extinction and habituation.
- Both Thorndike and Skinner performed experiments that led them to doubt the effectiveness of punishment. Skinner believed that punishment only temporarily suppressed behavior. He believed punishment temporarily put behavior in "reserve" to re-emerge once the punisher's suppressing effect was removed, a phenomenon known as compensatory recovery.
- Studies showed that punishment is effective if specific criteria are met during the experimental procedures meant to suppress behavior by using punishment. At least five factors were important to the effectiveness of punishment. These are intensity, delay, the interaction between the intensity of the punishment and the delay after which it is administered, schedule, and stimulus control.
- In children, physical punishment is also associated with adverse consequences. These include the generalization of fear eliciting stimuli, legitimizing violence, and the modeling of aggression. Physical punishment is also associated with detrimental effects on mental health, including depression, drug addiction, and altered brain development. Cultural spillover theory refers to the idea that physical punishment may result in blurred boundaries between the legitimate and criminal use of force.

Glossary

Compensatory recovery The process where an organism adapts to disruptions or changes by developing alternative strategies or behaviors to maintain function.

Contingent observation A technique in which an individual is removed from participation but still observes others engaging in reinforcing activities, promoting learning through indirect exposure.

Cultural spillover theory The idea that violence or aggression in one area of a society (such as within families) can spread into other areas (such as broader social interactions), influencing behavioral norms.

Planned ignoring A behavior intervention where attention to an undesirable behavior is intentionally withheld, reducing reinforcement for that behavior.

Prevention of preferred activities A behavior management method where access to enjoyable activities is restricted following undesired behavior, discouraging repetition of the unwanted action.

Time-out ribbons A strategy in which children wear ribbons indicating their access to reinforcement, and removal of the ribbon serves as a non-exclusionary time-out consequence.

Time-out A behavioral management technique where access to reinforcement is temporarily removed following an undesirable behavior to reduce its occurrence.

Module Summary

In the first chapter of this module, you learned that avoidance behavior, which includes active and passive avoidance, is adaptive in that it permits organisms to stay away from potentially dangerous or harmful stimuli. You also learned that the scientific study of avoidance behavior began with an experiment conducted by Vladimir Bekhterev, who conditioned human participants to remove their hands from a metal plate through which they received an electrical shock at the sound of a tone. This procedure differed from Pavlov's in that the participants learned to perform a response that permitted them to avoid the unconditioned stimulus. Pavlov's and Bekhterev's procedures were directly compared by W.J. Brogden and colleagues, who showed that a motor response conditioned to a CS can differ in quality depending on whether the aversive US is escapable or inescapable.

There are two types of avoidance procedures: the discriminated avoidance procedure, in which a conditioned stimulus signals the onset of an aversive stimulus, and the indiscriminate, or free operant, procedure, in which an external warning stimulus that signals an aversive stimulus is not given. In the 1960s, psychologists Martin Seligman and Steven Maier found that dogs that learned that there was nothing they could do to avoid a shock failed to learn an avoidance response. This phenomenon became known as learned helplessness.

Finally, you learned that animals possess species-specific defense reactions which permit them to escape predators and that psychologist Michael Fanselow proposed the predatory imminence continuum in which the extent to which the encounter with a predator is imminent determines which of three types of defensive behaviors (pre-encounter defensive behavior, post-encounter defense behavior, and circa strike defensive behaviors) are elicited.

In the second chapter, you learned about positive punishment, a procedure by which an aversive stimulus reduces the probability of the behavior it follows, and negative punishment, in which the loss of a privilege or removal of an appetitive stimulus minimizes the likelihood of the behavior it follows. You learned that whether a punishment is perceived as mild or severe is relative to the individual and the situation in which it is administered. You also learned that the effectiveness of punishment in controlling behavior has been put into question. However, studies have shown that the efficacy of punishers is related to their intensity, the delay after which they are administered, the schedule under which they are administered, and the environmental stimuli present when they are administered. Finally, you learned that punishment could have detrimental effects on the development of children.

Module 9

Application

Responding to Misbehavior: Alternatives to Physical Punishment

Physical punishment was found to have detrimental outcomes on children. For example, physical punishment is associated with increased aggressivity (Weiss et al., 1992) and mental health issues such as anxiety, depression, and drug addiction (Holmes and Robins, 1988). Therefore, parents and future parents need to learn about alternatives to punishment in exerting behavioral control over their children. Following is a list and description of several proposed alternatives (Ateah, Secco and Woodgate, 2003; Honig and Wittmer, 1991; Hyman, 1997). They can be remembered by the acronym D-RAMPART, which stands for **d**istraction, **r**eward positive behavior, **a**nticipate, **m**odeling self-control, **p**reserve self-esteem, **a**ge-appropriate consequences, **r**ules, and **t**eaching.

Distraction: When a child's behavior becomes troublesome, use distraction instead of constantly saying "no," which often frustrates both the parent and child and worsens the situation. For example, if the child screams for a particular object in a store, refocus the child's attention to another stimulus or interesting activity.

Reward positive behavior: Avoid paying too much attention to a child's misbehaviors. Instead, be attentive to the child's good behaviors, reward those with praise or special privileges, and encourage the child to repeat these behaviors in the future.

Anticipate: Anticipate situations in which you think the child will misbehave or is likely to get into trouble. For example, before embarking on a long car trip, inform the child that there will be plenty of stops along the way during which playtime will be permitted. Also, always put away dangerous objects, such as tools, with which the child may be tempted to play.

Modeling self-control: Children learn to react to situations by modeling their parents. Therefore, it is important for parents not to overreact to their children. When dealing with misbehavior, keep a low tone of voice and use a calm, rational approach to solving an issue that the child may have.

Preserve self-esteem: Show unconditional positive regard by criticizing the child's behavior but not the child. For example, say, "Mommy loves you but doesn't like it when you act like that" instead of "you get on my nerves," "you're annoying," or "you're lazy."

Age-appropriate consequences: Toddlers respond well to changes in tone of voice and to being redirected to other activities. For a school-age child, inform the child of the consequence of misbehavior, which may be limiting access to a toy or a game, and enact the consequence immediately following the misbehavior. Teens may have privileges taken away, such as using a cell phone, followed by a discussion about why the misbehavior

DOI: 10.4324/9781003491828-38

occurred. Teens respond well when they have input into the rules to be followed and the consequences for breaking them.

Rules: Parents need to set rules and explain why they exist. They must then enforce these rules by remaining empathetic to the child's feelings. However, the child must be able to distinguish between acceptable and unacceptable behavior and know what to expect if the rules are broken.

Teaching: A misbehaving child might not realize why a behavior is unacceptable. The parent must ensure the child understands the repercussions of their misbehavior and its impacts on other people.

Are You Thinking Critically?

1. Are there any circumstances under which physical punishment is warranted?
2. Are there any alternatives to punishment that you have found ineffective?
3. What other alternatives to physical punishment can you think of?

Module 10

Cognitive Psychology, Comparative Cognition, Memory, and Navigation

Introduction

Cognitive psychologists study mental processes such as problem-solving abilities, goal setting, memory, and planning. To behaviorists, postulating such unobservable constructs was unnecessary to explain behavior, a line of thinking that dominated psychology from the 1930s to the 1960s. The rise of cognitive psychology was marked by what is known as the cognitive revolution, which was inspired by the computer revolution and the information processing approach. This movement reached a turning point when linguist Noam Chomsky critiqued B. F. Skinner's book *Verbal Behavior*, which applied principles of operant conditioning to language acquisition. Comparative cognition is the comparative study of cognitive mechanisms across species. Comparative cognition originated with Charles Darwin, who believed in the continuity of intelligence from animals to humans. In Chapter 21, you will learn about the origins of cognitive psychology and some of the principles and studies in comparative cognition. Chapter 22 will teach you about memory, its different stages, stores, and subtypes. You will also learn about the various forms of amnesia, the mechanisms of memory formation, and how memory is experimentally investigated. Finally, you will learn how people find their way through the environment and some of the tasks devised to study animal spatial navigation.

DOI: 10.4324/9781003491828-39

21 The Surprisingly Complex Behavior of Animals

Cognitive Psychology and Comparative Cognition

Learning Objectives

1. Outline significant figures in cognitive psychology, highlighting their contributions to understanding mental processes.
2. Trace the evolution of cognitive psychology from skepticism about studying mental processes to the cognitive revolution in the 1960s.
3. Discuss Edward Tolman's early proposal of mental constructs in animal behavior.
4. Differentiate comparative cognition from cognitive ethology, emphasizing the avoidance of anthropomorphic errors and the application of Morgan's canon in attributing animal behavior to more straightforward explanations.
5. Examine the role of social learning and social transmission in animal behavior, noting the distinction between seemingly insightful behaviors and those acquired through shaping or stimulus-response associations.

Those "Smart" Animals

Source: IStock photo ID:170462856.

DOI: 10.4324/9781003491828-40

Saul and his friend Marina enjoy looking at online videos of city animals engaged in impressive behaviors. In one video, a magpie, a bird from the Corvidae family, is seen dropping stones into a bottle containing a low water level. This displaces the water and raises its level, making it possible for the magpie to drink from the bottle. In another video, cockatoos are seen opening garbage bins in several neighborhoods of Australia to get food scraps. As they watched, Saul turned to Marina and said, "This is definite evidence that non-human animals are intelligent and insightful; I would even say that they have problem-solving skills." "But these are human characteristics," exclaimed Marina. "So?" Saul replied. Marina answered, "Don't you remember what we learned in class last week?" "Oh yes!" Saul replied. Looking back at Marina, he remembered aloud, "We must avoid attributing the behavior of non-human animals to human characteristics. Intelligence, insightfulness, and problem-solving skills are all labels we use to point to characteristics we know are human." "What else?" Marina asked Saul. Saul replied, "The behavior of non-human animals should not be attributed to higher mental processes if simpler concepts can explain it." "Correct!" answered Marina, "We don't know the history of these animals. They may have learned these behaviors through shaping."

21.1 Cognitive Psychology

A Bit of History

Cognitive psychology studies mental processes such as remembering, perceiving, judging, reasoning, imagining, problem-solving, and other forms of knowing and awareness. Its beginnings can be traced back to psychologists Franciscus Donders (1818–1889), Wilhelm Wundt (1832–1920), and Hermann Ebbinghaus (1850–1909), who were among the first to dedicate themselves to the study of mental processes. Donders was interested in the speed of cognitive processes. In a famous experiment, he studied people's reaction times by asking them to press a button whenever a light was turned on (Donders, 1969). He then studied their choice reaction time by asking them to press a left button whenever a light on the left turned on and a right button whenever a light on the right came on. He found that participants took longer to press a button in the choice reaction time condition than in the reaction time condition. He attributed the extra time it took to press a button in the choice reaction time task to the time it took the participants to decide whether a left or right button press was required.

Wundt, often credited with establishing the first psychology laboratory, was interested in the structure of mental phenomena (Danziger, 1980). He and his student Bradford Titchener founded the psychological perspective known as *structuralism*, in which experiences are made up of combinations of essential elements, similarly to how molecules are constituted from combinations of atoms. In a method known as **analytic introspection**, they trained people to describe various stimuli by only referring to their basic elements.

Ebbinghaus studied the associations of events in memory and patterns of memory loss for information over time (Ebbinghaus, 1964). Using only himself as a subject, he experimented with studying lists of nonsense syllables such as "QAX," "ZUC," or "DAX," which, because they were devoid of meaning, could not easily be associated. He then tested how many syllables he could remember from the lists over 19 minutes to 31 days. He called the number of syllables he could remember from the lists "savings." He found that the most rapid memory loss for the syllables on the lists occurred during the first hour after learning, that 60% of the syllables were forgotten after 9 hours, and almost 70% were forgotten after 24 hours. He also found it more challenging to remember lists of nonsense syllables, which cannot easily be associated, than poems, which can be remembered by associations created between their elements.

Beginning in the early 1900s, behaviorists, influenced by John B. Watson's ideas, believed mentalistic constructs such as motivation, emotions, and conscious goal setting were unnecessary to understanding behavior. In addition, since they were unobservable, these behaviorists deemed them unworthy of scientific study (Watson, 1919).

The Cognitive Revolution

The behaviorist's point of view, championed by B.F. Skinner, dominated psychology until the 1960s, which marked the rise of cognitive psychology and what is often referred to as the **cognitive revolution.** The cognitive revolution was rooted in the advent of digital computers in the 1950s when many scientists wondered whether computers could be programmed to function like the human brain. This gave rise to the **information processing approach.** Within this approach, mental processes such as attention and memory occur by transmitting information through the brain. Proponents of this approach explored how humans processed incoming information (Broadbent, 1958; Treisman, 1964; Mackay, 1973). During the same period, psychologist Georges Miller (1920–2012) found that short-term memory was limited to seven bits of information (1956).

Despite the many important events that preceded it, the cognitive revolution is often attributed to linguist Noam Chomsky's reaction to Skinner's book *Verbal Behavior* (Skinner, 1957). In this book, Skinner argues that language acquisition is achieved through operant conditioning principles. In his book review, Chomsky argued that language was too complex to be explained through operant conditioning (1959).

Cognitive Maps

About 30 years before the so-called cognitive revolution, Edward C. Tolman (1886–1959) proposed that animals formed meaningful associations between environmental stimuli. He believed these associations led to the creation of **cognitive maps** of the environment, which permitted them to make rational decisions based on expectations, reason, and purpose. This meant that Tolman was not a behaviorist in the true sense of the term but that he believed that the study of behavior could be used to infer what was going on in an animal's mind. Hence, Tolman may have been one of the first cognitive psychologists. In a classic paper entitled "Cognitive Maps in Rats and Men," Tolman described different types of experiments which showed that the formation of cognitive maps was central to what is known as **latent learning** and **spatial orientation** (1948).

Latent Learning

Latent learning, or incidental learning, can be described as learning without intention, conscious effort, and reinforcers. Evidence of latent learning only manifests when the need to recall the information thus acquired arises. For example, after watching your friend play a video game on numerous occasions, you might be surprised at how good you are at it when playing it for the first time.

Latent learning was proposed by Blodgett, who performed an experiment showing that rats could learn the spatial layout of a maze's environment without the use of reinforcers (Blodgett, 1929). This experiment was replicated by Tolman and Honzik (1930) using the alley maze shown in Figure 21.1a. They ran three groups of rats on the maze, two control groups and one experimental group. One of the control groups was trained conventionally by being given daily trials in which they found a food reinforcer in a goal box at the end of the maze (HR). The second control group was permitted to explore the maze but never reinforced (HNR). The experimental group (HNR-R) was allowed to explore the maze without receiving any food until the 11th day of training. The dependent measure was the average number of errors, which consisted of the rats entering blind alleys.

The results of the experiment are shown in Figure 21.1b. As expected, the rats in the HR group, which were reinforced at the end of every trial, made progressively fewer errors across daily trials. The rats in the HNR group, who never received any food, made many errors, which remained consistent across trials. However, the number of errors committed by the rats in the HNR-R group remained high until the 11th trial, when they were finally rewarded for getting to the goal box. What was striking about this finding was that the number of errors they committed was lower than that of the rats in the HR group, which was reinforced on every trial. How can this be?

To explain these findings, Tolman suggested that during the unreinforced trials, the rats in the HNR-R learned about the spatial layout of the maze's environment by creating a cognitive map. This was not apparent during the unreinforced trials because the animals were not motivated by the prospect of finding food at the end of the maze. When food was suddenly made available, the rats could use the knowledge they acquired during the unreinforced trials to navigate the maze quickly.

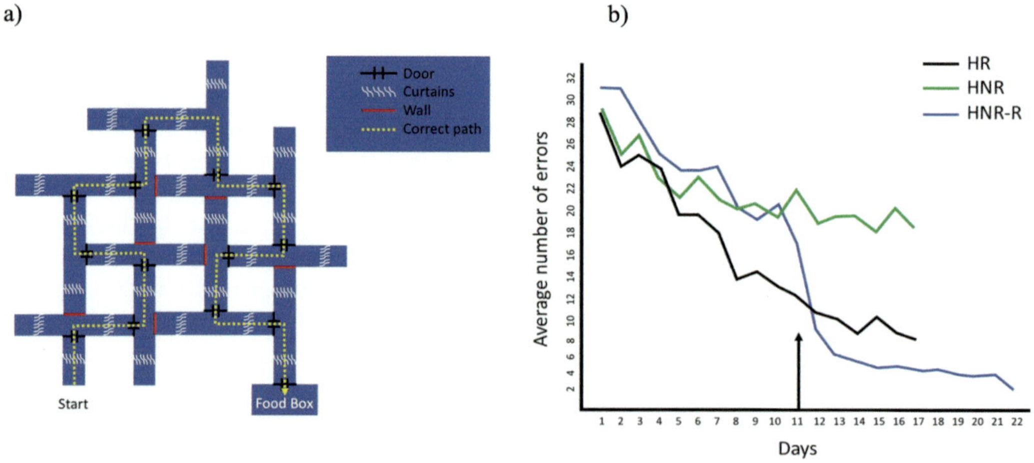

Figure 21.1 a) The type of maze used in the Tolman and Honzik (1930) latent learning experiment. b) Results of Tolman and Honzik (1930) for the rats who received the reinforcer in the goal box (HR), rats that never received the reinforcer (HNR), and rats that did not receive a reinforcer until day 11 (HNR-R).

Source: Modified from: Breedlove, S. M. (2015). *Principles of psychology*. Sunderland, MA: Sinauer Associates/Oxford University Press, Page 339.

Exploring an area such as a university campus without a specific goal can help you form a cognitive map, which can help you find specific locations, such as classrooms, when required on subsequent occasions. This is an example of latent learning.

Source: IStock photo ID:1323420737.

The results of Tolman and Honzik (1930) can be extrapolated to humans. For example, imagine that you decide to tour the grounds of a university to which you have been accepted for entry at the beginning of the next term. Since you have no classes to attend, you have no reason to visit one campus area more than another. You explore the area by making random turns down the maze-like paths, lined with buildings, that wind through the campus (such as in the photo above). At the beginning of the school year, when it comes time to find the location of your classes, you can easily do so. In contrast, the students who have yet to take such a tour spend much of their time searching for their classes and getting lost for their first few days of school. Their behavior is similar to that of the rats in the HR group in Tolman and Honzik (1930), who gradually learned to navigate the maze.

Hence, similarly to the HNR group in Tolman and Honzik (1930) that learned about the maze environment by being permitted to explore it without reinforcement (HNR), you learned about the campus's spatial layout without the goal of getting to a specific location. That is, during your random wanderings of the campus, you formed a cognitive map of the campus's environment. This only proved helpful when you needed to use the map to find your classes at the beginning of the term, a clear example of latent learning.

Focus On

The Debate Between Place and Response Learning

A debate raged about whether animals learned through stimulus-response (S-R) associations, as proposed by psychologist Clark Hull, or through the acquisition of cognitive maps, as suggested by Edward C. Tolman (1948). Tolman and others designed simple tasks (response and place) to settle this debate using the plus maze illustrated in Figure 21.2, on which rats were trained to find food at the end of either of two arms.

These tasks pitted S-R theory and cognitive map theory against each other (Tolman, Ritchie and Kalish, 1946b). In the response task (Figure 21.2a), rats were alternately released from the north (N) and south (S) positions. The food was in the maze's west arm (W) when the rats started from the N position but in the east arm (E) when the rats began from the S position. This arrangement promoted S-R learning because the rats could learn to get the food regardless of their starting point by making a right turn at the intersection in response to a local cue, such as a knot in the wood of the maze.

In the place task (Figure 21.2b), the starting point alternated between the N and S arms. However, the food was always at the end of the same arm. Contrary to the response task, a consistent turn, regardless of the start position, did not lead to the food. That is, a left turn led to the food in the W-arm from the S-arm but to the E-arm when started from the N-arm. To consistently get to the food, they had to learn to make a left turn when starting from the S-arm but to make a right turn when starting from the N-arm. According to Tolman, this required the formation of a cognitive map of the environment by which the location of the food was learned by associating it with extra-maze cues. Tolman found that the rats learned the place task faster than the response task, leading him to conclude that rats had a greater propensity for place learning than response learning.

Response and place learning were assessed simultaneously in the dual-solution task (Blodgett and McCutchan, 1948; Packard and McGaugh, 1996), which comprised a training and test phase. In the training phase, food was always at the end of the same arm, and the rats always started from the same arm, meaning they had to learn to make a right turn to get food (Figure 21.2c). Having learned this response, they were given a test during which food was located at the ends of both arms (Figure 21.2d). However, this time, they started from the arm opposite the one they had started from during training. They were considered response learners if they continued to make a right turn at the intersection, leading them to a place where food was not located during training, but considered place learners if they made a left turn at the intersection, a turn they had never learned to make, leading them to the place where the food was located during training.

Packard and McGaugh (1996) found that place learning was acquired faster than response learning, consistent with the cognitive map theory. They also found that the rats switched to response learning with extensive training. It is now known that response learning is more likely to occur with comprehensive training and distributed practice, in which training trials are separated by relatively long intervals and in environments devoid of extra-maze cues. In contrast, lower amounts of training and massed practice, in which training trials are relatively close in time and environments rich in extra-maze cues, are more conducive to place learning (Goodman, 2021).

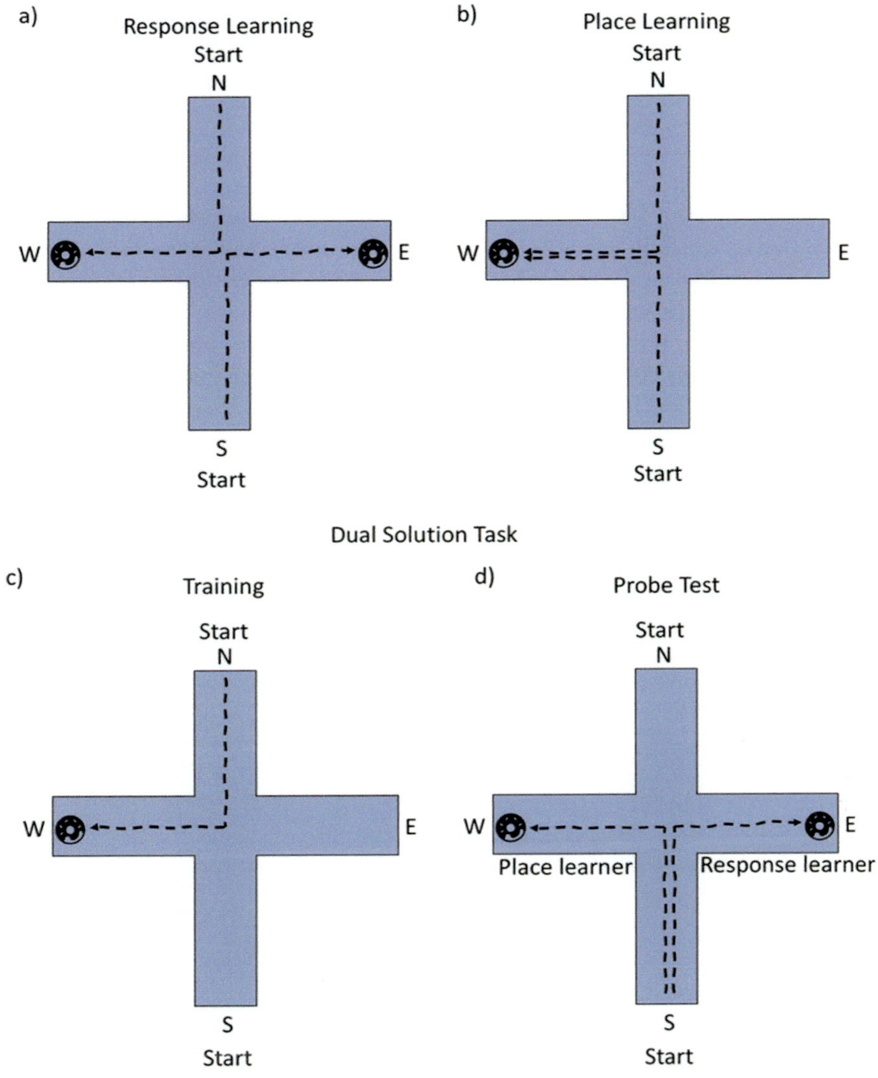

Figure 21.2 Tasks designed by Tolman, Ritchie and Kalish (1946b) to compare a) response learning and b) place learning. c) Dual-solution task in which animals are trained to find food on a maze by making a specific turn into one of the arms. d) In the test, rats were identified as place learners if they made a left turn to the food when starting from the arm opposite from the one used during training. They were identified as response learners if they made a right turn to the food when starting from the arm opposite from the one used during training. See text for details.

Source: Modified from Goodman, Jarid, Place vs. Response Learning: History, Controversy, and Neurobiology, *Frontiers in Behavioral Neuroscience*, 14, 2021, https://doi.org/10.3389/fnbeh.2020.598570 Figure 4.

Are You Thinking Critically?

1. Explain the nature of the debate between Hull and Tolman's ideas about S-R and cognitive map theory.
2. Describe the dual-solution task and what was learned from it.
3. What are the advantages of the dual-solution task over Tolman's tasks?

Spatial Orientation

Imagine that, while driving back home, you come to a newly erected roadblock, and the workers fail to put up detour signs for one reason or another. Fortunately, because of your knowledge of the city's layout and the location of your house within it, you can still make your way home by going down streets that you are unfamiliar with. Tolman wanted to find out whether rats could similarly find their way to a goal box they had previously learned to find at the end of a maze by using an unfamiliar path (Tolman, Ritchie and Kalish, 1946a).

He trained rats to find food in a goal box at the end of the maze, as shown in Figure 21.3a, by following the path indicated by letters A-G. A light bulb behind the goal box, the only light source in the room, illuminated the F-G alley. Once the rats learned to get to the goal box by making the necessary responses, Tolman wanted to find out if the rats could find their way if an alternate path blocked the original path. To do so, he placed a block at the end of the C-D alley, removed the alleys from D to G, and superimposed the sunburst maze, as shown in Figure 21.3b. The position of the goal box remained the same, but the light behind it was changed to a different color.

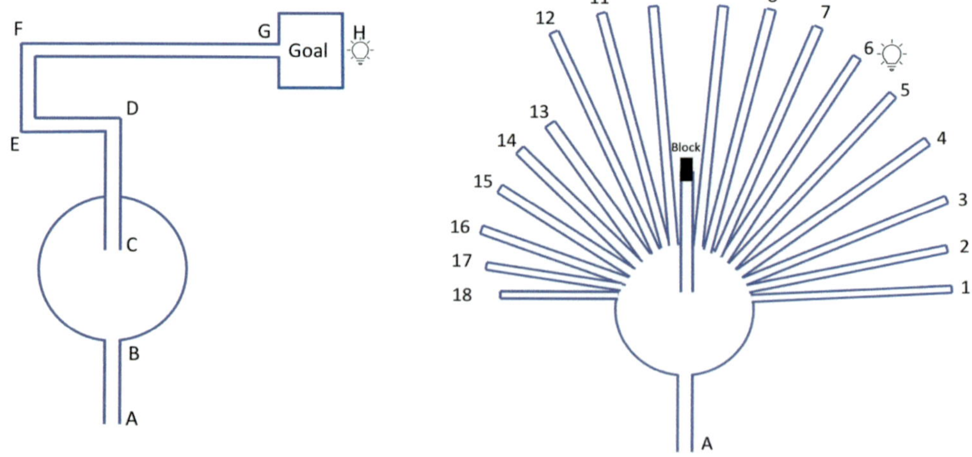

Figure 21.3 Maze used by Tolman, Ritchie and Kalish (1946a). a) Maze on which rats were trained to find the location of food following a path from A to G. b) The same maze as in A with a sunburst configuration superimposed to find out whether rats could still make their way to the goal box if the path from C to D were blocked. See text for details.

Source: Redrawn from Tolman, Ritchie and Kalish (1946a).

Tolman hypothesized that if the rats learned to get to the goal box by forming S-R associations, they would persist in going down the C-D alley or using the arms of the sunburst maze that were closest to it (i.e., arms 9 and 10). In contrast, if the rats had acquired a cognitive map of the environment, they would readily choose the arm that most directly led to the goal box after learning that the C-D alley was blocked. This is precisely what happened. Many of the 56 rats (36%) used in the experiment chose arm number 6, leading directly to the goal box.

Some of Tolman's critics claimed that the light had become a conditioned stimulus, which triggered the rats to run towards it once detected. Tolman responded to these critics by explaining that the light used in the test phase of the experiment was not the same as the one used in training. In addition, the angle by which the light was approached during training and testing differed. The approach was head-on from the F-G alley during training and from a 50-degree angle in arm number 6 during the test. Tolman also pointed out that the responses learned by the rats during training, which consisted of a series of turns away and towards the goal box, differed from the ones they performed during the test, which consisted of avoiding the C-D alley and going down arm number 6. Instead, Tolman suggested that the rats learned about the location or "place" of the goal box relative to the location of the light, which permitted them to orient and move towards it. Importantly, Tolman believed that acquiring a cognitive map led the rats to expect the goal box when they got to the light.

A Few Words on Latent Learning and Cognitive Maps

Many psychology textbooks stated that latent learning experiments provided incontrovertible evidence that learning did not require behaviors to be reinforced (Jensen, 2006). It is also taken as evidence that learning requires cognitive factors beyond the formation of stimulus-response associations and reinforcement. These ideas were generated by the results of the Tolman and Honzik (1930) experiment described previously, in which two of three groups of rats were given unreinforced preexposure trials to the maze shown in Figure 21.1a. Reinforcement for completing the maze throughout the experiment occurred only for one of the groups. This group gradually made fewer mistakes by not entering blind alleys across trials.

Remember that the rats in one of the other two groups that were given unreinforced preexposure trials received a reinforcer on day 11, after which the number of mistakes they made dropped drastically and remained low for the remainder of the trials. This sudden drop in the number of mistakes made by these rats was taken as evidence that they had acquired a cognitive map of the maze's environment. The acquisition of this map only became apparent once they received food to complete the maze. The argument is that reinforcement was unnecessary for learning since the rats' behavior in the maze during the preexposure trials was unreinforced with food (Tolman and Honzik, 1930).

However, you must know that this notion did not remain unchallenged (Jensen, 2006). A closer examination of Tolman's results (Figure 21.1b) shows that the groups' rats progressively made fewer mistakes from trials 1 to 5. Hence, the rats possibly began learning to navigate the maze through reinforcement during those first five trials. For example, walking into a blind alley may have become progressively less likely due to its aversive consequence (i.e., positive punishment). Therefore, when food was introduced on trial 11, the group that never received a food reinforcer until then may have already learned a series of stimulus-response associations. Food may have added a motivational factor or strengthened these already existing associations. Hence, it is possible that the suddenly enhanced performance of the rats on day 11 in that group may not have required the formation of a cognitive map.

Critical Thinking Spot Check 21.1

1. Name some of the early psychologists and their interests who were part of the early developments of cognitive psychology.
2. Describe the events that gave rise to the cognitive revolution.
3. How did Tolman determine that non-human animals could learn to navigate through the formation of cognitive maps?
4. Come up with examples of latent learning in your everyday life.

21.2 Comparative Cognition

What Is Comparative Cognition?

Comparative cognition is the area of *comparative psychology* engaged in studying cognitive processes across species. It mainly deals with the relationships between the cognitive capacities of humans and other animals (Beran et al., 2014) and how these cognitive capacities may have evolved (Chittka et al., 2012). The beginnings of comparative cognition date back to Charles Darwin, who believed that the cognitive skills of human and non-human animals differed more in degree than in kind (Darwin, 1871) (also see Chapter 9). Hence, comparative cognition addresses the possibility that specific cognitive capacities usually taken as distinctively human are, to some extent, present in other animals. This includes consciousness, self-awareness, problem-solving skills, creativity, language, and culture. In fact, comparative cognition applies the concepts used in the study of human cognition to the study of animals (Döring and Chittka, 2011).

The Anthropomorphic Error

Popular media widely report the seemingly intelligent behaviors of animals in cities. This includes videos of cockatoos lifting the lids of garbage bins to get food contents (Kim, 2021) and of a magpie dropping stones into a nearly empty bottle to raise the water level to the point where it can drink from it (Dharni, 2020). It is precisely these kinds of behaviors that are the focus of Saul and Marina's attention in the opening vignette of the chapter. Taking these behaviors as evidence of animals' capacity to reason and solve problems may be tempting. However, in doing so, one would be committing what is known as the anthropomorphic error (also known as anthropomorphic fallacy).

The **anthropomorphic error** refers to attributing human intelligence, insight, problem-solving, motives, and emotions to animals. This is the error that Saul commits before being corrected by Marina. In his book *Animal Intelligence*, Georges Romanes (1882), one of Darwin's most ardent supporters, provides a vast array of anecdotes of seemingly intelligent behaviors by animals ranging from protozoa to dogs recorded by unknown observers (see also Chapter 9). Romanes believed such anecdotes were evidence of the intent, emotions, and motives usually attributed to humans. The following is an example of such an anecdote.

> [Charlie, a dog,] had grown old and having some affliction in his legs which made walking difficult to him, he had sunk into a very stagnant sort of life, when a Scotch terrier was brought to live with us, and treated with much favour. All Charlie's old vigour revived upon the advent of this rival. He exhibited agonies of jealousy, and has since spent his life in following, watching, and imitating him. He insists on doing everything that Jack does. Although he had previously given up walking, he now makes a point of going out whenever Jack does so. Several times he has started with us, but finding that Jack was not of the party, has turned back and quietly gone home. In the same way, although before

he ate nothing but meat, he now eats any food that is also given to Jack; and if Jack is caressed he watches for some time, and then bursts out whining and barking.

(p. 442–443)

Cognitive Ethology Versus Comparative Cognition

In the field known as **cognitive ethology**, researchers are convinced that non-human animals have mental experiences, such as consciousness and self-awareness, that parallel those of humans (Griffin, 1992; Ristau, 2013). The more cautious scientists in comparative cognition avoid making such claims but concede that some animals may possess **primary consciousness**, defined by the ability to be aware of the present by integrating ongoing events with those stored in recent memory (Seth, Baars and Edelman, 2005). Comparative cognitive psychologists apply Morgan's canon to their explanations of animal behavior. Remember from Chapter 1 that Morgan's canon states that the behavior of animals should not be interpreted as a result of the operations of higher mental faculties if it can be construed as a result of some other faculty lower on the psychological scale. This is precisely what Marina reminded Saul about after he committed the anthropomorphic error.

Social Learning and Social Transmission

Some researchers have proposed that the seemingly intelligent behavior of animals in urban environments may be acquired through **social learning** and **social transmission** (Nielsen et al., 2012). Social learning is learning influenced by observing or interacting with others (Hoppitt and Laland, 2013). Social transmission refers to the spread of information or behaviors through a group of animals. Social transmission of information is thought to have significant adaptive value. For example, studies have shown that rats can learn that a particular food is safe to eat by smelling its odor in the breath of a conspecific (i.e., an animal of the same species) upon its return from a foraging trip (Galef, 1985). It has also been shown that this information can be held in memory for several weeks (Galef and Whiskin, 2003). The laboratory procedure to study socially transmitted food preferences is shown in Figure 21.4 (Bessières, Nicole and Bontempi, 2017).

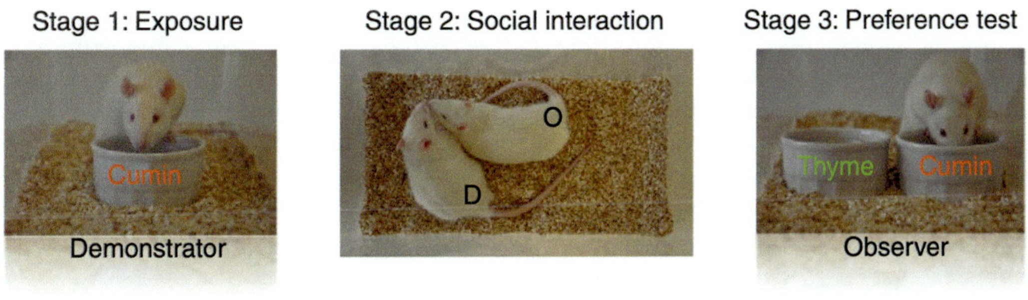

Figure 21.4 Socially transmitted food preference procedure. In Stage 1 (exposure), a rat (demonstrator) eats a flavored food (e.g., cumin). In Stage 2 (social interaction), a second rat (observer [O]) who was never exposed to the flavor (cumin) interacts with the demonstrator (D). In Stage 3 (preference test), the observer is given a choice between eating two flavored foods, the one eaten by the demonstrator (cumin) and another that was never eaten by the demonstrator (e.g., thyme). The observer usually eats significantly more of the food eaten by the demonstrator (i.e., cumin), suggesting that it has learned that the food is safe because it remembers smelling it on the demonstrator's rat breath.

Source: Bessières, B., Nicole, O., & Bontempi, B. (2017). Assessing recent and remote associative olfactory memory in rats using the social transmission of food preference paradigm. *Nat Protoc, 12*(7), 1415–1436.

Behavioral ecologist Barbara Klump and colleagues investigated the possibility that social transmission accounts for the spread of some of the surprising behaviors of animals you have seen in urban environments (2021). In one study, they investigated the garbage-bin opening behavior of cockatoos in the Sydney and Wollongong regions of Australia. To do so, they collected data on bin-opening sightings by surveying residents from these regions. The spatial distribution of the sightings across different suburbs between 2018 and late 2019 was plotted on a map. They collected 338 reports of bin-opening sightings across 44 suburbs. They found that the number of suburbs that reported sightings increased from 3 to 44 during that period.

To learn how the cockatoos achieved their feat of opening the bins, they marked some of the cockatoos where most of the sightings occurred and analyzed video clips of them opening garbage bins. They discovered that their bin-opening behavior consisted of five stages: pry, open, hold, walk, and flip (Figure 21.5). How each step in the sequence was executed was similar between individuals but became increasingly dissimilar with the geographical distance between neighborhoods.

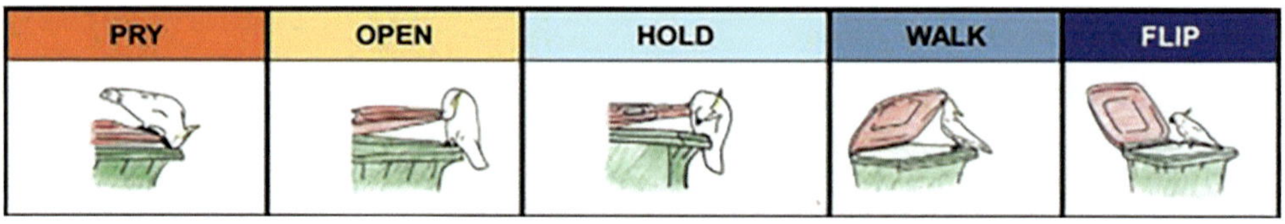

Figure 21.5 Bin-opening behavior of the cockatoos observed by Klump and colleagues (2021); see text for details.

Source: Klump, B. C., Martin, J. M., Wild, S., Hörsch, J. K., Major, R. E., & Aplin, L. M. (2021). Innovation and geographic spread of a complex foraging culture in an urban parrot. *Science, 373*(6553), 456–460.

They hypothesized that if learning to open the bins spread through social transmission, then new instances of bin opening should be more frequent in the suburbs close to where they were first observed due to the influence of informed birds flying into these suburbs because individuals that spend more time with each other have a greater opportunity to learn from each other (Coussi-Korbel and Fragaszy, 1995). They tested their hypothesis with a statistical technique that analyzes the spread of information or behaviors in social networks. Their analysis supported their hypothesis that the spread of the behavior was closely related to the proximity of the suburbs.

Insight

Another more controversial possibility is that the animals acquire impressive behaviors through **insight**. Learning by insight can be defined as the acquisition of an adaptive response not arrived at by trial and error but by the reorganization of behavior due to the sudden realization of the solution to a problem (Thorpe, 1963). Recall from the opening vignette that this is one of the human-like mental abilities that Saul attributes to the animals performing seemingly intelligent behaviors.

WOLFGANG KÖHLER'S MONKEYS

The first cases that appeared to be of insight learning in non-human animals were reported by psychologist Wolfgang Köhler (1887–1967) in 1927 while working at a laboratory in the Canary Islands. Köhler set up situations in which food was only indirectly accessible to animals (1925). He noticed that while dogs and cats persisted in walking up to the barrier in obviously futile attempts to get to the food, the chimpanzees, without trial and error, immediately adopted a circuitous path around the barrier to the food.

In a further experiment, Köhler placed a banana out of reach, outside of a chimpanzee's cage, and gave the monkey two sticks to play with. Without training, the monkey put the sticks together and retrieved the banana outside its cage. In another experiment, he hung bananas from the ceiling well out of reach of chimpanzees with wooden crates scattered throughout the room. Again, without being explicitly trained to do so (i.e., they were never trained for that specific purpose), the chimpanzees stacked up the crates, climbed on them, and retrieved the bananas. Since Köhler's experiments, reports of insightful behaviors have been demonstrated in various species (Waal, 2016).

INSIGHTFUL ROOKS?

The insightful problem-solving of rooks, a type of bird in the corvid family, was inferred in experiments that required them to use tools in various ways to collapse a platform that gave them access to a worm (Bird and Emery, 2009). This included selecting and dropping a stone of the correct size down a tube or inserting a stick into the tube to collapse the platform. It also included using and fashioning a hook to retrieve a basket containing the worm from through the tube. The complete list of tasks accomplished by the birds in the experiments is shown in Table 21.1. The defining feature of each of these experiments, which is why the different tasks were deemed to have been solved by insight, is that, similarly to Köhlers's chimpanzees, the birds were never explicitly trained to do so.

TOOL-USING COCKATOOS

In a relatively recent experiment, cockatoos were shown to have the capacity for composite tool use, meaning they could combine two different tools to complete a task (Osuna-Mascaró et al., 2022). Other than in humans, this ability has only been observed in chimpanzees that use a large stone as an anvil and a smaller stone as a hammer to crack the shells of nuts (Matsuzawa, 1994). In the first stage of the experiment, the cockatoos learned to drop a ball in a tube at one end of an apparatus to collapse a platform, resulting in a food reward delivery. In the second stage, the cockatoos were presented with a modified version of the apparatus, with a ball and a stick in front of it. Collapsing the platform to get the food would require them to pick up the ball and put it through a hole in the apparatus. The cockatoos would then have to pick up the stick, with which they would push the ball to one end of the apparatus, which would fall onto the collapsible platform, giving them access to the food. The cockatoos had never been trained to access the food in this way. The experimenters wanted to find out whether cockatoos would have the insight to solve the problem of getting the food in this way. Indeed, the experimenters found that all the cockatoos could solve the problem, with one of them solving it on its first try.

Table 21.1 The types of tasks solved by the rooks in the Bird and Emory (2009) experiments.

Type of task	*Task Description*	*Result*
Stone Size Test	The birds were given a choice between a small, medium, or large stone. Only the small stone fit into the tube.	The birds selected the small stone.
Stone Retrieval Test	The birds were given a choice between small, medium, or large stone located away from the apparatus. Only the small stone fit into the tube.	The birds only brought back a small stone.
Stone Orientation Test	The birds were given a choice between a long, thin stone and small, round stone. The birds had to orient the long, thin stone differently depending on tube size.	The birds selected the long, thin stone and oriented it according to tube size.
Stick Use Test	The birds were provided with a stick instead of stones.	The birds inserted the stick into the tube to collapse the platform.
Functional Tool Type Test	The birds were presented with 1) a functional long stick and non-functional large stone, and 2) a non-functional short stick and functional small stone.	The birds selected the functional tool regardless of type.
Metatool Test	The birds had to use a large stone to access either another large stone that did not fit into the tube or small stone that fit into the tube.	The birds used the large stone to gain access to the small stone that fit into the tube.
Stick Modification Test	The birds were given a tree branch with several side branches which had to be broken off to fit into the tube.	The birds broke off the side branches so that the branch fit into the tube.
Hook Use Test	The birds had to use a hook tool to pull out a basket with a worm inside from the tube.	The birds successfully pulled the basket out using the tool.
Functional Hook Test	The birds were given a choice of two hooks to retrieve a basket with a worm inside from the tube: one that was functional and one that was not functional.	The birds selected the functional hook.
Hook Manufacture Test	The birds were provided with a straight piece of wire to see if they fashioned it into a hook to retrieve a basket with a worm inside from the tube.	The birds were able to fashion a functional hook to retrieve the basket.

Insight or Shaping?

Remember from Chapter 9: animals can learn to perform a target behavior through shaping. Shaping through reinforcing behaviors by successive approximations can give rise to complex and impressive behaviors that may be interpreted as insightful. Some researchers have suggested that the behaviors displayed by the chimpanzees in Köhler's (1925) study would not have been observed if they had not first learned to push objects to a target and to climb on objects to reach other objects. When researchers replicated Köhler's (1925) findings using pigeons instead of chimpanzees, they found that only pigeons that were first trained to push a box towards a goal and to peck a suspended toy banana subsequently showed the seemingly insightful response of pushing a box under a banana, to then climb on it to peck the banana (Epstein et al., 1984). This raised the possibility that the pigeons were merely incited to perform previously learned responses. Their behavior might have been explained without resorting to a particular process, such as insight (Shettleworth, 2009a, 2010).

Others have also questioned the interpretation that insight was responsible for the rooks' ability in the study conducted by Bird and Emory (2009) described previously. For example, some researchers proposed that the pigeons achieved their feats through shaping by pointing out that the rooks were initially reinforced by the potentially accidental pushing of stone into the apparatus. They also pointed out that, in previous experiments, the same rooks learned to extract food from tubes by pushing objects through them (Lind, Ghirlanda and Enquist, 2009).

Critical Thinking Spot Check 21.2

1. Compare comparative ethology to cognitive cognition. What is the primary factor that can permit you to differentiate between them?
2. Describe and give an example of the anthropomorphic error.
3. What is the value of not committing the anthropomorphic error?
4. How would you explain city animals' seemingly intelligent and insightful behaviors without resorting to mental constructs?
5. Differentiate between social learning and social transmission.
6. Describe a study in which researchers believed that social learning could explain the behavior of city animals.

Chapter Summary

Each bullet point aligns directly with the learning objectives outlined at the beginning of the chapter.

- Cognitive psychology is the study of mental processes. Major figures in the history of cognitive psychology include Franciscus Donders, who studied the speed of mental processing by measuring people's reaction times to respond to stimuli; Wilhem Wundt and Edward Bradford Tichener, who believed that experiences were made up of essential elements and originated the concept of introspection and the school of thought known as structuralism; and Hermann Ebbinghaus, who explored the role played by associations in memory and patterns of memory loss over time.
- In the early 1900s, some psychologists rejected the idea that the goal of psychology should be the study of mental processes because they were unobservable and unnecessary in understanding behavior. This point of view dominated psychology until the cognitive revolution of the 1960s, which was influenced by the rise of computer science to give rise to the information processing approach. Another turning point in the cognitive revolution was Noam Chomsky's critique of Skinner's book *Verbal Behavior*.

- The idea that the behavior of animals can be explained by postulating a mental construct was proposed by psychologist Edward Tolman, a behaviorist, 30 years before the cognitive revolution. He proposed that animals can form cognitive maps of space, which they can use to navigate their environment. Tolman also suggested the concept of latent learning, in which information can be learned without any evidence until the information is required to perform a task. Tolman provided evidence of the contribution of cognitive maps and latent learning by giving rats tasks that required spatial orientation, such as finding their way to food on a maze even when the habitual path taken to it was blocked, requiring them to use an alternative path that was up to then not made available to them.
- Comparative cognition is a branch of psychology that compares cognitive processes across species. It differs from cognitive ethology in that, contrary to the field of comparative ethology, psychologists avoid committing anthropomorphic error, which refers to attributing human characteristics to animals. Comparative psychologists interpret their findings using Morgan's canon. Morgan's canon states that the behavior of non-human animals should not be attributed to higher mental processes if more straightforward concepts can explain it.
- Evidence shows that animals can learn complex behaviors through social learning and social transmission. Social learning is learning influenced by observing or interacting with others, while social transmission refers to the spread of information or behaviors through a group of organisms. Upon closer inspection, behaviors seemingly generated by insight have often been shown to have been acquired by shaping or a series of stimulus-response associations.

Glossary

Analytic introspection A method used in early psychology where individuals report their conscious experiences in detail to analyze thought processes.

Anthropomorphic error The mistaken attribution of human-like traits or reasoning to animals when interpreting their behaviors.

Cognitive ethology A branch of ethology that examines animal behavior in terms of cognitive processes such as memory, perception, and problem-solving.

Cognitive maps Mental representations of spatial environments that help organisms navigate and recall locations.

Cognitive psychology The scientific study of mental processes, including perception, memory, problem-solving, and decision-making.

Cognitive revolution A shift in psychology during the mid-20th century that moved away from behaviorism and emphasized mental processes in understanding behavior.

Comparative cognition The study of cognitive processes across different species to understand similarities and differences in learning and reasoning.

Information processing approach A framework in cognitive psychology that likens human thought processes to the functioning of computers, focusing on how information is encoded, stored, and retrieved.

Insight The sudden realization of a solution to a problem, often without trial-and-error learning, suggesting deeper cognitive processing.

Latent learning Learning that occurs but is not immediately demonstrated until there is motivation to express it.

Primary consciousness Basic awareness of sensory experiences and the immediate environment, often contrasted with higher-order reflective consciousness.

Social learning The process of acquiring behaviors and knowledge through observation and interaction with others.

Social transmission The spread of learned behaviors, ideas, or cultural practices through interaction within a group.

Spatial orientation The ability to understand and navigate one's position in physical space using cognitive and perceptual processes.

22 Tracing One's Path

Memory and Navigation

Learning Objectives

1. Define memory as the retention of experiences and explain the information processing approach's three stages of memory (encoding, storage, retrieval) and types of retrieval (recall, recognition, recollection), alongside potential memory failures due to interference.
2. Describe memory's three registers: sensory memory (iconic, echoic, haptic), short-term memory (including working memory), and long-term memory (declarative: episodic, semantic; nondeclarative: classical conditioning, emotional, procedural), noting vulnerability in short-term memory and the process of memory consolidation.
3. Discuss memory deficits resulting from brain damage or trauma, distinguishing between retrograde amnesia (loss of recent memories) and anterograde amnesia (inability to form new memories), and explain memory consolidation.
4. a) Describe memory tests such as delayed matching/non-matching to sample and novel object/place/context preference tests. b) Define navigation as animals' ability to find their way through environments, categorizing navigation into egocentric types.

A Case of Disorientation

IStock photo ID: 1180452321

DOI: 10.4324/9781003491828-41

Dachen is a 43-year-old office worker with difficulty orienting himself in his environment. As a teenager, Dachen relied on his older siblings, friends, and parents to accompany him wherever needed. If he tried to get anywhere by himself, he got lost. Today, Dachen can only get to work by following strict directions. He knows which bus to take but cannot remember its route. He knows how to get off the bus when he arrives at a square marked by an unmissable cathedral. After getting off the bus, he knew to immediately turn right on the sidewalk and walk for about 100 meters straight to the doors of the building where his office is located. Having to rely on such a strategy to get to work is often a source of stress for Dachen. One morning, his bus was unexpectedly sent on a detour, and his usual stop in the square was moved outside to a nearby street corner. Panic-stricken, he did not know what to do when the familiar square and cathedral never appeared, so he got off the bus at a random stop. Finding himself in a completely unfamiliar environment, he was unable to use any of the cues, such as the cathedral's steeple still visible towering over office buildings, to find his way to work. He tried to use his smartphone's mapping application, which added to his confusion. In desperation, he called his friend Mala, who was home on vacation. She asked Dachen to describe his environment and quickly figured out his location. She immediately set off to pick him up to drive him to work. Dachen's inability to orient and navigate his environment is known as topographical disorientation.

22.1 Fundamental Concepts in the Study of Memory

What Is Memory?

Memory refers to the process by which representations of experiences are retained. However, memory is about the past, present, and future. For example, you may think about the events that marked the wonderful trip you went on with your best friend over the summer, and you may mentally travel back in time, replaying the events as if they were occurring again. Remembering these events elicits the same positive emotions you felt during the trip. On the other hand, memories of events that did not go so well because of mistakes we made inform present behavior so that those mistakes are not repeated, thus avoiding future problems.

The Stages of Memory: Encoding, Storage, and Retrieval

According to the information processing approach (Broadbent, 1958), memory is defined as a three-stage process, as shown in Figure 22.1. **Encoding** refers to the process by which information is acquired to be stored in the brain. It includes the selection of information and its integration with existing memories. **Storage** refers to the maintenance of information over time. Memories are believed to be stored in patterns of connections between neurons called **engrams** (Hebb, 1949). However, it is essential to understand that engrams are not perfect records of experiences. Instead, they are believed to be imperfect packets of information used to reconstruct events in our minds. Human memories are malleable, meaning they can be transformed by new information or misleading questions about an event (Loftus, 1979). This fact about memories has led psychologist Elizabeth Loftus to question eyewitness testimonies' validity (2003). **Retrieval** refers to the process by which stored memories are accessed. Different forms of retrieval exist. **Recall** refers to the ability

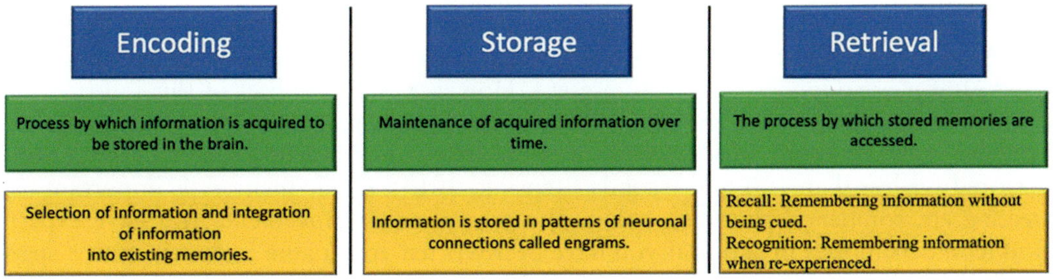

Figure 22.1 The three stages of memory according to the information processing approach (see text for details).

to remember information without being cued. Remembering what you had for breakfast when asked would be an example of recall. **Recognition** refers to remembering information when re-experiencing it. Correctly identifying your suitcase on an airport's baggage carousel is an example of recognition. **Recollection** refers to the process of reconstructing memories from partial memories or cues. Remembering something the teacher said in class by being reminded of the context in which she spoke, comments elicited by her words, or the content of an assignment would be an example of recollection.

FAILING TO REMEMBER

Not remembering information can be due to failure at any of the stages of memory processing. In the case of a failure to encode, it was shown that people fail to remember everyday objects' details if they are deemed unimportant (Nickerson and Adams, 1979). For example, try to remember the name of the company engraved on your house keys. It is not likely that you do, even if you have seen them thousands of times. You may also not have paid much attention to the instructions given by your teacher for an assignment, resulting in the information not being stored. Finally, you may not be able to remember information due to a failure in retrieval. This is best exemplified by the "tip-of-the-tongue" phenomenon, in which you know you know the information but cannot bring it to mind. In this case, you know that the information was encoded and stored because a cue in the memory permits retrieval.

Memory interference may also account for the failure to retrieve information. Two types of memory interference exist. **Retroactive interference** occurs when newly learned information interferes with remembering previously learned information. For example, you find that studying for your biology class after studying for your psychology class makes information from your psychology textbook more challenging to remember. In contrast, **proactive interference** occurs when previously learned information interferes with remembering new information.

The Registers of Memory

Memories are thought to be stored in the three different registers (or stores), shown in Figure 22.2. These are sensory memory, short-term memory, and long-term memory. We will now explore each one.

SENSORY MEMORY

Sensory memory refers to the persisting representation of a sensory stimulus for a brief period after it is no longer physically present. However, only a subset of this information is remembered if it becomes the focus of attention (Sperling, 1960). **Iconic memories** are persisting representations of visual information after it has faded. These representations are stored for less than 500 milliseconds (Rensink, 2014). Iconic memory is important for detecting environmental changes, such as the perception of movement. You have experienced iconic memories in action if you have ever written your name in the air with a sparkler. This experience is known as the sparkler's trail effect. **Echoic memories** are persisting representations of sounds after they have faded. These representations were found to persist for up to 10 seconds (Cowan, Saults and Nugent, 1997). Echoic memory is important for keeping track of speech during a conversation. You have experienced echoic memory if you ever asked someone to repeat a question but were able to answer it before the person finished repeating. This occurred because you processed the auditory information's persisting representation (or "echo"). **Haptic memories** are persisting representations of tactile details after they have faded. The duration of haptic memory is approximately two seconds (Shih, Dubrowski and Carnahan, 2009). Haptic memory is important for manipulating and recognizing objects by touch.

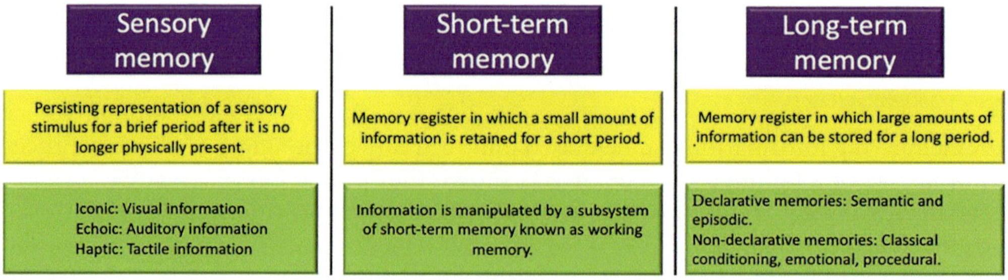

Figure 22.2 The registers of memory (see text for details).

SHORT-TERM MEMORY

Short-term memory refers to a memory store in which a small amount of information is retained for a short period. This information is manipulated by a subsystem of short-term memory known as **working memory**. This manipulation includes rehearsing information by mentally repeating it, such as when one tries to remember the names of key figures in the history of psychology for an exam, keeping track of the words of wisdom spoken by the teacher, or being able to get back to the page you were studying in your textbook before being interrupted by a text from your friend.

Psychologists Alan Baddeley and Graham Hitch (1974) and Baddeley (2007) developed a working memory model known as the **multicomponent model of** working memory. The model consists of four components: the visuospatial sketchpad, the phonological loop, the episodic buffer, and the central executive.

The visuospatial sketchpad temporarily stores visual and spatial information, such as remembering what someone looks like or visualizing the route to your classroom. The phonological loop rehearses verbal information through subvocalization (silently repeating information to yourself) and converts visual information into a phonological code. The episodic buffer integrates information from the visuospatial sketchpad and the phonological loop with a sense of time, permitting memories to be experienced as sequences of events. Finally, the central executive coordinates the activities of these components, allowing you to focus on a single task or switch from task to task. It also allows working memory to interact with long-term memory.

LONG-TERM MEMORY

Long-term memory refers to a memory register of potentially unlimited capacity for both the amount of information it can store and the time for which information is retained. As shown in Figure 22.3, there are two broad types of long-term memories: declarative and nondeclarative memories.

Declarative or explicit memories include memories of facts and life experiences. Memories of facts about the world are known as semantic memories, whereas memories of life experiences are known as **episodic memories** (Schacter, 1987; Squire and Zola, 1996). Retrieving semantic memories does not require you to mentally travel back in time to re-experience the event in which the fact was learned. For example, remembering a fact such as "the Alamo is in Texas" does not require you to remember the context in which the fact was learned (i.e., where you were, who was with you, who told you, and when). In contrast, episodic memories include the "when," "where," and "what" of personal experiences (Nyberg, McIntosh and Tulving, 1998; Tulving, 1983) and require you to mentally travel back in time, in your mind's eye, to re-experience an event (Tulving, 1983).

Nondeclarative memories, also known as *implicit memories*, do not require the conscious recollection of information but are made evident through task performance. There are many types of nondeclarative memories. Behaviors acquired through classical conditioning are

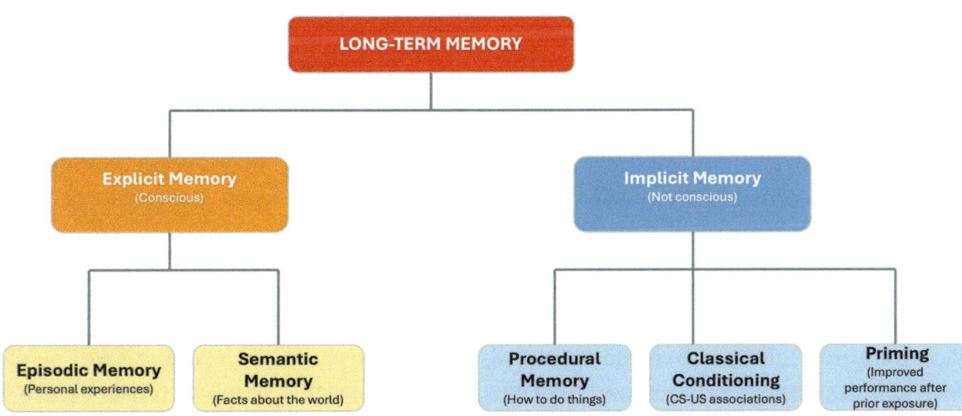

Figure 22.3 The types of long-term memories (see text for details).

Source: Okami, Paul. *Psychology: Contemporary Perspectives*. Oxford University Press Academic US, 2017. Figure 8.7.

examples of the expression of nondeclarative memories. Remember that the CS-US associations created during classical conditioning can occur without conscious awareness and that conditioned emotional or motor responses occur without conscious intent. Another type of nondeclarative memory is known as **procedural memory**. Procedural memory is a type of nondeclarative memory that leads to the performance of skills and habits or remembering how to do things like riding a bicycle or driving a car with a standard transmission, which also does not necessitate the conscious recollection of information (Cohen et al. 1997; Lum and Conti-Ramsden, 2013).

These are the behaviors acquired through habit or stimulus-response learning. Another type of procedural memory is priming, which refers to the change in the response to a word or object after encountering it. For example, you may complete a three-letter word stem such as S-T-A _ _ _ with STAIRS rather than STARS if the word STAIRS was part of a list of words presented to you on the previous day. You may also complete it with STAIRS if you were previously shown a picture of someone going up some stairs. In everyday life, priming might cause you to notice a particular make of car more frequently on the road after a friend has acquired one—no conscious recollection of having seen that car model previously is required.

Memory Consolidation

One of the defining characteristics of short-term memories is that they initially exist in an unstable and fragile state. The formation of short-term memories is vulnerable to disruptions. Just think about what happens if you get distracted while trying to memorize the list of key psychologists in the history of psychology, as mentioned previously. However, if permitted to rehearse the list uninterrupted enough mentally, you may remember it indefinitely. At this point, we may be able to say that the list of psychologists was stored in a more stable and lasting form.

The process by which memories go from being in an unstable and fragile state to a more stable and long-lasting form is known as **memory consolidation** (Squire et al., 2015). Elias Müller and Alfons Pilzecker of the University of Gottingen in Germany were the first to demonstrate memory consolidation experimentally (Müller and Pilzecker, 1900; Lechner, Squire and Byrne, 1999). In one experiment, participants learned a list of nonsense syllables such as SIE, FIET, and GEIM. The subjects were then made to learn a second list of nonsense syllables 34 seconds later. Six seconds after learning the first list, the subjects were asked to recall as many syllables of the first list as they could. They found that the participants could only correctly recall 23% of the syllables on the list. In a second condition, the participants also learned a list of syllables but did not have to learn a second one. In this condition, the participants could recall 48% of the syllables.

Müller and Pilzecker (1900) thought that the impaired recall of the list of syllables in the first condition occurred because the second list was learned too soon after learning the first and interfered with a process that solidified its memory. They hypothesized that if the participants were made to learn the second list once this process was completed, memory for the syllables on the first list would no longer be as vulnerable to interference. To test this hypothesis, they had participants learn a second list of syllables only 17 seconds after learning the first, which led to poor recall of the syllables on the first list. However, in another condition, the participants learned the second list six minutes after learning the first. In this condition, the participants' recall of the first list was relatively intact. They called the process by which learning the second list interfered with learning the first *retroactive inhibition* (today known as retroactive interference, as you read). They called the process that solidified the memory of the first list when enough time elapsed before learning the second list *memory consolidation*.

Amnesia

Amnesia refers to memory deficits resulting from brain damage or psychological trauma. Amnesia resulting from psychological trauma without brain damage is known as psychogenic or dissociative amnesia (Staniloiu and Markowitsch, 2012). There are two broad types of amnesia (Figure 22.4a): **retrograde** and **anterograde amnesia.** Retrograde amnesia refers to memory loss for information acquired before the event. Anterograde amnesia refers to an inability to form new memories after the event. Information acquired shortly before the event is often lost, but memories from remoter periods are preserved. This is known as **temporally graded retrograde amnesia.**

Much of what we know about the brain areas responsible for different types of memories comes from case studies of brain-damaged patients. The most famous of these cases is that of Henry Molaison (1926–2008), known as patient HM. In 1953, HM, who was 27 years old at the time, underwent bilateral surgical removal of the hippocampus (shown in Figure 22.4b) to relieve epileptic seizures. The surgery significantly reduced the frequency of his seizures but resulted in severe anterograde amnesia and temporally graded retrograde amnesia extending to his childhood (Scoville and Milner, 1957). This meant that he could no longer form new long-term memories and had a loss of memory for events extending from the time of his surgery back to his childhood. However, HM could remember information when permitted to rehearse, showing that his short-term memory was intact. Neurological testing of HM showed that brain damage HM sustained greatly affected his declarative memories (episodic and semantic) but left his nondeclarative memories (classical conditioning and procedural) intact. Hence, the case of HM showed that the hippocampus is only necessary for the processing of declarative memories, with nondeclarative memories being dependent on other brain areas.

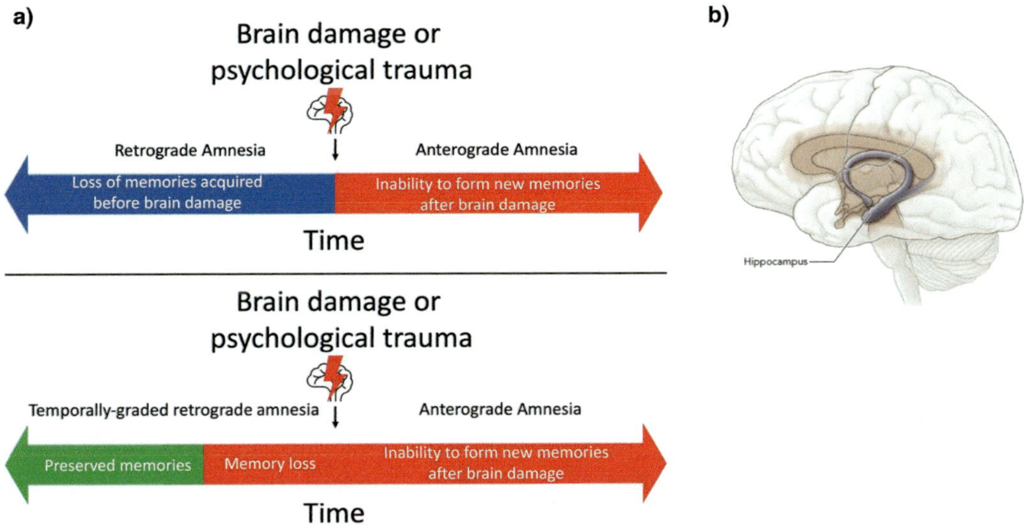

Figure 22.4 a) Patterns of retrograde amnesia. b) Location of the hippocampus in the brain.

Sources: Hippocampus (b) only: Source: Okami, Paul. *Psychology: Contemporary Perspectives*. Oxford University Press Academic US, 2017. Figure 8.8.

A THEORY OF MEMORY CONSOLIDATION

Remember that memory consolidation refers to the process by which short-term memories, which are stored in a fragile state, become stored in a more stable and long-lasting form within the brain. Remember also that the concept of memory consolidation was first experimentally demonstrated by Müller and Pilzecker (1900), who showed that learning a new list of syllables impaired the recall of the syllables on a previous list if it was learned shortly after learning the first list. However, learning a second list of syllables did not impair the recall of the syllables on the first list if it was learned after a longer period. This made scientists wonder whether memory consolidation could explain cases of temporally graded retrograde amnesia shown by certain brain damage patients.

Several theories of memory consolidation have been developed at different levels of analysis and complexity. However, a comprehensive review of these theories is beyond the scope of the present text. For more extensive coverage of these theories, I suggest taking a course in behavioral neuroscience or reading the relevant sections of a neuroscience textbook (Gaskin, 2020) or papers on the topic (Squire et al., 2015; Albo and Gräff, 2018; Takehara-Nishiuchi, 2021).

Here, we will focus on the most basic of these theories, known as the **standard model of memory consolidation**. According to the standard model (Alvarez and Squire, 1994), memory elements, including the cognitive, perceptual, and motor information that compose it, are encoded in groups of neurons, known as cortical modules, located in widespread areas of the cortex. Initially, the connections between these modules are weak, and the hippocampus needs to be maintained by repeatedly reactivating the memory. However, over time (weeks, months, or even years), the connections between the modules become strong enough to be sustained without the participation of the hippocampus. At this moment, the standard model proposes that the memory has been consolidated.

How does this theory explain temporally graded retrograde amnesia, in which memories acquired shortly before damage to the hippocampus are lost but in which remoter memories are preserved? The explanation is that shortly after acquisition, the connections between the cortical modules that compose the memory still need to be strengthened to be sustained without the participation of the hippocampus. In contrast, remoter memories are preserved because the connections between the modules in the cortex have become strong enough to be sustained without the participation of the hippocampus.

Critical Thinking Spot Check 22.1

1. Define memory and its different stages.
2. Name and compare the different types of retrieval processes and give an example of each.
3. Come up with everyday examples to differentiate between retroactive and proactive interference.
4. Name the different registers of memory and discuss their differences.
5. What is the value of knowing about the different registers of memory?
6. Differentiate the different types of long-term memories.
7. Define memory consolidation and how knowing about this process is important in understanding the patterns of memory loss in brain-damaged patients.

22.2 The Experimental Study of Memory

Commonly Used Memory Tests

Significant efforts to study memory in animals did not begin until the 1950s. The reason for this late start can be attributed to the influence of early behaviorists such as Watson and others, who believed that understanding the intelligence of animals required only the study of their ability to learn stimulus-response associations (Watson, 1913). They saw no need to attribute to animals complex cognitive processes when simpler processes can explain their behavior.

Today, a variety of memory tests that have been designed to study animals are available to researchers. The value of these tests goes beyond their use in comparing mnemonic abilities across species. They have also contributed and continue to contribute to our understanding of the neural processes that underlie different forms of memories. They are also commonly used to assess the efficacy of drugs to be used in the treatment of neurological disorders such as Alzheimer's disease and other forms of dementia (Souza Brocardo and Gil-Mohapel, 2012; Brodziak, Kolat and Rozyk-Myrta, 2014). In this section, you will learn about some of these tests.

The Delayed Matching and Non-Matching to Sample Tasks

The **delayed matching to sample task (DMS)** was developed in the late 1950s to assess short-term memory in pigeons (Blough, 1959; Konorski, 1959). The DMS consists of three stages: sample, delay, and choice. In one version of the test, pigeons were successively presented with two stimuli (a sample and a choice) on a pecking key. Each stimulus was presented for five seconds and could be differentiated by color, shape, or orientation. A delay determined by the experimenter separated the presentation of the stimuli. The pigeons were reinforced with food if they pecked the choice stimulus only when it matched the sample stimulus (Wasserman, 1976).

In another version of the test, pigeons were similarly presented with a sample stimulus followed by a delay. However, the pigeons were then presented with several choice stimuli, only one of which matched the sample stimulus, and the pigeons were reinforced to peck the one that matched the sample (Blough, 1959). In both test versions, the pigeon's performance was excellent if a short delay (e.g., one second) was imposed between the sample and test stimuli but degraded proportionally with the delay. It is important to note that the DMS also includes a long-term memory component. That is, animals must remember the rule of the task from trial to trial (i.e., "choose the matching choice stimulus"). Ever since these early studies, the DMS has been adapted to assess short-term memory in various species, including dolphins, rats, monkeys, and humans. It is widely used as a model for memory deficits induced by brain damage, drug abuse, dementia, and other psychiatric disorders.

An interesting aspect of the DMS is that correct responding involves not only the ability to remember but also the ability to withhold responding to a novel stimulus. This makes the test more difficult for animals and human babies, who naturally tend to be drawn to novelty. Fortunately, a test in which animals are reinforced for choosing the non-matching (novel) stimulus also exists. This test is the **delayed non-matching to sample task (DNMS)**. The performance of animals in the DNMS is superior to what is observed in the DMS, especially if novel stimuli are used on every trial (Mishkin and Delacour, 1975).

Similarly to the DMS task, the DNMS has been used in various species for the same purposes. For example, the DNMS test has been used to investigate monkeys' brain areas

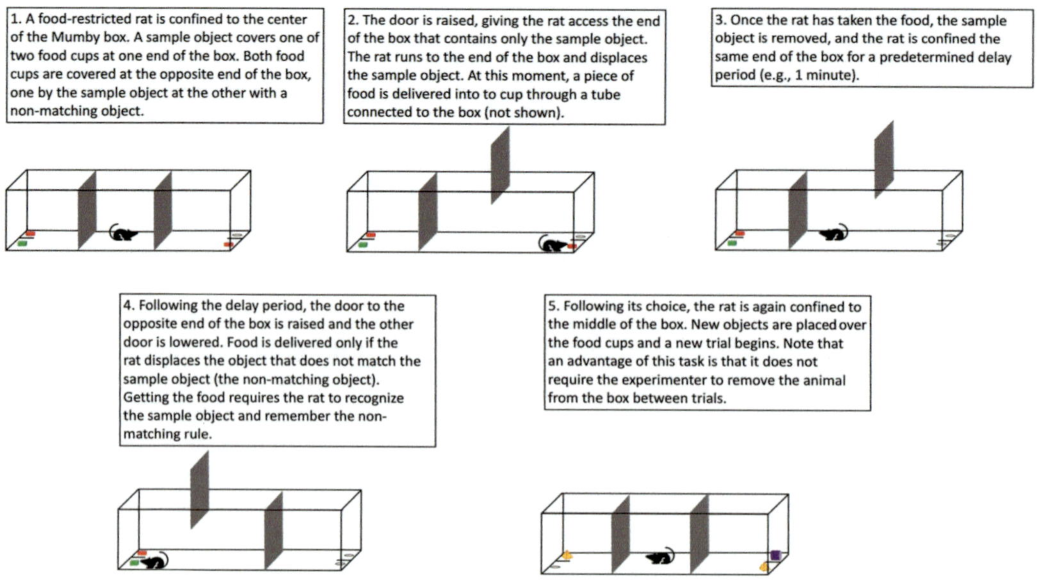

Figure 22.5 The DNMS was developed for rats (Mumby box) by Mumby and colleagues (1990).

involved in object-recognition memory (Meunier et al., 1993). In the sample phase, monkeys who received experimental brain damage were shown two objects, one covering a well containing food. Following a delay, the monkeys were presented with the same objects and were rewarded for displacing the object that did not cover the food during the sample phase. The results were that monkeys with intact brains and those with damage to the hippocampus performed well in the test but not those with damage to the perirhinal cortex.

Psychologist Dave G. Mumby and colleagues adapted the DNMS task to test object-recognition memory in rats by using what became known as the "Mumby box," shown in Figure 22.5 (Mumby, Pinel and Wood, 1990), which has since been used in several studies in which the neurobiological basis of object-recognition memory was investigated (Wood et al., 1993; Mumby and Pinel, 1994; Mumby et al., 1995; Kim et al., 1997; Clark et al., 2001).

Novelty-Preference Tests

Another way to assess object recognition memory in animals is the novel object preference test (NOP), which I referred to as the visual-paired comparison test (VPC) in Chapter 4 (Figure 4.4) in the context of habituation (Ennaceur and Delacour, 1988; Mumby et al., 2002; Gaskin, Tremblay and Mumby, 2003; Broadbent et al., 2010; Gaskin et al., 2010). I will describe it again here so that it can be compared with different versions of the procedure. In this test, an animal, usually a rat, is permitted to explore two identical objects in an open field (familiarization). After a delay predetermined by the experimenter, the rat is placed back into the open field, only this time a novel object (i.e., one that it has never seen before) is presented along with a copy of the one it has already seen. Because of their natural propensity to explore novelty, rats (and other animals) usually spend significantly more time exploring a novel object than one that it has already seen (familiar). This is taken as an indication that the rat has recognized the object it has already seen. The advantage of the NOP test over the DNMS test for rats is that it is easier to administer than the DNMS test. Another advantage is that it can test both short-term and long-term memory (Gaskin, Tremblay and Mumby, 2003).

In addition to testing object recognition memory (Figure 22.6 [top]), novelty-preference tests were adapted to assess memory for places and contexts. These tests take advantage of rats' propensity also to explore familiar objects that have been moved to a new place relative to the same environmental cues (Figure 22.6 [middle row]) and familiar objects that have been moved to a context containing no familiar cues (Figure 22.6 [bottom row]). The different versions of the test were thus created to determine which brain areas were involved in each of these types of memories (Mumby et al., 2002). It was found that the hippocampus, the region of the brain believed to participate in the formation of cognitive maps of space (see this chapter's "What in the Brain?" box), was necessary to recognize that an object has switched spatial locations (place test) and to recognize the context in which objects have been seen (context test). In contrast, in this study, the hippocampus was unimportant for object recognition (object test).

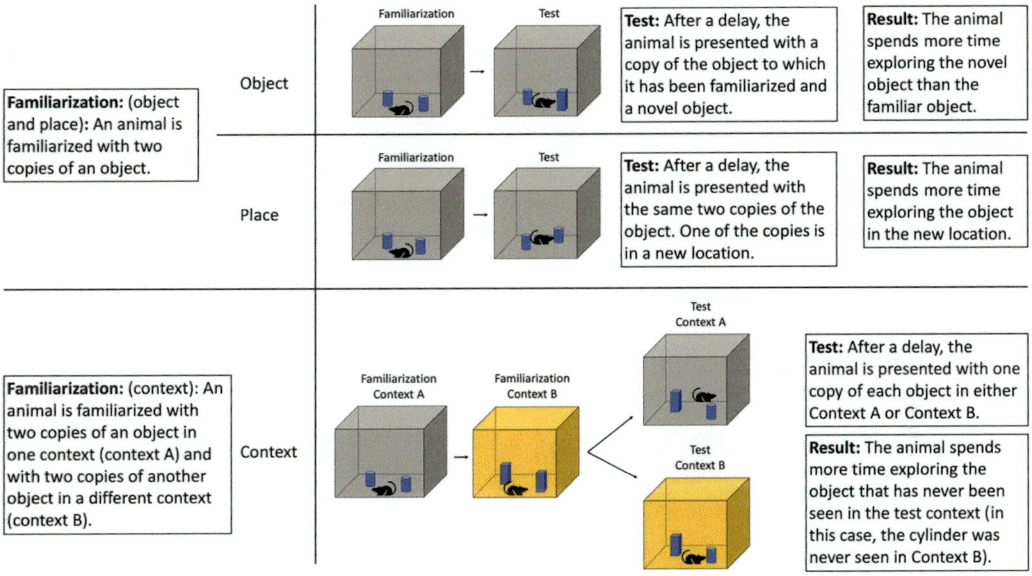

Figure 22.6 Three versions of the novelty preference test (see text for details).

Critical Thinking Spot Check 22.2

1. What is the purpose of using memory tests in animals?
2. Name and describe a test that assesses object recognition memory in animals. Describe different test versions as they were adapted for use with various animal species.

22.3 Navigation and Spatial Memory

What Is Navigation?

Navigation refers to using various environmental information to find one's way through an environment. The ability to successfully navigate one's environment is essential for survival.

For example, a bird leaving its nest or a rabbit leaving its den to forage for food must be able to find its way back. It must also be able to remember the location of predators to avoid them on future trips. It may be obvious to you that navigating is also important for people. For example, during the first few weeks of your college or university experience, you may have gotten lost on campus and had difficulty remembering the location of buildings and classrooms. However, by having to get to different locations for your classes or to various buildings to obtain various services, you gradually built a cognitive map of the campus to the point where finding any place became much easier. The neurobiological bases of the formation of cognitive maps of space have been, and continue to be, the focus of intense study (see this chapter's "What in the Brain? box").

Allocentric and Egocentric Navigation

ALLOCENTRIC NAVIGATION

Allocentric navigation, also known as *spatial navigation* or *piloting*, refers to the ability to find one's way by remembering the position of distal environmental cues or landmarks relative to each other. For example, the student in Figure 22.7a learned to get to the cafeteria building by knowing its location relative to the library and a tree. Allocentric navigation includes realizing the location of landmarks with respect to one's location as one moves through the environment. That is, coming from the opposite direction, she would still be able to accurately navigate to the cafeteria by realizing that from her new perspective, it would now be located behind the tree instead of in front of it and to the right of the library instead of to its left. Allocentric navigation can include the use of **beacons**, which are landmarks that signal the exact location of a goal. For example, the CN Tower in Toronto is a beacon that signals the location of the baseball stadium, which lies directly below it. That is, finding the CN Tower implies that you have also found the stadium. Beacons can also take the form of radio signals permitting rescuers to find their way to the site of a plane crash.

The CN Tower in Toronto (Canada) is a beacon that signals the location of the baseball stadium directly below it.

Source: IStock photo ID:483465910.

EGOCENTRIC NAVIGATION

Egocentric navigation, (also known as non-spatial or route-based navigation), is the ability to navigate by using the position of environmental cues with respect to one's location. That is, in egocentric navigation, turns are elicited by **signposts,** which are proximal landmarks encountered along a path that indicates a change in direction. For example, the student in Figure 22.7b has learned to get to her psychology class by walking straight to the security desk and making a right turn, followed by a left turn at the elevators and a right turn at the window. Notice that if she approaches the security desk from the opposite direction, she will be prone to making an incorrect right turn at the security desk.

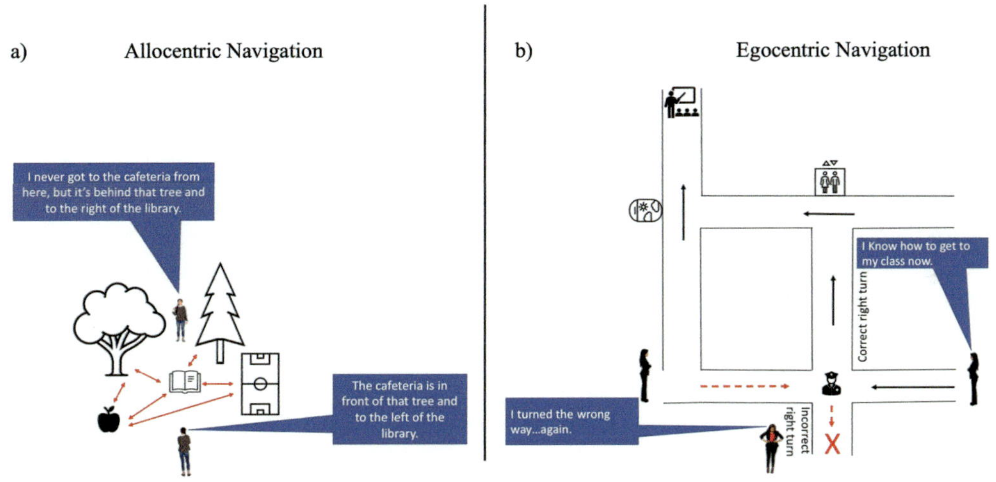

Figure 22.7 a) Allocentric navigation permits one to find her way by remembering relationships between distal landmarks, irrespective of her location. b) Egocentric navigation relies on the location of environmental cues relative to one's location.

TOPOGRAPHICAL DISORIENTATION

People who suffer from a disorder known as **topographical disorientation** may have great difficulty recognizing landmarks, recognizing their position relative to environmental cues, finding their way along previously familiar routes, and learning new routes. They may also be incapable of using maps for orientation. This is the case of Dachen in the opening vignette of the chapter. He was impaired at skills that constitute allocentric navigation described previously. For example, from the detoured bus stop, Dachen could see the cathedral's steeple towering over the buildings from a different perspective from when he got off the bus in the square. To most people who are not suffering from topographical disorientation, the steeple could still have been used as an effective beacon or landmark to find one's way. However, Dachen was unable to do this. His inability to use the mapping application on his smartphone was also characteristic of people suffering from this condition. He could only use the cathedral as a signpost indicating getting off the bus and turning right, an example of egocentric navigation.

Different subtypes of topographical disorientation are classified by the types of spatial impairments suffered by patients. It is also important to know that topographical disorientation can be developmental or acquired through brain damage. In Dachen's case, no obvious event in his life points to the possibility that he has sustained brain damage, making it likely that his topographical disorientation is developmental.

What in the Brain? Cognitive Mapping in the Brain

In their book *The Hippocampus as a Cognitive Map*, psychologists John O'Keefe and Lynn Nadel proposed that the hippocampus was necessary for forming cognitive maps of space in the brain (1978). According to them, these cognitive maps represented spatial relationships among environmental cues and were used for navigation. Later, evidence was found that the formation of cognitive maps of space involved the activity of several types of neurons across different brain areas. This evidence was primarily obtained through electrophysiological recordings of their activity as animals; typically, rats navigated through their environment. These neurons include place cells, head-direction cells, and grid cells.

Place Cells

Place cells were discovered in the hippocampuses of rats (O'Keefe and Dostrovsky, 1971). They increased their firing rate when an animal found itself in an area that contained familiar cues. Place cells are believed to be involved in animals' ability to locate themselves within their environment, thus contributing to their ability to navigate. Evidence of the existence of place cells has also been found in humans navigating through a virtual environment (Ekstrom et al., 2003).

Head-Direction Cells

Head-direction cells were discovered in the subiculum, thalamus, and striatum. Different populations of these cells fired when a rat pointed its head in particular directions. These neurons are believed to contribute to navigation by providing animals with heading information. They are also believed to play a role in the navigation of migratory birds (Takahashi et al., 2022). As for place cells, evidence for their existence in humans was found when their activity was detected as participants navigated through a virtual environment (Kim and Maguire, 2019).

Grid Cells

Grid cells were discovered in the entorhinal cortex. They fire at equal intervals with movement through the environment and are believed to provide metrics for the space traveled by animals, including humans (Jacobs et al., 2013; Whalley, 2013).

Putting It All Together

The discovery of place, grid, and head direction cells showed that the brain could form cognitive maps of space based on representations of location, distance, and direction, which animals could use to navigate the environment. All these neurons have been discovered in various animals, including humans, showing the continuity of spatial mapping abilities across species. It is important to realize that although we described the respective roles of these types of cells individually, it is likely that the formation of cognitive maps requires functional interactions between these different types of cells. These possible interactions are currently the focus of intense study (Morris and Derdikman, 2022; Sorscher et al., 2023).

Are You Thinking Critically?

1. Distinguish between the different types of neurons contributing to navigation by describing their functions.
2. Give an example of how the activity of each type of these neurons may be used in everyday life.
3. Why was the discovery of these types of neurons important?

Tasks Used to Assess Navigation

Allocentric Navigation (Spatial Navigation)

In the 1970s, David Olton devised a spatial memory task using an eight-arm radial maze consisting of an octagonal central platform with an arm radiating from each side (Figure 22.8a). In the standard version of the task, the maze is placed in the center of a room, which contains an array of spatial cues. A food pellet is placed at the end of each arm, and a hungry rat is placed at the maze's center and given free access to all arms. Rats learned to retrieve all the food pellets on the maze without returning to an arm they had already visited (Olton and Samuelson, 1976). This presumably occurs because the rats can hold the spatial location of the arms relative to the cues in the room in working memory. The radial maze can also be used to assess spatial long-term memory. The same four arms are baited across trials in the long-term memory version, whereas the remaining arms are always left empty. As in the working memory version, the rats eventually learn to never return to an arm from which they have retrieved the food within a trial (short-term memory). In addition, the rats learn never to enter the arms that have never been baited across trials (long-term memory). The experimenter can record the animal's location on the mazes manually. However, sophisticated software that tracks the animal's location via a video camera is commercially available (Figure 22.8b.).

Neuroscientist Richard Morris devised another widely used task to assess spatial learning (Morris, 1981; Morris et al., 1982). In the most used version of the task, the Morris water maze, a rat is put into a pool containing a submerged platform hidden by adding non-toxic paint or powdered milk to the water. The pool is in a room containing several spatial cues (Figure 22.9a). As with radial maze experiments, a computerized tracking system can record and trace an animal's path during every trial (Figure 22.9c).

Tracing the rats' paths within the pool reveals that when first placed in the pool, rats usually swim around in a circuitous path until they accidentally bump into the platform. Finding the platform is negatively reinforced by escaping the water by standing on the platform. After several trials, the rats readily reach the platform even if they are started from different locations in the pool (Figure 22.9b [top]). If the platform is moved to a new location after the rats have learned its original location, they spend more time in the quadrant of the pool where the platform used to be located relative to spatial cues (Figure 22.9b [middle]). Both findings indicate that the rats have learned to navigate to the platform by using spatial cues.

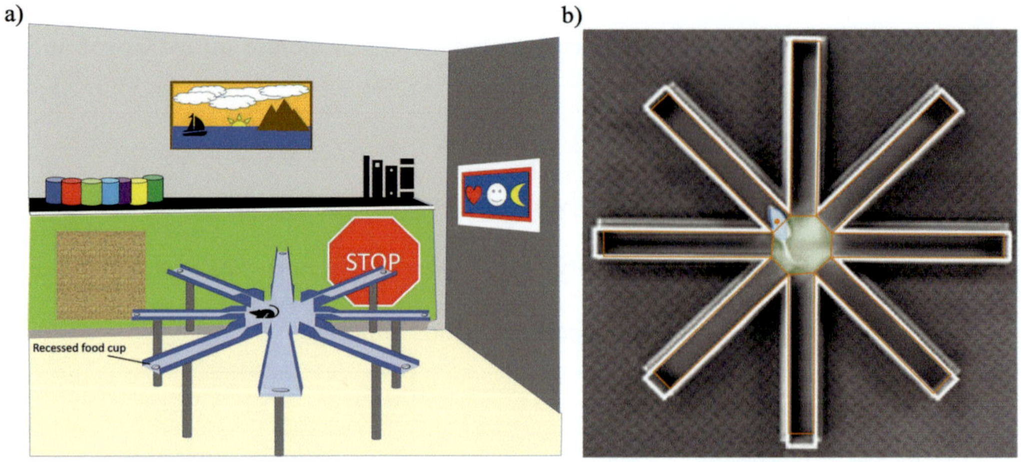

Figure 22.8 a) An eight-arm radial maze in a room containing an array of spatial cues. b) Image of a rat's location on a radial maze via a video tracking system (see text for details).

Source: Video tracking system image: Courtesy of Any Maze company website https://www.any-maze.com/applications/radial-arm-maze/.

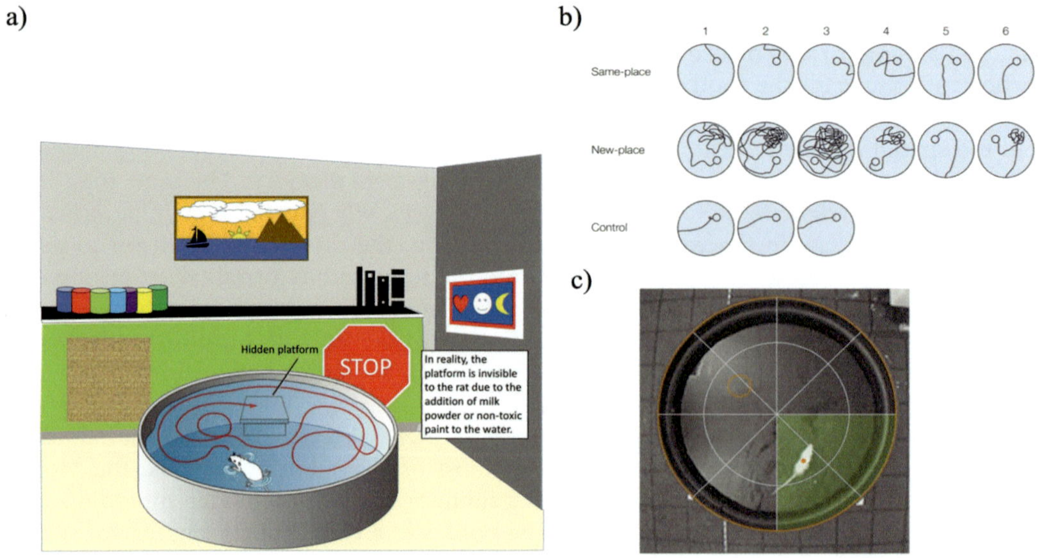

Figure 22.9 a) Morris water maze in a room containing an array of spatial cues. When first put into the pool, the rat takes a circuitous path and bumps into the platform by chance. b) (top [same-place]) Paths followed by individual rats when their starting location was changed from trial to trial with the platform remaining at the same place relative to spatial cues. (middle [new-place]) Paths followed by individual rats when the location of the platform was moved to a new location. Note that the rats spend more time in the quadrant of the pool where the platform used to be located, indicating that they remembered its location relative to spatial cues. (bottom [control]) The paths of rats for which both the starting location and the location of the platform remained the same. c) Image from a video tracking system.

Source: a) "Pool only" PhD, Mark F, B. et al. *Neuroscience: Exploring the Brain*. Wolters Kluwer Health (Figure 24.7) and b) Bouton, Mark E. *Learning and Behavior*. Available from: VitalSource Bookshelf (2nd Edition). Oxford University Press Academic US, 2016. Figure 8.34. c) Video tracking system image: Any Maze company website https://www.any-maze.com/applications/water-maze/.

Thus, this is an example of allocentric spatial learning. For control rats, the starting and platform locations remain the same (Figure 22.9b [bottom]).

In another condition (not shown), the rats always start from the same location, and the platform can always be reached by making a consistent turn (e.g., a left turn). In this situation, it cannot be immediately determined if the rats have learned the platform's location relative to spatial cues or allocentrically. This is because they may have learned to get to the platform egocentrically, that is, learning about the platform's location relative to their bodies instead of spatial cues. This can be tested by starting the rat from other pool locations. If the rat continues to make the same turn regardless of the platform's location, egocentric learning has occured.

Critical Thinking Spot Check 22.3

1. Name and describe the different types of tests used to study animal memory.
2. Explain allocentric and egocentric navigation and give examples of how you use each type of navigation in your everyday life.
3. Name and describe tasks used to test allocentric navigation in animals and how these tasks can be solved by using egocentric navigation.

Chapter Summary

Each bullet point aligns directly with the learning objectives outlined at the beginning of the chapter.

- Memory refers to the ability to retain representations of experiences. According to the information processing approach, memory comprises three stages: encoding, storage, and retrieval. Memories are believed to be stored in patterns of neural connections called engrams. Different forms of retrieval exist: recall, recognition, and recollection. The failure to remember might be caused by problems occurring at any of the stages of memory. Either retroactive or proactive interference may also cause it.
- In addition to being composed of three stages, memory can be stored in three registers. These are sensory memory, including iconic, echoic, and haptic memory; short-term memory, which includes working memory; and long-term memory, which provides declarative and nondeclarative memories. Declarative memories include episodic and semantic memories. Nondeclarative memories include classical conditioning, emotional memories, and procedural memories. Short-term memories are vulnerable to disruption. However, they can go from being in a fragile state to a long-lasting and stable form through memory consolidation.
- Brain damage and psychological trauma can result in a memory deficit known as amnesia. There are two different types of amnesia: retrograde amnesia and anterograde amnesia. Temporally graded retrograde amnesia occurs when recent memories are lost, but remote memories are preserved after brain damage. Temporally graded retrograde amnesia can be explained by the standard model of memory consolidation.
- A variety of memory tests exist. These include the delayed matching and non-matching to sample test and the novel object, place, or context preference tests. Navigation refers to an animal's ability to use various types of information to find its way through its environment. There are two broad types of navigation: allocentric navigation and egocentric navigation. Allocentric navigation has traditionally been tested in animals with the radial and the Morris water maze.

Glossary

Allocentric navigation Spatial orientation based on external landmarks rather than an egocentric perspective.
Anterograde amnesia A condition where individuals struggle to form new memories following brain damage.
Beacons Fixed landmarks used to guide navigation.
Declarative or explicit memories Memories that can be consciously recalled, such as facts or personal experiences.
Delayed matching to sample task (DMS) A test used in memory research where an individual must match a previously seen stimulus after a delay.
Delayed non-matching to sample task (DNMS): A memory test where individuals must select a novel stimulus instead of the one they previously saw.
Echoic memories Short-term auditory sensory memories that persist for a few seconds.
Egocentric navigation (also known as non-spatial or route-based navigation) The ability to navigate by using the position of environmental cues with respect to one's location.
Encoding The initial process of converting sensory input into a form that can be stored in memory.
Engrams Physical or neural representations of memories within the brain.
Episodic memories A type of explicit memory related to personal experiences and events.
Haptic memories Sensory memories related to touch, lasting only briefly.
Iconic memories Brief visual sensory memories lasting only milliseconds.
Memory consolidation The process of strengthening and stabilizing memories for long-term storage.
Memory The process of encoding, storing, and retrieving information over time.
Multicomponent model of working memory A framework describing working memory as consisting of multiple subsystems, including visuospatial and phonological components.
Navigation (non-spatial or route-based navigation) A method of finding one's way that relies on learned sequences of movements rather than spatial awareness.
Navigation The ability to move through and understand spatial environments using memory and perceptual cues.
Nondeclarative memories Memories that operate without conscious awareness, including skills and habits.
Proactive interference When previously learned information interferes with the acquisition of new memories.
Procedural memory A form of nondeclarative memory responsible for learning skills and habits, such as riding a bike.
Recall The ability to retrieve information without external cues.
Recognition Identifying previously learned information with the help of cues.
Recollection The reconstruction of memories with contextual and detailed information.
Retrieval The process of accessing stored information from memory.
Retroactive interference When new information disrupts the recall of older memories.
Retrograde amnesia A condition where individuals lose access to past memories, typically due to brain injury.
Signposts Environmental cues that indicate direction or location within an environment.
Standard model of memory consolidation A theory proposing that memories are initially dependent on the hippocampus before being transferred to long-term cortical storage.
Storage The retention of encoded information over time for later retrieval.
Temporally graded retrograde amnesia A form of amnesia where recent memories are more affected than older, well-consolidated ones.
Topographical disorientation A condition where individuals have difficulty recognizing familiar environments or navigating spatially.
Working memory A temporary storage system used for processing and manipulating information in real time.

Module Summary

In the first chapter of this module, we traced the beginnings of cognitive psychology and summarized the works and its historical figures. We then discussed the events that led to a significant turning point in the history of cognitive psychology, commonly known as the cognitive revolution of the 1960s. However, it was pointed out that it is interesting that the idea that the study of learning should include the study of mental constructs such as cognitive maps was first suggested by a behaviorist named Edward Tolman, who also proposed the related concept of latent learning. The first chapter of the present module also defined the branch of psychology known as comparative cognition. Researchers study the differences in cognitive processes that exist across species without committing what is known as the anthropomorphic error but by applying Morgan's canon. This differentiates comparative cognition from comparative ethology. Finally, we discussed the seemingly intelligent behaviors of animals and how they can be explained by social learning, shaping, or a series of stimulus-response associations rather than insight or problem-solving skills.

The second chapter of the module began with a discussion on memory. The different stages of memory were described, followed by a description of how memory lapses can be accounted for by disruptions in either one of these stages. This was followed by a discussion of the registers of memory and the different types of long-term memories, including those that are consciously retrieved and those retrieved unconsciously. This was followed by a discussion about how memories go from an initially fragile state to a more permanent and stable state through the process of memory consolidation. Different types of memory tests used for animals were also discussed. Finally, various ways people and animals navigate their environments were explained, and tasks used to test these abilities were discussed.

Module 10

Application

Mnemonics

What Are Mnemonics?

Mnemonics are methods used to assist memory. They usually work by creating associations between new information to be remembered and information already stored in long-term memory. This is known as elaborative rehearsal. A simple mnemonic could associate a password with a loved one's birth date or address. However, more complex mnemonics can be used to remember lists of words, concepts, digit combinations, people's names, and so on. Many different types of mnemonics exist, and students use them to improve their academic outcomes in many fields of study (Tamkin, 1988; Rubakovic and Steffen, 2011; Tullis and Qiu, 2022). Professional mnemonists also use them to impress audiences. Mnemonics are well worth exploring as their use can improve your grades. You can learn several types of mnemonics in memory champion Joshua Foer's *Moonwalking with Einstein: The Art and Science of Remembering Everything* (Foer, 2011) or in Lorayne and Lucas's older *Memory Book* (1974). However, to get you started immediately, a mnemonic known as the method of loci and a study that attests to its efficacy are described subsequently.

The Method of Loci

The method of loci is a mnemonic that consists of mentally linking to-be-remembered items to locations along a well-known route. The route can consist of a series of landmarks encountered on your way to school, the buildings you see as you make your way around campus, or the rooms in your home. In one study, college students were given a list of 12 grocery items (Table 1-M10 App, List 1) to remember using a chosen strategy (McCabe, 2015). The students were next asked to recall the items on the grocery list, and the percentage of students who remembered the list perfectly was recorded. The students were then asked to learn a second list of items after being taught the method of loci. This consisted of asking the students to draw a map of the college campus with 12 marked locations and asked to imagine walking through a route mapped out by these locations. They were then asked to remember a second list of items (Application Table 1-M10 App, List 2) by associating each item with locations along their campus route. For example, if the first building on their route was the library building, they could imagine that the top floor had a giant taco (the first item in List 2) sticking out of one of the windows. If the second building on their route was the gymnasium, they could imagine a bunch of carrots with legs running in and out of the building and so on for the other items. The method of loci works best when

DOI: 10.4324/9781003491828-42

Table 1-M10 App Lists of items to be remembered.

	List 1	*List 2*
1.	Eggs	Tacos
2.	Milk	Carrots
3.	Bread	Soda
4.	Sugar	Pretzels
5.	Apples	Juice
6.	Jelly	Ice cream
7.	Bacon	Chips
8.	Vinegar	Popsicles
9.	Hot dogs	Bagels
10.	Crackers	Pizza
11.	Cinnamon	Broccoli
12.	Grapes	Cheese

making associations that are out of the ordinary. This will make them more memorable. For example, it is easier to remember carrots with legs running out of a building than to associate the gym with carrots because they are both healthy. It was found that twice as many students demonstrated perfect recall of the list of items they were asked after learning the method of loci than the list they were asked to remember using a method of their choice. Now try the method of loci not just for remembering grocery lists but also for information that can be useful to your academic success, such as remembering the components or stages of a theory.

Are You Thinking Critically?

1. Describe how mnemonics work.
2. Why does the method of loci work best if the associations you make are out of the ordinary?
3. Research and compare the efficacy of different mnemonics. Does the effectiveness of mnemonics depend on the types of material to be remembered?

References

Abramson, L. Y., Metalsky, G. I., & Alloy, L. B. (1989). Hopelessness depression: a theory-based subtype of depression. *Psychol Rev*, *96*, 358–372. https://doi.org/10.1037/0033-295X.96.2.358

Abramson, L. Y., Seligman, M. E., & Teasdale, J. D. (1978). Learned helplessness in humans: critique and reformulation. *J Abnorm Psychol*, *87*(1), 49–74.

Ackerman, K. B., Samudre, M., & Allday, R. A. (2020). Practical components for getting the most from a token economy. *Teach Except Child*, *52*(4), 242–249. https://doi.org/10.1177/0040059919892022

Adamopoulou, E., & Moussiades, L. (2020). *An overview of chatbot technology*. Paper presented at the Artificial Intelligence Applications and Innovations, Cham.

Adibi, M., & Lampl, I. (2021). Sensory adaptation in the whisker-mediated tactile system: physiology, theory, and function. *Front Neurosci*, *15*, 770011. https://doi.org/10.3389/fnins.2021.770011

Afifi, T. O., Brownridge, D. A., Cox, B. J., & Sareen, J. (2006). Physical punishment, childhood abuse and psychiatric disorders. *Child Abuse Negl*, *30*(10), 1093–1103. https://doi.org/10.1016/j.chiabu.2006.04.006

Aggarwal, M., Akamine, Y., Liu, A. W., & Wickens, J. R. (2020). The nucleus accumbens and inhibition in the ventral tegmental area play a causal role in the Kamin blocking effect. *Eur J Neurosci*, *52*(3), 3087–3109. https://doi.org/10.1111/ejn.14732

Ainslie, G., & Herrnstein, R. J. (1981). Preference reversal and delayed reinforcement. *Anim Learn Behav*, *9*(4), 476–482. https://doi.org/10.3758/BF03209777

Alam, N., & Chaudhary, K. (2020). Repeated restraint stress potentiates methylphenidate and modafinil-induced behavioral sensitization in rats. *Naunyn Schmiedeberg's Arch Pharmacol*, *393*(5), 785–795. https://doi.org/10.1007/s00210-019-01790-4

Albo, Z., & Gräff, J. (2018). The mysteries of remote memory. *Philos Trans R Soc Lond B Biol Sci*, *373*(1742). https://doi.org/10.1098/rstb.2017.0029

Alessandri, J., & Lattal, K. A. (2021). Early-extinction effects on a force response of humans. *J Exp Anal Behav*, *115*(3), 667–678. https://doi.org/10.1002/jeab.683

Alferink, L. A., Critchfield, T. S., Hitt, J. L., & Higgins, W. J. (2009). Generality of the matching law as a descriptor of shot selection in basketball. *J Appl Behav Anal*, *42*(3), 595–608. https://doi.org/10.1901/jaba.2009.42-595

Ali, S., Hassan Bin Asad, M. H., Javed, M. A., Javed, T., Al-Kharaman, Y. M., Latif, M., . . . Hussain, I. (2022). A novel synthetic derivative of biaryl guanidine as a potential BACE1 inhibitor, to treat Alzheimer's disease: in-silico, in-vitro and in-vivo evaluation. *Pak J Pharm Sci*, *35*(5), 1339–1345. https://www.ncbi.nlm.nih.gov/pubmed/36451562

Allen, C. T., & Janiszewski, C. A. (1989). Assessing the role of contingency awareness in attitudinal conditioning with implications for advertising research. *J Market Res*, *26*(1), 30–43. https://doi.org/10.2307/3172667

Allen, K. D., & Hine, J. F. (2015). ABA applications in the prevention and treatment of medical problems. In J. K. Luiselli (Ed.), *Clinical and organizational applications of applied behavior analysis* (pp. 95–124). Springer.

Allison, J., & Timberlake, W. (1974). Instrumental and contingent saccharin licking in rats: response deprivation and reinforcement. *Learn Motivat*, *5*(2), 231–247. https://doi.org/10.1016/0023-9690(74)90029–0

Alvarez, P., & Squire, L. R. (1994). Memory consolidation and the medial temporal lobe: a simple network model. *Proc Natl Acad Sci USA*, *91*(15), 7041–7045. https://doi.org/10.1073/pnas.91.15.7041

American Psychiatric Association. (2013). *Diagnostic and statistical manual of mental disorders* (5th ed.). Washington, DC: American Psychiatric Association.

Amsel, A. (1958). The role of frustrative nonreward in noncontinuous reward situations. *Psychol Bull*, *55*(2), 102–119. https://doi.org/10.1037/h0043125

Andersson, M., & Simmons, L. W. (2006). Sexual selection and mate choice. *Trends Ecol Evol*, *21*(6), 296–302. https://doi.org/10.1016/j.tree.2006.03.015

Aparicio, C. F. (2001). Overmatching in rats: the barrier choice paradigm. *J Exp Anal Behav*, *75*(1), 93–106. https://doi.org/10.1901/jeab.2001.75-93

Arwas, S., Rolnick, A., & Lubow, R. E. (1989). Conditioned taste aversion in humans using motion-induced sickness as the US. *Behav Res Ther*, *27*(3), 295–301. https://doi.org/10.1016/0005-7967(89)90049–1

Asaad, W. F., Lauro, P. M., Perge, J. A., & Eskandar, E. N. (2017). Prefrontal neurons encode a solution to the credit-assignment problem. *J Neurosci*, *37*(29), 6995–7007. https://doi.org/10.1523/jneurosci.3311-16.2017

Ateah, C. A., Secco, M. L., & Woodgate, R. L. (2003). The risks and alternatives to physical punishment use with children. *J Pediatr Health Care*, *17*(3), 126–132. https://doi.org/10.1067/mph.2003.18

Athreya, A. P., Vande Voort, J. L., Shekunov, J., Rackley, S. J., Leffler, J. M., McKean, A. J., . . . Croarkin, P. E. (2022). Evidence for machine learning guided early prediction of acute outcomes in the treatment of depressed children and adolescents with antidepressants. *J Child Psychol Psychiatry*, *63*(11), 1347–1358. https://doi.org/10.1111/jcpp.13580

Austin, J. L., & Bevan, D. (2011). Using differential reinforcement of low rates to reduce children's requests for teacher attention. *J Appl Behav Anal*, *44*(3), 451–461. https://doi.org/10.1901/jaba.2011.44-451

Autor, S. M. (1960). *The strength of conditioned reinforcers as a function of frequency and probability of reinforcement*. Harvard University.

Axel Gorostiza, E., Colomb, J., & Brembs, B. (2015). A value-based behavioural choice underlies phototaxis in *Drosophila*. *bioRxiv*, 023846. https://doi.org/10.1101/023846

Ayers, E. D., & Powell, D. A. (2002). Multiple response measures during classical conditioning. *J Neurosci Methods*, *114*(1), 33–38. https://doi.org/10.1016/s0165-0270(01)00505–2

Azrin, N. H. (1960). Effects of punishment intensity during variable-interval reinforcement. *J Exp Anal Behav*, *3*, 123–142. https://doi.org/10.1901/jeab.1960.3-123

Azrin, N. H., & Holz, W. C. (1966). Punishment. In W. K. Honig (Ed.), *Operant behavior: areas of research and application* (pp. 213–270). New York, NY: Appleton-Century-Crofts.

Azrin, N. H., & Holz, W. C. (1966). Punishment. In W. K. Honig (Ed.), *Operant behavior: areas of research and application* (pp. 380–447). Appleton-Century-Crofts.

Azrin, N. H., Holz, W. C., & Hake, D. F. (1963). Fixed-ratio punishment. *J Exp Anal Behav*, *6*, 141–148. https://doi.org/10.1901/jeab.1963.6-141

Azrin, N. H., Hutchinson, R. R., & Hake, D. F. (1966). Extinction-induced aggression. *J Exp Anal Behav*, *9*(3), 191–204. https://doi.org/10.1901/jeab.1966.9-191

Baddeley, A. (2007). *Working memory, thought, and action*. Oxford University Press. https://doi.org/10.1093/acprof:oso/9780198528012.001.0001

Baddeley, A. D., & Hitch, G. J. (1974). Working memory. *Psychol Learn Motiv*, *8*, 47–89. https://doi.org/10.1016/S0079-7421(08)60452-1

Baerends, G. P., & Kruijt, J. P. (1973). Stimulus selection. In R. A. Hinde & J. Stevenson Hinde (Eds.), *Constraints on learning* (pp. 23–50). London: Academic Press.

Bahrick, L. E., Gogate, L. J., & Ruiz, I. (2002). Attention and memory for faces and actions in infancy: the salience of actions over faces in dynamic events. *Child Dev*, *73*, 1629–1643. https://doi.org/10.1111/1467-8624.00495

Bailey, R., Barrow, R., Carr, D., & McCarthy, C. (2013). *The SAGE handbook of philosophy of education*. SAGE Publications Ltd.

Balleine, B. W., & O'Doherty, J. P. (2010). Human and rodent homologies in action control: corticostriatal determinants of goal-directed and habitual action. *Neuropsychopharmacology*, *35*, 48–69.

Barajas Galindo, D. E., Vidal-Casariego, A., Calleja-Fernández, A., Hernández-Moreno, A., Pintor de la Maza, B., Pedraza-Lorenzo, M., . . . Ballesteros-Pomar, M. D. (2017). Appetite disorders in cancer patients: impact on nutritional status and quality of life. *Appetite*, *114*, 23–27. https://doi.org/10.1016/j.appet.2017.03.020

Barber, J. R., Chadwell, B. A., Garrett, N., Schmidt-French, B., & Conner, W. E. (2009). Naive bats discriminate arctiid moth warning sounds but generalize their aposematic meaning. *J Exp Biol*, *212*(Pt 14), 2141–2148. https://doi.org/10.1242/jeb.029991

Bargh, J. A. (1994). The four horsemen of automaticity: intention, awareness, efficiency, and control as separate issues. In R. Wyer & T. Srull (Eds.), *Handbook of social cognition* (pp. 1–2). Lawrence Erlbaum.

Bargh, J. A., Chen, M., & Burrows, L. (1996). Automaticity of social behavior: direct effects of trait construct and stereotype activation on action. *J Pers Soc Psychol*, *71*(2), 230–244. https://doi.org/10.1037/0022-3514.71.2.230

Barlow, D. H., & Durand, V. M. (1995). *Abnormal psychology: an integrative approach*. Belmont, CA: Thomson Brooks/Cole Publishing Co.

Baron, S. G., Gobbini, M. I., Engell, A. D., & Todorov, A. (2011). Amygdala and dorsomedial prefrontal cortex responses to appearance-based and behavior-based person impressions. *Soc Cogn Affect Neurosci*, *6*(5), 572–581. https://doi.org/10.1093/scan/nsq086

Barrett, D. (2007). *Waistland: a (r)evolutionary view of our weight and fitness crisis*. W. W. Norton.

Barrett, D. (2015). Supernormal stimuli in the media. In D. Barrett (Ed.), *Supernormal stimuli: how primal urges overran their evolutionary purpose* (pp. 131–154). Oxford University Press.

Barrett, S. P., Tichauer, M., Leyton, M., & Pihl, R. O. (2006). Nicotine increases alcohol self-administration in non-dependent male smokers. *Drug Alcohol Depend*, *81*(2), 197–204. https://doi.org/10.1016/j.drugalcdep.2005.06.009

Basile, A. G., & Toplak, M. E. (2015). Four converging measures of temporal discounting and their relationships with intelligence, executive functions, thinking dispositions, and behavioral outcomes. *Front Psychol*, *6*, 728. https://doi.org/10.3389/fpsyg.2015.00728

Baum, W. M. (1974). On two types of deviation from the matching law: bias and undermatching. *J Exp Anal Behav*, *22*(1), 231–242. https://doi.org/10.1901/jeab.1974.22-231

Baum, W. M. (2004). Molar and molecular views of choice. *Behav Process*, *66*(3), 349–359. https://doi.org/10.1016/j.beproc.2004.03.013

Baum, W. M. (2012). Mathematics and theory in behavior analysis: remarks on Catania (1981). The flight from experimental analysis. *Euro J Behav Anal*, *13*, 177–179. https://doi.org/10.1080/15021149.2012.11434417

Baum, W. M., & Aparicio, C. (1999). Optimality and concurrent variable-interval variable-ratio schedules. *J Exp Anal Behav*, *71*(1), 75–89. https://doi.org/10.1901/jeab.1999.71-75

Baumeister, R. F., Heatherton, T. F., & Tice, D. M. (1994). *Losing control: how and why people fail at self-regulation*. San Diego, CA: Academic Press.

Bayley, T. M., Dye, L., Jones, S., DeBono, M., & Hill, A. J. (2002). Food cravings and aversions during pregnancy: relationships with nausea and vomiting. *Appetite*, *38*(1), 45–51. https://doi.org/10.1006/appe.2002.0470

Beare, J. I. (2010). On memory and reminiscence Aristotle (ca. 350 b.c.). *Ann Neurosci*, *17*(2), 87–91. https://doi.org/10.5214/ans.0972-7531.1017208

Beck, A. T. (1976). *Cognitive therapy and the emotional disorders*. Oxford, England: International Universities Press.

Beeby, E., & White, K. G. (2013). Preference reversal between impulsive and self-control choice. *J Exp Anal Behav*, *99*(3), 260–276. https://doi.org/10.1002/jeab.23

Beecher, H. K. (1953). Analgesic power and the question of acute tolerance to narcotics in man. *J Pharmacol Exp Ther*, *108*(2), 158–167. https://www.ncbi.nlm.nih.gov/pubmed/13062086

Beilin, H., & Fireman, G. (1999). The foundation of Piaget's theories: mental and physical action. *Adv Child Dev Behav*, *27*, 221–246. https://doi.org/10.1016/s0065-2407(08)60140–8

Bejder, L., Samuels, A., Whitehead, H., Finn, H., & Allen, S. (2009). Impact assessment research: use and misuse of habituation, sensitisation and tolerance in describing wildlife responses to anthropogenic stimuli. *Marine Ecol Progress Ser*, 395, 177–185, 395. https://doi.org/10.3354/meps07979

Beran, M. J., Parrish, A. E., Perdue, B. M., & Washburn, D. A. (2014). Comparative cognition: past, present, and future. *Int J Compar Psychol*, *27*(1), 3–30.

Berlucchi, G., & Buchtel, H. A. (2009). Neuronal plasticity: historical roots and evolution of meaning. *Exp Brain Res*, *192*(3), 307–319. https://doi.org/10.1007/s00221-008-1611-6

Bernstein, I. L. (1978). Learned taste aversions in children receiving chemotherapy. *Science*, *200*(4347), 1302–1303. https://doi.org/10.1126/science.663613

Bernstein, I. L. (1985). Learned food aversions in the progression of cancer and its treatment. *Ann NY Acad Sci*, *443*, 365–380. https://doi.org/10.1111/j.1749-6632.1985.tb27086.x

Bernstein, I. L., & Webster, M. M. (1980). Learned taste aversions in humans. *Physiol Behav*, *25*(3), 363–366. https://doi.org/10.1016/0031-9384(80)90274–7
Berridge, K. C., & Robinson, T. E. (2016). Liking, wanting, and the incentive-sensitization theory of addiction. *Am Psychol*, *71*(8), 670–679. https://doi.org/10.1037/amp0000059
Bessières, B., Nicole, O., & Bontempi, B. (2017). Assessing recent and remote associative olfactory memory in rats using the social transmission of food preference paradigm. *Nat Protoc*, *12*(7), 1415–1436. https://doi.org/10.1038/nprot.2017.050
Betancur, C. (2011). Etiological heterogeneity in autism spectrum disorders: more than 100 genetic and genomic disorders and still counting. *Brain Res*, *1380*, 42–77. https://doi.org/10.1016/j.brainres.2010.11.078
Bickel, W. K., Athamneh, L. N., Basso, J. C., Mellis, A. M., DeHart, W. B., Craft, W. H., & Pope, D. (2019). Excessive discounting of delayed reinforcers as a trans-disease process: update on the state of the science. *Curr Opin Psychol*, *30*, 59–64. https://doi.org/10.1016/j.copsyc.2019.01.005
Biderman, N., Bakkour, A., & Shohamy, D. (2020). What are memories for? The hippocampus bridges past experience with future decisions. *Trends Cogn Sci*, *24*(7), 542–556. https://doi.org/10.1016/j.tics.2020.04.004
Bimpisidis, Z., Konig, N., & Wallen-Mackenzie, A. (2020). Two different real-time place preference paradigms using optogenetics within the ventral tegmental area of the mouse. *J Vis Exp* (156). https://doi.org/10.3791/60867
Bird, C. D., & Emery, N. J. (2009). Insightful problem solving and creative tool modification by captive nontool-using rooks. *Proc Natl Acad Sci USA*, *106*(25), 10370–10375. https://doi.org/10.1073/pnas.0901008106
Blaisdell, A. P., Gunther, L. M., & Miller, R. R. (1999). Recovery from blocking achieved by extinguishing the blocking CS. *Anim Learn Behav*, *27*(1), 63–76. https://doi.org/10.3758/bf03199432
Blanchard, R. J., & Blanchard, D. C. (1969). Crouching as an index of fear. *J Comp Physiol Psychol*, *67*(3), 370–375. https://doi.org/10.1037/h0026779
Blankenship, M. R., Finn, P. R., & Steinmetz, J. E. (2000). A characterization of approach and avoidance learning in high-alcohol-drinking (HAD) and low-alcohol-drinking (LAD) rats. *Alcohol Clin Exp Res*, *24*(12), 1778–1784.
Bleich, S. N., Wolfson, J. A., Vine, S., & Wang, Y. C. (2014). Diet-beverage consumption and caloric intake among US adults, overall and by body weight. *Am J Public Health*, *104*(3), e72–78. https://doi.org/10.2105/ajph.2013.301556
Bliss, T. V., & Lomo, T. (1973). Long-lasting potentiation of synaptic transmission in the dentate area of the anaesthetized rabbit following stimulation of the perforant path. *J Physiol*, *232*(2), 331–356. https://doi.org/10.1113/jphysiol.1973.sp010273
Blodgett, H. C. (1929). The effect of the introduction of reward upon the maze performance of rats. *Univ Calif Publ Psychol*, *4*, 113–134.
Blodgett, H. C., & McCutchan, K. (1948). Relative strength of place and response learning in the T maze. *J Compar Physiol Psychol*, *41*(1), 17–24. https://doi.org/10.1037/h0061366
Blough, D. S. (1959). Delayed matching in the pigeon. *J Exp Anal Behav*, 2(2), 151–160. https://doi.org/10.1901/jeab.1959.2-151
Boakes, R. A. (1977). Performance on learning to associate a stimulus with positive reinforcement. In H. Davis, & H. M. B. Hurwitz (Eds.), *Operant–Pavlovian interactions* (pp. 67–97). Hillsdale, NJ: Erlbaum.
Boe, E. E., & Church, R. M. (1967). Permanent effects of punishment during extinction. *J Comp Physiol Psychol*, *63*(3), 486–492. https://doi.org/10.1037/h0024632
Boeke, E. A., Moscarello, J. M., LeDoux, J. E., Phelps, E. A., & Hartley, C. A. (2017). Active avoidance: neural mechanisms and attenuation of Pavlovian conditioned responding. *J Neurosci*, *37*(18), 4808–4818. https://doi.org/10.1523/jneurosci.3261-16.2017
Bolles, R. C. (1970). Species-specific defense reactions and avoidance learning. *Psychol Rev*, *77*(1), 32–48. https://doi.org/10.1037/h0028589
Bolles, R. C., & Warren, J. (2014). The acquisition of bar press avoidance as a function of shock intensity. *Psychon Sci*, *3*, 297–298. https://doi.org/10.3758/BF03343145
Bonder, R., & Davis, C. (2022). Associations between food addiction and substance-use disorders: a critical overview of their overlapping patterns of consumption. *Curr Addict Rep*, *9*(4), 326–333. https://doi.org/10.1007/s40429-022-00443-6
Bootzin, R. R., & Perlis, M. L. (2010). Stimulus control therapy. In M. A. Michael Perlis & B. Kuhn (Eds.), *Behavioral treatments for sleep disorders* (p. 404). Academic Press.

Boring, E. G. (1950). *A history of experimental psychology* (2nd ed.). East Norwalk, CT: Appleton-Century-Crofts.

Borrero, J. C., Crisolo, S. S., Tu, Q., Rieland, W. A., Ross, N. A., Francisco, M. T., & Yamamoto, K. Y. (2007). An application of the matching law to social dynamics. *J Appl Behav Anal*, *40*(4), 589–601. https://doi.org/10.1901/jaba.2007.589-601

Bossert, J. M., Marchant, N. J., Calu, D. J., & Shaham, Y. (2013). The reinstatement model of drug relapse: recent neurobiological findings, emerging research topics, and translational research. *Psychopharmacology*, *229*(3), 453–476. https://doi.org/10.1007/s00213-013-3120-y

Boudreau, C. E., & Ferster, D. (2005). Short-term depression in thalamocortical synapses of cat primary visual cortex. *J Neurosci*, *25*(31), 7179–7190. https://doi.org/10.1523/jneurosci.1445-05.2005

Bouton, M. E. (1993). Context, time, and memory retrieval in the interference paradigms of Pavlovian learning. *Psychol Bull*, *114*(1), 80–99. https://doi.org/10.1037/0033-2909.114.1.80

Bouton, M. E., & Broomer, M. C. (2023). Learning to stop responding. *Behav Process*, 104830. https://doi.org/10.1016/j.beproc.2023.104830

Bouton, M. E., Todd, T. P., Vurbic, D., & Winterbauer, N. E. (2011). Renewal after the extinction of free operant behavior. *Learn Behav*, *39*(1), 57–67. https://doi.org/10.3758/s13420-011-0018-6

Bowers, R. I. (2020). Six clarifications for behaviour systems. *Behav Process*, *170*. https://doi.org/10.1016/j.beproc.2019.103987

Bowers, R. I., & Timberlake, W. (2018). Causal reasoning in rats' behaviour systems. *R Soc Open Sci*, *5*(7), 171448.

Boyes, A. (2018). *The healthy mind toolkit: simple strategies to get out of your own way and enjoy your life*. New York, NY: Penguin Putnam Inc.

Breland, K., & Breland, M. (1961). The misbehavior of organisms. *Am Psychol*, *16*, 681–684. https://doi.org/10.1037/h0040090

Brevers, D., Noël, X., Dan, B., & Nils, F. (2011). Sport superstition: mediation of psychological tension on non-professional sportsmen's superstitious rituals. *J Sport Behav*, *34*, 3–24.

Brickman, P., & Campbell, D. T. (1971). Hedonic relativism and planning the good society. In M. H. Appley (Ed.), *Adaptation-level theory: a symposium* (pp. 287–302). Academic Press

Brickman, P., Coates, D., & Janoff-Bulman, R. (1978). Lottery winners and accident victims: is happiness relative? *J Pers Soc Psychol*, *36*(8), 917–927. https://doi.org/10.1037//0022-3514.36.8.917

Broadbent, D. E. (1958). *Perception and communication*. Elmsford, NY: Pergamon Press.

Broadbent, N. J., Gaskin, S., Squire, L. R., & Clark, R. E. (2010). Object recognition memory and the rodent hippocampus. *Learn Mem*, *17*(1), 5–11. https://doi.org/10.1101/lm.1650110

Broberg, D. J., & Bernstein, I. L. (1987). Candy as a scapegoat in the prevention of food aversions in children receiving chemotherapy. *Cancer*, *60*(9), 2344–2347. https://doi.org/10.1002/1097-0142(19871101)60:9<2344::AID-CNCR2820600938>3.0.CO;2-8

Brocardo, P. S., & Gil-Mohapel, J. (2012). Studying learning and memory in animals: a look into cognitive function. In *The encyclopedia of child and adolescent development* (pp. 37–70). Wiley.

Brodziak, A., Kolat, E., & Rozyk-Myrta, A. (2014). In search of memory tests equivalent for experiments on animals and humans. *Med Sci Monit*, *20*, 2733–2739. https://doi.org/10.12659/MSM.891056

Brogden, W. J. (1939). Sensory pre-conditioning. *J Exp Psychol*, *25*(4), 323–332. https://doi.org/10.1037/h0058944

Brooks, D. C. (2000). Recent and remote extinction cues reduce spontaneous recovery. *Q J Exp Psychol B*, *53B*(1), 25–58. https://doi.org/10.1080/027249900392986

Brown, P. L., & Jenkins, H. M. (1968). Auto-shaping of the pigeon's key-peck. *J Exp Anal Behav*, *11*(1), 1–8. https://doi.org/10.1901/jeab.1968.11-1

Buckingham, H. W., & Finger, S. (1997). David Hartley's psychobiological associationism and the legacy of Aristotle. *J Hist Neurosci*, *6*(1), 21–37. https://doi.org/10.1080/09647049709525683

Buono, F., Sprong, M., Lloyd, D., Cutter, C., Printz Pereira, D., Sullivan, R., & Moore, B. (2017). Delay discounting of video game players: comparison of time duration among gamers. *Cyberpsychol Behav Soc Netw*, *20*. https://doi.org/10.1089/cyber.2016.0451

Cadoni, C., Pisanu, A., Solinas, M., Acquas, E., & Chiara, G. (2001). Behavioral sensitization after repeated exposure to Δ9-tetrahydrocannabinol and cross-sensitization with morphine. *Psychopharmacology*, *158*(3), 259–266. https://doi.org/10.1007/s002130100875

Cain, C. K., & LeDoux, J. E. (2007). Escape from fear: a detailed behavioral analysis of two atypical responses reinforced by CS termination. *J Exp Psychol Anim Behav Process*, *33*(4), 451–463. https://doi.org/10.1037/0097-7403.33.4.451
Cajal, S. R. Y., & Azoulay, L. (1995). *Histology of the nervous system of man and vertebrates* (N. Swanson & L. W. Swanson, Trans.). Oxford University Press. (Original work published 1909–1911).
Camarini, R., Marianno, P., & Rae, M. (2018). Chapter three—Social factors in ethanol sensitization. In M. F. Olive & S. E. Tomek (Eds.), *International review of neurobiology* (Vol. 140, pp. 53–80). Academic Press.
Campos, A. C., Fogaca, M. V., Aguiar, D. C., & Guimaraes, F. S. (2013). Animal models of anxiety disorders and stress. *Braz J Psychiatry*, *35*(Suppl. 2), S101–111. https://doi.org/10.1590/1516-4446-2013-1139
Capaldi, E. J. (1966). Partial reinforcement: a hypothesis of sequential effects. *Psychol Rev*, *73*(5), 459–477. https://doi.org/10.1037/h0023684
Carson, S. H. (2011). Creativity and psychopathology: a shared vulnerability model. *Can J Psychiatry*, *56*(3), 144–153. https://doi.org/10.1177/070674371105600304
Carson, S. H., Peterson, J. B., & Higgins, D. M. (2003). Decreased latent inhibition is associated with increased creative achievement in high-functioning individuals. *J Pers Soc Psychol*, *85*(3), 499–506. https://doi.org/10.1037/0022-3514.85.3.499
Catania, A. C. (1973). The concept of the operant in the analysis of behavior. *Behaviorism*, *1*(2), 103–116.
Cavalier, A. R., Ferretti, R. P., & Hodges, A. E. (1997). Self-management within a classroom token economy for students with learning disabilities. *Res Dev Disabil*, *18*(3), 167–178. https://doi.org/10.1016/s0891-4222(96)00045–5
Cecala, K. K., Noggle, W., & Burns, S. (2017). Negative phototaxis results from avoidance of light and temperature in stream salamander larvae. *J Herpetol*, *51*(2), 263–269, 267. https://doi.org/10.1670/16-083
Cengher, M., Ramazon, N. H., & Strohmeier, C. W. (2020). Using extinction to increase behavior: capitalizing on extinction-induced response variability to establish mands with autoclitic frames. *Anal Verbal Behav*, *36*(1), 102–114. https://doi.org/10.1007/s40616-019-00118-w
Centonze, D., Siracusano, A., Calabresi, P., & Bernardi, G. (2004). The project for a scientific psychology (1895): a Freudian anticipation of LTP-memory connection theory. *Brain Res Rev*, *46*(3), 310–314. https://doi.org/10.1016/j.brainresrev.2004.07.006
Chahrour, M., O'Roak, B. J., Santini, E., Samaco, R. C., Kleiman, R. J., & Manzini, M. C. (2016). Current perspectives in autism spectrum disorder: from genes to therapy. *J Neurosci*, *36*(45), 11402–11410. https://doi.org/10.1523/jneurosci.2335-16.2016
Chambers, K. C. (2018). Conditioned taste aversions. *World J Otorhinolaryngol Head Neck Surg*, *4*(1), 92–100. https://doi.org/10.1016/j.wjorl.2018.02.003
Chance, P. (1999). Thorndike's puzzle boxes and the origins of the experimental analysis of behavior. *J Exp Anal Behav*, *72*(3), 433–440. https://doi.org/10.1901/jeab.1999.72-433
Chapman, T., Rymer, T., & Pillay, N. (2012). Behavioural correlates of urbanisation in the Cape ground squirrel Xerus inauris. *Naturwissenschaften*, *99*(11), 893–902. https://doi.org/10.1007/s00114-012-0971-8
Cheungpasitporn, W., Thongprayoon, C., Edmonds, P. J., Srivali, N., Ungprasert, P., Kittanamongkolchai, W., & Erickson, S. B. (2015). Sugar and artificially sweetened soda consumption linked to hypertension: a systematic review and meta-analysis. *Clin Exp Hypertens*, *37*(7), 587–593. https://doi.org/10.3109/10641963.2015.1026044
Chezan, L. C., Drasgow, E., McWhorter, G. Z., Starkey, K. I. P., & Hurdle, B. M. (2019). Discrimination and generalization of negatively-reinforced mands in young children with autism spectrum disorder. *Behav Modif*, *43*(5), 656–687. https://doi.org/10.1177/0145445518781957
Chittka, L., Rossiter, S., Skorupski, P., & Fernando, C. (2012). What is comparable in comparative cognition? *Philos Trans R Soc Lond B Biol Sci*, *367*, 2677–2685. https://doi.org/10.1098/rstb.2012.0215
Chomsky, N. (1959). Verbal behavior, B. F. Skinner. *Language*, *35*(1), 26–58. https://doi.org/10.2307/411334
Chopra, D., Rehan, H. S., Sharma, V., & Mishra, R. (2016). Chemotherapy-induced adverse drug reactions in oncology patients: a prospective observational survey. *Indian J Med Paediatr Oncol*, *37*(1), 42–46. https://doi.org/10.4103/0971-5851.177015

Christian, K. M., & Thompson, R. F. (2003). Neural substrates of eyeblink conditioning: acquisition and retention. *Learn Mem*, *10*(6), 427–455. https://doi.org/10.1101/lm.59603

Clark, K. R. (2018). Learning theories: cognitivism. *Radiol Technol*, *90*(2), 176–179. https://www.ncbi.nlm.nih.gov/pubmed/30420575

Clark, R. E. (2004). The classical origins of Pavlov's conditioning. *Integr Physiol Behav Sci*, *39*, 279–294. https://doi.org/10.1007/BF02734167

Clark, R. E., Manns, J. R., & Squire, L. R. (2001). Trace and delay eyeblink conditioning: contrasting phenomena of declarative and nondeclarative memory. *Psychol Sci*, *12*(4), 304–308. https://doi.org/10.1111/1467-9280.00356

Clark, R. E., West, A. N., Zola, S. M., & Squire, L. R. (2001). Rats with lesions of the hippocampus are impaired on the delayed nonmatching-to-sample task†. *Hippocampus*, *11*(2), 176–186. https://doi.org/10.1002/hipo.1035

Clark, R. E., & Zola, S. (1998). Trace eyeblink classical conditioning in the monkey: a nonsurgical method and behavioral analysis. *Behav Neurosci*, *112*(5), 1062–1068. https://doi.org/10.1037//0735-7044.112.5.1062

Clear, J. (2018). *Atomic habits: an easy & proven way to build good habits & break bad ones: unabridged*. New York, NY: Penguin Audio.

Clower, W. T. (1998). Early contributions to the reflex chain hypothesis. *J Hist Neurosci*, *7*(1), 32–42. https://doi.org/10.1076/jhin.7.1.32.13099

Cohen, P. S. (1968). Punishment: the interactive effects of delay and intensity of shock. *J Exp Anal Behav*, *11*(6), 789–799. https://doi.org/10.1901/jeab.1968.11-789

Cohen, N. J., Poldrack, R. A., & Eichenbaum, H. (1997). Memory for items and memory for relations in the procedural/declarative memory framework. *Memory (Hove, England)*, *5*(1-2), 131–178. https://doi.org/10.1080/741941149

Colaizzi, J. M., Flagel, S. B., Joyner, M. A., Gearhardt, A. N., Stewart, J. L., & Paulus, M. P. (2020). Mapping sign-tracking and goal-tracking onto human behaviors. *Neurosci Biobehav Rev*, *111*, 84–94. https://doi.org/10.1016/j.neubiorev.2020.01.018

Cole, M. W., & Schneider, W. (2007). The cognitive control network: integrated cortical regions with dissociable functions. *Neuroimage*, *37*(1), 343–360. https://doi.org/10.1016/j.neuroimage.2007.03.071

Colwill, R. M., & Rescorla, R. A. (1985). Postconditioning devaluation of a reinforcer affects instrumental responding. *J Exp Psychol Anim Behav Process*, *11*(1), 120–132. https://doi.org/10.1037/0097-7403.11.1.120

Cong-Lem, N. (2022). Vygotsky's, Leontiev's and Engestrom's cultural-historical (activity) theories: overview, clarifications and implications. *Integr Psychol Behav Sci*, *56*(4), 1091–1112. https://doi.org/10.1007/s12124-022-09703-6

Coussi-Korbel, S., & Fragaszy, D. M. (1995). On the relation between social dynamics and social learning. *Anim Behav*, *50*(6), 1441–1453. https://doi.org/10.1016/0003-3472(95)80001–8

Cowan, N., Saults, J. S., & Nugent, L. D. (1997). The role of absolute and relative amounts of time in forgetting within immediate memory: the case of tone-pitch comparisons. *Psychon Bull Rev*, *4*(3), 393–397. https://doi.org/10.3758/BF03210799

Cowan, W. M., & Kandel, E. R. (2001). A brief history of synapses and synaptic transmission. In W. M. Cowan, T. C. Südhof, & C. F. Stevens (Eds.), *Synapses* (pp. 1–87). Johns Hopkins University Press.

Cox, D., Sosine, J., & Dallery, J. (2017). Application of the matching law to pitch selection in professional baseball. *J Appl Behav Anal*, *50*. https://doi.org/10.1002/jaba.381

Craig, W. (1917). Appetites and aversions as constituents of instincts. *Proc Natl Acad Sci USA*, *3*(12), 685–688. https://doi.org/10.1073/pnas.3.12.685

Crawford, L. L., & Domjan, M. (1996). Conditioned inhibition of social approach in male Japanese quail (Coturnix japonica) using visual exposure to a female. *Behav Process*, *36*(2), 163–169. https://doi.org/10.1016/0376-6357(95)00029–1

Crespi, L. P. (1942). Quantitative variation of incentive and performance in the white rat. *Am J Psychol*, *55*, 467–517. https://doi.org/10.2307/1417120

Creswell, K. G., & Skrzynski, C. J. (2021). The influence of smoking motivation on the associations among cigarette craving, attentional bias to smoking cues, and smoking behavior. *Nicotine Tobacco Res*, *23*(10), 1727–1734. https://doi.org/10.1093/ntr/ntab028

Critchfield, T. S., & Stilling, S. T. (2015). A matching law analysis of risk tolerance and gain–loss framing in football play selection. *Behav Anal Res Pract*, *15*(2), 112–121. https://doi.org/10.1037/bar0000011

Crowder, S. L., Hoogland, A. I., Welniak, T. L., LaFranchise, E. A., Carpenter, K. M., Li, D., . . . Jim, H. S. L. (2022). Metagenomics and chemotherapy-induced nausea: a roadmap for future research. *Cancer*, *128*(3), 461–470. https://doi.org/10.1002/cncr.33892

Cusato, B., & Domjan, M. (1998). Special efficacy of sexual conditioned stimuli that include species typical cues: tests with a conditioned stimuli preexposure design. *Learn Motivat*, *29*(2), 152–167. https://doi.org/10.1006/lmot.1997.0988

D'Alessio, M., Guarino, A., De Pascalis, V., & Zimbardo, P. G. (2003). Testing Zimbardo's stanford time perspective inventory (STPI)—short form. *Time Soc*, *12*(2–3), 333–347. https://doi.org/10.1177/0961463X030122010

Dalton, P. (2000). Psychophysical and behavioral characteristics of olfactory adaptation. *Chem Senses*, *25*(4), 487–492. https://doi.org/10.1093/chemse/25.4.487

Dang, J., Liu, X., Xiao, S., Mao, L., Chan, K. T., Li, C., Lin, M., Liu, Z., Luo, Y., Sun, Y., Wu, Y.-H., & Schiöth, H. B. (2020). The beauty of the zero: replications and extensions of the hidden-zero effect in delay discounting tasks. *Soc Psychol Pers Sci*, *12*(4), 544–549. https://doi.org/10.1177/1948550620929454 (Original work published 2021).

Daniels, A. C. (2005). *Other people's habits: how to use positive reinforcement to bring out the best in people around you*. Performance Management Publications.

Danziger, K. (1980). Wundt's psychological experiment in the light of his philosophy of science. *Psychol Res*, *42*, 109–122. https://doi.org/10.1007/BF00308696

Darling, N. (2007). Ecological systems theory: the person in the center of the circles. *Res Human Dev*, *4*(3–4), 203–217. https://doi.org/10.1080/15427600701663023

Darwin, C. (1859). *On the origin of species by means of natural selection, or preservation of favoured races in the struggle for life*. London: John Murray.

Darwin, C. (1871). *The descent of man, and selection in relation to sex* (Vol. 1). London, England: John Murray.

David, D., Cotet, C., Matu, S., Mogoase, C., & Stefan, S. (2018). 50 years of rational-emotive and cognitive-behavioral therapy: a systematic review and meta-analysis. *J Clin Psychol*, *74*(3), 304–318. https://doi.org/10.1002/jclp.22514

Davis, M. (1974). Sensitization of the rat startle response by noise. *J Comp Physiol Psychol*, *87*(3), 571–581. https://doi.org/10.1037/h0036976

Davis, M. (1984). The mammalian startle response. In R. Eaton (Ed.), *Neural mechanisms of startle behavior*. New York, NY: Plenum Publishing Corporation.

Davison, M. C., & Hunter, I. W. (1976). Performance on variable-interval schedules arranged singly and concurrently. *J Exp Anal Behav*, *25*(3), 335–345. https://doi.org/10.1901/jeab.1976.25-335

Dawes, C., Quinn, D., Bickerdike, A., O'Neill, C., Granger, K. T., Pereira, S. C., . . . Moran, P. M. (2022). Latent inhibition, aberrant salience, and schizotypy traits in cannabis users. *Schizophrenia Res Cogn*, *28*. https://doi.org/10.1016/j.scog.2021.100235

de Arriba-Perez, F., Garcia-Mendez, S., Gonzalez-Castano, F. J., & Costa-Montenegro, E. (2022). Automatic detection of cognitive impairment in elderly people using an entertainment chatbot with natural language processing capabilities. *J Ambient Intell Humaniz Comput*, 1–16. https://doi.org/10.1007/s12652-022-03849-2

de Brugada, I., González, F., Cándido, A., & Hall, G. (2021). Contextual control of the retardation of flavour aversion learning by preexposure to the unconditioned stimulus: acquisition or retrieval deficit? *Behav Process*, *188*, 104394. https://doi.org/10.1016/j.beproc.2021.104394

de Wit, H., & Stewart, J. (1981). Reinstatement of cocaine-reinforced responding in the rat. *Psychopharmacology*, *75*(2), 134–143. https://doi.org/10.1007/BF00432175

de Wit, S., Watson, P., Harsay, H. A., Cohen, M. X., van de Vijver, I., & Ridderinkhof, K. R. (2012). Corticostriatal connectivity underlies individual differences in the balance between habitual and goal-directed action control. *J Neurosci*, *32*(35), 12066–12075. https://doi.org/10.1523/jneurosci.1088-12.2012

Deitz, S. M., Repp, A. C., & Deitz, D. E. (1976). Reducing inappropriate classroom behaviour of retarded students through three procedures of differential reinforcement. *J Ment Defic Res*, *20*(3), 155–170. https://doi.org/10.1111/j.1365-2788.1976.tb00940.x

Descartes, R. (1986). *Discourse on method*. New York, NY: Macmillan and London: Collier Macmillan.

Devenport, L. D. (1998). Spontaneous recovery without interference: why remembering is adaptive. *Anim Learn Behav*, *26*(2), 172–181. https://doi.org/10.3758/BF03199210

Deweese, M. M., Versace, F., Kypriotakis, G., Dirba, D., Daniel, C. R., & Schembre, S. M. (2021). Satiety does not affect neuroaffective electrophysiological responses to food-related or emotional visual cues. *Behav Neurosci*, *135*(4), 571–580. https://doi.org/10.1037/bne0000467
Dharni, A. (2020). *Magpie uses stones to drink water just like the crow from the story we read as children.* https://www.indiatimes.com/trending/environment/video-magpie-uses-stones-to-drink-water-thirsty-crow-story-527642.html
Dickinson, A. (1985). Actions and habits: the development of behavioural autonomy. *Philos Trans R Soc Lond B Biol Sci*, *308*(1135), 67–78.
Dickinson, A., & Balleine, B. (2002). The role of learning in motivation. In H. Pashler, & R. Gallistel (Eds.), *Stevens' handbook of experimental psychology* (3rd ed., Vol. 3, pp. 497–533). John Wiley & Sons.
Dickinson, A., Campos, J., Varga, Z. I., & Balleine, B. (1996). Bidirectional instrumental conditioning. *Q J Exp Psychol B*, *49*(4), 289–306. https://doi.org/10.1080/713932637
Dickinson, A., & Dawson, G. R. (1987). Pavlovian processes in the motivational control of instrumental performance. *Q J Exp Psychol*, *39*(3b), 201–213. https://doi.org/10.1080/14640748708402264
Dickinson., A., Watt, A., & Griffiths. (1992). Free-operant acquisition with delayed reinforcement. *Q J Exp Psychol*, *45*, 241–258. https://doi.org/10.1080/14640749208401019
Dickman, S. J. (1990). Functional and dysfunctional impulsivity: personality and cognitive correlates. *J Pers Soc Psychol*, *58*(1), 95–102. https://doi.org/10.1037//0022-3514.58.1.95
Dickman, S. J. (1993). Impulsivity and information processing. In *The impulsive client: theory, research, and treatment* (pp. 151–184). Washington, DC: American Psychological Association.
Diehl, M. M., Bravo-Rivera, C., & Quirk, G. J. (2019). The study of active avoidance: a platform for discussion. *Neurosci Biobehav Rev*, *107*, 229–237. https://doi.org/10.1016/j.neubiorev.2019.09.010
Diener, E., Lucas, R. E., & Scollon, C. N. (2009). Beyond the hedonic treadmill: revising the adaptation theory of well-being. In E. Diener (Ed.), *The science of well-being: the collected works of Ed Diener* (pp. 103–118). Dordrecht: Springer Netherlands.
Diuk, C., Tsai, K., Wallis, J., Botvinick, M., & Niv, Y. (2013). Hierarchical learning induces two simultaneous, but separable, prediction errors in human basal ganglia. *J Neurosci*, *33*(13), 5797–5805. https://doi.org/10.1523/jneurosci.5445-12.2013
Domi, E., Xu, L., Toivainen, S., Nordeman, A., Gobbo, F., Venniro, M., . . . Heilig, M. (2021). A neural substrate of compulsive alcohol use. *Sci Adv*, *7*(34). https://doi.org/10.1126/sciadv.abg9045
Domjan, M., & Best, M. R. (1980). Interference with ingestional aversion learning produced by preexposure to the unconditioned stimulus: associative and nonassociative aspects. *Learn Motivat*, *11*(4), 522–537. https://doi.org/10.1016/0023-9690(80)90031–4
Domjan, M., & Gutierrez, G. (2019). The behavior system for sexual learning. *Behav Process*, *162*, 184–196. https://doi.org/10.1016/j.beproc.2019.01.013
Donders, F. C. (1969). On the speed of mental processes. *Acta Psychol (Amst)*, *30*, 412–431. https://doi.org/10.1016/0001-6918(69)90065–1
Döring, T., & Chittka, L. (2011). How human are insects, and does it matter? *Formosan Entomol*, *31*, 85–99.
Douglas, R. M., & Goddard, G. V. (1975). Long-term potentiation of the perforant path-granule cell synapse in the rat hippocampus. *Brain Res*, *86*(2), 205–215.
Dozois, D. J. A., & Beck, A. T. (2011). Cognitive therapy. In *Acceptance and mindfulness in cognitive behavior therapy: understanding and applying the new therapies* (pp. 26–56). Hoboken, NJ: John Wiley & Sons Inc.
Duhigg, C. a. (2014). *The power of habit: why we do what we do in life and business* (Random House Trade paperback ed.). New York, NY: Random House Trade Paperbacks.
Dunkelberger, B. S., Serway, C. N., & de Belle, J. S. (2008). A biological basis for animal model studies of learning and memory. In A. S. Benjamin, J. S. De Belle, B. Etnyre, & T. A. Polk (Eds.), *Advances in psychology* (Vol. 139, pp. 211–225). Elsevier.
Durrant, J., & Ensom, R. (2012). Physical punishment of children: lessons from 20 years of research. *CMAJ*, *184*(12), 1373–1377. https://doi.org/10.1503/cmaj.101314
Ebbinghaus, H. (1964). *Memory: a contribution to experimental psychology*. New York, NY: Dover Publications.
Edinger, J. D., Arnedt, J. T., Bertisch, S. M., Carney, C. E., Harrington, J. J., Lichstein, K. L., . . . Martin, J. L. (2021). Behavioral and psychological treatments for chronic insomnia disorder in

adults: an American Academy of Sleep Medicine clinical practice guideline. *J Clin Sleep Med*, *17*(2), 255–262. https://doi.org/10.5664/jcsm.8986

Eichstaedt, J. C., Smith, R. J., Merchant, R. M., Ungar, L. H., Crutchley, P., Preoţiuc-Pietro, D., . . . Schwartz, H. A. (2018). Facebook language predicts depression in medical records. *Proc Natl Acad Sci USA*, *115*(44), 11203–11208. https://doi.org/10.1073/pnas.1802331115

Eikelboom, R., & Stewart, J. (1982). Conditioning of drug-induced physiological responses. *Psychol Rev*, *89*(5), 507–528.

Eisenberger, R., Karpman, M., & Trattner, J. (1967). What is the necessary and sufficient condition for reinforcement in the contingency situation? *J Exp Psychol*, *74*(3), 342–350. https://doi.org/10.1037/h0024719

Eisner, T., & Grant, R. P. (1981). Toxicity, odor aversion, and "olfactory aposematism". *Science*, *213*(4506), 476. https://doi.org/10.1126/science.7244647

Ekstrom, A. D., Kahana, M. J., Caplan, J. B., Fields, T. A., Isham, E. A., Newman, E. L., & Fried, I. (2003). Cellular networks underlying human spatial navigation. *Nature*, *425*(6954), 184–188. https://doi.org/10.1038/nature01964

Elliott, S. (2015). *Ockham's Razors: a user's manual*. Cambridge: Cambridge University Press.

Elton, C. (1954). Research on rodent control by the bureau of animal population, September 1939 to July 1947. In D. Chitty (Ed.), *Control of rats and mice* (pp. 1–23). Oxford: Clarendon Press.

Ennaceur, A., & Delacour, J. (1988). A new one-trial test for neurobiological studies of memory in rats. 1: behavioral data. *Behav Brain Res*, *31*(1), 47–59. https://doi.org/10.1016/0166-4328(88)90157-x

Epstein, D. H., Preston, K. L., Stewart, J., & Shaham, Y. (2006). Toward a model of drug relapse: an assessment of the validity of the reinstatement procedure. *Psychopharmacology*, *189*(1), 1–16. https://doi.org/10.1007/s00213-006-0529-6

Epstein, R., Kirshnit, C. E., Lanza, R. P., & Rubin, L. C. (1984). 'Insight' in the pigeon: antecedents and determinants of an intelligent performance. *Nature*, *308*(5954), 61–62. https://doi.org/10.1038/308061a0

Ertel, W. (2018). *Introduction to artificial intelligence*. Springer.

Escobar, M., & Miller, R. (2004). A review of the empirical laws of basic learning in Pavlovian conditioning. *Int J Compar Psychol*, *17*(2), 279–303.

Esmorís-Arranz, F., Pardo-Vazquez, J., & Vázquez-García, G. (2003). Differential effects of forward or simultaneous conditioned stimulus-unconditioned stimulus intervals on the defensive behavior system of the Norway rat (Rattus Norvegicus). *J Exp Psychol Anim Behav Process*, *29*, 334–340. https://doi.org/10.1037/0097-7403.29.4.334

Estes, W. K. (1944). An experimental study of punishment. *Psychol Monogr*, *57*, i–40. https://doi.org/10.1037/h0093550

Etscorn, F., & Stephens, R. (1973). Establishment of conditioned taste aversions with a 24-hour CS-US interval. *Physiol Psychol*, *1*(3), 251–259. https://doi.org/10.3758/BF03326916

Everitt, B. J., Dickinson, A., & Robbins, T. W. (2001). The neuropsychological basis of addictive behaviour. *Brain Res Rev*, *36*(2–3), 129–138. https://doi.org/10.1016/s0165-0173(01)00088–1

Eysenck, S. B. G. (1993). The I_7: development of a measure of impulsivity and its relationship to the superfactors of personality. In *The impulsive client: theory, research, and treatment* (pp. 141–149). Washington, DC: American Psychological Association.

Fagan, J. F., & Detterman, D. K. (1992). The Fagan test of infant intelligence: a technical summary. *J Appl Dev Psychol*, *13*(2), 173–193. https://doi.org/10.1016/0193-3973(92)90028-G

Fairchild, L., & Erwin, W. M. (1977). Physical punishment by parent figures as a model of aggressive behavior in children. *J Genetic Psychol*, *130*(2), 279–284. https://doi.org/10.1080/00221325.1977.10533260

Falligant, J., Boomhower, S., & Pence, S. (2016). Application of the generalized matching law to point-after-touchdown conversions and kicker selection in college football. *Psychol Sport Exerc*, *26*. https://doi.org/10.1016/j.psychsport.2016.07.006

Falligant, J., Cero, I., Kranak, M., & Kurtz, P. (2021). Further application of the generalized matching law to multialternative sports contexts. *J Appl Behav Anal*, *54*(1), 389–402. https://doi.org/10.1002/jaba.757

Fan, J., Ma, C., & Zhong, Y. (2021). A selective overview of deep learning. *Stat Sci*, *36*(2), 264.

Fanselow, M. S. (1980). Conditional and unconditional components of post-shock freezing. *Pavlovian J Biol Sci*, *15*(4), 177–182. https://doi.org/10.1007/BF03001163

Fanselow, M. S. (1990). Factors governing one-trial contextual conditioning. *Anim Learn Behav, 18*(3), 264–270. https://doi.org/10.3758/BF03205285

Fanselow, M. S. (2022). Negative valence systems: sustained threat and the predatory imminence continuum. *Emerg Top Life Sci, 6*(5), 467–477. https://doi.org/10.1042/ETLS20220003

Fanselow, M. S., & Lester, L. S. (1988). A functional behavioristic approach to aversively motivated behavior: predatory imminence as a determinant of the topography of defensive behavior. In *Evolution and learning* (pp. 185–212). Hillsdale, NJ: Lawrence Erlbaum Associates, Inc.

Fanselow, M. S., Lester, L. S., & Helmstetter, F. J. (1988). Changes in feeding and foraging patterns as an antipredator defensive strategy: a laboratory simulation using aversive stimulation in a closed economy. *J Exp Anal Behav, 50*(3), 361–374. https://doi.org/10.1901/jeab.1988.50-361

Fanselow, M. S., & Sigmundi, R. A. (1982). The enhancement and reduction of defensive fighting by naloxone pretreatment. *Physiol Psychol, 10*(3), 313–316. https://doi.org/10.3758/BF03332956

Fareri, D. S., Chang, L. J., & Delgado, M. R. (2012). Effects of direct social experience on trust decisions and neural reward circuitry. *Front Neurosci, 6*, 148. https://doi.org/10.3389/fnins.2012.00148

Farrell, M. R., Ye, Q., Xie, Y., Esteban, J. S. D., & Mahler, S. V. (2022). Ventral pallidum GABA neurons bidirectionally control opioid relapse across rat behavioral models. *bioRxiv*, 2022.2002.2003.479042. https://doi.org/10.1101/2022.02.03.479042

Feijó, F. M., Ballard, C. R., Foletto, K. C., Batista, B. A. M., Neves, A. M., Ribeiro, M. F. M., & Bertoluci, M. C. (2013). Saccharin and aspartame, compared with sucrose, induce greater weight gain in adult Wistar rats, at similar total caloric intake levels. *Appetite, 60*(1), 203–207. https://doi.org/10.1016/j.appet.2012.10.009

FeldmanHall, O., Dunsmoor, J. E., Tompary, A., Hunter, L. E., Todorov, A., & Phelps, E. A. (2018). Stimulus generalization as a mechanism for learning to trust. *Proc Natl Acad Sci USA, 115*(7), E1690–E1697. https://doi.org/10.1073/pnas.1715227115

Feltmann, K., Giuliano, C., Everitt, B. J., Steensland, P., & Alsiö, J. (2018). The effects of the monoamine stabilizer (–)-OSU6162 on binge-like eating and cue-controlled food-seeking behavior in rats. *Neuropsychopharmacology, 43*(3), 617–626. https://doi.org/10.1038/npp.2017.215

Fernando, A. B., Urcelay, G. P., Mar, A. C., Dickinson, A., & Robbins, T. W. (2014). Safety signals as instrumental reinforcers during free-operant avoidance. *Learn Mem, 21*(9), 488–497. https://doi.org/10.1101/lm.034603.114

Ferreira, S. E., Abrahao, K. P., & Souza-Formigoni, M. L. O. (2013). Expression of behavioral sensitization to ethanol is increased by energy drink administration. *Pharmacol Biochem Behav, 110*, 245–248. https://doi.org/10.1016/j.pbb.2013.07.014

Finn, P. R., Kessler, D. N., & Hussong, A. M. (1994). Risk for alcoholism and classical conditioning to signals for punishment: evidence for a weak behavioral inhibition system? *J Abnorm Psychol, 103*(2), 293–301. https://doi.org/10.1037//0021-843x.103.2.293

Fitzwater, M. E., & Reisman, M. N. (1952). Comparisons of forward, simultaneous, backward, and pseudo-conditioning. *J Exp Psychol, 44*(3), 211–214. https://doi.org/10.1037/h0060495

Flaherty, C. F., & Checke, S. (1982). Anticipation of incentive gain. *Anim Learn Behav, 10*(2), 177–182. https://doi.org/10.3758/BF03212267

Flaherty, C. F., Turovsky, J., & Krauss, K. L. (1994). Relative hedonic value modulates anticipatory contrast. *Physiol Behav, 55*(6), 1047–1054. https://doi.org/10.1016/0031-9384(94)90386–7

Foer, J. (2011). *Moonwalking with Einstein: the art and science of remembering everything*. New York, NY: Penguin Press.

Foster, K. R., & Kokko, H. (2009). The evolution of superstitious and superstition-like behavior. *Proc Biol Sci, 276*(1654), 31–37. https://doi.org/10.1098/rspb.2008.0981

Franja, S., Elliston, K. G., & Ferguson, S. G. (2020). Body mass index and stimulus control: results from a real-world study of eating behaviour. *Appetite, 154*, Article 104783. https://doi.org/10.1016/j.appet.2020.104783

Fredrikson, M., Hugdahl, K., & Öhman, A. (1976). Electrodermal conditioning to potentially phobic stimuli in male and female subjects. *Biol Psychol, 4*(4), 305–314. https://doi.org/10.1016/0301-0511(76)90021–1

Freestone, D. M., & Balcı, F. (2019). Bayesian behavioral systems theory. *Behav Process, 168*, 103904. https://doi.org/10.1016/j.beproc.2019.103904

Futagi, Y., Toribe, Y., & Suzuki, Y. (2009). Neurological assessment of early infants. *Curr Pediatric Rev, 5*(2), 65–70. https://doi.org/10.2174/157339609788185730

Galef, B. G., Jr. (1985). Direct and indirect behavioral pathways to the social transmission of food avoidance. *Ann NY Acad Sci*, *443*, 203–215. https://doi.org/10.1111/j.1749-6632.1985.tb27074.x

Galef, B. G., Jr., & Whiskin, E. E. (2003). Socially transmitted food preferences can be used to study long-term memory in rats. *Learn Behav*, *31*(2), 160–164. https://doi.org/10.3758/bf03195978

Garcia, J., & Koelling, R. A. (1966). Relation of cue to consequence in avoidance learning. *Psychonomic Sci*, *4*(1), 123–124. https://doi.org/10.3758/BF03342209

Garcia, J., Ervin, F. R., & Koelling, R. A. (1966). Learning with prolonged delay of reinforcement. *Psychonomic Sci*, *5*, 121–122.

Garcia, J., Kimeldorf, D. J., & Koelling, R. A. (1955). Conditioned aversion to saccharin resulting from exposure to gamma radiation. *Science*, *122*(3160), 157–158. https://www.ncbi.nlm.nih.gov/pubmed/14396377

Gardiner, J. M., & Atema, J. (2007). Sharks need the lateral line to locate odor sources: rheotaxis and eddy chemotaxis. *J Exp Biol*, *210*(11), 1925–1934. https://doi.org/10.1242/jeb.000075

Garnham, A. (2017). *Artificial intelligence: an introduction*. Routledge.

Gaskin, S. (2020). *Behavioral neuroscience: essentials and beyond*. SAGE Publishing.

Gaskin, S., Chai, S. C., & White, N. M. (2005). Inactivation of the dorsal hippocampus does not affect learning during exploration of a novel environment. *Hippocampus*, *15*(8), 1085–1093. https://doi.org/10.1002/hipo.20127

Gaskin, S., Gamliel, A., Tardif, M., Cole, E., & Mumby, D. G. (2009). Incidental (unreinforced) and reinforced spatial learning in rats with ventral and dorsal lesions of the hippocampus. *Behav Brain Res*, *202*(1), 64–70. https://doi.org/10.1016/j.bbr.2009.03.016

Gaskin, S., Tardif, M., Cole, E., Piterkin, P., Kayello, L., & Mumby, D. G. (2010). Object familiarization and novel-object preference in rats. *Behav Process*, *83*(1), 61–71. https://doi.org/10.1016/j.beproc.2009.10.003

Gaskin, S., Tremblay, A., & Mumby, D. G. (2003). Retrograde and anterograde object recognition in rats with hippocampal lesions. *Hippocampus*, *13*(8), 962–969. https://doi.org/10.1002/hipo.10154

Gaskin, S., & White, N. M. (2010). Temporary inactivation of the dorsal entorhinal cortex impairs acquisition and retrieval of spatial information. *Neurobiol Learn Mem*, *93*(2), 203–207. https://doi.org/10.1016/j.nlm.2009.09.012

Gaskin, S., & White, N. M. (2013). Parallel processing of information about location in the amygdala, entorhinal cortex and hippocampus. *Hippocampus*, *23*(11), 1075–1083. https://doi.org/10.1002/hipo.22179

Gaspar, A., Hutka, B., Ernyey, A. J., Tajti, B. T., Varga, B. T., Zadori, Z. S., & Gyertyan, I. (2022). Performance of the intracerebroventricularly injected streptozotocin Alzheimer's disease model in a translationally relevant, aged and experienced rat population. *Sci Rep*, *12*(1), 20247. https://doi.org/10.1038/s41598-022-24292-5

Geiger, F., & Wolfgram, L. (2013). Overshadowing as prevention of anticipatory nausea and vomiting in pediatric cancer patients: study protocol for a randomized controlled trial. *Trials*, *14*(1), 103. https://doi.org/10.1186/1745-6215-14-103

Geller, I., & Seifter, J. (1960). The effects of meprobamate, barbiturates, d-amphetamine and promazine on experimentally induced conflict in the rat. *Psychopharmacologia*, *1*(6), 482–492. https://doi.org/10.1007/BF00429273

Gerevich, J., Bacskai, E., Farkas, L., & Danics, Z. (2005). A case report: Pavlovian conditioning as a risk factor of heroin 'overdose' death. *Harm Reduct J*, *2*, 11. https://doi.org/10.1186/1477-7517-2-11

Gilchrist, R. J., Gunter, L. M., Anderson, S. F., & Wynne, C. D. L. (2021). The click is not the trick: the efficacy of clickers and other reinforcement methods in training naïve dogs to perform new tasks. *PeerJ*, *9*, e10881. https://doi.org/10.7717/peerj.10881

Gillan, C. M., Papmeyer, M., Morein-Zamir, S., Sahakian, B. J., Fineberg, N. A., Robbins, T. W., & de Wit, S. (2011). Disruption in the balance between goal-directed behavior and habit learning in obsessive-compulsive disorder. *Am J Psychiatry*, *168*(7), 718–726. https://doi.org/10.1176/appi.ajp.2011.10071062

Gillaspy, J. A., Jr., Brinegar, J. L., & Bailey, R. E. (2014). Operant psychology makes a splash—in marine mammal training (1955–1965). *J Hist Behav Sci*, *50*(3), 231–248. https://doi.org/10.1002/jhbs.21664

Ginton, A., Urca, G., & Lubow, R. E. (1975). The effects of preexposure to a nonattended stimulus on subsequent learning: latent inhibition in adults. *Bull Psychonomic Soc*, *5*(1), 5–8. https://doi.org/10.3758/BF03336682

Gleeson, S., Ahlers, S. T., Mansbach, R. S., Foust, J. M., & Barrett, J. E. (1989). Behavioral studies with anxiolytic drugs: VI. Effects on punished responding of drugs interacting with serotonin receptor subtypes. *J Pharmacol Exp Therap*, *250*(3), 809–817.
Goldman-Rakic, P. S. (1995). Cellular basis of working memory. *Neuron*, *14*(3), 477–485. https://doi.org/10.1016/0896-6273(95)90304-6
Gonzalez-Gonzalez, C. S., Munoz-Cruz, V., Toledo-Delgado, P. A., & Nacimiento-Garcia, E. (2023). Personalized gamification for learning: a reactive chatbot architecture proposal. *Sensors (Basel)*, *23*(1). https://doi.org/10.3390/s23010545
Goodman, J. (2021). Place vs. response learning: history, controversy, and neurobiology. *Front Behav Neurosci*, *14*. https://doi.org/10.3389/fnbeh.2020.598570
Gormezano, I., Schneiderman, N., Deaux, E., & Fuentes, I. (1962). Nictitating membrane: classical conditioning and extinction in the Albino Rabbit. *Science*, *138*(3536), 33–34. https://doi.org/10.1126/science.138.3536.33
Gorn, G. J. (1982). The effects of music in advertising on choice behavior: a classical conditioning approach. *J Market*, *46*(1), 94–101. https://doi.org/10.1177/002224298204600109
Granger, K. T., Talwar, A., & Barnett, J. H. (2020). Latent inhibition and its potential as a biomarker for schizophrenia. *Biomark Neuropsychiatry*, *3*. https://doi.org/10.1016/j.bionps.2020.100025
Green, L., Myerson, J., & Ostaszewski, P. (1999). Amount of reward has opposite effects on the discounting of delayed and probabilistic outcomes. *J Exp Psychol Learn Mem Cogn*, *25*(2), 418–427. https://doi.org/10.1037/0278-7393.25.2.418
Griffin, D. R. (1992). *Animal minds*. Chicago, IL: University of Chicago Press.
Grigson, P. S. (1997). Conditioned taste aversions and drugs of abuse: a reinterpretation. *Behav Neurosci*, *111*(1), 129–136. https://www.ncbi.nlm.nih.gov/pubmed/9109631
Grigson, P. S. (2008). Reward comparison: the Achilles' heel and hope for addiction. *Drug Discov Today Dis Models*, *5*(4), 227–233. https://doi.org/10.1016/j.ddmod.2009.03.005
Griskevicius, V., Tybur, J. M., Delton, A. W., & Robertson, T. E. (2011). The influence of mortality and socioeconomic status on risk and delayed rewards: a life history theory approach. *J Pers Soc Psychol*, *100*(6), 1015–1026. https://doi.org/10.1037/a0022403
Groves, P. M., & Thompson, R. F. (1970). Habituation: a dual-process theory. *Psychol Rev*, *77*(5), 419–450. https://doi.org/10.1037/h0029810
Grow, L. L., Kelley, M. E., Roane, H. S., & Shillingsburg, M. A. (2008). Utility of extinction-induced response variability for the selection of mands. *J Appl Behav Anal*, *41*(1), 15–24. https://doi.org/10.1901/jaba.2008.41-15
Gulati, S., & Sondhi, V. (2018). Cerebral palsy: an overview. *Indian J Pediatr*, *85*(11), 1006–1016. https://doi.org/10.1007/s12098-017-2475-1
Guttman, N., & Kalish, H. I. (1956). Discriminability and stimulus generalization. *J Exp Psychol*, *51*(1), 79–88. https://doi.org/10.1037/h0046219
Ha, S., Sohn, I. J., Kim, N., Sim, H. J., & Cheon, K. A. (2015). Characteristics of brains in autism spectrum disorder: structure, function and connectivity across the lifespan. *Exp Neurobiol*, *24*(4), 273–284. https://doi.org/10.5607/en.2015.24.4.273
Hanson, H. M. (1957). Discrimination training effect on stimulus generalization gradient for spectrum stimuli. *Science*, *125*(3253), 888–889. https://doi.org/10.1126/science.125.3253.888
Harding, J. W., Wacker, D. P., Berg, W. K., Rick, G., & Lee, J. F. (2004). Promoting response variability and stimulus generalization in martial arts training. *J Appl Behav Anal*, *37*(2), 185–195. https://doi.org/10.1901/jaba.2004.37-185
Harris, J. D. (1943). Habituatory response decrement in the intact organism. *Psychol Bull*, *40*(6), 385–422. https://doi.org/10.1037/h0053918
Haushofer, J., & Fehr, E. (2014). On the psychology of poverty. *Science*, *344*(6186), 862–867. https://doi.org/10.1126/science.1232491
Hayes, S. C. (1989). Nonhumans have not yet shown stimulus equivalence. *J Exp Anal Behav*, *51*(3), 385–392. https://doi.org/10.1901/jeab.1989.51-385
Hearst, E., & Jenkins, H. M. (1974). *Sign-tracking: the stimulus-reinforcer relation and directed action*. Psychonomic Society.
Hebb, D. O. (1949). *The organization of behavior; a neuropsychological theory*. Oxford, England: Wiley.
Helson, H. (1948). Adaptation-level as a basis for a quantitative theory of frames of reference. *Psychol Rev*, *55*, 297–313. https://doi.org/10.1037/h0056721

Hemenway, D., Solnick, S., & Carter, J. (1994). Child-rearing violence. *Child Abuse Negl*, *18*(12), 1011–1020. https://doi.org/10.1016/0145-2134(94)90126–0
Herculano-Houzel, S. (2012). The remarkable, yet not extraordinary, human brain as a scaled-up primate brain and its associated cost. *Proc Natl Acad Sci USA*, *109*(Suppl. 1), 10661–10668. https://doi.org/10.1073/pnas.1201895109
Heron, W. T., & Skinner, B. F. (1939). An apparatus for the study of animal behavior. *Psychol Rec*, *3*, 166–176.
Herrera, B. M., & Lindgren, C. M. (2010). The genetics of obesity. *Curr Diabetes Rep*, *10*(6), 498–505. https://doi.org/10.1007/s11892-010-0153-z
Herrnstein, R. J. (1961). Relative and absolute strength of response as a function of frequency of reinforcement. *J Exp Anal Behav*, *4*, 267–272. https://doi.org/10.1901/jeab.1961.4-267
Herrnstein, R. J. (1964). Secondary reinforcement and rate of primary reinforcement. *J Exp Anal Behav*, *7*, 27–36. https://doi.org/10.1901/jeab.1964.7-27
Hilgard, E. R. (1931). Conditioned eyelid reactions to a light stimulus based on the reflex wink to sound. *Psychol Monogr*, *41*(1), i–50. https://doi.org/10.1037/h0093258
Hilgard, E. R., & Marquis, D. G. (1935). Acquisition, extinction, and retention of conditioned lid responses to light in dogs. *J Compar Psychol*, *19*(1), 29–58. https://doi.org/10.1037/h0057836
Hirsh, J., Morisano, D., & Peterson, J. (2008). Delay discounting: interactions between personality and cognitive ability. *J Res Pers*, *42*, 1646–1650. https://doi.org/10.1016/j.jrp.2008.07.005
Hobbes, T. (1968). *Leviathan*. Baltimore, MD: Penguin Books.
Hoch, H., McComas, J. J., Johnson, L., Faranda, N., & Guenther, S. L. (2002). The effects of magnitude and quality of reinforcement on choice responding during play activities. *J Appl Behav Anal*, *35*(2), 171–181. https://doi.org/10.1901/jaba.2002.35-171
Hofmann, S. G., Asnaani, A., Vonk, I. J., Sawyer, A. T., & Fang, A. (2012). The efficacy of cognitive behavioral therapy: a review of meta-analyses. *Cognit Ther Res*, *36*(5), 427–440. https://doi.org/10.1007/s10608-012-9476-1
Holland, P. C. (2018). Stimulus preexposure speeds or slows subsequent acquisition of associative learning depending on learning test procedures and response measure. *Learn Behav*, *46*(2), 134–156. https://doi.org/10.3758/s13420-017-0297-7
Holland, P. C., & Rescorla, R. A. (1975). Second-order conditioning with food unconditioned stimulus. *J Comp Physiol Psychol*, *88*(1), 459–467. https://doi.org/10.1037/h0076219
Holland, P. C., & Straub, J. J. (1979). Differential effects of two ways of devaluing the unconditioned stimulus after Pavlovian appetitive conditioning. *J Exp Psychol Anim Behav Process*, *5*(1), 65–78. https://doi.org/10.1037//0097-7403.5.1.65
Hollard, V., & Davison, M. C. (1971). Preference for qualitatively different reinforcers. *J Exp Anal Behav*, *16*(3), 375–380. https://doi.org/10.1901/jeab.1971.16-375
Holmes, S. J., & Robins, L. N. (1988). The role of parental disciplinary practices in the development of depression and alcoholism. *Psychiatry*, *51*(1), 24–36. https://doi.org/10.1080/00332747.1988.11024377
Holstein, S. E., Barkell, G. A., & Young, M. R. (2021). Caffeine increases alcohol self-administration, an effect that is independent of dopamine D2 receptor function. *Alcohol*, *91*, 61–73. https://doi.org/10.1016/j.alcohol.2020.12.004
Holt, D. D., Glodowski, K., Smits-Seemann, R. R., & Tiry, A. M. (2016). The domain effect in delay discounting: the roles of fungibility and perishability. *Behav Process*, *131*, 47–52. https://doi.org/10.1016/j.beproc.2016.08.006
Honig, A. S., & Wittmer, D. S. (1991). Socialization and discipline for infants and young children. *Early Child Dev Care*, *66*(1), 65–73. https://doi.org/10.1080/0300443910660106
Honig, W. K., & Slivka, R. M. (1964). Stimulus generalization of the effects of punishment. *J Exp Anal Behav*, *7*, 21–25. https://doi.org/10.1901/jeab.1964.7-21
Honig, W. K., & Urcuioli, P. J. (1981). The legacy of Guttman and Kalish (1956): twenty-five years of research on stimulus generalization. *J Exp Anal Behav*, *36*(3), 405–445. https://doi.org/10.1901/jeab.1981.36-405
Hoon, A., Dymond, S., Jackson, J. W., & Dixon, M. R. (2008). Contextual control of slot-machine gambling: replication and extension. *J Appl Behav Anal*, *41*(3), 467–470. https://doi.org/10.1901/jaba.2008.41-467
Hoppitt, W., & Laland, K. N. (2013). *Social learning: an introduction to mechanisms, methods, and models*. Princeton University Press.

Horn, C. C., Kimball, B. A., Wang, H., Kaus, J., Dienel, S., Nagy, A., . . . Andrews, P. L. R. (2013). Why can't rodents vomit? A comparative behavioral, anatomical, and physiological study. *PLoS One*, *8*(4), e60537. https://doi.org/10.1371/journal.pone.0060537

Hoxby, C., & Avery, C. (2013). The missing "one-offs": the hidden supply of high-achieving, low-income students. *Brook Papers Econ Activity*, *44*(1 (Spring)), 1–65. https://EconPapers.repec.org/RePEc:bin:bpeajo:v:44:y:2013:i:2013–01:p:1–65

Hsu, C.-L., & Lin, J. C.-C. (2023). Understanding the user satisfaction and loyalty of customer service chatbots. *J Retail Consum Serv*, *71*, 103211. https://doi.org/10.1016/j.jretconser.2022.103211

http://VH7QX3XE2P.search.serialssolutions.com/?V=1.0&L=VH7QX3XE2P&S=JCs&C=TC0000216164&T=marc&tab=BOOKS

http://www.myilibrary.com?id=232653

http://www.myilibrary.com?id=232653&ref=toc

http://www.myilibrary.com?id=801765

http://www.vlebooks.com/vleweb/product/openreader?id=none&isbn=9781410612403

https://public.ebookcentral.proquest.com/choice/publicfullrecord.aspx?p=227504

https://search.ebscohost.com/login.aspx?direct=true&scope=site&db=nlebk&db=nlabk&AN=1016404

https://search.ebscohost.com/login.aspx?direct=true&scope=site&db=nlebk&db=nlabk&AN=129646

https://www.taylorfrancis.com/books/e/9781135631918

https://www.taylorfrancis.com/books/e/9781315724256

https://www.taylorfrancis.com/books/e/9781317530404

https://www.taylorfrancis.com/books/e/9781410612403

https://www.vlebooks.com/vleweb/product/openreader?id=none&isbn=9781135631901

Huang, W., Hew, K. F., & Fryer, L. K. (2022). Chatbots for language learning—are they really useful? A systematic review of chatbot-supported language learning. *J Comput Assist Learn*, *38*(1), 237–257. https://doi.org/10.1111/jcal.12610

Hugdahl, K., & Ohman, A. (1977). Effects of instruction on acquisition and extinction of electrodermal responses to fear-relevant stimuli. *J Exp Psychol Hum Learn*, *3*(5), 608–618. https://www.ncbi.nlm.nih.gov/pubmed/894220

Hull, C. L. (1930). Knowledge and purpose as habit mechanisms. *Psychol Rev*, *37*(6), 511–525. https://doi.org/10.1037/h0072212

Hull, C. L. (1934). The concept of the habit-family hierarchy, and maze learning. Part I. *Psychol Rev,* 41, 33–54.

Hull, C. L. (1943). *Principles of behavior: an introduction to behavior theory*. Oxford, England: Appleton-Century.

Hultborn, H. (2006). Spinal reflexes, mechanisms and concepts: from Eccles to Lundberg and beyond. *Progress Neurobiol*, *78*(3–5), 215–232.

Hume, D. (1779). An enquiry concerning human understanding. In *Essays and treatises on several subjects, Vol. 2: Containing an enquiry concerning human understanding, a dissertation on the passions, an enquiry concerning the principles of morals, and the natural history of religion* (pp. 3–212). Unknown Publisher.

Humphrey, G. (1933). *The nature of learning in its relation to the living system*. Oxford, England: Harcourt, Brace.

Hyman, I. A. (1997). *The case against spanking: how to discipline your child without hitting*. San-Francisco, CA: Jossey-Bass.

Illescas-Huerta, E., Ramirez-Lugo, L., Sierra, R. O., Quillfeldt, J. A., & Sotres-Bayon, F. (2021). Conflict test battery for studying the act of facing threats in pursuit of rewards. *Front Neurosci*, *15*, 645769. https://doi.org/10.3389/fnins.2021.645769

Imamura, F., O'Connor, L., Ye, Z., Mursu, J., Hayashino, Y., Bhupathiraju, S. N., & Forouhi, N. G. (2015). Consumption of sugar sweetened beverages, artificially sweetened beverages, and fruit juice and incidence of type 2 diabetes: systematic review, meta-analysis, and estimation of population attributable fraction. *BMJ*, *351*, h3576. https://doi.org/10.1136/bmj.h3576

Innis, N. K. (1999). Edward C. Tolman's purposive behaviorism. In *Handbook of behaviorism* (pp. 97–117). San Diego, CA: Academic Press.

Ipser, J. C., Uhlmann, A., Taylor, P., Harvey, B. H., Wilson, D., & Stein, D. J. (2018). Distinct intrinsic functional brain network abnormalities in methamphetamine-dependent patients with and without a history of psychosis. *Addict Biol*, *23*(1), 347–358. https://doi.org/10.1111/adb.12478

Isaac, A. M. C. (2019). Realism without tears I: Müller's doctrine of specific nerve energies. *Stud Hist Philos Sci*, *78*, 83–92. https://doi.org/10.1016/j.shpsa.2019.01.002

Jackson, A. (2013). Animals and scientific research: the ethics that guide us. *Aust Vet J*, *91*(9), N27. https://doi.org/10.1111/avj.12107

Jacobs, J., Weidemann, C., Miller, J., Solway, A., Burke, J., Wei, X.-X., . . . Kahana, M. (2013). Direct recordings of grid-like neuronal activity in human spatial navigation. *Nat Neurosci*, *16*. https://doi.org/10.1038/nn.3466

Jacobsen, P. B., Bovbjerg, D. H., Schwartz, M. D., Andrykowski, M. A., Futterman, A. D., Gilewski, T., . . . Redd, W. H. (1993). Formation of food aversions in cancer patients receiving repeated infusions of chemotherapy. *Behav Res Ther*, *31*(8), 739–748. https://doi.org/10.1016/0005-7967(93)90004-e

James, W. (1890). *The principles of psychology* (Vol. II). New York, NY: Henry Holt and Company.

Jarvis, E. D. (2004). Learned birdsong and the neurobiology of human language. *Ann NY Acad Sci*, *1016*(1), 749–777. https://doi.org/10.1196/annals.1298.038

Jenkins, H. M. (1962). Resistance to extinction when partial reinforcement is followed by regular reinforcement. *J Exp Psychol*, *64*(5), 441–450. https://doi.org/10.1037/h0048700

Jenkins, H. M., & Harrison, R. H. (1962). Generalization gradients of inhibition following auditory discrimination learning. *J Exp Anal Behav*, *5*, 435–441. https://doi.org/10.1901/jeab.1962.5-435

Jenkins, H. M., & Moore, B. R. (1973). The form of the auto-shaped response with food or water reinforcers. *J Exp Anal Behav*, *20*(2), 163–181. https://doi.org/10.1901/jeab.1973.20-163

Jensen, J., Willeit, M., Zipursky, R. B., Savina, I., Smith, A. J., Menon, M., . . . Kapur, S. (2008). The formation of abnormal associations in schizophrenia: neural and behavioral evidence. *Neuropsychopharmacology*, *33*(3), 473–479. https://doi.org/10.1038/sj.npp.1301437

Jensen, R. (2006). Behaviorism, latent learning, and cognitive maps: needed revisions in introductory psychology textbooks. *Behav Anal*, *29*(2), 187–209. https://doi.org/10.1007/BF03392130

Johansen, J. P., Cain, C. K., Ostroff, L. E., & LeDoux, J. E. (2011). Molecular mechanisms of fear learning and memory. *Cell*, *147*(3), 509–524. https://doi.org/10.1016/j.cell.2011.10.009

Jones, M. C. (1991). A laboratory study of fear: the case of Peter. 1924. *J Genet Psychol*, *152*(4), 462–469. https://doi.org/10.1080/00221325.1991.9914707

Joseph, J. S., & Gray, M. J. (2008). Exposure therapy for posttraumatic stress disorder. *J Behav Anal Offender Victim Treatment Prev*, *1*, 69–79. https://doi.org/10.1037/h0100457

Kamin, L. J. (1968). "Attention-like" processes in classical conditioning. In M. R. Jones (Ed.), *Miami symposium on the prediction of behavior, 1967: aversive stimulation* (pp. 9–31). Coral Gables, FL: University of Miami Press.

Kamin, L. J. (1969a). Predictability, surprise, attention, and conditioning. In B. A. Campbell & R. M. Church (Eds.), *Punishment and aversive behavior* (pp. 279–296). New York, NY: Appleton-Century-Crofts.

Kamin, L. J. (1969b). Selective association and conditioning. In N. J. Mackintosh & W. K. Honig (Eds.), *Fundamental issues in associative learning. Proceedings of a symposium held at Dalhousie University, Halifax, June 1968* (pp. 42–64). Halifax: Dalhousie University Press.

Kandel, E. R. (2001). The molecular biology of memory storage: a dialogue between genes and synapses. *Science*, *294*(5544), 1030–1038. https://doi.org/10.1126/science.1067020

Karimi, S., Attarzadeh-Yazdi, G., Yazdi-Ravandi, S., Hesam, S., Azizi, P., Razavi, Y., & Haghparast, A. (2014). Forced swim stress but not exogenous corticosterone could induce the reinstatement of extinguished morphine conditioned place preference in rats: involvement of glucocorticoid receptors in the basolateral amygdala. *Behav Brain Res*, *264*, 43–50. https://doi.org/10.1016/j.bbr.2014.01.045

Kasprow, W. J., Schachtman, T. R., & Miller, R. R. (1987). The comparator hypothesis of conditioned response generation: manifest conditioned excitation and inhibition as a function of relative excitatory strengths of CS and conditioning context at the time of testing. *J Exp Psychol Anim Behav Process*, *13*(4), 395–406. https://www.ncbi.nlm.nih.gov/pubmed/3668477

Kassirer, J. P., & Kopelman, R. I. (1990). Cognition and connectionism. *Hosp Pract (Off Ed)*, *25*(2), 15, 23–16. https://doi.org/10.1080/21548331.1990.11703906
Katz, B., & Lattal, K. A. (2020). An experimental analysis of the extinction-induced response burst. *J Exp Anal Behav*, *114*(1), 24–46. https://doi.org/10.1002/jeab.611
Kehoe, E. J., & White, N. E. (2002). Extinction revisited: similarities between extinction and reductions in US intensity in classical conditioning of the rabbit's nictitating membrane response. *Anim Learn Behav*, *30*(2), 96–111. https://doi.org/10.3758/bf03192912
Keiner, C. (2005). Wartime rat control, rodent ecology, and the rise and fall of chemical rodenticides. *Endeavour*, *29*(3), 119–125. https://doi.org/10.1016/j.endeavour.2005.07.004
Kekic, M., McClelland, J., Bartholdy, S., Chamali, R., Campbell, I. C., & Schmidt, U. (2020). Bad things come to those who do not wait: temporal discounting is associated with compulsive overeating, eating disorder psychopathology and food addiction. *Front Psychiatry*, *10*, 978. https://doi.org/10.3389/fpsyt.2019.00978
Kelchen, R., Goldrick-Rab, S., & Hosch, B. (2017). The costs of college attendance: examining variation and consistency in institutional living cost allowances. *J Higher Educ*, *88*(6), 947–971. https://doi.org/10.1080/00221546.2016.1272092
Kelly, J. F., & Hake, D. F. (1970). An extinction-induced increase in an aggressive response with humans. *J Exp Anal Behav*, *14*(2), 153–164. https://doi.org/10.1901/jeab.1970.14-153
Kent, J. S., Kim, D. J., Newman, S. D., Bolbecker, A. R., O'Donnell, B. F., & Hetrick, W. P. (2020). Investigating cerebellar neural function in schizophrenia using delay eyeblink conditioning: a pilot fMRI study. *Psychiatry Res Neuroimag*, *304*, 111133. https://doi.org/10.1016/j.pscychresns.2020.111133
Khan, M. J., Jamil, B., & Sethi, A. (2020). Learning based on principles of cognitivism. *J Ayub Med Coll Abbottabad*, *32*(4), 585–587. https://www.ncbi.nlm.nih.gov/pubmed/33225671
Khantzian, E. J. (1985). The self-medication hypothesis of addictive disorders: focus on heroin and cocaine dependence. *Am J Psychiatry*, *142*(11), 1259–1264. https://doi.org/10.1176/ajp.142.11.1259
Kida, H., & Mitsushima, D. (2018). Mechanisms of motor learning mediated by synaptic plasticity in rat primary motor cortex. *Neurosci Res*, *128*, 14–18. https://doi.org/10.1016/j.neures.2017.09.008
Kim, C. K., Kalynchuk, L. E., Kornecook, T. J., Mumby, D. G., Dadgar, N. A., Pinel, J. P. J., & Weinberg, J. (1997). Object-recognition and spatial learning and memory in rats prenatally exposed to ethanol. *Behav Neurosci*, *111*(5), 985–995. https://doi.org/10.1037/0735-7044.111.5.985
Kim, M., & Maguire, E. A. (2019). Encoding of 3D head direction information in the human brain. *Hippocampus*, *29*(7), 619–629. https://doi.org/10.1002/hipo.23060
Kim, S. E. (2021). *Why Australia's trash bin–raiding cockatoos are the 'punks of the bird world'*. https://www.smithsonianmag.com/science-nature/cockatoos-learn-open-garbage-bins-observing-their-peers-180978248/
Kim, S.-J., Kim, H.-J., & Kim, K. (2020). Time perspectives and delay of gratification—the role of psychological distance toward the future and perceived possibility of getting a future reward. *Psychol Res Behav Manage*, *13*, 653–663. https://doi.org/10.2147/PRBM.S246443
Kirsch, I., Lynn, S. J., Vigorito, M., & Miller, R. R. (2004). The role of cognition in classical and operant conditioning. *J Clin Psychol*, *60*(4), 369–392. https://doi.org/10.1002/jclp.10251
Klump, B. C., Martin, J. M., Wild, S., Hörsch, J. K., Major, R. E., & Aplin, L. M. (2021). Innovation and geographic spread of a complex foraging culture in an urban parrot. *Science*, *373*(6553), 456–460. https://doi.org/10.1126/science.abe7808
Kohler, W. (1925). *The mentality of apes*. Oxford, England: Harcourt, Brace.
Köksal, F., Domjan, M., & Weisman, G. (1994). Blocking of the sexual conditioning of differentially effective conditioned stimulus objects. *Anim Learn Behav*, *22*(1), 103–111. https://doi.org/10.3758/BF03199962
Konorski, J. (1948). *Conditioned reflexes and neuron organization*. New York, NY: Cambridge University Press.
Konorski, J. (1959). A new method of physiological investigation of recent memory in animals. *Bull Pol Acad Sci Ser VI Biol Sci*, *7*(3), 115–117.
Konorski, J. (1967). *Integrative activity of the brain*. Chicago, IL: University of Chicago Press.
Koob, G. F. (2021). Drug addiction: hyperkatifeia/negative reinforcement as a framework for medications development. *Pharmacol Rev*, *73*(1), 163–201. https://doi.org/10.1124/pharmrev.120.000083

Koob, G. F., & Le Moal, M. (2008). Review. Neurobiological mechanisms for opponent motivational processes in addiction. *Philos Trans R Soc Lond B Biol Sci*, *363*(1507), 3113–3123. https://doi.org/10.1098/rstb.2008.0094

Kräplin, A., Höfler, M., Pooseh, S., Wolff, M., Krönke, K.-M., Goschke, T., . . . Smolka, M. N. (2020). Impulsive decision-making predicts the course of substance-related and addictive disorders. *Psychopharmacology*, *237*(9), 2709–2724. https://doi.org/10.1007/s00213-020-05567-z

Krypotos, A. M., Effting, M., Kindt, M., & Beckers, T. (2015). Avoidance learning: a review of theoretical models and recent developments. *Front Behav Neurosci*, *9*, 189. https://doi.org/10.3389/fnbeh.2015.00189

Kuhail, M. A., Alturki, N., Alramlawi, S., & Alhejori, K. (2023). Interacting with educational chatbots: a systematic review. *Educ Inf Technol*, *28*(1), 973–1018. https://doi.org/10.1007/s10639-022-11177-3

Kuhn, B. N., Kalivas, P. W., & Bobadilla, A.-C. (2019). Understanding addiction using animal models. *Front Behav Neurosci*, *14*. https://doi.org/10.3389/fnbeh.2019.00262

Kunin, D., Gaskin, S., Borjas, M. B., Smith, B. R., & Amit, Z. (2001). Differences in locomotor response to an inescapable novel environment predict sensitivity to aversive effects of amphetamine. *Behav Pharmacol*, *12*(1), 61–67. https://doi.org/10.1097/00008877-200102000-00007

Kunin, D., Gaskin, S., Rogan, F., Smith, B. R., & Amit, Z. (2000). Caffeine promotes ethanol drinking in rats. Examination using a limited-access free choice paradigm. *Alcohol*, *21*(3), 271–277. https://doi.org/10.1016/s0741-8329(00)00101–4

Kunin, D., Latendresse, M. W., Gaskin, S., Smith, B. R., & Amit, Z. (2000). Preexposure effects of nicotine and acetaldehyde on conditioned taste aversion induced by both drugs. *Pharmacol Biochem Behav*, *66*(4), 695–699. https://doi.org/10.1016/s0091-3057(00)00284–7

Kyonka, E. G. E., & Schutte, N. S. (2018). Probability discounting and gambling: a meta-analysis. *Addiction*, *113*(12), 2173–2181. https://doi.org/10.1111/add.14397

Lagerspetz, K. Y. H., & Vainio, L. A. (2006). Thermal behavior of crustaceans. *Biol Rev*, *81*(2), 237–258. https://doi.org/10.1017/S1464793105006998

Langenecker, S. A., Kling, L. R., Crane, N. A., Gorka, S. M., Nusslock, R., Damme, K. S. F., . . . Phan, K. L. (2020). Anticipation of monetary reward in amygdala, insula, caudate are predictors of pleasure sensitivity to d-Amphetamine administration. *Drug Alcohol Depend*, *206*, 107725. https://doi.org/10.1016/j.drugalcdep.2019.107725

Lashley, K. S. (1923). The behavioristic interpretation of consciousness. I. *Psychol Rev*, *30*(4), 237–272.

Lashley, K. S., & Wade, M. (1946). The Pavlovian theory of generalization. *Psychol Rev*, *53*, 72–87. https://doi.org/10.1037/h0059999

Lattal, K. A., Kuroda, T., & Cook, J. E. (2020). Early extinction effects following intermittent reinforcement: little evidence of extinction bursts. *J Exp Anal Behav*, *114*(1), 47–59. https://doi.org/10.1002/jeab.616

Lattal, K. A., & St. Peter Pipkin, C. (2009). Resurgence of previously reinforced responding: research and application. *Behav Anal Today*, *10*(2), 254–266. https://doi.org/10.1037/h0100669

LeDoux, J. E. (2000). Emotion circuits in the brain. *Annual Review of Neuroscience*, *23*(1), 155–184. https://doi.org/10.1146/annurev.neuro.23.1.155

Le Merrer, J., & Stephens, D. N. (2006). Food-induced behavioral sensitization, its cross-sensitization to cocaine and morphine, pharmacological blockade, and effect on food intake. *J Neurosci*, *26*(27), 7163. https://doi.org/10.1523/JNEUROSCI.5345-05.2006

Leaton, R. N. (1976). Long-term retention of the habituation of lick suppression and startle response produced by a single auditory stimulus. *J Exp Psychol Anim Behav Process*, *2*(3), 248–259. https://doi.org/10.1037//0097-7403.2.3.248

Lechner, H. A., Squire, L. R., & Byrne, J. H. (1999). 100 years of consolidation—remembering Müller and Pilzecker. *Learn Mem*, *6*(2), 77–87.

Lee, J. C. (2021). Second-order conditioning in humans. *Front Behav Neurosci*, *15*(146). https://doi.org/10.3389/fnbeh.2021.672628

Lepper, M. R., Greene, D., & Nisbett, R. E. (1973). Undermining children's intrinsic interest with extrinsic reward: a test of the "overjustification" hypothesis. *J Pers Soc Psychol*, *28*, 129–137. https://doi.org/10.1037/h0035519

Leung, H., & Shek, Y. W. E. (2020). Behavioral, cognitive–behavioral, and social learning approaches. In *The encyclopedia of child and adolescent development* (pp. 1–12).Wiley.

Leyton, M. (2022). Does stimulant drug–induced sensitization occur in primates? *J Psychiatry Neurosci*, *47*(2), E148. https://doi.org/10.1503/jpn.220055

Li, S., Tang, Z., Jin, N., Yang, Q., Liu, G., Liu, T., . . . Ma, L. (2022). Uncovering brain differences in preschoolers and young adolescents with autism spectrum disorder using deep learning. *Int J Neural Syst*, *32*(9), 2250044. https://doi.org/10.1142/s0129065722500447

Lieberman, D. A., McIntosh, D. C., & Thomas, G. V. (1979). Learning when reward is delayed: a marking hypothesis. *J Exp Psychol Anim Behav Process*, *5*(3), 224–242. https://doi.org/10.1037/0097-7403.5.3.224

Lim, S. M., Shiau, C. W. C., Cheng, L. J., & Lau, Y. (2022). Chatbot-delivered psychotherapy for adults with depressive and anxiety symptoms: a systematic review and meta-regression. *Behav Ther*, *53*(2), 334–347. https://doi.org/10.1016/j.beth.2021.09.007

Lima, S. L. (1998). Stress and decision making under the risk of predation: recent developments from behavioral, reproductive, and ecological perspectives. *Adv Study Behav*, *27*, 215–290.

Lind, J., Ghirlanda, S., & Enquist, M. (2009). Insight learning or shaping? *Proc Natl Acad Sci USA*, *106*(28), E76; author reply E77. https://doi.org/10.1073/pnas.0906120106

Liu, X. (2016). Chapter 22—Characterization of cue-induced reinstatement of nicotine-seeking behavior in smoking relapse: use of animal models. In V. R. Preedy (Ed.), *Neuropathology of drug addictions and substance misuse* (pp. 237–245). San Diego, CA: Academic Press.

Locke, J. (1948). An essay concerning human understanding, 1690. In *Readings in the history of psychology* (pp. 55–68). East Norwalk, CT: Appleton-Century-Crofts.

Loftus, E. F. (1979). The malleability of human memory: information introduced after we view an incident can transform memory. *Am Scientist*, *67*(3), 312–320. http://www.jstor.org/stable/27849223

Loftus, E. F. (2003). Our changeable memories: legal and practical implications. *Nat Rev Neurosci*, *4*(3), 231–234. https://doi.org/10.1038/nrn1054

Logue, A. W., Ophir, I., & Strauss, K. E. (1981). The acquisition of taste aversions in humans. *Behav Res Ther*, *19*(4), 319–333. https://doi.org/10.1016/0005-7967(81)90053-x

LoLordo, V. M. (2014). Selective associations. In *Mechanisms of learning and motivation* (pp. 367–398). Psychology Press.

Lømo, T. (2003). The discovery of long-term potentiation. *Philos Trans R Soc Lond B Biol Sci*, *358*(1432), 617–620. https://doi.org/10.1098/rstb.2002.1226

Lorayne, H., & Lucas, J. (1974). *The memory book*. New York, NY: Stein and Day.

Lorenz, K. Z. (1950). The comparative method in studying innate behavior patterns. In *Physiological mechanisms in animal behavior (Society's symposium IV)* (pp. 221–268). Oxford, England: Academic Press.

Lorenz, K. Z. (1958). The evolution of behavior. *Sci Am*, *199*(6), 67–82.

Lorenz, K. Z. (1982). *The foundations of ethology: the principal ideas and discoveries in animal behavior* (1st Touchstone ed.). New York, NY: Simon and Schuster.

Lorenz, K. Z., & Tinbergen, N. (1938). Taxis und Instinkthandlung in der Eirollbewegung der Graugans. [Directed and instinctive behavior in the egg rolling movements of the gray goose.]. *Zeitschrift Tierpsychologie*, 2, 1–29. https://doi.org/10.1111/j.1439-0310.1939.tb01558.x

Louis-Sylvestre, J., & Le Magnen, J. (1980). Fall in blood glucose level precedes meal onset in free-feeding rats. *Neurosci Biobehav Rev*, *4*(Suppl. 1), 13–15. https://doi.org/10.1016/0149-7634(80)90041-x

Lubow, R. E. (1989). *Latent inhibition and conditioned attention theory*. Cambridge: Cambridge University Press.

Lubow, R. E., & Gewirtz, J. C. (1995). Latent inhibition in humans: data, theory, and implications for schizophrenia. *Psychol Bull*, *117*(1), 87–103.

Lubow, R. E., & Moore, A. U. (1959). Latent inhibition: the effect of nonreinforced pre-exposure to the conditional stimulus. *J Comp Physiol Psychol*, *52*, 415–419. https://doi.org/10.1037/h0046700

Luiselli, J. K., Colozzi, G. A., Helfen, C. S., & Pollow, R. S. (1980). Differential reinforcement of incompatible behavior (DRI) in treating classroom management problems of developmentally disabled children. *Psychol Rec*, *30*(2), 261–270. https://doi.org/10.1007/BF03394676

Luiselli, J. K., & Reed, D. D. (2015). Chapter 21—Applied behavior analysis and sports performance. In H. S. Roane, J. L. Ringdahl, & T. S. Falcomata (Eds.), *Clinical and organizational applications of applied behavior analysis* (pp. 523–553). San Diego, CA: Academic Press.

Lum, J. A. G., & Conti-Ramsden, G. (2013). A review and meta-analysis of studies of declarative and procedural memory in specific language impairment. *Top Lang Disord*, *33*(4), 282–297. https://doi.org/10.1097/01.TLD.0000437939.01237.6a

Lund, B., & Ting, W. (2023). Chatting about ChatGPT: how may AI and GPT impact academia and libraries? *Library Hi Tech News*, *40*.

Lynn, S. K., Cnaani, J., & Papaj, D. R. (2005). Peak shift discrimination learning as a mechanism of signal evolution. *Evolution*, *59*(6), 1300–1305. www.jstor.org/stable/3448907

Mackay, D. G. (1973). Aspects of the theory of comprehension, memory and attention. *Q J Exp Psychol*, *25*(1), 22–40. https://doi.org/10.1080/14640747308400320

MacKillop, J., Amlung, M. T., Few, L. R., Ray, L. A., Sweet, L. H., & Munafò, M. R. (2011). Delayed reward discounting and addictive behavior: a meta-analysis. *Psychopharmacology (Berl)*, *216*(3), 305–321. https://doi.org/10.1007/s00213-011-2229-0

Mackintosh, N. J. (1976). Overshadowing and stimulus intensity. *Anim Learn Behav*, *4*(2), 186–192. https://doi.org/10.3758/bf03214033

Mackintosh, N. J., & Turner, C. (1971). Blocking as a function of novelty of CS and predictability of UCS. *Q J Exp Psychol*, *23*(4), 359–366. https://doi.org/10.1080/14640747108400245

MacMillan, H. L., Boyle, M. H., Wong, M. Y.-Y., Duku, E. K., Fleming, J. E., & Walsh, C. A. (1999). Slapping and spanking in childhood and its association with lifetime prevalence of psychiatric disorders in a general population sample. *Can Med Assoc J*, *161*(7), 805–809. https://www.cmaj.ca/content/cmaj/161/7/805.full.pdf

Macphail, E. M., & Bolhuis, J. J. (2001). The evolution of intelligence: adaptive specializations versus general process. *Biol Rev Camb Philos Soc*, *76*(3), 341–364. https://doi.org/10.1017/s146479310100570x

Madden, G. J., Petry, N. M., Badger, G. J., & Bickel, W. K. (1997). Impulsive and self-control choices in opioid-dependent patients and non-drug-using control patients: drug and monetary rewards. *Exp Clin Psychopharmacol*, *5*(3), 256–262. https://doi.org/10.1037/1064-1297.5.3.256

Magen, E., Dweck, C. S., & Gross, J. J. (2008). The hidden-zero effect: representing a single choice as an extended sequence reduces impulsive choice. *Psychol Sci*, *19*(7), 648–649. https://doi.org/10.1111/j.1467-9280.2008.02137.x

Maier, S. F., & Seligman, M. E. (2016). Learned helplessness at fifty: insights from neuroscience. *Psychol Rev*, *123*(4), 349–367. https://doi.org/10.1037/rev0000033

Malenka, R. C. (2003). The long-term potential of LTP. *Nat Rev Neurosci*, *4*(11), 923–926. https://doi.org/10.1038/nrn1258

Mallan, K. M., Lipp, O. V., & Cochrane, B. (2013). Slithering snakes, angry men and out-group members: what and whom are we evolved to fear? *Cogn Emot*, *27*(7), 1168–1180. https://doi.org/10.1080/02699931.2013.778195

Mancini, A. D., Bonanno, G. A., & Clark, A. E. (2011). Stepping off the hedonic treadmill: individual differences in response to major life events. *J Individ Differ*, *32*, 144–152. https://doi.org/10.1027/1614-0001/a000047

Mandal, J., & Parija, S. C. (2013). Ethics of involving animals in research. *Trop Parasitol*, *3*(1), 4–6. https://doi.org/10.4103/2229-5070.113884

Mansur, B. E., Rodrigues, J. R. V., & Mota, T. (2018). Bimodal patterning discrimination in harnessed honey bees. *Front Psychol*, *9*, 1529. https://doi.org/10.3389/fpsyg.2018.01529

Manza, P., Amandola, M., Tatineni, V., Li, C. R., & Leung, H. C. (2017). Response inhibition in Parkinson's disease: a meta-analysis of dopaminergic medication and disease duration effects. *NPJ Parkinsons Dis*, *3*, 23. https://doi.org/10.1038/s41531-017-0024-2

Marchetti, I., & Possel, P. (2022). Cognitive triad and depressive symptoms in adolescence: specificity and overlap. *Child Psychiatry Hum Dev*. https://doi.org/10.1007/s10578-022-01323-w

Marco-Pallarés, J., Mohammadi, B., Samii, A., & Münte, T. F. (2010). Brain activations reflect individual discount rates in intertemporal choice. *Brain Res*, *1320*, 123–129. https://doi.org/10.1016/j.brainres.2010.01.025

Marczinski, C. A., Fillmore, M. T., Bardgett, M. E., & Howard, M. A. (2011). Effects of energy drinks mixed with alcohol on behavioral control: risks for college students consuming trendy cocktails. *Alcohol Clin Exp Res*, *35*(7), 1282–1292. https://doi.org/10.1111/j.1530-0277.2011.01464.x

Martin, J. A. (1977). Effects of positive and negative adult-child interactions on children's task performance and task preferences. *J Exp Child Psychol*, *23*(3), 493–502. https://doi.org/10.1016/0022-0965(77)90041-8

Martin, N., & Morich, K. (2011). Unconscious mental processes in consumer choice: toward a new model of consumer behavior. *J Brand Manage*, *18*. https://doi.org/10.1057/bm.2011.10

Marx, I., Hacker, T., Yu, X., Cortese, S., & Sonuga-Barke, E. (2018). ADHD and the choice of small immediate over larger delayed rewards: a comparative meta-analysis of performance on simple choice-delay and temporal discounting paradigms. *J Attention Disord*, *25*(2), 171–187. https://doi.org/10.1177/1087054718772138

Matsuzawa, T. (1994). Field experiments on use of stone tools by chimpanzees in the wild. In *Chimpanzee cultures* (pp. 351–370). Cambridge, MA: Harvard University Press.

Mattes, R. D. (1994). Prevention of food aversions in cancer patients during treatment. *Nutr Cancer*, *21*(1), 13–24.

Mattes, R. D., Arnold, C., & Boraas, M. (1987). Management of learned food aversions in cancer patients receiving chemotherapy. *Cancer Treat Rep*, *71*(11), 1071–1078.

Mayer, J. (1955). Regulation of energy intake and the body weight: the glucostatic theory and the lipostatic hypothesis. *Ann N Y Acad Sci*, *63*(1), 15–43. https://doi.org/10.1111/j.1749-6632.1955.tb36543.x

Mazur, J. E. (1981). Optimization theory fails to predict performance of pigeons in a two-response situation. *Science*, *214*(4522), 823–825. https://doi.org/10.1126/science.7292017

Mazur, J. E. (1987). An adjusting procedure for studying delayed reinforcement. In *The effect of delay and of intervening events on reinforcement value* (pp. 55–73). Hillsdale, NJ: Lawrence Erlbaum Associates, Inc.

Mazur, J. E. (2006). Mathematical models and the experimental analysis of behavior. *J Exp Anal Behav*, *85*(2), 275–291. https://doi.org/10.1901/jeab.2006.65-05

McCabe, J. A. (2015). Location, location, location! Demonstrating the mnemonic benefit of the method of loci. *Teach Psychol*, *42*(2), 169–173. https://doi.org/10.1177/0098628315573143

McClure, S. M., Laibson, D. I., Loewenstein, G., & Cohen, J. D. (2004). Separate neural systems value immediate and delayed monetary rewards. *Science*, *306*(5695), 503–507. https://doi.org/10.1126/science.1100907

McCormick, D. A., & Thompson, R. F. (1984). Cerebellum: essential involvement in the classically conditioned eyelid response. *Science*, *223*(4633), 296–299. https://doi.org/10.1126/science.6701513

McDougall, W. (1914). The definition of the sexual instinct. *Proc R Soc Med*, *7*(Sect Psych), 65–88. https://www.ncbi.nlm.nih.gov/pubmed/19978253

McDougall, W. (1919). *An introduction to social psychology* (14th ed.). London: Methuen & Co. Ltd.

McLenon, J., & Rogers, M. A. M. (2019). The fear of needles: a systematic review and meta-analysis. *J Adv Nurs*, *75*(1), 30–42. https://doi.org/10.1111/jan.13818

Meehl, P. E. (1950). On the circularity of the law of effect. *Psychol Bull*, *47*(1), 52–75. https://doi.org/10.1037/h0058557

Meunier, M., Bachevalier, J., Mishkin, M., & Murray, E. A. (1993). Effects on visual recognition of combined and separate ablations of the entorhinal and perirhinal cortex in rhesus monkeys. *J Neurosci*, *13*(12), 5418–5432. https://doi.org/10.1523/jneurosci.13-12-05418.1993

Meyer, U., Chang, D. L., Feldon, J., & Yee, B. K. (2004). Expression of the CS- and US-pre-exposure effects in the conditioned taste aversion paradigm and their abolition following systemic amphetamine treatment in C57BL6/J mice. *Neuropsychopharmacology*, *29*(12), 2140–2148. https://doi.org/10.1038/sj.npp.1300522

Michael, J. (1975). *Behaviorism*, *3*(1), 33–44. http://www.jstor.org/stable/27758829

Miller, E. K., & Cohen, J. D. (2001). An integrative theory of prefrontal cortex function. *Annu Rev Neurosci*, *24*, 167–202. https://doi.org/10.1146/annurev.neuro.24.1.167

Miller, G. A. (1956). The magical number seven plus or minus two: some limits on our capacity for processing information. *Psychol Rev*, *63*(2), 81–97. https://www.ncbi.nlm.nih.gov/pubmed/13310704

Miller, R. R., Barnet, R. C., & Grahame, N. J. (1995). Assessment of the Rescorla-Wagner model. *Psychol Bull*, *117*(3), 363–386. https://doi.org/10.1037/0033-2909.117.3.363

Miller, R. R., & Matzel, L. D. (1988). The comparator hypothesis: a response rule for the expression of associations. In G. H. Bower (Ed.), *Psychology of learning and motivation* (Vol. 22, pp. 51–92). Academic Press.

Mineka, S., & Oehlberg, K. (2008). The relevance of recent developments in classical conditioning to understanding the etiology and maintenance of anxiety disorders. *Acta Psychol (Amst)*, *127*(3), 567–580. https://doi.org/10.1016/j.actpsy.2007.11.007

Mishkin, M., & Delacour, J. (1975). An analysis of short-term visual memory in the monkey. *J Exp Psychol Anim Behav Process*, *1*(4), 326–334. https://doi.org/10.1037//0097-7403.1.4.326

Moore, B. R. (2004). The evolution of learning. *Biol Rev*, *79*(2), 301–335. https://doi.org/10.1017/S1464793103006225

Morgan, D., & Lee, K. (1996). Extinction-induced response variability in humans. *Psychol Rec*, *46*, 145–159. https://doi.org/10.1007/BF03395168
Morisano, D., Hirsh, J. B., Peterson, J. B., Pihl, R. O., & Shore, B. M. (2010). Setting, elaborating, and reflecting on personal goals improves academic performance. *J Appl Psychol*, *95*(2), 255–264. https://doi.org/10.1037/a0018478
Morris, G., & Derdikman, D. (2022). The chicken and egg problem of grid cells and place cells. *Trends Cogn Sci*. https://doi.org/10.1016/j.tics.2022.11.003
Morris, J. S., Öhman, A., & Dolan, R. J. (1998). Conscious and unconscious emotional learning in the human amygdala. *Nature*, *393*, 467–470. https://doi.org/10.1038/30976
Morris, R. G. M. (1981). Spatial localization does not require the presence of local cues. *Learn Motivat*, *12*(2), 239–260. https://doi.org/10.1016/0023-9690(81)90020–5
Morris, R. G. M., Garrud, P., Rawlins, J. N., & O'Keefe, J. (1982). Place navigation impaired in rats with hippocampal lesions. *Nature*, *297*(5868), 681–683. https://doi.org/10.1038/297681a0
Morrow, J. D., Maren, S., & Robinson, T. E. (2011). Individual variation in the propensity to attribute incentive salience to an appetitive cue predicts the propensity to attribute motivational salience to an aversive cue. *Behav Brain Res*, *220*(1), 238–243. https://doi.org/10.1016/j.bbr.2011.02.013
Morse, W. H., & Skinner, B. F. (1958). Some factors involved in the stimulus control of operant behavior. *J Exp Anal Behav*, *1*, 103–107. https://doi.org/10.1901/jeab.1958.1-103
Moscovitch, A., & LoLordo, V. M. (1968). Role of safety in the Pavlovian backward fear conditioning procedure. *J Comp Physiol Psychol*, *66*(3), 673–678. https://doi.org/10.1037/h0026548
Mowrer, O. H. (1939). A stimulus-response analysis of anxiety and its role as a reinforcing agent. *Psychol Rev*, *46*(6), 553–565.
Mowrer, O. H. (1951). Two-factor learning theory: summary and comment. *Psychol Rev*, *58*(5), 350–354. https://doi.org/10.1037/h0058956
Mowrer, O. H., & Jones, H. (1945). Habit strength as a function of the pattern of reinforcement. *J Exp Psychol*, *35*(4), 293–311. https://doi.org/10.1037/h0056678
Mowrer, O. H., & Viek, P. (1948). An experimental analogue of fear from a sense of helplessness. *J Abnorm Psychol*, *43*(2), 193–200. https://doi.org/10.1037/h0057165
Moyer, J. R., Jr., Deyo, R. A., & Disterhoft, J. F. (1990). Hippocampectomy disrupts trace eye-blink conditioning in rabbits. *Behav Neurosci*, *104*(2), 243–252. https://doi.org/10.1037//0735-7044.104.2.243
Muench, C., Charlet, K., Balderston, N. L., Grillon, C., Heilig, M., Cortes, C. R., . . . Lohoff, F. W. (2021). Fear conditioning and extinction in alcohol dependence: evidence for abnormal amygdala reactivity. *Addict Biol*, *26*(1), e12835. https://doi.org/10.1111/adb.12835
Müller, G. E., & Pilzecker, A. (1900). *Experimentelle Beiträge zur Lehre vom Gedächtniss*. Leipzig: J.A. Barth.
Mumby, D. G., Gaskin, S., Glenn, M. J., Schramek, T. E., & Lehmann, H. (2002). Hippocampal damage and exploratory preferences in rats: memory for objects, places, and contexts. *Learn Mem*, *9*(2), 49–57. https://doi.org/10.1101/lm.41302
Mumby, D. G., Mana, M. J., Pinel, J. P., David, E., & Banks, K. (1995). Pyrithiamine-induced thiamine deficiency impairs object recognition in rats. *Behav Neurosci*, *109*(6), 1209–1214.
Mumby, D. G., & Pinel, J. P. (1994). Rhinal cortex lesions and object recognition in rats. *Behav Neurosci*, *108*(1), 11–18. https://doi.org/10.1037//0735-7044.108.1.11
Mumby, D. G., Pinel, J. P. J., & Wood, E. R. (1990). Nonrecurring-items delayed nonmatching-to-sample in rats: a new paradigm for testing nonspatial working memory. *Psychobiology*, *18*(3), 321–326. https://doi.org/10.3758/BF03327250
Naudé, G. P., Strickland, J. C., Reed, D. D., & Amlung, M. (2021). Delay discounting and neurocognitive performance in young adults with differential patterns of substance use: findings from the human connectome project. *Exp Clin Psychopharmacol*. https://doi.org/10.1037/pha0000469
Naylor, S., & Keogh, B. (1999). Constructivism in classroom: theory into practice. *J Sci Teach Educ*, *10*(2), 93–106. https://doi.org/10.1023/A:1009419914289
Neal, D. T., Wood, W., & Quinn, J. M. (2006). Habits—a repeat performance. *Curr Direct Psychol Sci*, *15*(4), 198–202. https://doi.org/10.1111/j.1467-8721.2006.00435.x
Neal, D. T., Wood, W., Wu, M., & Kurlander, D. (2011). The pull of the past:when do habits persist despite conflict with motives? *Pers Soc Psychol Bull*, *37*(11), 1428–1437. https://doi.org/10.1177/0146167211419863

Neef, N. A., Mace, F. C., Shea, M. C., & Shade, D. (1992). Effects of reinforcer rate and reinforcer quality on time allocation: extensions of matching theory to educational settings. *J Appl Behav Anal*, *25*(3), 691–699. https://doi.org/10.1901/jaba.1992.25-691
Neuringer, A., & Jensen, G. (2010). Operant variability and voluntary action. *Psychol Rev*, *117*(3), 972–993. https://doi.org/10.1037/a0019499
Nickerson, R. S., & Adams, M. J. (1979). Long-term memory for a common object. *Cogn Psychol*, *11*(3), 287–307. https://doi.org/10.1016/0010-0285(79)90013–6
Nielsen, M., Subiaul, F., Galef, B., Zentall, T., & Whiten, A. (2012). Social learning in humans and nonhuman animals: theoretical and empirical dissections. *J Compar Psychol (Washington, D.C.: 1983)*, *126*(2), 109–113. https://doi.org/10.1037/a0027758
Nist, A. N., & Shahan, T. A. (2021). The extinction burst: impact of reinforcement time and level of analysis on measured prevalence. *J Exp Anal Behav*, *116*(2), 131–148. https://doi.org/10.1002/jeab.714
Nyberg, L., McIntosh, A., & Tulving, E. (1998). Functional brain imaging of episodic and semantic memory with positron emission tomography. *J Mol Med, 76*, 48–53. https://doi.org/10.1007/s001090050189
Odum, A. L. (2011). Delay discounting: I'm a k, you're a k. *J Exp Anal Behav*, *96*(3), 427–439. https://doi.org/10.1901/jeab.2011.96-423
Odum, A. L., & Rainaud, C. P. (2003). Discounting of delayed hypothetical money, alcohol, and food. *Behav Process*, *64*(3), 305–313. https://doi.org/10.1016/s0376-6357(03)00145–1
Ohman, A., Eriksson, A., & Olofsson, C. (1975). One-trial learning and superior resistance to extinction of autonomic responses conditioned to potentially phobic stimuli. *J Comp Physiol Psychol*, *88*(2), 619–627. https://doi.org/10.1037/h0078388
Ohman, A., Erixon, G., & Lofberg, I. (1975). Phobias and preparedness: phobic versus neutral pictures as conditioned stimuli for human autonomic responses. *J Abnorm Psychol*, *84*(1), 41–45. https://doi.org/10.1037/h0076255
Öhman, A., Fredrikson, M., Hugdahl, K., & Rimmo, P. A. (1976). The premise of equipotentiality in human classical conditioning: conditioned electrodermal responses to potentially phobic stimuli. *J Exp Psychol Gen*, *105*(4), 313–337. https://doi.org/10.1037//0096-3445.105.4.313
Öhman, A., & Mineka, S. (2001). Fears, phobias, and preparedness: toward an evolved module of fear and fear learning. *Psychol Rev*, *108*(3), 483–522. https://doi.org/10.1037/0033-295x.108.3.483
O'Keefe, J., & Dostrovsky, J. (1971). The hippocampus as a spatial map. Preliminary evidence from unit activity in the freely-moving rat. *Brain Res*, *34*(1), 171–175. https://doi.org/10.1016/0006-8993(71)90358–1
O'Keefe, J., & Nadel, L. (1978). *The hippocampus as a cognitive map*. Oxford: Clarendon Press.
Olds, J., & Milner, P. (1954). Positive reinforcement produced by electrical stimulation of septal area and other regions of rat brain. *J Comp Physiol Psychol*, *47*(6), 419–427. https://doi.org/10.1037/h0058775
Olivetti Belardinelli, M. (2012). The debt of cognitive science to Ulric Neisser. *Cogn Process*, *13*(3), 189–191. https://doi.org/10.1007/s10339-012-0506-4
Olton, D. S., & Samuelson, R. J. (1976). Remembrance of places passed: spatial memory in rats. *J Exp Psychol Anim Behav Process*, *2*(2), 97–116. https://doi.org/10.1037/0097-7403.2.2.97
Ost, L. G., & Hugdahl, K. (1985). Acquisition of blood and dental phobia and anxiety response patterns in clinical patients. *Behav Res Ther*, *23*(1), 27–34. https://doi.org/10.1016/0005-7967(85)90139–1
Osuna-Mascaró, A. J., Mundry, R., Tebbich, S., Beck, S. R., & Auersperg, A. M. I. (2022). Innovative composite tool use by Goffin's cockatoos (Cacatua goffiniana). *Sci Rep*, *12*(1), 1510. https://doi.org/10.1038/s41598-022-05529-9
Oxoby, R., & Finnigan, H. (2007). Developing heuristic-based quality judgments: blocking in consumer choice. *Psychol Market*, *24*, 295–313. https://doi.org/10.1002/mar.20162
Packard, M. G., & McGaugh, J. L. (1996). Inactivation of hippocampus or caudate nucleus with lidocaine differentially affects expression of place and response learning. *Neurobiol Learn Mem*, *65*(1), 65–72. https://doi.org/10.1006/nlme.1996.0007
Papini, M. R., & Bitterman, M. E. (1990). The role of contingency in classical conditioning. *Psychol Rev*, *97*(3), 396–403. https://doi.org/10.1037/0033-295x.97.3.396
Paredes-Ramos, P., Diaz-Morales, J. V., Espinosa-Palencia, M., Coria-Avila, G. A., & Carrasco-Garcia, A. A. (2020). Clicker training accelerates learning of complex behaviors but reduces discriminative abilities of Yucatan Miniature Pigs. *Animals*, *10*(6), 959. https://doi.org/10.3390/ani10060959

Parylak, S. L., Cottone, P., Sabino, V., Rice, K. C., & Zorrilla, E. P. (2012). Effects of CB1 and CRF1 receptor antagonists on binge-like eating in rats with limited access to a sweet fat diet: lack of withdrawal-like responses. *Physiol Behav*, *107*(2), 231–242. https://doi.org/10.1016/j.physbeh.2012.06.017

Pavlov, I. P. (1902). *The work of the digestive glands: lectures by J.P. Pavlov*. London: C. Griffin.

Pavlov, I. P. (1927). *Conditioned reflexes: an investigation of the physiological activity of the cerebral cortex*. Oxford, England: Oxford University Press.

Peels, R. (2019). Replicability and replication in the humanities. *Res Integrity Peer Rev*, *4*(1), 2. https://doi.org/10.1186/s41073-018-0060-4

Pellegrino, R., Sinding, C., Wijk, R., & Hummel, T. (2017). Habituation and adaptation to odors in humans. *Physiol Behav*, *177*. https://doi.org/10.1016/j.physbeh.2017.04.006

Pelloux, Y., Dilleen, R., Economidou, D., Theobald, D., & Everitt, B. (2012). Reduced forebrain serotonin transmission is causally involved in the development of compulsive cocaine seeking in rats. *Neuropsychopharmacology*, *37*, 2505–2514. https://doi.org/10.1038/npp.2012.111

Perry, C. J., Zbukvic, I., Kim, J. H., & Lawrence, A. J. (2014). Role of cues and contexts on drug-seeking behaviour. *Br J Pharmacol*, *171*(20), 4636–4672. https://doi.org/10.1111/bph.12735

Peters, J., & Buchel, C. (2010). Neural representations of subjective reward value. *Behav Brain Res*, *213*(2), 135–141. https://doi.org/10.1016/j.bbr.2010.04.031

Peters, J., & Büchel, C. (2011). The neural mechanisms of inter-temporal decision-making: understanding variability. *Trends Cogn Sci*, *15*(5), 227–239. https://doi.org/10.1016/j.tics.2011.03.002

Petry, N. M. (2011). Contingency management: what it is and why psychiatrists should want to use it. *Psychiatrist*, *35*(5), 161–163. https://doi.org/10.1192/pb.bp.110.031831

Pinsker, H., Kupfermann, I., Castellucci, V., & Kandel, E. (1970). Habituation and dishabituation of the gill-withdrawal reflex in Aplysia. *Science*, *167*(3926), 1740–1742. https://doi.org/10.1126/science.167.3926.1740

Pliskoff, S. S., & Brown, T. G. (1976). Matching with a trio of concurrent variable-interval schedules of reinforcement. *J Exp Anal Behav*, *25*(1), 69–73. https://doi.org/10.1901/jeab.1976.25-69

Pokala, N., & Glater, E. E. (2018). Using optogenetics to understand neuronal mechanisms underlying behavior in *C. elegans*. *J Undergrad Neurosci Educ*, *16*(2), A152–A158. https://www.ncbi.nlm.nih.gov/pubmed/30057497

Polák, J., Rádlová, S., Janovcová, M., Flegr, J., Landová, E., & Frynta, D. (2020). Scary and nasty beasts: self-reported fear and disgust of common phobic animals. *Br J Psychol*, *111*(2), 297–321. https://doi.org/10.1111/bjop.12409

Poling, A., Austinn, J., Snycerski, S., Laraway, S. (2002). Nrgative punishment. In *Encyclopedia of psychotherapy* (Vol. 2). Elsevier.

Poling, A., Weeden, M. A., Redner, R., & Foster, T. M. (2011). Switch hitting in baseball: apparent rule-following, not matching. *J Exp Anal Behav*, *96*(2), 283–289. https://doi.org/10.1901/jeab.2011.96-283

Poulos, A. M., Mehta, N., Lu, B., Amir, D., Livingston, B., Santarelli, A., . . . Fanselow, M. S. (2016). Conditioning- and time-dependent increases in context fear and generalization. *Learn Mem*, *23*(7), 379–385. https://doi.org/10.1101/lm.041400.115

Premack, D. (1959). Toward empirical behavior laws: I. Positive reinforcement. *Psychol Rev*, *66*(4), 219–233. https://doi.org/10.1037/h0040891

Premack, D. (1962). Reversibility of the reinforcement relation. *Science (New York, N.Y.)*, *136*(3512), 255–257.

Pushparaj, A., Pryslawsky, Y., Forget, B., Yan, Y., & Le Foll, B. (2012). Extinction bursts in rats trained to self-administer nicotine or food in 1-h daily sessions. *Am J Transl Res*, *4*, 422–431.

Rachlin, H., Battalio, R., Kagel, J., & Green, L. (1981). Maximization theory in behavioral psychology. *Behav Brain Sci*, *4*(3), 371–388. https://doi.org/10.1017/S0140525X00009407

Rachlin, H., & Green, L. (1972). Commitment, choice and self-control. *J Exp Anal Behav*, *17*(1), 15–22. https://doi.org/10.1901/jeab.1972.17-15

Ramachandran, V. S., & Hirstein, W. (1999). The science of art: a neurological theory of aesthetic experience. *J Conscious Stud*, *6*(6–7), 15–51.

Randich, A., & LoLordo, V. M. (1979). Associative and nonassociative theories of the UCS preexposure phenomenon: implications for Pavlovian conditioning. *Psychol Bull*, *86*(3), 523–548. https://doi.org/10.1037/0033-2909.86.3.523

Rankin, C. H., Abrams, T., Barry, R. J., Bhatnagar, S., Clayton, D. F., Colombo, J., . . . Thompson, R. F. (2009). Habituation revisited: an updated and revised description of the behavioral characteristics of habituation. *Neurobiol Learn Mem*, *92*(2), 135–138. https://doi.org/10.1016/j.nlm.2008.09.012

Rasmussen, E. B., & Newland, M. C. (2009). Quantification of ethanol's antipunishment effect in humans using the generalized matching equation. *J Exp Anal Behav*, *92*(2), 161–180. https://doi.org/10.1901/jeab.2009.92-161

Razran, G. (1954). The conditioned evocation of attitudes (cognitive conditioning?). *J Exp Psychol*, *48*(4), 278–282. https://doi.org/10.1037/h0058778

Razran, G. (1958). Soviet psychology and psychophysiology. *Science*, *128*(3333), 1187–1194. https://doi.org/10.1126/science.128.3333.1187

Read, D., Olivola, C. Y., & Hardisty, D. J. (2017). The value of nothing: asymmetric attention to opportunity costs drives intertemporal decision making. *Manag Sci*, *63*(12), 4277–4297. https://doi.org/10.1287/mnsc.2016.2547

Reeb-Sutherland, B. C., & Fox, N. A. (2015). Eyeblink conditioning: a non-invasive biomarker for neurodevelopmental disorders. *J Autism Dev Disord*, *45*(2), 376–394. https://doi.org/10.1007/s10803-013-1905-9

Reed, D. D., & Kaplan, B. A. (2011). The matching law: a tutorial for practitioners. *Behav Anal Pract*, *4*(2), 15–24. https://doi.org/10.1007/BF03391780

Reissig, C. J., Strain, E. C., & Griffiths, R. R. (2009). Caffeinated energy drinks—a growing problem. *Drug Alcohol Depend*, *99*(1–3), 1–10. https://doi.org/10.1016/j.drugalcdep.2008.08.001

Renner, K. E. (1964). Delay of reinforcement: a historical review. *Psychol Bull*, *61*(5), 341–361. https://doi.org/10.1037/h0048335

Rensink, R. A. (2014). Limits to the usability of iconic memory. *Front Psychol*, *5*, 971. https://doi.org/10.3389/fpsyg.2014.00971

Rescorla, R. A. (1967). Pavlovian conditioning and its proper control procedures. *Psychol Rev*, *74*(1), 71–80. https://doi.org/10.1037/h0024109

Rescorla, R. A. (1997). Spontaneous recovery after Pavlovian conditioning with multiple outcomes. *Anim Learn Behav*, *25*(1), 99–107. https://doi.org/10.3758/BF03199028

Rescorla, R. A. (2004). Spontaneous recovery. *Learn Mem*, *11*(5), 501–509. https://doi.org/10.1101/lm.77504

Rescorla, R. A., & Solomon, R. L. (1967). Two-process learning theory: relationships between Pavlovian conditioning and instrumental learning. *Psychol Rev*, *74*(3), 151–182. https://doi.org/10.1037/h0024475

Rescorla, R. A., & Wagner, A. R. (1972). A theory of Pavlovian conditioning: variations on the effectiveness of reinforcement and non-reinforcement. In A. H. Black & W. F. E. Prokasy (Eds.), *Classical conditioning II: current research and theory* (pp. 64–99). New York, NY: Appleton-Century-Crofts.

Revillo, D. A., Arias, C., & Spear, N. E. (2013). The unconditioned stimulus pre-exposure effect in preweanling rats in taste aversion learning: role of the training context and injection cues. *Dev Psychobiol*, *55*(2), 193–204. https://doi.org/10.1002/dev.21011

Revusky, S. (1971). The role of interference in association over a delay. In W. K. Honig & P. H. R. James (Eds.), *Animal memory*. New York, NY: Academic Press.

Revusky, S. (1977). Learning as a general process with an emphasis on data from feeding experiments. In N. W. Milgram, L. Krames, & T. M. Alloway (Eds.), *Food aversion learning* (pp. 1–71). Boston, MA: Springer US.

Reynolds, B., & Schiffbauer, R. (2005). Delay of gratification and delay discounting: a unifying feedback model of delay-related impulsive behavior. *Psychol Rec*, *55*. https://doi.org/10.1007/BF03395520

Reynolds, G., Field, A. P., & Askew, C. (2017). Learning to fear a second-order stimulus following vicarious learning. *Cogn Emot*, *31*(3), 572–579. https://doi.org/10.1080/02699931.2015.1116978

Reynolds, G. S. (1961). Attention in the pigeon. *J Exp Anal Behav*, *4*(3), 203–208. https://doi.org/10.1901/jeab.1961.4-203

Reynolds, G. S. (1975). *A primer of operant conditioning*. Glenview, IL: Scott, Foresman.

Ribas-Fernandes, José J. F., Solway, A., Diuk, C., McGuire, Joseph T., Barto, Andrew G., Niv, Y., & Botvinick, Matthew M. (2011). A neural signature of hierarchical reinforcement learning. *Neuron*, *71*(2), 370–379. https://doi.org/10.1016/j.neuron.2011.05.042

Rioult-Pedotti, M. S., Friedman, D., Hess, G., & Donoghue, J. P. (1998). Strengthening of horizontal cortical connections following skill learning. *Nat Neurosci*, *1*(3), 230–234. https://doi.org/10.1038/678

Ristau, C. A. (2013). Cognitive ethology. *WIREs Cogn Sci*, *4*(5), 493–509. https://doi.org/10.1002/wcs.1239
Ritz, T., Meuret, A. E., & Ayala, E. S. (2010). The psychophysiology of blood-injection-injury phobia: looking beyond the diphasic response paradigm. *Int J Psychophysiol*, *78*(1), 50–67. https://doi.org/10.1016/j.ijpsycho.2010.05.007
Roane, H. S., Fisher, W. W., & Carr, J. E. (2016). Applied behavior analysis as treatment for autism spectrum disorder. *J Pediatr*, *175*, 27–32. https://doi.org/10.1016/j.jpeds.2016.04.023
Robbins, S. J. (1990). Mechanisms underlying spontaneous recovery in autoshaping. *J Exp Psychol Anim Behav Process*, *16*(3), 235–249. https://doi.org/10.1037/0097-7403.16.3.235
Robinson, T. E., & Berridge, K. C. (1993). The neural basis of drug craving: an incentive-sensitization theory of addiction. *Brain Res Rev*, *18*(3), 247–291. https://doi.org/10.1016/0165-0173(93)90013-p
Robinson, T. E., & Berridge, K. C. (2000). The psychology and neurobiology of addiction: an incentive-sensitization view. *Addiction*, *95*(Suppl. 2), S91–117. https://doi.org/10.1080/09652140050111681
Rodriguez, C. M. (2003). Parental discipline and abuse potential affects on child depression, anxiety, and attributions. *J Marriage Fam*, *65*(4), 809–817. http://www.jstor.org/stable/3599892
Rodriguez-Prieto, I., Fernández-Juricic, E., Martín, J., & Regis, Y. (2008). Antipredator behavior in blackbirds: habituation complements risk allocation. *Behav Ecol*, *20*(2), 371–377. https://doi.org/10.1093/beheco/arn151
Roesmann, K., Wiens, N., Winker, C., Rehbein, M. A., Wessing, I., & Junghoefer, M. (2020). Fear generalization of implicit conditioned facial features—behavioral and magnetoencephalographic correlates. *NeuroImage*, *205*, 116302. https://doi.org/10.1016/j.neuroimage.2019.116302
Romanes, G. J. (1882). *Animal intelligence*. London, Great Britain: Kegan Paul, Trench & Co.
Ross, C., & Neuringer, A. (2002). Reinforcement of variations and repetitions along three independent response dimensions. *Behav Process*, *57*(2–3), 199–209. https://doi.org/10.1016/s0376-6357(02)00014–1
Rotta, K., Kranak, M. P., & Poling, A. (2021). Spikes, tips, and points: matching in college volleyball attacks? *Behav Anal Res Pract*, *21*(1), 42–50. https://doi.org/10.1037/bar0000197
Rousseau, P. V., Matton, F., Lecuyer, R., & Lahaye, W. (2017). The moro reaction: more than a reflex, a ritualized behavior of nonverbal communication. *Infant Behav Dev*, *46*, 169–177. https://doi.org/10.1016/j.infbeh.2017.01.004
Rowlett, J. K., Lelas, S., Tornatzky, W., & Licata, S. C. (2006). Anti-conflict effects of benzodiazepines in rhesus monkeys: relationship with therapeutic doses in humans and role of GABAA receptors. *Psychopharmacology (Berl)*, *184*(2), 201–211. https://doi.org/10.1007/s00213-005-0228-8
Rubakovic, S., & Steffen, C. (2011). Mnemonics in dermatology. *Clin Dermatol*, *29*(5), 523–530. https://doi.org/10.1016/j.clindermatol.2010.09.019
Rutherford, A. (2000). Mary Cover Jones (1896–1987). *Feminist Psychol*, *27*(3).
Ryle, G. (1949). *The concept of mind*. Oxford, England: Barnes & Noble.
Samia, D. S. M., Nakagawa, S., Nomura, F., Rangel, T. F., & Blumstein, D. T. (2015). Increased tolerance to humans among disturbed wildlife. *Nat Commun*, *6*(1), 8877. https://doi.org/10.1038/ncomms9877
Samra, C. K., & Abdijadid, S. (2022). Specific phobia. In *StatPearls*. Treasure Island, FL: StatPearls Publishing.
Saunders, B. T., Yager, L. M., & Robinson, T. E. (2013). Cue-evoked cocaine "craving": role of dopamine in the accumbens core. *J Neurosci*, *33*(35), 13989–14000. https://doi.org/10.1523/JNEUROSCI.0450-13.2013
Schachtman, T., Walker, J., & Fowler, S. (2011). Effects of conditioning in advertising. In *Associative learning and conditioning theory: human and non-human applications*. https://doi.org/10.1093/acprof:oso/9780199735969.003.0157
Schacter, D. L. (1987). Implicit memory: history and current status. *J Exp Psychol Learn Mem Cogn*, *13*(3), 501–518. https://doi.org/10.1037/0278-7393.13.3.501
Schag, K., Teufel, M., Junne, F., Preissl, H., Hautzinger, M., Zipfel, S., & Giel, K. E. (2013). Impulsivity in binge eating disorder: food cues elicit increased reward responses and disinhibition. *PLoS One*, *8*(10), e76542. https://doi.org/10.1371/journal.pone.0076542
Schario, M. E., Bahner, C. A., Widenhofer, T. V., Rajaballey, J. I., & Thatcher, E. J. (2022). Chatbot-assisted care management. *Profess Case Manage*, *27*(1). https://journals.lww.com/professionalcasemanagementjournal/Fulltext/2022/01000/Chatbot_Assisted_Care_Management.6.aspx

Schippers, M. C., & Van Lange, P. A. M. (2006). The psychological benefits of superstitious rituals in top sport: a study among top sportspersons. *J Appl Soc Psychol*, *36*(10), 2532–2553. https://doi.org/10.1111/j.0021-9029.2006.00116.x
Schlosberg, H. (1937). The relationship between success and the laws of conditioning. *Psychol Rev*, *44*(5), 379–394. https://doi.org/10.1037/h0062249
Schneider, S. M., & Morris, E. K. (1987). A history of the term radical behaviorism: from Watson to Skinner. *Behav Anal*, *10*(1), 27–39. https://doi.org/10.1007/bf03392404
Schott, J. M., & Rossor, M. N. (2003). The grasp and other primitive reflexes. *J Neurol Neurosurg Psychiatry*, *74*(5), 558. https://doi.org/10.1136/jnnp.74.5.558
Schultz, W., Dayan, P., & Montague, P. R. (1997). A neural substrate of prediction and reward. *Science*, *275*(5306), 1593–1599. https://doi.org/10.1126/science.275.5306.1593
Scoville, W. B., & Milner, B. (1957). Loss of recent memory after bilateral hippocampal lesions. *J Neurol Neurosurg Psychiatry*, *20*(1), 11–21. https://doi.org/10.1136/jnnp.20.1.11
Seligman, M. E. P. (1970). On the generality of the laws of learning. *Psychol Rev*, *77*(5), 406–418. https://doi.org/10.1037/h0029790
Seligman, M. E. P. (1971). Phobias and preparedness. *Behav Ther*, *2*(3), 307–320. https://doi.org/10.1016/S0005-7894(71)80064-3
Seligman, M. E. P. (1975). *Helplessness: on depression, development, and death*. San Francisco, CA: W. H. Freeman.
Seligman, M. E. P. (2002). *Authentic happiness: using the new positive psychology to realize your potential for lasting fulfillment*. New York, NY: Free Press.
Seligman, M. E. P., & Maier, S. F. (1967). Failure to escape traumatic shock. *J Exp Psychol*, *74*(1), 1–9. https://doi.org/10.1037/h0024514
Seniuk, H. A., Vu, J. P., & Nosik, M. R. (2020). Application of the matching law to mixed martial arts. *J Appl Behav Anal*, *53*(2), 846–856. https://doi.org/10.1002/jaba.653
Seniuk, H. A., Williams, L., Reed, D., & Wright, J. (2015). An examination of matching with multiple response alternatives in professional hockey. *Behav Anal Res Pract*, *15*. https://doi.org/10.1037/bar0000019
Seth, A. K., Baars, B. J., & Edelman, D. B. (2005). Criteria for consciousness in humans and other mammals. *Conscious Cogn*, *14*(1), 119–139. https://doi.org/10.1016/j.concog.2004.08.006
Seymoure, B. M., Raymundo, A., McGraw, K. J., Owen McMillan, W., & Rutowski, R. L. (2018). Environment-dependent attack rates of cryptic and aposematic butterflies. *Curr Zool*, *64*(5), 663–669. https://doi.org/10.1093/cz/zox062
Shaham, Y., Shalev, U., Lu, L., de Wit, H., & Stewart, J. (2003). The reinstatement model of drug relapse: history, methodology and major findings. *Psychopharmacology*, *168*(1–2), 3–20. https://doi.org/10.1007/s00213-002-1224-x
Shahan, T. A., Sutton, G. M., Nist, A. N., & Davison, M. (2023). Aversive control versus stimulus control by punishment. *J Exp Anal Behav*, *119*(1), 104–116. https://doi.org/10.1002/jeab.805
Shalev, U., Highfield, D., Yap, J., & Shaham, Y. (2000). Stress and relapse to drug seeking in rats: studies on the generality of the effect. *Psychopharmacology*, *150*(3), 337–346. https://doi.org/10.1007/s002130000441
Shamosh, N. A., & Gray, J. R. (2008). Delay discounting and intelligence: a meta-analysis. *Intelligence*, *36*(4), 289–305. https://doi.org/10.1016/j.intell.2007.09.004
Sheldon, K. M., & Lyubomirsky, S. (2012). The challenge of staying happier: testing the Hedonic Adaptation Prevention model. *Pers Soc Psychol Bull*, *38*(5), 670–680. https://doi.org/10.1177/0146167212436400
Shettleworth, S. J. (2009a). Animal cognition: deconstructing avian insight. *Curr Biol*, *19*(22), R1039–1040. https://doi.org/10.1016/j.cub.2009.10.022
Shettleworth, S. J. (2009b). *Cognition, evolution, and behavior*. Oxford University Press.
Shettleworth, S. J. (2010). Clever animals and killjoy explanations in comparative psychology. *Trends Cogn Sci*, *14*(11), 477–481. https://doi.org/10.1016/j.tics.2010.07.002
Shih, R., Dubrowski, A., & Carnahan, H. (2009, 18–20 March). *Evidence for haptic memory*. Paper presented at the World Haptics 2009—third Joint EuroHaptics conference and Symposium on Haptic Interfaces for Virtual Environment and Teleoperator Systems.
Sidman, M. (1971). Reading and auditory-visual equivalences. *J Speech Hear Res*, *14*(1), 5–13. https://www.ncbi.nlm.nih.gov/pubmed/5550631

Sidman, M. (2006). The distinction between positive and negative reinforcement: some additional considerations. *Behav Anal*, *29*(1), 135–139. https://doi.org/10.1007/BF03392126
Siegel, S. (1975). Conditioning insulin effects. *J Compar Physiol Psychol*, *89*, 189–199. https://doi.org/10.1037/h0076811
Siegel, S. (2011). The Four-Loko effect. *Perspect Psychol Sci*, *6*(4), 357–362. https://doi.org/10.1177/1745691611409243
Siegel, S., Baptista, M. A., Kim, J. A., McDonald, R. V., & Weise-Kelly, L. (2000). Pavlovian psychopharmacology: the associative basis of tolerance. *Exp Clin Psychopharmacol*, *8*(3), 276–293. https://doi.org/10.1037//1064-1297.8.3.276
Siegel, S., Hinson, R. E., Krank, M. D., & McCully, J. (1982). Heroin "overdose" death: contribution of drug-associated environmental cues. *Science*, *216*(4544), 436–437. https://doi.org/10.1126/science.7200260
Sigafoos, J., Roche, L., O'Reilly, M. F., & Lancioni, G. E. (2021). Persistence of primitive reflexes in developmental disorders. *Curr Dev Disord Rep*, *8*(2), 98–105. https://doi.org/10.1007/s40474-021-00232-2
Silverman, K., Kaminski, B. J., Higgins, S. T., & Brady, J. V. (2011). Behavior analysis and treatment of drug addiction. In *Handbook of applied behavior analysis* (pp. 451–471). New York, NY: The Guilford Press.
Skinner, B. F. (1938). *The behavior of organisms: an experimental analysis*. Oxford, England and New York, NY: Appleton-Century.
Skinner, B. F. (1948). Superstition in the pigeon. *J Exp Psychol*, *38*(2), 168–172. https://doi.org/10.1037/h0055873
Skinner, B. F. (1951). How to teach animals. *Sci Am*, *185*(6), 26–29.
Skinner, B. F. (1953). *Science and human behavior*. Oxford, England: Macmillan and New York, NY: Free Press.
Skinner, B. F. (1956). A case history in scientific method. *Am Psychol*, *11*(5), 221–233. https://doi.org/10.1037/h0047662
Skinner, B. F. (1957). *Verbal behavior*. New York, NY and East Norwalk, CT: Appleton-Century-Crofts.
Skinner, B. F. (1969). *Contingencies of reinforcement*. East Norwalk, CT: Appleton-Century-Crofts.
Skinner, B. F. (1974). *About behaviorism*. Oxford, England: Alfred A. Knopf.
Small, W. S. (1901). Experimental study of the mental process of the rat. II. *Am J Psychol*, *12*(2), 206–239. https://doi.org/10.2307/1412534
Smith, B. R., Horan, J. T., Gaskin, S., & Amit, Z. (1999). Exposure to nicotine enhances acquisition of ethanol drinking by laboratory rats in a limited access paradigm. *Psychopharmacology (Berl)*, *142*(4), 408–412. https://doi.org/10.1007/s002130050906
Smith, J. (1991). The ethics of using animals in biomedical research: the findings of a working party of the Institute of Medical Ethics. *Bull Med Ethics*, *71*, 13–17. https://www.ncbi.nlm.nih.gov/pubmed/11659398
Smith, O. A. Jr., McFarland, W. L., & Taylor, E. (1961). Performance in a shock-avoidance conditioning situation interpreted as pseudoconditioning. *J Compar Physiol Psychol*, *54*(2), 154–157. https://doi.org/10.1037/h0043961
Sokolov, E. N. (1960). Neuronal models of the orienting reflex. In *The central nervous system and behavior*. New York, NY: Josiah Macy Jr. Foundation.
Sokolov, E. N. (1963). Higher nervous functions; the orienting reflex. *Annu Rev Physiol*, *25*, 545–580. https://doi.org/10.1146/annurev.ph.25.030163.002553
Solomon, P. R., Vander Schaaf, E. R., Thompson, R. F., & Weisz, D. J. (1986). Hippocampus and trace conditioning of the rabbit's classically conditioned nictitating membrane response. *Behav Neurosci*, *100*(5), 729–744. https://doi.org/10.1037//0735-7044.100.5.729
Solomon, R. L. (1980). The opponent-process theory of acquired motivation: the costs of pleasure and the benefits of pain. *Am Psychol*, *35*(8), 691–712. https://doi.org/10.1037//0003-066x.35.8.691
Solomon, R. L., & Corbit, J. D. (1974). An opponent-process theory of motivation. I. Temporal dynamics of affect. *Psychol Rev*, *81*(2), 119–145. https://doi.org/10.1037/h0036128
Solomon, R. L., Turner, L. H., & Lessac, M. S. (1968). Some effects of delay of punishment on resistance to temptation in dogs. *J Pers Soc Psychol*, *8*(3), 233–238. https://doi.org/10.1037/h0025567
Sorscher, B., Mel, G. C., Ocko, S. A., Giocomo, L. M., & Ganguli, S. (2023). A unified theory for the computational and mechanistic origins of grid cells. *Neuron*, *111*(1), 121–137 e113. https://doi.org/10.1016/j.neuron.2022.10.003
Spence, K. W. (1937). The differential response in animals to stimuli varying within a single dimension. *Psychol Rev*, *44*(5), 430–444. https://doi.org/10.1037/h0062885

Spence, K. W. (1947). The role of secondary reinforcement in delayed reward learning. *Psychol Rev*, *54*(1), 1–8. https://doi.org/10.1037/h0056533

Spence, K. W. (1956). *Behavior theory and conditioning*. New Haven, CT: Yale University Press.

Sperling, G. (1960). The information available in brief visual presentations. *Psychol Monogr General Appl*, *74*(11), 1–29. https://doi.org/10.1037/h0093759

Squire, L. R., Genzel, L., Wixted, J. T., & Morris, R. G. (2015). Memory consolidation. *Cold Spring Harb Perspect Biol*, *7*(8), a021766. https://doi.org/10.1101/cshperspect.a021766

Squire, L. R., & Zola, S. M. (1996). Structure and function of declarative and nondeclarative memory systems. *Proc Natl Acad Sci U S A*, *93*(24), 13515–13522. https://doi.org/10.1073/pnas.93.24.13515

Sripada, C. S., Gonzalez, R., Phan, K. L., & Liberzon, I. (2011). The neural correlates of intertemporal decision-making: contributions of subjective value, stimulus type, and trait impulsivity. *Hum Brain Mapp*, *32*(10), 1637–1648. https://doi.org/10.1002/hbm.21136

Staats, A. W., & Staats, C. K. (1958). Attitudes established by classical conditioning. *J Abnorm Psychol*, *57*(1), 37–40. https://doi.org/10.1037/h0042782

Staddon, J. E. (1968). Spaced responding and choice: a preliminary analysis. *J Exp Anal Behav*, *11*(6), 669–682. https://doi.org/10.1901/jeab.1968.11-669

Staddon, J. E., & Simmelhag, V. L. (1971). The "supersitition" experiment: a reexamination of its implications for the principles of adaptive behavior. *Psychol Rev*, *78*(1), 3–43. https://doi.org/10.1037/h0030305

Staniloiu, A., & Markowitsch, H. J. (2012). The remains of the day in dissociative amnesia. *Brain Sci*, *2*(2), 101–129. https://doi.org/10.3390/brainsci2020101

Steketee, J. D., & Kalivas, P. W. (2011). Drug wanting: behavioral sensitization and relapse to drug-seeking behavior. *Pharmacol Rev*, *63*(2), 348–365. https://doi.org/10.1124/pr.109.001933

Stephens, D. N., Ripley, T. L., Borlikova, G., Schubert, M., Albrecht, D., Hogarth, L., & Duka, T. (2005). Repeated ethanol exposure and withdrawal impairs human fear conditioning and depresses long-term potentiation in rat amygdala and hippocampus. *Biol Psychiatry*, *58*(5), 392–400. https://doi.org/10.1016/j.biopsych.2005.04.025

Stewart, J. (1983). Conditioned and unconditioned drug effects in relapse to opiate and stimulant drug self-administration. *Progress Neuro Psychopharmacol Biol Psychiatry*, *7*(4), 591–597. https://doi.org/10.1016/0278-5846(83)90030–1

Stojek, M. M. K., & MacKillop, J. (2017). Relative reinforcing value of food and delayed reward discounting in obesity and disordered eating: a systematic review. *Clin Psychol Rev*, *55*, 1–11. https://doi.org/10.1016/j.cpr.2017.04.007

Strapasson, B. A., & de Freitas Araujo, S. (2020). Methodological behaviorism: historical origins of a problematic concept (1923–1973). *Perspect Behav Sci*, *43*(2), 415–429. https://doi.org/10.1007/s40614-020-00253-z

Straus, M. A. (1991). Discipline and deviance: physical punishment of children and violence and other crime in adulthood. *Soc Probl*, *38*(2), 133–154. https://doi.org/10.2307/800524

Stuart, D. G., Schaefer, A. T., Massion, J., Graham, B. A., & Callister, R. J. (2014). Pioneers in CNS inhibition: 1. Ivan M. Sechenov, the first to clearly demonstrate inhibition arising in the brain. *Brain research*, *1548*, 20–48. https://doi.org/10.1016/j.brainres.2013.12.006

Suto, N., Wise, R. A., & Vezina, P. (2011). Dorsal as well as ventral striatal lesions affect levels of intravenous cocaine and morphine self-administration in rats. *Neurosci Lett*, *493*(1–2), 29–32. https://doi.org/10.1016/j.neulet.2011.02.011

Sweeney, M. M., & Shahan, T. A. (2013). Behavioral momentum and resurgence: effects of time in extinction and repeated resurgence tests. *Learn Behav*, *41*(4), 414–424. https://doi.org/10.3758/s13420-013-0116-8

Swithers, S. E., Laboy, A. F., Clark, K., Cooper, S., & Davidson, T. L. (2012). Experience with the high-intensity sweetener saccharin impairs glucose homeostasis and GLP-1 release in rats. *Behav Brain Res*, *233*(1), 1–14. https://doi.org/10.1016/j.bbr.2012.04.024

Takahashi, S., Hombe, T., Matsumoto, S., Ide, K., & Yoda, K. (2022). Head direction cells in a migratory bird prefer north. *Sci Adv*, *8*(5), eabl6848. https://doi.org/10.1126/sciadv.abl6848

Takehara-Nishiuchi, K. (2021). Neurobiology of systems memory consolidation. *Eur J Neurosci*, *54*(8), 6850–6863. https://doi.org/10.1111/ejn.14694

Tamkin, J. A. (1988). Medical Mnemonics. *Postgrad Med*, *83*(1), 114. https://doi.org/10.1080/00325481.1988.11700104

Tanner, R., Ferraro, R., Chartrand, T., Bettman, J., & Baaren, R. (2008). Of chameleons and consumption: the impact of mimicry on choice and preferences. *J Consum Res*, *34*, 754–766. https://doi.org/10.1086/522322

Temple, J. L. (2016). Behavioral sensitization of the reinforcing value of food: what food and drugs have in common. *Prev Med*, *92*, 90–99. https://doi.org/10.1016/j.ypmed.2016.06.022

Thomas, G. V., Lieberman, D. A., McIntosh, D. C., & Ronaldson, P. (1983). The role of marking when reward is delayed. *J Exp Psychol Anim Behav Process*, *9*(4), 401–411. https://doi.org/10.1037/0097-7403.9.4.401

Thompson, R. F. (1986). The neurobiology of learning and memory. *Science*, *233*(4767), 941–947. https://doi.org/10.1126/science.3738519

Thompson, R. F., & Steinmetz, J. E. (2009). The role of the cerebellum in classical conditioning of discrete behavioral responses. *Neuroscience*, *162*(3), 732–755. https://doi.org/10.1016/j.neuroscience.2009.01.041

Thorndike, E. L. (1898). Animal intelligence: an experimental study of the associative processes in animals. *Psychol Rev Monogr Suppl*, *2*(4), i–109. https://doi.org/10.1037/h0092987

Thorndike, E. L. (1932). *The fundamentals of learning*. New York, NY: Teachers College, Columbia University New York.

Thorpe, W. H. (1963). *Learning and instinct in animals* (2nd ed.). London: Methuen.

Thrailkill, E. A., Ameden, W. C., & Bouton, M. E. (2019). Resurgence in humans: reducing relapse by increasing generalization between treatment and testing. *J Exp Psychol Anim Learn Cogn*, *45*(3), 338–349. https://doi.org/10.1037/xan0000209

Timberlake, W. (1980). A Molar Equilibrium Theory of Learned Performance. In G. H. Bower (Ed.), *Psychology of learning and motivation* (Vol. 14, pp. 1–58). Academic Press.

Timberlake, W. (2000). Motivational modes in behavior systems. In *Handbook of contemporary learning theories* (pp. 165–220). Psychology Press.

Timberlake, W. (2001). Motivational modes in behavior systems. In *Handbook of contemporary learning theories* (pp. 155–209). Mahwah, NJ: Lawrence Erlbaum Associates Publishers.

Timberlake, W., & Allison, J. (1974). Response deprivation: an empirical approach to instrumental performance. *Psychol Rev*, *81*, 146–164. https://doi.org/10.1037/h0036101

Timberlake, W., & Grant, D. L. (1975). Auto-shaping in rats to the presentation of another rat predicting food. *Science*, *190*(4215), 690–692. https://doi.org/10.1126/science.190.4215.690

Timberlake, W., & Lucas, G. A. (1989). Behavior systems and learning: from misbehavior to general principles. In *Contemporary learning theories: instrumental conditioning theory and the impact of biological constraints on learning* (pp. 237–275). Hillsdale, NJ: Lawrence Erlbaum Associates, Inc.

Tinbergen, N. (1951). *The study of instinct*. New York, NY: Clarendon Press and Oxford University Press.

Tinbergen, N. (1952). The curious behavior of the stickleback. *Sci Am*, *187*(6), 22–26. https://doi.org/10.1038/scientificamerican1252-22

Tinbergen, N., & Perdeck, A. C. (1950). On the stimulus situation releasing the begging response in the newly hatched Herring Gull chick (Larus argentatus argentatus Pont.). *Behaviour*, *3*, 1–39. https://doi.org/10.1163/156853951X00197

Tolman, E. C. (1922). A new formula for behaviorism. *Psychol Rev*, *29*(1), 44–53. https://doi.org/10.1037/h0070289

Tolman, E. C. (1923). The nature of instinct. *Psychol Bull*, *20*, 200–218. https://doi.org/10.1037/h0070693

Tolman, E. C. (1948). Cognitive maps in rats and men. *Psychol Rev*, *55*(4), 189–208. https://doi.org/10.1037/h0061626

Tolman, E. C., & Honzik, C. H. (1930). Introduction and removal of reward, and maze performance in rats. *Univ Calif Publ Psychol*, *4*, 257–275.

Tolman, E. C., Ritchie, B. F., & Kalish, D. (1946a). Studies in spatial learning: orientation and the short-cut. *J Exp Psychol*, *36*, 13–24. https://doi.org/10.1037/h0053944

Tolman, E. C., Ritchie, B. F., & Kalish, D. (1946b). Studies in spatial learning; place learning versus response learning. *J Exp Psychol*, *36*, 221–229. https://doi.org/10.1037/h0060262

Tomoda, A., Suzuki, H., Rabi, K., Sheu, Y.-S., Polcari, A., & Teicher, M. H. (2009). Reduced prefrontal cortical gray matter volume in young adults exposed to harsh corporal punishment. *NeuroImage*, *47*(Suppl. 2), T66–T71. https://doi.org/10.1016/j.neuroimage.2009.03.005

Tornatzky, W., & Miczek, K. A. (1994). Behavioral and autonomic responses to intermittent social stress: differential protection by clonidine and metoprolol. *Psychopharmacology*, *116*(3), 346–356. https://doi.org/10.1007/BF02245339

Trappey, A., Trappey, C. V., Chang, C.-M., Tsai, M.-C., Kuo, R. R. T., & Lin, A. P. C. (2021). Virtual reality exposure therapy for driving phobia disorder (2): system refinement and verification. *Appl Sci*, *11*(1), 347. https://www.mdpi.com/2076-3417/11/1/347

Treisman, A. M. (1964). Selective attention in man. *Br Med Bull*, *20*(1), 12–16. https://doi.org/10.1093/oxfordjournals.bmb.a070274

Tropea, M. R., Sanfilippo, G., Giannino, F., Davi, V., Gulisano, W., & Puzzo, D. (2022). Innate preferences affect results of object recognition task in wild type and Alzheimer's disease mouse models. *J Alzheimers Dis*, *85*(3), 1343–1356. https://doi.org/10.3233/JAD-215209

Trosclair-Lasserre, N., Lerman, D., Call, N., Addison, L., & Kodak, T. (2008). Reinforcement magnitude: an evaluation of preference and reinforcer efficacy. *J Appl Behav Anal*, *41*, 203–220. https://doi.org/10.1901/jaba.2008.41-203

Tullis, J. G., & Qiu, J. (2022). Generating mnemonics boosts recall of chemistry information. *J Exp Psychol Appl*, *28*(1), 71–84. https://doi.org/10.1037/xap0000350

Tulving, E. (1983). *Elements of episodic memory*. Oxford University Press.

Tunstall, B. J., & Kearns, D. N. (2015). Sign-tracking predicts increased choice of cocaine over food in rats. *Behav Brain Res*, *281*, 222–228. https://doi.org/10.1016/j.bbr.2014.12.034

Turner, H. A., & Muller, P. A. (2004). Long-term effects of child corporal punishment on depressive symptoms in young adults: potential moderators and mediators. *J Fam Iss*, *25*(6), 761–782. https://doi.org/10.1177/0192513x03258313

Twitmyer, E. B. (1974). A study of the knee jerk. *J Exp Psychol*, *103*(6), 1047–1066. https://doi.org/10.1037/h0037386

Tzschentke, T. M. (2007). Measuring reward with the conditioned place preference (CPP) paradigm: update of the last decade. *Addict Biol*, *12*(3–4), 227–462. https://doi.org/10.1111/j.1369-1600.2007.00070.x

Virues-Ortega, J., Hurtado-Parrado, C., Cox, A. D., & Pear, J. J. (2014). Analysis of the interaction between experimental and applied behavior analysis. *J Appl Behav Anal*, *47*(2), 380–403. https://doi.org/10.1002/jaba.124

Vizcaino, E. J. V., Fernandez-Navarro, P., Blanco, C., Ponce, G., Navio, M., Moratti, S., & Rubio, G. (2013). Maintenance of attention and pathological gambling. *Psychol Addict Behav*, *27*(3), 861–867. https://doi.org/10.1037/a0032656

Vogel, J. R., Beer, B., & Clody, D. E. (1971). A simple and reliable conflict procedure for testing anti-anxiety agents. *Psychopharmacologia*, *21*(1), 1–7. https://doi.org/10.1007/bf00403989

Vollmer, T. R., & Bourret, J. (2000). An application of the matching law to evaluate the allocation of two- and three-point shots by college basketball players. *J Appl Behav Anal*, *33*(2), 137–150. https://doi.org/10.1901/jaba.2000.33-137

Vollmer, T. R., Iwata, B. A., Smith, R. G., & Rodgers, T. A. (1992). Reduction of multiple aberrant behaviors and concurrent development of self-care skills with differential reinforcement. *Res Dev Disabil*, *13*(3), 287–299. https://doi.org/10.1016/0891-4222(92)90030-a

Waal, F. B. M. d. (2016). *Are we smart enough to know how smart animals are?* (1st ed.). New York, NY: W.W. Norton & Company.

Ward, S. J., Walker, E. A., & Dykstra, L. A. (2007). Effect of cannabinoid CB1 receptor antagonist SR141716A and CB1 receptor knockout on cue-induced reinstatement of ensure and corn-oil seeking in mice. *Neuropsychopharmacology*, *32*(12), 2592–2600. https://doi.org/10.1038/sj.npp.1301384

Warner, L. H. (1932). The association span of the white rat. *Pedagogical Semin J Genetic Psychol*, *41*(1), 57–90. https://doi.org/10.1080/08856559.1932.9944143

Wasserman, E. A. (1976). Successive matching-to-sample in the pigeon: variations on a theme by Konorski. *Behav Res Methods Instrument*, *8*(3), 278–282. https://doi.org/10.3758/BF03201713

Watson, J. B. (1913). Psychology as the behaviorist views it. *Psychol Rev*, *20*(2), 158–177. https://doi.org/10.1037/h0074428

Watson, J. B. (1919). *Psychology from the standpoint of a behaviorist*. Philadelphia, PA: J B Lippincott Company.

Watson, J. B. (1930). *Behaviorism* (Rev. ed.). New York, NY: W.W. Norton & Co.

Watson, J. B., & Morgan, J. J. B. (1917). Emotional reactions and psychological experimentation. *Am J Psychol*, *28*(2), 163–174. https://doi.org/10.2307/1413718

Watson, J. B., & Rayner, R. (1920). Conditioned emotional reactions. *J Exp Psychol*, *3*(1), 1–14. https://doi.org/10.1037/h0069608

Watson, P., Wiers, R. W., Hommel, B., Gerdes, V. E. A., & de Wit, S. (2017). Stimulus control over action for food in obese versus healthy-weight individuals. *Front Psychol*, *8*, 580. https://doi.org/10.3389/fpsyg.2017.00580
Weiner, I., & Feldon, J. (1997). The switching model of latent inhibition: an update of neural substrates. *Behav Brain Res*, *88*(1), 11–25. https://doi.org/10.1016/s0166-4328(97)02314–0
Weingarten, H. P. (1985). Stimulus control of eating: implications for a two-factor theory of hunger. *Appetite*, 6(4), 387–401. https://doi.org/10.1016/S0195-6663(85)80006-4
Weiss, B., Dodge, K. A., Bates, J. E., & Pettit, G. S. (1992). Some consequences of early harsh discipline: child aggression and a maladaptive social information processing style. *Child Dev*, 63(6), 1321–1335. https://doi.org/10.1111/j.1467-8624.1992.tb01697.x
Welsh, J. P., & Oristaglio, J. T. (2016). Autism and classical eyeblink conditioning: performance changes of the conditioned response related to autism spectrum disorder diagnosis. *Front Psychiatry*, *7*, 137. https://doi.org/10.3389/fpsyt.2016.00137
Wendt, J., Hufenbach, M. C., Konig, J., & Hamm, A. O. (2020). Effects of verbal instructions and physical threat removal prior to extinction training on the return of conditioned fear. *Sci Rep*, *10*(1), 1202. https://doi.org/10.1038/s41598-020-57934-7
Wessa, M., & Flor, H. (2007). Failure of extinction of fear responses in posttraumatic stress disorder: evidence from second-order conditioning. *Am J Psychiatry*, *164*(11), 1684–1692. https://doi.org/10.1176/appi.ajp.2007.07030525
Whalley, K. (2013). Humans are on the grid. *Nat Rev Neurosci*, *14*(10), 667–667. https://doi.org/10.1038/nrn3588
White, K. S., & Cheung, V. (2021). Cognitive behavioral therapy for anxiety disorders. In *Handbook of cognitive behavioral therapy: applications* (Vol. 2, pp. 33–65). Washington, DC: American Psychological Association.
Wilder, D. A., Austin, J., & Casella, S. (2009). Applying behavior analysis in organizations: organizational behavior management. *Psychol Serv*, *6*, 202–211. https://doi.org/10.1037/a0015393
Wilkins, D. E., Hallett, M., & Wess, M. M. (1986). Audiogenic startle reflex of man and its relationship to startle syndromes a review. *Brain*, *109*(3), 561–573. https://doi.org/10.1093/brain/109.3.561
Winterbauer, N. E., & Bouton, M. E. (2010). Mechanisms of resurgence of an extinguished instrumental behavior. *J Exp Psychol Anim Behav Process*, *36*(3), 343–353. https://doi.org/10.1037/a0017365
Wise, R. A., & Hoffman, D. C. (1992). Localization of drug reward mechanisms by intracranial injections. *Synapse*, *10*(3), 247–263. https://doi.org/10.1002/syn.890100307
Wise, R. A., Murray, A., & Bozarth, M. A. (1990). Bromocriptine self-administration and bromocriptine-reinstatement of cocaine-trained and heroin-trained lever pressing in rats. *Psychopharmacology (Berl)*, *100*(3), 355–360. https://doi.org/10.1007/BF02244606
Wittgenstein, L. (1953). *Philosophical investigations. Philosophische Untersuchungen*. Oxford, England: Macmillan.
Wolfe, J. B. (1934). The effect of delayed reward upon learning in the white rat. *J Compar Psychol*, *17*(1), 1–21. https://doi.org/10.1037/h0070755
Wolfe, J. B. (1936). Effectiveness of token rewards for chimpanzees. *Compar Psychol Monogr*, *12*, 72–72.
Wolpe, J. (1958). *Psychotherapy by reciprocal inhibition*. Palo Alto, CA: Stanford University Press.
Wolpe, J. (1961). The systematic desensitization treatment of neuroses. *J Nerv Ment Dis*, *132*, 189–203. https://doi.org/10.1097/00005053-196103000-00001
Wolpe, J. (1982). *The practice of behavior therapy* (P. Press Ed. 3rd ed.).
Wood, E. R., Mumby, D. G., Pinel, J. P., & Phillips, A. G. (1993). Impaired object recognition memory in rats following ischemia-induced damage to the hippocampus. *Behav Neurosci*, *107*(1), 51–62. https://doi.org/10.1037//0735-7044.107.1.51
Wood, W., Quinn, J. M., & Kashy, D. A. (2002). Habits in everyday life: thought, emotion, and action. *J Pers Soc Psychol*, *83*(6), 1281–1297.
Woodruff-Pak, D. S. (2001). Eyeblink classical conditioning differentiates normal aging from Alzheimer's disease. *Integr Physiol Behav Sci*, *36*(2), 87–108. https://doi.org/10.1007/BF02734044
Woolley, K., & Fishbach, A. (2018). It's about time: earlier rewards increase intrinsic motivation. *J Pers Soc Psychol*, *114*, 877–890. https://doi.org/10.1037/pspa0000116

Yager, L. M., & Robinson, T. E. (2013). A classically conditioned cocaine cue acquires greater control over motivated behavior in rats prone to attribute incentive salience to a food cue. *Psychopharmacology (Berl)*, *226*(2), 217–228. https://doi.org/10.1007/s00213-012-2890-y

Yamaguchi, S., & Heisenberg, M. (2011). Photoreceptors and neural circuitry underlying phototaxis in insects. *Fly*, *5*(4), 333–336. https://doi.org/10.4161/fly.5.4.16419

Yan, W.-S., Chen, R.-T., Liu, M.-M., & Zheng, D.-H. (2021). Monetary reward discounting, inhibitory control, and trait impulsivity in young adults with internet gaming disorder and nicotine dependence. *Front Psychiatry*, *12*, 628933. https://doi.org/10.3389/fpsyt.2021.628933

Yau, J. O. Y., & McNally, G. P. (2018). Brain mechanisms controlling Pavlovian fear conditioning. *J Exp Psychol Anim Learn Cogn*, *44*(4), 341–357. https://doi.org/10.1037/xan0000181

Yi, R., Matusiewicz, A. K., & Tyson, A. (2016). Delay discounting and preference reversals by cigarette smokers. *Psychol Rec*, *66*(2), 235–242. https://doi.org/10.1007/s40732-016-0165-4

Yilmaz, K. (2011). The cognitive perspective on learning: its theoretical underpinnings and implications for classroom practices. *Clear House*, *84*, 204–212. https://doi.org/10.1080/00098655.2011.568989

Yogev, H., Sirota, P., Gutman, Y., & Hadar, U. (2004). Latent inhibition and overswitching in schizophrenia. *Schizophrenia Bull*, *30*(4), 713–726.

Yoon, N. A., & Diano, S. (2021). Hypothalamic glucose-sensing mechanisms. *Diabetologia*, *64*(5), 985–993. https://doi.org/10.1007/s00125-021-05395-6

Yu, L., Gao, J., Kong, Y., & Huang, L. (2023). Impact of perceived scarcity on delay of gratification: meditation effects of self-efficacy and self-control. *Curr Psychol*, 1–9. https://doi.org/10.1007/s12144-023-04455-x

Yu, Q., Li, E., Li, L., & Liang, W. (2020). Efficacy of interventions based on applied behavior analysis for autism spectrum disorder: a meta-analysis. *Psychiatry Investig*, *17*(5), 432–443. https://doi.org/10.30773/pi.2019.0229

Zehr, E. P., & Stein, R. B. (1999). What functions do reflexes serve during human locomotion? *Progress Neurobiol*, *58*(2), 185–205. https://doi.org/10.1016/S0301-0082(98)00081–1

Züst, M. A., Ruch, S., Wiest, R., & Henke, K. (2019). Implicit vocabulary learning during sleep is bound to slow-wave peaks. *Curr Biol*, *29*(4), 541–553.e547. https://doi.org/10.1016/j.cub.2018.12.038

Index

Note: Page numbers in *italics* indicate a figure and page numbers in **bold** indicate a table on the corresponding page.

For Product Safety Concerns and Information please contact our EU representative GPSR@taylorandfrancis.com Taylor & Francis Verlag GmbH, Kaufingerstraße 24, 80331 München, Germany